THE
Legal,
Ethical,
AND
Regulatory
Environment
OF
Business

Dawn D. Bennett-Alexander
University of Georgia

Linda F. Harrison
Georgia State University

Marsha E. Hass
College of Charleston

SOUTH-WESTERN College Publishing

An International Thomson Publishing Company

Publisher/Team Director:	Valerie Ashton
Acquisitions Editor:	Jeanne Busemeyer
Sponsoring Editor:	Christopher Will
Developmental Editor:	Kurt Gerdenich
Production Editor:	Sue Ellen Brown
Marketing Manager:	Scott Person
Production House:	Trejo Production
Cover Designer:	Ben Ross Design
Internal Designer:	Maureen McCutcheon Design
Illustrator:	Harvey Chan

LE63AA
Copyright ©1996
by South-Western Publishing
Cincinnati, OH

Library of Congress Cataloging-in-Publication Data
Bennett-Alexander, Dawn D.
      The legal, ethical, and regulatory environment of business / Dawn D. Bennett-
   Alexander, Linda F. Harrison, Marsha E. Hass.
         p.   cm.
      Includes index.
      ISBN 0-538-83728-4 (acid-free paper)
      1. Business enterprises—Law and legislation—United States.   2. Contracts
   United States.   3. Business law—United States. I. Harrison, Linda F. II. Hass,
   Marsha E., III. Title.
   KF1355.B46   1996
   346.73'07—dc20
   [347.3067]   95-16696
                                                                                      CIP

1 2 3 4 5 6 7 D1 10 9 8 7 6 5
Printed in the United States of America

This book is printed on acid-free paper that meets Environmental Protection Agency standards for recycled paper.

I(T)P
International Thomson Publishing
South-Western College Publishing is an ITP Company. The ITP trademark is used under license.

BRIEF CONTENTS

CONTENTS

Chapter 4

SOCIAL RESPONSIBILITY, ETHICS, AND WHITE-COLLAR CRIMES, *97*

Chapter 7

INTERNATIONAL LAW, *187*

Chapter 8

CHOOSING A FORM OF BUSINESS ORGANIZATION, *225*

Chapter 9

ENTREPRENEURSHIP: LEGAL ASPECTS OF THE NEW ENTERPRISE, *267*

Chapter 10

CONSIDERATIONS IN THE EMPLOYMENT RELATIONSHIP, *299*

Chapter 11

EMPLOYMENT LAW: WAGES, HOURS, SAFETY, WORKERS' COMPENSATION, AND LABOR LAW, *325*

Chapter 12

DISCRIMINATION IN EMPLOYMENT, *363*

Chapter 13

EMERGING ISSUES IN THE WORKPLACE, *405*

Chapter 15

INTELLECTUAL PROPERTY, *461*

Chapter 16

LIABILITY FOR PRODUCTS OR SERVICES, *501*

PREFACE

The textbook you now hold in your hands takes a new and innovative approach to teaching the legal environment of business. The book uses two characters, Ann and Bill, developing a business, to show you what you need to know about the legal environment of business. Ann and Bill are two college students who plan to form a business after graduating. They have worked during their undergraduate years to help put themselves through school, and will continue and expand the businesses after graduation. This is a new concept in the legal environment of business and is one quality that separates this book from other legal environment textbooks on the market. You will come to know Ann and Bill quite well.

Why do we discuss Ann and Bill in a legal environment textbook? At the suggestion of the American Assembly of Collegiate Schools of Business, colleges of business went from teaching a basic law course composed primarily of contracts to one which included a vast array of other legal concepts. With the new course, coverage of contracts went from comprising up to ten chapters of the course to no more than two, and in most cases only one. Coverage of other issues in the legal environment of business course now usually consists of no more than a single chapter on many other legal topics related to business.

Such exposure to a wider range of topics benefits you as students, but unfortunately you are no longer able to learn any one topic in the same depth once reserved for contracts. Many students feel frustrated because just as they are beginning to grasp one legal topic, it is time to move on to another, totally unrelated topic with little or no continuity in subject matter. They complain there is no link between the topics, making it more difficult to understand and digest the subject matter. They also say that most of the text covers topics in a way that made the topics seem isolated and distinct, when this is not the way things occur in the real world.

For professors, too, it is a problem, for dividing the law into discrete areas does not reflect the way in which they teach. Rarely are legal problems in business presented in such a singular, unrelated way. Rather, several matters may be involved at once.

We have consciously written the text with the specific purpose of arranging the subject matter so as to provide continuity and diminish that problem. To the seasoned professor the topic coverage and arrangement may seem somewhat unusual, but only in comparison with other texts' tables of contents, not with the way this book teaches. All of the subject matter is here and is probably more in keeping with how educators actually cover it. It is also more reflective of consideration for how the topics are likely to arise. For instance, agency considerations often arise in the context of tort actions committed by the agent, yet agency is often not covered until after torts, if at all.

In this text, Bill and Ann are the staples that provide you with continuity from one subject to another. They typify the average businessperson. Moreover, the text teaches the various areas of law through Bill and Ann's need to know for purposes of their business. The information will thus have a context as well as a unifying concept.

It is important to the concept of this textbook that it provide the principles of "black-letter law" as well as practical information you can apply once out in the real world. Theory is important also, as a vital and necessary part of understanding the law. All three—principles, application and theory—are included here.

The primary distinguishing aspects of this text are:

- its use of the characters Ann and Bill, which runs throughout the text

- the integration of subject matter into more realistic groupings,

- concern for consideration of principles, practices, and theory

- its inclusiveness, reflected in character names, chapter-end questions, and examples.

You will see Bill and Ann decide what type of business organization to create; decide how to finance it, hire and deal with employees, enter into agreements, handle torts in the business world, go public and handle securities matters, deal with environmental, antitrust, and multicultural considerations, and address a myriad of other legal situations businesspeople routinely confront. The story of how law affects business is told via Ann and Bill. Therefore, although the subject matter may change from chapter to chapter, they will always be present. In addition, while the basic subject matter stays much the same as other legal environment texts, its arrangement is innovative and more reflective of the ways professors actually teach and law really works in the business world.

When necessary, we provide more coverage to reflect the reality of the business world. For example, because it has so many different dimensions and because employment-related matters include about 80% of workplace-related litigation, there are four chapters addressing in some way these issues. Wage and hour considerations, for example, are quite different from workplace discrimination claims. And the latter are quite different from at-will considerations and workplace innovations like flextime and parental leave. Coverage therefore reflects that accordingly.

We feel the class in legal environment should not be simply an academic exercise. We take seriously our responsibility of teaching you the law, but we think that if we are to prepare you effectively for the workplace and the legal environment in which you will operate, we must also teach you how to avoid legal liability. That is a big part of what you will learn in this text—and one of the ways it is different from others.

In addition, this textbook comes to you with both learning and convenience in mind. Many others, in addition to the authors, have spent much time thinking about how students learn, how professors teach, and how to maximize both. We have come up with a dynamic set of supplementary materials that are geared to facilitating the learning process. In addition to Bill and Ann, we have included the following pedagogical tools and conveniences.

- Introductory chapter summaries outline that matters Ann and Bill will learn in the chapter.
- Learning objectives are stated at the beginning of the chapter.
- New terms are in boldface print.
- Term definitions appear in the page margin.
- An extensive new-term list is at the end of the chapter.
- Group exercises end chapters.
- Current event boxes bring issues to life.
- Generous use of information boxes, charts, and other graphics enhances and reinforces the subject matter
- Supplemental information from easily accessible sources shows how legal considerations in business arise in all sorts of situations all the time.

- Interesting and topical supplemental information draws the professor and the student together.
- The use of icons alerts you to issues that may have implications for the environment, international law, ethics, and so on.

All of this is in an effort to create a legal environment textbook that will best fit your needs as students and professors. We hope it works. We are very interested to know how you feel about the approach itself, as well as how it was executed. Don't hesitate to let us know what you think—thanks, and have fun with Bill and Ann.

Dawn D. Bennett-Alexander
302 Brooks Hall
Terry College of Business
University of Georgia
Athens, GA 30602-6255
706-542-4290; fax 706-542-4295
dawndba@uga.cc.uga.edu

Linda F. Harrison
College of Law
Georgia State University
P.O. Box 4037
Atlanta, GA 30303-4037
404-651-4159; fax 404-651-2092
lawlfh@landmark.gsu.edu

Marsha E. Hass
School of Business and Economics
College of Charleston
9 Liberty Street
Charleston, SC 29424-0001
803-953-5697; fax 803-792-5697
hassm@cofc.edu

ACKNOWLEDGMENTS

DDB-A   Jeanne Busemeyer deserves an incredibly big thank-you on the part of anyone who appreciates this book. It was Jeanne who had the foresight and determination to go after it and convince me to write it. It was Jeanne who ushered it through the process. Her intelligence, extensive knowledge and experience in the publishing process, and her insights gained in that process were immeasurably helpful. Jeanne is one of those angels who come to help us when we don't even know we need them. Thanks, Jeanne.

I also thank my coauthor, cohort, colleague, confidante, partner, and friend Linda F. Harrison, whose monomaniacal dedication to crisp, clean text is exceedingly only by her unfailing humor and inch-wide, mile-deep patter, which provided many a much-needed light moment during this undertaking.

I wish to thank my coauthor Marsha Hass for her active imagination and important contribution to the vision of this text.

My daughters, Jenniffer Dawn Bennett Alexander, Anne Alexis Bennett Alexander, and Tess Alexandra Bennett Harrison are thanked for their patience, love, understanding, and appreciation for what I try to contribute to the world for them and the world they will inherit.

Thanks to the likes of Billie Holiday, Earl Klugh, Muddy Waters, Bessie Smith, Vivaldi, Mozart, Beethoven, Phoebe Snow, Luther Vandross, and the many other musicians who played the sound track of my life as I wrote. Skylar O. Saveland, thanks for coming into my space and reconnecting me with the profound importance of the blues in the fabric of my life. Life is full of surprises and you are one of mine. Thanks for the purrs and the shoulder and lap time from PurrPuss, Amoré, Lumpkin, and Cappuccino as I sat at the computer writing; the songs and activity of the birds at the feeder outside my window as I wrote; and the peaceful, inspirational scenes provided for me out the bay window looking over my gardens as the seasons changed. All of this helps me so much to do what I do. Thanks also to Agatha Christie, Masterpiece Theater, the Discovery channel, Jessica Fletcher, and the authors of the slave narratives, all of whom provide me with often-needed respites and exaltation. Thanks also to my family and friends, both those here among us and those here no longer. You inspire me, lift me up, make me laugh, and give me a wonderful resting place in the warmth of your love. Thank you. Drake, here you are, buddy. Thanks for being one of my angels. Richard (Pop-Pop)

Harrison, you're a gem. Thanks for your confidence and encouragement. Thanks go to my students, one and all, who have influenced me over the years and made teaching both a joy and nonnegotiable for me. Thanks also to my department chair, Dr. Sandra G. Gustavson, and my dean, Dr. Alniemi, for being so supportive of my efforts.

LH thanks many times over to those responsible for making this book possible: dawn bennett-alexander for her faith in me, her support, and her ceaseless love; marsha hass for her vision; jeanne busemeyer for her firm but gentle editorial support; joan garner for being there for me; margaret nichols for teaching me how to be a grownup; derry drake for letting me be one of the boys; all of my students from whom i learn so much every time i teach them; and last, but not least, my three girls—jenniffer dawn, anne alexis, and tess alexandra, who keep me young at heart, free in spirit, and well with laughter.

ABOUT THE AUTHORS

Dawn D. Bennett-Alexander, Esq., is associate professor of legal studies and employment law at the University of Georgia Terry College of Business and an attorney admitted to practice in Washington, D.C., and six other federal jurisdictions. She is a cum laude graduate of Howard University School of Law and a magna cum laude graduate of Federal City College, now part of the University of the District of Columbia. She is cofounder and served as cochair from 1992 to 1994 of the Employment and Labor Law Section of the Academy of Legal Studies in Business, where she also coedited the section's newsletter; she was president of the Southeastern Academy of Legal Studies in Business during the 1992–93 term. Prior to coming to the University of Georgia, Bennett-Alexander taught legal studies and employment law at the University of North Florida from 1982–1988.

Prior to teaching, Bennett-Alexander worked at the Federal Labor Relations Authority, the White House Domestic Council, the U.S. Federal Trade Commission, and Antioch School of Law and was law clerk to the Honorable Julia Cooper Mack, at the highest court in D.C.: the D.C. Court of Appeals. Bennett-Alexander publishes widely in the employment law area and other fields of study and is founding partner at BJD Consulting, Diversity Consultants.

Linda F. Harrison, Esq., is instructor of legal research, writing and advocacy at Georgia State University School of Law, where she has taught since 1988. Prior to coming to Georgia State, Harrison served as assistant state attorney and division chief for the Duval (Fla.) County Office of the State Attorney. She is a graduate of American University College of Law and the University of North Florida.

Marsha E. Hass, Esq., is professor of legal studies at the College of Charleston and a member of the South Carolina bar. She is a cum laude graduate of Clemson University and holds the Master of Arts in Teaching (MAT), Master of Business Administration (MBA) and Juris Doctor (JD) degrees from the University of South Carolina. She served as president of the Southeastern Academy of Legal Studies in Business (ALSB) during 1993–94. She practiced law for eleven years and served as City Judge for Folly Beach, S.C. for two and one half years. She has published several articles in academic and practitioner journals in the area of employment law.

Chapter 1

INTRODUCTION TO LAW

Chapter Preview Summary

This chapter introduces you to Bill and Ann (see Preface). Because Bill and Ann will be running a business, much of which is affected by the law, this chapter introduces them to (1) the concept of law in our society as a structure within which people and businesses operate, (2) the different types of law our system recognizes, and (3) how law relates to business. The purpose of the chapter is to provide a background for the rights and responsibilities which will be discussed later in the text.

Chapter Objectives

In studying the chapter, you should learn:
- what law is
- the sources of our law
- what types of law our system recognizes
- what common law is
- how common law relates to precedent and stare decisis
- the different branches of law
- how administrative law relates to business
- the various areas of law
- the interplay between law, equity, morals, and justice

INTRODUCTION

ANN AND BILL

Ann is a 22-year-old senior marketing major at Brownsville State University, in Brownsville, Texas, near the Mexican border. She has worked her way through school by providing rug-cleaning services for local business owners. Bill is a 23-year-old senior accounting major who has worked his way through school by cleaning local homes and businesses.

One day one of Ann's clients asks whether Ann knows anyone who can replace the retiring cleaner who usually provided cleaning services for the business. Ann knows Bill from one of her classes, and she recommends him.

Soon Ann and Bill are working together fairly frequently. One of their joint assignments is at Denise's local garage. Denise is a college student whose business of repairing autos for other students had steadily grown to serve more and more customers. While Ann and Bill are cleaning Denise's garage, Denise asks whether they know how to dispose of some chemicals she has on hand. Bill and Ann handled the disposal, and eventually their business included not only cleaning carpets and buildings but also disposing of hazardous materials.

By the time Ann and Bill graduate, they have managed to build a steady and growing clientele. The two decide that they will engage in the business of cleaning and waste management.

law
limitations imposed upon society by government to protect, govern relationships, and provide predictability and security in our persons, possessions, and relationships

substantive law
laws that provide rights and responsibilities, upon pain of penalty in the form of liability or criminal sanctions

Our objective in this textbook is to teach you about **law** as it relates to the business world. In doing so, we will teach you about various types of **substantive law** that provide rights and remedies, such as business organizations, environmental law, and employment law. We will do that, in part, by having fictional businesspersons Bill and Ann set up and operate a cleaning and waste management business. You will be able to see, then, the interaction between law and business by accompanying Ann and Bill as they learn what they need to do to establish and run a business. Each chapter begins with an overview of the legal issues Ann and Bill must contend with in that chapter.

Before we begin journeying with Ann and Bill into the world of business, however, we must first establish a framework within which to operate. Before we begin discussing different types of specific laws, what those laws require, and how they work, we will first discuss the law in general. That is, we will discuss what it is designed to do, how it evolved to its present place in our system of government, and how it operates as a system within which all of the other things we discuss must operate. This overview chapter will acquaint you in a general way with some of the ideas that will make it easier for you to understand the rest of the information as we go along.

Law is something all of us have dealt with all of our lives, yet if you were now asked to define law, you would probably hesitate. Although we live with it every day, law can be difficult to define. We have taken law so much for granted that often we cannot readily think concretely about how deeply it affects our lives. But law forms the foundation of all of our business relationships and many of our personal ones. In fact, once we realize its impact, it can be difficult to think of anything in our lives that is not affected by law. This includes even the most personal areas of our lives.

Did you ever think about the fact that marriage is simply a legal concept? It has nothing to do with love itself, does it? The two often go hand in hand because in our society, as well as in many others, if we love someone we may decide that we wish to do even more. We want to formalize our feelings by way of the institution called marriage. But the institution itself is not based on feelings; it is based on law. Neither are the feelings based on the law. Nowhere in any state's marriage statute does it require that the parties love each other in order to marry. Witness the fact that many people love but do not marry, and many marry but do not love. Neither violates law. Then too, some love and cannot marry, such as those who are married to another, or who are too closely related by blood, or who are of the same gender (though the last is currently being challenged in courts across the United States). When we do something as personal as gaze starry-eyed at our beloved, we are not thinking about law, but still the law plays a large part in our relationship.

If the law plays that important a role in our personal lives, you can imagine how central it must be to our business relationships. We take for granted, for example, walking into a store and purchasing a compact disc or audiotape of music we want to listen to. But law governs everything from the contractual agreements that allowed the music to be in the store for you to purchase, to the warning label that may be on that tape or disc—and everything in between. Law governs the wages and hours of the store's employees, the way in which we pay for our purchase, the advertising the store owner may use to induce us to buy goods, the decibel level at which music may be played in the store, whether music may be played in the store at all because of copyright limitations, how the store finances its inventory, how it occupies the premises, what happens if your CD doesn't function correctly, and many other matters.

But what is the basis of this "law"? And what exactly is it? Is all law the same? Given that it affects almost everything we do, are there limitations on lawmaking? Those questions will be answered in this chapter. We will see how our law progressed to the present system, how the system affects businesspeople such as Ann and Bill, and how businesspeople can affect the laws to which they are subjected.

DEFINITION OF LAW

Law has been defined in a number of ways. Before reading further, stop and think of how you would define it. For our purposes, law is a system of limitations imposed by the government upon our actions in order to ensure order, safety, predictability, and control.

JURISPRUDENCE

jurisprudence
the study of various theories of law

Jurisprudence is the study of law, legal systems, and legal philosophy. Over the years, judicial philosophers have developed many different approaches to explain law and its role in society. While each has been the focus of volumes of study, a brief overview of a few of the more popular theories follows.

NATURAL LAW

natural law
legal philosophy that believes law is based on certain factors or morals that are universal, unchangeable, and dictated by God

The theory behind **natural law** is that a discoverable set of absolute right and wrong principles exists upon which our laws should be based. To the extent that laws reflect natural law—that is, the laws of nature, or God—laws are considered "good" ones. To the extent they do not, they are considered "bad."

A well-known example of natural law is the U.S. Declaration of Independence's statement that "We hold these Truths to be self-evident, that all Men are created equal, that they are endowed by their Creator with certain unalienable Rights, that among these are Life, Liberty, and the Pursuit of Happiness." The statement specifically says that the truths are self-evident, and that all men are endowed with certain unalienable rights. This is natural law at work. In the view of the signers, it was without question that the statement was true and that all other laws were to flow from this natural law. Of course, the logical questions are, Who determines what those natural laws are? And how can we be sure?

For instance, at the time the Declaration of Independence was written, the authors most assuredly intended that natural law dictated that the self-evident truths applied only to men, not women. Further, not even all men were being referred to. As a compromise, the U.S. Constitution later dictated that slaves be counted as three-fifths of a person. Later still, after the Thirteenth Amendment to the Constitution abolished slavery, free blacks were written and interpreted into the Constitution. Ironically, what was deemed to be self-evident was actually very limited, though it was considered the natural order of things at that time.

LEGAL POSITIVISM

The theory of **legal positivism** is based on law as issued by a governing figure, or sovereign. In legal positivism, the law derives its status as law not from some natural order of things that dictates what should be right and just and fair, but, rather, from the fact that it has been enacted by the sovereign with power to make and enforce law. This law may or may not be just or fair. Of course, that no real guidelines exist for judging the law, except that the sovereign issued it, can be problematic.

legal positivism
legal philosophy that believes the law is that which the sovereign says it is

It is this theory that "justified" the restriction on, and eventual extermination of, millions of Jews, Pentecostals, gays and lesbians, and others during the Holocaust as ordered by Hitler, because Hitler was, for all practical purposes, the sovereign. Many of the German officers tried for their crimes at the Nuremberg trials offered as their explanation that they did not do anything wrong or should not be held responsible for their acts, because they were ordered to do what they did. In short, legal positivism argues say that because the law was made by the sovereign, it is law and therefore must be obeyed.

LEGAL REALISM

legal realism
legal philosophy that considers sociology, economics, politics, or other factors in deciding the law

For **legal realists**, actual experience is the key to what law is. Legal realists believe that what is actually done is important, as opposed to what the law says should be done. The drawback to this theory, for some, is that it follows rather than leads. Legal realism does not establish law as a guideline to be followed, but instead makes law follow what people actually do. For legal realists, the outcome of a lawsuit is more important than the reasoning behind the outcome. For instance, if the reality was that most people smoked marijuana, then it should be deemed legal, rather than deeming it illegal because it is somehow viewed as immoral and then holding violators responsible for transgressing the law. A well-known example coming close to legal realism was the repeal of Prohibition in the early part of the 20th century. Because it turned out to be virtually impossible to stop people from drinking alcohol under the law, the law was repealed.

SOCIOLOGICAL THEORY

sociological theory
philosophy of law
stateing that
law is a reflection
of constantly
competing interests
of society

The **sociological theory** of jurisprudence is based on the idea that society's ideas change over time and law should reflect a compromise between the changing, often conflicting, interests of society. For instance, we are currently witnessing a change in society's treatment of children. Previously, children were taught to be passive appendages of their parents and to be seen and not heard. They had no real legal life of their own. Recently, however, we have seen a movement away from such attitudes. A young boy was recently permitted to divorce his parents because the court found it in his best interest to do so. Blacks experienced a similar change in status after *Brown v. Board of Education of Topeka, Kansas*[1] in 1954 and after the Civil Rights Act of 1964. Both were significant in moving America away from its discriminatory treatment of blacks and toward equality. Women underwent (and are still undergoing) a similar change, in which their status and rights are changing. Society is also experiencing such change regarding gays and lesbians, with the advent of new laws extending to them protection from discrimination in employment and other protections.

Some think that sociological theory is not a good way to view law because it makes law too fluid and, some would say, "wishy-washy." Keep in mind that the U.S. Constitution is the oldest continuous constitution in existence. There have been many, many societal changes during its more than 200-year history, yet it is still a healthy and viable document. If it were so inflexible, it would not have been able to withstand more than 200 years of social change. Whether we determine our legal theory fits neatly into one category or another is not nearly as important as the fact that we have for our laws a framework we respect and are able to live with as a society.

SOURCES OF LAW

Where do our laws come from? What yardstick do we measure them by to make sure they are permissible as law? To whom do the laws apply? These questions are answered by looking at the sources of our laws.

THE CONSTITUTION

The primary source of reference for our laws is our federal Constitution. It provides the structure within which all other laws are made. Under the Supremacy Clause of the Constitution (see Box 1–1), the Constitution is deemed the supreme law of the land. Any law made must be consistent with the Constitution and may not be at odds with it. Under the Constitution's Tenth Amendment (see Box 1–1), states may pass laws in areas not left to the federal government, but the Supremacy Clause requires that their laws still be consistent with the federal Constitution. States may even have their own constitutions, and virtually all do, but again, state constitutions must be consistent with the U.S. Constitution.

Under our Constitution, we have a **tripartite system** of government. It consists of three separate and independent branches: the executive, the legislative, and the judicial. As you can see from Box 1–2 on page 9, each branch has its own article in the Constitution, setting forth its powers. None is more powerful than any other, and each has powers that act as checks on the power of the other branches to act. The legislative branch—the U.S. Congress—enacts statutes in the areas carved out for it by the Constitution. The executive branch, headed by the president as chief executive, is responsible for executing, or carrying out, laws. The judicial branch, headed by the U.S. Supreme Court, has authority to interpret laws and to make sure that challenged laws are not unconstitutional.

Each of the three branches has its own powers, but when exercised, those powers also act as **checks and balances** of the other branches. That is, each of the branches has some way of influencing the others so that no one branch has the ability to operate completely

tripartite system
the system of government that comprises three branches: legislative, executive, and judicial

checks and balances
powers one branch of government has over another as a limitation on the powers of the respective branches

1-1 LEGAL EXCERPTS

Article IV and the Tenth Amendment to the U.S. Constitution

This Constitution, and the Laws of the United States which shall be made in Pursuance thereof . . . shall be the supreme Law of the Land; and the Judges in every State shall be bound thereby, any Thing in the Constitution or Laws of any State to the Contrary notwithstanding.

Article IV of the U.S. Constitution

The powers not delegated to the United States by the Constitution, nor prohibited by it to the States, are reserved to the States respectively, or to the people.

Tenth Amendment to the U.S. Constitution

alone and to the exclusion of the other branches. Together, the three branches have an impact on the laws that govern us, though the power to actually legislate resides with Congress alone.

Congress makes laws, and the president is responsible for executing Congress's laws, but the president also has the power to veto Congress's laws. The Supreme Court has responsibility for interpreting the Constitution, but in doing so, it has the authority to declare Congress's laws and the president's acts unconstitutional. The executive and legislative branches counterbalance the judicial branch in that the president nominates U.S. Supreme Court justices, but nominated justices can be appointed only with the advice and consent of the Senate. Congress can also reject Supreme Court interpretation of law by passing a law that has the effect of overturning a Court decision. In addition, as mentioned earlier, each state has its own constitution, which while being quite different from the federal Constitution, must still be in conformity with it.

TREATIES

In addition to the U.S. and state constitutions, we must also obey treaties made with other groups (e.g., Native Americans) or countries (e.g., the migratory bird treaty with Canada). Basically, treaties are contracts between countries; they cover matters of international sig-

1–2   LEGAL EXCERPTS

Articles I, II, and III of the U.S. Constitution

All legislative Powers herein granted shall be vested in a Congress of the United States, which shall consist of a Senate and House of Representatives.

Article I of the U.S. Constitution

The executive Power shall be vested in a President of the United States of America.

Article II of the U.S. Constitution

The judicial Power of the United States, shall be vested in one supreme Court, and in such inferior Courts as the Congress may from time to time ordain and establish.

Article III of the U.S. Constitution

nificance. An example is the recent North American Free Trade Agreement (NAFTA), governing trade and environmental matters between the United States, Mexico, and Canada. Another is the General Agreement on Tariffs and Trade (GATT), addressing trade relationships between the United States and other countries. All treaties must be consistent with the U.S. Constitution, and laws enacted may not violate treaties with which they may interface.

STATUTES

When most of us think of law, we think of legislative, or **statutory law**, that is, laws enacted by the U.S. Congress or by state legislatures. Such laws may govern any area the legislature is free to act upon. The U.S. Constitution specifically tells Congress in Article I the areas in which it may legislate. The Constitution also sets forth which areas are to be left to the states to address. States generally address those areas through state legislatures, which enact state laws for their respective states much the way the U.S. Congress enacts federal laws for the country. Examples of state legislation would be laws concerning education or marriage. Local legislative bodies also exist, such as city or

statutory law
laws, known as statutes, passed by a legislative body

town councils, which pass local **ordinances** affecting their immediate areas, such as housing occupancy limitations or hours of operation of bars.

Judges play a part in statutory law in that their interpretation of a statute becomes a part of what that statute means. When passed, some laws are much like a skeleton. Judges flesh out that skeleton by their decisions regarding the interpretation to be accorded the law. The law may say a person is not permitted to kill another human being. But what does that mean? What if the killing was done in self-defense? What if it was done in order to protect the perpetrator's child? What if it was done in war? What if it was an accident? What if it was done to prevent starvation? Again, the law provides the skeleton, but judicial decisions interpreting the legislature's intent in passing the law become an important part of the law.

COMMON LAW

common law
judge-made law and law based on the custom and tradition brought from England by the colonists

Another source of law is the **common law**. After the Norman conquest in 1066, and long before there were statutes and legislatures, judges of the king's court traveled with the king from place to place deciding cases based on common sense and custom. Of course, that approach did not provide a good deal of predictability for the parties involved, because each case was decided on its own, with no real guidelines.

stare decisis
requirement that prior similar cases be used to determine issues now before the court

Eventually judges began to write down their decisions in Year Books read by other judges. The common law is also called judge-made law because much of it comes from cases decided by judges based on those judges' interpretations of situations brought before them.

precedent
judicial decisions that must be looked to in later, similar cases

This body of law came to America with the new settlers on the *Mayflower* and formed the basis for Colonial law until there were legislatures and until statutes were enacted in this new land. In that sense, the common law is also very much derived from British law. Today, the common law is still an important source of law, though many of our common law principles have been codified into statutory law. The system of looking to previously decided cases evolved into a bedrock legal principle still alive in our system today: **stare decisis**, meaning to abide by or adhere to previous decisions, which are called **precedent**.

JUDICIAL LAW

Judicial law is a product of this system. Under this principle, as we discussed, judges' (also called "the court") decisions become an important part of the law. Once a decision is rendered by a court, that decision becomes precedent for that court jurisdiction. If a similar situation arises in the same jurisdiction, stare decisis generally dictates that the court base its present decision upon precedent. If the facts of the case before the court are substantially the same, that is, **on all fours**, then the present case must be decided consistently with precedent. If, however, the facts of the present case can be distinguished in some significant way from precedent, then it may be argued that the previous case is not really precedent and therefore need not be followed. U.S. Supreme Court decisions must be followed by all courts.

Our law is flexible enough that as times change, precedent can change to accommodate social change. For instance, the Topeka, Kans., case of *Brown v. Board of Education* referred to previously changed prior law permitting racial segregation in public schools by deciding that separate meant inherently unequal, and laws allowing such schemes could not stand.

Often, if business owners such as Bill and Ann think that a case they are involved in may result in a decision adverse to their interests and that the type of case is likely to arise again in the future, they will settle the case rather than allow it to go to court. They do so because they do not want the case to go to court and become precedent, which must then be followed in subsequent cases. Judicial decisions, which then become precedent, are a significant source of law.

ADMINISTRATIVE LAW

Administrative law is also a significant source of law. It comprises the rules and regulations made by administrative agencies as well as the laws that govern the process. Agencies are created by the government to conduct business on its behalf. Much of administrative law consists of rules and regulations enacted by administrative agencies rather than statutory law passed by a legislature. However, if administrative agencies have promulgated the rules and regulations pursuant to legitimate delegations of authority from the legislature through the *enabling statutes* creating the agencies, those rules and regulations must be complied with just as laws must. For instance, if an Interstate

judicial law
law derived from cases decided by judges

on all fours
facts before the court are the same in all significant aspects as precedent, thus requiring the precedent be applied in the present case

administrative law
the law that regulates federal and state agencies and how they conduct their business within constitutional guidelines, as well as the body of quasi-legislative enactments of the agency

Commerce Commission regulation requires that trucks be equipped with certain types of mud flaps, then Bill and Ann must equip their delivery truck with such mud flaps or be subject to the penalty imposed for violation of the regulation.

The fact that the agency acted in a *quasi-legislative* capacity in promulgating the regulation does not make the regulation any less effective as a dictate to be followed. We must say the agency acted in a quasi-legislative capacity because under the Constitution, only Congress has the power to legislate. Therefore, when it delegates some of its authority to an agency so as to permit that agency to act and the agency promulgates rules and regulations under that authority, the agency is not actually making law, though it is acting as if it does. The term *quasi* means *like*, or *as if*. The agency rules and regulations, while not actual legislative or statutory law, are similar to it.

Agencies may also act in a quasi-judicial capacity, meaning they have the power, if granted by enabling statute, to hear disputes involving agency regulations. Such agency decisions also become a sort of quasi-judicial law. In addition, as a business owner who may be subject to an agency's rules and regulations, Bill and Ann must know how to provide input into agencies' workings so that they have a means whereby their business interests may be heard and represented. Ordinarily it is our elected representatives who pass laws, and we express to our legislators our position regarding the laws. Hopefully, they vote accordingly.

This does not work the same way for agency heads making regulations. Rather than being elected to represent our interests, agency heads are instead generally appointed by the president with the advice and consent of the Senate. Ann and Bill may indirectly impact the quasi-legislative regulations by asking their senators to vote to approve only the appointment of agency heads whose decisions will be in their best interest. But they can also participate in the agency's regulatory process by providing input when they are notified of proposed rules to be promulgated. The **Administrative Procedures Act** dictates how agencies conduct their business in order to ensure due process in their actions. Box 1–3, "The Administrative Process in Action," gives an example of the effect of agency regulations on something as commonplace as a dry-cleaning business.

Administrative Procedures Act
the federal law governing the operation of agencies to ensure proper due process and uniform conduct of business among the agencies

1–3   LAW IN THE REAL WORLD

The Administrative Process in Action

Ronald Kantor doesn't have high-minded ideas about the environment. To him, clean means green—as in dollars.

Kantor is owner of Leather-Rich Inc., in Oconomowoc, Wis., a dry-cleaning business that specializes in leather. He opened a new plant in a 29,000-square-foot building equipped with the latest machinery to clean clothing without spewing chemicals into the air, water, or soil.

Regulations by states and the Environmental Protection Agency covering proper use and disposal of dry-cleaning fluids have tightened as concern about the environment has increased. In some states, dry cleaners have been sued because of solvent leaks or [for causing] air pollution.

"The laws were changing to meet the needs of society," Kantor says. "I felt that if I were to put into a business real money—and we're talking a couple million dollars—I had to do things to protect my investment. We can't sell our business or even pass it on to our children without the worry that the business will be sued for past transgressions."

To avoid such problems, Kantor hired an environmental lawyer, worked with a builder and a manufacturer, and came up with "a plant that's built for the future."

Starting from the ground and working up, Kantor had the floor dug out to a depth of three feet; then he put down a heavy plastic liner, covered it with sand, and laid pipes over that. The liner is there to protect the soil and groundwater in the event a pipe breaks and spills chemicals. "This plant sits on an aquifer," Kantor says. "We had to protect the water."

Eight dry-cleaning machines use a "dry-to-dry" system in which all the solvents used are encapsulated within the machinery, cooled, and extracted from garments before they're removed. "The whole dry-cleaning machine is completely enclosed," Kantor says. "No stacks release fumes to the atmosphere." Other machinery removes volatile gases from the water, so that whatever goes into the sewer system is clean. "Our neighbors, their children, our customers can all rest assured we're doing everything we can," he says.

But it's expensive. The sad truth, he says, is, "there are trade-offs. The environmental things we're talking about cost money."

Source: "The Administrative Process in Action," January 31, 1994, *USA Today*. ©1994, *USA Today*. Reprinted with permission.

EXECUTIVE ORDERS

executive order
the edicts issued by
the president or
governor that are
much like law

Executive orders issued by the president (or the governor of a state, at the state level), act much like administrative law. That is, the chief executive does not have the constitutional authority to pass laws, but does have the power to issue executive orders that are much like law. As another check and balance, however, an executive order can be overridden by the legislative body. A recent, widely known situation in which such overriding was highlighted occurred when President Bill Clinton was considering issuing an executive order to lift the ban on gays in the military. Congress threatened to enact legislation that would counteract that executive order if Congress felt the executive order went too far in lifting the ban.

Executive Order 11246 is one of the more well-known executive orders, which most people consider law. It prohibits discrimination in employment on the basis of race, color, gender, national origin, or religion on the part of all employers who contract with the federal government to provide goods or services valued at $10,000 or more. That order was probably the one that required the notation "We are an equal employment opportunity employer" to appear at the bottom of your college or university stationery. Again, the fact that the chief executive does not have legislative power as Congress does, does not diminish the reality that executive orders have much the same impact and function as a source of law.

JUSTICE AND MORALS

Notice that nowhere in our list of sources of law do references to morals and justice appear. While many of our laws may be in conformity with our morals or our own set of personal values as to what is right and wrong based on religion, family training, peer influences, community standards, and so on, morals, justice, and law may be quite different. Morals and justice are our own personal matters. Law is not. We may choose our own morals. We may not choose the law—except in terms of when we vote for legislators who will hopefully vote in line with our views. We may attempt to regulate morals through law, but morals actually are our own to choose. Law may attempt to dictate morals, for instance, concerning matters like whether we should drink alcoholic beverages or have abortions even though it may be legal to do so. However, for the most part, law and morals are separate.

Justice generally involves our feeling about how well the law has accomplished what we feel it set out to do. It can also involve how well we feel the responsibility and repercussions of doing an act fit the act done. If a law says we cannot murder and evidence points to someone committing that heinous act, we feel justice is served if the perpetrator is convicted and sentenced to a fitting punishment.

However, it is entirely possible for us to comply with the law, yet still feel as if justice has not been served. For instance, millions watched television in horror as then-President Ronald Reagan was shot by John Hinckley, yet Hinckley was determined to be incompetent at the time of the shooting and sentenced to a hospital rather than prison. Many felt that because they saw Hinckley shoot the president, justice would only be served if he was convicted and sentenced to prison. While morality and justice may be a source from which legislators operate to vote their consciences on legislation, morals and justice are not, per se, sources of law.

CLASSIFICATIONS OF LAW

You may not have given much thought to the differences in laws, but laws fall into distinct categories. Law can be classified as *civil* or *criminal*, *substantive* or *procedural*, *public* or *private*, and *legal* or *equitable*.

CIVIL AND CRIMINAL LAW

You are probably most familiar with civil and criminal law. **Civil law** is the type of law that permits people to generally recover money damages for noncriminal actions that occur, such as car accidents or defamation of character. **Criminal law** addresses actions that violate criminal statutes and, instead of money damages awarded to the victim, generally result in punishment for the perpetrator.

civil law
law governing noncriminal violations of law

criminal law
law governing criminal matters

SUBSTANTIVE AND PROCEDURAL LAW

Substantive law provides rights and remedies, and it dictates what kinds of actions we can and cannot engage in. For example, laws regarding trade secrets would provide Ann and Bill with a right to sue someone who has intentionally taken their closely guarded trade

procedural law
laws and regulations governing the exercise of substantive rights provided by law

public law
law dealing with the government in its operations or the relationship between the government and its citizens

private law
law involving rights between private citizens

plaintiff
party who initiates civil legal proceedings

defendant
the one who is sued in a lawsuit

summons
legal document issued by a court, demanding that a party under the court's jurisdiction submit to the court's authority

secrets for his or her own purposes. **Procedural law**, on the other hand, provides rules and regulations for how to proceed in enforcing substantive rights provided by law. Among other things, procedural rules govern in which court Ann and Bill would bring an action, what the requirements of bringing the case would be, what motions they could file in the case, what cost they would have to pay to file the case, or on what basis the case could be dismissed.

PUBLIC AND PRIVATE LAW

Public law addresses areas such as criminal law and civil rights laws, which deal with people's interacting with the government or the government's interest on behalf of its people. For instance, when a criminal law is violated, it is the government that brings the case—on behalf of the people of the state or federal government—in order to protect the interest of society. If Bill and Ann illegally dumped toxic waste, they would be prosecuted under public law.

Private law, on the other hand, involves areas like torts, contracts, or property law, which involve private parties and/or the government, and not just the interest of the state. If the case is to be brought, it is brought by the party interested in pursuing it. If Bill and Ann want to sue someone who untruthfully said that the cleaning products used in their business were adulterated and not as effective as they should be, it would involve private law and the tort of disparagement. Bill and Ann, not the state, would bring the case if they wanted to pursue the matter.

Public law may involve involuntary litigation, whereas private law is completely voluntary on the part of the **plaintiff**—the party bringing the case. Once the court has jurisdiction over the **defendant** being sued, the case is not voluntary on the part of the defendant, because the defendant must answer the court's **summons**. If, for example, a person is murdered or raped, the state, through its state attorney, makes a prosecutorial decision either alone or with the help of the grand jury regarding whether to go forward with the case. The case can proceed whether or not the victim (or, in the case of murder, the victim's family) wishes to go forward. The litigation is involuntary in the sense that it can proceed regardless of the wishes of the injured party. Not so with private law. In private law, the only way in which the case will go forward is if the injured party proceeds. If Bill and Ann did not want to bring the disparagement case, no cause of action would be filed.

LAW AND EQUITY

In addition to the legal recourse we have discussed until now, **equity** stands outside the strict parameters of the law to provide relief when legal remedies are not available (see Box 1–4). For instance, if Ann and Bill's next-door neighbor wants to build a brick wall on his own property and it is within the zoning laws to do so but doing so would block the ocean view of the office Ann and Bill have built, a court of equity might be able to help. Because there is no actual illegality here, there is no basis for going to a court of law. People's actions do not always fit into neat compartments, and therefore courts of equity stand ready to look into offering relief when all legal remedies are unavailing. Whereas courts of law and courts of equity were actually physically separate at one time in our history, they no longer are, and in most jurisdictions a judge may hear both types of actions in the same case. Jury trials are generally not permitted in equity cases.

equity
the area of law that goes beyond legalities and instead addresses the fairness of situations

AREAS OF LAW

Although, in general, law is a set of rules we must follow, the law is divided into several distinct areas, each with separate considerations. Broad categories of law exist: criminal law and civil law. Acts committed under these categories are called **crimes** and **torts**, respectively. Crimes are violations of criminal law. Torts are noncontract violations of civil law. Under the broad concept of civil law, in addition to the torts, there are also the concepts of property and contracts. The latter two areas usually involve personal agreements of some kind between the parties, and violation of the agreements does not result in torts, but rather, generally breaches of contract. Civil actions involve noncriminal matters of law, but some facts that support torts may also result in crimes.

crime
a violation of criminal law, which may result in incarceration or a fine or both

tort
noncontractual, noncriminal violations of civil law

CIVIL AND CRIMINAL LAW

Civil law violations and crimes are both violations of law (or, in the case of contracts, agreements), but the two are quite different in their purposes and effect (see Box 1–5). Criminal law is made to punish perpetrators, deter further violations, and exact retribution from the criminal. Civil law is designed to make whole again those who have suffered injury at the hands of another. In certain types of civil cases, punitive damages may be imposed for the sake of punishing the liable

1-4   CONCEPT SUMMARY

Comparison of Law and Equity

Law	Equity
Jury trial in most cases	Jury trial generally not permitted
Money damages	Usually nonmonetary remedies
Law governs cases	Equitable principles/maxims govern cases
Stare decisis is used	Courts more free to fashion unique remedy suited to facts
Need legal relief	Must allege remedy at law is insufficient

party and to act as a deterrent to others. Convictions under criminal law result in incarceration in jail or prison, restitution, and/or fines. Tort liability generally results in financial liability on the part of the *tortfeasor*—the one who committed the tort.

As mentioned previously, criminal cases are brought (at times involuntarily on the part of the victim) by the state, whereas tort cases are voluntarily brought by the injured party. Crimes are divided into **felonies** and **misdemeanors**, with the latter being less serious and sometimes resulting, upon conviction, in jail time of less than a year.

Felonies are serious criminal offenses, and convictions result in prison time of a year or more and loss of civil rights such as voting and the right to possess firearms. Either felonies or misdemeanors may involve fines. Torts usually do not have the same type of degree division, though there may be gradations in the tort of negligence such as gross negligence or simple negligence.

The victim of a crime may receive no compensation for harm done (though many states have victim restitution or reimbursement programs), but rather may see the perpetrator put behind bars. The injured party in a tort case generally receives money damages to compensate for the harm suffered or damage done. Criminal cases are

felony
serious crimes resulting in prison time of a year or more

misdemeanor
less serious crimes, sometimes resulting in jail time of less than a year or a fine

1–5   CONCEPT SUMMARY

Comparison of Civil and Criminal Law

Criminal Law	Civil Law
Intent is to punish	Intent is to make injured party whole
Perpetrator is violator	Tortfeasor/breaching party is violator
Results in conviction	Results in liability
Violater fined, incarcerated	Liable party pays damages
Case brought by state	Case brought by private party
Interest of society at stake	Interest of private party at stake
Felonies or misdemeanors	Usually no degrees of torts
Loss of civil rights upon conviction	No loss of civil rights
Possible restitution if convicted	Liability imposed if liable

brought on behalf of the state to protect society. Tort cases are brought on behalf of private parties to protect individual interests.

TORT LAW

Just as there are many different types of crimes, there are also many different types of torts. They vary from state to state, for this area was left to the states under the Constitution. Most torts are derived from the common law and, as such, are called common law torts. However, even where this is so, many of the torts have been codified into statutes, and new torts have been created by statute or judicial law.

Some typical common law torts are assault, battery, intentional or negligent infliction of emotional distress, defamation, false imprisonment, invasion of privacy, and negligence. Business torts include disparagement; false advertising; trademark, patent, and copyright infringement, and interference with contractual relations. Each tort has its own requirements, which must be met in order to impose liability on the tortfeasor.

The underlying basis for tort relief is that people have a right to the protection of their person, property, business, and reputation. Those who cause injury to one or more of those protected interests should take responsibility for their actions. With business tortfeasors, there are additional considerations, such as that businesses are generally in a better position to pay for their torts because they can pass the cost on to consumers as a cost of doing business spread out over many people.

CONTRACTS

contract
lawful agreement between two or more competent parties

consideration
a bargained-for legal detriment exchanged between parties

legal detriment
either doing something one has no legal obligation to do or not doing something one has a legal right to do if one wishes

Civil law also includes the area of contracts. **Contracts** are voluntary, binding agreements people or businesses enter into in order to obtain something to which they are not otherwise entitled. For instance, if Bill and Ann wish to obtain cleaning equipment, they would not be entitled to get it from a supplier simply because they want it. Rather, they must negotiate with the equipment dealer to allow the purchase, agree on the terms, and in exchange, pay an agreed price. Bill and Ann are entering into an agreement to obtain something they would not otherwise be entitled to receive. The agreement, if it meets all necessary requirements, is called a contract. A contract must be supported by consideration. Consideration is a bargained-for **legal detriment** exchanged between the parties.

Failure of one of the parties to the contract to perform as agreed results in *breach of contract* for which money or other remedies may be decided by a court. Those who breach a contract must be willing to pay the cost of doing so. Generally, that means putting the non-breaching party in the position that party would have been in had there been no breach.

PROPERTY

bailment
relationship created when the owner or legal possessor of personal property gives possession over to another for a period of time for a specific purpose

Property law is an area of civil law. It governs the acquisition of title to both real and personal property and covers the rules for proper transfer of property, whether for purposes of sale, by will, by gift, as a **bailment**, or as an original owner (such as wild game one has trapped or killed). It may or may not be governed by contract. For instance, a contract would govern a sale of property, but not a gift of property or the finding of lost property. A bailment is the legal relationship created when a person gives possession of property over to another for a specific purpose, such as to loan it to another, have another repair it, or to have another look after it while the person is away, say, on vacation.

Again, while the three areas of torts, contracts, and property have distinct subject matter, they all involve civil matters rather than criminal. Between the two large areas—civil and criminal—lies virtually every cause of action that arises under our law.

SUMMARY

The legal structure within which business operates is broad and far-reaching. It influences in some way or another nearly every business decision we make. The structure within which we make business decisions includes the various jurisprudential theories of law, the U.S. Constitution and its many business-related provisions, treaties, the common law, statutes, executive orders, and judicial decisions.

Law is divided into criminal and civil law, with the latter being further divided into torts, contracts, and property law. Further, law may be public or private, substantive or procedural. Knowing the background and structure within which we make legal and business decisions will help Ann and Bill to make better and more effective choices in business matters.

CHAPTER TERMS

administrative law	executive order
Administrative Procedures Act	felony
bailment	judicial law
checks and balances	jurisprudence
civil law	law
common law	legal detriment
consideration	legal positivism
contract	legal realism
crime	misdemeanor
criminal law	natural law
defendant	on all fours
equity	ordinance

plaintiff	stare decisis
precedent	statutory law
private law	substantive law
procedural law	summons
public law	tort
sociological theory	tripartite system

CHAPTER-END QUESTIONS

1. List five sources of law.
2. List and explain three theories of jurisprudence.
3. Distinguish between precedent and stare decisis.
4. Our tripartite system of government consists of three branches: _____, _____, and _____.
5. All but which of the following is an attribute of criminal law?
   a. punishment
   b. make-whole relief
   c. involuntary litigation
   d. public law
6. _____ law provides rights and remedies; while _____ law provides a method for pursuing those rights.
7. Jettie Robinson was rear-ended by Bunn Liles at a busy intersection. At the time of the accident, Bunn was driving a delivery truck for Ratliff Shipping Inc. Jettie decides to sue for the damages she sustained. Discuss what kind of case Jettie's attorney would likely bring, against whom, and why.
8. Bill and Ann hear that new regulations will be issued requiring them to have more protective gear for their employees. They do not think such a regulation will be good. What can they do?
9. List three differences between law and equity.
10. When Dennis tries to determine in which court he should sue Loretta for disparaging his business, Dennis is dealing with procedural law. True or false?

11. The constitutional provision that states that the Constitution is the supreme law of the land is called the

   a. supremacy clause.
   b. due process clause.
   c. equal protection clause.
   d. interstate commerce clause.

12. Srabanti tells Brett that if he breaches his contract with her, it will be a tort. Is Srabanti correct?

GROUP EXERCISE

Have each group choose a current article from a newspaper or magazine. The article can be about virtually anything. Have the group discuss the different aspects of law that they derive in the article, using as many of the chapter topics as possible and telling how the aspect they have chosen relates to the topic they have connected it to. Students can even extrapolate on the article's legal implications. For instance, in an article on a football game, students may discuss who may be sued if a fan was hurt during the game, whether the game rules come under public or private "law," and what recourse there would be if a star player decided to quit just before the game.

REFERENCES

1 347 US 483 (1954).

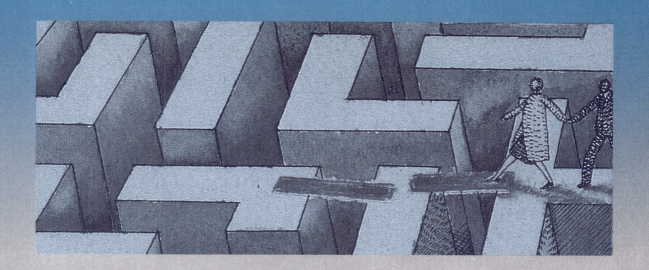

Chapter 2

IMPORTANT LEGAL CONCEPTS AND CONSTITUTIONAL PRINCIPLES

Chapter Preview Summary

This chapter introduces Bill and Ann to several of the important legal and constitutional concepts that underlie many of the discussions of legal matters in this text. Concepts such as due process, equal protection, police power, ethics, and the adversarial system are introduced and explained so that Ann and Bill will understand more about the context and infrastructure in which businesses operate.

Chapter Objectives

In studying the chapter, you should learn:
- how the adversarial system works
- what police power is and what it regulates
- what constitutes due process and equal protection
- what is meant by equal protection of the law
- what interstate commerce is and what it is used for
- what is meant by preemption of an area by Congress
- how taxation is used to impact and regulate business
- the role of ethics in the legal system

INTRODUCTION

Now that you know a bit about the general background of the law, including different theories of law, the origin of our law, and the sources of law, it is a good idea to know a few of the broad underlying considerations that operate within the law. It has been mentioned several times that the U.S. Constitution is the standard by which all of our laws must be judged. Within the Constitution, there are a few important basic legal concepts with which you should be familiar because they underlie or are components of virtually all laws in some way or another.

IMPORTANT LEGAL CONCEPTS

The following are legal concepts you will need to know and consider, as appropriate, during further legal discussions in the text.

ADVERSARIAL SYSTEM

adversarial system
system of litigation in which cases are handled by attorneys on each side of the case who represent the interest of their client

Our legal system is based upon an **adversarial system** in which it is thought that the most effective way to dispose of legal cases is to have the parties positioned at odds with each other so that the issues will be sharpened by the debate and each more forcefully advocated by one whose only position is the protection of that advocate's client's interest. Despite this important foundation in our system, nonadversarial systems of dispute resolution are gaining in popularity as litigation costs escalate and litigation time lengthens.

 Nonadversarial alternative systems to litigation differ in that both parties come seeking a joint solution as quickly as possible. It can be a win–win situation, rather than a someone-must-lose-and-someone-must-win proposition. We discuss in Chapter 3 the subject of adversarial litigation as well as these alternative methods of dispute, but Box 2–1, "ABA Nixes Mandatory Court-Annexed Arbitration," notes that lawyers will not exchange the adversarial system for nonadversarial concepts anytime soon—at least not in the federal sector.

2–1 LAW IN THE REAL WORLD

ABA Nixes Mandatory Court-Annexed Arbitration

Lawyers of the American Bar Association [ABA], meeting for their 1994 annual convention in New Orleans in August, put the ABA on record against any federal legislation providing for mandatory arbitration programs in federal courts. While the ABA has gone on record in the past in support of alternative dispute resolution {ADR} programs, including court-annexed arbitration, the delegates objected strongly to the mandatory nature of the arbitration programs envisioned for the federal courts in HR 1102, a measure that was passed by the House of Representatives last year but is now stalled in the Senate Judiciary Committee.

Mandatory court-annexed arbitration programs require that certain classes of claims go to arbitration as a prerequisite to trial. Such programs are not new. Three federal district courts began pilot programs in 1978. The pilot programs were later expanded to 10 courts. In 1988, Congress gave legislative sanction for the first time to the 10 existing programs and authorized 10 additional voluntary programs.

HR 1102 would require federal district courts to adopt arbitration procedures for claims seeking money damages not in excess of $150,000. Some of the pilot programs have had cutoff figures of $100,000 and $150,000.

Opponents of mandatory arbitration programs, representing the state bars of Arkansas, Georgia, Mississippi, and South Dakota, mustered support from a federal district court judge and a federal procedure authority of the University of Texas law school. They said that while voluntary ADR may be a "fine complement" to the federal evidentiary process, compelled arbitration amounts to doing away with the right to trial. "The ABA should reject such a measure on principle."

The judge said that the mandatory court-annexed arbitration is a "bad idea" for the federal courts. First, he said, the cutoff figure of $100,000 or $150,000 dictates that the burden of mandatory arbitration programs will fall on litigants with small claims. Second, those litigants with the least financial resources will be forced to bear an extra layer of mandatory procedure before exercising their right to a federal trial. Finally, he said, Article III of the U.S. Constitution envisions dispute resolution by a life-tenured judge.

Judge Shapiro disagreed that mandatory arbitration programs harm the poor. She stressed [that] the most famous of the court-annexed ex-

continued on next page

perimental programs is only "presumptively mandatory," because lawyers have the right to refuse to go to arbitration in some circumstances. The right to go to trial is not totally foreclosed in any case, she said.

The delegates voted loudly by voice to condemn mandatory arbitration for any class of claims in federal court.

Source: Excerpted with permission from *United States Law Week*, 63 LW 2098 (August 16, 1994). ©1994 by the Bureau of National Affairs, Inc. (800-372-1033).

POLICE POWER

police power
constitutional power of a state to legislate for the health, safety, welfare, and morals of its citizens

Under the concept of **police power**, states have broad authority to enact legislation to regulate for the health, safety, welfare, and morals of their citizens. As previously mentioned, this leaves the states free to regulate such matters as drinking alcohol in public, child welfare, business licensing, and zoning, which may affect Bill and Ann's business. The state may exercise its police power for very broad reasons, in virtually any permissible area, as long as the argument can be made that such exercise is for the health, safety, welfare, or morals of its citizens.

It is under the state's police power that the state may require among other things, that:

- Bill and Ann have a license to conduct business.

- Bill and Ann's business be located only in certain areas of the city.

- Ann and Bill may operate the business only during certain hours of the day.

- Ann and Bill have bathrooms for customer and employee use.

- The outside of Bill and Ann's business establishment meet certain aesthetic requirements (for instance, the preservation of a certain neighborhood's character, such as the Georgetown area in Washington, D.C., or the antebellum look of Madison, Georgia).

- Bill and Ann provide their employees minimum rest breaks during work.

2–2   APPLICATIONS

Police Power: Regulating Student Housing

Pursuant to its police powers, Prince Georges County, Md., passed a "mini-dorm" zoning ordinance regulating rental of residential property to three or more students pursuing higher education, but not other groups of similar size. The ordinance defined a "mini-dormitory" as "an off-campus residence, located in a building that is or was originally constructed as a one-family, two-family, or three-family dwelling which houses at least three but not more than five individuals, all or part of whom are unrelated to one another by blood, adoption or marriage and who are registered full- time or part-time students at an institution of higher learning." Such dormitories were subjected to various prohibitions and restrictions under the ordinance.

 The ordinance was struck down as not rationally related to the legitimate governmental purpose of controlling parking, noise, and litter and was therefore found to have violated the Fourteenth Amendment's Equal Protection Clause.

Kirsch v. Prince Georges County, Md., Md. Ct. App., No. 111, 6/25/93

Police power is broad, but it is not absolute. For instance, it has been used to uphold a state's power to regulate nude dancing in bars, but not prohibit such dancing as an ongoing business concern altogether. Box 2–2, "Police Power: Regulating Student Housing," gives an example of how police power can influence you as a student.

DUE PROCESS OF LAW

In passing laws, the federal and state governments must ensure its citizens due process of law as well as equal protection of the laws. **Due process of law** is the legal process which is reasonable under the circumstances. It includes, at a minimum, **notice** and the **opportunity to be heard** when there is the possibility that a person will lose life, liberty, property, or some right to which the person is entitled.

 As an example of due process, one could not be sentenced to prison for life for a criminal law violation without first being notified of the charges and given an opportunity to be heard. In a criminal

due process of law
constitutional requirement that all laws be fair rather than arbitrary and provide both notice and an effective opportunity to be heard before the taking of life, liberty or property

notice
due process of law right to be made aware that there is a possibility of loss due to some act of the government

opportunity to be heard
due process of law right to give input to the government after receiving notice that the government may cause a loss of liberty, rights, economic position, etc.

indictment
grand jury's decision that a prosecutor has enough evidence to try a suspect for a crime

information
prosecutor's notification to the suspect that the suspect is charged with committing a crime

notice of proposed rule making
administrative law requirement that before a rule or regulation can be promulgated, notice must be given in the official organ of administrative agencies in the state or national government

Federal Register
official publication organ of federal agencies, in which the latter publish their business such as rules and regulations

procedural due process
constitutional requirement that government provide appropriate notice and an opportunity to be heard before taking life, liberty, or property

case, the required notice is usually an **indictment** or **information**. The opportunity to be heard in a criminal case takes the form of a trial at which the defendant is represented by an attorney, is able to face his or her accuser, and has the right to present evidence and testimony and to cross-examine witnesses.

The Fifth Amendment to the U.S. Constitution requires this of federal laws, and the Fourteenth Amendment made the requirement applicable to state laws. It is now recognized that the laws passed at any level of government (federal, city, county, state) must meet this requirement. Due process is a limitation on governmental action, not on private action.

However, not all legal matters will have the same potential loss involved, and as such will not be subject to the same level of due process. In an administrative setting in which an agency is considering issuing regulations, the process that is due to those potentially affected by the regulations may be simply a **notice of proposed rule making** published in the *Federal Register*. That notice may have as its opportunity to be heard the solicitation of letters from the public commenting on the proposed rules. Because there is as yet no loss to be suffered, the same type of process is not due to those who may be affected by a rule as one who is accused of violating the rule. The *Federal Register* is the official publication the federal government uses to offer notice to the public of the regulatory business of federal agencies.

Later, if the regulation is promulgated and Bill and Ann are given a citation for violating the regulation, then due process may involve both a formal notice of citation from the agency specifically to Bill and Ann as the violators and an opportunity to have an administrative hearing at which evidence is presented. This is different from a general notice in the *Federal Register* and an opportunity to be heard by sending a letter to the agency. Notice that when more is at risk, more due process is required before the law or its penalties can be imposed. Due process is rooted in the Constitution and in our belief that people have a right to be protected from governmental excesses. Box 2–3, "Due Process for Music Groups and Distributors," shows how much of an impact this protection can have on something as seemingly far-fetched as music groups, which, in addition to being recreational for the listener, are made up of businesspeople nevertheless.

Due process must be fair, both substantively and procedurally. **Procedural due process** deals with making sure that a person is

2-3 APPLICATIONS

Due Process for Music Groups and Distributors

Washington state had an "erotic sound recordings" statute to regulate the availability of obscenity to minors. Under the statute, a prosecutor who deems erotic a recording that is being sold, distributed, or exhibited in the state applies to the court for a hearing to determine the issue. Notice of the hearing is immediately served upon the dealer, distributor, or exhibitor of the material, and the court holds a hearing not later than five days from the service of notice to determine whether the [material] is erotic within the meaning of the statute. Musical groups claimed [both] that the lack of timely and adequate notice [before] the initial hearing to determine whether a particular sound recording is erotic denies due process because not all interested parties are given timely notice or adequate notice concerning which recordings have been adjudged to be erotic and that five days' notice does not provide sufficient time for adequate legal preparation to defend the recording.

The court agreed. It said that only one dealer or distributor is notified of the initial hearing, yet that initial determination by the court applies prospectively and is binding on all dealers and distributors in the entire state. The determination becomes statewide legislation that affects the rights of nonparties who received [neither] notice nor opportunity to respond and therefore is a violation of due process.

The music groups also argued that the initial judicial determination of *erotic* in a later criminal prosecution is a violation of due process also, because the elements of the crime must be proved beyond a reasonable doubt, but the initial determination could be used to make the determination for a later criminal case, when the defendant was not even a party to the civil proceedings and had not been afforded the opportunity to litigate the issue of obscenity in some forum before being convicted of selling obscene materials. Since there was not proper due process, the law was struck down.

Soundgarden v. Eikenberry, 123 Wash. 2d 750 (1994)

---

substantive due process
constitutional requirement that laws be fair if they are to deprive a person of rights

not deprived of life, liberty, or property without a fair proceeding. **Substantive due process** addresses the fairness of the law itself, or its application, if it could deprive a person of personal or property rights.

EQUAL PROTECTION OF LAW

equal protection
constitutional requirement that government treat those similarly situated equally, but if treated differently, the difference be supportable by a legitimate state interest

Equal protection is the constitutional concept requiring that all people (including businesses and noncitizens) be treated equally, that is, comparably, under the law, unless there is a justifiable reason not to do so. The concept comes into play whenever one group of people alleges that a law or regulation treats them differently from others similarly situated and thus that that law denies them the equal protection of the law. Even though equal protection of the law is required, again, if it can be shown that the law's basis for differentiating is justified, then the law will be allowed. In other words, the law may treat people differently, but only when it can be shown that there is a good reason for doing so.

Constitutional due process and equal protection both are limitations on a government's powers and as such affect only actions of the federal, state, or local government. They are not theories that can be used to challenge the actions of private parties unless it can be shown that a private party acted in ways that can be shown to be, for the most part, action on the part of the state. For instance, if the government has granted a utility the right to conduct business the government usually would engage in as a governmental act, then the utility's actions can be argued to be those of the state. Otherwise, due process and equal protection are concepts applied only to the actions of a government.

compelling state interest
strongest justification for a state to be able to legitimately deny one's constitutional right to equal protection

strict scrutiny
heightened level of court analysis of laws creating classifications that treat similarly situated people differently

Different standards exist that must be applied to justify differences in treatment among groups under a law, depending on what the basis for the difference in treatment is. For instance, if the difference is based on someone's race, then the state must show a **compelling state interest** in enacting the law. This is a very high standard, which subjects the challenged law to **strict scrutiny** by the courts. The law is justified only if it serves a compelling state interest and is narrowly drawn to effectuate that interest. No race-related classification has ever survived a strict-scrutiny test. For example, say Bill is African-American and challenged a law that said he could not receive a business license because he is African-American. The law would be subjected to strict scrutiny, and the state would be required to show a compelling state interest in having such a law.

Rational Basis Test

If a difference in treatment or classification is based on business or economic interests, then the state need show only a **rational basis** for the law. In analyzing the law, the court subjects it to a minimum **rational basis test** to see whether the law is rationally related to achieving the statutory purpose set forth in the law. Box 2–4, "Rational Basis for Unlimited Punitive Damages against Business," provides some insight. For instance, if Ann and Bill challenged a law that said they must have a certain number of trucks before they could be licensed to carry hazardous waste and if no such requirement exists for other types of businesses, the requirement would be analyzed under the rational basis test. The rational basis test is the least burdensome test, and it is fairly easy for a state to pass. In the *Minnesota v. Clover Leaf Creamery Company* case, the rational basis test is used.

rational basis
theory a government can use when denying to a business the equal protection of the law

rational basis test
test a court uses to analyze whether denial of equal protection to a business is legal

2–4 APPLICATIONS

Rational Basis for Unlimited Punitive Damages against Business

In order to punish and deter the defendant, a Georgia statute provides that in product liability cases unlimited punitive damages may be awarded, though there may be only one such punishment meted out to a product liability defendant regardless of the number of causes of action [that] may arise from [the defendant's] conduct. Since the purpose is to punish the defendant who has the potential to greatly damage society at large, rather than to provide a windfall to the plaintiff, 75% of awards of punitive damages arising out of product liability cases—less costs and reasonable attorneys' fees—must be paid into the treasury of the state to benefit all the citizens of Georgia. In nonproduct liability cases—except when the defendant acted with specific intent to harm—punitive damages are limited to a $250,000 maximum.

The court held the law did not violate the Equal Protection Clause in treating product liability defendants differently [from] other tort defendants [because] there was a potential for greater harm to society in product liability cases than in other cases.

Mack Trucks, Inc. v. Conkle, 263 Ga.539 (1993)

MINNESOTA V. CLOVER LEAF CREAMERY COMPANY
449 US 456 (1981)

A dairy, six companies that produced or leased plastic container manufacturing equipment, and a trade association for the plastics industry sued the state of Minnesota after the latter passed a law banning the retail sale of milk in nonreturnable plastic jugs but not in glass containers or nonrefillable paperboard containers. The parties alleged that Minnesota's statute, among other things, violated the equal protection and due process clauses. The trial court and Minnesota Supreme Court found the law violated the due process and equal protection clauses, but the U.S. Supreme Court reversed, holding that the Minnesota law that discriminated against plastic containers was supported by a rational basis.

Brennan, J.: The parties agree that the standard of review applicable to this case under the Equal Protection Clause is the familiar rational basis test. Moreover, they agree that the purposes of the act cited by the legislature—promoting resource conservation, easing solid waste disposal problems, and conserving energy—are legitimate state purposes. Thus the controversy in this case centers on the narrow issue [of] whether the legislative classification between plastic and nonplastic nonreturnables is rationally related to the achievement of the statutory purposes.

The state identifies four reasons why the classification between plastic and nonplastic nonreturnables is rationally related to the articulated statutory purposes. If any one of the four substantiates the state's claim, we must sustain the act.

Although the parties challenging legislation under the Equal Protection Clause may introduce evidence supporting their claim that it is irrational, they cannot prevail so long as it is evident from all the considerations presented to the legislature and [from] others of which we may take judicial notice that the question is at least debatable. Where there is evidence before the legislature reasonably supporting the classification, litigants may not procure invalidation of the legislation merely by tendering evidence that the legislature was mistaken.

Among the reasons identified by the state why the classification between plastic and nonplastic returnables is rationally related to the articulated statutory purposes, the state argues that the elimination of the popular plastic milk jug will encourage the use of environmentally superior containers. There is no serious doubt that the plastic containers consume energy resources and require solid waste disposal or that refillable bottles and plastic pouches are environmentally superior. Citing evidence that the plastic jug is the most popular, and the gallon paperboard carton the most cumbersome and least well regarded package in the industry, the state argues that the ban on plastic nonreturnables will buy time during which environmentally preferable alternatives may be further developed and promoted.

We find the state's approach fully supportable. The Equal Protection Clause does not deny Minnesota the authority to ban one type of milk container conceded to cause environmental problems merely because another type, already established in the market, is permitted to continue in use. The Equal Protection Clause is satisfied by our conclusion that the legislature could rationally have decided that the ban on the plastic nonreturnable milk jugs might foster greater use of environmentally desirable alternatives. The act may not be a sensible means of conserving energy, but it is up to legislatures, not courts, to decide on the wisdom of legislation. REVERSED

Case Questions

1. What was Minnesota's rational basis for differentiating between the types of containers?

2. Despite the court's opinion, are you persuaded there was a rational basis between the law and the basis for unequal treatment between plastic milk containers and those of glass or nonrefillable paperboard? Why or why not?

3. As a businessperson adversely affected by a law permitting unequal treatment, how do you think you would feel about it, and what would you wish could be done?

WYGANT V. JACKSON BOARD OF EDUCATION
476 US 267 (1986)

The board of education's collective bargaining agreement required that in layoffs, those with most seniority would be retained except that there could not be a lesser percentage of minority personnel laid off than the current percentage employed at the time of the layoff. Under the provision, there were times when minority teachers with lesser seniority than white teachers were retained, while white teachers were laid off. The white teachers sued, alleging violation of the Equal Protection Clause, among other things. The lower courts upheld the claim, but the Supreme Court reversed.

Powell, J.: Can a school board, consistent with the Equal Protection Clause, extend preferential protection against layoffs to some of its employees because of their race or national origin? The teachers' central claim is that they were laid off because of their race—in violation of the Equal Protection Clause of the Fourteenth Amendment. Any preference based on racial or ethnic criteria must necessarily receive a most searching examination to make sure that it does not conflict with constitutional guarantees. There are two prongs to this examination. First, any racial classification "must be justified by a compelling governmental interest." Second, the means chosen by the state to effectuate its purpose must be "narrowly tailored to the achievement of that goal."

The Court of Appeals held that the board's interest in providing minority role models for its minority students, as an attempt to alleviate the effects of societal discrimination, was sufficiently important to justify the racial classification embodied in the layoff provision. The court discerned a need for more minority faculty role models by finding that the percentage of minority teachers was [smaller] than the percentage of minority students.

Societal discrimination alone is not sufficient to justify a racial classification. It is too amorphous a basis for imposing a racially classified remedy. Rather, there must be some showing of prior discrimination by the governmental unit involved before allowing limited use of racial classifications in order to remedy such discrimination. The role model theory employed has no logical stopping point. No one doubts that there has been serious racial discrimination in this country. But as the basis for imposing discriminatory *legal* remedies that work against innocent people, societal discrimination is insufficient and overexpansive.

In order to remedy the effects of prior discrimination, it may be necessary to take race into account. As part of this nation's dedication to eradicating racial discrimination, innocent persons may be called upon to bear some of the burden of the remedy. Here the means chosen to achieve the board's asserted purposes is that of laying off nonminority teachers with greater seniority in order to retain minority teachers with less seniority. We have previously expressed concern over the burden that a preferential-layoff scheme imposes on innocent parties because the [scheme] disrupts settled expectations in a way that general hiring goals do not. We therefore hold that as a means of accomplishing purposes that otherwise may be legitimate, the board's layoff plan is not sufficiently narrowly tailored. Other, less intrusive means of accomplishing similar purposes—such as adoption of hiring goals—are available. The board's selection of layoffs as the means to accomplish even a valid purpose cannot satisfy the demands of the Equal Protection Clause. REVERSED

Case Questions

1. Can you see the difference between the use of the heavier burden of the strict-scrutiny test here and the lighter burden of the rational basis test in the case before? Explain.

2. Can you understand why one type of discriminatory treatment would require a heavier burden of scrutiny than another? Discuss.

3. Would hiring goals have been helpful in this situation, as the court suggested, if layoffs had been accomplished according to seniority and few minority teachers would have sufficient seniority to protect them from layoff because discrimination had kept them from being hired until recently? Explain.

Compelling State Interest Test

compelling state interest test

test used by courts to determine whether a state may deny a person the constitutional right to equal protection of the law

In the following case, the U.S. Supreme Court analyzed an employer's discriminatory layoff policy for teachers under the **compelling state interest test**. See if you can understand the difference between this and the rational basis test covered earlier.

REGULATION OF INTERSTATE COMMERCE

Regulation of interstate commerce is in the power of Congress to regulate commerce among and between the several states. The Constitution did not give the federal government police power to regulate for the general welfare of its citizens. That was left to the states. However, it did give Congress the power to regulate interstate commerce. One of the most important functions of interstate commerce has been to provide Congress the power, much like police power, to regulate in areas where it would otherwise not have the authority.

For instance, through its power over interstate commerce, Congress has been able to enact laws regulating minimum wages and hours; collective bargaining; child labor; the environment; and discrimination in employment, education, public accommodations, and housing. States generally enact such laws under their police power, but Congress does so by way of its power over interstate commerce. As you can see, this is one of the most important provisions for Ann and Bill to know about and understand concerning the federal government's power to regulate business.

It should be noted that Congress can also cause regulation to occur in areas it would otherwise have no power to do so. For instance, although the legal age for alcohol consumption is regulated by states, Congress was able to greatly influence states to raise the minimum drinking age to 21 by stating that it would withhold from states federal funds for highways if a state's law permitted drinking before age 21. Because for most states federal funds represent a significant source of revenues, the threat was an effective tool for Congress. It was able to do indirectly what it could not do directly: through the use of its power over interstate commerce. Box 2–5, "The Commerce Clause and the Americans with Disabilities Act," demonstrates how Congress prohibited discrimination against disabled persons through its expansive use of this power.

TAXATION

Closely akin to the regulation of interstate commerce regarding business is Congress's power to tax and—through taxing—to regulate important business areas it would otherwise not be able to regulate. For instance, while Congress cannot likely tell employers they must hire returning homemakers coming into the workplace, Congress can tell employers it would offer tax incentives if they did so.

The same can be said for the hard-core unemployed or for the developing businesses in certain areas such as production of energy-saving devices during the energy crisis of the 1970s. Business owners who know they will get a dollar-for-dollar tax write-off for engaging in certain activities are much more likely to undertake them.

2–5   APPLICATIONS

The Commerce Clause and the Americans with Disabilities Act

A restaurant that came under the public accommodations provision of the Americans with Disabilities Act [ADA] challenged the law as being unconstitutional. The law, enacted pursuant to the Commerce Clause of the U.S. Constitution, requires existing places of public accommodation to remove architectural barriers to access, when such removal is "readily achievable." This includes rearranging tables and chairs, installing small ramps, installing grab bars in rest rooms, and repositioning shelves and telephones. The ADA provided an 18-month notice period for businesses to comply with its requirements, and no liability was imposed before the end of that period. Small businesses were given even lengthier notice. The court found that the law was constitutional, as the U.S. Supreme Court had consistently held that Congress is empowered under the Commerce Clause to regulate not only interstate activities but also intrastate activities that substantially affect interstate commerce.

Pinnock v. International House of Pancakes Franchisee, DC S. Calif., No. 92–1370–R (CM), 11/8/93

An owner may not want to hire a homemaker reentering the workplace after a long hiatus from employment, but may not mind doing so if all of the monies spent to retrain the entering employee can be written off. Thus, Congress has been able to influence regulation in areas where it had little or no power to do so itself. This is an important tool for business regulation.

PREEMPTION

preemption
right of the federal legislature to be the only body to enact legislation in a given area, to the exclusion of the states

Congress has determined that it will be the only body that can make law in certain areas. This is called **preemption**. If Congress totally preempts an area, then states may not pass laws in that subject area. Interstate commerce is one such area Congress has preempted.

Because of the importance of commerce between and among the states and because of Congress's concern that interstate commerce not be interfered with in any way, Congress preempted the area, determining that interstate commerce should not be subjected to the laws of the individual states, but only to federal law. Thus, though we have 50 states, no one has to worry about a state's closing off its borders or enacting legislation placing a burden on commerce between the states. Box 2–6, "Old Joe Camel and Preemption," shows how states and the federal government can have different interests that are played out in a preemption dispute.

ETHICS

The theme of ethics runs throughout this text. In fact, ethics is so important an area that a separate chapter is devoted to it. However, keep in mind that while ethics and morals may constitute the basis of many of our laws, ethics is generally thought to pick up where the law leaves off. Whereas law is that set of rules imposed upon us by the government regarding how we are to conduct ourselves, ethics represents our own set of personal rules covering how we are to conduct ourselves and our business affairs.

As you will see in the chapter on ethics, many businesses have made a commitment to be responsible by establishing and living by their own set of business or corporate ethics. Unfortunately, such has not always been the case. We have seen increasing examples of bad ethical decisions ever since the Watergate break-in of the Democratic National Committee in the '70s, which resulted in President Richard

2–6   APPLICATIONS

Old Joe Camel and Preemption

A lawsuit was brought challenging an advertising campaign for Camel cigarettes featuring a cartoon character, Old Joe Camel. The suit alleged that the advertising campaign had successfully targeted teenagers and encouraged them to smoke Camel cigarettes. The action also alleged that the cigarette manufacturer, R. J. Reynolds Co., "caused the advertisements of Camel cigarettes without any warning that cigarettes pose a health hazard." It was alleged that these actions were a violation of the Federal Cigarette Labeling and Advertising Act and also constituted an unlawful and unfair business practice under the California Business and Professions Code. In California it is unlawful to sell or furnish cigarettes to minors and for minors to buy them. The narrow issue of the case was whether, notwithstanding that prohibition against the sale of cigarettes to minors, attempts in California to regulate or prohibit advertisement of cigarettes to minors are preempted by federal law. The court held that the state claim was not preempted by the Federal Cigarette Labeling and Advertising Act, and thus, the state could pursue its action against the Reynolds Co.

Mangini v. R.J. Reynolds Tobacco Co., 7 Cal.4th 1057 (1994)

M. Nixon's resigning his office as chief executive of the United States. As a result of that one incident, state bar associations began instituting ethics sections as a part of lawyers' bar examinations, and law, business, medical, and other professional schools began incorporating the study of ethics into their curricula.

Later, highly publicized business ethics violations further highlighted the need for such information. Codes of ethics have increasingly been adopted by businesses, schools, and government agencies to impose rules for conducting business, but there are still gray areas calling for personal judgment. Our hope is that each student will adopt a set of personal business ethics that places a high value on treating others well and respectfully while still making a profit. Box 2–7, "Tobacco Killed My Family," provides an interesting view of this, from an unlikely perspective. See how you feel about it.

2–7   LAW IN THE REAL WORLD

Tobacco Killed My Family

A long as special interest money continues to influence politicians, the death toll from cigarettes will continue . . .

When my older brother, R. J. Reynolds III, died recently from emphysema caused by his smoking addiction, the story was trumpeted by newspapers and broadcast media around the world. But when our father, R. J. Reynolds Jr., died from precisely the same cause in 1964, his cigarette addiction went virtually unnoticed.

There's some irony in the fact that two R. J. Reynoldses, as well as several other family members, have died from cigarette smoking.

There's further irony in the fact that a Food and Drug Administration panel concluded this week what research had been showing all along—that the nicotine contained in cigarettes is an addictive drug.

Who, exactly, is to blame? It's easy to point to the tobacco companies, whose billions spent annually on manipulative and deceptive advertisements have helped influence millions of teenagers and children to smoke.

It's an obvious call to point to the tobacco companies' CEOs, who testified under oath that they did not believe nicotine to be addictive and that they would *never* tamper with nicotine levels.

And it's easy to point to the industry's outrageous abuses of freedom of speech, such as the full-page ads proclaiming that smoking is a matter of choice. (*What* choice? According to Dr. C. Everett Koop's report, nicotine is as addictive as heroin.)

But there looms an even greater culprit than the tobacco companies: Our government's system of allowing the special interests to influence the votes of our elected officials [by means of] campaign contributions is perhaps the greatest evil in our government today.

New studies show that officials who receive big tobacco contributions do tend to vote against legislation to regulate cigarettes. And tobacco has been contributing. In recent years, the cigarette industry has been donating millions to the campaign funds of politicians at [both the] federal and state levels.

Corporations never spend large amounts of money without expecting something in return. What does the tobacco industry hope to gain? First, it has managed to keep cigarette advertising legal, when it should have been banned long ago, as France, Canada, and other nations have done. The industry can no longer plausibly use the freedom of speech argument to justify its ads' continued association of smoking with positive images of health, sports, success, and being "a real person."

Simply put, tobacco ads are outrageous lies. The attractive models on cigarette billboards are role models that our children see daily and look up to. In fact, those ads are the tobacco industry's greatest means of holding onto the gradually waning public acceptance of smoking.

Another result of the [industry's] lobbying and campaign contributions is that the United States has the lowest tax on cigarettes of any industrialized nation in the world—proof that the special interests have far too much influence over policy. Our average state and federal tax on cigarettes is 52 cents per pack versus $3.26 in Canada, $4.07 in Denmark, $3.24 in England, and about $2 per pack in many other countries.

With a recent study informing us that the direct medical costs of smoking are over $2 per pack, a $2 tax on cigarettes is the *minimum* [that] should now be considered.

While the cigarette companies plaintively ask, "Why single out tobacco?" the answer is simple: Cigarettes are the only products [that] when used as intended, cause widespread addiction, disease, and death. Other products, like alcohol, are not necessarily harmful when used as intended. Cigarettes are, and that's why tobacco should be singled out and regulated much more tightly.

The core issue here is getting rid of the tobacco lobby and the government's tolerance of the special interests, which makes it all possible. If we don't, we will continue to decline as a nation. If we do, there is hope. And one day, we might really have a smoke-free society.

Patrick Reynolds, founder of Citizens for a Smokefree America, Los Angeles, is the grandson of the founder of R. J. Reynolds tobacco company.

Source: *USA Today*, August 4, 1994, p. 9A. Reprinted with permission of Patrick Reynolds, President, Citizens for a Smoke-free Society, Los Angeles.

SUMMARY

The legal structure within which business operates is broad and far-reaching. It affects in some way or another nearly every business decision Bill and Ann will make. Important legal concepts such as due process, equal protection, and regulation of interstate commerce make up a very strong part of the framework for law and for business.

Knowing the background and structure within which legal and business decisions are made will help Ann and Bill do a better job of running their business in a manner less likely to cause violations of law and help them better understand business restrictions.

CHAPTER TERMS

adversarial system

compelling state interest

compelling state interest test

due process of law

equal protection

Federal Register

indictment

information

notice

notice of proposed rule making

opportunity to be heard

police power

preemption

procedural due process

rational basis

rational basis test

strict scrutiny

substantive due process

CHAPTER-END QUESTIONS

1. If a legislature passes a law that discriminates between people based on race, the test that is used to determine the validity of the law is the
   a. rational basis test.
   b. deep pockets test.
   c. strict-scrutiny test.
   d. respondeat superior test.

2. Kasimir works as an accountant at a large corporation. One day when Kasimir comes in to work, there is a "pink slip" on his desk telling him he is terminated from his position, effective immediately. Kasimir feels that his summary dismissal is unfair and a violation of due process. Kasimir is correct. (True or False)

3. It is possible for Congress to legislate in an area without actually having power to do so directly. (True or False) Give an example.

4. Chris and Linda are co-owners of a women's bookstore. They decide that since many women work and also have families to care for, it will better serve their clientele if they keep their store open

24 hours a day. To keep down the cost of policing the streets at night, the city passes an ordinance prohibiting all businesses except gas stations, bars, and health care facilities from staying open 24 hours a day. (a) Can the city legally pass such an ordinance? (b) If it can, what can Chris and Linda do about it?

5. A state legislature passed a law requiring that businesses that manufactured birdhouses for retail sale paint the exterior of the houses with weatherproof paint. The purpose of the law was to better preserve the houses in order to induce birds to repopulate the state after severe weather. The law did not apply to hobbyists who made and sold birdhouses. If birdhouse manufacturers challenged the law under the Equal Protection Clause, saying it put an unfair financial burden on them, and not on hobbyist manufacturers, for no good reason, the analysis the court would use to determine the issue would be the

   a. rational basis test.
   b. strict-scrutiny test.
   c. supremacy doctrine.
   d. deep pockets theory.

6. Geraldo calls his state representative in Tallahassee, Fla., to complain loudly about the law being debated that would require all items being shipped out of the state by whatever means bear a stamp saying, "From Florida! The land of Sunshine!" Geraldo, a computer manufacturer, does a great deal of shipping. He complains that the new requirement would place a significant burden on his business and would be a burden on interstate commerce as well, which he says, is _____ by the federal government and therefore not allowed to be the subject of state legislation.

7. The federal government determines it wishes to encourage valuing diversity in society. As a part of its plan, it passes a law providing that an employer of 15 or more employees that can show it has met certain specified diversity guidelines set forth in the legislation will receive a tax deduction of up to 30% of the demonstrated cost of instituting the employer's diversity initiative. Zapix Inc. is outraged and argues that the federal government cannot regulate the workplace in this way. Is Zapix correct? Why or why not?

8. Drew's Putt-Putt Golf Range is concerned about a new regulation passed by its state's department of public safety, which requires that all ranges put up a protective barrier to prevent errant golf

balls from harming people. In order to comply with the law, Drew's would be required to spend thousands of dollars. Drew's knew nothing about the regulation before its promulgation. Does Drew's have any recourse? Explain.

9. In response to recent research showing that domestic violence tended to be more frequent during the televising of professional football games, a city passes an ordinance stating that football games cannot be shown on television in commercial establishments such as bars, lounges, auto repair garages, and stores. A group of bar owners whose business depended on crowds of football fans challenges the ordinance. The owners say it is a denial of equal protection for the state to prohibit the playing of televised football only in commercial establishments. Analyze the business owners' argument under the appropriate test and discuss.

10. The same business owners as in question number 9 also argue that the ordinance is an unlawful use of the government's police power. Discuss.

GROUP EXERCISE

Assign one of the chapter's important legal concepts to each group. Have each group come up with an example of a real or hypothetical situation involving the topic assigned to it. For instance, recent political discussions of welfare system reform may be used as an example of due process or equal protection, or the issue of gays in the military may be used as an example of equal protection or compelling state interest. In reporting to the class, students should explain how their topic involves the important legal or constitutional principle they have chosen.

Chapter 3

RESOLVING LEGAL DISPUTES

Chapter Preview Summary

In this chapter Bill and Ann learn about the legal system within which they will run their business. The chapter explains what happens if a legal dispute arises between Bill and Ann or between them and their customers, vendors, or anyone else they do business with. Finally, Bill and Ann will learn how a case proceeds through court, if that is the means of resolving the dispute, and what other options are available if it is not.

Chapter Objectives

In studying the chapter, you should learn:
- the American court system
- the way a case proceeds through court
- the alternatives that exist to resolve disputes through means other than litigation
- the administrative hearing process

INTRODUCTION

No matter how hard Bill and Ann try to avoid them, if they are in business, disputes will arise. The disputes may be with the person who installed the wrong color or pattern of carpet in Bill and Ann's offices, the person who delivered the wrong type of coffee for the office coffee service, the printer who mistakenly put the wrong address on their stationery, the client who does not like the job they have done, or the window washer who slips and falls on soapy water while cleaning their windows. (See Box 3–1, "Trouble in Foley Square.")

When a dispute arises, Bill and Ann will need to reach a resolution. Hopefully, it can be done without resort to litigation, but that may not be possible. In order for them to be in the best position to avoid conflicts and to understand what to do when conflicts arise, Bill and Ann need to understand dispute resolution—both litigation and its alternatives.

Very few complaints that are brought to an attorney are actually filed with a court, and few cases that are filed with a court are actually brought to trial. (See Box 3–2, "1991—U.S. District Courts Cases Filed versus Cases Tried," on page 50.) In fact, Bill and Ann will be relieved to learn that most legal disputes between private individuals are resolved or settled without any intervention by a court at all.

However, for those cases that do require court intervention, the legal system is designed to ensure two things: fairness and impartiality. That is, the rules that govern the legal system are for the benefit of both parties, and the requirement that the system be impartial ensures that neither side has any built-in advantage over the other. Of course, we know that such does not always appear to be the case, but it represents the design and intent of the structure. In Chapters 1 and 2 you were introduced to an overview of different aspects of law. This chapter addresses some of those issues in more depth.

3–1   LAW IN THE REAL WORLD

Trouble in Foley Square

Many lament that litigation in America, particularly in the historic federal court at Foley Square in Manhattan, is very different today from what it was in the 1950s. What has brought about this change in the years since I was a boy, aspiring to practice here? To begin with, the sheer numbers of lawyers now admitted to practice in the Manhattan federal court have overwhelmed the powerful sense of collegiality and pride that obtained in the halcyon days of the '50s.

In 1958, there were about 600 lawyers admitted to our rolls. Today, we admit 3,000 per year. At that annual rate, more than 50,000 lawyers will be authorized to practice before the court just after the turn of the century.

Such crowding has caused a loss of focus and discipline among lawyers and has led to a regrettable reduction of quality in their legal papers, arguments, and professional manners.

Litigants now routinely challenge the hiring, admission, suspension, firing, tenure, retirement, pension, discipline, and promotion decisions—or nondecisions—of businesses, unions, corporations, universities, clubs, government agencies, cities, towns, the armed forces, and myriad other organizations at every level of life in the nation, on the grounds of race, age, sex, gender preference, disability, or national origin. These cases, rarely settled, are characterized by high levels of acrimony and subjective claims of victimization; they are immensely time-consuming; and [they] are controlled by legal standards that, lacking sufficient precision, are overgeneralized and of marginal use.

The economics of going to court chagrin and alarm the nation's business community, whose competitiveness in global markets is damaged by a degree of litigiousness in America that is simply unheard-of in the rest of the world.

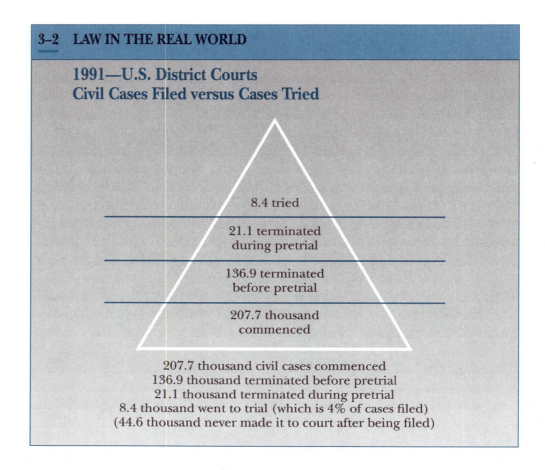

3–2 LAW IN THE REAL WORLD

**1991—U.S. District Courts
Civil Cases Filed versus Cases Tried**

8.4 tried

21.1 terminated
during pretrial

136.9 terminated
before pretrial

207.7 thousand
commenced

207.7 thousand civil cases commenced
136.9 thousand terminated before pretrial
21.1 thousand terminated during pretrial
8.4 thousand went to trial (which is 4% of cases filed)
(44.6 thousand never made it to court after being filed)

STRUCTURE OF THE COURT SYSTEM

OVERVIEW

Article III, Section 1, of the U.S. Constitution vests the judicial power of the United States in "one supreme Court, and in such inferior Courts as the Congress may . . . establish." State constitutions establish and grant power to state courts. (See Box 3–3, "The Roles of the Courts.")

Both the federal and the state court systems are hierarchical. At the lowest level are the trial courts, which have fact-finding as their primary function. At the trial court level, a jury generally hears the ev-

3–3 **BLACK LETTER LAW**

The Roles of the Courts

Trial Court

- The trial court hears witnesses and views evidence.
- The trial court judge decides issues of law; the jury decides questions of fact. (When there is no jury, the trial court judge decides both the questions of law and the questions of fact.)

Intermediate Court of Appeals

- The intermediate court of appeals reviews the written record and exhibits from the trial court.
- When an issue raises a question of law, the intermediate court of appeals may substitute its judgment for the judgment of the trial court judge; when an issue raises a question of fact, the appellate court must defer to the decision of the finder of fact (the jury or, if there was no jury, the trial judge).

Supreme, or Highest, Court

- Like the intermediate court of appeals, the supreme court reviews the written record and exhibits from the trial court.
- Like the intermediate court of appeals, it has broad powers to review questions of law: it determines whether the trial court and intermediate court of appeals applied the right law correctly. Its power to review factual issues is, however, very limited. Like the intermediate court of appeals, it can determine only whether there is sufficient evidence to support the decision of the jury or, if there was no jury, the decision of the trial court judge.

idence (though a judge may sit without a jury if none is requested or allowed, as we shall discuss later), and the court then enters a **judgment**.

At the next level are the intermediate courts of appeal, that is, courts between trial court and the supreme court. These courts hear the majority of **appeals** to decide whether the trial court applied the correct law and whether there was sufficient evidence to support the

judgment
judge's formal determination of a controversy, which details the outcome, how outcome was arrived at, and its consequences

appeal
taking a case that has been decided by a court to the next-highest level for a review of the decision

legal brief
written statement of
facts and law
supporting one side
of a case and
presented to a court

oral argument
verbal presentation
by attorneys in court
aimed at persuading
a judge of their view

federal district court
court established by
federal law

original jurisdiction
jurisdiction of an
appellate court to try
a case

specialized courts
courts created for
handling specific
types of cases,
e.g., United States
Tax Court

circuit
jurisdictional area of
a court

jurisdiction
authority of a court
over parties and
subject matter to
hear and determine
legal disputes

verdict. Unlike trial courts, the intermediate courts do not conduct trials. There are no witnesses, and decisions are based solely on the record below and the written **legal briefs** and **oral arguments** of the attorneys.

At the highest level are the state supreme courts and the Supreme Court of the United States. The primary function of the supreme courts is to make final interpretations of law that end up being the final authority on legal interpretation. The supreme courts hear only cases that involve issues of great public importance or cases in which different court divisions have applied conflicting laws. Like the intermediate courts, they do not hear evidence, but rely on the record as well as attorneys' written legal briefs and oral arguments.

FEDERAL COURTS

Unlike the state courts, which differ from state to state, the federal court system is uniform throughout the country, so we begin with that system. In the federal court system, a case is heard initially in a **federal district court**, which is the primary trial court in the federal system. Federal district courts have **original jurisdiction** over most federal questions and have the power to review the decisions of some administrative agencies. Each state has at least one district court, and some states have several. Cases are tried before a single judge. Cases that are not heard in the district courts are heard in one of several **specialized courts**, such as the United States Tax Court or the United States Court of Claims.

Appeals from the decisions of the district courts are heard by the *United States Court of Appeals*. The jurisdictional area of a Court of Appeals is called a **circuit**. There are currently 13 circuits: 11 numbered circuits, the District of Columbia Circuit, and the Court of Appeals for the Federal Circuit. (See Box 3–4, "Diagram of Federal Circuit Court System.")

The Court of Appeals for the Federal Circuit, created in 1982, has **jurisdiction** for both claims against the federal government and for patent matters. It also hears appeals from decisions of the U.S. Trademark Patent Office and the International Trade Commission, as well as from the Court of International Trade and the United States Claims Court (mainly concerning tax matters). A three-judge panel normally hears cases in the Courts of Appeals. (See Box 3–5, "The Federal Court System," on page 54.)

3–4   LEGAL EXCERPTS

Diagram of Federal Circuit Court System

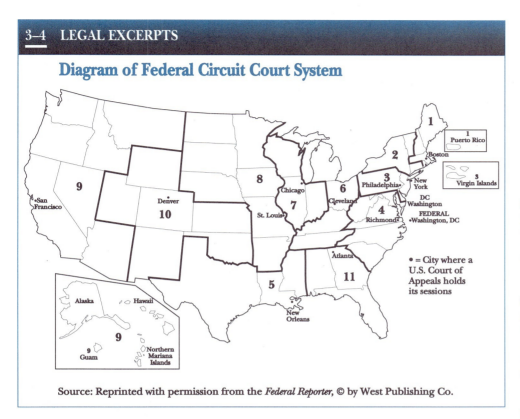

Source: Reprinted with permission from the *Federal Reporter,* © by West Publishing Co.

The highest federal court is the *United States Supreme Court,* and it is the final **appellate court**. Each case that comes before the Supreme Court is heard by all nine justices. Each year the Supreme Court receives more than 5,000 requests for review (**writs of certiorari**). Of the approximately 160 cases it actually hears, about two-thirds are appeals from the United States Court of Appeals, and about one-third from state courts. (See Box 3–6, "Too Few Judges, Too Many Cases.")

Federal Subject Matter Jurisdiction

Jurisdiction of federal courts exists in **federal question** cases and in cases with **diversity of citizenship** of the parties. Whenever a case is based on a federal law, a federal treaty, or the federal Constitution, it raises a so-called federal question. Included also in this group are

appellate court
courts above the trial level that hear cases on review from lower courts

writ of certiorari
order directing a lower court to send the record of a case to an appellate court for review

federal question jurisdiction
judicial power of the United States extending to cases arising under the Constitution, the laws of the United States, and treaties

diversity of citizenship jurisdiction
jurisdiction of federal courts based on controversy between citizens of different states and amount involved

3–5 CONCEPT SUMMARY	
The Federal Court System	
Court of Final Appeals	United States Supreme Court
Courts of Intermediate Appeals	United States Court of Appeals United States Court of Appeals for the Federal Circuit
Courts of Original Jurisdiction	U.S. Tax Court U.S. District Courts U.S. Court of International Trade U.S. Claims Court

There are 92 district courts in the 50 states. There are districts courts also in Washington, D.C., Puerto Rico, the Virgin Islands, the Canal Zone, and Guam.

cases in which the Supreme Court has original jurisdiction or in which federal law provides for the exclusive jurisdiction of federal courts—for example, cases involving bankruptcy, patent and copyright law, federal criminal law, maritime claims, and claims arising under the Securities Exchange Act.

Federal courts also have jurisdiction in all matters, other than divorce, in which the parties are citizens of different states or of foreign countries and the amount in controversy is at least $50,000 (diversity jurisdiction), even though the matter is a state rather than a federal matter. Bill and Ann may prefer to go to federal rather than state court with a state-based claim because they may wish to have, say, a jury that is not drawn from such a localized area or a jury that may be less likely to shrink from granting large sums of money if liability is found. There may also be a larger caseload in the local courts— causing a longer waiting period—or the federal court's procedures may simply be more appealing to the litigant.

In a federal question case, a federal court decides according to federal law. In a diversity of citizenship case, it applies the law of the state where it sits. In federal question cases, it is bound by the law of the appellate federal courts. In diversity of citizenship cases, it is bound by the legislation and case law of the highest court of that state.

3–6 LAW IN THE REAL WORLD

Too Few Judges, Too Many Cases

The U.S. federal court system is too small for the job [before it], [for it has] too few judges and too many cases. A proposal, made by Judge Stephen Reinhardt of the Ninth Circuit Court of Appeals, that Congress double the size of the court of appeals, points out that many cases simply do not get the full attention that they deserve, largely because of the procedural shortcuts necessary to handle the current caseload. Justice Reinhardt points out that the cost of operating the judicial system is only three-tenths of 1% [0.003%] of the federal budget. By comparison, one Stealth bomber costs almost as much, and the entire judicial system could operate for 15 years on the cost of a single space station.

Source: "Too Few Judge, Too Many Cases." Justice Stephen Reinhardt, *ABA Journal*, ©1993, American Bar Association. Reprinted by permission of the *ABA Journal*.

Responding to Justice Reinhardt is Justice Gerald Tjoflat, chief judge of the Eleventh Circuit Court of Appeals, who titles his article "More Judges, Less Justice":

Bigger is not always better. The problem for most circuits is not that they have too few judges, but that they have too many. As the number of judges in a circuit grows, the productivity of individual judges goes down; the clarity and stability of the circuit's law suffer; and the legal environment [becomes] inhospitable to individual rights.

Source: "More Judges, Less Justice," Justice Gerald Tjoflat, *ABA Journal*, ©1993, American Bar Association. Reprinted by permission of the *ABA Journal*.

Limitations of Federal Courts

case, or controversy
two expressions used interchangeably to describe situations sufficiently defined as to be within the power of the court to decide

ripeness
on the facts and procedurally, the case's realness and readiness for determination by the court

standing
qualification to sue or defend because of having a personal stake in the outcome of a case

political questions
issues that do not present a case or controversy, but rather a dispute between two branches of government or within a single branch of government

Federal jurisdiction is limited by several requirements. First, every case must present a **case or controversy**. Second, the case must be **ripe** for decision. Third, a plaintiff must have **standing** to sue, that is, the plaintiff must be directly concerned by the case.

A case or controversy requirement means that every case must represent an actual and not a hypothetical issue. Courts do not issue advisory opinions. Bill and Ann cannot, therefore, challenge a law by going to court and having the court determine the validity of the law without Ann and Bill's first violating the law.

For instance, suppose a new regulation required Ann and Bill to hire only licensed window washers, and they believe the regulation is unfair and costs them undue expenses. In order to challenge the law, Bill and Ann would actually need to hire unlicensed window washers, be given a citation for violating the regulation, have an administrative hearing, and eventually go to court. They could not, instead, simply go to the court and ask what would happen if they hired unlicensed window washers. The issues of ripeness and standing are related. If an issue is not ripe or a plaintiff does not have standing, then the issue is an abstract question, and the case does not provide the necessary case or controversy to allow the court to hear it.

In addition, federal courts do not consider **political questions**. The definition of what constitutes a political question changes with time and circumstance. For example, questions related to the inner workings of the legislature and the executive branches, once deemed political questions, have been subject to judicial review.

For example, in *Powell v. McCormack*, 395 U.S. 486 (1969), members of the House of Representatives refused to seat Adam Clayton Powell, a black legislator who had been elected to the House of Representatives 90th Congress. Essentially, the argument advanced by the defendants was that whether a member is seated or not is solely within the discretion of the House and is not subject to review by the judiciary, because it represents a political question. The court disagreed, stating that the qualifications are stated in the Constitution, the interpretation of the Constitution was a judicial function, and therefore the case was subject to the Court's review. Absent a showing by the House that he was not constitutionally qualified, Powell had to be seated.

3–7   CONCEPT SUMMARY

The State Court System

State Supreme Court
Court of final resort. Some states call it the Court of Appeals, Supreme Court, or Supreme Court of Appeals.

Intermediate Appellate Courts
Currently 37 of the 50 states have intermediate appellate courts, which constitute an intermediate appellate tribunal between the trial court and the court of final resort. A majority of cases are decided finally by these appellate courts. Other states have appeals to the state supreme court as a matter of right.

Superior Courts
Highest trial court with general jurisdiction. Some states call it the Circuit Court, District Court of Common Pleas, or, in New York State, the Supreme Court. May have specialized branches like probate court and family court.

County Court of Limited Jurisdiction
These courts, sometimes called Common Pleas or District Courts, have limited jurisdiction in both civil and criminal cases.

Municipal Court
In some cities, it is customary to have less important cases tried by both civil and criminal municipal magistrates.

STATE COURTS

All of the states have a judicial hierarchy that consists of two or more levels of courts (see Box 3–7, "The State Court System"). The lowest levels consist of **courts of limited jurisdiction**, such as municipal, city, county, traffic, and small claims courts. They exist to relieve the burden of the courts of general jurisdiction (see Box 3–8, "Record State Caseloads in 1990").

court of limited jurisdiction
court limited by statute in one or more respects as to what types of cases it may handle

3–8   LAW IN THE REAL WORLD

Record State Caseloads in 1990

State court caseloads reached an all-time high in 1990 when more than 100 million were filed. The case breakdown is 18.4 million civil, 13 million criminal, 1.5 million juvenile, 67.5 million traffic or other ordinance violations, and 238,000 appellate. By way of comparison, the number of criminal and civil filings in state courts—31.4 million—is more than 100 times greater than the number of federal court filings, which was 280,000 in 1990. Since 1984, criminal caseloads have increased 33%, civil caseloads by 30%, juvenile caseloads by 28%, and traffic by 12%. In contrast, the national population has increased by only 5% during the same time period.

Source: "Record State Caseloads in 1990," Henry J. Reske, August 1992, *ABA Journal.* ©1992, American Bar Association. Reprinted by permission of the *ABA Journal.*

court of general jurisdiction
court without limit as concerns the amount in controversy, the nature of the penalty it may adjudge, or the type of case it may consider within a broad jurisdictional area

At the next level are **courts of general jurisdiction**. These courts have the power to review decisions of the courts of limited jurisdiction and of original jurisdiction over claims arising under state law. Designation of these courts is often confusing, for it varies from state to state. Usually they are called district courts, circuit courts, superior courts, courts of common pleas, or, in New York State, the supreme court. Some states have specialized courts—on the same level as courts of general jurisdiction—that are used to handle specialized areas of the law. There are, for example, family and domestic relations courts, probate courts, and surrogate courts.

About one-half of the states have intermediate courts. These courts hear appeals as of right from the state courts of general jurisdiction, and the bulk of their caseload consists of criminal appeals. Because of their heavy workload, many are divided into specific divisions.

Final appellate jurisdiction, whether states have two or three levels, is the state supreme court. Such courts review the decisions of the state trial courts and the courts of appeal, and they are the final arbiters of the state's constitutional, statutory, and common law. (See Box 3–9, "Budget Cuts and Courts.")

State courts possess general jurisdiction to hear most matters except when exclusive federal jurisdiction is in effect. That is, their jurisdiction extends to all persons and to all subject matters. (See Box 3–10, "Subject Matter Jurisdiction of the Federal and State Courts," on page 61.)

Small Claims Court

One of the avenues open to resolve certain disputes is small claims court. These courts are created by state law and may also be called municipal courts, justice of the peace courts, or county courts. Their purpose is to allow a party to sue a defendant with less of the formality of regular court and with less cost. The universal limitation on small claims court is that the amount one can seek in damages is limited, although not all jurisdictions have the same limitations. Generally, the range is between $200 (e.g., Georgia) and $5,000 (e.g., Nevada, Tennessee, and Virginia).

The basic approach to small claims court allows a party to go to the local courthouse, file a complaint with the clerk for a nominal fee, have the defendant served with a notice of the complaint, get a court date, attend the hearing, and have a judgment rendered by the judge or other presiding party. All of this takes place without the assistance of a lawyer and without anything other than a layperson's knowledge of the court system and the rules of procedure. No lawyers are necessary, and in some instances, no lawyers are permitted to attend. The particulars of each state's procedures are available from the clerk of the court in that jurisdiction.

For example, some states require the parties to attend without a lawyer, some states require certain documentation to be attached to the complaint, and some states require that the defendant respond to the plaintiff's complaint in writing. Other states simply allow defendants to appear on the court date and present their side of the case, some states require that service to the defendant be made by registered mail, and still others allow a nonprofessional server (such as a friend who is willing) to serve the defendant with notice of the complaint. Although these particular procedures vary from state to state, the substance of small claims courts is consistent throughout the 50 states.

3-9 LAW IN THE REAL WORLD

Budget Cuts and Courts

The following two examples illustrate how the justice system is not immune from the state budget shortages. Until recently, Mississippi had the most underfunded state court system in the U.S. Judges could not even afford clerks and secretaries. It had the poorest justice system in the nation. There was no court of appeals, no administrative office of the courts, and no money to provide secretaries or law clerks for trial judges. With annual salaries of $67,000, trial judges were the worst paid in the nation.

Due to the recent influx of tax revenues from casino gambling and the lobbying efforts of Mississippi Bar Association President Grady Tollison, however, the state's courts will begin receiving dramatic new funds. Since a chain of gambling operations opened in 1992, about $38 million in additional tax revenues has poured into state coffers. A chunk of the money will go to the courts. The changes are dramatic. A five-member state court of appeals will be created with $1.1 million to hear cases assigned to it by the Supreme Court. Currently, cases are appealed directly to the Supreme Court, resulting in three to five years from appeal to decision. An administrative office will open, and trial judges' salaries will increase from $67,000 to $82,000, with an additional $20,000 to pay support staff.

Source: "Mississippi Changing," by Mark Curriden, September 1993, *ABA Journal*, ©1993. American Bar Association. Reprinted by permission of the *ABA Journal*.

Mississippi is not the only state with budget shortages which affect the judicial system. At least four state court systems have asked or required judges to take time off without pay or to give up paid leave in budget cut efforts. In 1992, justices in California were asked to take a few days of unpaid furlough; in Maryland, five days of leave time was deducted from [each of] the state's judges; in Rhode Island, all state employees, including judges, were required to take three days of furlough; and in Maine, courts were closed two days in May and for more than a week in July to reduce the costs of the state budgets.

Source: "Unpaid Leave for Judges," by Don J. DeBenedictis, April 1992, ©1992. American Bar Association. Reprinted by permission of the *ABA Journal*.

3–10   CONCEPT SUMMARY

Subject Matter Jurisdiction of the Federal and State Courts

Subject Matter Jurisdiction of the Federal Courts
- Cases arising under the Constitution
- Cases arising under a treaty
- Cases arising under federal statutes
- Cases in which the United States is itself a party
- Cases involving state law if the dispute is between citizens of different states or between a state and a citizen of a different state

Subject Matter Jurisdiction of the State Courts
State courts generally have jurisdiction over anything the Constitution or statutes permit. State jurisdiction includes:
- Cases arising under the U.S. Constitution and certain federal statutes
- Cases arising under a state's own constitution, statutes, or common law

LITIGATION AS A MEANS OF DISPUTE RESOLUTION

A CIVIL CASE

The procedural rules governing how a civil or criminal case is to be brought vary from state to state. They are known as procedural rules, and there are rules for both civil procedure and criminal procedure. For federal courts, there are also federal rules of civil and criminal procedure, which are uniform for all federal courts. Although the procedures can vary from state to state, most states have some general similarities that can be discussed. (See Box 3–11, "Overview of Civil Litigation from Filing to Trial.")

Aside from the actual event causing the dispute, a civil case usually begins when a client contacts a lawyer about some matter that needs resolution. That matter may be a pending lawsuit, or the client may wish to begin a lawsuit of his or her own. If the lawyer decides to take the case, a **retainer** is usually signed by the client, which formally retains the services of the lawyer on behalf of the client. In some cases, a **contingency fee arrangement** may be made. A contingency fee is

retainer
amount paid to an attorney to take a case

contingency fee arrangement
arrangement allowing plaintiff to pay attorney a certain percentage of judgment awarded if plaintiff wins suit

generally arrived at by a formula in which the amount is unspecified because it is a percentage of the award, whether by settlement or verdict. For example, in a personal injury case, a contingency fee might be one-third of the award if no lawsuit is necessary; it might be 40% if a lawsuit is necessary. The more difficult it is to establish liability, the higher the contingency fee.

The attorney then investigates the matter and, if possible, enters into negotiations to settle. If a settlement can be reached at this point, then the matter is ended. If not, then the attorney will begin to file formal documents with the court, and if the case is pursued through means of a trial, litigation begins.

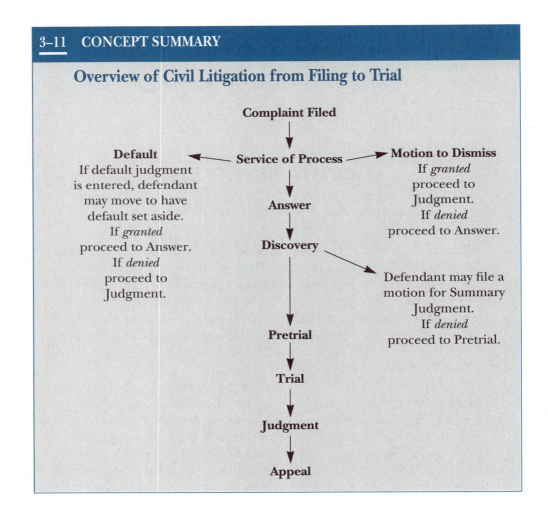

3–11   CONCEPT SUMMARY

Overview of Civil Litigation from Filing to Trial

Complaint Filed

Default ◄— **Service of Process** —► **Motion to Dismiss**

Default
If default judgment is entered, defendant may move to have default set aside. If *granted* proceed to Answer. If *denied* proceed to Judgment.

Answer

Motion to Dismiss
If *granted* proceed to Judgment. If *denied* proceed to Answer.

Discovery

Defendant may file a motion for Summary Judgment. If *denied* proceed to Pretrial.

Pretrial

Trial

Judgment

Appeal

PURSUING A CASE THROUGH TRIAL

Filing the Pleadings

Pleadings consist of all the documents filed by both parties prior to the pretrial phase of litigation. Usually, the **pleadings** consist of a complaint, summons, answer, reply, and motions.

A **complaint** is the document the plaintiff files stating the court's jurisdiction to hear the case, the facts being alleged, and, usually, the relief being sought. It names the party or parties being sued. Filing the lawsuit establishes the date the case officially begins, and all deadlines in the case stem from that date.

As discussed in Chapter 1, the summons is the notice the court sends to the party being sued. It notifies the party that a complaint has been filed, and it gives the party a certain amount of time to respond with an answer. Service of process (delivery of the summons and complaint) officially notifies the defendant of the lawsuit and gives the court personal jurisdiction over the defendant, which is necessary to impose judgment.

The **answer** is the defendant's response to the complaint. The answer responds specifically to each allegation and either denies or affirms it. The defendant may, along with the answer, file a counterclaim, cross-claim, or affirmative defense.

A **counterclaim** is a claim asserted by the defendant against the plaintiff. It is a suit within a suit. In a counterclaim, the defendant feels there may be harm done by the plaintiff that the plaintiff should be liable for, even though the plaintiff is the one who is suing the defendant. For instance, if Bill and Ann are sued by a plaintiff cleaning product manufacturer for their failure to pay for cleaning products delivered, Bill and Ann may, in turn, countersue the manufacturer for failure of the product to clean as represented.

When two or more persons are sued and made defendants in an action and one of the defendants believes another defendant should bear the liability, the first defendant can file a **cross-claim** against the second. For example, Bill and Ann are sued, along with their cleaning product manufacturer, for harm done to antique floors they clean. Bill and Ann may file a cross-claim against the manufacturer if they believe that any damages owed to the floor's owner were caused by the cleaning product manufacturer rather than their negligence.

In response to plaintiff's complaint, defendants may allege in their complaint an **affirmative defense**. An affirmative defense says

pleadings
in civil cases, litigants' written statements of their claims and responses in forms prescribed by a court

complaint
initial pleading alleging a violation of civil law

answer
defendant's response to plaintiff's complaint

counterclaim
lawsuit filed against the opposing party

cross-claim
lawsuit brought by one defendant against another defendant

affirmative defense
defense that may defeat the original claim, such as self-defense or assumption of the risk

that even if all of the allegations are true, the defendant has a defense to the claim and should prevail. Affirmative defenses are defined by substantive law. For example, a civil action for battery can be defeated by affirmation of self-defense; a negligence action can be defeated by proving assumption of the risk (where it still exists). These are all concepts you will learn in Chapter 5.

During this period, as with pretrial and trial, either party may motion the court. A **motion** is a request that the court grant relief favorable to the party who filed the motion, called the **moving party**. If a motion is filed, the court notifies the nonmoving party and grants each side a chance to be heard on the issue.

One such often used motion is the motion to dismiss. A motion to dismiss is generally granted when the court finds that the moving party's complaint is insufficient to state a claim upon which relief may be granted. In such a case, the moving party is entitled to dismissal as a matter of law. The purpose of motions to dismiss is to promote the expeditious resolution of disputes and to curb frivolous litigation. Once the motion to dismiss has been granted, the case is completed (unless the dismissal is appealed).

If the defendant raises new allegations in an answer, the plaintiff may file a reply. A **reply** admits or denies the new facts. Those denials, admissions, and motions filed during the pleadings form the basis, or outline, of the issues to be litigated. Once either party admits an issue, that issue will not be litigated. Only disputed facts form the basis of a suit. (See Box 3–12, "Sample Complaint for Specific Performance.")

Pretrial

Pretrial is the period before trial but after the pleadings, in which the parties use discovery procedures to investigate their case. The rules of **discovery** attempt to remove trial by ambush by eliminating any surprises in the evidence. Discovery makes it possible for both sides of a lawsuit to be informed about witnesses and evidence that will be presented. Discovery also helps reveal whether a defense exists that may either lead to dismissal of the case, thereby saving time and expense, or may lead to early settlement. Discovery can also lead to information that can strengthen a case. There are several discovery tools available.

A **deposition** is a statement made by a witness under oath outside of court while being questioned (or examined) by both parties to the litigation. Depositions are taken in order to probe a witness's memory

motion
formal request by an attorney that a court decide a matter

moving party
the party who makes a motion to the court

reply
plaintiff's response to defendant's answer

pretrial
time period between filing of pleadings and trial, during which discovery is completed

discovery
learning in advance of trial an adversary's position on issues raised in the pleadings

deposition
sworn testimony of witness or party prior to trial, given before court reporter, for later use in court

3–12   LEGAL EXCERPTS

Sample Complaint for Specific Performance

[Title of Court and Cause]

1. [Allegation of jurisdiction, which tells the judge the case is in the right court.]
2. On or about [date], plaintiffs Bill Jones and Ann Smith and defendant Ace Properties Inc. entered into an agreement in writing, a copy of which is hereto annexed as Exhibit A.
3. In accord with the provisions of that agreement plaintiffs Jones and Smith tendered to defendant Ace Properties Inc. the purchase price and requested a conveyance of the land, but defendant refused to accept the tender and refused to make the conveyance.
4. Plaintiffs Jones and Smith now offer to pay the purchase price.

Wherefore plaintiffs demand (1) that the defendant be required specifically to perform said agreement, (2) damages in the sum of one thousand dollars, and (3) that if specific performance is not granted, plaintiffs have judgment against defendant in the amount of [_____] dollars.

Attorney for Plaintiff

Source: Reprinted with permission from *West's Federal Forms*, Robt. Meisenholder, Vol. 2B, Section 1713-2200 (1983). ©West Publishing Company.

about facts known to the witness while memory is still fresh. Such depositions can be used by a witness to refresh memory at trial, and discrepancies between a witness's deposition testimony and trial testimony can be used to discredit or impeach a witness.

A **request for production of documents**, tangible items, or entry to property for inspection is a discovery tool whereby documents and other relevant evidence in the possession of one party may be freely examined by the other party.

request for production of documents discovery tool whereby relevant evidence is produced for examination by the opposing party

interrogatories
written questions about the case sent to opposing party or witness for answers and for return to sending attorney

voir dire
questioning of prospective jurors by lawyers to determine who will sit on jury

challenges
objections to prospective jurors sitting on jury

peremptory strikes
objections to prospective jurors made without explanation; usually limited to criminal cases

challenge for cause
prospective juror does not meet statutory qualifications or is personally unfit for jury service

Interrogatories are written questions submitted to an opposing party, and, like depositions, the answers must be sworn to under oath.

Upon motion, an opposing party can request that a party submit to a medical examination by a doctor chosen by the opposing party. Such examinations can be physical or psychological. (See Box 3–13, "Sample Plaintiff's Interrogatory for Gender Discrimination.")

Jury or Non-Jury

Jury selection, also called **voir dire** (to speak the truth), is the process by which the triers of fact are chosen. The purpose of the process is to seat a fair and impartial jury that will listen to the case with an open mind and determine the facts accordingly.

If a party is entitled to a trial by jury, generally that right can be waived by the parties. If they so waive, then the trial judge not only decides the law but also is the trier of fact for the case.

If a jury is not waived, then jury selection proceeds. **Challenges** to a juror can be made for cause or by using **peremptory strikes**. A **challenge for cause** is made when, as a matter of law, a juror cannot sit on the jury because that juror cannot be fair and impartial. For example, a juror may be stricken for cause by being related to or having close acquaintance with a person who is an integral part of the trial, such as a witness, the judge, or an attorney.

A peremptory strike is generally used when the potential juror does not fit the profile of jurors who the attorney feels would most benefit the client. For example, in a trial involving a landlord/tenant dispute, the attorney for the landlord would want to strike any tenants on the jury who would possibly be sympathetic to the tenant's case. An attorney could remove such jurors by using a peremptory strike.

Unlike challenges for cause, peremptory strikes are limited in number. Also unlike challenges for cause, peremptory strikes can be used for any reason, subject to constitutional limitations. No reason has to be disclosed when using a peremptory strike, unless it is subject to a *Batson* challenge as outlined below.

In addition, the Supreme Court recently ruled that *Batson* applies to gender-based challenges, when it ruled in *J.E.B. v. Alabama*, 114 S.Ct. 1419 (1994), a case in which the state used 9 of its 10 peremptory challenges to remove male jurors in a paternity and child support trial. What qualifies for race-based classifications? For example, is it a racial classification when a black juror is excluded because of living in a high-crime area and is suspected of being predisposed against the

3–13   LEGAL EXCERPTS

Sample Plaintiff's Interrogatory for Gender Discrimination

[Names of court and parties, description of action, introduction, and usual formal parts omitted.]

General Employment

1. When did X begin hiring production employees for its Truck Plant?

2. What recruitment sources were utilized to secure these employees?

3. What instructions were given by X to recruitment sources concerning the type of employee desired for production work at the _____ Truck Plant?

Job Requirements

4. Does X have any height or weight requirements in effect at any of its other plants or facilities?

5. Does Motor Company contend that the _____-pound weight requirement is significantly related to successful job performance for any job classifications at the _____ Truck Plant?

Female Employment

6. How many females have applied for production work at the _____ Truck Plant since hiring began?

7. List the name, address, and telephone number, if available, of all females who have applied for such production work, and state the reason each was denied employment. [Date, signature, certificate of mailing, or form of admission of receipt of copy omitted.]

police? Is a juror who is a member of the National Association for the Advancement of Colored People (NAACP) impermissibly excluded on the basis of race if the trial is politically based?

State courts are not immune from putting flesh on the *Batson* skeleton. The Minnesota Supreme Court has refused to extend *Batson v. Kentucky* to strikes exercised on the basis of religion in *Minnesota v. Davis*. (See Box 3–14, "*Batson* and the Straight-Face Test.")

BATSON V. KENTUCKY
476 US 79 (1986)

Batson, an African-American, was convicted of burglary and receipt of stolen goods by an all-white jury. During the voir dire, the judge excused several jurors for cause. The prosecutor struck the remaining four African-Americans by using his peremptory strikes. Batson moved to discharge the jury, claiming that the prosecutor's removal of the African-Americans violated his rights to a jury drawn from a cross section of the community under the Sixth and Fourteenth Amendments and that the exclusion violated his Equal Protection rights under the Fourteenth Amendment. The trial judge ruled that the prosecutor could use his peremptories to strike anyone he liked, thereby denying the defendant's motion by reasoning that the fair cross section referred to the panel as a whole and not to the specific jurors chosen from that panel. On appeal, the Kentucky Supreme Court affirmed Batson's conviction, and Batson appealed to the U.S. Supreme Court, which reversed.

Powell, J.: More than a century ago, the Court decided that the state denies a black defendant equal protection of the laws when it puts him on trial before a jury from which members of his race have been purposefully excluded. That decision laid the foundation for the court's unceasing efforts to eradicate racial discrimination in the procedures used to select the venire from which individual jurors are drawn.

A defendant has no right to a "**petit jury** composed in whole or in part of persons of his own race." But the defendant does have a right to be tried by a jury whose members are selected pursuant to nondis-criminatory criteria.

The harm from discriminatory jury selection extends beyond that inflicted on the defendant and the excluded juror to touch the entire community. Selection procedures that purposefully exclude black persons from juries undermine public confidence in the fairness of our system of justice.

Accordingly, the component of the jury selection at issue here—the state's privilege to strike individual jurors through peremptory challenges—is subject to the commands of the Equal Protection Clause. Although a prosecutor ordinarily is entitled to exercise peremptory challenges "for any reason at all, so long as that reason is related to a view concerning the outcome" of the case to be tried, the Equal Protection Clause forbids a prosecutor to challenge potential jurors solely on account of their race or on the assumption that black jurors as a group will be unable to impartially consider the state's case against a black defendant.

In order to make a **prima facie case**, the defendant must show that he is a member of a cognizable racial group, that the prosecutor has exercised peremptory challenges to remove from the venire members of the defendant's race, and that facts and other relevant circumstances raise an inference that the prosecutor used that practice to exclude [certain members of] the venire from the petit jury on account of their race. Once the defendant makes a prima facie showing, the burden shifts to the state to come forward with a neutral explanation for challenging black jurors. The prosecutor may not rebut the defendant's prima facie case of discrimination by stating merely that he challenged jurors of the defendant's race on the assumption—or his intuitive judgment—that they would be partial to the defendant because of their shared race, nor may the prosecutor rebut the defendant's case merely by denying that he had a discriminatory motive or "[affirming] [this] good faith in making the individual selections."

The standard we adopt under the federal Constitution is designed to ensure that the state does not use peremptory challenges to strike any black juror because of his race. We have no reason to believe that prosecutors will not fulfill their duty to exercise their challenges only for legitimate purpose. REVERSED

petit jury
the jury that hears a case in court

prima facie case
proof of evidence of each element in a cause of action

continued on next page

Case Questions

1. In his concurring opinion, Justice Marshall argues that the use of peremptory challenges should be discontinued altogether in order to further eliminate the individual bias of the prosecutor. In light of the fact that *Batson* has been extended to apply both to prosecutors and defense attorneys, is this suggestion legitimate? Discuss.

2. Aren't all groups "cognizable"? Where do you see *Batson* ending?

3. In the dissent to *Batson*, Justice Rehnquist and Chief Justice Burger argue that rather than neutralizing the jury selection, *Batson* will make everyone more race conscious by requiring detailed explanations from potential jurors on their race and national origin, so that judges can keep a record of group compositions that may be challenged. Is this overburdening the court, or does it ensure that no groups are discriminated against based on stereotypes? Explain.

opening statement
statements by lawyers at beginning of trial outlining case and what they expect evidence to prove

direct examination
first examination of one's own witness at trial

cross-examination
examination of a witness by the opposing side

closing argument
argument made by lawyers at close of the evidence urging judge or jury to reach the decision each side desires

Trial

After the jury is sworn in, the trial begins. A trial consists of several parts, all interrelated. First, the lawyers have the opportunity to make an **opening statement**. Opening statements are narratives that present each side's theory of the case to the jury. After both sides have given their opening statement (though the defendant may reserve his or her opening statement until presentation of the defendant's case), the plaintiff presents the plaintiff's side of the case by calling witnesses and introducing evidence into the trial. When a plaintiff's witness testifies for the plaintiff, the questions and answers are called **direct examination**. After such direct examination, the witness is tendered to the defense, and the questions and answers then given are called **cross-examination**. Rebuttal testimony may be provided on redirect examination or recross-examination. After all the witnesses have testified and the evidence has been admitted, the defense presents its side of the case, using the same format and procedure as for the plaintiff.

Once all the evidence has been presented, both sides (generally plaintiff first) have the opportunity to present to the jurors their **closing argument**, which is a summary of the evidence and the law. It

3–14   LAW IN THE REAL WORLD

Batson and the Straight-Face Test

In his concurrence to *Batson v. Kentucky*, Justice Byron White predicted that "much litigation would be necessary to spell out the contours" of the opinion's equal protection pronouncements. Since then, post-*Batson* litigation has become a thriving cottage industry. The *Batson* decision made it unconstitutional to use peremptory challenges to reject jurors on the basis of race. Clarifying *Batson* has become almost an annual event for the Court, which in 1991 alone handed down three such decisions. This doesn't include the lower courts, which are left with interpreting *Batson* challenges on bases other than race.

The Supreme Court has held that *Batson* challenges can apply to criminal defendants even if they are not members of the excluded race (*Powers v. Ohio*, 111 S.Ct. 1364 [1991]; [that they] protect Hispanics and other "cognizable" groups (*Hernandez v. New York* (111 S.Ct. 1859 [1991]); that *Batson* challenges can be used against criminal defendants as well as by them (*Georgia v. McCollum* (112 S.Ct. 2348 [1992]); and that *Batson* applies to civil cases (*Edmonson v. Leesville Concrete Co.*, 111 S.Ct. 2077 [1991]).

Source: *Batson* and the Straight-Face Test," by Stephanie B. Goldberg, August 1992, ©1992. American Bar Association. Reprinted by permission of the *ABA Journal*.

is during the closing argument that the lawyers will try to persuade jurors that the evidence admitted during the trial and the law given to them by the judge during the jury instructions will require them to reach a verdict for their respective client.

In most civil cases the burden of proof required is **preponderance of the evidence**. This means that the jury feels the evidence shows that the defendant more likely than not did act as alleged by plaintiff. In more serious civil cases, the burden of proof on the plaintiff is, instead, **clear and convincing evidence** to show that the events occurred as alleged. The heavier burden is imposed because of the more serious nature of an offense. For instance, say Ann and Bill are being sued for injuries sustained by someone who fell when they negligently failed to put out a sign that said "slippery when wet." The required

preponderance of the evidence
usual burden of proof that plaintiff must bear in a civil case, showing it was more likely than not that events occurred as plaintiff alleges

clear and convincing evidence
burden of proof that plaintiff must carry in more serious civil cases in which there has been loss of life or heavy property damage, showing clearly that events occurred as plaintiff alleges

proof would be the preponderance burden. If, however, Ann and Bill failed to safely dispose of toxic waste and several people were killed as a result, the burden on the families to show Bill and Ann's negligence would instead be the burden of clear and convincing evidence.

Appeal

The party against whom a judgment has been entered may move to have the judgment set aside. The two most common devices to achieve this are the **judgment notwithstanding the verdict (jnov)** and a **motion for a new trial**.

Generally, a jnov must be filed within 10 days after judgment has been entered, and it asks that the judgment be set aside. And generally, a jnov is granted if the weight of the evidence is contrary to the jury's verdict.

Generally, a motion for a new trial also must be filed within 10 days of the entry of judgment. Typically, this motion alleges procedural errors (e.g., improper argument by opposing counsel, improperly admitted or excluded evidence, or prejudicial jury instructions), a verdict contrary to law, excessive or inadequate damages, or other grounds.

If neither motion is successful, the losing party may choose to appeal the decision. The party seeking the appeal is known as the **appellant** (or **petitioner**), and the party who must defend against the appeal is known as the **appellee** (or **respondent**).

The rules for an appeal generally require the appellant to file with the court that will hear the appeal a notice of appeal within a specific time limit after the court enters the judgment on the trial verdict. After giving notice of the appeal to the appellate court and to the appellee, the appellant must comply with appellate court rules, which generally require the filing of a **brief**. A brief is a written document outlining the points of error that the appellant alleges were made in the trial, along with whatever exhibits are relevant. Once a copy of the appellant's brief has been filed with the court and a copy served to the appellee, the appellee then responds by filing an answer brief, which argues that the trial court was correct and that the verdict should stand.

The appellate court, in addition to reading the briefs filed in the case, may wish to hear the arguments and ask questions of the lawyers. This process, known as **oral** (or **appellate**) **argument**, is usually requested by all appellants, but is granted in only a few cases the court

---

judgment notwithstanding the verdict
judgment given in favor of side that lost by verdict

motion for new trial
request to judge, made by the losing party, that new trial be granted because of error committed during trial

appellant (or petitioner)
one who brings an appeal of a lower court decision

appellee (or respondent)
one against whom an appeal is sought

brief
written document outlining the points of error that the appellant alleges were made in the trial, along with relevant exhibits

deems to be significant in some way. If granted, each party is given a specific time period (usually no more than 30 minutes) in which to present arguments and respond to questions from the justices.

Unlike at trial, the justices, as many appellate judges are called, do not render their opinion about the case immediately following oral arguments. Instead, they consider the case among themselves for as long as it takes to reach a decision, and sometime in the future the parties are notified of that decision. If the decision comes from a court of last resort, or the highest court that can hear the case (for example, the state supreme court), then that decision is the final decision. If the court is an intermediate appellate court, the losing party may choose to appeal the decision to the highest court. If so, then the appellate process begins again.

REMEDIES

One of the primary differences between law and equity is the **remedy** that is allowed at the conclusion of a case. In law, a party is entitled to monetary damages. In equity, a party is entitled to nonmonetary relief.

remedy
award of money damage or order to do or refrain from doing something

Legal Damages

Three types of *legal* (i.e., monetary) *damages* exist: compensatory, punitive, and nominal.

Compensatory damages are intended to pay for the actual harm caused to the injured party. What a party is entitled to be compensated for depends on the type of action that is brought. For example, in an action for breach of contract, compensatory damages are for the actual loss suffered because of the defendant's breach of (noncompliance with) the contract. In a tort action, however, compensatory damages are intended to cover a wider variety of injuries, such as pain and suffering, physical and mental impairment, or injury to reputation, in addition to the actual loss suffered by the injured party.

compensatory damages
money given by defendant to plaintiff to compensate for injury

Injuries that are caused by a defendant indirectly may also be recovered under compensatory damages. Such indirect damages are called **consequential damages** and are limited to injuries that are a natural and probable consequences of the defendant's act, which the defendant was aware of. A defendant is not required to pay avoidable or speculative damages.

consequential damages
damages arising from circumstances that could have been anticipated

punitive damages
damages awarded in a civil case to punish wrongdoer

nominal damages
damages awarded as acknowledgment that legal right was invaded, but little harm done

liquidated damages
damages predetermined by the parties before breach

equitable remedies
remedy beyond law, applying equitable principles

decree
the decision of a court of equity

specific performance
equitable remedy ordering party to perform contractual obligation

injunction
court order directing something to be done or not to be done

accounting
requirement that one who has fiduciary duty to another account for all money entrusted to a fiduciary

mandatory injunction
court order that a thing be done

Punitive damages have as their purpose both punishment and deterrence. They are damages over and above what is necessary to make the party whole. Punitive damages are intended to reflect society's reaction to the harm inflicted by the defendant. Punitive damages are generally not available in contract actions, unless specifically authorized by statute.

Nominal damages are awarded when the plaintiff has proven that the defendant was at fault, but has failed to prove that any actual loss occurred as a result of that fault. Nominal damages are usually awarded in the amount of $1.

Liquidated Damages

Liquidated damages are used in contract law to specify the predetermined amount of damages that a defendant will be liable for in case of breach. The amount is specified in the contract and generally includes consequential damages. Although the amount need not be exact, the liquidated damage amount cannot be so much in excess of actual damages suffered by the nonbreaching party until it acts as punitive damages, for punitive damages generally are not allowed in contract actions. (See Box 3–15, "Liquidated Damages Clause Sample.")

Equitable Remedies

An **equitable remedy** will only be awarded when a monetary remedy will not resolve the dispute. Equitable remedies take the form of court orders, called **decrees**, to do or refrain from doing something specific. Three common types of decrees are **specific performance**, **injunction**, and **accounting**.

Specific performance is a decree ordering a party to specifically perform the obligations of a contract. As a general rule, specific performance is ordered only in cases involving the sale of unique or one-of-a-kind goods. Specific performance is most often ordered in real property cases because of the belief that each piece of real estate is unique from all others.

An injunction is a court order to do or stop doing a particular thing. When an injunction is issued, it generally enjoins, (i.e., prevents) a party from continuing to do a harmful act, such as pollute or create noise. A **mandatory injunction** is a court order requiring an affirmative act, such as providing a zoning ordinance.

3–15   BLACK LETTER LAW

Liquidated Damages Clause Sample

Liquidated Damages for Delay in Delivery or Other Breach of Contract

In the event that seller does not make shipments as above agreed through no fault of buyer, damages to buyer would be substantial but speculative and difficult to ascertain, and, accordingly, seller agrees to pay to buyer as liquidated damages for each day that the [goods] [are] not shipped as agreed $_____.

Source: Reprinted with permission from *Nichols Cyclopedia of Legal Forms Annotated*, published by Clark, Boardman Callaghan, 155 Pfingsten Road, Deerfield, IL 60015. Toll free 800-221-9428.

Injunctions are issued in three phases. First, a **temporary restraining order** may be issued. This is an extraordinary measure issued by a judge without notice to the other party, and it is of very limited duration (usually a few days). Next, a **preliminary injunction** halts the harmful act temporarily after both sides have an opportunity to be heard and the complaining party has established both likelihood of success on the merits and that there will be irreparable harm if the injunction is not ordered. If, after a full trial the harm is held to exist, a **permanent injunction** may be ordered by the court.

In cases involving misuse of funds held in trust, the court may order an accounting, which requires the defendant to account for use of the monies in question.

A CRIMINAL CASE

This textbook deals with civil law for the most part, but it is still important for you to know the basic structure of the criminal law system. More and more business crimes are being created, with serious repercussions for those like Ann and Bill who own businesses or for those who make decisions for owners. A basic knowledge of criminal law is therefore helpful.

For the defendant, a criminal case usually begins with an arrest. An arrest occurs when a person is taken into custody, usually by a law

temporary restraining order injunction granted without a hearing, usually on a showing of urgency

preliminary injunction injunction granted after hearing before a judge in advance of trial, to last until the granting or denial of a permanent injunction

permanent injunction injunction granted as part of a judgment after full determination of rights of the parties

grand jury
panel of citizens convened to determine whether a prosecutor has enough evidence to cause an indictment to be issued against a person who allegedly committed a crime

arrest warrant
legal document issued by a judge indicating enough evidence has been presented to have defendant arrested for and charged with a crime

search warrant
legal document issued by a judge indicating enough evidence has been presented to show probable cause that evidence of a crime will be found on premises the warrant is issued for

enforcement officer, to answer for a crime. The arrest may be made either on the scene, or following an investigation that may be short or lengthy, or after the convening of a **grand jury**, or pursuant to an arrest warrant. An **arrest warrant** is a court order commanding that a law enforcement officer take into custody the individual named in the warrant to appear before a court. In a criminal case, the parties involved are the defendant and a government entity, represented by either federal or state prosecutors.

Constitutional Protections

When arrested, a person is in the custody of the state and is no longer free. Custody gives rise to constitutional considerations, namely the Fourth, Fifth, Sixth, and Eighth amendments to the U.S. Constitution, which impose limitations on the government in dealing with people (and, sometimes, businesses). (See Box 3–16, "Constitutional Amendments.")

Under the Fourth Amendment, a person is protected against unreasonable searches and seizures by the police. Usually, in order to conduct a lawful search, the government needs a **search warrant**. A search warrant is a sworn affidavit stating the probable cause (the basis for belief that a crime has occurred, which makes a search necessary) and describing both the places to search and the objects to be seized. Absent a warrant, the government is allowed to search only if certain exceptions exist.

The Fifth Amendment gives an individual protection from compulsory self-incrimination. You've probably heard the expression "I plead the Fifth." It means the person doesn't want to testify in response to a question because the answer may tend to incriminate that testifier. (See Box 3–17, "The Miranda Warnings," on page 78.) Fifth Amendment protection is limited, however. For example, one person cannot use the Fifth Amendment to refuse to appear in a lineup, provide fingerprints, or give blood, hair, skin, breath, voice, or other body samples, even though such might be incriminating.

The Sixth Amendment provides the right to legal counsel through all of the important phases of the criminal process. It also provides for a speedy trial, the right to subpoena favorable witnesses, the right to confront and cross-examine adverse witnesses, and the right to an impartial jury drawn from the jurisdiction where the crime allegedly occurred.

3–16 BLACK LETTER LAW

Constitutional Amendments

Amendment IV

The right of the people to be secure in their persons, houses, papers, and effects, against unreasonable searches and seizures, shall not be violated; and no Warrants shall issue, but upon probable cause, supported by Oath or affirmation, and particularly describing the place to be searched, and the persons or things to be seized.

Amendment V

No person shall be held to answer for a capital, or otherwise infamous crime, unless on a presentment or indictment of a Grand Jury, except in cases arising in the land or naval forces, or in the Militia, when in actual service in time of War or public danger; nor shall any person be subject for the same offense to be twice put in jeopardy of life or limb; nor shall be compelled in any criminal case to be a witness against himself, nor be deprived of life, liberty, or property, without due process of law; nor shall private property be taken for public use, without just compensation.

Amendment VI

In all criminal prosecutions, the accused shall enjoy the right to a speedy and public trial, by an impartial jury of the State and district wherein the crime shall have been committed, which district shall have been previously ascertained by law, and to be informed of the nature and cause of the accusation; to be confronted with the witnesses against him; to have compulsory process for obtaining witnesses in his favor, and to have the assistance of counsel for his defense.

Amendment VIII

Excessive bail shall not be required, nor excessive fines imposed, nor cruel and unusual punishments inflicted.

The Eighth Amendment requires that bail not be excessive, and it prohibits cruel and unusual punishment. All criminal defendants are entitled to reasonable bail; however, most jurisdictions deny bail to a criminal defendant charged with a capital crime, meaning one for which a possible sentence is death.

The procedures and practices of law enforcement throughout the legal process must ensure that the foregoing rights are protected for each individual. Evidence obtained in violation of those amendments is subject to exclusion from trial. We have often seen this portrayed on television shows or in the movies: the police violate the constitutional rights of a suspect in order to obtain evidence tending to prove the suspect's guilt, and then the evidence cannot be used by the prosecutor bringing the case. The purpose of the rule is to prevent police officers, as representatives of the government, from violating people's rights. If the police know the evidence cannot be used, they are less likely to violate a person's constitutional rights just to get that evidence. It can be frustrating at times, but our constitutional rights must remain inviolate if they are worth anything. Even though it sometimes seems the defendant may have "gotten off on a technicality," constitutional principles are not so easily dismissed. The law takes the position that a conviction based on violation of a defendant's constitutional rights is unconstitutional and cannot stand—despite the defendant's guilt or innocence.

3–17   BLACK LETTER LAW

The Miranda Warnings

The Miranda warnings hold that when a person is taken into custody or otherwise deprived of freedom in any significant way and is subjected to questioning—known as custodial interrogation—that person must be advised of certain rights. They are that:

1. the person has the right to remain silent;
2. anything the person says can be used against the person in a court of law;
3. the person has the right to consult a lawyer;
4. if the person cannot afford a lawyer but desires one, one will be appointed for the person prior to any questioning;
5. the person can stop speaking at any time, even after the interrogation has begun.

These rights apply only to in-custody interrogation by law enforcement personnel.

Applications to Business

Under the Fourth Amendment, businesses enjoy the same protections from unwarranted searches as do individuals, with the exception of so-called highly regulated businesses, which are defined as those having a decreased expectation of privacy. Given the purposes of the Occupational Safety and Health Administration, the Food and Drug Administration, the Environmental Protection Agency, and other government agencies, warrantless searches are sometimes necessary and justified. Otherwise, businesses have the same expectations and rights to privacy that ordinary people do.

Under the Fifth Amendment, most business records can be subpoenaed for use in court as evidence against a business. Since the Fifth Amendment is a personal right, it does not protect ordinary business records. However, if the records are truly private, such as a personal diary kept at work, an individual might be able to assert a Fifth Amendment right. However, corporate records kept in the ordinary course of business are not so protected.

Under the Sixth Amendment, business criminal defendants (in the person of agents or officers of the business) have a right to counsel just as any other individual does. The fact that they represent a business does not take away their constitutional right to counsel.

A Criminal Trial

Once a criminal case proceeds to trial, the trial is conducted in much the same manner as a civil suit, with the primary distinction being at the conclusion of the trial, when the defendant is judged either not guilty (acquitted) or guilty. The burden of proof in a criminal trial is termed guilt **beyond a reasonable doubt**. That is, to convict a defendant, a jury must be convinced beyond all reasonable doubt that the evidence shows defendant committed the crime as charged.

Occasionally, a jury is unable to reach a verdict, and that results in a mistrial, or **hung jury**, in which case the government has the opportunity to retry the case. If a jury renders a verdict of guilty, then the defendant can appeal to a higher court. If the jury acquits the defendant, then the government generally does not have the right to appeal; nor can it retry the case. The doctrine of **double jeopardy** prevents the government from retrying a defendant on the same charges twice, and the doctrine is protected by the Fifth Amendment of the Constitution.

beyond a reasonable doubt
prosecutor's burden of proof in criminal cases

hung jury
in a criminal case, a jury that is unable to decide guilt or innocence of defendant

double jeopardy
a doctrine that defendant cannot be tried twice for same crime

In addition to those constitutional protections, a defendant has the right to other constitutional protections, including the right to a speedy trial, the right to face one's accuser, and the right to know of any evidence tending to point to the defendant's innocence (exculpatory evidence).

The vast majority of criminal appeals are initiated by defendants unhappy with the results of their case and hoping that some appellate court will make a more favorable decision. All 50 states provide some form of appeal or review of criminal convictions. Indigent defendants (those who cannot afford counsel) are entitled to appointed counsel for the first appeal.

information
legal document in which prosecutor charges defendant with crime

indictment
decision of grand jury that prosecutor has enough evidence to charge and try defendant for a crime

Few appeals are initiated by the prosecutor, because of the problem of double jeopardy. Most states allow only pretrial and post-conviction appeals by the prosecutor, such as an appeal of a motion to dismiss or dismissals involving technicalities in the **indictment** or **information**. Box 3–18, "Constitutional Fairness?" illustrates a recent example of the prosecution abandoning its usual rule of not retrying cases after losing the first time. See if you can understand why an exception was made in this case.

ALTERNATIVE DISPUTE RESOLUTION

Not every dispute that Bill and Ann become involved in will end up in litigation. Hopefully, most will not. Not only is litigation costly and time-consuming, but it simply is not necessary for the resolution of every disagreement. For some conflicts it would be like using a sledgehammer to kill a fly. Litigation is the heavy artillery of the conflict resolution arena and should be used most judiciously. Ideally, it should be used only as a means of last resort. For those conflicts that do not need litigation, several alternatives exist. Together these mechanisms have come to be known as **alternative dispute resolution**, or **ADR**.

alternative dispute resolution
nonlitigation ways of resolving legal disputes

Ann and Bill can use three main mechanisms to resolve disputes without resort to litigation: *conciliation*, *mediation*, and *arbitration*. Unless the state or local law in a given jurisdiction has a prescribed means by which ADR must be pursued, it is very flexible and the mechanisms need not be used in any particular order, though they have a natural logic. Because they offer to the court and the parties considerable cost savings, time saving, and privacy, they have grown increasingly popular during the recent past.

3–18   LAW IN THE REAL WORLD

Constitutional Fairness?

Byron de la Beckwith was tried for the murder of Medger Evers twice in 1964 by all white juries and was acquitted both times. Beckwith went on with his life, that is, until the Mississippi Supreme Court decided he could be charged a third time—nearly 30 years after the murder.

Beckwith, now a 74-year-old white supremacist, was reindicted in 1990 for the 1963 murder of Evers, the 37-year-old field secretary of the NAACP (National Association for the Advancement of Colored People) who was shot in the back outside his Jackson, Mississippi, home. Prosecutors reopened the case after a newspaper disclosed that the Mississippi Sovereignty Commission, a defunct state agency dedicated to preserving segregation, secretly helped the defense select the jury in at least one of Beckwith's trials.

Beckwith argued that the 21-year period between the last mistrial and the dropping of charges should warrant a dismissal. He further argued that a fair trial after so much time would be impossible because of the dimming of memories and the loss of witnesses who have died or disappeared. In addition, Beckwith argues that to retry him would place him in double jeopardy, since jeopardy attached when the first jury was sworn in and ended when the charges were dropped in 1969.

However, prosecutors contend that the passage of time has no legal or constitutional bearing on the status of the case. There is no statute of limitations for murder; the right to a speedy trial no longer applies once charges have been dropped; and jeopardy doesn't attach until a defendant has been convicted or acquitted on the merits.

Apparently, the Mississippi Supreme Court agreed with the prosecution, as it allowed Beckwith to be tried for a third time. This time, he was convicted and is currently serving his sentence for the 1964 murder of Medger Evers. Is this fair?

Source: "New Trial for a White Supremacist?" by Mark Hansen, January 1993, *ABA Journal*, ©1993 American Bar Association. Printed with permission of the *ABA Journal*.

CONCILIATION

conciliation
the principle by
which parties with a
dispute attempt to
resolve it by trying to
reach an agreement
between themselves

It may seem too simple to even discuss, but the very first thing Ann and Bill should do when involved in a conflict is to attempt **conciliation**. It is the simplest, cheapest thing to do, and if it is successful, nothing else need be done and the conflict can end at this point. Conciliation is important enough that it has been written into some statutes. For instance, under the statutory scheme of Title VII of the Civil Rights Act of 1964, by law the parties must first attempt to conciliate claims of employment discrimination before proceeding further.

Conciliation simply involves the parties talking to each other either orally or by letter in an effort to reach a resolution of the conflict. Conciliation costs nothing, and nothing is lost if the parties do not eventually reach a satisfactory resolution. It is surprising how many people who have conflicts skip this step and go directly to litigation. Many times they find after filing suit that the matter may have been handled without legal intervention. Again, if conciliation does not work, the parties can move on to the next step and nothing is lost.

MEDIATION

mediation
disinterested third
party attempts to talk
with disputing
parties to try to help
them reach a
resolution

Whereas conciliation occurs between the parties to the conflict and without the intervention of a third party, **mediation**, for the first time, brings into the conflict an outsider. The purpose of the third party is to try to get the original parties to reach a resolution on their own. Have you ever had a conflict with one of your parents in which your other parent or a friend talks to each of you separately, trying to get you to see the other person's side or to look at things a different way in order to resolve the conflict? That is, essentially, mediation. Mediation is most beneficial when the parties wish to continue an ongoing relationship but simply need help with a current conflict.

For instance, say Bill and Ann have a disagreement over the terms of an agreement with the national distributor of a commodity needed in their business. If that national distributor is the best place from which they can purchase the needed merchandise, Bill and Ann and the distributor are essentially locked in this relationship together. They need to preserve their relationship, yet still resolve the dispute between them. Rather than resort to the adversarial path of litigation, which rarely preserves a relationship between parties, they are prime candidates for mediation.

Under mediation, a third party is brought into a conflict to try to assist the parties themselves in resolving it. Let's say you have a conflict with your roommate over the roommate's bringing overnight guests into the apartment you share. The mediation can be as informal as getting someone whom you and your roommate both trust to mediate the conflict. On the other hand, it can be as formal as the national baseball teams' calling on the assistance of the Federal Mediation and Conciliation Service to have someone come in to help try to end their dispute. There are no formal requirements for who can mediate disputes, but formal structures are in place for those who wish to take advantage of them.

The *Federal Mediation and Conciliation Service* (FMCS) is a government agency that can be called upon to perform mediation. The agency maintains a roster of mediators. Parties seeking the services of a federal mediator notify FMCS and either request a mediator they both know and trust or request a list of mediators' names. The list also gives the mediators' backgrounds, names the previous mediations they have conducted, and offers other pertinent information that can be used by the parties to evaluate an individual mediator's suitability for their purposes. Each party strikes names from the list until the parties decide on one that is mutually satisfactory. Arrangements are then made for the mediator to enter the negotiation. Many private mediation organizations now exist also, in addition to attorneys who offer ADR as part of their services.

Most often, the mediator engages in a type of "shuttle diplomacy" whereby the mediator goes back and forth between the two parties, listening to each one's concerns and trying to find a way for both to get what they want. The uninvolved third party can "hear" the parties' concerns better than the opposition can, because the third party is not involved in the dispute and does not evaluate information with an eye toward trying to gain an advantage or keep from either being embarrassed or appearing weak.

Some courts, in attempts to lighten their caseload, relieve court docket congestion, decrease the wait time for court dates for litigants, decrease the cost of dispute resolution, and free themselves for those matters that truly need court disposition, have instituted some form of ADR program. The programs vary from jurisdiction to jurisdiction, but may be a variation involving, for example, required use of **court-annexed ADR** for certain types of cases, optional use of ADR, use of ADR with the option of proceeding to court if the parties are not satisfied, or required use of ADR for cases that involve only certain subject

court-annexed ADR
ADR done as part of a courts procedures

matter, issues, or monetary amounts. If the resolution proposed is not satisfactory to the parties, they may proceed to the next ADR mechanism.

ARBITRATION

arbitration
mechanism by which disinterested third party hears dispute between parties and makes a decision based on the findings

binding arbitration
agreement in advance to be bound by an arbitrator's decision

nonbinding arbitration
agreement to arbitrate a conflict, but not to be bound by the arbitrator's decision

award
decision by an arbitrator

Arbitration also involves intervention by a disinterested third party into a dispute, but the purpose is quite different. In mediation the third party tries to get the parties to reach a resolution on their own. In arbitration the role of the third party is to listen to the concerns and evidence given by both parties and then to impose a decision on them, much like a judge does. The parties will not be resolving their own conflict, but instead contractually agree between themselves to have a resolution imposed by an outsider to the conflict.

Arbitration may be **binding** or **nonbinding**. If the arbitration is binding, the parties agree to abide by the decision reached (called an **award**) by the arbitrator and not take the case to court. If it is nonbinding, then the party not satisfied with the arbitrator's decision can pursue litigation. In binding arbitration, the arbitrator's award is virtually final and can be reviewed by a court of law only for reasons involving unconstitutionality, abuse or fraud in the arbitrator's decision, and like matters attacking the validity of the award itself.

However, parties who simply do not like the award cannot decide to use the courts as another bite at the apple. They have contractually agreed to be bound by the arbitrator's decision, and the courts take such agreement seriously. Arbitrators' awards can thus be even more powerful than those of a court, for a court is subject to review by higher courts on appeal. This is an interesting point, considering there is generally no requirement that an arbitrator be a lawyer, have any legal training, or make awards that are consistent, as with the concept of stare decisis in legal cases.

In more than 20 state and federal districts, court-annexed arbitration programs have been adopted to help shorten court dockets. Under most of the statutes, cases filed for litigation are reviewed for arbitration potential. If, for instance, they fit the profile of involving less than a certain amount of money, the judge to whom the case is assigned refers the case to arbitration. Most systems have a roster of arbitrators—in many cases, attorneys—who hear cases and render an award. Under most schemes, parties must participate in court-annexed arbitration, but they may proceed with litigation if they demand a trial within a certain amount of time after the arbitrator's award.

The American Arbitration Association (AAA), the most popular national arbitration organization, maintains a roster of arbitrators anyone can consult to choose an arbitrator. Those on the roster have met certain requirements, such as experience with arbitrating disputes. Much like with mediators, at a client's request the AAA will send to the parties a list of arbitrators. Each party reviews the list, striking the names of those persons they do not want until agreement is finally reached. Arrangements for scheduling and for paying for the arbitrator's services are made with the arbitrator directly by the parties. The cost of the arbitrator's services is usually split equally between the parties by prior agreement. AAA handles about 55,000 commercial arbitrations per year. U.S. Arbitration and Mediation is another organization that also offers ADR services.

It is possible for arbitrators to sit to hear conflicts in panels of three or more, rather than singly. Generally, panels comprise an odd number of arbitrators so that the decision will not be evenly split. When there is more than one arbitrator, generally the majority rules. Although arbitration proceedings are like trials in that each party presents evidence and witnesses supportive of its claims, the rules are generally more relaxed and the structure less formal than in court.

Most collective bargaining agreements between labor unions and employers contain a provision for binding arbitration, requiring that contract disputes be handled by an arbitrator rather than a court. This is called *labor arbitration*. It permits the parties to the collective bargaining agreement to dispose of disagreements arising under the contract without resort to the time-consuming method of litigating every disagreement.

Commercial arbitration addresses virtually all disputes to be arbitrated other than labor, and it includes employer-employee disputes when no union or collective bargaining agreement is in effect.

Arbitrators can be found who specialize in certain areas, such as securities conflicts, marital conflicts, environmental conflicts, and sports conflicts. Within the past several years, as the costs of litigation have risen and the number of litigants has increased, the courts and the legal system have become much more amenable to ADR than they once were. The *Federal Arbitration Act* applies to commercial agreements that affect interstate commerce and make arbitrators' awards in such cases legally enforceable. State laws make other arbitrators' awards (those not affecting interstate commerce) enforceable, though states vary in their commitment to ADR. In addition, some specific statutes contain arbitration provisions. For instance, there is a Securities and Exchange Commission rule that securities disputes be handled by arbitration if possible.

Some states have done the same thing with disputes between customers and car manufacturers, for example. The Better Business Bureau has an automobile arbitration program that allows car owners to negotiate with manufacturers free of charge and receive a decision within ten days. Owners who do not like the decision are not bound, though automobile manufacturers are.

Despite its advantages, ADR has not always been favored, and at one time, in fact, courts were downright hostile to the idea. Logic won out in time, however. In the following case, the Supreme Court discusses its change of heart.

OTHER ALTERNATIVES

In addition to the mechanisms previously described, parties may also use several other alternatives developed in recent years.

Mock Trials

mock trial
a pretend trial presented before a group of people to see how they react to presentation of evidence before actual presentation in court

An attorney may wish to use this to determine how a jury might react to the attorney's case. The attorney assembles a mock jury made up of ordinary citizens, presents the case as if in court, and then requests that the mock jury make a decision. Hearing the decision and questioning the mock jury about its thought process can be very instructive for the attorney in deciding how best to proceed with the case from that point.

Minitrials

minitrial
presentation of conflict before businesspeople, as a way to enhance settlements and avoid trial

Minitrials are used for business cases and are presented before top business executives rather than ordinary citizens. The lawyers for both sides assemble a panel consisting of a neutral adviser and high-ranking business executives who have settlement authority from each business. Agreements vary, but generally the parties consider the problem as one of a business nature rather than a legal nature. They then go into settlement negotiations afterward. There have been instances in which large, complex cases have been settled quickly after a minitrial, whereas litigation may have dragged on for years.

RODRIGUEZ DE QUIJAS ET AL. V. SHEARSON/AMERICAN EXPRESS

490 US 477 (1989)

Even though a group of securities investors signed customer agreements requiring that account disputes be settled by binding arbitration (unless the agreement was found unenforceable under federal or state law), when their investments went bad, they brought suit in court alleging fraudulent and unauthorized transaction in violation of the Securities Act of 1933 and the Securities and Exchange Act of 1934. The U.S. Supreme Court held that the agreement to arbitrate securities claims is binding and that the courts were not the only forum in which securities disputes are to be resolved.

Kennedy, J.: The Court's characterization of the arbitration process in *Wilko v. Swan*, 346 U.S. 427 (1953), is pervaded by "the old judicial hostility to arbitration." That view has been steadily eroded over the years. The erosion intensified in our most recent decisions upholding agreements to arbitrate federal claims raised under the Securities Exchange Act of 1934, under the Racketeer-Influenced and Corrupt Organizations (RICO) statutes, and under the antitrust laws. See also *Dean Witter Reynolds Inc. v. Byrd*, 470 U.S. 213 (1985) (federal arbitration statute "requires that we rigorously enforce agreements to arbitrate"), and *Moses H. Cone Memorial Hospital v. Mercury Construction Corp.*, 460 U.S. 1 (1983) ("[Q]uestions of arbitrability must be addressed with a healthy regard for the federal policy favoring arbitration"). The shift in the Court's views on arbitration away from those adopted in *Wilko* is shown by the flat statement in *Mitsubishi Motors Corp. v. Soler Chrysler-Plymouth, Inc.*, 473 U.S. 614 (1985): "By agreeing to arbitrate a statutory claim, a party does not forgo the substantive rights afforded by the statute; it only submits to their resolution in an arbitral, rather than a judicial forum." To the extent that *Wilko* rested on suspicion of arbitration as a method of weakening the protections afforded in the substantive law to would-be complainants, it has fallen far out of step with our current strong endorsement of the federal statutes favoring this method of resolving disputes.

continued on next page

In *Shearson/American Express, Inc. v. McMahon*, 482 U.S. 220 (1987), we stressed the strong language of the Arbitration Act, which declares as a matter of federal law that arbitration agreements "shall be valid, irrevocable, and enforceable, save upon such grounds as exist at law or in equity for the revocation of any contract" (9 USC Sec. 2). Under that statute, the party opposing arbitration carries the burden of showing that Congress intended in a separate statute to preclude a waiver of judicial remedies or that such a waiver of judicial remedies inherently conflicts with the underlying purposes of that other statute. But there is nothing in the record before us, or in the facts of which we can take judicial notice, to indicate that the arbitral system would not afford the plaintiff the rights to which he is entitled. Petitioners have not carried their burden of showing that arbitration agreements are not enforceable under the Securities Act. AFFIRMED

Case Questions

1. Do you agree with the court that "by agreeing to arbitrate a statutory claim, a party does not forgo the substantive rights afforded by the statute; it only submits to their resolution in an arbitral, rather than a judicial forum"? Why or why not?

2. If arbitration awards can be reviewed only by a court for reasons such as fraud or collusion on the part of the arbitrator, unconstitutionality, and the like aren't the courts virtually foreclosed to the parties?

Regulatory Negotiation

This mechanism is used by administrative agencies wishing to avoid protracted litigation with interested groups over regulations the agency wants to institute. The agency meets with the groups before formally proposing the regulations—often with a third party such as a mediator present—and attempts to negotiate the provisions of the regulations. In this way a challenge is less likely once the regulations are promulgated. The Environmental Protection Agency has used regulatory negotiation for air- and water-quality regulations.

regulatory negotiation mediation between agency and interested constituents concerning regulations the agency contemplates promulgating

Summary Jury Trial

Some jurisdictions provide for summary jury trials after cases have been filed, if the case will require a great deal of time for trial and is unlikely to be settled by negotiation. Without telling participants that their decision is not binding, a small jury (of about 6 people) is chosen just as a regular jury would be, the case is presented in summary fashion by the parties, and the jury renders a verdict. Based on the jury's input, the parties are urged to negotiate a settlement.

Alternatives to dispute resolution have become an important aspect of resolving conflicts—and an almost necessary adjunct to litigation. With the rising cost of attorneys' fees, court costs, witness fees, and other expenses associated with litigation, it is only fitting that these mechanisms continue to grow in popularity and use.

ADMINISTRATIVE ADJUDICATION

One of the other forums for resolving specific kinds disputes is the administrative process. Administrative law addresses the regulations promulgated by administrative agencies pursuant to authority given them by the state or federal legislature.

As previously discussed under the tripartite system of government set up by the Constitution, government power resides with the legislative (Congress), judicial (courts), and executory (president) branches of government. For practical reasons, each individual branch may not be able to fully exercise each of its powers itself. It therefore grants some of its authority to an agency it creates for that purpose. As discussed in Chapter 1, the legislation that creates an agency is called an enabling statute. The statute creates the agency, tells what its powers are, and sets forth the authority by which the agency is created.

An agency may be granted whichever of the three types of authority it needs in order to carry out its mission. As mentioned in Chapter 1, since the ultimate power actually is granted to a branch of government, an agency may exercise a power like another branch but it cannot actually have such authority. Instead, it has quasi-powers, meaning "like" powers or "as-if" powers.

Because the Constitution actually granted legislative authority only to Congress under the tripartite system, only Congress can actually legislate. However, congress may grant some of its authority, on a limited basis, to an agency it creates, if the power is a necessary part of the mission of the agency. Agencies may be given *quasi-judicial authority* to adjudicate matters of controversy generally arising from the exercise of alleged violations of the regulations. Agencies also have executive powers to carry out agency business. Agencies' powers vary from agency to agency, because each is given authority to do only what it is designed to do.

An agency may be granted *quasi-legislative authority* to issue regulations in pursuance of its authority to enforce a particular law. For instance, Congress has power over interstate commerce. In an effort to exercise that power, it created the U.S. Department of Transportation to be responsible for safety on highways. As a part of that, and pursuant to the exercise of its quasi-legislative powers, the agency may promulgate regulations determining the appropriate size and placement of mud flaps on trucks to ensure the adequate protection of other vehicles from unsafe splashes. The agency's regulations, while not actually law, have the effect of law. If a truck driver is found to be in violation of the regulation and contests the citation, the agency would hold a hearing pursuant to its quasi-judicial power. Many statutes permit the agency decision to be appealed up through the agency and then in court under judicial review.

administrative law judge (ALJ)
one who acts as judge in administrative agency hearings

During the agency's hearing process, the proceeding is generally much less formal than a court hearing. The agency has **administrative law judges (ALJs)**, who hear and decide the issues brought before the agency. The rules of evidence for administrative hearings are more relaxed than in a court of law, for there is no jury sitting. Most agencies have an internal appeals process in which aggrieved parties may have their issues heard by a higher level of the agency administration, up to and including the agency heads. If the party still does not agree with the agency's determination, the party can request judicial review in an appropriate court, as set forth in the enabling statute. It should be noted, however, that like many court dockets, agency dockets are backlogged, agency personnel numbers are being cut back, and administrative agencies suffer from chronic allegations of government inertia and inefficiency.

Before a claimant can bring an administrative determination into a court of law for **judicial review** of an agency's decision, the claimant must **exhaust administrative remedies**. That is, the claimant must show that all procedures set forth in the agency's regulations for review of decisions have been complied with and that there is now only the court as a resort for relief.

When a court hears administrative matters on judicial review, it must give the agency great latitude in conducting agency business. The court generally does not sit to substitute its judgment for the agency's—because the agency generally is considered the expert in the area—but courts also are not there simply to rubber-stamp agency decisions, either. Most statutes grant **limited review** in the sense that the court can overturn the agency's decision only if that decision has been arbitrary, capricious, or otherwise not in accordance with law. However, some statutes give courts the power of **de novo review**. That is, the case that comes to court after going through the administrative process can be tried again, this time in court, as if it had not yet been tried at all.

SUMMARY

While we hope that Ann and Bill will be able to avoid business disputes and litigation, such is highly unlikely. In the event that they do encounter them, there are several alternatives to litigation open to them. If they are successful, it will save them time and money, yet still end with a satisfactory solution. Several different alternatives exist from which parties may choose, all of which are less costly and time-consuming than suing in court. Ann and Bill can choose from conciliation, mediation, arbitration, minitrial, mock trial, summary jury trial, and regulatory mediation.

If litigation is necessary as a last resort, it is available, and we have seen how a litigant progresses through the court system from beginning to end, with an eye toward fairness and objectivity to all those involved. For those matters appropriate for administrative determination, Ann and Bill can proceed through an agency's quasi-judicial process. If they are unable to avoid disputes, at least there are several alternatives from which to choose in resolving them.

judicial review
review of an agency decision by a court of law

exhaust administrative remedies
go through all agency procedures before taking agency decision to court

limited review
review by court of agency decision to ensure decision was not arbitrary, capricious, or otherwise not in accordance with law

de novo review
court review of agency decision by court's having a new look at the case through holding a trial

CHAPTER TERMS

accounting

administrative law judge (ALJ)

affirmative defense

alternative dispute resolution

answer

appeal

appellant (or petitioner)

appellate court

appellee (or respondent)

arbitration

arrest warrant

award

beyond a reasonable doubt

binding arbitration

case, or controversy

challenge for cause

circuit

challenges

clear and convincing
   evidence

closing argument

compensatory damages

complaint

conciliation

consequential damages

contingency fee arrangement

counterclaim

court-annexed ADR

court of general jurisdiction

court of limited jurisdiction

cross-claim

cross-examination

de novo review

decree

deposition

direct examination

discovery

diversity of citizenship
   jurisdiction

double jeopardy

equitable remedies

exhaust administrative remedies

federal district court

federal question jurisdiction

grand jury

hung jury

indictment

information

injunction

interrogatories

judgment

judgment notwithstanding
   verdict

judicial review

jurisdiction

legal brief

limited review

liquidated damages

mandatory injunction

mediation

minitrial

mock trial

motion

motion for new trial

moving party

nominal damages

nonbinding arbitration

opening statement

oral arguments

original jurisdiction

peremptory strikes

permanent injunction

petit jury

pleadings

political questions

preliminary injunction

preponderance of the evidence

pretrial

prima facie case

punitive damages

regulatory negotiation

remedy

reply

request for production of
   documents

retainer

ripeness

search warrant

specialized courts

specific performance

standing

temporary restraining order

voir dire

writ of certiorari

CHAPTER-END QUESTIONS

1. List four differences between civil and criminal cases.

2. Khadiszha is raped one night by a clothing store employee while she is trying on clothes just before the store's closing. Khadiszha wants two things: money for her injuries and that the perpetrator be punished for what he did. Khadiszha's friend Regine tells her that if she wants to receive compensation for her injuries, she should allow the case to be prosecuted, and as part of the decision, if the perpetrator is found guilty, he will have to pay. Is Regine's advice good advice? Explain.

3. The Pacific Coast Fishing Commission (PCFC), which regulates the fishing industry in the Pacific Northwest, has had reports of several deaths of fishers lately. In virtually all of the deaths, the fishers were not wearing safety equipment while on the fishing boats. The PCFC decides that it must act. It thinks it would be best to require fishing boats to carry safety equipment and have the fishers wear the equipment or risk a citation. The PCFC is

also aware that many of the fishers have been in the business for generations and fish the way they were taught. Many are also small family-owned businesses that barely make a living at fishing. Being required to purchase and wear safety equipment will cause a rather heated debate within the fishing community. Before PCFC promulgates the regulations, are there ways it can try to avoid the suspected outcome?

4. Xie Xianging (pronounced "Zhang Zhow-zing") is stopped at a red light at a busy intersection. Monty rear-ends Xie Xianging, causing her a severe case of whiplash. Xie Xianging has little money for a lawyer, but wishes to have the cost of her injuries and car damages paid for by Monty. What would you suggest to Xie Xianging?

5. Chad, a train engineer, is on duty when a train he is operating is involved in an accident that kills 3 and injures 175 passengers. The passengers sue the railroad company, alleging that Chad operated the train negligently, thereby causing the accident, because he was under the influence of an illegal drug. In deciding the case, the court will likely impose what standard upon the jury hearing the case?

6. During the voir dire for a civil case involving computer software infringement, Rachel, the attorney for the software company, tries to strike from the jury anyone who has ever used a computer because she thinks such persons would be predisposed to think that copying software is no big deal because virtually everyone does it. Rachel's attempts to strike prospective jurors will likely be done on the basis of which types of strike? Will she likely be successful in striking all the computer users from the jury?

7. Ralph is riding in his automobile when Becky runs a red light and crashes her truck into the side of Ralph's car, causing him severe injury. Ralph is from Georgia and Becky is from Florida. Ralph sues Becky for $115,000 for his injuries, pain and suffering, loss of wages, and so forth. Ralph brings the case in federal court. Becky's attorney argues that the federal court has no jurisdiction over this state claim of negligence. Who is correct? Why?

8. Barton alleged that he had a contract with Ace Motor Co. to purchase a car and that Ace sold the car to someone else. Barton was able to purchase an identical car at Bowers Motor Co. for the same price he was to purchase it from Ace. Barton argues that since Ace breached the contract with him, he is entitled to com-

pensatory damages. Barton is awarded $1 in damages. Is he correct about the compensatory damages? Explain.

9. Alvarez Nursery and Garden Supply is involved in a dispute with one of its seed suppliers. The matter goes to arbitration, and the three-arbitrator panel determines that Alvarez loses. Alvarez declares that since only two of the three arbitrators support the award, the decision cannot be imposed on her. Is she correct? Explain.

10. Dawn takes her great-great-grandmother's sewing machine, which has been in her family for over a hundred years, to Charlie's Sew 'n' Vac Repair & Used Electronics Shop for servicing. When Dawn returns to pick up the machine at the agreed time, she is told that it was sold. Charlie offers to pay Dawn the price of a similar machine. Dawn refuses the offer. Explain the alternatives Dawn has for relief.

11. In a jury trial, once a case is finished being presented and the jury completes deliberations, the jury returns with a judgment. (True or False)

12. The process by which the lawyers determine who sits on the jury is called

    a. discovery.
    b. voir dire.
    c. counterclaim.
    d. interrogatory.

GROUP EXERCISE

Have the class as a whole come up with a legal dispute of its own design or one that students may have seen in the news—preferably one that has not yet been resolved. Have the class divide into groups, and assign each group to handle the dispute in a different way. One group will try conciliation, another mediation, and so on. See how the situations work themselves out. Which worked best? Why? In the alternative, visit a courtroom with a case in progress. How did it compare with what you learned in this chapter?

Chapter 4

SOCIAL RESPONSIBILITY, ETHICS, AND WHITE-COLLAR CRIMES

Chapter Preview Summary

In this chapter Ann and Bill are introduced to the concepts of ethics and corporate social responsibility and are given an overview of white-collar crimes. The purpose of the chapter is to provide them with a sense of their responsibilities over and above what the law may provide as a floor, or minimum. When Ann and Bill begin to act as a business as a means of making profit, they should not do so without due consideration to the social and ethical consequences of their decisions. This chapter will provide with an overview of how our economic system of free competition affects our legal system, an introduction to the importance of ethical analysis and considerations in decision making, and a summary of white-collar crime.

Chapter Objectives

In studying the chapter, you should learn:
- **what the concept of social responsibility is and how it has evolved**
- **about profit maximizing and social responsibility**
- **how ethical considerations affect long-term business decisions**
- **that corporate officers/managers can be held criminally responsible for business decisions**

INTRODUCTION

One of the most important concepts in this text concerns the ethics and social responsibility of Bill and Ann's business. In fact, we hope you will try to apply what you learn in this chapter to each of the remaining chapters. We want you to see ethical considerations lurking behind every word, every law, and every management decision.

In last previous chapters you learned about many of the legal concepts and important legal considerations that underlie the law. The law provides a sort of floor below which Bill and Ann's actions may not go without causing legal liability attaching. Ethics and social responsibility are thought of by many as being the considerations *above* the floor provided by the law.

Many in Ann and Bill's position believe that if they make business decisions that are profitable and legal, they have satisfied whatever responsibility they may have to society. However, the concepts of social responsibility and ethics may require them to make decisions that perhaps turn out to be unprofitable or less profitable in order to contribute to the well-being of society as a whole.

This chapter also discusses the escalating problem of white-collar crime, meaning, crime committed by and against business. Included within this discussion is the separate consideration of computer crime.

ETHICS

ethics
principles of operating in the world that are over and above what is required by law

morality
personal opinions concerning right or wrong

business ethics
the study of what is right or wrong; good or bad human conduct in business

Ethics, from the Greek word *ethos*, meaning character or custom, suggests two basic concerns: (1) individual character, including what it means to be a good person, and (2) the social rules that govern and limit our conduct—rules concerning right and wrong, called **morality**. *Morality* often refers to individual conduct and values; *ethics* usually refers to the study of that behavior. But in everyday language, *ethics* and *morals* are used interchangeably to describe what we call "bad" people and "wrong" actions.

Business ethics concerns itself with how humans act while conducting a business, that is, the motivation behind the decisions made that affect the business. Business can mean everything from a corner grocery store to a multinational enterprise. And a businessperson can be anyone, from the sole owner of that grocery store to the president or CEO of that multinational corporation. For the purposes of this chapter, the word **business** encompasses any organization whose objective is to provide goods or services for profit, and *businesspeople* means those who are responsible for planning, organizing, or directing the work of a business.

The most powerful argument for ethics in business is success. Ethical businesses are successful. Of course, ethicality in business is no assurance of success, and there are, for certain, unethical businesses that are quite successful. However, in any system based on trust, a few deceivers will prosper. The point of doing business is to do well by providing the best service or product at a reasonable cost.

business
any organization whose objective it is to provide services or goods for profit

ETHICS AND LAW

The lawfulness of actions does not automatically make such actions morally or ethically right. Although the law should reflect the moral values embedded in a society, it cannot account for every aspect of human conduct. Therefore, the law should be looked at as the floor above which lies moral conduct. But obeying the law doesn't always make one moral.

As an illustration of this point, think back to the letter written by Dr. Martin Luther King Jr. from the Birmingham jail where he was incarcerated for attempting to desegregate in the South. King explained that he could follow the decision handed down in *Brown v. Board of Education* because that law was morally correct, but he could not follow the Jim Crow laws of Alabama because those laws were immoral, even though they too were laws.

Another example of morally questionable laws are the Good Samaritan laws, which are codified in almost all of the 50 states. These laws state that there is no duty to render aid to a person in need, unless you have a preexisting relationship with that person that is recognized by law, such as a teacher to a student or a doctor to a patient. However, if you accept the premise that it would be morally wrong to allow a person to suffer if, at no cost or inconvenience to yourself, you could render aid to that person, then there is a question of whether following the Good Samaritan law would be morally correct. The two examples show that acting lawfully may not equal acting morally, and they illustrate clearly how moral conduct can slip through the cracks of the legal floor.

THEORIES OF ETHICS

Many people believe that morality, and therefore ethics, boils down to religion. As you saw in Chapter 1, others believe that that which is right or wrong is only a function of what a particular society takes to be right or wrong. Certain theories of ethics spring from philosophy and are applicable to the study of business and ethics. Let's discuss a few.

Egoism

egoism
the doctrine that an act is morally right only if it furthers one's own best interest

Egoism contends that an act is morally right if it produces for the individual (or, in our context, a business) a greater ratio of good to evil in the long run than any other alternative will. For example, egoism would dictate that companies support policies of nonsmoking campaigns only to the extent that the companies further their own self-interest and that companies have no obligation toward others. Even self-sacrificial acts are viewed as egotistical and are seen as being done for the purpose of satisfying self-interest.

Utilitarianism

utilitarianism
the doctrine that we should always act to produce the most good for the most people

Utilitarianism contends that we should always act to produce the greatest possible balance of good over bad for everyone affected by our action. For utilitarians, no action is in itself objectionable. An action is objectionable only if it leads to a lesser amount of total good than could otherwise have been brought about. Like egoism, utilitarianism focuses on the result of an action, and not on the action itself.

For example, although breaking a promise generally produces unhappiness, there can be circumstances when breaking a promise can cause more good than keeping it. In such a circumstance, a utilitarian would break the promise. In a business context, consider the following example. Suppose the government suspected that a certain pollutant caused a certain type of lung disease, so it enacted legislation requiring factories that had that pollutant in their atmosphere to install expensive equipment to reduce the amount of that pollutant. One plant requests it be exempt from the law so that it can perform research at the plant that would determine the precise cause of that lung disease. The government indeed waives the requirement for that plant, in essence potentially exposing plant workers to the lung disease in question. Utilitarians would say that if the experiment maximizes the good of society, then the government waiver is just. Critics of utilitarianism would disagree.

Good Will

The preceding two theories are known as consequentialist theories; that is, they reduce morality to a concern with consequences. The following two theories are called, predictably, nonconsequentialist theories, because they contend that right and wrong can be determined by looking at the action absent any result the action might bring about.

The first of these is good will. **Will** is the capacity to act from principle. **Good will** contends that for an action to be moral, it must be motivated by a sense of duty to be fair and honest. Any other motivation, although it produces similar results, is immoral. Duty comes from the creation of the **categorical imperative**. Simply stated, a categorical imperative is a universal truth. A universal truth is simply a maxim that cannot be contradicted. Can you think of any categorical imperatives?

Well, for one example, we can look at the nature of a promise. The universal truth about promises is that they be kept, categorically, that is, that they are binding on everyone. Compared to a **hypothetical imperative**, which tells us what to do if we want a certain result, a categorical imperative requires adhesion to the maxim regardless of result.

To put this theory in a business context, good will would state that it is always wrong to misrepresent a product; such deliberate misconduct is always wrong. To use the example from the utilitarian discussion, it would be wrong to expose plant workers to the potential lung disease, even if it meant advancing our medical knowledge.

Prima Facie Obligations

This nonconsequentialist theory maintains that all of our moral obligations are prima facie ones. A **prima facie obligation** is simply an obligation that can be outweighed by other more important obligations, depending on the circumstances under which they arise.

Consider this famous example: A murderer comes to your door and demands to know where your friend is so that he can kill your friend. Your friend is upstairs hiding in your attic. If you exercised the categorical imperative theory, then you would be obligated to tell the murderer the truth, because truth telling is a categorical imperative

will
the capacity to act from principle

good will
theory stating that only when we act from duty do we have moral worth

categorical imperative
a universal truth lacking contradictions

hypothetical imperative
what to do to obtain a certain result or particular outcome

prima facie obligation
obligation that can be overridden by a more important consideration or obligation

that cannot be concerned with the result. Under the prima facie theory, however, you have a genuine obligation to tell the truth, but it is a prima facie one, that is, one outweighed by other moral factors. Most people would say that you have a moral obligation to protect your friend that outweighs the moral obligation to tell the truth in this case.

In a business context, a manufacturing company may consider that its obligation is to install pollution control devices in its plant to protect workers rather than start a day care facility for workers' children, even though the cost of both is the same. The company may have a stronger duty to respect its employment-related obligations than to make its employees happy in other ways. In other words, there is a stronger duty to not violate people's rights or, otherwise, injure them than there is to assist them or otherwise promote their well-being.

CORPORATE ETHICS

corporate culture
management philosophy of a business regarding ethics

No generally applied ethical standards exist for ordinary business operations. The management of each business, therefore, has to develop its own philosophy for how to treat customers, suppliers, employees, and each other. This is commonly referred to as **corporate culture**. More fully stated, corporate culture develops from beliefs that company managers have about how they should manage themselves, other employees, and how they should conduct their business. The corporate culture is formed by the ways people get ahead in the company. What behavior is rewarded? How are employees who engage in legal but unethical behavior treated? Are codes of ethics communicated to each employee? Is there training in ethical behavior? Even with all that is known about corporate culture, the real question is whether ethics can be taught.

Can Ethics Be Taught?

As a result of events during the 1980s and early 1990s, ethics has become a buzzword in businesses, in business schools, and in the business and lay media. There appears to be widespread concern over the apparent lack of ethics by the managers of U.S. businesses, resulting in a push by corporate leaders to have ethics covered in business schools. However, widespread disagreement exists over whether ethics can be taught. Many critics feel that whatever values a person holds will be learned early in life at home, in school, or in church. The argument that ethics cannot be taught may or may not be valid.

Your authors, however, do believe ethics can be taught from an academic standpoint. Even though we are not attempting to teach you right from wrong, we can help you to become more aware of ethical issues and to learn to be sensitive to ethical considerations implicit in decision making. Throughout this book, and throughout your business career, you will encounter many legalistic situations. It is important that you always try to consider the ethical implications therein. Many times, doing so has the extra benefit of better positioning you to avoid legal liability.

Do Corporations Have Ethics?

A number of writers point out that in a society such as the United States, cultural differences make an agreed-upon set of ethics difficult, if not impossible, to achieve. Those same critics also point out that corporations are not human, but are instead artificial legal beings and, as such, do not have ethics in the normal sense. They argue that corporations consist of individuals who have vastly different ethical views due to different backgrounds and religions. Therefore, they argue, since a corporation operates through its board of directors, it cannot have corporate ethics, but instead it represents a collection of individual ethics.

 Whether or not a corporation has ethics or can be said to have ethics may not be important. What is important is the perception of the public which consists of the corporation's investors and consumers. If the latter two groups believe that corporations should have ethics and that a particular corporation has not acted ethically, then investors may stop investing in that company and consumers may stop consuming goods made by the company. Thus, corporations must heed this and either act ethically or pay the consequences.

SOCIAL RESPONSIBILITY

"To realize its full promise in the world of tomorrow, American business and industry—or, at least, the vast portion of it—will have to make social goals as central to its decisions as economic goals; and

social responsibility responsibility of a corporation to act as a good citizen in the community in which it exists

leadership in our corporations will increasingly recognize this responsibility and accept it."[1]

Just what social responsibility does a corporation have? Is its responsibility to be construed narrowly as merely profit making? Or is it broader, to include refraining from harming society and contributing actively and directly to the public good?

PROFIT MAXIMIZATION

Traditional economic theory argues that businesses should operate to maximize profits, and in doing so, the result would be the optimum allocation of society's scarce resources. Obviously, spending money on "socially responsible" issues could decrease profits, thus arguably distorting the optimum allocation of resources.

Conservative economists argue that regulation of business (especially in socially responsible areas) distorts a market economy in such a way that the true costs of the regulations can never be measured. Further, they argue that regulation would be better done at the end of

---

4-1   LAW IN THE REAL WORLD

Ethical Dilemma: What Do You Think?

The area around Love Canal, near Niagara Falls, New York, was used as a toxic dumping site from 1947 to 1952 by Hooker Chem-icals and Plastics Corp., a subsidiary of Occidental Petroleum. The company sold the poisoned area to the Niagara Falls Board of Education in 1953. Homes were built on and around the site. In 1976 the toxic wastes began to take their toll on life and property. There were extremely high incidences of cancer, residents' hair falling out, and the contracting of strange skin diseases. Primarily through the efforts of mothers in the area who were concerned about what was happening to their children, the name Love Canal became a symbol of environmental pollution. Occidental Petro-leum and Hooker Chemicals refused to accept any liability for the damages, of whatever kind, created by their use of the canal as a toxic sewer.

the system by government through the implementation of a tax, rather than through the imposition of inefficient regulations such as the requirement of emission controls or employment discrimination laws. The question of whether businesses should be profit maximizers (and not be socially responsible) has evoked an enormous amount of discussion. However, as you can see from Box 4–2, acting ethically does not automatically mean profits suffer. Sometimes there is a benefit. See if you agree.

BUSINESSES AS CITIZENS

The rival position to the conservative economists says simply that business has other obligations in addition to pursuing profits. These critics agree that profit making is one goal of a corporation, but that there are other responsibilities that arise as a result of the enormous social and economic power that corporations possess. They argue that business does not operate in a vacuum, but that business's actions have ramifications throughout society. As a result, they claim, although investors in businesses expect those businesses to pursue profit, they do not expect them to do so at the expense of the larger society.

Recently, it appears that we have reached a consensus that businesses, such as that of Ann and Bill, are citizens of the communities in which they are located, as are the employees and other people who live in that community. Support for this concept is supported by the Internal Revenue Code, which allows charitable deductions for contributions to community activities of certain types. Many businesses encourage managers to join community groups. Some businesses even go so far as to require their employees to join civic-minded community organizations. Some bar associations and law firms give special treatment to lawyers who offer pro bono services for those who cannot afford lawyers. These businesses obviously perceive benefits (either in the short run or the long run) in being seen and perceived by the general public as socially responsible. Can you think of other benefits?

ULTRA VIRES ACTS

Another reason many businesses in the past did not engage in socially responsible activities was that the law required that incorporated busi-

4-2   LAW IN THE REAL WORLD

Sometimes It "Ain't All Bad"

Recently the following message was on the noticeably smaller carton (made of 90% recycled paper) containing a new laser printer cartridge:

This smaller package is part of HP [Hewlett-Packard]'s commitment to the environment. It continues to provide the necessary protection for maintaining the integrity of the product while reducing mass by over 35%.

What message does the notation send to consumers? Is there a cost benefit to the company from making the switch to less packaging? If so, do you think it is worth it?

Source: Hewlett-Packard Co., Palo Alto, CA 94304.

nesses engage only in activities that led directly to profits for their owners. Socially responsible activities were declared to be **ultra vires** or "outside the power" of the corporation.

ultra vires
acts outside the power of the corporation

Since a corporation is an artificial legal being (entity) whose owners (shareholders) are usually not its managers or on its board of directors, this legal concept required boards of directors and managers to stay on a path directly related to profits and shareholder interests. If a corporation decided, for instance, to contribute funds or land to a charity, any shareholder who disagreed with the contribution could argue that the act was ultra vires and, therefore, not legally permissible. Today, the concept of ultra vires acts, while not dead and buried, is rarely used to challenge socially responsible acts, and any attempt to do so would likely be unsuccessful in the courts.

APPLICATIONS OF ETHICAL ANALYSIS

With the emphasis on profits, it is fairly obvious that managers and business owners will try to make decisions that are profitable. When the dimension of ethics is added to the decision-making process, managers are forced to look beyond profits and what is best for the busi-

4–3   LAW IN THE REAL WORLD

Ethical Dilemma: What Would You Do?

The Tylenol Crisis

In 1982 in Chicago, five people died from ingesting Tylenol Extra Strength Capsules. Although the tampering was localized to the Chicago area, Johnson & Johnson, the makers of Tylenol, pulled 31 million bottles of Tylenol from shelves nationwide and notified 500,000 doctors and hospitals about the contaminated capsules. Consumers were offered the opportunity to replace the capsules with tablets for free, and Johnson & Johnson reported all known information to the public as it became known to them. The handling of this crisis is often cited as a reason why consumer confidence continued in Johnson & Johnson products. This company is viewed as a good corporate citizen. What would you have done in the situation?

ness to how the decision will affect others including consumers and the community.

There are numerous situations wherein all of the alternatives seem to be negative and you end up trying to minimize your losses or the negative effects. No one ethical test can give you a right or wrong answer. Your own sense of right and wrong will help you appreciate and understand the alternatives and their ethical implications.

Recognition of the ethical considerations of the possible alternatives cannot help but make your decision-making process better from an ethical and social responsibility standpoint, but there may be an even more important reason to consider the ethics of your actions. As mentioned earlier, most of our criminal laws have an ethical basis. Therefore if your action is not ethical, it may also be illegal now or may become illegal in the future.

WHITE-COLLAR CRIMES

 It would be impossible to list and explain all of the crimes that may be committed by and against businesses; by listening to the news and

white-collar crimes
crimes committed
against or by a
business

reading current news stories you know that the list is long. Because many of the crimes are committed in the business context, we refer to most business crimes as **white-collar crimes**. Many white-collar crimes are not violent and do not target specific victims; hence society has treated these crimes differently from other, or so-called blue-collar crimes.

Today the distinction has become less meaningful as we realize just how dangerous and cruel white-collar crime can be. For example, we now recognize that a business that chooses to dump its toxic wastes into a city's storm drains can cause illness, brain damage, and even death to great numbers of people, animals, flora, and fish.

Although we cannot imprison a corporation, we can send corporate officers and managers to prison if they participated in the crime or should have known that a crime was being committed. The theory

---

4–4   LAW IN THE REAL WORLD

Ethical Dilemma: What Do You Think?

Assume that Bill has decided to hire an employee. The salary range has been determined to be $20,000–$22,000. Bill conducts the interviews and selects the best-qualified candidate. When asked what salary would be acceptable, the candidate (who has not been told the salary range) responds with a figure of $18,000. If profits are Bill's only concern, he would pay exactly what the applicant asked: $18,000. If ethics were the only determinant, perhaps he would want to pay what he thought the job was worth ($20,000–$22,000). How much do you think Bill should pay the employee? Why?

Now, assume Ann is hiring two people. Assume the two have equivalent qualifications. When asked salary requirements, one responds $18,000 and one responds $21,500. Does Ann pay them what they asked, resulting in one's making $3,500 less than the other? Would it make a difference if Ann knew that one of the applicants was from a poor family and had large educational loans, while the other did not? Should it make a difference?

4–5   LAW IN THE REAL WORLD

Ethical Dilemma: Discuss the Business and Other Implications

Dow Corning chemical company allegedly concealed complaints from medical doctors about its silicone breast implants that later caused various medical problems in women with implants.

behind holding corporate officers and managers liable is similar to respondeat superior: We hold the corporate executives and managers liable for crimes committed by corporate employees over whom they exercised control or could have exercised control. If we did not hold a CEO and other high-level officers and managers liable for the acts of their employees, then those executives could delegate their duties to subordinates and possibly avoid liability. See if you agree with the *Park* decision on the next page.

This case has been criticized due to the several levels of management found in large corporations today. Many corporate executives in the Fortune 500 companies feel they cannot be expected to take care of the myriad small details of daily operation. In other words, critics of the *Park* case believe it is not fair to convict an executive of a crime when that executive had in good faith ordered the appropriate subordinates to comply with the law. In other words, no criminal intent is shown. However, under that theory, only the lower-level employees actually responsible for the physical labor would be responsible. This would, or could, provide a disincentive for corporate officers to act ethically and within the law. In addition, it totally ignores the fact that employees work for corporations and do what they are told to do or suffer the repercussions. Does it seem fair to allow a corporation to back away from its responsibilities this way? Why or why not?

Those who agree with the decision believe that ultimately, top management has to be accountable. What do you believe? If you agree that Park should not be convicted, how would you hold a corporation responsible for its acts, which can be carried out only by people?

UNITED STATES V. JOHN PARK
421 US 658 (1975)

In April 1970, the Food and Drug Administration (FDA) notified Acme Markets of rodent infestation in their Baltimore warehouse, which had caused food shipped to Acme stores to be altered in violation of the Food and Drug Act. Park, Acme's president and CEO, was responsible for the entire operation of the company, including sanitation. Park ordered his subordinates to clean up the warehouse. In 1972, however, Acme received another letter from the FDA complaining that the warehouse still had the same conditions and that they had existed for a long time. The government then brought suit against Acme and Park, alleging violations of the Food and Drug Act, which prohibits the alteration of food with filthy, putrid, or decomposed substances. Acme pled guilty, but Park went to trial. He argued that he was responsible for sanitation, but that he was not guilty because he had ordered his subordinates to clean up the warehouse and they had failed to do so. He also testified that he could not have done anything more than he did to get the warehouse cleaned up and therefore he should not be held liable. Park was convicted, but it was reversed on appeal. The U.S. Supreme Court, however, ordered the case reversed.

Burger, J.: The government establishes a prima facie case when it introduces evidence sufficient to warrant a finding that the defendant had, by reason of his position in the corporation, responsibility and authority either to prevent in the first place, or promptly to correct, the violation complained of. The record in this case reveals that the jury could not have failed to be aware that the main issue was not respondent's position in the corporate hierarchy, but rather his accountability, because of the responsibility and authority of his position, for conditions which give rise to the charges against him. We are satisfied that the act imposes the highest standard of care and permits conviction of responsible corporate officials who, in light of this standard of care, have the power to prevent or correct violations of its provisions. **REVERSED**

Case Questions

1. Do you think Park should have been convicted? Explain.

2. Do you think Park's argument that he had done all he could do is a good one? Why or why not?

3. What is the biggest concern you have with this case?

4–6   BLACK LETTER LAW

Crimes against Business

Arson is the unlawful burning of a building. Because of the great potential for harm, no one is allowed to burn any home or office building, even when no claim for insurance is involved. When an insurance claim is involved, another crime—defrauding an insurance company—may be involved.

Burglary is the breaking and entering into a building at night with the intent to commit a felony. It is more serious if the building is also a dwelling place. The felony may be theft, but also may involve rape or any other felony.

Embezzlement involves the theft of property entrusted to a person. One of the necessary elements is possession of the property prior to the unlawful taking.

Evasion of income taxes is a federal and/or state crime. While it is legal to undertake business strategies that minimize taxes by taking advantage of certain planning devices or loopholes in the law, it is a crime to willfully evade income taxes.

Shoplifting is the theft of inventory from a retail establishment. Generally, before intent can be established the person stealing the property must pass through the checkout area without paying. When property is concealed, it is presumed that the person intends to steal the property.

Theft by computer is a relatively new crime, and statutory law has been enacted in most states to cover money or goods obtained through the fraudulent or illegal use of computers.

COMPUTER CRIMES

The growth of computer use in the business environment has brought with it an explosion of computer-related crimes and ethical dilemmas never before considered—or even dreamed of. The law has been slow to catch up with this new form of criminal behavior and questionable ethics, but as computer crimes continue to escalate, so too will methods of dealing with it.

What makes it such a challenge for law enforcement is that computers tend to leave a paperless trail and do not fit traditional notions of "taking" and "trespass" that laws have traditionally prohibited. For example, if you simply "use" the computer of your employer, have you deprived the employer of use of the property or in any way removed it? Probably under the old rules, no. If you simply enter a computer program and copy personal information, have you deprived anyone of their property? Was there a "taking" in the traditional sense? Again, probably not. What is needed in the computer arena is either the redefinition of the elements of crimes as they exist or the creation of new laws that take into consideration the level of sophistication of computer criminals. What, for instance, do you call something of great value that exists only as electrical impulses? Goods? Services? Knowledge? Following are some of the new rules that have come upon the scene to help deal with computer-related criminal behavior.

FEDERAL LAWS

The Access Device and Computer Fraud and Abuse Act of 1984 outlaws:

1. obtaining classified information from a computer without authorization and with intent or reason to believe that it is to be used to injure the United States;

2. obtaining from a computer without authorization information that is protected by the Right to Financial Privacy Act or contained in the consumer files of a credit reporting agency; and

3. interfering with the operations of a government computer.

The Comprehensive Crime Control Act of 1984 contained a section on the use of computers in credit card fraud and outlines penalties for violations.

4–7   LAW IN THE REAL WORLD

$50-Million Phone Bill Tied to Stolen Cards

An MCI employee has been charged with running up a $50-million bill by using other customers' long-distance calling cards. MCI said that Ivy James Lay, a switch technician in Cary, N.C., was arrested last week by the Secret Service. He's free on bond.

The company says more than 60,000 calling card numbers were stolen in what may be the largest and most sophisticated case of phone fraud yet uncovered, says an MCI spokeswoman. Customers will not be charged.

The Secret Service says Lay designed computer software so to divert and hold calling card numbers from a variety of carriers—including MCI, Sprint, and AT&T—that route calls through MCI equipment.

Those numbers were sold to computer hackers in the United States and Europe, who resold them to other users. MCI and AT&T suspected fraud last spring. The companies called the Secret Service after identifying Lay as a suspect.

"If suddenly 50 calls show up in a 15-minute period to a Third World country that you haven't called before, we're going to suspect something . . . especially if all those calls are from a pay phone in New York City," Aun [a spokeswoman] said. Fraud costs the long-distance industry $2 billion to $5 billion annually, Aun says.

Source: *USA Today*, October 4, 1994. ©1994, *USA Today*. Reprinted by permission.

     The Computer Fraud and Abuse Act of 1986 established as federal crimes computer fraud, destruction, and password trafficking.

STATE LAW

Nearly every state has attempted to deal with computer crimes in one of two ways: by changing the elements of existing crimes to encompass the nontangible property nature of computer crime or by creating new crimes that contemplate the variety of computer crimes being committed. Under either approach, most of the state statutes

4–8   BLACK LETTER LAW

Electronic Export Violation?

Can you violate export laws by entering a secret encryption code on the Internet? U.S. authorities think so, and they are investigating Phillip Zimmerman for just such charges.

In 1991, Zimmerman invented an encryption code that is unbreakable. (An encryption code scrambles computer messages.) Someone, not him, he claims, entered it on the Internet, and within light-seconds Internet users put it on their computers. It works on an algorithm and, unlike the old cryptography which had only one key to unravel, Zimmerman's encryption code requires two keys, one for the sender and one for the receiver. This makes the code impossible to decipher, not even by the government.

Which is exactly why he invented it. Zimmerman believes that everyone should have the right to private conversations, even on the Internet. The government's plans to require the "chipper clip" to be placed in every computer so that every encryption code could be deciphered (under court order) prompted Zimmerman to hole up for six months and create his "Pretty Good Privacy" (as he has named it) code.

The problem is that it is now being used by people whom the police deem undesirables. PGP has been used by a pedophile to keep secret his diary, by drug traffickers to encode their books, and by terrorists to send secret messages. The fear among businesses is that employees will encrypt their e-mail messages, which employers routinely read for personal information. Even the government has said that the PGP code is unbreakable.

Source: *The Wall Street Journal*, 4/28/94.

4–9   BLACK LETTER LAW

Eavesdropping on Workplace Communication Systems

Electronic mail, or e-mail, is fast becoming a workplace feature. Consequently, privacy issues surrounding who can access an employee's e-mail are beginning to emerge as well. Unresolved is exactly what laws currently in existence will be used to decide issues of workplace employee privacy.

The Fourth Amendment to the U.S. Constitution protects employees from intrusions by the government, but this does not protect against intrusions by private employers. The Federal Electronic Communications Privacy Act (ECPA), originally designed to prevent wiretapping and telephone eavesdropping, was amended in 1986 to account for the newer forms of technology, such as e-mail, cellular phones, and fax machines and other data communications, but it contains a specific exception for devices provided by an employer for use by an employee. So far, this act has been interpreted to allow employers to listen to employee's phone conversations to monitor unauthorized use, but it has not specifically interpreted this act for e-mail interception.

Likewise, voice-mail presents a different issue. While the ECPA allows monitoring of live conversations, once the call is identified as nonbusiness related, the employer is supposed to hang up. However, for voice-mail use, most employees are told to make up a personal identification number which only they know, that allows them to access their messages, leading the employee to conclude that their messages are only accessible by use of that number. This is not true for most voice-mail systems, and employers can access that number as well. The question is, if an employee is not told of the employer's ability to access the number, is there a legitimate expectation of privacy in those messages? Only time will tell, but these and other issues are winding their way through the world, "as we speak!"

cover (1) computer trespass (unauthorized access), (2) damage to computers or software (introduction of viruses), (3) theft or misappropriation of computer services, and (4) unauthorized obtaining or disseminating of information via computer.

ETHICAL PROBLEMS

 Taking a ride on the information superhighway has blurred all the lines concerning what is ethical behavior and what is not. Not only is business being generated by the use of Internet, e-mail, and on-line services, but it's being conducted on these highways as well. But what are the rules? Where are the written contracts that lawyers have relied on forever? What laws will govern conflicts that arise between users? These and other questions are just beginning to be fleshed out. If one thing is clear, however, it's that this is going to be a long ride over uncharted territory and may be much like going where no one has gone before. How much existing law will be useful in resolving conflicts is anybody's guess.

4–10   BLACK LETTER LAW

Is It Criminal to Dispense Law via Bulletin Boards?

A brief inquiry on Prodigy has bar associations pondering this question: Is giving legal advice on computer bulletin boards practicing law without a license?

One New Jersey lawyer may soon find out. He responded to a question placed on the bulletin board about a contract in Texas. Donald Dickson, the New Jersey lawyer, responded, as he routinely does. The problem is, Dickson is not licensed in Texas. The question is, Can he answer the legal question posed?

Experts disagree on this one. Although some attorneys say it depends on exactly what the question, and the answer are, Dickson believes his responses don't amount to legal advice because his answers are generic and usually advise the questioner to get the advice of a lawyer in [the appropriate] jurisdiction. Most experts say that the more specific the advice becomes, the closer it gets to the attorney-client relationship and to the unauthorized practice of law.

Dickson defends his practice by saying he is not engaging in the unauthorized practice of law, but rather, is trying to encourage people to trust lawyers enough to seek personal advice.

Source: *ABA Journal,* June 1993.

SUMMARY

This chapter has discussed the development and importance of the concept of social responsibility. A relatively new notion, social responsibility has gone from a disfavored economic concept denounced by conservative economists to one that is generally accepted today. The evolution of otherwise ultra vires acts now allows socially responsible acts, which are no longer subject to serious legal challenge.

Ethics is important to law and management decision making for two reasons. First, most laws have an ethical basis. Second, juries view any evidence from their personal perspectives, which usually include some implicit assumptions about what is fair, right, and just. Despite the importance of ethics to law, legal cases are decided by application of legal principles and precedent, which may or may not lead to what appears to be ethical decisions.

To aid in their decision making, Ann and Bill need to consider the ethical implications of the various possible alternatives available in each situation. Ethical analysis can be aided by the use of ethical thought or tests.

Ethics also appears to be the basis for many of our criminal laws. Therefore, Ann and Bill need to pay attention to societal trends in order to anticipate how their actions might be judged in the future. Because most laws are ethically based, Ann and Bill can probably minimize any criminal liability by acting ethically.

CHAPTER TERMS

business
business ethics
categorical imperative
corporate culture
egoism
ethics
good will
hypothetical imperative

morality
prima facie obligation
social responsibility
ultra vires
utilitarianism
white-collar crime
will

CHAPTER-END QUESTIONS

1. Give two examples of "socially responsible" actions by companies in your local area or state.
2. Explain an ultra vires act. How has this concept changed?

3. Explain utilitarianism and good will.

4. Analyze the following situation using the four theories of ethics:

   You are employed by a shampoo company whose sales have fallen off. In a brainstorming session, the R&D department shows some data that say that most women judge the right amount of shampoo by how much lather is produced when they apply the shampoo to their head. The chemist suggests that the company alter the formula so that less lather is produced, thereby forcing women to use more shampoo in order to produce the same amount of lather. Would this be an acceptable way to increase sales? Discuss.

   Another suggestion is made to decrease the size of the bottle slightly. Would this be an acceptable way to increase sales? Discuss.

   Which of the two is more acceptable? Why?

5. Explain why ethics is important to business.

6. Explain how an act could be legal but not ethical.

7. Faith, a college student, starts a note-taking service for students at her college. She pays students to take copious notes of lectures and then has the notes transcribed, word processed, and duplicated for sale. The lecture notes are available within 24 hours of class. Faith sells the notes on a daily or semester basis. Assume this business is legal. Is it ethical? Discuss.

8. Consider the different ethical choices in the following scenario. In recommending the relocation of a high-polluting industry, the company economist advises relocating to an economically poor country, because, he argues, the costs of health-impairing pollution depend on the earnings lost from increased injury and death. So the poorer the country, the lower the cost of pollution.

9. A female employee fought for and won additional compensation for herself and all the women in her company under the equal-pay-for-equal-work law. On the heels of that victory, and before the awards had been made, a male coworker suggested that because the company had agreed that women had been underpaid, the female employee ought to insist that the firm pay back wages, as well as increase future earnings. When she approached management with this idea, management indignantly offered three reasons why her suggestion was outrageous. First, the past decisions had been made by management personnel who no longer worked at the company; second, to pay all the women back pay would affect the company's profit picture and require that all workers' pay be decreased in order to afford the women's in-

crease; and third, under the theory of back pay, the company would be obligated to seek out any woman who had ever worked there and then make compensation. What are the ethical issues here?

10. Johns-Manville Corp. failed to put warning labels on asbestos products even though the company knew from its own studies the danger of inhaling asbestos. What are the ethical considerations?

GROUP EXERCISE

Have each group choose a type of business (government, computer industry, education, environmental, manufacturing, etc.). Now do some digging in sources such as newspapers and periodicals to see if the groups can come up with ways that businesses in those industries have done things the group thinks are ethical. As an example, say the government group finds that an agency requires all workers to periodically report conflicts of interest or sums of money they receive from other agencies for consulting.

Alternative 2: Come up with ways you think a business could operate more ethically.

Alternative 3: Think up some ethical dilemmas you are aware of. Have each group discuss them. Then gather to see how each of the groups handled the dilemma. Topics might include selling cigarettes shown to have a link with cancer and other health problems; developing scientific processes that would lead to genetic alterations in humans and possibly to couples' choosing the type of child they wish to have; not requiring seat belts for children on planes, because there have yet to be enough injuries and deaths to justify the added installation cost that would devolve to everyone; advertising in inviting ways cigarettes, liquor, and foods that are known to have a deleterious effect on health, which would cause rising health care costs for everyone by creating health problems that are avoidable; in a multiple pregnancy, allowing hospitals to perform procedures that abort one or more of the fetuses so that the others may be born healthy, because of knowing that if all are allowed to live, all will have serious health problems.

REFERENCES

1 Quoted in Bernard D. Nossiter, *The Mythmakers: An Essay on Power and Wealth* (Boston: Houghton Mifflin), 1964, p.100.

Chapter 5

TORTS

Chapter Preview Summary

In this chapter Ann and Bill learn about the liability they incur for civil wrongs that may result through either negligence, strict liability, or intentional torts. They also learn the defenses against those actions, and, therefore, how to avoid liability in those areas. Further business owner liability and warranties are covered in Chapter 16.

Chapter Objectives

In studying the chapter, you should learn:
• what torts are
• what the characteristics are of various torts
• the underlying basis for the different classes of torts
• which defenses can be used for which torts
• who has liability for torts

INTRODUCTION

Fortunately (or unfortunately, depending on which side they are on), Bill and Ann have available to them a system for addressing torts. As we discussed in Chapters 1 and 3, torts are civil wrongs. That is, they are violations of law that are civil rather than criminal in nature. The plaintiff sues usually in order to be compensated for losses involved in the tort committed against him or her. In this chapter Ann and Bill see what torts are available to them when a wrong is committed against them. Learning the torts will also help them learn what kinds of situations they should avoid in order to lessen possible liability for tortious activity as business owners.

STRICT LIABILITY

strict liability
liability regardless
of fault

If Ann and Bill engage in an activity that is extremely serious, with great potential for harming others, and someone is, in fact, harmed by their act, then they will be strictly liable to the person for the harm done. **Strict liability** means that Ann and Bill can offer no defense to avoid liability except in a case in which the person harmed was harmed after voluntarily assuming the risk of engaging in the activity despite knowing it would be harmful. Being careful and exercising appropriate care do not constitute a defense to a strict liability tort.

Because there is virtually no way for Bill and Ann to avoid liability once it is shown that they engaged in the activity and the activity is a strict liability offense, what constitutes a strict liability offense is defined by statute rather than being a common law offense. States may define any activity they wish as a strict liability offense, but the activities traditionally included in most liability statutes are the keeping of wild animals and engaging in ultrahazardous activity such as the blasting of explosives. These are so serious that if it is shown that Bill and Ann engaged in either and someone is harmed as a result, they are responsible for the consequences regardless of whether they were careful or whether they intended harm to result.

KLEIN V. PRYODYNE CORP.

117 Wash. 2d 1 (1991)

An aerial fireworks contractor who put on public fireworks displays contracted to provide fireworks for a Fourth of July celebration at a state fair. Two spectators were injured when a mortar was knocked into a horizontal position and discharged into the crowd. They brought suit alleging that the appropriate standard of review was strict liability for the activity they alleged was abnormally dangerous. The court agreed.

Guy, J.: Section 519 of the Restatement (Second) of Torts provides that anyone carrying on "abnormally dangerous activity" is strictly liable for ensuing damages. Section 520 lists six factors that are to be considered in determining whether an activity is abnormally dangerous: "(a) existence of a high degree of risk of harm to the person, land, or chattel [personal property] of others; (b) likelihood that the harm that results from it will be great; (c) inability to eliminate the risk by the exercise of reasonable care; (d) extent to which the activity is not a matter of common usage; (e) inappropriateness of the activity to the place where it is carried on; and (f) extent to which its value to the community is outweighed by its dangerous attributes." Any one of these factors is not sufficient of itself, and ordinarily several of them are required for strict liability. The essential question is whether the risk created is so unusual as to justify the imposition of strict liability for the harm that results from it, even though it may be carried on with all reasonable care.

The factors in clauses (a), (b), and (c) are all present in the case of firework displays. With fireworks, risk is always present and no matter how much care is exercised, pyrotechnicians cannot entirely eliminate the high risk inherent in setting off fireworks near crowds.

As for factor (d), although fireworks are common on the Fourth of July, relatively few persons conduct public fireworks displays, and thus, presenting public displays is not a matter of common usage. The location—factor (e)—is not an issue here, because although some

continued on next page

locations, such as over water, may be safer, the fairgrounds is an appropriate place for a fireworks show. Regarding factor (f), the county has a long tradition of fireworks on the Fourth of July. That tradition suggests that we as a society have decided the value of fireworks on the day celebrating our national independence outweighs the risk of injury.

Four of the six factors for determining whether an activity is abnormally dangerous are present here. We therefore hold that conducting public fireworks displays is an abnormally dangerous activity justifying the imposition of strict liability.

Case Questions

1. Do you agree with the court's decision? Why or why not?

2. Does it seem consistent for the court to say we as a society have deemed fireworks on the Fourth of July to be appropriate as a way to celebrate our country's independence and then to hold the pyrotechnicians strictly liable for the harm caused, despite the fact that they may have been as careful as possible? Explain.

3. Discuss what you think the effect such a decision would likely have on those in the business of dealing with fireworks. Discuss the effect on the public.

NEGLIGENCE

negligence
failure to meet the standard of care of a reasonable person under the circumstances

Recovery for accidental injuries is addressed through **negligence** (often called personal injury) actions (see Box 5–1, "Negligence"). When Ann and Bill fail to meet a standard of reasonable care appropriate for the circumstances and someone is injured as a result, they can be sued by the injured party for negligence. Generally, the standard for judging the behavior of the tortfeasor is that of a reasonable person under the particular circumstances. Ann and Bill's truck driver is held to the standard of a reasonable driver driving under similar circumstances. Their window cleaners are held to the standard of reasonable window cleaners. Their waste disposers are held to the standard of reasonable waste disposers. If any one of them has an accident while performing their job and the injured person sues, the

5–1   BLACK LETTER LAW

Negligence

Negligence—failure to meet standard of reasonable care owed to another, resulting in harm to that other. Proof requires a duty, breach of duty, proximate cause, and damages. *A customer slips and falls in Ann and Bill's office when Ann and Bill fail to up water they spilled on the floor.*

court will examine whether the tortfeasor acted as a reasonable person under the circumstances. If the person did, there is no liability; if not, liability for negligence is imposed.

Four requirements must exist before a plaintiff can prove negligence: duty, breach of duty, proximate cause, and damages. Let's say Ann and Bill's workers are cleaning windows when their scaffold falls and injures a passerby. In order to recover in court, the passerby must show that the workers had a duty to build the scaffold in a way that it would not come apart and injure others; that the workers breached the duty by building an unsafe scaffold, which then fell when used; and that the passerby was injured, because of the workers' failure to build the scaffold so that it would not come undone. If the foregoing can be shown, then the passerby would be able to recover for the injuries sustained as a result of the workers' failure to meet the standard of reasonable care under the circumstances.

DEFENSES

It is possible for Bill and Ann to defend against the negligence suit by showing that the passerby contributed to the injury either by doing a negligent act himself (**contributory negligence**) or by voluntarily assuming the risk (**assumption of the risk**) by virtue of knowing that the risk of the scaffold's falling existed and walking under the scaffold anyway. The contributory negligence may have occurred when the passerby pushed on the scaffold and thus assisted in its fall. If either of these defenses was shown, it would be a defense to the negligence action brought by the passerby, preventing passerby from recovering from Ann and Bill.

contributory negligence
plaintiff's engaging in an act of negligence that contributes to the harm arising from negligence by another

assumption of the risk
knowing a risk is present and deciding to take a chance anyway

comparative negligence
comparing the plaintiff's negligence with the defendant's negligence and deducting from plaintiff's award a percentage equal to plaintiff's share of the responsibility

Because a finding that the passerby was contributorily negligent would relieve Ann and Bill of liability, some states have passed **comparative negligence** statutes. In jurisdictions with comparative negligence statutes, once Ann and Bill showed that the passerby was contributorily negligent, the passerby would be able to then show that his negligence accounted for only a certain percentage of the harm that resulted to him, and thus the rest of it should be the responsibility of Bill and Ann.

If the passerby were to receive $100,000 for his injuries and it were found through comparative negligence that he was responsible for, say, 30% of the injuries because of his own negligence, then his recovery would amount to the $100,000 minus 30% of $100,000 ($30,000), or $70,000. If the jurisdiction has no comparative negligence statute and passerby was found to be contributorily negligent, passerby would recover nothing. Some statutes restrict plaintiff's coverage to nothing if the amount of liability attributable to the plaintiff is over 49% or 50%, for the attributable amount of his liability would then outweigh the negligence of the tortfeasor.

PROXIMATE CAUSE

proximate cause
legal cause of negligence for which law will impose liability

Before leaving negligence, a word of explanation is in order about **proximate cause**. By having laws against negligence, our legal system wishes to ensure that people conduct themselves safely, reasonably, and in ways that do not present an unreasonable risk to others. The law therefore holds us responsible for foreseeable injuries to others resulting from our acts. That is, if we can foresee that our conduct presents an unreasonable risk of harm to others, we should not engage in such conduct. For instance, we should not drink and drive because we realize that to do so presents an unreasonable risk of harm to others who may be on the highway with us (or harm to ourselves!).

Proximate cause is the way the law cuts off the consequences of our actions so that we are not responsible for every single act that flowed from our breach of duty, but only those that are foreseeable and should have been contemplated. In this way, strict liability is different from negligence, because under strict liability, the tortfeasor is responsible for all harm that results from the tortfeasor's actions. In negligence, the tortfeasor is responsible only for the harm that was the proximate or legal cause of the tortfeasor's actions. Although the tortfeasor's act may have been the actual cause of harm to a plaintiff, it may not be the proximate or legal cause, because the law cuts off liability past the point where it is foreseeable. Sound confusing? See if you think so after considering the following example.

Ann and Bill are washing department store display windows for a client. Ordinarily, they put up caution signs around a site where they are working to let people know they should be careful of the soapy water on the ground, which may make it slippery. However, one time they forget to put the signs up. Steve comes by and slips on the soapy water, falls, and is injured. As Steve is slipping, he grabs onto Gale, a passerby, to try to steady himself. Gale, carrying a small child, screams because she does not know why she is being grabbed. Gale falls and is injured also. The child falls out of Gale's arms and in a panic, runs into the street. Richard, a pedestrian across the street, seeing the child in the street and hearing Gale's scream, has a heart attack. As Richard drops to the ground, he falls against an art shop wall. Leslie, browsing in the shop, is injured when Richard's fall causes a painting Leslie is standing near to fall on her head and injure her.

Whew! Convoluted enough for you? Let's see if we can tell what proximate cause will decide where the liability lies and who can recover. The actual cause of everyone's injuries is the negligence of Bill and Ann in not putting up the sign that would have cautioned pedestrians to walk around the soapy wetness or be cautious in walking through it. Because they did not do so, Steve slipped and began a chain of events that directly caused the final injury to Leslie in the art shop across the street. But the law will likely not hold Bill and Ann liable for all of the injuries even though their negligence was the actual cause. The reason is that the law wants to keep us from presenting unreasonable risks of harm that are foreseeable from our not acting reasonably. What should that include here? Steve's slipping? Gale's falling? The child's falling? Richard's heart attack? Leslie's being bonked on the head by a picture falling off the wall in an art shop across the street?

You would probably think that Steve and Gale's injuries constituted pretty foreseeable harm that would be likely to result from Ann and Bill's failure to put up adequate warning signs. However, you probably think that Richard's heart attack from seeing the child in the street and Leslie's subsequent head injury due to Richard's fall are not the kinds of foreseeable consequences the law had in mind when it held Bill and Ann responsible for adequately warning people of the slippery surface. Failure to put up a sign is not really related to that kind of injury, you probably think.

Well, you're right. Though Ann and Bill's actions were the actual cause of all of the injuries, they were not the proximate or legal cause of the injuries to Richard and Leslie because those were not the kind of harms foreseeable from a failure to warn. Proximate cause is merely a way the law has so it can cut off the liability for which a tortfeasor will be responsible when it gets too far away from the harm the law was trying to prevent.

INTENTIONAL TORTS

intentional tort
torts based on the intentional acts of others

If the civil wrong that happens to Bill and Ann, or that they commit, is not a strict-liability offense or an unintentional accident, then it is an **intentional tort**. Intentional torts are civil wrongs that occur because of an intentional act of some sort on the part of the tortfeasor. What the intentional act must be depends on the kind of intentional tort committed. There are several. In order to hold a tortfeasor liable for an intentional tort, the plaintiff must show that the act needed for the tort was committed and that it was intentional rather than an accident. Whether injury must be shown, as in negligence, depends on the type of tort. Some require a showing of injury, some do not. The intent required is the intent to do the act that results in the harm rather than an intent to harm. (See Box 5–2, "Selected Common Law Intentional Torts.")

INTENTIONAL TORTS AGAINST PROPERTY

Personal Property

trespass to personal property
intentionally interfering with possession and control of someone's personal property

conversion
intentional exercise of dominion and control over the personal property of another

Torts against personal property consist mainly of trespass to personal property and conversion. **Trespass to personal property** is unlawful interference with the possession and control of another's goods. **Conversion** is unlawful exercise of dominion and control over the goods of another. Sound similar? They are. Think of them as being on a continuum, with trespass being the less serious offense, and conversion the more serious. The line is not always clear that delimits when the tort is one or the other. The more serious the interference with the rights of the property's possessor, the more likely the action is to be deemed conversion rather than trespass.

5–2   BLACK LETTER LAW

Selected Common Law Intentional Torts

Assault—intentionally putting another in fear and/or apprehension of an immediate offensive bodily touching. *Bill or Ann points a gun at a customer who walks up to the counter.*

Battery—intentional , unwanted touching of the body of another. *Bill or Ann slaps a client during a meeting.*

Conversion—intentionally exercising dominion and control over someone else's personal property. *Ann and Bill's employee takes equipment home from the job in order to perform jobs "on the side" during the weekend and in the evenings.*

Defamation—intentionally making untrue statements about someone to a third person, which has the effect of lessening the discussed person's reputation in the community. *In front of other employees, Ann or Bill accuses an innocent employee of stealing money from the cash register.*

False Imprisonment—intentionally putting someone in a confined space from which there is no viable means of exit. *Ann or Bill locks an employee in a supply closet.*

Intentional infliction of emotional distress—intentionally doing an outrageous act toward another, which goes beyond all bounds of common decency and causes the victim severe emotional distress; actually not recognized at common law, but only fairly recently. *Ann is frustrated at being given the runaround by a delinquent customer. She cannot locate the customer and in an effort to do so, calls his mother. Ann pretends to be a doctor in the local hospital's emergency room, telling the mother the customer's child has been in a serious accident and the hospital needs the customer's phone number in order to notify him. The grandmother, extremely upset about the "accident," gives Ann the number. The mother later discovers this was only a trick to allow Bill and Ann to locate their delinquent customer.*

Trespass—intentionally coming onto the land of another. *Ann and Bill take a shortcut across a neighboring field to get to the road more quickly.*

The real difference lies in the remedy. The remedy for trespass of personal property is to give the property back to its owner and have the trespasser pay damages for both any harm caused the property and the loss of its use while it was out of the owner's possession.

Conversion is a more serious intrusion into the possessory rights of the owner, and the remedy is a forced sale. That is, the converter pays the owner the value of the good, rather than give the good itself back to the owner. The converter is then entitled to the goods, rather like the signs in stores saying, "You break it, you've bought it." The interference with control can come from a taking of the property from the owner or from a possession that starts out lawfully but becomes unlawful because of not being returned in a timely fashion.

Real Property

trespass to real property
intentionally coming onto the land of another

Anyone who intentionally comes onto Bill and Ann's land or real estate without permission has committed the tort of **trespass to real property**. It does not matter whether the trespasser intended to come onto the property or did so accidentally. The tort is for the protection of the integrity of one's land, and the reason for a trespasser's entering is not important in establishing the tort, beyond intent. In addition, no harm need be proved to establish the tort of trespass to real property, but, of course, without harm, damages will be minimal.

INTENTIONAL TORTS AGAINST PERSON

assault
intentionally putting a person in fear and/or apprehension of an immediate harmful or offensive bodily touching

battery
intentional unpermitted or offensive touching of the body of another

There are several torts that do not involve property, but, rather, involve one's person. Most will sound familiar to you, though you may not know the actual legal specifics of the torts.

Assault—Assault is intentionally putting of a person in fear and/or apprehension of an immediate harmful or offensive bodily touching. An assault is *not*, by definition, an attempted battery. An assault is a tort complete in itself. The victim need not actually be afraid but be merely apprehensive because of perceiving that the unwanted touching is about to occur.

Battery—Battery is the intentional, unwanted touching of the body (or something closely attached to it such as a hat or cane) of another. No harm need actually come about as a result of the battery. It is one's bodily integrity that is being protected, that is, the right not to be touched unless you want to be. The touching need not be hitting or punching. How hard the touch is or whether it draws blood or breaks bones is a matter more of damages than of making out a prima facie case. The tort of battery does not include the usual touching that occurs in daily life such as being jostled on a crowded elevator or bus. However, it can include such if the expected touching is exceeded. Being jostled on a crowded bus is not the same act as someone intentionally "copping a feel" for sexual gratification in the same circumstance. The touching can start off as permitted, then exceed the permission and become unpermitted, for example, in a company picnic touch football game in which one of the players gets carried away and becomes unnecessarily rough in tackling an opponent, or when petting turns into rape.

Defamation—Everyone is entitled to maintain the integrity of their reputation. Defamation is the act of intentionally making an untrue statement about another, in the presence of a third party, which lessens that person's reputation in the community. If the statement is either written or widely broadcast by a source such as television or radio, it is called **libel**. If the statement is made orally, it is called **slander**. Because one of the elements of defamation is that the statement made be untrue, truth is an absolute defense to defamation and the tortfeasor is not liable.

Some statements have a **qualified privilege** if used correctly, such as recommendations by an ex-employer to a prospective employer about an employee who had worked for the ex-employer. If the statements by the ex-employer are made correctly, they are protected from a defamation suit by the ex-employee. This will be discussed further in the section on employment at will.

Other statements are absolutely privileged because of the importance of the process in which the statements are made. For instance, legislators speaking on the floor of the legislature have **absolute privilege** to say what they want and cannot successfully be sued for such statements: This is because of the importance of the legislative process and so that legislators need not worry about being sued while engaging in the important work of the legislature.

False Imprisonment—False imprisonment consists of intentionally putting a person in a confined space with no reasonable means of exit. This tort is most commonly used today by store owners who detain people they believe shoplifted. When it turns out that the person has no stolen items, sometimes in turn the detainee sues the shopkeeper for false imprisonment.

Because the law recognizes store owners' need to detain those suspected of stealing, a store can defend by using the **shopkeeper's rule**. Under the rule, the shopkeeper has a conditional privilege to hold a person suspected of shoplifting. The conditions are that the person

defamation
intentionally making false statements about someone to a third person, which has the effect of lessening the victim's reputation in the community

libel
written defamation

slander
oral defamation

qualified privilege
no liability for engaging in certain behavior as long as the behavior follows prescribed guidelines

absolute privilege
privilege given to engage in certain behavior for which no liability attaches regardless of why the behavior is done

false imprisonment
intentionally confining someone to a place with no reasonable means of exit

shopkeeper's rule
a shopkeeper's conditional privilege to hold a suspected shoplifter in order to investigate, if the suspicion is reasonable, the time is reasonable, and the person receives reasonable treatment

intentional infliction of emotional distress
intentionally doing an act that goes outside all bounds of common decency, thereby causing serious emotional distress to another

invasion of privacy
interfering with someone's legitimate expectation of privacy through one of the four recognized means

intrusion upon seclusion
intentionally coming into someone's private space, photographing the person there, tapping the person's phone, or listening to the person's conversations

appropriation of name or likeness
intentionally using a picture, drawing, or name of someone without the person's permission, generally for economic gain or advantage

false light
intentionally publishing something about someone that puts the person in a false light, even though the actual publication may be true

be held for the charges based on a reasonable suspicion that the person stole something, that the person be held for only a reasonable time, and that the person be questioned in a reasonable way. If those three conditions are met, then even if the suspect did not steal anything, the shopkeeper is not liable for false imprisonment.

Intentional infliction of emotional distress—This tort covers the intentional activity a person engages in that goes beyond all bounds of common decency and causes serious emotional distress to another. It is hard to define because it varies so much from state to state. A community standard is used to determine whether an act goes beyond all bounds of common decency, and so can vary widely. What is shocking in Iowa may not be shocking in New York, and vice versa. This tort would probably cover a situation in which Bill and Ann had come to clean the building of a client, but played a trick on the client by shouting that the building was about to collapse and everyone should clear out. Later, after everyone has cleared out, Bill and Ann tell the client it was only a joke.

Invasion of privacy—This actually consists of several torts. **Intrusion upon seclusion** means intentionally intruding into a space someone has a right to consider private. For instance, say Bill and Ann suspect an employee of stealing equipment, and they break into the employee's house to search for it. Invasion of privacy can also include such intrusions as wiretapping, taking unwanted photos in a private place, and intrusive telephoning. You may recall that in the fall of 1994 a stir was created when a German newspaper published nude photos of Britain's Prince Charles drying off after a bath. The pictures had been taken with a powerful telephoto lens while the prince was in his bathroom. Box 5–3 ("Rest Room Videos") reports on a restaurant owner's troubles in this area.

Appropriation of someone's name or likeness—Let's say Ann and Bill use a picture of publishing mogul John H. Johnson in one of their advertisements as if Johnson were endorsing their cleaning services, when, in fact, he has not. Johnson would be able to sue Ann and Bill for appropriation of his name or likeness as an invasion of his privacy.

False light means engaging in behavior that puts another in an unfavorable light that is not true. For instance, in their workplace newsletter, Bill and Ann run a big headline stating, "Equipment Stolen!" and underneath is a picture of one of their employees. Close by on the page is a smaller article saying the employee pictured is being honored as employee of the month. Anyone glancing at the paper thinks the pictured employee is the one who stole the equipment. The employee would be able to recover from Bill and Ann for false light.

The last privacy action is called **publication of private facts**. It involves one's widely disseminating certain information about someone that, though true, is highly private and need not be publicized. In a classic case, a store owner was owed money by a doctor and the doctor would not pay. The store owner put a sign in his store window saying the doctor was a deadbeat. It did not constitute defamation because it was a true statement, yet it was private information that others had no right or need to know. The doctor would be able to sue the store owner for publication of private facts.

publication of private facts intentionally publishing information about someone that is a private matter

---

5–3   LAW IN THE REAL WORLD

Rest Room Videos

The owner of a local pizzeria was sentenced to six months in a detention center—with the balance of a 10-year sentence to be served on probation—for videotaping women using a restaurant bathroom.

Stephen DeLoach, 30, of Doraville, Ga., was arrested as he entered Mazzio's Pizza carrying videotapes used to record the women through a small camera installed behind a hole in the rest room ceiling, almost directly above a toilet stall. The camera was connected to a video recorder in a restaurant office.

Two of DeLoach's victims—both former Mazzio's employees—made statements. "We were raped of our dignity," one of the women said. "I'm just ill about the whole situation. It's not fair."

The other victim said she has developed a fear of being watched in rest rooms. "I look on the ceilings, I look behind the toilet," she said. "What happened is disgraceful, disgusting."

DeLoach said, "I had a sexual problem and I didn't recognize it. I never meant to hurt anybody."

Query: Aside from the criminal case of invading the privacy of another, which DeLoach was sentenced for, do you think the women DeLoach videotaped have a good case for civil invasion of privacy? Explain.

DREJZA V. VACARRO
No. 92-CV-1281 (DC Ct. App. 8/25/94)

A rape victim sued a police officer for intentional infliction of emotional distress because of the way he treated her after she was raped. The court found the officer's acts sufficiently outrageous to constitute the tort.

Schwelb, J.: This is an action for intentional infliction of emotional distress brought by a rape victim against the police detective assigned to investigate the rape. Some of the detective's more extreme alleged conduct included tossing the distraught victim's undergarments at her while telling her to take her "little panties home" and later joking and snickering about her lack of virginity. He allegedly acted as though the victim's ordeal was insignificant and her complaints unreasonable and bullied her into an initial decision not to press charges against the rapist.

To succeed on such a claim, a plaintiff must show (1) extreme outrageous conduct on the part of the defendant that (2) intentionally or recklessly (3) causes the plaintiff severe emotional distress. The dispositive issue lies in whether the detective's alleged conduct was sufficiently "extreme or outrageous" or, more precisely, whether an impartial jury could reasonably so view it.

The requirement of outrageousness is not an easy one to meet. The conduct must be "so outrageous in character, and so extreme in degree, as to go beyond all possible bounds of decency, and to be regarded as atrocious, and utterly intolerable in a civilized community" (*Restatement [Second] of Torts,* Section 46, comment [d]). Moreover, the nature of the conduct must be considered in the milieu in which it took place.

The detective was dealing with a woman who was in an extraordinarily vulnerable condition. An hour or so before the first interview, as the detective well knew, she had endured a violent rape. Acts that are not generally considered outrageous may become so when the actor knows the other person is peculiarly susceptible to emotional distress.

In this case the detective was also aware that as a result of her ordeal—in her own home where she thought she was safe—she had probably been severely traumatized.

In his role as the detective to whom the victim was taken by other police officers, he was the specialist in sex crimes. He was an official, the victim could reasonably suppose, who could be trusted to assist her and investigate her complaint in a professional and helpful manner. If the victim's account of her encounter is credited, then instead of helping and reassuring her, the detective abused the authority of his office to ridicule, bully, humiliate, and insult her. An impartial trier of fact could reasonably find that any woman who has been raped a short time earlier is thereby rendered peculiarly susceptible to emotional injury. REVERSED

Dissent, Terry, J.: My colleagues are well on the way to creating a new tort of not being nice to a victim of crime. Common decency is a moral, not a legal duty. The detective may be a lout and a boor or worse, but he is no tortfeasor.

Case Questions

1. How can an employer such as Bill and Ann prevent liability from attaching for the sort of activity described here?

2. Do you agree with the majority, or with the dissent? Why?

3. Does the police officer's action seem outrageous enough to you to be considered as intentional infliction of emotional distress? Why or why not?

BUSINESS TORTS

Many of the common law torts can be used for business-related litigation. As we have seen, a negligence action, for instance, may be brought against Ann and Bill if their truck driver accidentally runs into another vehicle. However, over the years, several torts specifically related to the business setting have been developed (see Box 5–4, "Selected Business-Related Torts"). Business-related torts include disparagement, interference with contractual or business relations, palming off (sometimes known as passing off), theft of trade secrets, and infringement of trademarks, trade names, patents, and copyrights. The infringement torts are mentioned only briefly here, but will be discussed in greater detail in Chapter 15.

Disparagement—Disparagement, also known as **injurious falsehood**, is the making of false statements about the quality or ownership of someone's goods. It can be thought of as a defamation against someone's property rather than person. If someone told Bill and Ann's customers that Bill and Ann used cleaning products that had been watered down and lost their effectiveness, Bill and Ann would be able to sue for disparagement. Ann and Bill would be successful if they could show they did not use watered-down products (i.e., that the disparager's statement was false) and that they were injured or otherwise damaged by the statements.

Intentional Interference with Contractual Relations—Bill and Ann can use this tort when someone intentionally interferes with either an existing or a prospective contract they have with another party. For instance, Bill and Ann's competitor, in an effort to gain an advantage, tells a cleaning products supplier of Bill and Ann's that Bill and Ann can no longer pay their bills. Because of that, the supplier stops supplying Bill and Ann's needs—in violation of contract. It would constitute an intentional interference with contractual relations, and Bill and Ann could sue their competitor for the damages they suffered as a result of the competitor's interference with their contract.

Theft of Trade Secrets—If Ann and Bill have either a particular way they clean windows that makes them shine more or a special formula they use to get out stubborn stains, and they keep this matter secret from the general public, they have a trade secret. Ann and Bill could sue for theft of trade secrets if someone who took their secret to use for their own business or to sell to someone else. In order to be successful, they must show that they actually did keep the matter secret and it was not general knowledge throughout the business. This

---

disparagement
intentionally making false statements about the quality or ownership of someone's goods

injurious falsehood
another term for disparagement

intentional interference with contractual relations
intentionally interfering with either established or prospective contractual relations between two or more parties

theft of trade secrets
intentionally taking information that is a business secret and using it for one's own purposes

5–4   BLACK LETTER LAW

Selected Business-Related Torts

Disparagement—intentionally misrepresenting the quality or title of another's goods or services. *Bill and Ann falsely tell others that their competitor is using inferior cleaning products.*

Interference with contractual or business relations—intentionally performing an act that interferes with the contractual relations between parties to a contract. Results in causing one of the parties to refrain from performing as agreed. *Ann tells the creditor of her competitor that the competitor cannot pay bills, and the creditor decides not to extend further credit to the competitor as agreed.*

Palming off—seller sells products as one brand, when it is actually another, generally inferior, brand. *Bill and Ann sell XYZ cleaning compound as the more well-known ABC brand. They are palming off goods on the unsuspecting buyer.*

Theft of trade secrets—theft of a business owner's particular recipe, method of manufacturing, or list of customers that is kept closely guarded and is not public information, even within the company. *Bill and Ann have a cleaning product they make to use for special cleaning jobs, and their employee appropriates and sells to a competitor that secret "recipe" for the product.*

Infringements of trademark, trade name—Trademarks are distinctive marks, mottoes, devices, or implements a manufacturer stamps, prints, or otherwise affixes on goods produced. It is infringement if someone uses another's trademark or trade name without permission. Service marks are used by those who provide services rather than goods, for instance, an airline's logo or symbol. These can be infringed also. *Ann and Bill manufacture cleaning products and attach Procter & Gamble Co.'s moon and stars logo without that company's permission.*

Patent infringement—Patents are granted by the government so that an inventor can have exclusive right to use, make, or sell an invention for a period of seventeen years. Infringement occurs if someone else makes the patented item without permission. *Ann and Bill own the patent to a cleaning product. One of their employees quits and begins manufacturing the product without Ann and Bill's permission.*

Copyright infringement—Copyright protection is granted by the government to authors of certain literary or artistic productions (such as books or music) for a period of the life of the author plus 50 years.

continued on next page

> Infringement occurs if, without permission of the author, a person uses or copies in substantial part the form of expression of the copyright holder's idea. *Ann and Bill take an employee's copyrighted material on how to clean certain hard-to-clean surfaces and publish it under their own name and with no permission from the employee.*

palming off
passing off someone else's goods as one's own

trademark infringement
using the trademark registered to another without permission

patent infringement
making a product for which an exclusive patent has been given to another

copyright infringement
using the original, copyrighted written material of someone else without permission

tort is often used by employers when employees leave, taking information with them that they might then use for their own purposes, financial gain, or economic advantage.

Palming Off—In palming off, Bill and Ann would pass off their competitor's goods as their own so that buyers think they are buying one thing when, in fact, they are buying another.

Trademark Infringement—This involves using another's registered trademark, service mark, logo, or other distinctive mark without the owner's permission. (See Box 5–5, Trends: Corporate Logos Sabotaged and Resold.")

Patent Infringement—Patent infringement consists of making, without the permission of the patent holder, an item patented by that patent holder.

Copyright Infringement—This is the use—without permission—of songs, literary pieces, computer programs, dances, and other such items that have been copyrighted by the creator.

Trademark, patent, and copyright will be discussed in greater detail in Chapter 15.

RESPONSIBILITY FOR TORTIOUS ACTIVITY

respondeat superior
legal theory allowing an employer to be liable for torts committed by an employee within scope of employment

An important part of torts committed in the business setting is the concept of **respondeat superior**. Generally everyone is responsible for torts he or she commits. Through the theory of respondeat superior, however, the law also imposes upon Bill and Ann, as business owners, liability for torts that are committed by their employees within the scope of the employment, even though it was the employees, not Bill or Ann, who committed the torts.

For instance, if their company's waste dump truck accidentally runs into another vehicle while making a delivery, in addition to suing

U.S. HEALTHCARE INC. V. BLUE CROSS OF GREATER PHILADELPHIA

898 F.2d 914 (3d. Cir. 1990)

Blue Cross and U.S. Healthcare (a health maintenance organization, or HMO), large health insurers, engaged in an advertising war with each other. The HMO brought suit against Blue Cross alleging commercial disparagement, defamation, and tortious interference with contractual relations. Blue Cross counterclaimed on the same theories, arguing that its ads were entitled to heightened constitutional protection under the First Amendment. The court did not agree.

Scirica, J.: It started in 1986 when Blue Cross launched what it termed a deliberately "aggressive and provocative" advertising campaign calculated to increase the attractiveness of its products—in particular its Personal Choice product designed to compete with the HMO—at the expense of HMO products. The Blue Cross campaign included direct mail, television, radio, and print advertisements. The HMO embarked on its own campaign that not only highlighted the positive characteristics of its own product but also featured anti–Blue Cross advertisements.

Although the speech here does discuss costs and consequences of competing health insurance and health care delivery programs, some of the advertisements capable of defamatory meaning here add little information and even fewer ideas to the marketplace of health care thought. It is important to note that we do not have a situation in which a corporation addresses an issue of public concern involving a competitor, but does so with speech that is neither commercial nor chill resistant. REVERSED

Case Questions

1. Why do you think Blue Cross would attempt to have its allegedly defamatory speech treated as protected speech under the Constitution?

2. Should defamation or disparagement be protected as free speech? Does doing so necessarily prevent liability from attaching?

Trends: Corporate Logos Sabotaged and Resold

Andy Warhol must be grinning in his grave. Three decades after he made pop art out of Campbell's soup cans, corporate logos are again being mischievously subverted. See that kid in the McDonald's baseball cap? Read between the golden arches: those letters spell *marijuana*. That Adidas-style T shirt? It says *sadist*. A designer water spelled backwards becomes a state of mind (*naive*), and everyday motor oil (Pennzoil) turns into a hallucinogen (*peyote*). Same typefaces—very different messages. "There's so many corporate logos cluttering up your life," says Steve Dukich, whose Seattle band Steel Wool co-opted the Brillo-pad design for its T-shirts. "This is a way to personalize it."

Skateboarders spread this visual sampling way back in the late '80s. The fad spread among ravers, hip-hop kids and media-addicted suburban youth. At The Alley, a counterculture boutique in Chicago, one of the popular summer T-shirts sports a familiar orange cereal box with a boy pouring marijuana leaves into a bowl of "Weedies."

Not amused by satirical infringement of its trademark, Ford issued a cease-and-desist order last year to a line of clothing called Fuct that swiped Ford's familiar blue-and-white oval. Adidas is cracking down on underground designers who replace the company's trefoil logo with a pot leaf. That's OK: logo mania will soon fade into the next big thing. Hot T's at The Alley feature serial killers, Kurt Cobain's [lead singer of the rock group Nirvana] death certificate, and slogans like *Surf Satan*. Cool, dude.

Source: *Newsweek*, August 15, 1994. ©1994, Newsweek, Inc. All rights reserved. Reprinted by permission.

the driver, the accident victim may sue Ann and Bill (or their corporation) as the owners of the business to which the truck belongs. Respondeat superior involves **vicarious liability**. That is, as business owners, Bill and Ann are legally responsible for the torts committed by another—their employee—if that employee was working for them and acting within the scope of the employment at the time of the accident. In Box 5–5, "You Make the Call," several actual situations are presented for you to decide whether the employer should be liable for an employee's actions through respondeat superior.

vicarious liability
liability imposed based on legal relationship between tortfeasor and employer rather than upon the liable party committing the tort

DEFENSES TO TORTS

Even if a tortfeasor engages in tortious activity, she may be able to defend the actions and thus avoid liability. With intentional torts, the tortfeasor can show that there was no intent to do the act that resulted in the harm (i.e., it was an accident), the victim gave **consent** to the activity, or the activity was done in **defense of oneself or others**. For instance, if a person sues Ann for battery, alleging Ann hit that person, but Ann can show that she hit the accuser because the accuser was attacking Bill and Ann was trying to protect Bill, then Ann may be relieved of liability.

consent
giving someone permission to do an act

self-defense
using appropriate force to protect oneself from an unpermitted touching by another

Defenses to negligence may include showing that the standard of care appropriate under the circumstances was complied with or that the victim contributed to the harm by engaging in negligent activity (contributory negligence). Defendants can also allege voluntary assumption of the risk, that is, that the plaintiff knew a certain risk was involved in the activity and decided to engage in the activity anyway. For instance, people have sued baseball park owners when they were injured by balls that hit them while they attended games. When they are harmed by the ball and sue for damages, the owner defends against the action by alleging that signs were posted in the area warning of the possibility of injury from balls, so the plaintiff knew of the potential risk and still voluntarily assumed the risk of sitting in the area. This relieves the park owners of liability.

Because strict-liability offenses are so dangerous, they can generally be defended against only by proving the event did not take place, no injury occurred, or the victim voluntarily assumed the risk involved that resulted in the injury. It does no good in a strict-liability action to show that defendant used due care, because it is irrelevant to strict liability.

5–6   LAW IN THE REAL WORLD

You Make the Call

The following scenarios are from recent newspaper reports. After reading each one, make a determination as to whether you think the employer would be vicariously liable for the acts committed by the employee.

A. Two grocery store employees saw a customer slap her son in the face while in the store. They called the police, who came into the store, handcuffed the mother, and charged her with felony cruelty to children. The charges were later dropped because of the prosecutor's inability to prove the mother caused the boy excessive pain as required by the statute. If the mother sues the grocery store and the employees, should the store be held vicariously liable for the actions of its two employees?

B. A high school teacher provided a group of eight teenagers with 15 cases of beer for a spring break trip to Florida. While walking along a road near the beach in Florida, one of the students was killed when struck by a car. The autopsy found the student's blood-alcohol content at the time was 0.13 percent—higher than the state's legal presumption of intoxication. If the parents of the deceased teen sue the school system for the wrongful death of their child because of the teacher's actions, should the school be held liable?

C. An employer set up a hidden video camera to discover why the coffee had been tasting "funny." The videotape revealed a worker urinating into the communal coffee pot. The employee had been feuding with coworkers. If an employee who drank the coffee becomes ill and sues the employer, should the employer be held liable?

DAMAGES

We discussed in Chapter 3 the matter of one's recovery of damages—under the law—for injuries caused by others. If the torts spoken of in this chapter are proven to the satisfaction of the court, the plaintiff may be able to recover compensatory damages; injunctive relief; damages for loss of wages, pain, and suffering; prospective earnings; or any other type of damages that may be appropriate.

Because recovery for injuries or other losses is the main object of civil suits, the victim will want to maximize chances of recovery for those losses. For instance, Ann and Bill will generally be in a better financial position to make the victim whole than will the truck driver who was working for them. Under the **deep-pockets theory**, victims sue the person who has the most money. Ann and Bill, as owners of the business, likely have more money, or "deeper pockets," than their truck driver employee and would likely be the ones sued.

deep-pockets theory plaintiff's suing of business owner, who is thought to have more money to pay a judgment for tort committed by the owner's employee in the course of business

SUMMARY

Torts are civil wrongs for which Bill and Ann may sue to receive compensation for injuries. Alternatively, if Bill and Ann commit torts themselves, they are liable to the person injured. The law of torts exists to compensate the injured rather than punish the tortfeasor, but punitive damages are available in some cases to discourage certain activity.

Ann and Bill should ensure that they, as well as their employees, do not engage in activity that might cause injury to the person, property, or economic interest of others.

CHAPTER TERMS

absolute privilege	contributory negligence
appropriation of name or likeness	conversion
assault	copyright infringement
assumption of the risk	deep-pockets theory
battery	defamation
comparative negligence	disparagement
consent	false imprisonment

false light	publication of private facts
injurious falsehood	qualified privilege
intentional infliction	respondeat superior
of emotional distress	self-defense
intentional interference with	shopkeeper's rule
contractual relations	slander
intentional tort	strict liability
intrusion upon seclusion	theft of trade secrets
invasion of privacy	trademark infringement
libel	trespass to personal
negligence	property
palming off	trespass to real property
patent infringement	vicarious liability
proximate cause	

CHAPTER-END QUESTIONS

1. Roscoe erects a home-size golf driving range in his backyard, complete with a 10-foot-by-10-foot mesh screen to prevent the balls from going too far. One day while practicing his swing, one of the balls goes over the screen and crashes through the window of his next-door neighbor's office, injuring both his neighbor E.J. and a client in E.J.'s office at the time. When Roscoe is sued by E.J. and the client, what are the likely grounds, and what will Roscoe's response likely be?

2. As Cindy Ho is walking to work one day, she sees that Botticelli's Glassworks workers are installing a plate glass window at Puck's Deli. The rope they are using to help lift the glass does not seem to Cindy to be very strong, but she does not want to be late for work and so hurries through the workers and underneath the glass, rather than around it. The rope breaks, the glass falls, and Cindy is injured. Will Cindy be able to recover from Botticelli's Glassworks? Discuss.

3. Would it change your answer if the facts in number 2 were changed as follows? The rope is fine, but when Cindy walks under the glass, it falls and she is injured. As it turns out, the reason the

glass fell was that Cindy teasingly pinched one of the workers as she was going by, he lost his grip on the glass, and it fell, injuring Cindy.

4. As part of a promotion for their window washing services, Ann and Bill feature in front of their office Bessie the elephant, who, while dancing, takes water into her trunk and sprays it on the window, which is then washed by Linda, an employee. Bessie is tame and highly trained, and she has been performing in front of people for years as a dancer. Bessie's trainer is present, and as a precaution, Bessie's hind leg is chained to a parking meter. Half an hour into the promotion, Bessie breaks the chain, moves away from the window—dragging the parking meter behind—and runs down the street, crushing cars, pedestrians, shop windows, and small children. Upon seeing this, Linda has a heart attack. All of the injured parties sue Ann and Bill. Are Ann and Bill liable? Discuss.

5. If one of the people injured by Bessie's attack in number 4 sued Bill and Ann for battery because his car was crushed as he watched from inside the barber shop during a haircut, he could recover. (True or False)

6. While Matthew is asleep on the bus that's taking employees on a company picnic, Maria, whom Matthew barely knows, kisses him. Matthew finds this out upon arrival after he awakens and the other employees tease him about it. If Matthew wanted to bring an action against Maria, it would likely be for

    a. assault.
    b. battery.
    c. intrusion upon seclusion.
    d. intentional infliction of emotional distress.

7. Ceilie, who is pregnant, comes into the Athletic Outlet sporting goods store to look for a left-handed catcher's mitt for her daughter Tess. In the store, Ceilie is approached by two store personnel who grab her arms and loudly tell her to give them the basketball they say she has hidden under her clothing. Ceilie denies the allegation, and the employees drag her to the back of the store where she is detained for three hours. Eventually, they discover Ceilie's pregnancy. What likely happens if Ceilie sues for false imprisonment?

8. Carlton drives a delivery truck for Purvis Inc. Unknown to Purvis, Carlton has been driving the truck home at the end of the day for

his personal use. If Purvis sues Carlton, it will likely be for
_____. Why?

9. Robert, owner of Robert's Inc., one of Bill and Ann's commercial customers, is not satisfied with the cleaning his building has received. He complains to Ruby, the crew leader responsible for the building. The discussion becomes heated and Ruby ends up punching Robert in the face. When Robert sues Bill and Ann for the injuries he received, they defend by saying that they were not involved in the dispute and are therefore not responsible. Is this a good defense? Explain.

10. Another name for injurious falsehood is _____.

11. Manuel opens up a new business, called Delightful Donuts! because of his deliciously light secret recipe. Delightful Donuts! is an instant hit based on its light, delicious, melt-in-your-mouth delicacies. Because he doesn't want anyone else to know his recipe, Manuel comes into the shop every morning before the other employees and makes up the dough for the day. One morning Deborah, an employee of Delightful Donuts! sneaks in and watches while Manuel makes the dough. A few weeks later Deborah quits working for Manuel and opens her own doughnut shop on the other side of town. Deborah's recipe is the one Manuel uses for his doughnuts. Is there anything Manuel can do? Explain.

12. During the building of her magnificent mansion, Mariko visits the site and falls over the railing that runs along the balcony of the building's second story. Will Mariko likely be successful if she sues the contractor on the basis of strict liability? Why or why not?

13. Assume we are still dealing with Mariko and her house from question number 12 above. After the specifications for the house have been furnished to the contractor, the contract has been signed, and the contractor has begun to build the house, Mariko demands that the contractor add beneath her bedroom floor certain heating coils to heat the floor, as well as floor lights to light her path to the bathroom during the night. These additions were not in the original agreement. The contractor refuses. Is this a breach of contract? Why or why not? Does Mariko have any recourse? Explain.

GROUP EXERCISE

As business owners, Ann and Bill will be responsible for the torts their employees commit within the scope of employment. Have groups come up with a policy for Bill and Ann to implement so that employees aware of the owners' efforts to minimize employees' committing torts. Have the class vote on which is the best policy to accomplish the task.

Chapter 6

CONTRACTS

Chapter Preview Summary

In this chapter Ann and Bill learn what it takes to enter into legally enforceable agreements with those with whom they wish to do business. The contracts can cover anything from hiring their employees to ordering cleaning supplies, from purchasing trucks for their business to catering their holiday party, from renting or buying a building for their business to buying employee uniforms, or anything else in between. Bill and Ann will learn how to avoid problems with contracts and what to do when contracts need to be enforced.

Chapter Objectives

In studying the chapter, you should learn:
- the requirements for a valid contract
- how to enforce contracts
- which contracts must be in writing in order to be enforced
- remedies available for breach of contract

INTRODUCTION

Entered into any good contracts lately? Ann and Bill would not be able to run their business without entering into them. Anytime we have someone perform a service for us (unless it is a gift or favor) or we buy things, a contract is formed. So though you may think you haven't entered into a contract lately, you probably have. You did so when you made provisions to attend the school where you are studying and when you took clothes to the cleaners, purchased groceries, had your electricity connected, arranged for cable TV, filled your gas tank at the local pump last time, or purchased this book.

As we discussed briefly in Chapter 1, a contract is an enforceable promise, or set of promises, and the law recognizes its enforcement or a remedy for nonperformance. A contract includes a bargained-for legal detriment (with its concomitant benefit) exchanged between the parties. If there had been no gas in the pump but the station owners still demanded that you pay, or if you took your groceries and left the store without paying, or if your agreements went awry in any other way, then you would quickly realize that you and the party you had a contract with had a set of expectations about what should and should not be done. If you entered into the contract correctly, you would be able to enforce it against the party that did not perform. Of course, if you did not perform, the other party would be able to sue you to enforce the contract.

You can see how important contracts would be to Ann and Bill. As business owners, they must purchase goods and services on a regular basis, enter into contracts to perform services for others, and be paid for such services as a source of business revenue. They need some type of redress when they perform work for others whose payment is not forthcoming or when they order goods or services that do not arrive as scheduled. The way in which they deal with these problems is through the law of contracts.

breach of contract

party to contract does not perform as agreed

Failure of one of the parties to the contract to perform as agreed results in **breach of contract**, for which monetary compensation or other remedies may be given by a court. Generally, this involves putting the nonbreaching party in the position that party would have been in had there been no breach.

In order to be able to recover for breach of contract, the parties to the contract must first meet all the requirements for a valid contract to exist (see Box 6–1, "Requirements for Valid, Enforceable Contract"). That is, they must have *legal* subject matter of the con-

6–1   CONCEPT SUMMARY

Requirements for Valid, Enforceable Contract

- Mutual assent (offer and acceptance)
- Consideration
- Legality
- Capacity
- Compliance with the Statute of Frauds and Parol Evidence Rule (i.e., the contract must be in writing if required by the Statute of Frauds, and under the Parol Evidence Rule, only those provisions in writing will be enforced.

tract, have *capacity* to enter into contracts, exchange between themselves either *consideration* or something of agreed value and have *mutual assent*, meaning true agreement between the parties as to the contract's terms. Mutual agreement consists of both an offer by the *offeror* initiating the contract and acceptance by the *offeree* to whom the offer is made.

Contractual capacity ensures that those who enter into agreements understand the nature and effect of their agreements. Therefore, those under the legal age of contracting (generally, legal age is 18 in most states), those who are intoxicated, and those who are otherwise mentally incompetent lack capacity.

Legality refers to the contract's subject matter being legally cognizable. Generally, if it is illegal to do a thing, then it is illegal to contract to have the thing done. For instance, gambling contracts in states where gambling is illegal, agreements to charge a borrower more than the legal rate of interest on a loan, and agreements to commit crimes all lack legality.

Consideration ensures that parties to the contract actually bind themselves to something by having them exchange both an agreed-upon legal detriment and benefits. That is, either the parties agree to do something they do not have to agree to do, or they agree to forbear doing something they could do if they wish to in order to give another a benefit that the other would not otherwise be entitled to. In the simple contract for buying a piece of equipment for their business, for instance, Bill and Ann agree to exchange money (that they otherwise would not have to give the supplier) for a piece of equipment the supplier would not have to give them in the absence of an agreement to do so.

This description gives you an overview of the factors important to valid contracts. Before we go into more detail about each of these requirements, it is helpful to know that the law of contract is derived from two sources that must be kept in mind constantly.

SOURCES OF CONTRACT LAW

Restatement of Contracts
compilation of states' contract law into one source with suggested approaches that states can adopt if they wish, in whole or in part

There are two sets of laws that govern contracts. Each state has its own common law of contracts. You can imagine how unwieldy this must be in an era when interstate commerce is such an important part of our lives. In any given home or business, you may find goods from virtually all 50 states—brought there by a contract of some sort. Rather than know what the law is in each state, states' contract laws have been gathered in a compilation called the **Restatement of Contracts**.

The Restatement is a compilation of the most common approaches to states' common law of contracts. It is not in and of itself law, but rather a collection of the most common approaches to contract law, which states can either adopt in whole or in part, or even modify as they see fit. The Restatement brings a measure of consistency to the various state laws governing contracts thereby making it easier to deal with the interstate nature of many business transactions. Since most contract law in the Restatement comes from the common law, the terms common law of contracts and common law tend to be used interchangeably to refer to contract law contained in the Restatement.

Uniform Commercial Code (UCC)
compilation of state laws covering commercial transactions including contracts, with a suggested approach, creating uniformity

The other source of contract law is the **Uniform Commercial Code**, or **UCC**. Article 2 of the UCC covers the sale of goods defined as tangible, movable personal property. The UCC tends to simplify contract law as it relates to sales of goods and tailors the law of contracts to fit that specific relationship.

The Restatement and the UCC, which have been adopted in some form by all states, except Louisiana, together cover all contract actions. Generally, sales of goods are covered by the UCC, and land and service contracts are covered by the Restatement or common law. For the most part, our discussion addresses the common law of contracts except when there are UCC rules you should be aware of.

CLASSIFICATION OF CONTRACTS

VALID, VOID, VOIDABLE, UNENFORCEABLE

As stated previously, a valid contract is one that meets each of the four requirements discussed in Chapter 1: mutual assent, consideration, legality, and capacity. In order for the rights to exist that devolve to a contract, the contract has to be **valid**.

If a contract meets the requirements except either that it is required to be in writing and is not or that part of an agreement reached orally before or at the time of contracting is not put into the written agreement (whether or not the agreement was *required* to be in writing), then the contract will be **unenforceable**.

If a contract meets the requirements except that one or both of the parties was not of legal age or there was **fraud in the inducement** as the basis for a party to enter the contract, then the contract is **voidable**.

If the contract does not have legal subject matter or there was **fraud in the execution** in entering into the agreement, then the contract does not actually exist at all. It is called a **void** contract—otherwise an oxymoron, for a void contract is not a contract at all. Void contracts have no legal force and effect and therefore cannot be enforced when the nonbreaching party sues for breach of contract.

EXECUTORY, EXECUTED

When a contract has been fully performed, it is known as an **executed contract**. When a contract has not yet been performed, it is known as an **executory contract**; it has legal status as a contract, but simply has not yet been performed by the parties. It is possible for a contract to be partially executed, in that some of it has been performed and some not yet performed. For instance, if Ann and Bill take out a bank loan, the bank's duty has been executed because the bank has given them the money. Bill and Ann's duties are executory, because they must repay, generally on a monthly basis. Once they complete repayment, the contract will be executed on their part.

valid contract
a contract that meets the requirements of mutual assent, consideration, capacity, and legality

unenforceable contract
a contract that is not in writing as required or will not otherwise enforced by the court

fraud in the inducement
intentional misrepresentation of material facts about a matter in order to induce a party to enter into an agreement

fraud in the execution
intentional misrepresentation that a writing is something other than the contract it actually is

void contract
an agreement that has no legal effect because it lacks legality

voidable contract
a contract that one of the parties may opt not to go through with, without fault

executed contract
one that has been performed

executory contract
a contract that has been made but not yet performed

unilateral contract
agreement in which one party promises to do something if the other party does an act

bilateral contract
agreement in which both parties promise something

UNILATERAL, BILATERAL

Remember that a contract is a set of promises for which the law will recognize a remedy for nonperformance. If one party *promises* to do something if the other party *does* something, it is a **unilateral contract**. If the party *promises* that she will do something if the other *promises* to do something, it is a bilateral contract. A promise in exchange for an act is a unilateral contract; a promise for a promise is a **bilateral contract**.

 For example, Jan says to Pedro, "I promise to give you $400 if you drive my car to Malibu from San Francisco." This creates a unilateral contract when the car reaches Malibu, and Jan must pay Pedro. Say, instead, that Jan says to Pedro, "I promise to give you $400 if you promise to drive my car to Malibu from San Francisco." This would create a bilateral contract as soon as Pedro accepts the offer by agreeing. Of course, if Jan later takes back his promise and decides not to have Pedro make the trip, then this issue becomes quite important. If Jan had made a unilateral offer and Pedro had not yet accepted by driving the car, there would be no contract whereby Pedro could sue for breach.

If Jan's offer was bilateral and a contract was formed as soon as Pedro agreed, Jan would be in breach of the contract if he attempted to take back the offer. In fact, the offer became a contract upon Pedro's acceptance of the bilateral offer. When it is unclear what the parties intended, the default is to bilateral contracts. However, the law will recognize unilateral contracts if the parties so intend.

EXPRESS, IMPLIED-IN-FACT, AND IMPLIED-IN-LAW CONTRACTS

express contract
a contract that parties actually discuss and that may or may not be committed to writing

implied-in-fact contracts
contracts gathered from the acts of parties exhibiting an intent to contract

This categorization deals with how contracts come about, that is, how they are entered into by the parties. Contacts can be express, implied in fact, or implied in law.

If the parties to a contract actually discuss the matter, then it is an **express contract**. Express contracts may be either written or oral. That is, the parties can discuss the contract and either commit it to writing or not, and it is still an express contract.

The vast majority of contracts are actually contracts **implied in fact**. A contract implied in fact is made when the parties enter into the agreement by their actions, rather than because they have actually discussed the matter of entering into a contract. For instance, driving by, Ann and Bill see a dirty plate glass window in a store. They get out of their truck, stand in front of the window, hold up their window-cleaning gear with a questioning look, and point to the window. The owner, inside the building, sees them and nods his head. By their actions the parties have entered into a contract to have Bill and Ann clean the windows.

It would also be an implied-in-fact contract if Ann and Bill are sitting in a bar drinking club soda, and they look at the bartender and point to their glasses. In that setting their actions are understood to mean they wish the bartender to give them another of whatever they had been drinking. By their actions, they have entered into a contract to have the bartender bring them the drinks and to be willing to pay for them. In neither of these cases have the parties actually discussed entering into a contract, and they certainly haven't committed anything to writing; yet it is an enforceable agreement nonetheless—as a contract implied in fact—because of the actions of the parties.

Contacts implied in law are not really contracts at all. Rather, they are the law's way of imposing liability when someone receives a benefit in circumstances under which they would ordinarily be required to pay. The law prevents the beneficiary from being unjustly enriched at the expense of the provider of the benefit by imposing on the beneficiary a duty to pay to the person who performed the service the reasonable value of the benefit.

For instance, a doctor is driving along and sees someone lying in the road, injured and unconscious. The doctor takes the person to the nearest hospital, administers whatever medical attention is needed, and thereafter sends a bill for the services. There is no contract, for there was no mutual assent, the injured party being unconscious and unable to communicate. However, we would ordinarily expect that if we received needed medical services, we would have to pay for them. In this case, it isn't fair to let the injured party who received needed medical care get out of paying for the services by simply saying, "I never agreed to anything, so there is no contract."

To keep the doctor from being left empty-handed, the law will require the injured party to pay the doctor at least reasonable value for the services. This is a recovery in **quantum meruit**, based on a contract implied in law. It is also called a **quasi contract**. It is like a con-

implied-in-law contracts
contracts imposed by law upon parties in an effort to prevent unjust enrichment by one party at the expense of the other

quantum meruit
payment of reasonable value of services or goods imposed by law in a transaction where one would otherwise be unjustly enriched by not being required to pay because an element of a valid contract is missing

quasi contract
appears to be a contract, but generally lacks mutual assent; another name for contracts implied in law

tract but is not a contract because it does not meet the requirements of a valid contract, there being no mutual assent, at the very least.

Rather than let the injured party receive a benefit that party would not otherwise have been entitled to receive for free, the court will require the injured party to pay at least reasonable value for the services. The doctor does not get to charge the normal contract price, but neither is the doctor left empty-handed. The patient does not have to pay the usual contract amount, but only the reasonable value of what was received.

REMEDIES

If a contract is not performed as agreed, the nonbreaching party is generally entitled to remedies for breach. As previously discussed in Chapter 3, such remedies can take the form of legal remedies or equitable remedies. The goal in breach-of-contract actions is to put the nonbreaching party in the position that party would have been in had there been no breach. Several kinds of remedies can be used together in order to make the nonbreaching party whole. Monetary damages may be the most likely way to make the nonbreaching party whole, but if not, then equitable remedies may be used as appropriate. Punitive damages are generally not awarded in breach-of-contract actions. However, if the breach was malicious, fraudulent, or connected with a tort, they may be awarded.

REQUIREMENTS FOR A VALID CONTRACT

restitution
giving back something one party gave other under contract

rescission
contract undone by parties or by court order

There are four requirements for a valid contract. If they are all present and the contract is in the correct form, the contract is enforceable. The four requirements for validity are mutual assent, capacity, consideration, and legality.

MUTUAL ASSENT

Mutual assent is the combination of a valid offer by an offeror and an acceptance of the offer by the offeree. In order for the offer to set up

STAMBOVSKY V. ACKLEY
169 A.2d 254, 572 NYS2d 672 (Sup. Ct. NY, App. Div. 1991)

A home buyer later discovered that the home he purchased had been widely reputed to be haunted with poltergeists. The seller had not told this to the buyer. When the buyer found out, he brought an action for **restitution** to have the court rescind the purchase agreement. The court of appeals granted **rescission**.

Rubin, J.: Whether the source of the spectral apparitions seen by the seller and her family are parapsychic or psychogenic, having reported their presence in both *Reader's Digest* and the local press, the seller is estopped to deny the existence and, as a matter of law, the house is haunted. More to the point, however, no divination is required to conclude that it is the seller's promotional efforts in publicizing her close encounters with these spirits that fostered the home's reputation in the community. In 1989, the house was included in a five-room walking tour of Nyack, N.Y., and described as "a riverfront Victorian (with ghost)." The impact of this reputation thus created goes to the very essence of the bargain between the parties, greatly impairing both the value of the property and its potential for resale.

The doctrine of caveat emptor [buyer beware] requires that a buyer act prudently to assess the fitness and value of a purchase and operates to bar the purchaser who fails to exercise due care from seeking the equitable remedy of rescission. Here, however, the purchaser is not a member of the local community, and the record indicates he met his obligation to conduct an inspection of the premises and a search of available public records with respect to the title. The most meticulous inspection and search would not reveal the presence of poltergeists at the premises or unearth the property's ghoulish reputation in the community. Therefore there is no sound policy reason to deny the purchaser relief for failing to discover a state of affairs that the most prudent purchaser would not be expected to even contemplate. Nondisclosure, under these circumstances, constitutes a basis for rescission as a matter of equity. REVERSED

continued on next page

Case Questions

1. Do you think rescission was appropriate here? Why or why not?

2. Do you think the court was correct in holding that the house was haunted "as a matter of law," meaning no proof to the contrary could be offered? Explain.

3. Can you understand why sometimes a remedy at law is insufficient? Discuss.

in the offeree the power to conclude a contract by accepting the offer, the offer must meet certain requirements.

Offer

offeror
one who gives an offer

offeree
one who receives an offer

An offer is the communication by the **offeror** to create a contract upon acceptance by the **offeree**. In order for an offer to be sufficient to create a contract by its acceptance, it must meet certain requirements.

Requirements

In order to be sufficient to create a contract upon acceptance, the offer must contain *definiteness of terms*, *intent*, and *communication*. Definiteness of terms ensures that the parties understand exactly what it is that is being offered. Anything the parties wish to have as part of the contract should be included in the offer. For the UCC, that means—at a minimum—quantity, quality, and price. If other terms are left out, it is not fatal, because they can be filled in by UCC provisions. For instance, if there is no term for delivery, the UCC states that delivery will take place at the seller's place of business, or if none exists, the seller's home. For non-UCC contracts, all pertinent terms of the offer should be included, as the Restatement does not contain **gap-filling** provisions the way the UCC does.

gap filling
UCC concept of court or parties being able to fill in blanks in a contract when UCC provides rules for such

Intent ensures that the offeror intended to make an offer and was not merely joking, or angry, or in the midst of great excitement. Generally, courts examine the *objective intent* actually demonstrated by the offeror to determine intent rather than the *subjective intent* of what was in the offeror's head. What an offeror says or does is considered, not what the offeror was thinking. If an offeror looks serious and appears to be making an offer, then it matters little that in the offeror's mind it was only a joke.

Communication of the offer must be made to the offeree by the offeror or the offeror's agent. It is not sufficient for the offeree to simply hear about the offer and respond to it.

Termination of Offers

In order for an offer to create a contract by acceptance by the offeree, the offer must still be alive and viable when the offeree accepts. There are several factors affecting the viability of the offer. If one of these factors is present, the offer is terminated, is no longer in existence when accepted by the offeree, and therefore does not create a contract. Thus, when the offeree accepts, the offeree is accepting nothing and is not creating a contract that can then be enforced. The factors that terminate the offer are set forth in Box 6–2, "Factors Terminating an Offer."

Acceptance

General

Acceptance must be by the intended offeree or the offeree's agent, or no contract is created. An offeror can make the terms of acceptance whatever the offerer wants them to be. The offeror, who has complete control over the offer, can require that acceptance be at midnight in front of the double-barreled cannon in the town square, with the football linebacker–offeree wearing green fishnet stockings and a polka-dot dress, if the offeror so wishes. If the linebacker is to accept the offer, it must be as the offeror specified in order to be effective to create a contract.

The acceptance must be an unequivocal acceptance of the contract terms offered by the offeror and can be direct or indirect. Direct acceptance occurs when the offeree simply communicates to the offeror the wish to enter into the contract. Indirect acceptance occurs through the offeror's doing some act consistent with acceptance, such as sending a check for the agreed amount by the time specified.

Under a theory called the **mailbox rule** or the **deposited acceptance rule**, unless otherwise agreed, an acceptance is effective when it is sent, if it is sent correctly. That is, if the offeror specified how acceptance must be made (by mail, fax, etc.), then it is effective as soon as it is sent that way, even though something may happen to delay its

rejection
offeree's nonacceptance of an offer

revocation
offeror's rescinding an offer

option contract
contract of offeror's promising to keep offer open for a stated period

merchant's firm offer
merchant's statement in signed writing that offer will remain open for a stated period, not to exceed 90 days

mailbox, or deposited acceptance, rule
rule that once an acceptance is deposited in the system used for communication, it is a valid acceptance and creates a contract

6–2   CONCEPT SUMMARY

Factors Terminating an Offer

The seven factors that will terminate an offer form the pneumonic DDRRIIL. Keep in mind that the offer has been made and one of these factors occurs before it is accepted.

Destruction of the subject matter: the subject matter of the contract is destroyed through no fault of the parties.

Death or incapacity: The death or incapacity of either party immediately terminates the offer.

Rejection: If the offeree declines to accept the offer, the offer is terminated. If the offer is under the Restatement and the offeree changes the terms of the offer in any way, it is considered to be a **counteroffer**, which terminates the original offer and creates a new offer by the old offeree, who now becomes the offeror.

Revocation: The offeror takes back the offer. The general rule is that an offer can be revoked anytime prior to acceptance by the offeree unless it meets one of the three exceptions. The *exceptions* are as follows.

1. If the offeree has given the offeror an *option contract*, then the offeror cannot revoke the offer for the period covered by the option. An option contract is an agreement that the offeror will hold the offer open for the offeree for a certain time period. The consideration given for the option is not a down payment unless the offeror makes it so. If the offeree decides not to accept the offer, the consideration for the option need not be returned to the offeree. It is not a part of the contract price, but rather a separate contract addressing only the offer being kept open.

2. *Unilateral offer upon which performance has begun:* Unilateral offers are accepted and create contracts by the offeree's performing completely the requested act. Because the general rule is that an offer can be revoked anytime prior to acceptance, it would be theoretically possible that someone begins performance of a unilateral offer, and in the middle of the performance, the offeror revokes the offer. Because the offeree has not yet accepted by completing performance of the requested act, the offer can be revoked.

The law provides that if the offeree has accomplished substantially begun performance of the requested act, the offeror's power to revoke is suspended until the performance is finished or the time has come for the performance to be completed, even if it is not.

3. *Merchant's firm offer:* This is a UCC concept. A merchant is one who deals in goods of the kind being dealt with in the contract. If a merchant gives written, signed assurances that an offer will be held open for a speci-

fied time, then even without consideration to hold the offer open as needed with an option contract, the offer must remain open during that time and cannot be revoked.

Incapacity: If either of the parties becomes incapacitated while the offer is pending then the offer is terminated and has no legal significance.

Illegality: If, after an offer is made but before it is accepted, the subject matter of the offer becomes illegal, the offer is terminated. An example would be if a liquor distiller had made an offer to a bar to sell it certain liquor, and before the offer was accepted, the sale of liquor was made illegal by Prohibition. The outstanding offer to the bar owner would immediately be terminated. The bar owner would not be able to successfully sue the distiller for not delivering even if the bar owner had accepted the terminated offer.

Lapse of stated or reasonable time: If the offeror specifies a time within which the offer must be accepted, it must be accepted within that time or the offer is terminated. If no time is given in the offer, then the law will impose a reasonable time based on the circumstances. At the end of that time, if the offer is not accepted, it lapses and is no longer an outstanding offer that can be accepted to create a contract.

reaching the offeror. It may even be lost altogether. A contract is still created, however, because it was created when the acceptance was sent.

An **acceptance after a prior rejection** occurs when the offeree first rejects the offer, then later decides to accept it. The first communication to reach the offeror is effective. In this case, acceptance is not effective when sent but would be effective only if it were the first to reach the offeror.

acceptance after a prior rejection
an offer that is initially rejected, then later accepted by the offeree

Generally, silence by the offeree after being given an offer does not constitute acceptance. The offeror cannot make offeree's silence into acceptance by saying something like, "If I don't hear from you by 12 o'clock, we have a contract." Of course, this is not so if the parties have a contract, a previous relationship, or a history of making silence an acceptance.

UCC

Under the Restatement the offeree's acceptance of an offer must be unequivocal and be a mirror image of the offer. If it is not—and

acceptance with varied terms
UCC concept allowing offeree to vary the terms of an original offer without terminating it

proposals for addition to the contract
new terms added to an original offer by offeree

any terms are changed by the offeree—it is considered to be a counteroffer, which terminates the offer. Under the UCC, however, changes to the offer are considered counteroffers only if the offeree so states. Otherwise, the offeree is said to have given an **acceptance with varied terms**. Unlike the counteroffer, the acceptance with varied terms does not have the effect of terminating the original offer.

If the acceptance with varied terms is a definite and seasonable acceptance not conditioned on the offeror's acceptance of the offeree's varied terms (remember that it is the *offeror* who has complete control over the offer), then there is a contract between the parties as to the original offer. The varied terms will be considered as **proposals for addition to the contract**, which must be negotiated into the contract in order to become a part of it.

If the acceptance is neither definite nor seasonable, then there is no acceptance and no contract. Seasonable means the offer was accepted within the time set forth by the offeror, or, if none is given, then a reasonable time based on the circumstances. Definiteness addresses the overall impression that the offer is being accepted rather than rejected.

For instance, if a retailer offers to sell Bill and Ann a new truck for $6,000, deliverable on Friday, and Bill and Ann respond that they would like to buy the truck but wish it delivered Tuesday, they have changed the terms of the original offer, but their acceptance is definite in that it expresses a wish to enter into the contract, but with a change in the time of delivery. This is an acceptance with varied terms because it differs from the original, and it is under the UCC because it is a sale of goods. The parties thus have a contract for the truck, and must simply work out the delivery date. When thinking about buyers' being bound to something they may not want, just remember that the buyer had the right to reject in the first place. However, once she gives a definite and seasonable acceptance, there is a contract.

In order to determine what the terms of the contract will be, the determination must be made whether the varied terms are *different* or *additional*. If the varied terms are *different*, in that they change what is actually in the offer to something else (Bill and Ann say they accept the offer but they want it Tuesday, not Friday), then the varied terms will have to be negotiated into the contract, or the original offer stands.

Additional terms leave what is in the original offer but add something to it. If the terms are additional, we must look to see if the offer is between merchants or nonmerchants. If it is between nonmerchants the rule is the same as for different terms. That is, the original offer will stand unless the additional terms are negotiated into the contract. If the additional terms are between merchants, then the varied terms automatically become a part of the contract *unless* (1) the offer is expressly limited to its terms, (2) the offeror objects to the different terms within ten days of receiving them, or (3) the newly proposed terms materially alter the original offer. If any of these occurs, the varied terms are treated as proposals for addition to the contract, which must be negotiated in different terms, that is, as in order to become a part of it.

Genuineness of Assent

Closely aligned with the matter of the method whereby acceptance is accomplished is the issue of whether the agreement reached between the parties is, in fact, legitimate. Oftentimes it may appear so, but it is not so in actuality. For instance, a seller's name may appear on a deed to property, yet it was put there only because the buyer exerted duress on the seller by threatening to expose a private matter if the seller did not comply by signing the deed. (See Box 6–3 for other "Challenges to Mutual Assent.")

CONSIDERATION

Consideration is the thing of value exchanged between the parties to a contract. If there is no consideration between the parties, there is no binding contract. Consideration is often defined as bargained-for legal detriment exchanged between parties. The law does not really deal with value except as value is agreed to between the parties. That is, unless fraud is involved, the parties can agree to consideration of as little or as much as they want. In order to determine what is being used as consideration in a contract, put the contract in the form of the following sentence: "In exchange for _____, I will give you/do _____." You will then easily see what is being given as consideration when it otherwise may seem confusing.

Adequate Consideration

Consideration is usually money on one side of the contract (for instance, Bill and Ann pay money to buy a new piece of equipment), but it need not be. Consideration can be anything the parties decide it is. In order to qualify as adequate consideration to create a binding contract, the party giving the consideration must suffer a legal detriment and the party receiving it receives a legal benefit.

6–3   CONCEPT SUMMARY

Challenges to Mutual Assent

duress
exertion of pressure on a party to influence that party to enter into a contract

Duress This is the exertion of pressure through threats or actual use of physical force; economic disadvantage, exposure of private matters, and so forth, to get a party to enter into a contract. The contract is *voidable* by the party experiencing the duress. The contract is *void* if threat of deadly force is used (gun, knife, etc.) to obtain assent. *Bill and Ann's signature conveying to Shelby the deed to their premises is obtained by Shelby's threatening to start false rumors about Bill and Ann's relationship.*

undue influence
presumption created in the case of a dominant-subservient relationship, opportunity for the dominant party to influence the subservient party, and a contract that tends to favor the dominant party

Undue influence A rebuttable presumption of undue influence arises when it is shown that the accused party had a dominant relationship with the other party to the contract, who was subservient; and that there was opportunity to exert undue influence over the subservient party; and that there is a contract that appears to give an unreasonable advantage to the dominant party. If the presumption is not rebutted, the subservient party will be able to avoid the contract. Dominant-subservient relationships include doctor and patient, priest and parishioner, and attorney and client. *Bill's 87-year-old grandmother signs the deed to her $650,000 house over to her doctor, who is the only one who comes to visit the ill, bedridden patient, who lives alone. The deed conveys the property to the doctor for $2,500. The contract deeding the house is voidable at the option of Bill's grandmother.*

mutual mistake
misunderstanding in which both parties think they are agreeing to the same contract terms, but unbeknownst to them, they are agreeing to different terms

Mutual mistake Both parties believe they are agreeing to something, when, in fact, neither has the same thing in mind. *Ann agrees to clean Tony's building for $2,500 per month for the next six months. Ann thought Tony was talking about his building on 3d and Vine. Tony was actually talking about his building on 16th and U. The 16th and U Street building is much larger and more complicated to clean than the building Ann had in mind. The parties have experienced a mutual mistake, and the contract may be rescinded.*

unilateral mistake
mistake that one party makes in contracting, but of which the other party is unaware

Unilateral mistake The mistake is made by one party to the contract and the other party is unaware of the mistake. The contract is enforceable as stated and the offeror making the mistake must bear the burden. Remember that it is the objective intent that governs, not the subjective intent. It is what the offeror actually said and did, not what was on his mind to do that the court gives effect to. *Jane offered to sell Bill her blue truck, but meant to offer the black truck.* The contract is for the blue truck. If the mistake is made by only one party to the contract and the other knows of the mistake, the court will not allow the party who does not realize the mistake to be taken advantage of. The contract will be on the terms both were aware of. *When Tony offers to have Ann and Bill clean his building, he knows that Ann does not realize that he has a new, bigger building that he wants her to clean, so he doesn't tell her, but agrees to have her "clean his building" for a* *much lower price than it should be for all the square footage his new building has. The court would enforce the contract for the building both knew Tony owned, rather than the one only he knew about, but Ann did not.*

Mutual ignorance Both parties are aware that they do not know all they need to know before contracting, and they contract anyway. Both are bound to the contract even though things turn out differently than the parties thought it would. Of course, again, if one party has superior knowledge, that party will not be allowed to use it to disadvantage the other. *While shopping for office furniture at a secondhand store, Bill and Ann come across an interesting painting they wish to buy. The store owner does not to know who the artist is, and neither do Bill and Ann. They purchase the painting for $5. They later discover the painting is an original Vivaldi worth $2.5 million. The store owner would not be able to get the painting back. Neither party knew the artist, both knew they did not know, and both decided to contract about the painting anyway. The court will not force Bill and Ann to give up the painting, which now turns out to be worth so much more.*

Unconscionability No undue influence or pressure has been exerted on a party to the contract in the traditional sense, but there is a disadvantage involved in the contract, preventing the court from wanting to enforce it. This is a UCC concept. *Bill and Ann contract with their poor, Hispanic clients to sell them cleaning products on a monthly basis. Unknown to the clients, who usually cannot read English, the written agreement says the buyers can have their home taken by Bill and Ann for failure to pay for the cleaning products within ten days of receipt. The courts would most likely not allow such a provision to be enforced.*

Fraud See previous discussion in this chapter.

mutual ignorance
a case of both parties' knowing they do not know one or more factors about the subject matter of a contract, but entering into a contract about it anyway

unconscionability
UCC concept of refusal of a court to give force and effect to a contract that seems grossly unfair to one of the parties

A **legal detriment** is one's doing something one does not have to do, or not doing something one could do if one wanted to. The latter is called **forbearance**. The legal detriment could be giving someone money you have no legal obligation to give in the absence of the agreement. It could just as well be promising to clean someone's garage, repair a car, cook a meal, give a plane ride, or anything legal the parties decide. Forbearance would be agreeing *not* to do something one would otherwise have a legal right to do if one wished—for instance, promising not to smoke or drink until age 25. A **legal benefit** is gaining something one would not otherwise be entitled to in the absence of an agreement.

Note that the terms *detriment* and *benefit* do not have their usual lay meanings, that is, that a detriment is always a disadvantage or negative, and a benefit always an advantage or positive. The term *legal* in

forbearance
not doing something one could legally do if one wanted to

legal benefit
obtaining a benefit to which one is not otherwise entitled in the absence of contract

front of both of the other terms limits their meaning to the contractual context of gaining or losing something because one has agreed to do so. As such, something may actually be a benefit, but is considered for contracting purposes to be a legal detriment.

If Ann and Bill contract with their employees to pay the employees a bonus if they do not smoke while in Ann and Bills' employ, that would be an actual benefit to the lungs and general health of the employees, for they would not be subject to the ill effects of smoking. However, the employees have a legal right to smoke if they wish, so in giving the right away to Bill and Ann via contract, they would thereby suffer a legal detriment.

The employees would also gain a legal benefit because they would receive money (the bonus) they would not otherwise be entitled to receive. Bill and Ann, who would seem to gain nothing by having their employees not smoke, actually receive a legal benefit because they are gaining something they would not be entitled to in the absence of an agreement (employees' not smoking). They also suffer a legal detriment in that they must pay out money they would not otherwise have to pay in the absence of an agreement to the contrary.

Some kinds of consideration do not qualify as adequate consideration to create a binding contract. They lack one of the requirements of the three-pronged definition given earlier. That is, they will not be bargained for, will not be a legal detriment, or there will be no exchange between the parties. If consideration is lacking, then no contract is formed. When the party sues for breach of contract, the party will lose because there is no contract to enforce without the essential element of adequate consideration.

Inadequate Consideration

past consideration
the giving of something of value prior to a party's agreeing to give something in return under a contract

Past consideration is not adequate consideration to support a promise, and therefore it will not create a contract. Past consideration is something that has already taken place serving as the basis for consideration. Because it has already taken place, the bargaining element is not met, and it is not adequate consideration to support a promise.

Let's say Bill's dog is almost run over by a truck, but Naybor rescues the dog and the dog is safe. When Bill hears, he is so grateful that he tells Naybor, "Thank you so much for rescuing Spot. I really owe you one. In fact, come by tomorrow after work and I'll give you a $50 reward." Naybor comes by the next evening, but Bill, irritated with Spot for chewing up his new shoes, refuses to pay Naybor the $50. If Naybor sues Bill for breach of contract, who wins?

Bill wins. Even though Bill promised Naybor the money, the promise is not supported by adequate consideration because the consideration was for something that had already taken place. The dog had already been rescued. The "contract" said, "In consideration of your rescuing my dog, I will give you $50, Naybor." Because the rescue had already taken place, it is past consideration and fails as consideration sufficient to bind the contract.

 If the promise is based merely upon a moral obligation, it will not be adequate consideration to support a promise. Let's say an employee of Bill and Ann's is injured on the job. They feel close to the employee, know the employee is putting three kids through college, and know that workers' compensation payments will not be sufficient to support the employee's family. They tell the employee they will pay $10,000 in yearly installments for five years. They do so for two years, then stop when times get tough for their business. The ex-employee sues for breach of contract.

Our contract's sentence will read, "In consideration of our feelings about you as a valued employee and your family obligations, we will give you $10,000 per year for five years." The feelings that make Ann and Bill want to pay the money are only a moral obligation on their part, not a legal obligation. Under workers' compensation statutes, once the employee receives workers' compensation benefits, the employer's obligation is ended. There is therefore no legal obligation here, but only a moral obligation, and it is insufficient to support the contract. The employee would therefore not win in a suit against Ann and Bill.

If the act the party is to do is based on a **preexisting legal** or **contractual obligation**, then it will not be adequate consideration to support a contract. The preexisting obligation may be based either on law or on contract. Legal obligations arise from laws while contractual obligations arise from contract.

 Assume Ann and Bill have a valued employee who contracted to work for them for a year, but is being wooed away by another company after only six months. Ann and Bill say that if the employee stays, they will pay a bonus of $2,500 at the end of the year. The employee stays, but at the end of the year they refuse to pay. Who wins if the employee sues Ann and Bill for breach of contract?

Ann and Bill win. Their promise to pay the $2,500 is not supported by adequate consideration, and therefore the contract fails. "In consideration of your fulfilling your already-existing contract to work for us for a year, we will give you $2,500." The employee suffers no legal detriment because the employee is promising only to do

preexisting contractual or legal obligation
a legal requirement imposed by law or contract, which exists prior to the time a party agrees by contract to do what is already required

something there is already a contractual obligation to do. When you think about how it seems unfair because Ann and Bill promised the bonus, don't forget to think too about the promise the employee had already made to Bill and Ann before entering into the new agreement to charge more for the same thing that had already been promised.

gratuitous promise
promise to give someone something without receiving anything in return

Gratuitous promises will also not support a contract. Promising to give something such as a gift is not an *exchange*, which our definition requires there to be, and therefore, such a contract fails for lack of consideration. If Bill promises to give Ann a party on her 25th birthday but later decides not to, Ann cannot successfully sue Bill for breach of contract. No consideration supports his promise. It was merely gratuitous. If Ann moves in reliance on Bill's promise and based on his promise contracts with a florist, band, caterer, hotel, paper goods store, and dressmaker, paying down payments on all of those contracts in order to secure performance, then she will be able to get back from Bill what she has paid out in reliance on his promise by using **promissory estoppel**. Promissory estoppel can be thought of as a sort of substitute for consideration when actual consideration is not present but when injustice would result otherwise.

promissory estoppel
court order prohibiting the use of the lack of consideration defense by someone who made a promise knowing it would likely be relied upon when the party moves, to their detriment, in reliance on the promise

Ann would be able to recover the amounts she paid out, but no more. She cannot enforce the contract, because there is no contract. But the court will not allow her to be left holding the bag if she moved only in justifiable reliance on Bill's promise and Bill had reason to know she would do so. Because Bill set up the situation and Ann relied on Bill's promise—to her detriment (by spending money she would not have otherwise spent for the promised party)—the court will stop Bill from being able to use lack of consideration as a defense to a breach of contract action taken by Ann. (See Box 6–4, "Not Adequate as Consideration.")

CAPACITY

Contracts are voluntary agreements entered into by parties, and it is important to ensure that the parties understand what they are doing. Capacity deals with whether parties entering into a contract are of at least minimal age or have the mental ability to be able to comprehend what they have done by agreeing to be bound. In addressing capacity, the law protects three groups in particular: infants, incompetents, and the intoxicated.

Infants are those younger than the legal age for contracting in the state—generally 18 years of age. Bill and Ann have to be very careful

<u>6–4</u>   **CONCEPT SUMMARY**

Not Adequate as Consideration

- Gratuitous promises
- Past consideration
- Preexisting legal or contractual obligation
- Moral obligation

when dealing with minors. The law is set up to favor them, and if Bill and Ann are not careful, they can get left holding the bag. The contracts of parties younger than the legal age for contracting are voidable at those parties' option and at only their option. They may **disaffirm**, or get out of, a contract anytime before reaching the age of majority, or within a short time thereafter. If they do not wish to disaffirm a contract, they can **ratify** it by continuing the contract after reaching the age of majority, in which case the contract will be binding.

Disaffirmance and ratification can be made directly or indirectly. Direct disaffirmance consists of the minor's telling the other party to the contract that the minor no longer wishes to be a part of the contract. Indirect disaffirmance is the minor's doing something at odds with continuing the contract, such as no longer making payments on a car contracted for. Ratification can be either direct or indirect also. That is, the minor, upon reaching the age of majority or within a short time thereafter, can inform the other party of a wish to continue the contract or can simply engage in behavior consistent with doing so, such as continuing the car payments after reaching age 18.

In most states, a minor who disaffirms a contract has the right to get back whatever it is that that minor gave under the contract. The minor's only responsibility is to give back whatever is left of what was received under the contract regardless of the condition of the consideration. If the car is wrecked, the minor gives back a wrecked car. The minor is entitled to full repayment of whatever it is that was given under the contract regardless of the status of the minor's return of her own consideration.

If a minor contracts for **necessaries**—usually considered to mean food, clothing or shelter—then decides to disaffirm, the minor can

disaffirm
exert the legal right to get out of a contract

ratify
perform acts or say words evidencing a wish to go through with a contract despite the legal right not to do so

necessaries
food, clothing, or shelter contracted for by one lacking capacity

do so, but the other party is entitled to receive reasonable value for whatever was provided the minor. The law feels that because the other party has provided the minor with necessaries, that party should not be left empty-handed and should receive some sort of compensation. Recovery is in quantum meruit, so that it is not the contract price or market value but, rather, the reasonable value of the necessaries.

In the case of incompetents, the law requires only that the parties to the contract be able to know and understand what they are doing by entering into the contract. The incompetent party need not be declared incompetent by a court. In fact, if such is indeed the case, the contract is void, not voidable. Rather, incompetent parties need only show they were incapable of understanding the nature and extent of their actions. If, however, an incompetent ratifies during a lucid moment, the contract will be fully enforceable. How one shows a party was having a lucid moment is a matter of factual proof. Only the incompetent has a right to disaffirm the contract, and if the contract is for necessaries, the incompetent party can be made to pay reasonable value.

Intoxicants include those whose mental faculties are voluntarily or involuntarily temporarily impaired due to drugs or alcohol. They lack capacity to enter into contracts and can disaffirm them if made. Intoxicants can also ratify upon becoming sober, in which case the contract becomes enforceable. They too are responsible for the reasonable value of necessaries provided them.

LEGALITY

In order for a contract to be legal, what it proposes to do must be legal. If it is not, the contract is void. Interestingly enough, so-called contracts to kill people ("There is a contract out on his life") are not contracts at all, because it is illegal to commit murder.

Generally, anything that is illegal to do is illegal to contract to do or have done. The law singles out certain kinds of contracts, such as those for illegally high interest rates on noncorporate loans (usury), gambling, and unlicensed professionals as illustrative of illegality. For instance, a person who is not licensed to practice law but who performs legal services for a client would not be able to collect the fee for services from the client, because it is illegal to contract to perform legal services if one is not a lawyer. The law closes the courts to unlicensed practitioners, so they will be less likely to engage in unlicensed practice if they know they cannot sue on contracts for their services.

When parties enter into an illegal agreement and one of them does not perform as agreed and then sues the other for breach of contract, the court generally leaves the parties where it finds them. It does not enforce the agreement, because to do so would encourage parties to continue to make illegal agreements.

Neither will the courts enforce agreements that violate public policy. That is, the agreements go against the court's determination of the underlying policies of statutes or closely held beliefs the court takes notice of. In the following case, a California court was called upon to determine whether surrogacy agreements, in which one woman agrees to bear a child for another, violated public policy.

ENFORCEABILITY OF CONTRACTS

Although not a requirement for validity, another requirement exists for contracts to be fully effective. In order for a contract to be not only valid but also enforceable, some contracts are required to be in writing. Others not required to be in writing have requirements imposed upon them if, in fact, they are in writing. The distinction is purely legal rather than practical. After all, what good is a contract's validity if it cannot be enforced? Nonetheless, the law makes a distinction, so that what we ultimately hope for is a valid, enforceable contract. The previous information addressed the former requirement. The information that follows addresses the latter requirement.

STATUTE OF FRAUDS

Certain kinds of contracts must be in writing in order to be enforced in court. Because the law decided that certain kinds of things were likely to be lied about by parties to a contract (or memory was conveniently uncertain), the Statute of Frauds was created. It requires that contracts about these things be in writing if the parties wish to enforce them. Remember, contracts about matters within the Statute of Frauds are legal and may be valid, but they simply cannot be enforced in a court of law if they are not in writing—for what it's worth. If a contract is one of those required to be written under the Statute of Frauds, we say it is within the statute. If a contract is within the statute, it must be in writing to be enforceable. If it is not in writing, check to see if there is an exception that may apply to make the contract enforceable even though there is no writing. Do not, however, use an ex-

Statute of Frauds
law requiring that certain contracts be in writing to be enforced

JOHNSON V. CALVERT
5Cal. 4th 84, 851 P.2d 776 (Calif. 1993)

A married couple wanted a child, but the wife had undergone a hysterectomy. The couple entered into an agreement with a woman who contracted to carry in her womb a fetus created by the sperm and egg of the couple and to relinquish all rights to the child at its birth in exchange for $10,000. After relations deteriorated between the two sides during the pregnancy, the couple went to court seeking to be declared the legal parents of the unborn child. The surrogate filed to be declared the mother. In deciding the matter, the court had to make a determination as to the legitimacy of the contract between the parties. It decided the contract did not violate public policy.

Panelli, J.: The surrogacy contract does not violate public policy. The parties voluntarily agreed to participate in in vitro fertilization and related medical procedures before the child was conceived; at the time Anna [the surrogate mother] entered into the contract, therefore, she was not vulnerable to financial inducements to part with her own expected offspring. Anna was not the genetic mother of the child. The payments to Anna under the contract were meant to compensate her for her services in gestating the fetus and undergoing labor, rather than for giving up "parental" rights to the child.

It has been suggested that gestational surrogacy may run afoul of prohibitions on involuntary servitude. We see no potential for that evil in the contract at issue here, and extrinsic evidence of coercion or duress is utterly lacking. The contract specifically said that all parties agreed that the pregnant woman had the absolute right to abort or not.

Anna and some commentators have expressed concern that surrogacy contracts tend to exploit or dehumanize women, especially women of lower economic status. Although common sense suggests that women of lesser means serve as surrogates more often than do wealthy women, there has been no proof that surrogacy contracts exploit poor women to any greater degree than economic necessity in general exploits them by inducing them to accept lower-paid or otherwise undesirable employment.

The argument that a woman cannot knowingly and intelligently agree to gestate and deliver a baby for intending parents carries overtones of the reasoning that for centuries prevented women from attaining equal economic rights and professional status under the law. To resurrect this view is both to foreclose a personal and economic choice on the part of the surrogate and to deny intending parents what may be their only means of procreating a child of their own genes. AFFIRMED

Case Questions

1. Do you agree with the court that surrogacy contracts do not violate public policy? Discuss.

2. What do you think of the argument the court said some people made about the exploitation of women? Does it make sense to you?

3. What factors should the court consider in determining whether contracts are void as against public policy?

ception to the writing requirement until and unless you are certain that no sufficient writing exists.

Contracts within the Statute of Frauds

The following types of contracts fall within the Statue of Frauds.

Contracts made in contemplation of marriage: As unromantic as it may sound, if parties agree to certain things as a prerequisite to marriage ("If you marry me, I'll give you $10,000"), then the agreement is enforceable only if it is in writing.

Contracts for an interest in land: These must be in writing to be enforceable. They include leases of longer than a year, sales of real estate, and mortgages. If the agreement is not in writing but the buyer moves onto the property, makes improvements, and has paid part of the purchase price, the law allows the agreement to be enforced even without the writing. This is the **part performance exception**.

Contracts that, by their terms, are incapable of being performed within a year from the time they are made: These too must be in writing to be en-

part performance exception
enforceability of an oral contract for land if the party moves on, makes improvements and pays part of the consideration

forceable. The time starts to run when the contract is made, not when it is to be performed. Whether it is capable of being performed is not a function of the substantive performance itself but, rather, what the agreement language says about the *time* of performance.

If, for instance, the agreement says "Jeanne will come work for Ann and Bill for two years," then the contract is incapable of being performed within one year and must be in writing to be enforced. However, if the agreement says Jeanne is to work on a project and "has up to two years to finish it," then by its terms the contract is capable of being performed within a year from the time it was made and need not be in writing to be enforced. If Jeanne leaves the project without finishing it, Bill and Ann would be able to sue to enforce the contract even though it is not in writing. By its terms the contract was capable of being performed within a year from the time it was made.

Agreements in which an estate executor agrees to be personally bound to pay the decedent's debts must be in writing to be enforceable. If Ann died and Bill as her estate executor under her will, out of deference to their friendship, told one of Ann's personal creditors that if the assets of Ann's estate were insufficient to pay the debt to the creditor, he (Bill) would make good on the debt himself, then in order for the creditor to successfully sue Bill if Bill doesn't pay, the agreement between Bill and the creditor would have to be in writing.

Suretyship agreements must be in writing to be enforced. **Surety** agreements are legal relationships formed when one agrees to help strengthen another's credit by agreeing to pay if the debtor does not. What such agreements are actually saying is, "Give the other party the contract's benefit, and if the party doesn't pay, I will." This is perfectly legal, as you well know if your parents did this so you could get a car or borrow money for your tuition. But if it is to be enforced in court when the debtor doesn't pay and the creditor turns to the surety for payment, it must be in writing.

When the promise is "give it and I'll pay," such as when one orders flowers from the florist to be sent to someone, this is a primary promise, not a secondary one, and it need not be in writing to be enforced. Also, if the real purpose of the promise is to benefit the surety (the one making the promise to pay if the primary party does not), then under the **main purpose doctrine**, the promise is enforceable even though oral.

Say Bill and Ann are having an office building constructed. The electrician working on the building tells them it will not be possible to

surety
one who agrees to be responsible for debtor's debts if debtor does not pay

main purpose doctrine
enforceability of an otherwise unenforceable oral surety contract if the main reason one acts as a surety is for one's own personal advantage rather than that of the debtor

finish the work because the electrical supplier refuses to extend any further credit to the electrician. Without the electrician's finishing, everything else on the building will be held up. Bill and Ann approach the supplier, they ask that the electrician be given what is needed to finish, and they promise to pay if the electrician doesn't. This promise really isn't being made for the electrician's benefit but, rather, for Bill and Ann's. Therefore, technically they are sureties, but the law will allow their promise to be enforceable even though oral, because it is really for their own benefit that the promise was made.

Contracts for the sale of goods of $500 or more must be in writing to be enforceable. This is a UCC rule. It has four exceptions.

1. *Specially manufactured goods upon which performance has begun.* This applies when goods have been specially ordered orally, the maker has begun to make them, and then the buyer backs out of the deal. The law permits the nonbreaching party to recover on such an oral contract for $500 or more, even though it should have been in writing. For instance, say Bill and Ann order by phone $650 worth of business stationery, pencils, pens, business cards, and magnets, all with their company logo on them. After the printer begins to make up the order, they cancel. Even though such a contract is required to be in writing (because it is for more than $500) and is not, it will be enforced anyway, because it involved specially manufactured goods and the printer had begun performance.

2. *Part performance.* If one of the parties partially performs the contract, then the contract will be enforceable to the extent it was performed. For example, say Bill and Ann orally ordered 100 new brooms, 100 new mops, 100 new dustpans, and 100 new vacuum cleaners, for a total of $2,500. Half of the order was delivered, and Ann and Bill accepted it but then refused to go through with the rest of the contract. Because the contract involved more than $500, it was required to be in writing before the seller could sue Ann and Bill to enforce the agreement. It was not in writing, however. Bill and Ann accepted half the goods, and they must now pay for the half they accepted. The contract for the other half is still unenforceable because the contract is enforceable only up to the amount of that partially performed.

If the contract is not able to be divided because of its nature, it will be enforceable in its entirety. If Bill and Ann had orally ordered a new $650 television set for their employee lounge, sent a $50 down payment, and then backed out of the contract, the contract for the television set would be enforceable.

3. *Admissions in court documents.* Sometimes parties to an oral contract admit in court documents that they entered into a contract, but because they know oral contracts involving $500 or more must be in writing, they think they have a defense. Or they may agree that they had a contract, but for a lesser amount than is being alleged. If, in the court documents, the parties admit to contracts, then they are liable for the amount admitted to, though no more.

4. *Written confirmation between merchants.* This is a merchants-only rule under the UCC. If a merchant orally contracts to buy goods costing $500 or more, then a written confirmation is sent after the oral agreement, the written confirmation binds both of them unless the receiver objects to the terms of the written confirmation within ten days of receiving it. This generally covers situations in which the parties agree orally, but the written confirmation differs from the oral agreement. The party receiving the written confirmation has a duty to look at it to make sure it accurately reflects the oral agreement; otherwise, that party is bound to the writing even though it does not accurately reflect the oral argument.

The Writing Requirement

The writing requirement is not that the parties actually have a written contract in the traditional sense. There must simply be something in writing, signed by the party who is being sued, that gives evidence of the material terms of the contract. If more than one writing is involved, each must be able to relate to the others without explanation. It is conceivable that a canceled check is a sufficient writing for Statute of Frauds purposes.

Let's say Bill and Ann entered into an oral contract to purchase a parcel of land for a new office building. Half the price was paid by check as a down payment, but the seller breached the contract. Bill and Ann sue, and the seller defends by pleading the Statute of Frauds, that is, that it was an oral contract for the sale of land and is therefore unenforceable. Bill and Ann have in hand the canceled check showing the seller's name as the payee (seller), their name as drawer of the check (buyer), the amount, the signature of the buyer on the back as endorsement of the check, and a memo notation on the lower left of the front of the check saying, "½ the payment for 'Plot 40, Plat 63, Clarke County, GA.'" Thus it is clear that they paid the check to the breaching seller for the piece of land legally described in the check. The seller's signature (the party to be charged, i.e., the party being sued) is represented on the back of the check as an endorsement, and even the date is there. This writing would be sufficient for Statute of Frauds purposes, even though it is not a written contract.

PAROL EVIDENCE RULE

Sometimes when parties enter into a written agreement, it is at the end of a negotiating period during which there have been several conversations, letters, or other correspondence about the matter contracted for. However, once the parties commit the agreement to writing, that writing should include all points the parties wish to have covered. In fact, the Parol Evidence Rule ensures this.

The Parol Evidence Rule provides that if there is a valid, written, integrated contract between the parties, then evidence of prior or contemporaneous agreements will not be permitted to vary or alter the contract's terms. In other words, if the parties to a contract commit the contract to writing as the sole agreement between them but do not include in it some point they agreed on orally before signing the contract, then the point is lost. Contracts are to be enforced as written.

If a written contract is to govern the relationship between parties, then anything the parties want in the contract and agree to before signing the contract should be there. This rule does not apply to agreements made after parties enter into the contract, which later agreements may modify the written contract.

As with the Statute of Frauds, with the Parol Evidence Rule the issue is not whether there is, in fact, a contract. Rather, the issue is, What were the terms agreed to before the parties signed the contract? If one of the parties to the written contract sues for something agreed to between the parties but not included in the contract, the court cannot enforce that part of the agreement if a party sues for breach. Bill and Ann must make sure they include in the written contract before signing it everything agreed upon, or they run the risk that they will not be able to sue for breach if it is not included.

Bill and Ann enter into an agreement to purchase certain equipment, with the seller to deliver it at their warehouse. Before they sign the agreement, Bill and Ann realize it does not contain a provision stating where the equipment is to be delivered. They mention it to the seller, who says not to worry—he knows where it should be delivered to and he'll be the one making the delivery. They do not write it into the contract.

It turns out that the equipment is not delivered. The seller says the equipment is at the seller's warehouse waiting for Bill and Ann to come and get it. Bill and Ann sue for breach of contract, alleging the seller did not deliver the equipment as promised. The written contract, however, had no provision saying seller would deliver it. Because it was not included in the written contract, having been merely agreed to before the contract was signed, Bill and Ann will not be able to introduce evidence in court showing they made such an agreement with the seller. Only the terms of the written contract will be enforced. Because the contract does not say seller is to deliver, Ann and Bill lose. Make sure to get all of it in writing!

CONTRACTS INVOLVING THIRD PARTIES

Until now we have talked only about the offeror's and offeree's being involved in a contract. However, there is the possibility that others may be involved at some point. In those cases, the issue becomes whether the third party has any rights in the contract, either to sue for breach or to demand performance. Resolution of those issues depends on the type of relationship the third party has to the contract. The ways in which a third party can be involved in a contract are by assignment or as a third-party beneficiary.

ASSIGNMENT CONTRACTS

assignment
transfer of contract rights to one not a party to the contract

delegation
transfer of contract duties to one not a party to the contract

Once a contract is formed, rights and obligations accrue to both sides. If Ann and Bill contract to dispose of hazardous waste for Heather, then Ann and Bill have the right to receive payment and the obligation to dispose of the waste. Heather has the right to have the waste disposed and the obligation to pay. If either side decides to allow someone else to receive its benefit in the contract, it is done by an **assignment**. If the duties are transferred to a third party to perform, it is called a **delegation**.

Actually, the word *assignment* is used in a dual sense. It means giving one's rights in a contract over to a third party not originally involved in the contract and, more generically, the relationship that transfers the rights and duties in a contract to someone else not originally in the contract. That is, when contract rights and duties are

6–5   CONCEPT SUMMARY

Assignment of Contract

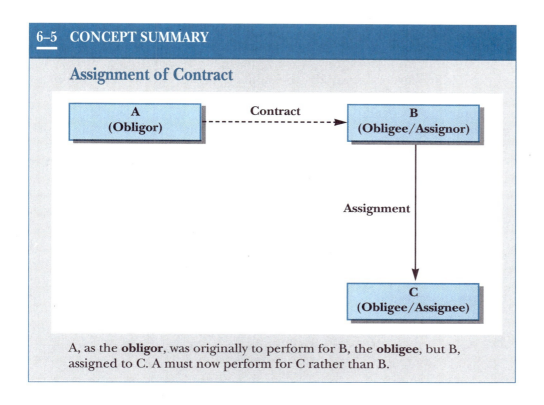

A, as the **obligor**, was originally to perform for B, the **obligee**, but B, assigned to C. A must now perform for C rather than B.

transferred to a third party, it is known as an assignment, even though technically, the giving over of duties to another is actually a delegation. See Box 6–5, "Assignment of Contract," to see the relationship formed when this occurs.

Either party to a contract can assign contract rights to a third party, and generally can do so without permission of the original obligor (the one who is to perform) in the contract. The obligor who was to perform for the original party must now perform, instead, for the third party, called the **assignee**. The one who assigns rights in a contract is called the **assignor**. Virtually any contract may be assigned as long as the contract is not too personal or does not substantially change the obligation of the obligor. The obligor who must now perform for the assignee may not refuse to perform simply because the assignee was not originally a party to the contract. However, if the obligation is too personal or if assigning the contract changes the obligor's duties under the contract by making performance more burdensome, the obligor can refuse to perform.

obligor
one obligated to perform under a contract

obligee
one who receives another's performance under a contract

assignee
one who receives transferred contract rights

assignor
one who transfers contract rights to another

Let's say Bill and Ann contracted to clean Brenda's office building. Brenda later assigns her rights in the contract to Lynette, so that Bill and Ann must now clean Lynette's office building. If the two buildings are substantially the same, Bill and Ann cannot refuse to perform for Lynette under the assigned contract. However, Brenda's building is 2,400 square feet and Lynette's is 5,600 square feet, so Bill and Ann's duties under the contract would be substantially more burdensome than they were under the agreement with Brenda. If they refused to clean Lynette's building, they would not be liable for breach.

There are no formalities to assigning a contract, and no consideration is necessary. However, if no consideration is given and the assignor chooses to take back the assignment, the assignee has no recourse. The assignment is an agreement between the assignor and assignee, but it is not considered to be a contract between them. Instead, when an assignment is made, the assignor is also making implied warranties that certain facts are true. If they turn out not to be true, the assignee can sue for breach of warranty. Warranties are mainly that an assignor does, in fact, have rights to assign under the contract and will not do anything to interfere with the assignee's right to receive benefits under the contract.

When a contract is assigned, the assignee steps into the shoes of the assignor and has the same rights the assignor had under the contract. This means that the assignee is also subject to any defenses to nonperformance that the obligor may have against the original party to the contract—now the assignor. The assignee gets no greater rights under an assignment than the original party had.

For instance, if Brenda had not paid as agreed, for the office cleaning referred to earlier, then Ann and Bill would not have to perform for Lynette, the assignee (assuming the buildings were comparable and the assignment thus valid). Lynette would have to go against Brenda on the grounds of breach of warranty for engaging in activity (nonpayment of the contract price) that adversely impacted Lynette's rights under the assignment (i.e., because the price was not paid, Lynette could not get her building cleaned). Ann and Bill's defense of nonpayment would be good against Lynette's breach of contract action when Lynette sues after Ann and Bill do not clean her building.

An assignable contract need not have the permission of the other party to the contract to be assigned, but notice should be given to the obligor by the assignee or assignor as soon as possible after assignment so that the obligor will not perform for the original party (now assignor).

Although the obligor's permission is not necessary for a valid assignment, if the obligor does give permission, so that now all three parties involved agree to the assignment, it is called a **novation**. A novation takes the assignor out of the contract altogether and substitutes the assignee in the assignor's place. The assignor no longer has any part in the contract. This can be very important, because an assignment does not otherwise relieve the assignor of contractual responsibilities. If the obligor does not perform for the assignee, the assignee can still look to the assignor. If there is a novation, the assignor is totally out of the picture.

novation agreement between obligor, assignor, and assignee to allow assignor to be released from a contract and the assignee be put in the assignor's place

THIRD-PARTY BENEFICIARY CONTRACTS

Unlike assignments which have third parties entering the contract only after the contract is made, **third-party beneficiary contracts** include third parties from the outset. That is, the contract itself is made for the benefit of a third-party. By its design, the contract is between the offeror and offeree, but it is for the benefit of the third-party beneficiary. Third-party beneficiaries have rights in the contract from the time it is made, and their rights cannot be abridged without their consent.

third-party beneficiary contract contract entered into between two parties for the benefit of a third person

A very simple but familiar example would be having flowers sent. Suppose Ann decides to send flowers to Bill on the occasion of their first anniversary in business. Ann calls the florist and orders the flowers. The flowers are not to be sent to her but, rather, to Bill. From the outset and by design, the contract is between the Ann and the florist for the benefit of Bill.

The contract between Ann and the florist you are already familiar with. It is just a regular contract, with regular contract remedies if something should go wrong. However, with the third-party contract portion, the question often arises as to the rights of Bill, since he was not involved in making the contract if something goes wrong with the performance he is to receive. For example, the flowers do not arrive or they arrive wilted or dead. Does Bill, who wasn't involved in the contract, have the right to sue the florist? The answer is yes. Bill is a third-party beneficiary and has the right to sue the florist-obligor for breach of contract if something goes wrong.

donor
one who gives a gift

donee beneficiary
one who is to
receive benefits
under a third-party
beneficiary contract
as a gift from a party
to the contract

**third-party creditor
beneficiary**
one who is to receive
benefits under a
contract as
repayment of an
obligation of a party
to the contract

The other question is, Who else can Bill sue? Can he also sue Ann? That depends on what the relationship is between Ann and Bill relative to the flowers. If the flowers are a gift, then Ann is a **donor** and Bill is a **donee beneficiary**. A donor is the one who gives a gift, and a donee is the one who receives a gift from a donor. But there is no contract between the two, and a gift is not supported by consideration, so there is no basis for a donee to sue a donor. Thus Bill could not sue Ann if this was a gift. Bill could sue only the florist.

If, instead, Ann was sending the flowers to Bill to repay a debt between the two based on a previous obligation, Ann would be the debtor and Bill would be the creditor. In a creditor-debtor situation, the creditor can sue the debtor for nonpayment or incomplete payment. If Ann was sending the flowers to Bill to repay a debt, Bill is a **third-party creditor beneficiary**. If something goes wrong with the flowers, Bill can sue either the florist who was contractually obligated to provide fresh flowers or Ann, who owed him a debt but something has caused its nonrepayment.

CONTRACT PERFORMANCE

condition precedent
act that must take
place before the duty
of a party to perform
under a contract
arises

**condition
subsequent**
act which ends the
duty of a party to
perform under a
contract

Ideally, a party to a contract is supposed to perform the specified duties as soon as the time to perform arises. If the duty has a **condition precedent** to performance, then the performing party need not perform until the condition has been met, for the condition's being met precedes performance by the performing party. For instance, say Bill and Ann agree to be responsible for cleaning all government buildings in Atlanta if the 1996 Olympics are to be held in Atlanta. If the 1996 Olympics are not scheduled to be held in Atlanta, Ann and Bill have no responsibility to clean the buildings. When the city was indeed granted the right to host the Olympics, Bill and Ann had a duty to perform.

If the condition is a **condition subsequent**, then performance is due until and unless the condition is met. Sounds strange, doesn't it? Conditions subsequent are more prevalent than you may realize. Let's say Bill and Ann deed a piece of property to their alma mater, the University of Georgia, "only so long as the land is used for purposes of teaching the business curriculum." The university would be allowed to keep the property unless the condition of not using it for business education purposes is met.

Most conditions are **concurrent conditions**. That is, performance by both parties takes place virtually simultaneously. When you go to the store to buy groceries, you pay for them then and there, and the store gives you the groceries then and there.

concurrent conditions acts on the part of each party to a contract—that must take place at the same time in order for the parties' duties to perform arise

SUMMARY

Contracts will be an important part of Ann and Bill's business. In this chapter they have learned what is required in order for them to have valid, enforceable contracts, what to do if others breach their contracts, how not to breach contracts, how third parties come into contracts, what kinds of contracts must be in writing to be enforced, and how they must perform in order to avoid liability. If Ann and Bill follow the rules closely, they will greatly lessen the possibility of legal problems in the area of contracts.

CHAPTER TERMS

acceptance after prior rejection

acceptance with varied terms

assignee

assignment

assignor

bilateral contract

concurrent conditions

condition precedent

condition subsequent

delegation

disaffirm

donee beneficiary

donor

duress

executed contract

executory contract

express contract

forbearance

fraud in the execution

fraud in the inducement

gap filling

gratuitous promise

implied-in-fact contracts

legal benefit

mailbox, or deposited
   acceptance rule

main purpose doctrine

merchant's firm offer

mutual ignorance

mutual mistake

necessaries

novation

obligee

obligor

offeree

offeror

option contract

part performance exception

past consideration

preexisting contractual or
   legal obligation

promissory estoppel

proposals for the addition
   to the contract

quantum meruit

quasi contract

ratify

rejection

rescission

Restatement of Contracts

restitution

revocation

Statute of Frauds

third-party beneficiary contract

third-party creditor beneficiary

unconscionability

undue influence

unenforceable contract

Uniform Commercial Code
   (UCC)

unilateral contract

unilateral mistake

valid contract

void contract

voidable contract

CHAPTER-END QUESTIONS

1. On July 1, 1994, André, a computer engineer, orally contracts with Cooder Construction Company to provide computer support services for innovations Cooder wishes to institute. Under the contract, André is to provide services for Cooder from January 2, 1995, to September 1, 1995. André begins the work as stipulated, but is terminated by Cooder without explanation on April 11, 1995. When André sues Cooder Construction Company for breach of contract, Cooder's defense is that the contract is not enforceable because it was oral. Is this a good defense? Explain.

2. Linda organizes an office betting pool at her workplace for the NCAA basketball tournament. Gambling is illegal in the state. Everyone contributes $25, winner take all. When Chris wins the pool, Linda refuses to give Chris the winnings—well over $1,200. Chris sues Linda for breach of contract but loses. Explain.

3. The agreement between Chris and Linda in number 2, above, is
   a. void.
   b. voidable.

c. valid.

d. unconscionable.

4. In agreements such as number 2, when a party sues for breach of contact, the court will _____.

5. On March 4 Gloria calls Sheffield Inc. to inquire about cleaning services for her office building. Kim Sung gives Gloria an offer over the phone and says he will send the contract over for her to sign. When Gloria receives the contract on March 6, she immediately signs it and puts it in the mail. A few hours later Gloria finds out she can have the work done more cheaply by another firm, and she faxes a rejection to Sheffield. Sheffield receives the signed contract on March 12. As per the contract, Sheffield employees show up on March 15 to clean Gloria's office building. Gloria refuses to let them enter the premises, saying there is no contract between Gloria and Sheffield because she rejected the offer. If Sheffield sues Gloria for breach of contract, who wins? Why?

6. Weinstein Inc. orders four Lear jets from Johnson Aerospace Co. for an agreed price of $295,000 per jet. The contract for the purchase of the jets is 10 pages long, with complete specifications as to instrumentality, capacity, interior decor, and so forth. When Weinstein gets ready to sign the contract, company representatives notice that the color stipulated for the cloth on one jet's seats is #301, Meadow Green. The color is supposed to be #306 Forest Green. Weinstein calls Johnson to discuss the matter and signs the contract after Johnson says the seats would be Forest Green. Satisfied that the seats would be the correct color, Weinstein signs the contract as is, but does not note the change on the contract. When the jets are delivered, the seats are Meadow Green not Forest Green. When Weinstein sues Johnson, what happens?

7. Bill and Ann have been trying to get a contract with a very large, very prestigious account. Unbeknownst to them, their friend Ku mentioned them to the owner of the company they had been trying to deal with. They then received a call from the owner asking if they could take on the account, which they agreed to do. When they called Ku to tell him the good news, Ku told them of his conversation with the owner. They tell Ku they are so thankful for what he did that they want to give $50,000 to his favorite charity. When Ku later calls to give them the name of the charity,

they say they have decided not to give the money. When Ku sues Ann and Bill for breach of contract, who wins and why?

8. A promise for a promise is a

   a. unilateral contract.
   b. bilateral contract.
   c. executed contract.
   d. voidable contract.

9. When Jekyll goes to paint Hyde's house at the time agreed, Hyde refuses to allow Jekyll in to do the painting. If Hyde sues Jekyll for breach of contract for failure to paint his house, Jekyll can likely successfully defend on the basis of _____.

10. Sarafina enters into a contract with Biceps Store weight-training facility to use the facility for one year. After five months, Sarafina feels she has become too muscular and no longer wishes to train. Sarafina assigns her rights in the contract to Alice. When Alice comes to Biceps Store to train, the store refuses to allow her to do so, saying it has not entered into a contract with her. What are Alice's rights, if any?

GROUP EXERCISE

Have each group decide on some type of agreement the members would like to enter into. After the decision is made, have two groups come together to negotiate one group's contract. The group then meets with another group and has that group negotiate its contract. Each group will have met with one group to negotiate its own contract and one to negotiate the contract of another group. How does it work out? Were all matters in the contract carefully considered? Were the parties willing to compromise if necessary?

Chapter 7

INTERNATIONAL LAW

Chapter Preview Summary

The purpose of this chapter is to introduce concepts involving the international marketplace. Assume Bill and Ann have been looking to expand into the international marketplace both by exporting products and by offering their services to other countries. They should know the ways that international business must be conducted, the international rules and organizations they will encounter in conducting business in another country, the U.S. rules and regulations that have to be adhered to, the ways products can be marketed, and the protections offered to businesses that deal in foreign markets. The primary sources of international law, such as treaties, custom, and organizations, are also introduced.

Chapter Objectives

In studying the chapter, you should learn:
- the sources of international law
- international business regulations
- about the General Agreement on Tariffs and Trade
- U.S. export regulations
- ways to conduct business
- how to license a product
- why multinational corporations are heavily regulated
- about unfair trade practices

INTRODUCTION

 Most successful U.S. businesses seek to expand their markets. (See Box 7–1, "95% of World Population Lives outside the U.S.A.") One of their options is to expand into the international marketplace. If Bill and Ann have been successful in this country, the next logical step would be to increase profits by expanding their sales market. (See Box 7–2, "Top 20 Importers of U.S. Products—1993.")

7–1   LAW IN THE REAL WORLD

95% of World Population Lives outside the U.S.A.

Country	Population	Percentage of World Population
North America*	279,000	5.1%
Asia	3,046,000	56.2
Africa	817,000	15
South America, Latin America, Caribbean	458,000	8.4
Europe	502,000	9.2
Former USSR	293,000	5.4
Oceania and Australia	27,000	.4
Antarctica	uninhabited	0
1993 Total Population	**5,423,000**	
United States	256,561,239	

Source: *The World Almanac and Book of Facts—1994.*

7–2   LAW IN THE REAL WORLD

Top 20 Importers of U.S. Products—1993 (in billions)

Canada	$100.1
Japan	47.9
Mexico	41.6
United Kingdom	26.3
Germany	18.9
Taiwan	16.2
South Korea	14.7
France	13.2
Netherlands	12.8
Singapore	11.6
Hong Kong	9.8
Belgium	8.8
China	8.7
Australia	8.2
Switzerland	6.8
Saudi Arabia	6.6
Italy	6.4
Malaysia	6.0
Brazil	6.0
Venezuela	4.5

Source: Reprinted by permission, *Nation's Business*, May 1994, p. 23. ©1994. U.S. Chamber of Commerce.

Selling a product on the international market involves more than just shipping that product to another country.

Shipment of Bill and Ann's products to a market in another country requires their knowledge of export regulations. However, there is more involved than knowledge of export regulations. Whether a company's dealings are with a large multinational enterprise (for which there are special considerations covered in this chapter) or a relatively small business, competition for international dollars has prompted enactment of rules and regulations that attempt to ensure that only companies that meet international standards for quality can be involved in international business. If Ann and Bill are to compete, then, on the international market, those quality standards must become part of their daily operations of the business. (See Box 7–3, "Quality Standards the World Agrees On.")

Because of increased awareness of the importance of respecting multiculturalism, U.S. businesses must also ensure that neither their products, their salespeople, nor their sales techniques offend international buyers. In order to do this effectively, Ann and Bill must be educated about both the ultimate international business environment they will deal with and their targeted consumers.

To give an understanding of the choices available to Ann and Bill, this chapter presents the traditional business aspects of international law, as well as the emerging multicultural considerations connected with doing business across geographic boundaries.

DEFINING THE SCOPE OF THE INTERNATIONAL LEGAL ENVIRONMENT

International law, by definition, involves the study of many different legal systems other than our own. Those various legal systems apply a variety of mechanisms to regulate business and resolve conflicts. However, that is too wide a scope for our purposes. For this chapter, we limit our study to the sources of international law, international and U.S. regulation of world trade, methods of conducting international business, multinational enterprises, resolution of international disputes, and remedies for unfair trade practices.

SOURCES OF INTERNATIONAL LAW

The primary sources of international law include custom, treaties and other agreements, and organizations. Each of these has its own special considerations, which will be discussed.

Custom

custom
a principle or practice that has developed over a course of dealing that is so well recognized that it becomes binding on the parties to the custom

A **custom** is a principle or practice that has developed over a course of dealing; the practice is so well recognized that it becomes binding on the parties to the custom. The *United Nations International Court of Justice (the World Court)* defines a custom as "evidence of a general practice accepted as law." Many such customs have become the sub-

7–3   LAW IN THE REAL WORLD

Quality Standards the World Agrees On

In American business there's a quickening interest in the series of international standards known as ISO 9000. More and more firms have come to realize that meeting those standards not only can ease entry into the export markets but can lead to significant cost savings.

ISO 9000 certification signifies that a company has fully documented its quality-control procedures, whatever they are, and is abiding by them. (Thus the ISO mantra: Say what you do, do what you say.) ISO certification can bring significant savings by sharply reducing the need for quality audits and inspections of incoming products. "ISO keeps employees involved and aware," reports Tim Barry of American Saw, "and ISO has been a major marketing advantage. We've picked up a bundle of new clients in the U.S. and Europe."

Source: Reprinted by permission, *Nation's Business*, May 1994. ©1994. U.S. Chamber of Commerce.

ject of treaties so as to codify the rules. Any practice left uncodified is still subject to court interpretation as to whether that practice is so well recognized that it has become a custom.

Treaties and Other Agreements

Treaties regulate a large segment of international business. A **treaty** is simply a negotiated contract between parties who happen to be nations. In addition to regulating the subject matter of the treaty, treaties often provide a structure for resolving conflicts that may arise under the treaty. (See Box 7–4, "North American Free Trade Agreement.")

treaty
a negotiated contract between parties who happen to be nations

Other types of agreements include *conventions*, *protocols*, and executive orders, none of which have the force of a treaty, but each of which may be used to further clarify a sovereignty's position.

Sometimes nations are party to multiple treaties that may conflict with one another. This problem was addressed by the *Vienna Convention on the Law of Treaties*, adopted in 1969 (effective 1980). The convention codified the entire law of treaties, and it established rules to be applied in interpreting treaties.

7–4   LEGAL EXCERPTS

North American Free Trade Agreement

Mexico and Canada are major export markets. The North American Free Trade Agreement (NAFTA) provides significant new benefits and opportunities in Mexico and Canada for U.S. industries. From the top 36 U.S. manufacturing sectors and small businesses which export into these countries, a reported $280 billion in exports was generated in 1993. In fact, since Mexico began opening up its markets in 1986, U.S. merchandise exports to Mexico have increased 228%, reaching $40.6 billion in 1992. [The number of] U.S. jobs generated by these exports has also increased, from 274,000 in 1986 to an estimated 700,000 in 1992. Merchandise exports to Canada support another 1.5 million U.S. jobs. By 1995, it is estimated that NAFTA will create another 200,000 high-wage jobs related to exports to Mexico.

Exports are expected to increase because of NAFTA's reduction in tariff barriers and incentives for North American production. NAFTA's main provisions:

- Eliminate Mexican tariff barriers, thereby providing significant new access to U.S. industries and increasing the competitive edge to North American companies over non-North American countries.

- Eliminate Mexican tariffs on 50% of current U.S. industrial exports, and within 5 years 65% of industrial exports; all others will be eliminated within 10 years.

- Eliminate all tariffs on semiconductors.

- Allow U.S. companies to compete for Mexican and Canadian government procurement contracts in such areas as the state oil monopolies and national electricity commission, thereby benefiting U.S. exporters of oil and gas field equipment, construction equipment, telecommunications equipment, and building materials.

- Open "services" to competitive bidding by U.S. suppliers—the first time an international government procurement agreement includes such.

- Require substantial North American input in labor and materials in order for a product to receive zero duty treatment, thereby benefiting such U.S. industries as textiles and apparel, which must contain North American yarn, and the automotive industry, which requires passenger vehicles to contain North American parts.

For import-sensitive industries, NAFTA provides adjustment periods, during which U.S. tariffs will be gradually phased out, ranging from 6 years for textile imports to 10 years for building materials and Mexican leather imports.

Other provisions in NAFTA are seen as important breakthroughs. For the first time, Mexico will protect such trade secrets as production processes, customer lists, and formulas—critical for the protection of high-tech, high-paid U.S. jobs. Canada will drop compulsory licensing for pharmaceuticals. U.S. environmental health, safety, and workplace standards are maintained under NAFTA. NAFTA is said to have created the biggest marketplace in the world: a $6.5-trillion market with 370 million customers.

Source: NAFTA, "Opportunities for U.S. Industries," U.S. Dept. of Commerce, October 1993.

Organizations

Organizations are formed by agreement and may be local, regional, or international. Regional organizations consist of groups of nations whose purpose it is to regulate business within that region. Examples of such regional organizations are the *European Common Market (ECM)*, *Andean Common Market (ANCOM)*, *Organization of Petroleum Exporting Countries (OPEC)*, *Association of Southeast Asian Nations (ASEAN)*, and *Gulf Cooperation Council*. (See Box 7–5, "The European Common Market.")

International organizations are larger in scope than local or regional organizations and are efforts by the world communities to regulate business worldwide. Such international organizations include the International Monetary Fund (IMF), the General Agreement on Tariffs and Trade (GATT), and the United Nations (UN).

organization
an international body that is recognized by most countries as having rule-making capabilities to which those nations adhere

INTERNATIONAL REGULATION OF WORLD TRADE

After World War II the Truman and Marshall Plans opened up the world as a marketplace for everyone. Reconstruction of much of Europe and Japan allowed for all developed nations to contribute. The

7–5   LEGAL EXCERPTS

The European Common Market

The European Common Market, officially known as the European Community (EC), was formed in 1957 for the purpose of building a foundation for economic and political cooperation and to make possible an eventual federation of Europe. Post–World War II economic chaos and the descent of what he called the Iron Curtain led Winston Churchill to declare in 1946, "We must create a sort of United States of Europe."

The primary purpose of the Treaty of Rome, which established the EC, was to create a common market with common customs tariffs and common economic, agricultural, transportation, and nuclear policies between its member nations, which currently number 12. Although to some extent still 12 separate markets, the EC has made strides toward its goal of a unified marketplace.

The EC is well on its way to forming a single internal market with a common monetary policy and currency and similar policies on the environment, immigration, and foreign relations. The EC and the seven European Free Trade Area (EFTA) member countries are also negotiating an expanded European Economic Area (EEA) of 19 nations.

The importance of the EC to world trade, particularly the United States, cannot be overstated. In 1988, imports into the EC amounted to $458.6 billion, with $79.6 billion coming from the United States (23.7% of U.S. exports); exports from the EC amounted to $430.8 billion worldwide, with $84.4 billion worth of goods flowing into the United States (19.6% of EC exports). In 1989, total U.S.-EC trade amounted to $171.7 billion, with the trade balance in favor of the United States for the first time since 1982. By 1992, the trade balance had increased to $17 billion, while exports from the United States to the EC totaled $103 billion.

The United States and the EC are each other's most significant sources of direct investment as well. By 1989, the EC had $194 billion invested in the United States, and the United States had $127 billion invested in the EC.

increased access for U.S. businesses, plus the desire of other nations to engage in world trade, led to creation of international agreements to promote and regulate world business.

One such organization—the Coordinating Committee for Multilateral Export Controls (COCOM)—in a move that reflects the changing landscape of the international political scene, was disbanded on April 1, 1994. COCOM had been an international cartel of Western nations that controlled the export of goods determined to be strategic for certain purposes to politically sensitive locations. That cold war organization, consisting of the United States and other member nations, voted to formally disband as a result of the demise of the Communist political party. It left the 17 member nations to set their own individual rules about export to former Soviet countries.

The General Agreement on Tariff and Trade (GATT)

GATT, in force since 1947, is the only **multilateral instrument** that lays down agreed rules for international trade. It is currently subscribed to by 104 nations (China is not a member), which together account for nearly 90% of world trade. About two-thirds of the member countries are in the early stages of economic development.

The principal objective of GATT is to liberalize international trade and place it on a secure basis, thereby contributing to the economic growth, development, and welfare of the world's peoples. It acts both as a code of rules and as a forum in which countries can discuss solutions to their trade problems and negotiate the reduction of various restrictive trade measures. Those negotiations, called **rounds**, occur every few years and take years to complete. The Uruguay Round began in 1986, concluded on April 15, 1994, and as of May 1994, had been ratified by 109 of its 125 member nations. Effective January 1, 1995, GATT was replaced by the World Trade Organization. (See Box 7–6, "Uruguay Rounds Conclude Three Years Late.")

GATT attempts to impose nondiscriminatory principles on its members by requiring equal treatment of all member countries. That principle, known as **most-favored-nation (MFN) status**, imposes a duty on member nations to exact the same tariffs on every country and requires that the importing country treat imported goods from member nations as though they are domestic goods. (See Box 7–7, "China's Most-Favored-Nation Status Renewed.") **Tariffs** are charges imposed on a product when the product is imported into a country. The

GATT
(General Agreement on Tariffs and Trade) agreement between the United States and several other countries about trading among the nations
multilateral instrument·
agreement between several nations

rounds
conferences held to rework GATT

most-favored-nation status
status given to countries allowing them to enjoy import duties no higher than those of the most favored nation

tariffs
charges imposed on a product when imported into a country

7–6   LAW IN THE REAL WORLD

Uruguay Rounds Conclude Three Years Late

Culminating more than seven years of arduous and often bitter bargaining, ministers from 109 countries signed a far-reaching trade liberalization agreement aimed at stimulating exports and slashing tariffs around the world. This round reduced tariffs by about 40% and included for the first time such areas as agriculture, textiles, and financial services. Left unresolved was whether China would be able to become a founding member of the World Trade Organization [WTO]—the successor to GATT—scheduled to take effect in January 1995. China never became a member of GATT. Some member nations contend that China must open up its domestic economy before becoming eligible for membership.

GATT has estimated that the accord will increase global economy by $235 billion a year. The WTO, in replacing the 47-year-old GATT, will join the IMF and the World Bank as the main watchdogs of the global economy. The new body will have far greater authority than GATT to bring order to world commerce.

The accord deals with a new area—services—in an effort to liberalize trade in banking, insurance, and tourism. Rules were tightened to prevent "dumping" of goods and to protect intellectual property. The backbone of this accord is market access, the opening up of economies to more foreign products. This was accomplished by cutting tariffs on industrial and farm goods by an average of 40%. Although development experts insist that poor African and Caribbean countries will suffer, for the dominant countries of the world, the agreement is considered good news.

Note: GATT was finally approved by Congress on December 2, 1994, after a hotly contested debate which alternately described GATT as good for America and as the last nail in the coffin of direct labor-content employment in the United States. Most opponents of GATT cite the conspicuous absence of environmental protections in GATT, as compared with the same protections included in the NAFTA agreement. Also cited by opponents are the lack of protections for workers' rights and the surrender of U.S. sovereignty to international trade bureaucrats created by the World Trade Organization, which was created by GATT to settle trade disputes. Proponents, on the other hand, applauded GATT as an economic boost and argued that GATT would boost the world's economy by increasing trade and creating 1.4 billion jobs within the United States within 10 years.

Source: *New York Times,* April 16, 1994.

7–7   LAW IN THE REAL WORLD

China's Most-Favored-Nation Status Renewed

In May 1994, President Clinton granted China most-favored-nation trading status once again. This represented an about-face on the issue from where he stood as a presidential candidate in 1992. It was then that he assailed President Bush, who had continued China's most-favored-nation status while ignoring China's human rights abuses. Then-Governor Clinton vowed, if elected, to link China's most-favored-nation status to human rights conditions and stated that only if China improved significantly would [its] most-favored-nation status continue.

However, when faced squarely with the issue, President Clinton de-linked human rights from trade, stating exactly those reasons cited by Bush, i.e., that it is more effective to work with a regime to [which] you have acted hospitably, than to revoke most-favored-nation status and then try to put pressure on an unfriendly regime.

Human rights advocates expressed deep disappointment at Clinton's decision and attributed his actions to chasing the dollar, rather than placing human beings above U.S. business concerns. Advocates had hoped that Clinton would remain firm in his insistence that China clean up [its] abuses. Advocates fear that granting most-favored-nation status removes any possibility of forcing China to improve in that area and insist that now that China has seen an about-face, [it] will be even more hesitant to improve human rights in China.

Source: *Los Angeles Times*, May 27, 1994.

higher the tariff on **imports**, the more expensive the imported goods are, and the less likely buyers are to purchase such imported goods over domestic goods that have no such tariffs imposed upon them.

Most-favored-nation status therefore becomes very important to a country if it wishes to have its goods readily accepted and bought in another country's markets. GATT ensures that one country's products will not have an advantage over those of another due to differences in tariffs imposed.

 There are certain nontariff barriers to free trade that create exceptions to GATT. However, GATT's rounds are continuously at work to remove them. (See Box 7–8, "'Buy American' Violates GATT.")

import
a foreign-produced good or service that is sold in the domestic country

7–8   LAW IN THE REAL WORLD

"Buy American" Violates GATT

The Buy American Act (BAA) began as a Depression-era "device to foster and protect American industry, American workers, and American invested capital." Legislative history describes the law as "primarily . . . an employment measure conceived in the notion that American money should maintain American labor in its moment of crisis and exigency." Today the Buy American Act continues to shape the way in which government contracts are awarded.

Passed on March 3, 1933, the BAA mandates that "only such unmanufactured articles, materials, and supplies as have been mined or produced in the United States, and only such manufactured articles, materials, and supplies as have been manufactured in the United States substantially all from articles, materials, or supplies mined, produced, or manufactured, . . . , in the United States, shall be acquired for public use." Buy-American restrictions are also placed on government construction projects.

Products meeting these criteria are known as domestic end products, for which the determining factor is the location of the manufacturing or mining process rather than the nationality of the contractor. If the end product is manufactured in the United States and at least 50% of its cost can be attributed to domestic components, the goods will be deemed domestic end products.

Recognizing that it is not always possible to use domestic end products, the BAA carved out exceptions for some items, but many BAA restrictions are embedded in specific appropriations bills which mandate that only domestic materials be used. An example of such a mandate was a provision, inserted into a [piece of] National Science Foundation (NSF) appropriations legislation, that no appropriations "may be obligated for procurement of a multibeam bathymetric sonar mapping system manufactured outside of the United States." The effect of the addition was to steer the procurement award away from Atlas Electroniks (Atlas), a German solar-mapping manufacturer and the leading candidate to sell such items to the NSF, and toward Seabeam, a Massachusetts producer.

Atlas complained to Economic Community (EC) officials, and a complaint was launched at the GATT meeting. Although the GATT Agreement on Government Procurement permits some foreign contractors to bid on U.S. government contracts, last year a GATT panel determined that the U.S. procurement action against Atlas inserted into the appropriations bill violated GATT. EC officials allege that, as in this case, Americans have so many exceptions to the way government contracts are awarded that the result is "they are doing a lot less than they claim" toward allowing foreign contractors to bid.

Government procurement represents 20% of all U.S. consumption. In 1990, federal procurement was estimated at $424 billion, while states spent $674 billion on goods and services.

Source: *National Law Journal*, Monday, July 26, 1993, pp. 23–27. Reprinted with permission of Professor William H. Lash, George Mason University School of Law, and the *National Law Journal*. ©1994, New York Law Publishing Company.

Organization for Economic Cooperation and Development (OECD)

The OECD is a 24-nation intergovernmental organization established in 1960 as the successor to the international body that had administered the Marshall Plan. (The Marshall Plan was the agreement made by the industrialized nations to rebuild war-torn Europe after the end of World War II.) The principal purpose of the OECD is to coordinate the key economic policies of the major industrialized countries. The OECD consists of Australia, Canada, Japan, New Zealand, the United States, and the Western European nations.

ISO 9000

Soon to be a major force in regulating international trade with the European Community is the imposition of ISO 9000 (pronounced ICE-o nine thousand and derived from the Greek *isos*, meaning "equal"). ISO 9000 is a series of rules drawn up by the International Organization for Standardization, an international body in Geneva, Switzerland. Founded in 1947, the International Organization for Standardization is a nonprofit group composed of industrial-standard-setting bodies from 92 countries.

The organization sets, but does not enforce, international norms for everything from paper sizes to screw threads to film speed. ISO 9000 concentrates on procedures, controls, and documentation and is designed to assure the international business community that the highest level of quality control is practiced by ISO 9000–approved businesses. The assumption is that better quality control ensures better-quality products.

Although already adopted by 24,000 European sites in 60 European countries, as of late 1992 ISO 9000 had certified only 400 U.S. companies. Between 1991 and 1992, the increase in the number of U.S. companies seeking ISO 9000 certification increased 150%,[1] and the trend to seek certification is growing among small and midsized firms.[2] (See Box 7–9, "Hot New Seal of Quality.")

U.S. REGULATION OF WORLD TRADE

It is unlikely that until their company becomes large enough to expand its production, Ann and Bill will have any interaction with the international organizations that regulate business. However, before they can export products, they will have to apply for a specific kind of export license determined by an evaluation of the type of product Ann and Bill produce. Although many previously restricted technological products have been lifted from the export restriction list, certain products still require special permission to export.

The primary statutory scheme regulating the exportation of goods (not services) to foreign countries is the **Export Administration Act (EAA)**. The EAA grants authority to the U.S. Department of Commerce—through the **Office of Export Administration (OEA)**—to control the flow of **exports** to foreign countries. The EAA cites three reasons for controlling exports: to protect national security, to promote foreign policy, and to prevent a short supply of goods in the United States. The Department of Commerce uses a scheme of licenses to control exports from the United States.

Most U.S. exports require only a general license from the OEA. No application is required and no specific documents are issued or needed to sell most products outside the United States. A validated export license is a specific grant of authority by the Department of Commerce to an individual to export a particular commodity or technology. This type of license must be applied for by the exporter, must be approved by Commerce on a case-by-case basis, and is granted for a specific period of time.

The EAA is the most widely applicable export control. But, there are, in addition, more specific export controls. For example, the *Nuclear Proliferation Act* and the *Atomic Energy Act* (1954) control exportation of nuclear material. The *Arms Export Control Act* controls exportation of weapons to foreign countries.

7–9   LAW IN THE REAL WORLD

Hot New Seal of Quality

What is ISO 9000? Dial-a-horoscope? A foreign sports car? A new galaxy? No, try again: ISO 9000 is a standard of quality management, hugely popular in Europe, that is rapidly taking hold in the United States and around the globe.

DuPont, General Electric, Eastman Kodak, British Telecom, and Phillips Electronics are among the big-name companies that are urging—or even coercing—suppliers to adopt ISO 9000 (say it ICE-o nine thousand). GE's plastics business, for instance, commanded 340 vendors to meet the standard by June (1994). Declares GE's general manager of global sourcing: "There is absolutely no negotiation. If you want to work with us, you have to get it."

"It" is a certificate awarded by one of many independent auditors, attesting that your factory, laboratory, or office has met quality management requirements determined by the International Standardization Organization. The ISO 9000 standards provide a framework for showing customers how you test products, train employees, keep records, and fix defects. ISO 9000 is a set of generally accepted accounting principles for documenting quality procedures. With certificates issued worldwide and estimated at more than 30,000, the standard is rapidly becoming an internationally recognized system, comprehensible to buyers and sellers. The drive for ISO registration can often cost upwards of $200,000 per site.

In the United States, the biggest problem surrounding ISO 9000 is ignorance. Nearly two-thirds of executives at midsize manufacturers either have never heard of ISO 9000 or think it will have no impact on their companies. Other managers cling to the wrong impression that an ISO certificate is a prerequisite for doing business in the European Community. But it is steamrolling through Europe, where about 17,000 certificates have been issued in Britain alone compared with about 1,300 in the United States. ISO is not an acronym in any language. It is an official nickname, derived from *isos*, a Greek word meaning "equal." ISO has been adopted by 60 countries, including the United States, Japan, Canada, and the 12 members of the European Community.

ISO makes no demands or assurances about the quality of a company's products. But many companies insist that ISO is worth chasing, because it helps them run their businesses more efficiently and because their customers are demanding it.

Source: *Fortune*, June 28, 1993. ©1994 Time Inc. All rights reserved.

REGULATION BY FEDERAL AGENCIES

In addition to the statutory schemes designed to control exports, a variety of federal agencies regulate exports.

U.S. Trade Representative

The Office of the U.S. Trade Representative (USTR) is a cabinet-level office with the rank of ambassador. The USTR formulates trade policy for the United States. In addition to other duties, the USTR is the official U.S. representative in all activities concerning GATT.

U.S. Customs Service

The U.S. Customs Service is housed within the U.S. Department of the Treasury. In terms of international business, the office is charged with the responsibility of collecting customs duties, export taxes, fees, and penalties owed for imported merchandise. It also enforces copyrights and patent and trademark provisions.

International Trade Administration

The International Trade Administration (ITA) is located within the Department of Commerce. ITA promotes world trade and strengthens the position of the United States in international trade and investments. It also assists the International Trade Commission when the latter investigates charges of unfair trade practices.

International Trade Commission

The International Trade Commission (ITC) is an independent agency that imposes tariffs and import quotas on industries. The ITC advises the President on and investigates issues such as the balance of trade between imports and exports, economic impact in the United States of any proposed trade agreements, and effects of foreign competition on the United States. The ITC also investigates charges of unfair trade practices, and it recommends appropriate action to remedy proven violations.

METHODS OF CONDUCTING INTERNATIONAL BUSINESS

After Bill and Ann's decision to enter the international market, there remains the decision about how to market their product in another country. If a buyer has contacted the business directly, then a simple **direct sale** may be the answer. If Ann and Bill have not been approached and do not have the capital to venture into the market unguided, they may wish to sell their product to an export company that specializes in marketing their type of product. If their products have name recognition all their own, then Ann and Bill may wish to license their products, or, conversely, they may wish to become a licensee for another company's product. Which method Ann and Bill decide upon will be based upon specific considerations.

direct sale
the sale of goods arranged directly between the buyer and the seller

Direct Sales

The sale of a domestically manufactured good to a foreign purchaser, or export, is the most common and direct way to conduct international trade. The manufacturer or seller is the *exporter*; the purchaser is the *importer*.

In addition to the export regulations that may affect direct sales, a common body of international sales law has developed, known as the *UN Convention on the International Sale of Goods (CISG, or the Vienna Convention)*. The CISG treaty has been adopted by over two dozen countries, including the United States (1988). The treaty applies to the sale of goods between parties whose places of business are in different nations and who have agreed to the terms of the convention.

The Vienna Convention regulates such items as contract formation, delivery obligations and risk of loss, buyer's and seller's remedies, and excuses for nonperformance. The convention applies only to the sale of certain goods. It does not apply to, among other things, household goods purchased for personal use. It is applicable only between merchants doing business.

While direct sales may be the simplest way to market goods internationally, it may well be one of the riskiest. If disagreements arise between the buyer in one country and the seller in another because of contract disputes, nondelivery, delivery of nonconforming goods, nonpayment of goods, or the like, the problem may take on horrendous proportions due to the language barrier, difficulty in communications, and the inconvenience of suing. The CISG is not perfect, but it does offer some comfort to a merchant doing business with another merchant from a signatory country. (See Box 7–10, "Product Take-Backs.")

Indirect Export Sales (Distribution through Export Companies)

Ann and Bill may not have been contacted directly by a potential buyer, but may still wish to enter the international market. Because of the financial risk of direct sales exporting, they may wish to export products through the use of intermediaries known as an *export trading company (ETC)*, and *export management company (EMC)*. Both provide the service of exporting a seller's product to an overseas market. The main difference between an ETC and an EMC is size. An EMC generally is smaller and usually handles only one product or type of product; an ETC generally handles more types of goods. Another difference is that an ETC takes title to the goods while the goods are still in this country, thereby providing the seller with revenue upon sale to the ETC. The seller retains title when dealing with an EMC.

Export trading companies are regulated through the *Export Trading Company Act*, which encourages formation of ETCs by allowing banks to be involved in setting up ETCs, and by reducing an ETCs antitrust liability.

Licensing Agreements

license
an agreement giving the licensee permission to produce or distribute the licenser's product under the licenser's name

A **license** is an agreement (contract) that gives the licensee permission to use, produce, or distribute the licenser's product, information, or invention under the licenser's name. A license agreement is a document or certificate that generally states the terms of the license, including the conditions of its use, assistance the licenser may provide the licensee, compensation arrangements (royalties), the law that will govern, and the method for resolving disputes. The licensee is the party to whom the license is granted. The licenser is the party granting such permission.

Licensing is most often used when a trademark, patent, copyright, technology, or trade secret is involved. The value in licensing a product is that it creates much less financial risk compared with other forms of investment. The drawbacks in licensing are that the licenser can lose control over the product and risks the disclosure of secrets to the licenser's competitors.

7–10   LAW IN THE REAL WORLD

Product Take-Backs

A new approach to regulating the environment has emerged within the last five years with significant international implications. The approach calls for direct regulation of products of manufacturing activities instead of regulating only localized emissions and wastes associated with manufacturing activities. Any manufacturer selling in markets that have product-oriented environmental restrictions is certain to be affected. These developments hold the promise of raising environmental standards for all global manufacturers while carrying the potential of erecting trade barriers.

A German law, effective January 1991, imposes strict packaging "take-back" requirements on manufacturers, importers, and retailers doing business there. Several types of packaging materials are regulated, including transport packaging, secondary packaging, sales packaging, and beverage containers.

Transport packaging is defined as any packaging material that is used by a manufacturer or importer to protect a product during transit, such as drums, canisters, pallets, and crates. In addition to being required to take it back, the manufacturer or importer is required to dispose of it outside the public waste disposal system, by either reuse or recycling.

Secondary packaging is defined as packaging material used to deter product theft or designed for use in vending machines, advertisements, or promotions, e.g., blister packs or cartons. Retailers are required to remove this packaging at the point of sale or allow the consumer to return it to the retailer.

Sales packaging is the packaging used by the consumer to transport and protect the product up to the point of use, such as bags, wrappers, cups, cartons, and bottles. Retailers and mail-order establishments are required to collect sales packaging from the consumer. In turn, manufacturers, importers, and distributors are required to take back the sales packaging from the retailers and reuse or recycle it outside the municipal waste system.

Prompted by the German model, take-back laws have been emerging in other countries. Austria has followed the German model, while Canada, Belgium, the Netherlands, and Sweden have other required take-back laws.

Source: *National Law Journal*, 2/7/94, p. 32. Reprinted with permission of David J. Hayes and Judith King Boyle and the *National Law Journal*. ©1994, New York Law Publishing Company.

Protection from such disclosures can be obtained by filing for an international trademark through the *International Union for the Protection of Industrial Property (the Paris Convention)*, a treaty that provides for trademark protection and protects trademarks and patents from unfair use provided the country in which the goods are marketed honors the Paris Convention.

The Services Area

In addition to products, licensing is also used by service industries. A license from the owner of a trademark or trade name—in the form of an identified set of procedures for conducting a specific business or service, which permits another to sell a product or service pertaining to that trademark or trade name—is called a **franchise**. The franchisee is the renter or buyer or recipient of the franchise license. The franchisor means the grantor of the license. Franchising means conducting the business of selling or servicing franchises. Franchising operations such as McDonald's, Pizza Hut, and other fast-food chains and convenience stores use such licensing agreements.

During the past few decades, the services sector of business has become the dominant employer and producer of income in all developed and many developing countries. Although no commonly accepted definition of the services sector exists, it is generally agreed that it covers such services as transportation, communication, banking, finance, insurance, business and professional, community, social, and personal services. (See Box 7–11, "Historical Background of Merchandising.")

This expansion has prompted GATT to begin talks with the intention of establishing international trade agreements for services much like the agreements produced for trade of goods. Progress was made on this issue during the Uruguay Rounds.

Joint Venture

An international **joint venture** occurs between two or more companies—one of which is not located in the country targeted as a market—that contribute assets for conducting the business. The usual scenario is that Ann and Bill's business, for example, forms a joint venture with a business located in the country in which they wish to do business. Because of the complexity of setting up a joint venture and the strict rules some countries have in place regarding involve-

franchise
a licensed business that uses the name of the franchisor's product in the business

joint venture
a commercial enterprise organized by the participants who control and share its profits and losses

7–11   BLACK LETTER LAW

Historical Background of Merchandising

Although it is difficult to pinpoint exactly when merchandising first began, it is certain that the licensing of properties for use on products to help sell these products is not a truly modern phenomenon. The general concept of merchandising has been around for hundreds of years. It was not until the 1970s, however, that merchandising, as we know it today, really made a major impact on the marketplace.

The earliest example of licensing of properties for use on products dates back to the Middle Ages, when the Popes granted warrants, or licenses, to local entrepreneurs, who collected taxes (royalties) for the Vatican. The next known instance of merchandising dates back to the 1770s, when two enterprising ladies of British nobility permitted their names to be used in association with a line of facial cosmetics in return for a royalty based on sales of the line of cosmetics. Subsequent milestones in merchandising's early history have included the following:

1904	Buster Brown
1913	Theodore Roosevelt licensed the teddy bear
1918	Raggedy Ann (Raggedy Andy followed 2 years later)
1928	Mickey Mouse
1929	Buck Rogers
1930	The Lone Ranger
1930	Shirley Temple dolls
1940	Hopalong Cassidy
1950	Zorro, Annie Oakley, and Howdy Doody
1955	Davy Crockett
1960	Batman and Robin

Source: Reprinted with permission. This material originally appeared in *The Law of Merchandise and Character Licensing*, by Gregory J. Battersby and Charles Grimes, and is available from Clark Boardman Callaghan, 155 Pfingsten Road, Deerfield, IL 60015 (800-323-1336).

ment by the foreign investors (in this case, Ann and Bill) in the joint venture, this type of international business should not be initiated without consulting legal counsel in both jurisdictions.

However, there are substantial benefits to be considered in operating a joint venture. First, the foreign company can use its contacts, distributors, and knowledge of the foreign market. Second, the U.S. partner can decrease its risk of operation and limit its costs of doing business internationally.

MULTINATIONAL ENTERPRISES

multinational enterprise
an enterprise that is directed from its countries of origin (or home countries) and engages in economically significant activities within other states, known as host countries

A **multinational enterprise** (MNE, also known as a multinational or transnational corporation) is an enterprise that is directed from its countries of origin (or home countries) and that engages in economically significant activities within other countries, known as host countries.[3] The difference between a multinational enterprise and any other form of doing business is the former's ability to exercise market power and influence in host countries by "remote control."[4] In addition, the MNE is designed to be controlled by the home country while the effects of the business decisions take place in the host country, without any input from the host country. That is, Bill and Ann would direct from here in the United States the international business located in the host country.

Regulation of the Multinational Enterprise

During the decade of the 70s, multinational enterprises came under intense scrutiny because of the emergence of the political power of Third World countries. The enormous impact of large multinational enterprises on the economic stability of less developed countries (LDCs) was being viewed as a new form of colonialism, that is, a variation of the form of business that had operated LDCs for centuries. Those countries then developed regional and national rules that began to regulate MNEs in ways expected to be more beneficial to the host countries rather than to the MNEs.

The *United Nations Commission on Transnational Corporations* was established to develop a code of conduct for MNEs. Of particular concern were areas such as the economic relations between the MNE and the host country, the impact of MNE operations on the balance of payments, the transfer of technology from the parent company to the local affiliate, the MNE's impact on labor and employment in the host country, and the MNE's influence on the people and environment of the local community.

Industrialized nations also got into the debate by forming the *Organization for Economic Cooperation and Development (OECD)*. This organization, consisting of the countries of Western Europe, the United

States, Canada, Australia, and Japan, adopted provisions that regulated many facets of an MNE's relationship with its host country. Although the codes are subscribed to voluntarily, they have had deep impact on the ways MNEs conduct business worldwide.

In addition, individual countries and regional organizations have enacted legislation exerting greater control over foreign investment through MNEs. Most of that legislation contains three main provisions: a limit on defense-related industry, partnership with a local owner who has 50% or more ownership interest, and specific goals for the MNE and the host country, meaning the sharing or transfer of technology to the host country. For example, Latin America developed the *Commission of the Andean Pact*, which has as its basis a requirement that MNEs sell off, over a period of time, a portion of their interests so that there can be greater local control.

Expropriation and Nationalization

On occasion, a corporation has had its property **nationalized** or **expropriated** by the government in whose country it is operating. Expropriation is the taking of the business by the host government; nationalization is having the government run the business once it is taken. There is also **confiscation**, in which the host government takes the property and does not compensate the owner. This occurs for various reasons, most notable of which are independence or revolution.

International law universally recognizes the right of a country to seize businesses from private investors for reasons the country considers a public purpose, such as the social or economic welfare of the country. The issue that arises from nationalization is the extent of payment for the taking of the business. Since no international standards exist for determining what is "reasonable" when property is nationalized, often the sum paid is less than the stated value of the company. (Expropriations are excluded here because companies are not compensated for expropriations, although these terms are often used interchangeably.)

To protect against government expropriation or nationalization, Ann and Bill can ensure against losses in one of several ways. First, they may use the insurance offered by the *Overseas Private Investment Corporation (OPIC)*, the *Import-Export Bank*, or the *Foreign Credit Insurance Association*. Second, they may use a private insurance company that offers such coverage. Third, they may attempt to ensure nonexpropriation through specific clauses that may be present in the

expropriation
the takeover of private property by a government without paying the owner for the property

nationalization
the takeover of private property by a government that pays the owner for the property

confiscation
the takeover of private property by a government that does not compensate the owner

local government's investment codes. Last, Ann and Bill may attempt to protect their investment by referring to an agreed-upon treaty that guarantees the standard for "reasonableness" regarding compensation.

Act-of-State Doctrine and Sovereign Immunity

act-of-state doctrine
a legal doctrine prohibiting the courts of one country from ruling on the legality of the acts of another country

The **act-of-state doctrine** bars the judicial examination of certain acts of a foreign government (such as expropriation) and applies to private parties as long as an act of state was involved and the act was for a public purpose.

sovereign immunity
freedom of a sovereignty from suit in another country without its consent, except for suits involving its commercial activity

Under the **doctrine of sovereign immunity**, a foreign government is immune from the jurisdiction of the U.S. courts. There are two exceptions to this rule. First, when immunity is waived (i.e., when the government has agreed to be sued), there is no sovereign immunity. Second, where the country is engaged in purely commercial activity (such as a contract between a country and a private company to purchase a product from the private company), there is no immunity.

Both of these doctrines have as their purpose the desire to keep the U.S. courts out of the realm of political foreign policy best left to the executive branches of government.

RESOLUTION OF INTERNATIONAL DISPUTES

There is no such thing as international commercial litigation as such. What does exist is litigation that takes place in the courts of a particular country, subject to its rules, which attempts to resolve disputes between litigants from different countries. Often, however, most international commercial contracts entered into between merchants contain an arbitration clause, which states that prior to or in lieu of litigation, the parties will submit their dispute to an agreed-upon arbitration board. This section of the chapter examines both arbitration and international litigation as they most commonly occur.

Arbitration

If the contracting parties choose to include an arbitration clause, the clause usually designates the arbitration board to be used. Although there are numerous boards available, one of three major boards is often selected: the *International Chamber of Commerce (ICC)*, the *American Arbitration Association (AAA)*, or the *United Nations Commission on*

BANCO NACIONAL DE CUBA V. SABATTINO
376 U.S. 398 (1964)

Farr, Whitlock & Co., an American commodity broker, entered into an agreement with Compañia Azucarera Vertientes de Cuba (C.A.V.), which was a Cuban corporation largely owned by American stockholders, to purchase sugar produced in Cuba. After the sugar was loaded onto a ship for transport to the United States, the Cuban government seized the shipment of sugar. Farr, Whitlock & Co. was forced to repurchase the shipment of sugar from the Cuban government. C.A.V. sued the Banco Nacional de Cuba (an arm of the Cuban government) to stop payment on the check paid to it by Farr, Whitlock & Co., alleging that the sugar belonged to C.A.V. The issue was whether the act-of-state doctrine barred any action by the U.S. courts. The district court held that the seizure was not an act of state, and the court of appeals agreed with the district court. Banco Nacional de Cuba appealed to the U.S. Supreme Court.

Harlan, J.: The classic American statement of the act-of-state doctrine, which appears to have taken root in England as early as 1674, is found in *Underhill v. Hernandez*, which stated that:

Every sovereign State is bound to respect the independence of every other sovereign State, and the courts of one country will not sit in judgment on the acts of the government of another done within its own territory. Redress of grievances by reason of such acts must be obtained through the means open to be availed of by sovereign powers as between themselves.

The outcome of this case, therefore, turns upon whether any of the contentions urged by the respondents against the application of the act-of-state doctrine in the premises is acceptable: that the act-of-state doctrine does not apply to acts of state which violate international law, as is claimed to be the case here.

Rather than laying down or reaffirming an inflexible, all-encompassing rule in this case, we decide only that the judicial branch will not examine the validity of a taking of property within its own territory by a foreign sovereign government in the absence of a treaty or other

continued on next page

unambiguous agreement regarding controlling legal principles, even if the complaint alleges that the taking violates customary international law.

There are few if any issues in international law today on which opinion seems to be so divided as the limitations on a state's power to expropriate the property of aliens. There is, of course, authority—in international judicial and arbitral decisions, in the expressions of national governments, and among commentators—for the view that a taking is improper under international law if it is without provision for prompt, adequate, and effective compensation. However, Communist countries, . . . , commonly recognize no obligation on the part of the taking country. Certain representatives of the newly independent and underdeveloped countries have questioned whether rules of state responsibility toward aliens can bind nations that have not consented to them, and it is argued that the traditionally articulated standards governing expropriation of property reflect "imperialist" interests and are inappropriate to the circumstances of emergent states.

The disagreement as to relevant international law standards reflects an even more basic divergence between the national interests of capital importing and capital exporting nations and between the social ideologies of those countries that favor state control of a considerable portion of the means of production and those that adhere to a free enterprise system. It is difficult to imagine the courts of this country embarking on adjudication in an area which touches more sensitively the practical and ideological goals of the various members of the community of nations.

We find the respondent's countervailing arguments quite unpersuasive. Their basic contention is that the United States could make a significant contribution to the growth of international law, whose importance would be magnified by the relative paucity of decisional law by international bodies. But given the fluidity of present world conditions, the effectiveness of such an approach is highly conjectural. Moreover, it rests upon the sanguine presupposition that the decision of the courts of the world's major capital exporting country and principal exponent of the free enterprise system would be accepted as disinterested expressions of sound legal principle by those adhering to widely different ideologies.

However offensive to the public policy of this country and its constituent states an expropriation of this kind may be, we conclude that both the national interest and progress toward the goal of establishing the rule of law among nations are best served by maintaining intact the act-of-state doctrine in this realm of its application. REVERSED

Case Questions

1. What detriment could occur from having a court judgment that rules an expropriation invalid while negotiations for compensation were being undertaken by another branch of government?

2. What do you think of the argument noted by the court that some emerging nations might balk at the suggestion that they honor agreements made by their imperialist rulers, once those imperialists are overthrown?

3. Do you agree with the opinion in number 2? Why or why not?

International Trade Law (UNCITRAL). Each of these boards has specific rules governing arbitration proceedings, but the rules are far less restrictive than court proceedings, and generally, the cost of arbitration is much less than litigation. Arbitration is the preferred method of dispute resolution for most merchants.

Arbitration is unique in that it can be structured in almost any way that accommodates the needs of the parties. Following is an illustration of just such an accommodation. (See Box 7–12, "The Iran-U.S. Claims Tribunal.")

Litigation

If arbitration does not apply to a dispute, or the parties choose to litigate, then three scenarios generally arise. First, there is **multinational litigation**, which consists of concurrent proceedings in more than one jurisdiction, involving the same parties or arising out of the same factual litigation.

Second, a party can proceed in one jurisdiction on an issue that is actually ancillary to the main proceeding that is occurring in another

multinational litigation
litigation involving litigants of different countries

7–12   BLACK LETTER LAW

The Iran-U.S. Claims Tribunal

The Iran-U.S. Claims Tribunal ("Tribunal") is a unique commercial dispute resolution body that derives its entire identity and reason for being from the seizure and holding as hostage of a number of the members of the staff of the U.S. embassy in Teheran in 1979. With the subsequent release of the hostages under a negotiated agreement usually referred to as the Algiers Accords, the United States and Iran agreed to submit a large number of commercial claims growing out of contracts made during the regime of the deposed Shah of Iran.

[T]he Tribunal is scheduled to go out of business as soon as all the claims are arbitrated, something that will probably occur before the end of the century. Nonetheless, it provides a very good example of how arbitration, properly structured and organized, can serve as a helpful bridge between two countries who otherwise find very little to agree upon.

The claims are paid out of monies formerly held by banks, mainly in the United States, that were sequestered by the president of the United States shortly after the U.S. embassy was seized. Under the accords, these monies were placed in a security account.

[A] total of 3,835 claims were filed, over 2,700 of which were designated as small claims (amounts in controversy of less than $250,000). As of mid-1991, the Tribunal had adjudicated approximately three-quarters of the individual cases pending before it.

Source: *International Commercial Agreements: A Primer on Drafting, Negotiating, and Resolving Disputes*, 2d ed., by William F. Fox Jr. Reprinted with permission. Kluwer Law and Taxation Publishers.

jurisdiction, such as an action to freeze the assets of the defendant pending the outcome of the main litigation.

Third, the party may be faced with choosing the forum in which to bring action. That decision may be guided by whether the party should proceed in country X, where the opponents' assets are located, or country Y, where litigation is quicker or cheaper. These choices should be left up to a trained adviser who is familiar with all the ramifications of the choice made.

UNFAIR TRADE PRACTICES AND THEIR REMEDIES

Companies that do business with businesses in the United States sometimes engage in unfair trade practices. Such trade practices can be accomplished in several ways, explained later. If they are found to exist, they are most often redressed through the imposition of additional **tariffs** or **import duties** on a product or by seizing the goods. The remedy imposed depends on the type of unfair trade practice.

import duties
charges imposed on goods coming into one country from another

Dumping

Dumping occurs when a product is sold for less money in the United States or other countries into which it is imported than it is sold for in the home country it comes from. Dumping is harmful because it can undercut the competition's ability to compete in the same market. In addition, by forcing those competing companies out of business, it creates a monopoly for the importers. When competitors are injured, a tariff is imposed to make up for the advantage in price that was gained by dumping.

dumping
the sale of goods in a foreign market for a price that is lower than the price of the goods sold in the home market

The *International Trade Administration* is the agency that determines whether there is a lower price in the foreign market; the *International Trade Commission* determines whether there is injury to competing domestic companies. If both of these conditions exist, then an antidumping tariff is imposed on the importer.

Countervailing Duty

If a foreign government pays a subsidy to a manufacturer in that country to produce a product and that product is then imported into the United States, then a **countervailing duty** may be imposed on the product. A duty is an amount imposed upon importation of a product, much like a tariff. For example, if Japan pays a subsidy to a Japanese car manufacturer to manufacture cars and those cars are then imported into the United States, then a countervailing duty may be imposed on the cars.

countervailing duty
a duty imposed on products manufactured with the help of foreign government subsidies, which are sold for less money in the domestic market, thereby hurting the businesses that are competing in the domestic market

This additional duty is designed to make up for the competitive edge gained by the reduction in cost to produce the item and caused by the subsidy. The reasoning behind the countervailing duty is that by subsidizing the manufacture of products, products can be sold for less in the foreign (U.S.) market, thus competing unfairly with unsubsidized goods in that market. Examples of government subsidies are tax rebates, loans, training and research, or tax credits.

The duty of imposing such tariffs is divided between the ITA and the ITC. The ITA determines whether a government subsidy exists and if so, how much and in what form. The ITC finds whether a domestic company is suffering because of the subsidized product. If so, then a countervailing duty is imposed.

Gray Market Goods

gray market goods
goods manufactured in a country other than the United States, bearing a valid U.S. trademark, and imported into the United States without the consent of the U.S. trademark holder

When foreign trademark rights are given to a manufacturer by a U.S. trademark holder, there is usually a requirement made that those goods be sold only in that foreign country, and not in the United States. **Gray market goods** are goods manufactured in a country other than the United States and bearing a valid U.S. trademark, which are imported into the United States without the consent of the American trademark holder. They are distinguished from counterfeit goods in that the use of the U.S. trademark is authorized by the holder of the foreign trademark. Gray market goods are subject to seizure upon entering this country without permission.

MULTICULTURAL IMPLICATIONS

Aside from the various legal aspects of international business that Ann and Bill must consider, there is the very important issue of multicultural implications. By this we mean the implications Bill and Ann must consider when dealing with cultures different from theirs. You can imagine the importance of such factors when Bill and Ann are doing business outside the United States.

Throughout the text we emphasize that good business practices and maximization of profits require businesspeople to deal with everyone respectfully and considerately. This should be done not only because it is the right thing to do, but for the more practical reason that it maximizes profits and production. However, such has not always been a part of what was considered good business practices for many businesses. Bill and Ann and other business owners who ignore this important area do so at their peril. (See Box 7–13, "Cultural Differences, on page 219.")

A policy of respect and consideration has manifestations that may seem surprising. Of course it means such things as not discriminating

U.S. V. SAM'S WHOLESALE CLUB
992 F.2d 508 (5th Cir. 1993)

Sam's is a retail outlet that has purchased a shipment of watches with a Rolex trademark from an importer who alleged that it is licensed to import such watches. After completion of the purchase with the importer, but before the watches were sold in the retail store, the watches were seized by customs officials. The owner of the trademark (Rolex USA) alleged that the watches were sold in the United States without its permission and were gray market goods. Sam's disagrees, basing its argument on the fact that both the U.S. and foreign trademarks (Rolex USA and Bienne, respectively) are owned by the same person or business (the Wilsdorf Foundation) or are subject to common ownership or control (by Rolex Geneva). If true, this would exclude Sam's from section 526 of the Tariff Act, which prohibits the importation of any merchandise bearing a trademark owned by a citizen or corporation created or organized in the United States and registered with the Patent Office. The following is the court's response, by Judge DeMoss.

There are two questions which must be answered in response to Sam's allegations. First, are the foreign and domestic trademarks owned by the same company? If not, then the second question is, Are the two companies under common control? If the answer to either of these questions is yes, then Sam's is correct in asserting that the goods in question are not gray market goods, because under the Tariff Act, they have been purchased from the owner of the trademark.

The first question is answered by looking at the relationship between the domestic trademark owner and the foreign trademark owner. Bienne is the owner of the "Rolex" trademark. Rolex Geneva is authorized by Bienne to register this mark and has authorized "Rolex USA" to be the owner of the rights to the Rolex mark in the United States. However, the fact that Bienne has allowed another company (Rolex Geneva) to issue its trademark does not mean that Rolex Geneva becomes the trademark owner; nor does it mean that Bienne and Rolex Geneva are common owners of the trademark. Under American trademark law, the fact that Rolex Geneva's name is on the

continued on next page

watch does not indicate that Rolex Geneva owns the Rolex mark. The court therefore concluded that Bienne has always owned the Rolex mark, that Rolex Geneva is authorized to license the use of the Rolex trademark, and that it authorized Rolex USA to be the owner of the rights to the Rolex trademark in the United States. Therefore, the importer must obtain permission from Rolex USA to sell the watches in the United States.

The second question was also answered negatively for Sam's. Since the court did not find common ownership, the court examined Sam's allegation that the two companies were under common control. Common control means effective control in policy and operations based on the Rolex empire. Sam's contended that because the two companies performed essential functions in the manufacturing and selling of Rolex watches, they operated as one company. The court disagreed, stating that common control means more of a parent/subsidiary relationship or one where a common owner exercised control over both organizations. The relationship between Bienne and Rolex USA was that of a successful business relationship. The fact that Bienne manufactured the movements of the watches, which are then placed in casings and distributed by Rolex Geneva worldwide, did not give proof that Rolex USA and Bienne are under common control of Rolex Geneva. AFFIRMED

Case Questions

1. What is the effect of not recognizing the practical workings of companies that form foundations and other licensing companies, but that insist that the parent trademark appear on all products?

2. Other than asking the importer, how is a purchaser able to determine whether goods are properly imported?

3. Should there be an exclusion for purchasers who have made inquiry and been told that the goods are legally imported, but whose purchased goods are seized by customs because they are, in fact, illegally imported?

against customers, clients, employees, and suppliers based on factors other than those relevant to the relationship they have with the business. That is, there should be no discrimination based on gender, race, national origin, and so on. However, in the international business realm, it also means considering the cultural factors connected with the country and people with whom Bill and Ann will be doing business rather than assuming that everyone is the way Americans are. Factors to be considered include the language, customs, and mores of the people of the targeted country. Failure to consider such factors can have, and has had, disastrous results.

- Chevrolet entered the South American to market to sell its Chevy Nova automobile. The automaker did not discover until it was too late that in Spanish, "no va" means "doesn't run."

- When it tried in Africa to market its baby food with the famous Gerber baby on the jar label, the Gerber baby food company did not realize that in many African countries, what is pictured on the front of the jar is what is inside. As you can imagine, there was not much of a market for eating pureed white babies.

- Dr Pepper had a major surprise on its hands when it realized, only after marketing its soft drink in Europe, that in many European countries, "pepper" is a slang word for a prostitute.

We are also becoming increasingly aware that business deals can be won or lost based on innocent social gaffes. Although they may be innocent, they are often avoidable through a small but worthwhile investment in time and effort. Checking up on the customs and mores of a country before entering into business relations with its people minimizes problems significantly.

For instance, the Japanese have different concepts of personal physical space, and touching people without permission is unacceptable, even though it usually presents no problem for most Americans. The Japanese have 17 different rules about the simple matter of exchanging business cards, including that a card should not be written upon by the receiver or put in the recipient's wallet, which is considered dirty. In some Middle Eastern countries it is totally unacceptable to touch someone with one's right hand or to have the bottom of one's shoe face another person.

As early as is feasible, Bill and Ann should do as much checking as possible with a wide range of sources, including embassies, books, sources located in the country, and travel and business consultants. The reality is that in many countries, Americans are considered to be rude and condescending. Bill and Ann should make sure as early as possible that actions they take regarding conducting negotiations and business in the other country do not indicate a disregard for the people with whom they wish to establish a lasting business relationship.

7–13   LAW IN THE REAL WORLD

Cultural Differences

The following is only a sprinkling of the kinds of differences which may exist in different countries other than the United States, and even within cultures within the United States. See if any surprise you.

- "Don't squat when waiting for a bus or a person. Don't spit in public. Don't point at people with your fingers. Don't make noise. Don't laugh loudly. Don't yell or call to people from a distance. Don't pick your teeth, pick your nose, blow your nose, pick at your ears, rub your eyes, or rub dirt off your skin. Don't scratch, take off your shoes, burp, stretch, or hum."

From a list of tips to travelers abroad, issued by the Chinese government. Newsweek, September 13, 1994.

- Japanese culture promotes a tremendous sense of identity and group belonging. Creating ambiguity is almost a social obligation and an unconscious process that often lead foreigners to draw false conclusions based on Japanese appearances. *Managing Cultural Differences*, 3d ed., Harris and Moran, at 3.
- In Saudi Arabia, the protocol is to use the first meeting for social acquaintance, warm-up, or trust building, and not as a time to conduct serious business. Ibid.
- In matters of recruitment and selection, Asian managers often rely on family and friends whom they can trust or have obligations to, while Western managers use more objective measures of competency. Ibid.
- When doing business in Indonesia, handshaking with either sex is perfectly acceptable, but using the left hand for this purpose is strictly "taboo"; in other cultures, handshakes are avoided, and some form of bow is preferred. Ibid.
- Leaving the office in America requires one to say "Good night" or "See you tomorrow." Leaving the office in Japan is a procedure requiring exquisite timing and style. Generally speaking, no one should leave before his or her boss. But since everyone in a corporation has a

boss, except the chairman, no one moves until something happens way up the line. Because chairmen could die in their chairs (thereby trapping everybody for an eternity of twenty-four-hour paper shuffling), elaborate rituals have been developed to break up the workforce at the end of the day. A supervisor will remember an urgent appointment for drinks with a supplier; a department head will discover in his wallet tickets to the ballet; a section chief will receive a call from a dying mother. Pretty soon, it's "okay" to split. Most Japanese offices are empty by 10 pm. *Japan-Think/Ameri-Think: An Irreverent Guide to Understanding the Cultural Differences between Us*, Robert J. Collins, Penguin Books, 1992, p. 59.

- In working with Hispanic Americans, [there are often] problems dealing with conflicts over sex roles. In their traditional culture, men are expected to be strong, dominant, and the provider for the family, whereas women are expected to be nurturant, submissive to the male, and self-sacrificing. *Counseling the Culturally Different: Theory and Practice*, 2d ed., Derald Wing Sue and David Sue, John Wiley & Sons, 1990, p. 233.

SUMMARY

If Bill and Ann are to maximize their potential as a business, it is highly likely that they will decide to deal in some way with customers outside the borders of the United States. If they do, they must be aware of the myriad rules and regulations that govern doing business internationally. The ways they choose to operate in the international arena will be based on their own individual considerations regarding the safety and political stability of the country they wish to do business with, the ease with which they will be able to communicate with customers in the other country, language differences, access to the litigation process, and regulations governing the kinds of goods sold and how business is to be conducted in another country if the business is with outsiders.

Once Bill and Ann determine that the effort to go outside the borders of the United States is worth their while economically, then making certain they become familiar with and understand the culture they are dealing with is an important factor in conducting business. Covering all the bases, in terms of both the laws and the culture, will go a long way toward ensuring their international success.

CHAPTER TERMS

act-of-state doctrine	joint venture
confiscation	license
countervailing duty	multinational enterprise
custom	most-favored-nation status
direct sale	multilateral instrument
dumping	multinational litigation
export	nationalization
expropriation	organization
franchise	rounds
GATT	sovereign immunity
gray market goods	tariffs
import	treaty
import duties	

CHAPTER-END QUESTIONS

1. _____ consists of groups of nations whose purpose is to regulate business within that region.

2. What is a custom, as it relates to international law? Explain.

3. Rondon Inc. is concerned that the political situation in a Southeast Asian country to which it wishes to export its goods is so unstable that a problem may arise. What kinds of problems should Rondon be concerned about? Explain.

4. In Africa while on a trip to Rwanda, Suellen sees some wonderful embroidered African dresses, shirts, and pants she decides would sell well in her hometown of Atlanta and other U.S. cities. Suellen finds a Rwandan entrepreneur who has several people working to make the outfits. Suellen arranges with the entrepreneur to have an agreed-upon amount of the clothing sent to her in the United States. The clothing sells so well that Suellen eventually decides she wants to arrange to go into business on her own and cut out the middleperson entrepreneur. If she does so, what must she consider?

5. Ling Tsu Inc. has a successful cartoon caricature logo that has been so successful that clothing manufacturers have asked to put it on popular clothing items they sell. Part of the appeal of the cartoon is a special secret paint Ling Tsu had developed especially for the cartoon to enhance its character. Several of the companies that request to be licensed to use the cartoon are outside the United States. Discuss what Ling Tsu's most pressing concerns should be when deciding whether to grant a license to the outside companies.

6. MicroCorp. is exporting its goods for the first time. A rather large shipment is involved, and because of cash flow considerations, the company needs to have as much cash as possible. If MicroCorp. decides to export its goods through an exporting company, which type would be best? Why?

7. If a country other than the United States sells its goods in the United States for less than it sells them in its own country, this is called

    a. rounds.
    b. custom.
    c. dumping.
    d. a direct sale.

8. A business that wishes to extend its restaurant chain operations into another country will likely make arrangements by way of

    a. import duties.
    b. countervailing duties.
    c. license.
    d. franchise.

9. A countervailing duty may be placed upon gray market goods imported into this country when it is found that the country of origin has subsidized the exporter by way of

    a. providing subsidies.
    b. tax credits.
    c. training and research.
    d. all of the above.

10. The purpose of the General Agreement on Tariffs and Trade is to impose tariffs on goods shipped between countries signatory to the agreement. (True or False)

GROUP EXERCISE

BIG Corp, whose home country is an industrialized nation, has been operating a MNE in the host country of Shawa, an undeveloped nation, for the past 50 years. During this time BIG has conducted unlimited harvesting of Shawa's major crop and exported it primarily to BIG's home country. BIG received huge concessions by Shawa when it opened its operations 50 years ago. Shawa has consistently complained over the past 20 years about the amount of pollution BIG creates in Shawa as a result of its manufacturing operations, and of BIG's use of child labor and substandard wages paid to Shawa workers. Thus far, BIG has refused to heed any of Shawa's warnings or requests by its workers to change its policies.

Divide yourselves into four groups. One group represents the BIG Corp.; one represents the government of the home country of BIG; one represents the employees of the BIG Corp. in the host country; and one represents the host government. Discuss the pros and cons of expropriation, nationalization, confiscation, and cooperation.

REFERENCES

1   *Electronic Business* (October 1992, Special Quality Issue).
2   *Business Wire*, March 12, 1993.
3   "The Legal Effects of Codes of Conduct for Multinational Enterprises," p. 4, Hans W. Baade, in *Legal Problems of Codes of Conduct for Multinational Enterprises*, Norbert Horn, ed., Vol. 1, 1980.
4   Ibid.

Chapter 8

CHOOSING A FORM OF BUSINESS ORGANIZATION

Chapter Preview Summary

In this chapter Bill and Ann are exposed to the various ways in which a business can be organized to carry on its activities. The advantages and disadvantages of each type of business organization, as well as external factors that may affect their choice of ways to organize the business are presented. We will see what Ann and Bill's business would look like if it begins as a sole proprietorship, if the business hires employees, and if it expands to a form of multiple ownership (e.g., partnership, closely held corporation, etc.). We will see how the legal form of a business affects business decision making and will learn the impact that legal form has on events that occur in the ordinary course of business.

Chapter Objectives

In studying the chapter, you should learn:
- the various forms of business organizations
- the advantages of each form of business
- the disadvantages of each form of business
- the external factors that may affect the choice of business organization

INTRODUCTION

Ann and Bill need to learn how to operate as a legally recognized business. Not every business form is the same. People choose to have their businesses organized in different ways for many different reasons. There may be financial considerations, emotional considerations, personality considerations, or liability considerations. Before Ann and Bill can choose what is best for them, they need to know what is available. In this chapter they learn the different forms in which a business can operate and the advantages and disadvantages of each. Knowing this will help them greatly in making the right choice of form for their own business.

FORMS OF BUSINESS ORGANIZATIONS

There are many legal forms of business from which to choose. Some of them have been in existence for a long time. Others are relatively new, having been developed to maximize the use of available tax benefits or to minimize liability. Popularity of the various forms closely parallels changes in the tax laws.

When Ann and Bill were operating their own individual businesses, they were doing so as sole proprietors. Of course, they had to comply with the law, but they did not have to answer to anyone except themselves. Unless they hired employees, they owed no formal (legal) duties to anyone other than their customers/clients (and creditors). If they expanded the business by hiring employees or by adding an additional owner(s), they would have to assume certain responsibilities (legal duties) to others.

SOLE PROPRIETORSHIP

sole proprietorship
business owned and controlled exclusively by one person

The first option available for a business owner's consideration is that of operating as a sole proprietor. A **sole proprietorship** is a business owned and controlled exclusively by one person. The proprietor may or may not be the operator or manager of the business. While the owner may hire others to work for the sole proprietorship, the proprietor is the only owner. The business assets of a sole proprietor belong to the sole proprietor, just as do personal assets. The proprietor is the business and the business is the proprietor. Sole ownership may be right for either small or large businesses—anything from the mom-and-pop corner grocery store to the Wal-Mart stores chain, whose Sam Walton was for many years the sole owner.

For this part of the chapter, we will use Ann and her ongoing cleaning business as the basis for discussion. Assume that Ann began operating as a sole proprietor, working from her home on weekends and in the evenings after work. As business picks up, Ann and the answering machine can no longer handle the volume of calls. Ann is faced with several options. She can hire an employee(s), quit her other job, or add co-owners by way of a partnership or a corporation. Quitting her job will result in the immediate loss of income, benefits, and so on. Adding an employee will result in an immediate cost to the new business (i.e., wages, benefits, and required withholdings). Doing both at once would be doubly expensive. Any of these decisions will allow the business to operate in Ann's absence, to conduct more business, and perhaps to enjoy the benefits of specialization of labor.

Adding a co-owner will probably result in an infusion of operating capital; adding employees would represent an additional business expense. Thus Ann may be forced to make the decision based solely on the state of the business's financial situation unless funds for business expansion are readily available. This is, perhaps, an example of the old saying that "it takes money to make money." As Ann considers expansion, it becomes apparent that expansion is expensive.

Adding an employee will cost the business more than just the employee's wages. Several major pieces of legislation regulate the employment relationship. The Fair Labor Standards Act regulates child labor, minimum wages, overtime, and the like. Among other things under Internal Revenue Service (IRS) rules, employers are required to match the employee's FICA (Social Security) contribution. The federal government also requires payment of unemployment taxes. States generally require workers' compensation payments. Employees add considerably more to an employer's costs than payment of their wages.

Advantages

A sole proprietorship can be started with few legal formalities. To become a sole proprietor, Ann would need to simply obtain the necessary business licenses and begin operating. Ann would have 100% control over the business. The ease of start-up and the idea of being self-employed as well as being "the boss" are seen as the main advantages of a sole proprietorship.

Disadvantages

Several disadvantages are worth noting. First, as a sole proprietor, Ann has unlimited personal liability for any debts or liabilities incurred by the business. This means that there is no one with whom Ann shares responsibility for the debts of the business. Further, payment of the debts is not limited to the assets of the sole proprietorship alone. Because the sole proprietorship is not incorporated, in addition to using Ann's business assets to satisfy debts, creditors may also use Ann's personal assets. Simply closing the business and walking away is not an option. As a sole proprietor, Ann *is* the business, and Ann's creditors can cause or force a bankruptcy proceeding, either voluntary or involuntary.

Such unlimited liability for business debts is problematic if Ann has a spouse or family to support or extensive personal holdings she does not want to put in jeopardy. Ann's decision regarding forms of business with unlimited liability depends on several factors involving the specific business in which Ann will be engaged. For instance, will the business be high risk? Is the risk only financial (loss of money) or would it include possible bodily injury? Can consumers be personally injured by the product or service? Answering yes to any of those questions puts Ann in the position of needing protection for her personal assets because of the risk to them that is presented by the nature of her business.

A second disadvantage is that the ability to raise financial capital for the business may be more limited in a sole proprietorship than in a partnership or a corporation. In order to raise funds as a sole proprietor, Ann must generally depend on banks, friends, or relatives. Being in business alone, she would have no business partner to contribute capital. Unless Ann has a good deal of money, or access to it, this may present a problem.

A third disadvantage is that a sole proprietor generally has to be a "Jack or Jill of all trades" or be financially able to hire others with the needed business skills (e.g., typing, sales, production, accounting and bookkeeping, marketing). Ann can hire another person to operate the business or may personally operate the business. In order to hire another person, Ann must be financially able to do so.

A fourth disadvantage of the sole proprietorship is said to be that it "dies with the owner." Therefore, it has a duration limited to the life of the proprietor. This is technically correct, but many small businesses are not limited by the death of the owner because they are conveyed through a will to a spouse or other family member or sold by the heirs as an ongoing business. When the assets of a sole proprietorship are sold or conveyed by will, there often arises the problem of **valuation**. Valuation of a small business consists of determining what it is worth, either for estate tax purposes or for a sale. Unlike other assets, which may have easily established market values, sole proprietorships are difficult to valuate due to the contribution of the owner (sole proprietor).

valuation
determination of the worth of business

Nowadays, there are financial experts in the area of valuation, and computer software has been developed to aid in the valuation. Overall, the transferability of a sole proprietorship is probably no more difficult than that of a partnership interest or of an interest in a closely held corporation. However, if Ann is not concerned about passing the business on, this disadvantage matters little.

Ann will report business income and expenses on IRS Schedule C as part of her individual tax return. The profit, if any, will be taxed at individual rates. Likewise, any loss will also be reported on Ann's individual return. Under state law, certain businesses (usually those that have four or more employees) are required to obtain workers' compensation insurance. Health and dental insurance, retirement plans, and other employee benefits all are potential costs connected with the decision to add an employee. Those costs can often make the effective, or real, cost of an employee fully one-third higher than payment of the wages alone.

CO-OWNERS

If Ann decides to take someone on as a co-owner, she must decide whether she wants an investor who will provide money without active participation in management (limited partner or inactive shareholder) or whether she wants a working co-owner, who will actively participate in the day-to-day decisions (general partner or active shareholder). Keep in mind that some people will tell you they "just want to invest," but they then end up wanting to participate in decision making.

Thus, legal advice and help in creation of the agreement are crucial so that there will be an enforceable, legal contract delineating the rights and responsibilities of the parties. It may end up being a partnership agreement, an investment contract (similar to a loan arrangement), or an incorporation with bylaws. In states that have passed appropriate legislation, limited-liability companies and limited-liability partnerships are also viable options.

PARTNERSHIP

partnership
a voluntary agreement between two or more people to work together for profit

The second option for Ann to consider is to form a **partnership** with one or more people. The Uniform Partnership Act defines a partnership as "the association of two or more persons to carry on as co-owners a business for profit, whether or not the persons intend to form a partnership." Therefore, rather than operate alone, Ann can have others come into the business and form a partnership. There are different kinds of partnerships: primarily general and limited.

General Partnership

general partnership
a partnership in which all the partners are able to fully participate in the decision making and running of the partnership

A general partnership is the basic kind of partnership that comes to mind when most people think of the term *partnership*. Each partner has an equal say in the liabilities and the assets of the partnership, as well as a say in the running of the business, unless otherwise agreed. There are other considerations also, as follows.

Advantages

Capital   The principal advantage of a general partnership is that the addition of one or more persons as co-owners may alleviate the difficulty of raising capital found in the sole proprietorship. That is, each of the partners could contribute capital to operate the partnership rather than Ann's being totally responsible for financing the business.

Human Capital versus Investment   When correctly formed, co-ownership may alleviate the human capital problem of the sole proprietorship by allowing for the specialization of labor. However, many times partners are chosen merely for their financial contributions, not their expertise.

One factor to consider in the formation of a partnership is the combining of human capital so that people with talent and skill in particular areas can concentrate in their area, thus alleviating the necessity of paying out more money to hire others with the needed expertise or skills. If the partnership does not offer the opportunity for specialization of labor, it might be better to remain a sole proprietor and try to raise capital some other way.

Profit-and-Loss Sharing   It will also be advantageous for Ann to be able to share the losses of the business with other partners rather than her paying for them alone. Partners share equally in partnership profits and losses unless the partnership agreement provides otherwise.

Disadvantages

Liability for Acts of Other Partners   Just as with a sole proprietorship arrangement, there are disadvantages to the partnership form of business organization. First and foremost is that each partner is an agent of the partnership and the other partners for the purpose of partnership business. Under the Revised Uniform Partnership Act, Ann will be **jointly and severally liable** for the partnership obligations (both in contract and in tort) deemed to be within the scope of the partnership.

A partnership does not eliminate the disadvantage of unlimited personal liability for partnership obligations that the sole proprietorship had. This is perhaps even more important when one is in business with others through whom one may incur vicarious liability. Ann may be liable for the other partners' contracts or tortious acts, and if the partnership assets do not satisfy a judgment, Ann's personal assets may be used to do so.

It is arguable that the partnership form of business presents an even bigger disadvantage to personal liability because all the partners have unlimited liability for partnership obligations and are said to be jointly and severally liable. Thus, any one partner may be required to pay the entire partnership debt or be liable for torts committed by other partners within the scope of the partnership. An innocent partner could, however, seek **contribution** from the partners responsible for the debt or tort. Contribution means that the debt will be shared between the partners, each partner being responsible for an agreed-upon proportionate share. **Marshaling of assets** requires that creditors proceed against partnership assets first, but if the partnership debt remains unsatisfied, then the personal property of the partners is at risk.

Partnership Agreement   There are no legal formalities in forming a partnership, but it is not advisable to enter into one without a comprehensive partnership agreement. A partnership is in many ways similar to a marriage. In fact, it is a business marriage—of sorts. Therefore, like a marriage, the partnership relationship should not be

joint and several liability liability imposed on individual involved in tort or contract breach, or on all of the persons liable

contribution the sharing of payment for a debt among the persons liable for it

marshaling of assets collection of assets, their arrangement in order of priority, and then division of the assets to pay claims

entered into unadvisedly. Ann's selection of a partner is of critical importance.

Writing Requirement   Generally there is no requirement that a partnership agreement be in writing, but it should be. Because of the vicarious and unlimited liability involved, the agreement should be drafted by an attorney. Rather than a standardized agreement, Ann should have an agreement tailored specifically for the partnership and the way it will conduct business.

The partnership agreement should specify, among other things, the form in which capital is to be contributed by partners, the voting powers of partners, the extent of the powers of the general partners, how profits and losses will be split among the partners, and what should happen upon **dissociation** of a partner or **dissolution** of the partnership. Thus, one of the disadvantages of a partnership is the necessity for and the cost of a detailed, written partnership agreement. However, it will be money well spent, for it can save so much trouble later.

In most cases each partner should consult an attorney, and the partnership should have a separate attorney. This is to ensure unbiased legal opinions that are free from conflicts of interest. It sounds expensive and it probably should be, for it is far superior to a canned partnership agreement straight from the word processor. The latter may be cheaper in the short run, but could result in litigation later.

Right to Participate in Management   Unless otherwise agreed, all partners have a right to participate equally in management. This is often cited as one of the disadvantages of the partnership form of business. As a practicality, most partnerships have a designated managing partner, who assumes responsibility for the day-to-day operation of the partnership business. Even with a written partnership agreement in which managing partner has been designated, still the partners must agree on partnership matters because unanimous agreement is required for important partnership matters.

Transfer of Partnership Interest and Dissolution   The transferability of a partnership interest is similar to that of the sole proprietorship, due to problems in valuation of the interest. Like a sole proprietorship, a partnership has a limited duration and may be dissolved upon changes in the relationship of the partners. The Revised Uniform Partnership Act (RUPA) defines a partner's leaving the partnership as a dissociation, which may be rightful or wrongful. Thus, when any of the partners dies, the partnership suffers a dissociation, which may or

dissociation
the term used by the RUPA when a partner leaves (rightfully or wrongfully) a partnership; may or may not be followed by a dissolution

dissolution
the ending of a partnership

may not be followed by a dissolution. The Revised Uniform Partnership Act provides, however, that when partners enter and leave, the partnership is not legally dissolved.[1]

Legal Status of Partnership   A partnership is now viewed as a separate legal being or business organization. It is an association of people for profit-making purposes. Section 201 of RUPA provides that for most purposes, such as ownership of property, a partnership is considered an "entity, and not just an aggregate of the partners." However, a partnership does not pay taxes. Rather, the partnership files an informational tax return reporting partnership income and expenses. Partnership profits and losses are reported on the individual tax returns of each partner. Thus, when a partner enters or leaves the partnership, the resulting partnership is different from the previous partnership and the previous partnership is considered (technically) dissolved. The entity theory of partnership adopted by RUPA is consistent with the concept of dissociation.

Because a partnership is a voluntary association, there must be unanimous agreement to admit a new partner. An exception to that general rule might occur under is a partnership agreement that specifically provides otherwise. Unanimity is also generally required in the making of all basic partnership decisions such as dissolution or changing the nature of the partnership.

LIMITED PARTNERSHIP

The third option for Ann to consider is formation of a **limited partnership**. A limited partnership is composed of at least one general partner, who manages the partnership, and one or more limited partners, who invest in the partnership. General partners have unlimited personal liability as in an ordinary partnership, but the limited partners are treated more like shareholders in a corporation. In the event of partnership liability, limited partners ordinarily risk only their financial investment in the business.

limited partnership
an unincorporated association, or firm, in which the limited partners are relieved from liability beyond the amount of capital they contributed

Partnership Name

Limited partners cannot normally include their names as part of the partnership name, because in doing so, the unsuspecting public would be put at a disadvantage. The public assumes that when one's name is a part of a partnership name, one is a general partner with unlimited liability. It would be misleading, therefore, to allow creditors to think that limited partners were general partners, because limited partners are not normally liable beyond the amount of their investment in the event liability is attached to the partnership.

Ann might consider a limited partnership in which the limited partners make investments but do not participate in day-to-day management of the business. This form of business is much like a closely held corporation with the limited partners having rights similar to shareholders. Because of Uniform Limited Partnership Act (ULPA) restrictions, limited partners generally cannot participate in management. Thus by definition, most limited partnership interests are treated as securities and are regulated by state or federal securities laws (discussed later in this chapter). Like a corporation, a limited partnership must be registered with the state. Because most limited partnership interests are in the form of securities, they are highly regulated by the states or the Securities and Exchange Commission. It is usually easier and cheaper to form a general partnership or a closely held corporation than a limited partnership.

Right to Participate in Management of the Partnership

Typically, and for similar reasons, limited partners are also prohibited from participating in the active management of the partnership. The Revised Limited Partnership Act provides that limited partners can participate in management so long as they notify all creditors that might otherwise rely on them that they are limited partners and therefore would not be held personally liable if anything goes wrong.

If Ann were the only general partner, then management would be the same as in a sole proprietorship and Ann would have complete control. However, the limited partnership form of business is highly regulated, and most states have used the Uniform Limited Partnership Act and, more recently, the Revised Uniform Limited Partnership Act as the bases for their laws.

If the limited partnership had several general partners, the advantages and disadvantages of an ordinary partnership would apply. The only real difference to the general partners would be that strict legal formalities would have to be in place in order to operate as a limited partnership. These restrictions are probably more important to limited partners than to general partners, who always have control and always have unlimited personal liability. Most states require that a partnership be registered with the appropriate state office and that all partners (general and limited) be listed on the registration statement.[2]

Ann should consult either an attorney, a certified public accountant (CPA), or a tax attorney prior to deciding whether forming a limited partnership is in her best interest. Potential investors (limited partners) are affected by the tax treatment of their limited partnership interests. If there are no investors, there is no need to form a limited partnership.

Transferability and Duration

Transferability of interests in limited partnerships is usually restricted by state laws or by the limited partnership agreement. The duration of the limited partnership is not ordinarily affected by the entry, exit, or death of limited partners, but could be affected by the entry, exit, or death of any of the general partners.

A limited partnership may be worthwhile for Ann to look into if she has people interested in joining the partnership for business investment purposes, but who do not want to deal with the partnership as a business affair to be managed on an everyday basis. Therefore, we assume that Ann will not form a limited partnership. Instead, Ann forms either a general partnership or a limited liability partnership.

Unlike a general partnership, a limited liability partnership conveys limited personal liability for employees' or other partners' acts in which the partner did not participate or supervise. In other words, a partner is always liable for acts that that partner commits, but vicarious liability (liability for the acts of others) is restricted to acts of employees supervised by the partner. This amounts to the same liability as that on the part of a shareholder in a corporation. Although legislation providing for limited liability partnerships has not been passed in every state, it is expected that this form of business will become very popular.

LIMITED LIABILITY PARTNERSHIPS

The newest form of partnership is the registered **limited liability partnership**. In 1994, the Big Six accounting firms changed to this form in an effort to limit liability in tort for professional malpractice. Under this form, the general partners are jointly liable in contract, but are liable in tort only for their own negligence or that of those directly under their control.

Before a registered limited liability partnership is possible, the state in which the partnership is to be formed must have passed legislation providing for this new form of partnership. The legislation usu-

limited liability partnership
new form of business organization that allows the partners to escape joint and several liability in tort

8–1   LAW IN THE REAL WORLD

Accounting Firm Becomes Limited Liability Partnership

July 27, 1994

Dear Faculty Members and Friends of Ernst & Young:

Change to LLP Status

On August 1, Ernst & Young will become a limited liability partnership (LLP). Other than adding the initials LLP after our name, there will be no changes in the firm's organization, personnel, or service to our clients. We are sharing this news with you in advance of our conversion to an LLP because you are important to us and to the development of future members of our profession.

Similar to the corporate form of business organization, an LLP generally limits the liability of its owners to their capital invested in the firm for liabilities arising from services performed by the firm. An LLP will not diminish the ability of plaintiffs to recover damages from the firm itself or from the individuals who directly caused the loss; nor will it reduce our legal or insurance expenses.

The other Big Six firms—as well as many other firms—are changing to LLPs. We carefully considered other organizational options for protecting partners' personal assets, including professional corporations, limited liability companies, limited partnerships, and general corporations. We concluded that an LLP is the most appropriate option.

LLPS do not reduce the need for liability reform in the United States, which remains a high priority for our firm. All U.S. businesses—not just professional services firms—are subject to abuse through our nation's tort system, particularly because of its inherently unfair "joint and several liability" standard—and the related unjust targeting of so-called "deep pockets."

Ernst & Young is financially strong and secure. Regardless of our form of organization, our high standards for quality work and client satisfaction will remain unaffected. If you have any questions about Ernst & Young or LLPs, please write or give me a call.

Sincerely,

Charles B. Eldridge
National Director of Recruiting and University Relations

Source: Courtesy of Ernst & Young. Used with permission.

ally consists of an amendment to the state's version of the uniform partnership act. In Box 8–1, a letter from Ernst & Young announces the firm's conversion to the limited liability partnership form of business.

JOINT VENTURE

As you saw in the previous chapter, a joint venture resembles a partnership. Unlike a partnership, which has the connotation of an ongoing business, a joint venture is usually a combination of businesses that join together temporarily for a special project, such as building a shopping center. Although the businesses are not considered partners in any other respect, partnership law is generally applied to such relationships. Thus Ann would have to choose an initial form of business and then look for a "joint venturer."

This type of business organization is advantageous when the joint venturers do not want to go into a permanent business, but need a form of business organization for only a specific duration of time or for a special project. Because Ann plans to stay in business permanently, this would not be a likely choice for the form of Ann's business organization.

CORPORATIONS

Whereas the other forms of business organization discussed so far have placed the ownership and the running of the business in the same hands (except in the case of the limited partnership), the corporate form of business actually creates a separate legal entity—separate and apart from its owners. If Ann decides to incorporate there are several choices available in most states. Ann can form a close corporation (under statutory close corporation laws), an ordinary C corporation, an S corporation (under IRS rules), or a limited liability company. (Most so-called regular corporations are designated as **C corporations**.)

Corporations are purely creatures of state statutes, and each state has its own corporate statutes dictating how corporations are formed and what powers they have. Most states have used the Model Business Corporation Act as a starting point. Model Acts and Uniform Acts are different in that one expects legislation based on uniform acts to be very similar in each state, whereas legislation based on model acts can result in very different results from state to state.

C corporation
an artificial person or legal entity—created by or under the authority of the laws of a state, sometimes composed of a single person and the successors, but ordinarily consisting of numerous individuals—which is regarded in law as having a personality and existence distinct from that of its members

Advantages

Legal Status of Corporations

A corporation is an artificial legal being, which separates business ownership from governance and liability. A corporation is a separate legal being that can sue and can be sued. Those who own the corporation are shareholders, and those who govern it are members of the board of directors. Corporate officers carry out the business of the board. Corporate debts are the obligation of the corporation but not the shareholders personally, unless the shareholders have signed in an individual capacity and agreed to be liable for corporate debts.

Corporate Ownership and Governance

board of directors
the group that governs a corporation

corporate veil
legal protection provided for corporations that protects them as legal entities separate from their owners

While sole proprietors and partners own and manage their businesses, corporations are owned by shareholders and governed by a **board of directors**. Even though they own the corporation, shareholders normally do not participate directly in the governance of the corporation. Rather, they do so indirectly by voting for members of the board of directors.

The Corporate Veil

Protection from personal liability is sometimes referred to as limited liability. The separate legal status of a corporation as a business organization acts as a **corporate veil**—a shield that prevents creditors from reaching the personal assets of stockholders. As we have seen, there is no such shield separate and apart from their business organization for partners in a general partnership, or for the general partners in a limited partnership, or for a sole proprietor.

In order to enjoy the protection of the corporate veil, efforts must be made to keep the corporation separate from the individuals who own it. This means that the shareholders should make an effort to keep their personal lives and assets separate from those of the corporation by using separate bank accounts, bookkeeping, and so on. Assuming that this is done, when the business fails or owes money, its creditors can normally look only to corporate assets for satisfaction of their claims.

Duration of the Corporation

The third most cited advantage of the corporate form of business is that the corporation has an unlimited duration, sometimes called per-

8–2   CONCEPT SUMMARY

Corporate Terminology

A **public** corporation is one set up by a government; a **private** corporation is set up by individuals.

A **close** or closed corporation is a corporation with total ownership in a few hands.

A corporation is **domestic** in the state in which it was incorporated; a corporation is **foreign** in all other states.

An **eleemosynary** corporation is a charitable corporation.

A corporation that is **closely held** is not traded on any recognized exchanges.

A corporation that is **publicly traded** is traded on one of the national exchanges.

public corporation
one held by the government

private corporation
one held by private citizens rather than the government

close corporation
one whose stock is held by only a few people

domestic corporation
a corporation operating in the state of its incorporation

foreign corporation
a corporation operating in a state other than the state of its incorporation

eleemosynary
a corporation set up for charitable purposes

closely held corporation
a corporation whose shares are held by only a few shareholders

publicly traded
securities trading on one of the national stock exchanges

statutory close corporation
corporation whose voting shares are held by a single or close-knit group of shareholders

petual life. In the case of a large corporation, such as General Motors, this may be true. However, the majority of corporations are small, and many are **closely held** by family members or close friends. The duration of the closely held corporation and the transferability of its stock can be greatly affected by the death of the CEO. As mentioned previously, valuations of small or closely held businesses are difficult. The difference between corporations such as General Motors and a mom-and-pop corporation makes comparison of the advantages and disadvantages difficult.

Identity Protection

A rarely mentioned advantage of incorporating is that the business name will receive a form of identity protection. No other corporation in the same state of incorporation will be allowed to choose the same name or one that is so similar that consumers would be confused.

Disadvantages

Management

Corporate status would be disadvantageous for Ann as a way of doing business if Ann wanted sole control of the business. A corporation is governed by a board of directors that meets periodically to set policy for the corporation. The board of directors has a fiduciary duty to the corporation and its shareholders and must act in the best interests of those shareholders.

Day-to-day operation of a corporation is carried on by its corporate officers: president, vice president, and so forth. The officers are hired by and responsible to the board of directors. Depending on Ann's position as a member of the board of directors, a shareholder, or an officer, there would be limitations and restrictions on what she could do, unlike in the case of a sole proprietorship, in which all the decisions are left to the discretion of the business owner, or in the case of a partnership, in which management may be shared.

Other disadvantages of incorporating are the start-up formalities, the costs associated with incorporation, and double taxation. However, many states now have simple incorporation forms that are mainly fill-in-the-blanks. Some states still require an attorney's signature. Even in those states though, a small-business incorporation

8-3   APPLICATIONS

Incorporating Tip

Even including the filing fees and attorney's fees, Ann and Bill could incorporate in many states for about $500 each. South Carolina law requires a new corporation to have $1,000 in assets, of which $500 must be in cash. Ann and Bill would be allowed to pay the filing fees and attorney's fees with that $500. This should not be an onerous requirement for someone going into business.

Corporations govern themselves internally by use of a document called bylaws. Corporate bylaws and forms may be obtained in reasonably priced kits that help laypersons through the initial corporate formalities such as calling the first board of directors meeting and the first stockholders' meeting. Various tax elections and resolutions are also included, with instructions.

should not be as expensive as a thorough partnership agreement. There usually are state filing fees attached to incorporation. (See Box 8–3, "Incorporating Tip.")

Double Taxation of Corporations

Double taxation refers to the fact that a corporation pays taxes on its profits. The profits are then subject to taxation again as personal income when they are distributed as dividends to the shareholders or are accumulated in the corporation without a business purpose. The IRS takes the position that such undistributed profits can be taxed as income to the shareholders even though not actually received by them.

TYPES OF CORPORATIONS

The limited liability offered by a C corporation may appeal to Ann and Bill if they want the more formalized structure a C corporation reflects and the separate business organization identity. Protection from liability can be a powerful inducement when most of the alternatives considered so far have been characterized by unlimited business and personal liability.

Statutory Close Corporation

Some states provide special laws for **statutory close corporations.** The laws allow Ann and Bill, as owners of a closely held corporation, to do away with the formalities usually required of corporations, such as having a board of directors and holding annual shareholder meetings. Thus the business is essentially allowed to operate as a sole proprietorship (if only one shareholder) or a partnership (if more than one shareholder).

S Corporation

Corporations are often referred to as C corporations or **S corporations**. A C corporation is the regular corporation type just discussed. An S corporation actually refers to an IRS tax election that allows the corporation to be taxed as a partnership (subject only to personal income taxation). The corporation itself would not be a taxpaying entity. Taxes flow through the corporation to the shareholder(s). Profits are taxed at the individual income tax rate, not the corporate rate.

S corporation
a small business corporation that may elect to have its undistributed taxable income taxed to its shareholders

Obviously, this would not be a popular election for Ann and Bill unless their individual tax rates are lower than the corporate tax rates or the corporation expects a loss. Not all corporations qualify for an S election. (See Box 8–4, "S Election Requirements.")

Professional Corporation (PC)

professional corporation (PC)
a business organization composed of professionals who require a license to practice

Many professionals, whether practicing as sole practitioners or as partners, have converted their practice to a **professional corporation**. This is a special form of incorporation that allows professionals the tax advantages of doing business in the corporate form. However, only licensed professionals can be shareholders in the corporation. In states where this is allowed, it does not seem to change the concept of liability of the professionals in their professional capacity. Professionals continue to have unlimited personal liability for professional negligence or malpractice, rather than being allowed to avoid liability for their negligence through the corporate structure.

The law takes the position that when professionals deliver professional services, they should not be able to avoid liability for negligent delivery of those services through the use of the corporate shield, which would otherwise prevent liability from attaching. Since Ann and Bill are not licensed professionals, this is likely not a business organization available or suited to their business enterprise.

8–4	CONCEPT SUMMARY

S Election Requirements

S corporations have rather stringent ownership restrictions:
- no more than 35 shareholders
- shareholders must be natural persons or limited trusts/estates
- only one class of stock allowed

Neither can S corporations specially allocate the component profits and losses of the business. All items of income and expense are generally allocated on a per-share, per-day basis.

Shareholder Rights

Fiduciary Duties

Under a closely held corporation, including S corporations and limited liability companies (in which Ann and Bill were the majority stockholders), a limited partnership (in which Ann and Bill were the general partners), or a general or limited liability partnership, Ann and Bill would owe **fiduciary** duties to the limited partners, the minority stockholders, or the other general partners. Fiduciary duties are the highest duties under the law and generally require honesty and fair dealing. In decision making, the best interests of the limited partners, minority stockholders, or partnership must be taken into account rather than one's own personal interest.

In closely held corporations, the majority shareholders (Bill and Ann) owe the corporation and the minority shareholders a fiduciary duty because of the imbalance of power. Because the majority shareholders can (and usually do) make decisions that affect all of the shareholders, the majority must take into account the best interests of the minority shareholders. A majority shareholder cannot dominate a corporation for an illegal purpose, loot the corporation, or otherwise act to the detriment of the minority shareholders or the creditors.

fiduciary
one who has the responsibility to act for and on behalf of another's interest rather than that one's own, in making decisions

The Corporate Veil in Smaller Settings

As we discussed, a corporation is an artificial legal being and as such should be separate from its owners. By this is meant that it should be distinguishable from its owners. When it is, the law provides the corporate owners/shareholders with a corporate veil to protect them from liability for corporate debts in excess of their contribution paid for shares in the corporation. This is especially important for smaller or more closely held corporations whose corporate existence may be closely tied to that of its owners, and the two may even become indistinguishable. If this happens, corporate protection can be lost and the corporate veil pierced.

Ann and Bill should have separate bank accounts that reflect separately the corporate transactions and their personal business. Thus, there will not be a commingling of personal and corporate funds. Personal bills should be paid from personal accounts, not corporate accounts. When the owners of a corporation do not observe these corporate formalities, they are treating the corporation as their alter egos. Such practice can be, and often is, the basis for setting aside or

pierce the corporate veil
court goes behind the corporate identity shield and imposes personal liability on shareholders for corporate debts

piercing the corporate veil and imposing unlimited personal liability on the owners who were active in management.

The owners of a corporation may loot a corporation by withdrawing funds via excessive salaries, large or numerous perquisites (perks), or employment of friends or family members for work not really performed or work unnecessary to the business. When this results in creditors' not being paid, the corporate veil may be pierced and any owners who are active in management may be held personally liable to the creditors.

Minority Shareholder Rights

Minority shareholders may have other legal rights in closely held corporations. Many states provide for the minority shareholders to have **preemptive** rights. This is the right of first refusal to buy a portion of any new stock issued by the corporation. They are entitled to buy the same percentage of any new issue of stock as they currently hold. Thus, after the issue of stock, they will own the same percentage of stock as before the issue, and their ownership will not be diluted.

Minority shareholders do not have to exercise their preemptive right to purchase the additional shares, but they must be given a good faith option to do so. Thus, any plan by the majority shareholders to issue new stock for the express purpose of diluting the ownership of minority shareholders is illegal when the majority knows or has reason to know that the minority shareholders will not be able to exercise their preemptive rights. As an old legal maxim goes, "What you cannot do directly, you cannot do indirectly."

Many states also offer minority shareholders the right to **cumulative voting** in elections of the company's board of directors. Shareholders are given a number of votes equal to the number of board of director members to be voted on times the number of shares they own. Usually, corporate voting is like any other voting: one share, one vote. This is known as **straight voting**. Cumulative voting works quite differently.

Let's assume there are three shareholders who own a total of 100 shares. Ann owns 60 shares, Bill owns 20 shares, and Hunter owns 20 shares. The bylaws provide for a three-person board of directors. Ann nominates herself for seat number one. Bill and Hunter nominate Hunter. They cast their votes. Ann votes for herself (60 votes), and Bill and Hunter vote for Hunter (40 votes). Ann is elected. Ann nomi-

preemptive rights
the right of first refusal that a shareholder has in the buying of a portion of new stock issued by the corporation

cumulative voting
voting in which shareholders have total votes equal to the number of board members to be elected times the number of shares owned

straight voting
voting in which shareholders get to cast the same number of votes as they have shares in the corporation

nates her brother for seat number two. Again, Bill and Hunter nominate Hunter. Ann's brother is elected by a vote of 60-40. Ann nominates a friend for seat number three. Again, the vote is 60-40, with Ann's friend elected. The board is now complete, and Bill and Hunter have no representation on the board.

In cumulative voting, shareholders are allowed to accumulate votes and cast them all at one time. Assume the same facts, but assume that the election will be conducted using cumulative voting. With three seats on the board, Ann will have a cumulative total of 180 (3 × 60) votes. Bill and Hunter will each have 60 (3 × 20) votes. The formula requires that votes be cast for all three seats.

If Ann wants to be elected to the board, she will end up distributing her votes in a manner that results in her winning two of the three seats. Bill and Hunter, with their cumulative votes, will then be able to elect their candidate to one of the seats. As the number of the seats on the board of directors increases, the formula allows an increasing number of seats to be elected by the minority shareholders through cumulative voting, but the minority shareholders will be able to elect only a minority, never a majority, of the seats.

The purpose behind cumulative voting is to ensure that minority shareholders at least have a voice in corporate governance. If we assume that most directors are honest and act in good faith, the minority member of the board can be an effective voice. If not, at least there will be a paper trail to prove breach of fiduciary duty, should one occur.

A third shareholder right is the **right to inspect** the corporate books and records at reasonable times and at reasonable places for legitimate purposes. When a shareholder asks to exercise inspection rights, the corporation will initially decide whether there is a legitimate purpose behind the request. If not, the court, not the corporation, will make the decision as to whether the request is reasonable and for a legitimate purpose.

Minority shareholders may also be afforded **appraisal rights**. When the majority makes a major decision, such as deciding to dispose of a major corporate asset, dissenting minority shareholders can vote no in writing and ask to be bought out at fair market value the day before the sale or disposition of the asset. This allows minority shareholders to salvage their investment in the corporation. Obviously, the action must be objectionable to the minority shareholder or somehow endangers the investment of the minority or the shareholder would not exercise this right.

right to inspect
the shareholders' right to see the corporate books for legitimate purposes

appraisal rights
the right of a dissenting minority shareholder to vote no in writing and ask to be bought out at fair market value the day before the sale or disposition of assets as voted by the majority

As you have probably realized, the discussion of shareholder rights has centered on small, closely held, non–publicly traded corporations. Corporations that are publicly traded are highly regulated under various state and federal securities laws to be discussed shortly. In many large, publicly traded corporations there is generally no majority shareholder, and thus all shareholders are minority shareholders. A 10% equity interest in a corporation such as General Motors Corp. would represent an enormous block of stock.

Dividend Rights

Securities are usually purchased for the periodic income (payment of dividends) associated with many types of securities. Bonds pay interest. Stocks pay dividends. Most consumers understand interest, but dividend rights are often misunderstood. No shareholder has a right to a dividend unless the board of directors has declared and authorized the dividend. Once declared, dividends become a debt of the corporation. Dividends cannot be paid unless there are funds available and the payment of the dividend would not cause the corporation to become insolvent.

Many investors and consumers purchase stock because of a company's record of giving dividends, and they depend on those dividends for income. When the corporation experiences hard times or decides to accumulate funds (and not pay dividends) for legitimate corporate purposes (such as plant expansion or purchase of capital equipment), such shareholders are without a remedy.

The IRS has taken the position that a corporation may not accumulate large sums of cash (and not pay dividends) unless the corporation has a legitimate purpose to do so. When dividends are paid, the recipients must pay income tax on them. This is the double taxation connected with the corporate form of business. Some corporations attempt to postpone dividends in order to avoid or postpone income taxes having to be paid by recipients.

business judgment rule
directors will not be held liable for losses suffered by a corporation if they have used due diligence in making the decision resulting in the loss

Business Judgment Rule

Historically, the **business judgment rule** has protected members of corporate boards of directors from liability for poor business decisions. The rule acts very much like the duty of the majority shareholder in small corporations to treat minority shareholders fairly. In this instance, the duty runs from the board to the shareholders. As you might guess, sometimes business decisions turn out to be wrong or unprofitable. Sometimes external forces may turn a good decision into a poor one. In the past, the business judgment rule basically provided that when the board acted in good faith, it would be protected from liability for poor decisions. The burden of proof was on the shareholders to prove a board's lack of good faith.

Today, the protection afforded by the rule appears to have eroded, and the burden of proof appears to have been shifted. During the 1980s, courts began to require that a board of directors prove good faith (by showing the members made a reasonable investigation before the decision) and that it show it acted in the best interests of the shareholders, as opposed to the board itself or the company management. With some of the decisions made by certain savings and loans that resulted in their bailout by government and hundreds of cases brought by the Resolution Trust Corporation— established to handle the cases and oversee the industry—you can imagine why the rule shifted somewhat. It was difficult to believe that board members had the best interests of shareholders and the corporation at heart when they authorized expensive office furnishings, gold office bathroom fixtures, trips to exotic places, and other questionable outlays that resulted in massive losses in the savings and loan industry. However, because of that widespread industrial debacle, virtually all savings and loans' losses came under scrutiny. Many, whose policies had been in place for years, found themselves in court trying to justify themselves to the Resolution Trust Corporation and a judge. As the following case shows, however, the business judgment rule was still applicable when it seemed appropriate.

REGULATION OF SECURITIES

If Ann and Bill decide to incorporate the business, they may issue stock in the corporation to raise funds. They will have to comply with their state's securities laws (**blue-sky laws**) or the federal Securities Act of 1933, one of which will probably be applicable unless the stock issue falls under a recognized exemption. Although many people consider the term *stock* to be synonymous with the term **security**, the two are not synonymous.

A security is any investment in a common enterprise from which the purchaser or holder expects or hopes to make a profit mostly

blue-sky laws
state securities laws

security
any investment in a common enterprise from which the purchaser or holder expects or hopes to make a profit mostly from the efforts of others

RESOLUTION TRUST CORPORATION V. EASON ET AL.

17 F.3d 1126 (8th Cir. 1994)

The Resolution Trust Corporation (RTC) brought this action seeking $12 million in damages from officers and directors of the First Federal Savings and Loan Association of Fayetteville, Ark. (S&L). RTC alleged the officers and directors were negligent and breached their fiduciary duty by approving $12 million in loans which later failed. RTC alleged that the S&L's policy of deciding whether to underwrite loans in which it pooled its resources with other banks for the total amount of the loan was negligent in that the S&L would make the lending decision based on the determination of the lead lender in the pool or on its personal knowledge of the applicant. The RTC alleged it was a violation of the business judgment rule for the S&L not to perform its own independent analysis of the loan application. The lower court held for the S&L, and the decision was affirmed.

Bright, J.: In this case, and regarding the business judgment rule, the trial court instructed the jury:

The defendants contend that they are not liable for any losses resulting from the loans in question because their acts and decisions were protected by the business judgment rule. The business judgment rule is a presumption that in making a business decision, the directors or officers of a corporation acted on an informed basis, in good faith, and in an honest belief that the action taken was in the best interest of the company. This rule is based on the assumption that the directors and officers of the corporation are better equipped than the court or the jury to make business judgments or decisions.

A director or officer may rely on the protections of the business judgment rule if:

(1) The director or officer is disinterested and has acted in good faith. The term *disinterested* means that the director or officer must not be personally interested, financially or otherwise, in the transaction at issue; and

(2) The director or officer had fulfilled his duty to inform himself of all material information reasonably available to him prior to making the business decision.

You are instructed that in this case, the plaintiff does not contend that defendants were personally interested, financially or otherwise, in any of the loans which are the subject matter of this lawsuit or that they acted in bad faith. Thus, if you find from a preponderance of the evidence that a defendant has met the requirements set forth in subparagraph (2) above, your verdict shall be for such defendant unless you find that the plaintiff has rebutted the presumption created by the business judgment rule by showing that no person with ordinary, sound business judgment would have, as an officer or director of the corporation, assented to the action taken.

To invoke the business judgment rule, directors must show (1) that they were disinterested and that their conduct otherwise met the test of business judgment and (2) that they informed themselves of all material information reasonably available to them before making a business decision and, having become so informed, acted with requisite care in discharging their duties.

Here, the officers followed customary underwriting practices that had been found acceptable by the Federal Home Loan Bank Board during its audit. After the audit, the S&L received a grade of B (on an A–F scale) for its loan practices, and there were handwritten notes by the bank examiner next to two of the loans in question saying they were excellent investments. There was also evidence of a proposed rulemaking from the Federal Home Loan Bank Board codifying the approval of the practice of relying on the lead lender's verification of information submitted in support of participation proposals. Experienced board members testified that the practice of relying on the lead lender's verification of the borrower was the usual banking custom locally and nationally.

After carefully reviewing the record, we determine that the officers introduced enough evidence concerning their underwriting practices to justify the instruction, and there was no error in giving the instruction to the jury. AFFIRMED

Case Questions

1. Does it seem to you that a practice that permits a lending institution to make loan decisions based on someone else's analysis of the applicant's data is a solid basis for good business judgment? Explain.

continued on next page

2. What, if anything, do you think is lost by directors' using the method of decision making based on someone else's analysis? Gained?

3. Based on what you have learned about the business judgment rule, which approach do you think Bill and Ann should take in making business decisions if they form a corporation and are on the board of directors? Why?

from the efforts of others. Common examples of securities are stocks, bonds, investment contracts, and limited partnership interests. There are several examples that a layperson would probably not consider a security. For example, time-shares in condominiums/vacation plans and membership in some country clubs have been held to be securities. The definition of a security is broad and has become even broader in recent years. The 1933 and 1934 Securities Acts are the two most important federal laws regulating securities.

The 1933 Securities Act

The 1933 Securities Act was passed after the crash of the stock market in 1929 and was an attempt to restore investor confidence in the markets. The main purpose of the law is to provide for potential investors the disclosure of accurate information about the issue and the company issuing the security. This is accomplished by the filing of a **registration** statement with the Securities and Exchange Commission (SEC). The act requires that the statement's questions be answered fully and truthfully and be organized so as not to be misleading. There can be massive civil liability if any of the information is misleading, contains misstatements of fact, or omits information that a reasonable investor would consider material.

The first 20 items on the registration statement constitute the information contained in the **prospectus** given to all purchasers of securities. Because the required information in the prospectus is what the investor will see, it must be written clearly and nonmisleading. Of course, it must be accurate. The general rule says that the issuance of all securities must be registered—unless exempted from registration—and that no security can be sold until its registration is effective.

registration
the process of disclosing to the SEC or state security agency requested information about a security being offered to the public

prospectus
information provided to prospective buyers about a security being offered to the public

Registration is an expensive process and constrains a company from issuing securities until the registration statement becomes effective (a minimum of 20 days after filing). The fact that a corporation has complied with the provisions of the 1933 act does not guarantee that the company's stock is a good investment. Compliance with the act ensures only that investors have access to truthful, nonmisleading information about the company and the stock issue.

The fraud provisions of the 1933 act apply to all issues, whether or not the issue was registered or required to be registered under the 1933 act. Under those provisions, any material misstatements or omissions of material facts in connection with the issue of securities can result in criminal as well as civil liability for a large number of participants (including the issuer, the board of directors, company officers, experts, and underwriters). The issuer itself is held strictly liable, and there is no defense available. The others are held to a negligence standard and can present a defense called **due diligence**. This assumes, of course, that those others were not aware of and did not participate in the fraud. Successful use of the due diligence defense requires a reasonable investigation of the information provided and that after the investigation there is no reason to believe there are any misstatements or omissions of material facts.

While a company waits for its registration statement to become effective, the market may fall. Due to the importance of timing in the financial markets, as well as the expense involved in registration, companies often attempt to structure an issue so that it will qualify for one of the allowable **exemptions**.

due diligence
board of directors members' using care and good faith in making decisions for the corporation

exemptions
securities that, by statute, do not have to be registered with the SEC

Registration Exemptions

Exemptions under the 1933 act have changed over time, but they are still based on the original exemptions, which fall into three categories. The first one, Rule 147, is known as the *intrastate exemption*. It is based on the fact that the stock to be issued will be purchased by residents of the same state where the company is incorporated. Residents cannot resell the stock for at least a nine-month period. In addition, the state where the stock is issued must be the same as the one in which the issuer does 80% of its business, where 80% of its assets are located, and where 80% of the proceeds from the sale of the stock will be used. This is known as the **80% rule**. The intrastate exemption has been liberalized. Originally, all of the purchasers and the issuer had to reside in the same state—the 100% rule.

80% rule
exemption from SEC registration requirements for offerings in which at least 80% of the investors are from the state, 80% of the issuer's assets are there, and 80% of the proceeds from the issue will be there

The second category of exemptions, the *small-offering exemption,* is based on an offering of a relatively small dollar amount. Regulation A applies to issues of stock not exceeding $1.5 million in a 12-month period. Regulation D provides two more exemptions. Rule 504 provides an exemption when the issue does not exceed $500,000 in any 12-month period. Rule 505 has a limit of $5 million in any 12-month period and provides that no more than 35 nonaccredited purchasers may buy (a nonaccredited investor has less than $100,000 annual income); there is no limit on the number of accredited purchasers. The early form of the small-issue exemption was based solely on the dollar amount of the issue.

The third category of exemptions is known as the *private placement exemption,* Rule 506, and applies when the issue is limited to 35 nonaccredited investors. There is no limit on accredited investors (those who earn more than $100,000 a year), and there is no dollar amount limit on Rule 506. Originally, the private placement exemption protected unsophisticated investors by requiring that all potential purchasers be insiders, who would have access to and the ability to understand (sophistication) the financial information found in the registration statement. Thus, unsophisticated investors were ineligible potential investors. The number of "sophisticated" investors was also limited to 35.

Today, the private placement exemption still exists, but the notion of sophistication has been replaced by an income ($200,000 annual minimum) or net worth requirement. Investors who meet the income/net worth requirement are called accredited investors. Presumably, those making a lot of money are sophisticated (and more able to bear the risks involved in any investment). In reality, however, that may not be true. Those with high incomes (e.g., sports players, actors, doctors) are often the most likely victims of securities fraud. Presumably, Congress and the SEC feel that these "accredited" persons are able to protect themselves by hiring someone who is "sophisticated." Section 4(6) allows the sale of up to $5 million of securities to accredited investors. Section 4(6) is an example of the combination of the dollar limitation found in the small-offering rule and the requirement of accredited buyers found in the private placement exemption.

When a company issues stock under a federal exemption, it may still have to comply with state law. Laws vary from state to state, so Bill and Ann should be sure they are complying with whatever laws are in effect. Many of the states have modeled their laws after the federal law, and therefore most of the state laws are disclosure laws. However, in some instances, monies must be put into escrow—that is, held by a third party, such as a bank.

An attorney specializing in business law should be able to advise Bill and Ann, or they can call the state attorney general's office or the secretary of state's office for advice. Securities laws are very complex and we have only scratched the surface. Since Bill and Ann are going into business on only a small scale until they graduate from college, it appears that neither of them would need to issue stock at this point.

The 1934 Securities Act

The 1934 Securities Act covers the resale rather than the initial issuance of securities and may apply irrespective of whether a security was registered under the 1933 act. The 1934 act requires the disclosure of important information that is material to investors. The information required for disclosure under the act essentially updates the information that would be in a registration statement under the 1933 act.

Registration under the 1934 act is required of every corporation whose securities are traded on one of the national exchanges and every corporation that has 500 or more shareholders and $5 million or more in assets and that trades equity securities in an over-the-counter market. As you can see, most closely held corporations will not meet these requirements. By definition an S corporation can have only 35 shareholders and therefore does not qualify. Therefore, keep in mind that state laws and regulations govern most of the small, closely held corporations and that these vary greatly from state to state. Businesspersons would be well advised to seek the counsel of a professional (attorney, CPA, etc.) in the states in which they intend to conduct business.

Section 10 requires that companies with securities under the 1934 act make periodic reports to the SEC. These reports essentially update the information that would be found in a registration statement. The **current report** (monthly) is an **8K**, which covers material happenings in the current month. The **quarterly report**, **10Q**, reports any material financial changes during the current quarter. The **annual report**, **10K**, contains audited financial statements for the year and other material information about the corporation.

Proxy solicitations are also governed by the 1934 act. A proxy is a written authorization of voting rights. Each time there is a corporate

8K report
the monthly report corporations must make to the SEC to update their securities registration

10Q report
the quarterly report corporations must file with the SEC to update material aspects of their securities registration statement

annual report
the yearly report corporations must make to the SEC, with an audited financial statement and other pertinent information regarding their business transactions

proxy
written authorization given by a shareholder permitting someone to vote for him or her when the shareholder is not present to do so

quorum

minimum number of
people necessary to
be present to
conduct corporate
business

meeting in which a vote will take place, those who are unable to attend may vote by proxy if the corporate bylaws so permit. Generally, management solicits proxies, so that there will be enough shares represented to ensure a **quorum**. A quorum is the minimum number of persons or shares necessary to be present or represented in order to lawfully conduct corporate business. The quorum may consist of persons in attendance, persons not in attendance but represented by proxies, or both. The 1934 act regulates the solicitation of proxies so that shareholders can make an intelligent decision about how they wish to vote and to whom they wish to give their proxies. Consistent with the purpose of the securities laws, this represents another form of required disclosure. A proxy solicitation should disclose the issues to be voted on, the identity of and important information concerning the solicitor (usually the CEO/management), management's stand on each issue, and a choice of the way the shareholder wishes the proxy holder to vote.

tender offer

an offer, usually
public, to purchase a
certain amount of
stock at a set price
(generally above
market price);
generally precedes a
takeover (hostile or
friendly) of one
company by another
company or
individual

Section 13 regulates **tender offers**. A tender offer is an offer, usually public, to purchase a certain amount of stock at a set price (generally above market price). Often, a tender offer precedes a takeover (hostile or friendly) of one company by another company or individual. A company that owns 5% of another company's stock must file with the SEC and disclose all material information about the acquiring company or person. With that disclosure, potential sellers will have information to base an intelligent decision about whether or not to sell. Not all purchases of stock lead to a takeover; some are merely investments by one company in another. When the purchases are for the purpose of takeover, both the SEC and the Federal Trade Commission must be notified. (Mergers must be evaluated for legality under the antitrust laws.)

Section 10 is the major fraud section of the 1934 act. Under this section, Rule 10-b-5 is the most well-known antifraud provision (see Box 8–5, "Rule 10-b-5"). In fact, it is probably the most famous of the SEC provisions for laypeople and the one any of us are most likely to be familiar with. It is the rule that forms the basis for most of the securities fraud cases we read about in the press.

In 1984, Congress enacted the Insider Trading Sanctions Act. The legislation followed a series of cases in which the SEC had been unsuccessful in proving alleged insider trading as violations of Rule 10-b-5. While it does not define insider trading, it does provide both criminal (fines and jail terms) and civil (treble damages) sanctions.

8–5 LEGAL EXCERPTS

Rule 10-b-5

It shall be unlawful for any person, directly or indirectly, by the use of any means or instrumentality of interstate commerce, or of the mails or any facility or any national securities exchange,

 (a) To employ any device, scheme, or artifice to defraud;

 (b) To make any untrue statement of a material fact or to omit to state a material fact necessary in order to make the statements made, in the light of the circumstances under which they were made, not misleading; or

 (c) To engaged in any act, practices, or course of business which operates or would operate as a fraud or deceit upon any person, in connection with the purchase or sale of any security. 17 CFR §240, 10-b-5

Section 16 covers **short-swing trades**. Section 16-a defines **insiders** as 10% shareholders, officers, and directors. Section 16-b prohibits those insiders from trading in company shares **and** from making a profit (it does not prohibit a loss) during any six-month period. If you buy in January and sell in March and make a profit, you would violate Section 16 if you were an insider. The SEC requires that transactions by insiders be reported to the SEC. Any illegal profits must be paid over to the corporation. It does not matter in which order the transactions occur (buying or selling). Simply put, insiders cannot trade in their company's stock twice in a six-month period.

In 1977, Congress passed the Foreign Corrupt Practices Act amending the 1934 Securities Act. The Foreign Corrupt Practices Act applies to the same companies covered under the 1934 act. When most people think of this act, they think the major thrust concerns bribery. While Section 103 does cover bribery and makes it a violation of the act, Section 102 is the more important section. Section 102 requires companies covered by the act to have sufficient internal controls in place to account for the disposition of material corporate assets. Thus any bribe, if a material amount of money, would have to be disclosed.

short-swing trade
trade of a security within six months of purchase

insider
10% shareholder or officer or director of a corporation

8-6   APPLICATIONS

Corporate Characteristics

The case of *Morrissey v. Commissioner* (296 U.S. 344 [1935]) determined that there were six factors that were characteristic of a corporation: associates, profit motive, centralized management, continuity of life, free transferability of ownership interests, and limitation of personal liability. Because associates and the profit motive are present in both corporations and partnerships, these characteristics were not found to be the determining ones. Thus, the last four characteristics were found to be determinative in distinguishing a corporation from a noncorporation (i.e., partnership): centralized management, continuity of life, free transferability of ownership interests, and limitation of personal liability.

LIMITED LIABILITY COMPANIES

limited liability company
new form of business organization that offers limited liability to its members and taxation as a partnership if certain conditions are met

One of the newest forms of business Ann should consider is the **limited liability company**. As of 1994, 40 states had enacted legislation allowing businesses to operate under this innovative form. Under it, the members of a company are co-proprietors who are not personally liable merely due to membership. They are held liable only for their negligence or the negligence of someone under their direction and control. Thus, the members are treated similarly to shareholders in a corporation (or the same as the tort liability of the members of a registered limited liability partnership).

If structured properly, the limited liability company will be taxed as a partnership by the IRS. Thus, the owners of the limited liability company appear to have the best of both forms of business (the advantages of taxation available to an S corporation, without the restrictions placed on S corporations by the IRS). The requirements for favorable tax treatment by the IRS are given in Box 8–6, "Corporate Characteristics."

A limited liability company is essentially an S corporation without most of the restrictions placed on S corporations. As its name implies, limited liability is an important feature. Equally important, when properly organized, a limited liability company is treated by the federal tax laws as a partnership. This seems to combine the advantages of a corporation (limited liability, increased sources of financial capital, specialization of labor) with the advantages of a partnership (lower tax rates, flow through of profits and losses to the "partners") without adding the disadvantages of either.

Since there has been so little history or litigation in this area, it is difficult to predict whether it will be the business form of the future as some writers have predicted. It does appear that it will be a competitive form of business in those states in which it is allowed. An important issue may arise regarding the way a state that does not provide for or recognize this form of business would treat a limited liability company from another state. Some states have already decided to tax this new form of business as a corporation for state tax purposes. That measure therefore removes one of the incentives associated with this form of business. Some states have decided that professionals cannot use this form of business; thus professionals would have to operate in another form.

FRANCHISES

For Bill and Ann's purposes, the franchise, like the joint venture, is not an optimal form of business organization. However, it is a very popular way for many people to get into business. Under a franchise, the franchisor who has developed a successful business sells, leases, or licenses its business plan to a franchisee or buyer who wishes to enter the business. There are start-up fees (like a buy-in) as well as ongoing royalty fees that must be paid by the franchisee to the franchisor. Franchises are subject to Federal Trade Commission disclosure rules, and they face the possibility of additional federal legislation in the near future.

Since Ann and Bill are just starting their business, becoming a franchisor may be possible in the future if the business is one that can be repeated and is successful. They would likely not want to be franchisees unless there were a franchisor with a business like theirs whose name and reputation they would want to buy into and be associated with.

EXTERNAL FACTORS

As we have seen, businesses can be operated in many different forms. These include the sole proprietorship, general partnership, limited partnership, limited liability partnership, C corporation, statutory close corporation, S corporation, professional corporation (professional association), limited liability company, joint venture, and franchise. In order to decide which form is appropriate for any particular business at any point in time, one must consider several external factors. These include the nature or classification of the business itself, the tax laws currently in effect or on the horizon, and the potential for legal liability.

NATURE AND CLASSIFICATIONS OF BUSINESS

Businesses can be classified as service businesses (e.g., dry cleaners), professional service businesses (e.g., accountants), trade businesses (e.g., plumbers), retail businesses (e.g., department stores), manufacturing businesses (e.g., automakers), or a mix of businesses (e.g., manufacturing and retailing). Different types of businesses incur different types and levels of risk. The type and level of risk associated with the type of business may have an effect on the choice of business form.

When a real estate deal goes bad or falls through, there is a possibility of financial liability. When the food in a restaurant is tainted, there is the possibility of personal injury or product liability. While the nature and classification of the business alone do not dictate any particular form of business, when taken together with other factors, some forms of business may be more advisable than others.

For instance, accountants and lawyers have historically operated their businesses—sometimes called professional practices—as sole proprietorships or partnerships. More recently, many have formed professional corporations (professional associations) in those states that allow it. Plumbers have also operated in sole proprietorships or partnerships. Manufacturers, like General Motors Corp., have traditionally used the corporate form. Start-up costs can be a factor. For instance, a manufacturing process may need a large amount of financial capital and might be described as capital-intensive. This would seem to indicate that a sole proprietorship might not offer the opportunity to raise the needed funds, whereas partnerships (both general and

8–7   APPLICATIONS

Business Liability

If Ann and Bill were going to operate a charter fishing service, we would probably say that it could be a high-risk business. Anglers could slip and fall in the boat or get fishhooks stuck in themselves instead of the fish. The boat could even sink! One might therefore assume that Ann and Bill would definitely form a corporation to protect themselves from personal liability for the personal injury or death of an angler.

Assume that an angler is hurt and that the boat's crew consisted of a hired captain and hired first mate. If the angler sues and the crew members were negligent, the corporate veil would probably protect Bill and Ann and any other shareholders. All that the injured angler could get would be the corporate assets.

However, if we assume that Ann or Bill is the captain, we may find a radically different result. If the injured angler can prove the injury was a result of Ann or Bill's negligence, Ann or Bill may be held personally liable also because everyone is liable for the torts he or she personally commits. Thus the corporate veil does not really protect Ann or Bill from personal liability. The angler's attorney will bring suit against all of the possible defendants, including the defendant with the deepest pocket, which may include Ann or Bill as an individual as well as an agent of the corporation.

If we look at the issue of limited personal liability for corporate liability or for corporate debts, the answer is—for all practical purposes—the same. If the corporation involved is a small business in which Ann and Bill are the majority stockholders, a bank will probably demand that they sign the bank loan note as the corporate president or an officer and as individuals. By signing in an individual capacity, Bill and Ann are personally liable for the bank note and loan. If the corporation is unable to pay, Ann and Bill will have to pay from their personal assets. Therefore, in many instances, the idea of limited liability is only wishful thinking.

limited), corporations (both C and S), limited liability companies, or even joint ventures would make the fund-raising easier.

BENEFITS, PROFITS, LOSSES, AND TAX LAWS

Another factor to consider is that of benefits. Typically, the IRS has made certain tax benefits available to corporations. The tax treatment of those benefits has helped to make the corporate form of business organization very popular.

Corporate taxation became especially beneficial due to the enhanced retirement plan contributions that used to be available to corporations compared with those available to partnerships. Since 1960, however, the retirement plan contribution options available to a corporation have become greatly circumscribed, whereas the retirement plan contribution options available to a partnership have been expanded. Presently, there is little substantive difference between the amounts a partner versus a stockholder can set aside as retirement plan contributions in a qualified retirement plan, given the same profits and employees. Thus the form of doing business is no longer driven by the availability of retirement plan contribution options. The Tax Reform Act of 1986 effectively ended the tax shelter era, and since the mid 1980s, the incentive to form a corporation has diminished due to the availability of favorable tax treatment in other forms of business.

START-UP COSTS AND TAXATION

If a business will be solely service oriented, such as a repair business, its start-up costs will probably not be large, and practically any form of business would be appropriate. By adding tax considerations we may begin to get a sharper picture. Thus, other factors being even, Ann might or might not choose to do business as a C corporation based solely on the tax rates in effect.

PROJECTED LEVEL OF PROFIT AND TAXATION

The decision as to whether Bill and Ann would choose one form of business over another could depend on the projected level of profit. The sole proprietorship, partnership (general, limited, and limited li-

8–8   APPLICATIONS

Actual Losses versus Paper Losses

When a business spends more than it takes in, it is said to have a loss. In that instance, the loss is a cash loss. A paper loss occurs when a business takes in more than it spends in cash, but after depreciation allowances are added to expenses, the business shows a loss.

Depreciation is an accounting term that reflects a fall in value or a reduction in worth of an asset that has a limited useful life. No actual cash is expended each year, but an allowance is granted by the IRS to reflect the loss in value of the asset.

ability), S corporation, and limited liability company would all allow taxation at the currently lower rates if profits exceed $50,000. Remember, however, that the limited partnership, S corporation, limited liability partnership, and limited liability company are highly regulated, and only those businesses that can meet the requirements qualify. Sometimes the fact that we project business losses—actual or paper—makes the C corporation undesirable from a tax minimization viewpoint (see Box 8–8, "Actual Losses versus Paper Losses"). Since we see many C corporations, there must be factors other than tax considerations at work.

APPLICATIONS

Following are several hypothetical situations. Observe how the form of business affects the results. For each situation, try to formulate your own answer prior to reading the explanation that follows the hypothesis.

HYPOTHESIS 1

Bill, who is too busy to make a bank deposit before lunch, asks his employee to make the bank deposit on his way to lunch. Assume that the employee is in his personal car (not one belonging to Bill) and that he negligently sideswipes a car on a narrow street, causing property damage and personal injury to the other driver. Who can be held liable?

No matter what the form of business, the employee can be held liable for his tort. If Bill is operating as a sole proprietor, both the employee and Bill (the employer) may be held liable. Under respondeat superior, Bill would liable for the negligent torts of his employee committed within the scope of employment. Bill cannot argue that the employee is not within the scope, because when he asked the employee to make the bank deposit, Bill extended the scope of employment through the lunch break. As a practical matter, most injured people will seek a deep-pocket defendant (generally the employer) if vicarious liability will apply.

If Bill is operating as the general partner in a partnership, the result is the same as under a sole proprietorship. If there is another general partner, both partners may be held liable, although the victim can collect only once. If one of the partners is forced to pay, he would be entitled to contribution from the other partner. If Bill is operating as a limited partner, he will not face liability (except to the extent of his capital contribution). If Bill is a general partner in a limited liability partnership, it has to be determined whether he was in control or he was the supervisor of the employee involved in the wreck, such that personal liability attaches. This is usually interpreted to mean supervision of work (such as supervising a junior accountant on a tax return or audit), not driving.

If Bill is operating as a corporation (C or S) or as a limited liability company, he cannot, normally, be held personally liable. The corporation, as employer, may be held liable under respondeat superior.

HYPOTHESIS 2

Bill's business is very profitable. How are taxes affected by the legal form of business?

If Bill is operating as a sole proprietor or as a partner in any of the forms of partnership or as a shareholder in an S corporation or a limited liability company, all of the profits he receives are taxable as individual income. Individual tax rates vary with income, and corporate dividends are taxed again at the individual rate. Thus the legal form of business can, and does, affect the amount of taxes due on income.

HYPOTHESIS 3

Bill's company produces "kidgets." These toys are very popular with children. Kidgets were designed and manufactured with the safety of children in mind, but somehow a child is injured while playing with a kidget. Who can be held liable?

If Bill is operating as a sole proprietor or a general partner, he may be held personally liable to the injured child. If he is operating in an S or C corporation, in a limited liability company, or in a limited liability partnership, the company, and not Bill, will normally be held liable.

HYPOTHESIS 4

One of the employees at Bill's company illegally dumps used oil into the storm drain outside the company gate. Who may be held criminally liable?

The company itself can be held criminally liable and fined, under any form of business. The issue of whether Bill can be held criminally liable rests upon his participation in or knowledge of the illegal dumping. If Bill is in a responsible or high position in the company, the trend is that he may be held criminally liable. Of course, the employee may be held liable for his crime.

HYPOTHESIS 5

Bill's company experiences several years of poor business. Ultimately, the business cannot pay its debts as the debts come due. Who can be held liable to the creditors?

If the company is a sole proprietorship or a general partnership, Bill may be held personally liable for the business debts. If the business is operating as an S or C corporation, as a limited liability company, or as a limited liability partnership, Bill is not, normally, held personally liable, and the creditors can seek payment only from the business and the business assets.

HYPOTHESIS 6

Bill's company is in so much debt it decides to declare bankruptcy. How is bankruptcy affected by the legal form of business?

If Bill is operating as a sole proprietorship, he may choose to file bankruptcy under Chapter 7 (individual bankruptcy) or Chapter 13 (wage earner bankruptcy). If the business is a corporation, it can file under Chapter 7 or Chapter 11 (reorganization). Many businesses attempt to reorganize under Chapter 11 because they may be able to emerge from bankruptcy as a viable concern. If it is decided that the sale of the business is the only viable alternative, it is usually more beneficial to sell the business as a going concern. Good will has an economic value and will be lost if the business is closed and only assets are sold.

SUMMARY

Entrepreneurs like Ann and Bill have a choice of several business organizations as a way of conducting their business activities. Business forms include sole proprietorship, partnership, limited partnership, limited liability partnership, C corporation, statutory close corporation, professional corporation, S corporation, limited liability company, joint venture, and franchise. Each of the types of business organization has advantages and disadvantages.

The main factors to consider are legal formalities, costs of creation, availability of limited liability, tax treatment by the IRS, duration, transferability, and valuation. However, more important than all of these may be the needs that drive Bill and Ann, in addition to personal considerations as to how much they want control over their enterprise and how much they feel they can risk. Now that they are aware of the various types of business organizations, they can choose more wisely the organization right for them.

CHAPTER TERMS

annual report	close corporation
appraisal rights	closely held corporation
blue-sky laws	contribution
board of directors	corporate veil
business judgment rule	cumulative voting
C corporation	dissociation

dissolution	preemptive right
domestic corporation	private corporation
due diligence	professional corporation (PC)
8K report	prospectus
80% rule	proxy
eleemosynary	public corporation
exemptions	publicly traded
fiduciary	quorum
foreign corporation	registration
general partnership	S corporation
insider	security
joint and several liability	short-swing trade
limited liability company	sole proprietorship
limited liability partnership	statutory close corporation
limited partnership	straight voting
marshaling of assets	10Q report
partnership	tender offer
pierce the corporate veil	valuation

CHAPTER-END QUESTIONS

1. Explain the liability of a general partner in each type of partnership.

2. Explain the liability of a shareholder in each type of corporation.

3. Explain what a fiduciary duty is and who is affected by it.

4. Megan and Serita are minority shareholders in the Satprep Corporation. They are very unhappy with the way things are being done in the corporation and the decisions that are being made. Megan says that as minority shareholders, however, they can do nothing and they have no rights against the majority shareholders. Is Megan correct? Explain.

5. Securities laws are for the purpose of preventing people from buying into unwise investment schemes. (True or False) Explain.

6. List and explain the exemptions available under the 1933 Securities Act.

7. List and explain the reporting requirements under the 1934 Securities Act.

8. Explain what the Foreign Corrupt Practices Act covers.

9. Arturo is sued by some of the shareholders of Wyzenheim Inc. Arturo was a director for Wyzenheim during a time when the board voted to invest in a venture that turned out badly and caused the corporation a loss. The investment looked sound when the board analyzed the necessary factors, but the loss was significant and the shareholders are upset. Is there anything Arturo can use as a defense to the shareholders' suit?

10. Write a paragraph advising Bill and Ann about the factors involved in a choice of business form.

11. What legal form of business organization do you believe Ann and Bill should choose for their new business? Why?

GROUP EXERCISE

Assume that you are considering going into business with several friends at your college. You have decided to form a business that will offer house-sitting services. Included in the service will be someone who will physically be present in the house to water plants, take care of pets, and perform related services as the need arises. What legal form of business would your group choose and why?

REFERENCES

1 §601, 701 & 801, Revised Uniform Partnership Act (1994).
2 §201 Revised Uniform Partnership Act (1985).

Chapter 9

ENTREPRENEURSHIP: LEGAL
ASPECTS OF THE NEW ENTERPRISE

Chapter Preview Summary

Now that Bill and Ann have a basic understanding and overview of the legal environment of business, this chapter will begin to help them understand the nuts and bolts of the legal issues involved in operating a business as they consider its legal implications.

Chapter Objectives

In studying this chapter, you should learn:
- the sources of business advice
- how a business name is protected by the law
- that a business must be accessible to the disabled
- what an environmental audit is
- the various ways that real estate can be held
- what a business license is
- what a federal tax identification number is
- why a business should maintain its own bank accounts
- why a business should establish internal controls
- what the law requires regarding issuance of securities

INTRODUCTION

Usually, students learn about the law in big, broad generalities. This is necessary because course coverage must be limited in order to fit as much as possible into the time allotted. However, sometimes students come away without having gained real appreciation of how the law actually works and what the law requires them to do on a practical basis. This chapter addresses that problem by providing practical information about what comes into play when a business like Ann and Bill's starts up.

The majority of new businesses fail for one reason or other within a year after their establishment. We want to minimize the possibility of this happening to Ann and Bill by ensuring that before they begin to operate, they have a real appreciation of what they are in for.

SOURCES OF INFORMATION

Before opening their new business, Ann and Bill realize they should seek advice on exactly what might be involved in its start-up. They check around and discover several sources of advice for aspiring entrepreneurs. Small businesses, which provide the bulk of jobs in this country, are helped by the federal government's Small Business Administration (SBA). The SBA has 750 Small Business Development Centers (SBDCs) located in cities throughout the United States. The centers are usually affiliated with colleges and universities. A list of SBDC offices is available from the SBA. The offices are willing to help small firms, and they offer a wide array of services, from loans to free and nominal-cost education.

If there is no SBDC nearby, another excellent source of information and help is the Service Core of Retired Executives (SCORE). A list of SCORE offices is available by calling 800-634-0245.

A third source of information can probably be found by contacting professors of business at any local college or community college. Business professors will be able to provide valuable information for new entrepreneurs. Many of them routinely offer consulting services as part of their professional commitments. Frequently, college business classes undertake projects in which students offer free assistance to local businesses in need of short-term expertise. Contacting a local institution of higher education should put Ann and Bill in contact with the appropriate connections.

Should none of the foregoing be available in their locality, perhaps there is either a local attorney who handles business matters or a local CPA. The SBA, SBDC, and SCORE offices often sponsor seminars to give instruction in and develop entrepreneurship. Virtually every town has a chamber of commerce. Chambers of commerce are associations of businesses in an area and often sponsor programs or provide information or referral for new businesses.

THE BUSINESS PLAN

Where there is local access to an SBDC, help can be obtained to formulate a **business plan**. A business plan outlines all aspects of a business and how it conducts its business, including obtaining needed funds. The plan is generally developed when a business wishes a loan from a bank or other investor. While help would be of great assistance, a business plan should be developed for new or aspiring entrepreneurs whether or not help is available.

business plan
a plan that outlines important aspects of a business, generally used to determine feasibility of extending credit to the business

A business plan is an essential first step in the planning process. Going through the steps in developing a business plan should be very helpful in determining what the initial needs and goals of the business will be. In developing the plan, Ann and Bill must explain their business concepts, analyze their potential markets, and plan the ways they will reach those markets. The process can help them decide on a name for their businesses, help them choose a location, and determine how much capital they will need for start-up. (See Box 9–1, "Sample Business Plan Outline" on pages 270–271.)

FINANCING THE NEW ENTERPRISE

After their capital needs are determined, if Ann and Bill do not have all the money they need to start up the business the way they would like to, they will have to decide on ways to finance their new business. They can try any alternative—from saving until they get enough money, to borrowing from friends and family, to borrowing from banks, savings and loans, venture capital firms, or other sources. What they decide to do depends on what they want and the requirements of the process.

If Ann or Bill or both decide to run the business as a sole proprietorship or partnership, capital will be raised through the use of per-

9–1 APPLICATIONS

Sample Business Plan Outline

I. Cover Letter
   A. Dollar amount requested
   B. Terms and timing
   C. Type and price of securities

II. Summary
   A. Business description
      1. Name
      2. Location and plant description
      3. Product
      4. Market competition
      5. Management expertise
   B. Business goals
   C. Summary of financial needs and application of funds
   D. Earnings projections and potential return to investors

III. Market Analysis
   A. Description of total market
   B. Industry trends
   C. Target market
   D. Competition

IV. Products or Services
   A. Description of product line
   B. Proprietary position: patents, copyrights, and legal and technical considerations
   C. Comparison to competitor's products

V. Manufacturing Process (if applicable)
   A. Materials
   B. Source of supply
   C. Production methods

VI. Marketing Strategy
   A. Overall strategy
   B. Pricing policy
   C. Methods of selling, distributing, and servicing products

VII. Management Plans
   A. Form of business organization
   B. Board of directors composition
   C. Officers: organization chart and responsibilities
   D. Résumés of key personnel
   E. Staffing plan/number of employees

F. Facilities plan/planned capital improvements
G. Operating plan/schedule of upcoming work for the next one to two years
VIII. Financial Data
A. Financial statements (five year to present)
B. Five-year financial projections (first year by quarters; remaining years annually)
1. Profit-and-loss statements
2. Balance sheets
3. Cash flow charts
4. Capital expenditure estimates
C. Explanation of projections
D. Key business ratios
E. Explanation of use and effect of new funds
F. Potential return to investors; comparison with average return in the industry as a whole

Source: "Financing a Small Business: From *Small Business Reporter*, Bank of America.

sonal assets, loans from friends or family, loans from venture capital firms, or loans from local banks or the SBA. The SBDC and SCORE can help Ann and Bill with the financial process, including—if they wish—the SBA loan applications.

In order to qualify for an SBA loan, Ann and Bill must be unable to obtain credit through local banking channels. Because they are both college students who must work in order to put themselves through school, they will both probably qualify for an SBA loan in terms of need. The challenge lies in convincing the SBA they are good candidates for a loan. In any event, their loan applications must start at local banks. In addition, it would probably be a good idea to consult an attorney or a CPA or both as they start the planning process.

LEGAL ISSUES: START-UP

As Ann and Bill develop their business plans, they will be choosing a name and a location and making lease-or-purchase decisions about the location and necessary equipment. All of these decisions have legal implications in addition to the obvious business or financial decisions. Ask any marketing specialist about the importance of name selection, and you will be told that it is very important (second only to location! location! location!).

CHOOSING THE BUSINESS NAME

The choice of a business name will say a lot about the business. The law requires that you select a name that is unique in the sense that it generally cannot be the name of a business already in existence in the area or one already reserved by a business in the area. Businesses receive protection for their names in several ways.

Common Law Protection

Under common law, a business acquires trade-name protection by establishing that the name has been exclusively used for an extensive period of time, that the name has acquired secondary meaning in the minds of consumers, and that the use of a similar name would lead to confusion in the minds of consumers. Obviously, Bill and Ann's choice of business name cannot receive common law protection until the name has been in use for a number of years and has become associated with the business and Ann and Bill. One of the best examples of secondary meaning is the name McDonald's and the image of the golden arches. They mean fast food to everyone. Of course, the risk of this method is that during the time the name is being established without protection, another business might come into existence and use one of the other ways to protect the name.

Therefore, before choosing a name, it would be best to conduct a little research. Bill and Ann should check local telephone books, call the appropriate state office, and check with the local chamber of commerce. They would hate to spend money promoting or advertising their business only to have another business challenge their name. And, of course, that is a two-way street. If Ann and Bill have a business name they would like to protect, they need to be vigilant, notifying any new business with a similar name that they object to the use of a name that is the same as or similar to theirs. If necessary, they may have to file a lawsuit to enforce their exclusive right to the name. Since it is the very identity of their business that is at stake, it would probably be an undertaking well worth the effort.

Lanham Act Protection

The major source of statutory trade-name protection is under Section 43(a) of the Lanham Act. Under the Lanham Act, in order to receive statutory protection for a business name, Bill and Ann should choose a name that is distinctive (fanciful, suggestive, or arbitrary), but not one that is generic (in common usage or that represent certain companies or types of products). Distinctive names do not have to prove secondary meaning. Development of secondary meaning is the other basis for protection. If Bill or Ann's last name is Smith, it would be difficult, but not impossible, to claim exclusive rights to it. However, via advertising, Mrs. Smith's Pies has taken on secondary meaning and is protected. McDonald's has received protection for its name as well.

However, both common law protection and statutory protection can be lost by allowing the name to become commonly used or generic. Aspirin has probably lost its distinctiveness and is now a generic term for acetylsalicylic acid. To prevent this from happening to it, Xerox Corp. periodically spends great sums of money on advertising that asks consumers not to misuse its name as a collective noun for copiers or as a verb, such as in the expression to "xerox" something.

Many national companies have had problems with name protection. When Esso wanted to go international, it discovered a conflict. It then developed the name Exxon. The change was accomplished through advertising and the changing of signs at the local stations— all at great expense. Coca-Cola is one of many companies that has been actively protecting its name and trademark. When you ask for a coke, Coca-Cola wants you to get a Coke, not a Pepsi or other cola drink. Many fast-food chains are now being very clear about what they serve, due to the insistence of soft drink companies. So when you order fries and a coke, the server will probably say, "We serve Pepsi. Is that OK?" Now you know why.

Protection by Incorporation

If Ann and Bill decide to incorporate their new business, they may be able to reserve a corporate name until they file the incorporation papers. Before the state allows a name reservation, a clerk checks the state corporations list for any names similar to the one requested. If the choice is too close ("deceptively similar"), the state will not allow them to use the name they request. For example, let's say Ann would like to name her business Clean Care Inc. When she calls the secretary of state's office, she is told that the name is too similar to Klean Kare Inc., which is being used by another local company in the business of housecleaning. What if the other business is a lawn service? Can you see that consumers might not be as confused?

If Ann and Bill plan to do business in a large area or interstate, it would be advisable to look into trade-name protection under the Lanham Act. By using this federal law, Ann and Bill can get trademark protection in advance of initial use. This is a new provision and acts much like a name or mark reservation would on the state level. Under the old provisions of the Lanham Act, a business had to show actual use before it could receive protection. Therefore, while a business was spending time and money developing advertising and marketing strategy, some other business could beat it to the market and the use of the name or mark would be lost.

The Yellow Pages

Another name-connected issue that Bill and Ann might want to consider is yellow pages placement. This is done alphabetically by category. Once a name has been chosen, it will be difficult to change. Consumers looking in the yellow pages generally start at the beginning of a category. That's why so many companies have names such as "AAA Party Rentals" or "A Reel Adventure." Being close to the beginning of a category is an important consideration, especially for new businesses and those that cannot afford large display ads. Even for a small business, a sizable ad distinguishing it from the others in the section can cost upwards of $4000 per month. If the placement is a good one and the business gets lots of calls from people who found it in the yellow pages, then obviously, the expense is well worth it.

THE BUSINESS LOCATION

Once Ann and Bill have determined their business name, they will then need to select both a permanent mailing address and a location from which they will operate. They will need to do this before they can order business checks, obtain business licenses, have business checks printed, and arrange for utilities and other services. If the business is retail, there are obvious marketing implications, but there are also legal implications connected with the location decision.

Zoning Laws

The most important initial legal implication will be zoning. Most cities have enacted land-use plans that restrict real property uses. Real property law differs from state to state and from city to city. Different types of businesses are allowed or disallowed in different areas. Sometimes it is obvious from a simple look at the street; other times it is necessary to check the zoning ordinances at the local zoning office. There are some businesses that may be operated from a residence, but many are not allowed to do so. Zoning can affect where a business is located, how the business building looks, what advertising the business can have outside letting people know it is there, what kinds of things can be done on the premises, and so on.

It is no coincidence that you do not generally see department stores in the middle of residential districts or cement factories downtown. It is as a result of zoning regulations. If an area is zoned strictly residential, then Bill and Ann would not be able to locate their business there, no matter how much they wanted to. On the other hand, they also don't have to worry about a lot of children running around getting in the way of their trucks, if they are located in an industrially zoned area.

In-Home Offices

If Ann and Bill plan to operate from their house or apartment, they will probably need to obtain an exception or special permission from the zoning office. Houses and apartments may be zoned for residential use only. Most zoning boards grant an exception for nonintrusive businesses that do not require excessive traffic or negatively affect the neighborhood. In many instances, off-street parking for two or three cars must be available if the business will have customers/clients who come to the business. Businesses that serve customers/clients at the customer's places of business or at the customer's homes would not normally require parking for customers. However, if there are employees, parking may present a problem.

For example, because Ann operates a rug cleaning business, she will be going to clients' houses rather than have clients coming to her. It is very unlikely that the zoning board or Ann's neighbors would object to this type of business being run from Ann's home. If, instead, Ann is an attorney, then clients will be coming to her place of business. Because a single attorney can see only one client at a time, Ann would probably be granted an exception by the zoning board. However, she will probably not be allowed to display a business sign—or at least not a large one. It is no coincidence that attorneys located in residential districts have only a shingle over their door, discreetly giving their name and the notation "attorney-at-law." As you can see, zoning boards allow only those in-home businesses that can be operated without affecting the residential nature of the neighborhood.

Accessibility Considerations under the ADA

A third issue Ann and Bill must consider when making a location decision is accessibility by the disabled. The Americans with Disabilities Act requires that businesses that are open to the public be accessible to people with disabilities. (See Box 9–2, "ADA Public Accessibility Provisions.") This means that as they look at property, Bill and Ann must keep accessibility in mind. Are there steps to be negotiated? Is there space for a wheelchair ramp? Are doors (exterior and interior) wide enough for wheelchairs? Can the bathroom accommodate a wheelchair? Most such accommodations can be made relatively inexpensively, but Ann and Bill must take them into account as they negotiate a lease or sale price. Tax laws provide certain tax credits for renovations by small businesses, and Bill and Ann should look into this.

Environmental Concerns

The fourth location consideration concerns the environment. A business's waste management needs obviously depend on the type of business being operated and on the services available from the city or county. Cities and counties typically collect waste twice a week and regulate how much waste (and sometimes what kinds of waste) may be left outside businesses. Businesses that generate so-called excessive amounts of waste or hazardous waste often have to contract with private collectors in order to meet city or county waste management codes. Therefore, their site must be accessible to the trucks sent to collect such waste.

environmental audit
an investigation of a premises to see if there are any existing or potential environmental problems

If Ann and Bill plan to purchase real property, it would be advisable to have someone do an **environmental audit** of the property. Under the Comprehensive Environmental Response, Compensation, and Liability Act (CERCLA) and Superfund, all owners in the chain of title may be liable for cleanup costs. An environmental audit should uncover any potential liability, and it can be used to show good faith in the innocent-owner defense to liability under Superfund.

9-2   LEGAL EXCERPTS

ADA Public Accessibility Provisions
42 USCA§12182

(a) General rule

No individual shall be discriminated against on the basis of disability in the full and equal enjoyment of goods, services, facilities, privileges, advantages, or accommodations of any place of public accommodation by any person who owns, leases (or leases to), or operates a place of public accommodation.

(b) Construction

  (1) General prohibition

    (A) Activities

      (i) Denial of participation

It shall be discriminatory to subject an individual or class of individuals on the basis of disability or disabilities of such individual or class, directly, or through contractual, licensing, or other arrangements, to a denial of the opportunity of the individual or class to participate in or benefit from the goods, services, facilities, privileges, advantages, or accommodations of an entity.

  (2) Specific prohibitions

    (A) Discrimination

For purposes of subsection (a) of this section, discrimination includes:

      (i) the imposition or application of eligibility criteria that screen out or tend to screen out an individual with a disability or any class of individuals with disabilities from fully and equally enjoying any goods, services, facilities, privileges, advantages, or accommodations, unless such criteria can be shown to be necessary for the provision of the goods, services, facilities, privileges, advantages, or accommodations being offered;

      (ii) a failure to make reasonable modifications in policies, practices, or procedures, when such modifications are necessary to afford such goods, services, facilities, privileges, advantages, or accommodations to individuals with disabilities, unless the entity can demonstrate that making such modifications would fundamentally alter

continued on next page

the nature of such goods, services, facilities, privileges, advantages, or accommodations;

(iii) a failure to take such steps as may be necessary to ensure that no individual with a disability is excluded, denied services, segregated or deprived of auxiliary aids and services, unless the entity can demonstrate that taking such steps would fundamentally alter the nature of the good, service, facility, privilege, advantage, or accommodation being offered or would result in an undue burden;

(iv) a failure to remove architectural barriers, and communication barriers that are structural in nature, in existing facilities, and transportation barriers in existing vehicles and rail passenger cars used by an establishment for transporting individuals (not including barriers that can only be removed through the retrofitting of vehicles or rail passenger cars by the installation of a hydraulic or other lift), where such removal is readily achievable; and

(v) where an entity can demonstrate that the removal of a barrier under clause (iv) is not readily achievable, a failure to make such goods, services, facilities, privileges, advantages, or accommodations available through alternative methods if such methods are readily achievable.

If the history of the property indicates a potential environmental problem, Bill and Ann would be wise to engage environmental engineers to properly evaluate the risks prior to entering into a contract to purchase the property. If it appears there is contamination that will have to be removed or cleaned up, such removal or cleanup costs and duties must be factored into the contract price. Environmental cleanup is usually very expensive, and when an environmental audit detects a problem, many buyers simply walk away to pursue other sites.

Lease versus Purchase

One of the first decisions Bill and Ann have to make about their new location is whether they will rent or purchase it. If they intend to purchase it, the issues become how the property will be held and what interest will be held. The law of property has different estates that owners can hold and different ways they can own them.

What Interest in Real Estate Is Owned

Bill and Ann could want to own the property outright, without restrictions, thereby gaining the power to sell it, rent it, will it upon their death, or mortgage it. This arrangement is called a **fee simple absolute**. If there was a condition to their owning the property, such as the seller's transferring it to them only on condition that it be used for business purposes, then this would be a **conditional fee simple**. Ann and Bill would be able to deal with the property only consistent with the condition placed upon it, and if they failed, the property would revert to the original transferor or the transferor's designee.

If Bill and Ann received the property for only their lifetime, they would own a **life estate**, which they would not be able to treat as totally belonging to them. They would have to act consistently with having only a lifetime interest in the property. They therefore could not will it away or sell to anyone any interest other than one that ended upon the measuring life. In addition, they could not act inconsistently with the use being made of the property, or it would be considered committing **waste**, and they could be liable to those who take after them.

How real estate is held   In addition to what Bill and Ann hold is the matter of how they hold it. The property can be held individually in only one of their names, or it can be held jointly in both names. Even if they hold jointly, there are different ways to do it. They can hold as **joint tenants with right of survivorship** or as **tenants in common**. If they hold as joint tenants with right of survivorship, Bill and Ann would each own an undivided interest in the property, and when one died, the other would be entitled to the deceased's share. If they hold as tenants in common, they would each hold an undivided interest in the property, but upon the death of one of them, the decedent's property could go to whomever they wished, rather than to the other owner. If Bill and Ann were married, they could hold the property as **tenants by the entirety**. This is joint tenants with right of survivorship for married couples only.

If Bill and Ann owned the property jointly, neither could do anything significant to the property without the consent of the other. Ann could not sell, mortgage, lease, or otherwise dispose of "her" share of the property without Bill's consent, because each owns an

---

fee simple absolute
unconditional ownership of real estate in perpetuity

conditional fee simple
ownership of real estate based on a condition that the owner must comply with or forfeit the property

life estate
real estate conveyed for a time period measured by the life of the transferee or some other party

waste
life tenant doing an act inconsistent with the interest of those to take after the life estate is ended

joint tenant with right of survivorship
more than one person's owning property that will go to the other owners upon their death

tenants in common
more than one person's owning property that can be willed to someone other than the other owners upon their deaths

tenants by the entirety
married couple owning property as joint tenants

undivided interest in the property. So even if they owned the property in equal proportions (though it need not be that way), Bill would own an undivided interest in Ann's share, and she in his.

Leaseholds

tenant from period to period
one who leases a premises from one date to another (e.g., from 1/1/95 to 12/31/96)

tenant at will
one who leases a premises with no set time period of occupancy

tenant for a stated period
one who leases a premises for a given time period (e.g., 5 years)

tenant at sufferance
one who overstays a lease period

If Ann and Bill leased the property, they would not have the rights of ownership but only the rights of possession. They would be tenants on the landlord's property. They would have the right to exclusive possession, except as otherwise agreed in the lease (such as giving the landlord the right to come onto the premises for pest control, for making repairs, in emergencies, etc.). The landlord would have the right to own the property and to collect rent.

If they leased, Ann and Bill could be **tenants from period to period**, **tenants at will**, or **tenants for a stated period**. If they were tenants for a stated period, their lease would simply state they had, for example, a five-year lease. If they were tenants from period to period, their lease would state they were to be in possession of the premises from, say, January 1, 1995, to December 31, 2000. Both types of lease would cover five-year periods, but they would have different legal significance in terms of notice to be given at the end of the lease. If no time period was established, Ann and Bill would be tenants at will, who could leave whenever they wanted. If they overstayed their lease, they would be **tenants at sufferance**, subject to the landlord's will.

Other Considerations

As always, tax laws can also play an important part in Bill and Ann's location decision. Leasing property is a deductible business expense, but Ann and Bill will not build up any equity in the property. Purchasing property allows them to build up equity while deducting expenses for mortgage interest and depreciation. Of course, purchasing usually requires a large down payment and a sufficient credit history to qualify them for a loan and mortgage. Ann and Bill's accountant can help them with the decision about leasing versus purchasing the property.

BUSINESS LICENSES

Once they have decided on a potential location, Ann and Bill must secure the necessary business licenses and permits required to open the business. (See Box 9–3, "Sample Business License.") License re-

9-3 LAW IN THE REAL WORLD

Sample Business License

Athens-Clarke County, Georgia Government

Business License Tax

LICENSE NUMBER: 95-00000   TAX NUMBER: 00-000-0000

CONTROL NUMBER: 8703

PERIOD ENDING:

1995   LOCATION 179 ST JAMES DR

CLASSIFICATION MISCELLANEOUS PERSONAL SERVICES   CLASS 729

NOT TRANSFERABLE

ABC CONSULTING
123 MAIN STREET
ANYTOWN   GA 30600

ATHENS
CLARKE
COUNTY

MUST BE POSTED IN A CONSPICUOUS LOCATION AND EXPOSED TO VIEW AT ALL TIMES

Any person required by the Business License Tax Ordinance to register a
business shall notify the Department of Finance Business License Tax
Office in writing within 30 days of the following changes:
(a) any change of address of the business, in which case the same
    business tax receipt shall be valid at the new location;
(b) any change of ownership, in which case the transfer shall be
    treated as the termination of one business and the establishment of
    a new business for the purposes of this ordinance;
(c) the termination of any business.

quirements vary from business to business and locality to locality, but
almost always include at least one business license. This is usually a
revenue-producing license for the city and/or county in which Ann
and Bill will operate their businesses; it is based on the classification
of the business and the gross receipts. License fees usually cover gross
receipts from the particular area, and thus business revenue records
must be segregated and kept by government area so that the fee owed
to each government unit can be determined.

It is sometimes difficult to determine just how many of these business licenses a business will need. Most townships, cities, and counties
take the position that if you do business in their area, you must obtain
a business license. For example, if Ann and Bill are cleaning houses,

they might need to obtain a license from each of the government entities they might go into to clean, such as a city or a county. If Bill is a CPA and clients all come to his office, he may need licenses only from the city and county in which his office is located. As you can see, this can be very confusing for a new business.

Another fact to keep in mind is that before a government agency issues a business license, a government employee usually visits the site to confirm compliance with the zoning laws and to certify that the site meets the building codes currently in effect. This means the employee will inspect the plumbing and the electrical wiring to make sure they are up to code standards and can carry a commercial load, if necessary. Unwary entrepreneurs have often signed leases or bought property only to find that the property cannot be used for business purposes without extensive, and possibly expensive, renovations.

OTHER LICENSES AND PERMITS

According to the nature of the business, there may be other licenses or permits required. For example, restaurants need health certificates, and most states require liquor licenses before alcoholic beverages can be sold. Businesses that will emit air or water pollutants need environmental permits, which may be federal, state, and local. As you can see, the number of licenses and permits is highly dependent on the nature of the business. Ann and Bill might consider asking others already operating in the same field of business what licenses and permits they hold. A good idea is for them to join a trade association in their field of business. Local members of the association are generally helpful to other members. Joining a national association, while clearly beneficial for national requirements, may not be sufficient to keep them abreast of current local requirements.

FEDERAL AND STATE TAX IDENTIFICATION NUMBERS

As they go into business, it is advisable for Bill and Ann to maintain a business bank account separate from their personal accounts. In order to open a business account, Ann and Bill will often be asked for a federal tax identification number. If the business is not incorporated, a Social Security number can be used to open the accounts. However, for other purposes, Ann and Bill will probably need a federal tax ID number. For example, the IRS and most state tax commissions require the payment of various business-related taxes for which a federal tax identification number is required. An attorney or accountant can help them obtain these numbers, or they can call the IRS and their state (and perhaps local) tax commission.

BUSINESS RECORDS

Business records have to be set up in a manner that allows the business to track the various taxes due all of the government agencies. If the business will have an employee, it will be subject to, among other things, federal withholding, state withholding, FICA (Social Security), and unemployment taxes. If Ann and Bill are involved in retail sales, they may have to collect state and local sales taxes. Many businesses are subject to other taxes such as special state and local taxes on accommodations or food and beverages. Can you think of other taxes imposed on various businesses?

 As pointed out, it is advisable to maintain separate business banking accounts so that the required record keeping is easier. Professionals (accountants, attorneys, etc.) who handle other people's money may be required by law to keep those funds in separate accounts known as escrow or trust accounts. Such accounts are generally subject to random audits by a professional certification board or licensing authority. In these professions, there are generally severe repercussions if the professional **commingles** personal funds with clients' funds.

commingle to place funds received in a professional capacity with the professional's personal funds

BUSINESS BANKING ACCOUNTS

When Ann and Bill open their bank accounts, they will be operating under the law of **negotiable instruments**. This law involves Articles 3 and 4 of the Uniform Commercial Code (UCC) and has been passed in all states. When Ann and Bill open a checking account, there will be a contract with the bank stating that the bank will honor (pay) checks that Ann or Bill writes on their accounts when there are sufficient funds in the account. Ann and Bill may be able to arrange to have their bank cover (pay) checks even when there is not enough money in the account, but unless the bank has agreed to that provision, it is under no duty to pay overdrafts. In either case, Ann and Bill will incur special charges when they write a check for which they do

negotiable instrument legal document, meeting certain requirements and representing a right of the holder of the instrument to receive money or goods

not have sufficient funds in the account. When the bank does not honor a check, it returns it as unpaid (bounced). Remember, writing a bad check (one without sufficient funds to pay the check) is a crime in most states.

Liability on Negotiable Instruments

Under the UCC no one is liable on a check unless his or her signature appears on it. On the checks written by Ann or Bill on their account, each would sign the check at the bottom as the drawer and as a representative of the business, so that it is clear that they are signing in a business, rather than a personal, capacity. (See Box 9–4, "Examples of Signatures in Various Business Capacities.") On checks that are payable to Ann or Bill, either could sign the back of the check as an endorser. If the check is made payable to both of them, each must endorse the check in order to negotiate it. If the check is signed by Ann or Bill in a business capacity, any liability on the check would accrue to the business rather than to Ann or Bill in a personal capacity.

A bank is supposed to know the signature of its customer (Ann and Bill) and is not supposed to pay any check from their account without Ann or Bill's signature or pay checks with a forged version of their signature. If the bank does, it must usually bear the risk of loss. The bank is also usually liable when it pays over a forged endorsement, unless the forgery is Ann or Bill's fault.

You might be wondering how the forgery of someone else's endorsement could be your fault. Assume Joe defrauds Bill after convincing Bill to give Joe a check by claiming to represent the American Cancer Society when in fact Joe does not. Joe, the imposter endorses the check Bill gave him, and the check is then paid by Bill's bank. Under the UCC's **imposter rule**, Bill will bear the loss because he could have best prevented this loss by asking for identification to make sure Joe, in fact, represented the American Cancer Society.

When a business gives an employee check-signing privileges, the business will bear the loss if the employee embezzles money by writing checks to fictitious payees (people or businesses that do not exist) and then endorsing and cashing those checks for personal benefit. This is known as the UCC's **fictitious payee rule**. If an employee (such as a supervisor) tells the company payroll department to pay wages to a fictitious employee and the company payroll department writes a check that is then forged by the supervisor, the company will bear the

imposter rule
the rule that one who gives a negotiable instrument to someone who turns out to be an imposter is still responsible for payment of the negotiable instrument

fictitious payee rule
the rule that one is liable on a negotiable instrument written on one's account, if it was written by someone in one's employ or control, to a nonexistent person and cashed by the maker

---

9–4   LAW IN THE REAL WORLD

Examples of Signatures in Various Business Capacities

A. Ann & Bill's Clean 'n Shine Inc.

_____

by Ann Smith, President

B. _____, President
Ann & Bill's Clean 'n Shine Inc.

C. _____
As agent for Ann & Bill's Clean 'n Shine

---

loss, not the bank. The supervisor was responsible for the loss, and the company is in a better position to prevent such a loss than is the bank.

Internal Controls

A company can reduce the risk of loss by requiring that employees be bonded (insured) for this type of loss and by carefully checking the history and background of prospective employees. Many owners of small businesses give check-writing powers to bookkeepers, secretaries, or partners. There are obvious risks in allowing others access to bank accounts.

Should a company decide to give an employee check-writing privileges, the company should have established sufficient internal controls to prevent embezzlement. One easy rule to remember is not to allow anyone who can write checks, other than yourself, to also balance or reconcile the monthly statement. In addition, invoice numbers should be written on all checks to make transactions easy to verify. Thus, if bank statements are reviewed in a timely manner, any wrongdoing should be able to be caught within a month. In fact, failure to do so can result in liability the bank might otherwise be responsible for.

ACQUISITION OF BUSINESS EQUIPMENT

In order to conduct business, most businesses need a telephone (and perhaps a fax machine). Business lines generally cost two to three times the cost of personal telephone lines. Dedicated fax lines sometimes cost less than a business line. Unless the business is leasing telephone equipment, there are usually no long-term contracts to sign. Many companies now also offer voice mail numbers, which can be used as sort of telephone mailboxes, so that a client need not even know that the operation is as small as it may be. Telephone mailboxes have a recorded message that allows the caller to personally leave a message for the receiver if the receiver is on the phone or otherwise unavailable; they can also route the message elsewhere. Such lines can usually be maintained for any length of time. There is also computer software that can take care of this for relatively inexpensive cost.

Yellow pages advertising is usually handled by a subsidiary of the local telephone carrier or even a yellow pages competitor of the local telephone company. Ordinarily, Bill and Ann cannot place a yellow page ad or even get a listing without installing and paying for at least one business line. Yellow pages advertising requires relatively short-term contracts that are the same length as the use of the telephone book (normally a year). Should Bill and Ann become unable to pay for the yellow page ad with the Bell system company (thus breaching its contract), they would have to give up the use of the number in the ad.

LEASE VERSUS PURCHASE

When setting up their business, Ann and Bill will need to decide whether to lease or purchase business equipment such as computers, telephones, cash registers, furniture, and fixtures. An accountant can offer advice about the tax ramifications of leasing versus purchasing. Often the out-of-pocket expense will be less by leasing, but Bill and Ann would not build up any equity, would not be able to take deductions for depreciation expense, and may have nothing at the end of the lease. On the other hand, because of today's rapid changes in technology, purchasing for the long term may not have the advantages it seems to have at first blush.

Requirements for Acquisition

Under either alternative, Bill and Ann will be entering into long-term lease contracts or if not paying by cash or credit card, entering into a **secured transaction** by signing **promissory notes** and **security agreements**. A security agreement gives the creditor (the seller or the bank) a security interest (the right to repossess) in the collateral (equipment) should the company default on the loan payments. If Ann and Bill should default on a lease or promissory note, they may be held liable for the remainder of the lease payments or for the outstanding loan amount after the collateral is sold and the costs of repossession are paid. Liability will depend on how the lease or note was signed and whether or not the business is incorporated.

Liability on Acquisition Agreements

As we discussed in Chapter 8, liability is sometimes referred to as **joint and several liability**. Joint liability means just what it says. When two or more people are held liable for the same debt, we call it **joint liability**. If one of the two can be made to pay the entire debt, we call the liability **several**. In legalese, the term *several* means "individual." Thus, when a person agrees to be jointly and severally liable with another person on a loan, the person can be made to pay the entire amount of the debt. If she does pay, then she may seek contribution from the other person(s) who did not pay. However, as a practical matter, the fact that one of the signers was asked to pay the entire amount is often a signal that the other person(s) may be unable to pay.

As we saw in Box 9–4 regarding business signatures and their liability, if the business is incorporated and the note or contract was signed only as president of the company, the signer will not be held personally liable. If the note or contract was not signed as a company officer, but instead as an individual, then that individual may be held personally liable. Owners of sole proprietorships are personally liable on leases and notes they have signed. Partners may be held personally liable even when they have not signed, as long as the leases and notes were in the ordinary scope of the partnership business.

BUSINESS INSURANCE

Assuming that Ann and Bill lease or purchase equipment, lease or purchase the location where they will operate, plan to hire an em-

---

secured transaction
credit transaction in which creditor obtains from debtor an agreement to use debtor's personal property as collateral to be taken by creditor in the event debtor defaults on the loan

promissory note
a note containing a creditor's unconditional promise to repay a loan

security agreement
agreement creating a secured transaction that gives creditor a security interest in debtor's goods upon default on a loan

joint and several liability
liability as an individual, as well as jointly with another

joint liability
liability in which more than one party is responsible for contract breach or tortious activity

several liability
individual liability for an act resulting in need to compensate another

merchant
under the UCC, one who deals in goods of the kind under contract

implied warranty of merchantability
UCC warranty arising upon a merchant's sale of goods that the goods will be of fair and average quality and do what such goods should do

implied warranty of fitness for a particular purpose
UCC warranty arising from the sale of goods that the goods will perform as the seller represented they would, knowing the particular purpose for which the goods would be used

insurable interest
a legal interest in property that permits one to purchase insurance on the property

ployee, plan to use their automobiles in their businesses, or enter into loans to finance their businesses, they will want to consult an expert in the insurance field. Businesses will need insurance coverage in all areas, including property loss, liability coverage, health, life, or even loss of income due to a hazard or disability.

INSURABLE INTERESTS

All property (real and personal) in which there is an **insurable interest** may be insured. An insurable interest is defined as a real financial interest in another person or object. In other words, a person or business must stand to lose (money) by the loss or destruction of the property or person. This is to prevent the insurance contract from becoming a form of gambling. If you could insure strangers on a plane, you might be inclined to buy insurance much like you would a lottery ticket. Others might even be inclined to blow up a plane in order to collect. Thus, before purchasing insurance, the insurance company satisfies itself that the purchaser of the insurance has an interest in the thing or person being insured, such that the purchaser will suffer an economic loss should there be a loss that must be compensated by the insurance company.

REPLACEMENT VALUE VERSUS FAIR MARKET VALUE

Hazard insurance covers losses from fires and other casualties, but it usually excludes flood and earthquake coverage, which must be purchased separately. Ann and Bill may purchase hazard insurance on property they are buying or leasing. Many commercial leases, most mortgages, and most secured transactions require that hazard insurance be obtained on the property or collateral. In the event of a loss, the insurance proceeds are used to pay off the lease or the loan. If there is any money left, it will belong to Ann or Bill. Hazard insurance can cover either the replacement value or the fair market value (depreciated value) of the property (collateral). Replacement value coverage is more expensive than depreciated value coverage.

Ann and Bill can keep their premiums lower by contracting for a large deductible. This is the amount of the loss that Ann or Bill agree to bear should their property be lost or destroyed. Generally, the larger the deductible, the smaller the premium. However, if Ann and Bill are not financially able to meet the deductible because it is too high, then the insurance has not really accomplished its purpose, because it will not kick in until the deductible is paid.

As you know, automobiles must be insured in most states. If Ann or Bill will drive a car in the business or allow an employee to drive within the scope of employment, Ann and Bill will want to obtain adequate insurance for protection from losses in the event of an accident.

Professionals, such as attorneys and accountants, usually purchase a type of insurance covering errors and omissions. Essentially, this type protects professionals in the event they are negligent. It is expensive insurance and has been rising due to the number of lawsuits against professionals in which the jury found the professionals liable for millions of dollars.

BULK TRANSFERS

Instead of starting a business, Bill and Ann could buy a going concern or a business already in existence. If they decide to do this, they must comply with Article 6 of the UCC, which covers the law of **bulk transfers**. A bulk transfer occurs when one buys an ongoing business or the major part of the materials, supplies, merchandise, or other inventory of a business that sells from stock or inventory.[1] The purpose of Article 6 is primarily to protect the creditors of the seller, but compliance also protects the buyer. In the sale of a business, the buyer and seller negotiate a sale price. The price generally reflects who is to be responsible for paying the seller's creditors (business debts or even personal debts if business assets are collateral).

bulk transfer
a transfer of virtually all of a seller's interest in materials, supplies, merchandise, or other inventory

In cases in which the buyer assumes (agrees to pay) the business debts and liabilities, the sale price would be lower than if the seller had retained responsibility for the business debts. The buyer will have title to and possession of the stock, inventory, and equipment, all or some of which may be collateral under various secured transactions between the seller and various creditors. The creditors need to know of the sale so that they can take the necessary steps to protect themselves. The notice provisions in Article 6 accomplish that.

Article 6 provides two alternatives for notification of the seller's creditors. The first is public notice achieved through publication in a newspaper of general circulation once a week for two weeks. The notice must show the names and addresses of the seller and buyer, give the effective date of the transfer, and state whether the new enterprise assumes the debts of the seller.

The second alternative, which is the one most commonly chosen, basically requires that when a bulk sale occurs, the buyer must require the seller (under oath) to provide a list of existing creditors and to prepare a schedule of property to be transferred. The buyer then sends notice to each creditor. The sale will be ineffective against creditors unless they are notified by certified mail at least ten days prior to the sale. The notice must state notice of the bulk sale, the names and addresses of the seller and buyer, and whether or not all of the debts of the seller are to be paid in full as they fall due.

If the debts are not to be assumed, the notice must state whether the debts are to be paid by the seller at the transfer. Obviously, it is in the best interest of the buyer to ensure that these provisions are met and to agree to a price that reflects how creditors are to be paid. If not, the buyer may have to pay creditors that were not paid by the seller and seek indemnification from the seller.

FRANCHISES

When starting a new business, Ann or Bill might consider entering into an agreement with a franchisor, such as McDonald's. A franchise is a business arrangement in which one party (the franchisee) buys the right to market the goods or services as developed by a second party (the franchisor) and use the franchisor's name. There is currently no uniformity in this area except for the Federal Trade Commission Franchise Disclosure Rules, which are similar to the Securities and Exchange Commission disclosure rules. Instead, franchisors must comply with the laws in every state where they sell or operate franchises. In essence, the rules require franchisors that are charging more than a stipulated dollar investment to disclose (truthfully) the number of franchises, the probable profitability (based on other franchises) of the franchise, and so on.

Such rules are helpful but not a guarantee of success. It is best to retain counsel and talk to other franchisees of the same company as well as those of other companies prior to making any financial investment. The advantage of franchises consists in the name recognition and uniformity already established by the franchise holder. After all, everyone knows McDonald's as soon as the arches go up, but who knows anything about Kathy's Burger Barn when it first opens its doors?

BANKRUPTCY

The last consideration we want to discuss may seem out of place in a chapter on starting up a business, but **bankruptcy** occurs usually in the first two years of a business. As you probably know, bankruptcy is a federal law that allows debtors to legally discharge their debts while it provides for a fair and orderly distribution of available assets to creditors. Current bankruptcy law allows individuals as well as companies to file for bankruptcy if they cannot pay debts as the debts come due. The law does not require that debtors' liabilities exceed their assets. Bankruptcy is usually voluntary, but under certain conditions, people and businesses can be brought into bankruptcy involuntarily.

Chapter 7 bankruptcies provide for straight bankruptcies. This means that the assets are collected and sold. The cash proceeds are then distributed to creditors. Both individuals and companies may use Chapter 7. Under Chapter 7, there are exemptions, which vary from state to state. Exemptions consist of property that can be excluded from being liquidated for bankruptcy purposes. Some interesting things are included in lists of exemptions. (See Box 9–5, "Bankruptcy Exemptions.") Due to generous exemptions, a few states allow debtors to keep considerably more property than other states allow. People have moved into these states in anticipation of bankruptcy proceedings. Many, including most creditors, feel that the current bankruptcy laws are too lenient and, thus, unfair to creditors.

Chapter 11 bankruptcy is often referred to as a reorganization. Its provisions allow a company (not an individual) to file for bankruptcy protection while attempting to reorganize its financial affairs. During that period, bargaining with the creditors, renegotiation of contracts, restructuring of debts, or sale of the company can occur. Hopefully, the company will emerge from Chapter 11 and be successful. A good example is the oil company Texaco Inc., which filed for Chapter 11 protection after it lost a huge lawsuit to Pennzoil. Texaco emerged from bankruptcy a healthy company.

Chapter 13 is known as wage earner bankruptcy and applies to those who are employed as wage earners or are self-employed. Under Chapter 13 the debtor arranges a plan to repay creditors usually over an extended period of time. The plan must be court approved. At the end of the period, the debtor emerges from bankruptcy. The major advantage of this chapter is protection from creditors.

bankruptcy
the process of having property liquidated in order to pay off debts one cannot otherwise repay

Chapter 7 bankruptcy
in which the bankrupt's assets are collected, sold, and creditors paid from the proceeds

Chapter 11 bankruptcy
also called reorganization; company permitted to file for bankruptcy protection while attempting to reorganize its financial affairs

Chapter 13 bankruptcy
also called wage earner bankruptcy; debtor arranges a court-approved plan to repay creditors over an extended period

9–5 CONCEPT SUMMARY

Bankruptcy Exemptions

(1) The debtor's aggregate interest, not to exceed $7,500 in value, in real property or personal property that the debtor or a dependent of the debtor uses as a residence, in a cooperative that owns property that the debtor or a dependent of the debtor uses as a residence, or in a burial plot for the debtor or a dependent of the debtor.

(2) The debtor's interest, not to exceed $1,200 in value, in one motor vehicle.

(3) The debtor's interest, not to exceed $200 in value in any particular item or $4,000 in aggregate value, in household furnishings, household goods, wearing apparel, appliances, books, animals, crops, or musical instruments that are held primarily for the personal, family, or household use of the debtor or a dependent of the debtor.

(4) The debtor's aggregate interest, not to exceed $500 in value, in jewelry held primarily for the personal, family, or household use of the debtor or a dependent of the debtor.

(5) The debtor's aggregate interest in any property, not to exceed $7,500 in value, plus $400, plus up to $3,750 of any unused amount of the exemption provided under paragraph 1 of this subsection.

(6) The debtor's aggregate interest, not to exceed $750 in value, in any implements, professional books, or tools of the trade of the debtor or the trade of a dependent of debtor.

(7) Any unmatured life insurance contract owned by the debtor, other than a credit life insurance contract.

(8) The debtor's aggregate interest, not to exceed in value $4,000, less any amount of property of the estate transferred in the manner specified in section 542(d) of this title, in any accrued dividend or interest under, or loan value of, any unmatured life insurance contract owned by the debtor under which the insured is the debtor or an individual of whom the debtor is a dependent.

(9) Professionally prescribed health aids for the debtor or a dependent of the debtor.

(10) The debtor's right to receive:
    (A) a Social Security benefit, unemployment compensation, or a local public assistance benefit;
    (B) a veteran's benefit;

(C) a disability, illness, or unemployment benefit;

(D) alimony, support, or separate maintenance, to the extent reasonably necessary for the support of the debtor and any dependent of the debtor;

(E) a payment under a stock bonus, pension, profit-sharing, annuity, or similar plan or contract on account of illness, disability, death, age, or length of service, to the extent reasonably necessary for the support of the debtor and any dependent of the debtor, unless:

   (i) such plan or contract was established by or under the auspices of an insider that employed the debtor at the time the debtor's rights under such plan or contract arose;

   (ii) such payment is on account of age or length of service; and

   (iii) such plan or contract does not qualify under section 401 (a), 403 (a), 403 (b.), 408, or 409 of the Internal Revenue Code of 1986 (26 U.S.C. 401 [a], 403 [a], 403 [b], 408, or 409).

(11) The debtor's right to receive, or property that is traceable to:

(A) an award under a crime victim's reparation law;

(B) a payment on account of the wrongful death of an individual of whom the debtor was a dependent, to the extent reasonably necessary for the support of the debtor and any dependent of the debtor;

(C) a payment under a life insurance contract that insured the life of an individual of whom the debtor was a dependent on the date of such individual's death, to the extent reasonably necessary for the support of the debtor and any dependent of the debtor;

(D) a payment, not to exceed $7,500, on account of personal bodily injury, not including pain and suffering or compensation for actual pecuniary loss, of the debtor or an individual of whom the debtor is a dependent; or

(E) a payment in compensation of loss of future earnings of the debtor or an individual of whom the debtor is or was a dependent, to the extent reasonably necessary for the support of the debtor and any dependent of the debtor.

(e) A waiver of an exemption executed in favor of a creditor that holds an unsecured claim against the debtor is unen-

continued on next page

forceable in a case under this title with respect to such claim against property that the debtor may exempt under subsection (b) of this section. A waiver by the debtor of a power under subsection (f) or (h) of this section to avoid a transfer, under subsection (g) or (i) of this section to exempt property, or under subsection (i) of this section to recover property or to preserve a transfer is unenforceable in a case under this title.

(c) Notwithstanding any waiver of exemptions, the debtor may avoid the fixing of a lien on an interest of the debtor in property to the extent that such lien impairs an exemption to which the debtor would have been entitled under subsection (b) of this section, if such lien is:

(1) a judicial lien; or

(2) a nonpossessory, nonpurchase-money security interest in any:

(A) books, animals, crops, musical instruments, or jewelry that is held primarily for the personal, family, or household use of the debtor or a dependent of the debtor;

(B) implements, professional books, or tools of the trade of the debtor or the trade of a dependent of the debtor; or

(C) professionally prescribed health aids for the debtor or a dependent of the debtor.

The Chapter 7 bankruptcy concept is similar to a **composition of creditors**. In a composition, an attorney usually contacts the creditors to discuss the debtor's inability to pay. If the debtor files Chapter 7, most creditors get nothing, so they usually negotiate a settlement for much less than they are due. This can be done outside bankruptcy, and therefore there is no record of bankruptcy, which would otherwise threaten the debtor's credit rating.

composition of creditors
debtor who cannot repay as promised contacts creditors in an attempt to reach an agreement about repayment without using bankruptcy

SUMMARY

Starting a new business is not easy. People generally choose to start a business because there is something they want to do or to bring to the public. As this chapter demonstrates, it is not that simple. Not only must business entrepreneurs know the actual aspects of the thing they want to do; but they must also know the information required to position themselves to be able to do it as a business. Making jam as gifts for friends who enjoy them tremendously is one thing. Opening a store to sell the jams to the public is quite another.

A business must comply with the rules and regulations under which the state allows it to act as an ongoing business concern. Every business is different, but certain accepted principles must be considered. They include developing a business plan, arranging financing, choosing a name, selecting a location, obtaining business licenses and permits, opening bank accounts, purchasing or leasing equipment, and arranging for insurance. New business owners face a growing list of rules and regulations. Such restrictions begin with business licenses and hopefully, do not conclude with bankruptcy.

CHAPTER TERMS

bankruptcy	composition of creditors
bulk transfer	conditional fee simple
business plan	environmental audit
Chapter 7 bankruptcy	fee simple absolute
Chapter 11 bankruptcy	fictitious payee rule
Chapter 13 bankruptcy	implied warranty of fitness
commingle	for a particular purpose

implied warranty of
  merchantability

imposter rule

insurable interest

joint and several liability

joint liability

joint tenant with right
  of survivorship

life estate

merchant

negotiable instruments

promissory note

secured transaction

security agreement

several liability

tenant at sufferance

tenant at will

tenant for a stated period

tenant from period
  to period

tenants by the entirety

tenants in common

waste

CHAPTER-END QUESTIONS

1. What protections are available to protect a business's trade name, and why is it important to do so?

2. Ziggy owns a piece of property as a single owner in fee simple absolute. Ziggy wants to build an apartment building on the site in order to generate income. The builder Ziggy commissions tells him the apartment building cannot be built because the property is zoned for industrial use. Ziggy says that because he owns the property as a fee simple absolute, he should be able to do whatever he wants on the property. Is Ziggy correct? Explain.

3. How do environmental laws affect business location decisions?

4. How does the ADA affect business location decisions?

5. What will happen if a business cannot pay for its business equipment (defaults on either a secured transaction or purchase on credit or a lease of equipment)?

6. When are the bulk transfer laws applicable? What do they require?

7. What is bankruptcy? Explain the three types of bankruptcy.

8. What is a business license?

9. Explain joint and several liability.

10. Bill and Ann purchased some cleaning equipment and supplies from Lumpkin Cleaning Supply Co. They had told the sales representative that they needed a product to clean gasoline off garage floors. The equipment was to be a scrubber that could handle the job. When Bill and Ann tried out the products on one of their cleaning jobs, the scrubber pad came off, along with the handle by which the machine was held and guided. The cleaner did not get the gasoline off the floor. What rights do Bill and Ann have under the UCC?

11. What is a franchise? Give three examples.

12. Kimmis tries to raise money for a new product he wants to create and manufacture. To do so, he sells interests in his company to his friends, all of whom are located in Chippewa, N.Y., where Kimmis's company is incorporated and where the product will be manufactured and distributed. One of the friends to whom Kimmis offers to sell an interest tells Kimmis she will not make the purchase because Kimmis has not registered his securities with the Securities and Exchange Commission as required. Kimmis tells her that she need have no fear, because the securities do not have to be registered. Who is correct?

GROUP EXERCISE

In groups, help Ann and Bill select the names for their businesses. Assume that Ann will be cleaning houses and offices and that Bill will be cleaning up construction sites. Decide whether Ann and Bill should operate out of their homes/apartments or lease/purchase office space and equipment. Have groups keep a list of facts that must be known to make such decisions.

REFERENCES

1 UCC Article 6 §6-102.

Chapter 10

CONSIDERATIONS IN THE EMPLOYMENT RELATIONSHIP

Chapter Preview Summary

In this chapter, Bill and Ann learn the different ways in which they can have employees work for them and what they must know in dealing with those relationships as employment relationships. More detail is provided regarding the work relationships recognized by law and the legal liability that attaches to those relationships.

Chapter Objectives

In studying the chapter, you should learn:
- the types of employment relationships recognized by law
- the factors used to determine whether a worker is an employee
- employer's liability for torts of contracts entered into by those in the employer's employ
- what employment at will involves and when it applies
- the exceptions to the at-will doctrine
- the provisions of the Model Employment Termination Act
- about issues related to defamation in employment

INTRODUCTION

Once Bill and Ann decide that the work necessary can no longer be done by them alone, they must contract with someone to help. There are many ways that someone can be brought in to assist a business owner, and in this chapter we examine the relationship formed when Bill and Ann hire someone to work for or with them. They can hire someone as an employee, an independent contractor, or an agent. Each type of hire is governed by its own rules and regulations. The primary legal issues arising involve contracts and torts. That is, what rights and responsibilities are there between Bill and Ann and those working for them? between the worker and third parties? And what happens if the worker commits a civil wrong while in the scope of employment with Bill and Ann.

TYPES OF EMPLOYMENT RELATIONSHIPS

The liability that attaches to torts committed and contracts entered into by someone in an employment relationship depends on the type of employment relationship that exists. As you will see, it can be of utmost importance to determine the relationship properly, as it can mean the difference between Ann and Bill's being liable for the worker's actions or not liable for those actions. This matter also has great importance for payment of Social Security tax, workers' compensation, federal withholding tax, unemployment compensation, employment discrimination laws, and other matters to be discussed later in the text.

INDEPENDENT CONTRACTOR

independent contractor
one who is employed by a principal to perform work the independent contractor has the expertise and authority to direct

principal
one who employs an independent contractor; one for whom an agent acts

If Ann and Bill have a job to be done for which they wish to hire someone with a particular expertise who can do the job without their direction, they probably want to hire an **independent contractor**. Independent contractors contract to work with the person who hires them (called the **principal**), but they do not take from the principal direction regarding how to accomplish their task. The two would, of course, consult on the specifics of what Bill and Ann want done, the time frame for doing it, the cost, and so forth. But actual accomplishment of the job is left up to the independent contractor. Most attorneys, CPAs, real estate agents, insurance agents, and interior decorators, among others, are independent contractors.

For instance, if Ann and Bill wanted to have an interior decorator renovate the offices they are moving into, the parties would decide on: an overall price; what Bill and Ann want to have done; and the colors, fabrics, and so on that will be used, but the work of renovating the premises would be left up to the decorator. Even the choice of colors and fabrics can be left to a decorator if Bill and Ann so choose. The significant factor is that the independent contractor is left alone to exercise professional judgment in executing the job. For instance, the attorney and CPA Bill and Ann hire will be independent contractors, with Bill and Ann as their principal.

Torts

If an independent contractor commits a tort while within the scope of an endeavor, liability for the tort rests with the independent contractor, not with the principal for whom the contractor worked. For instance, if while working on Ann and Bill's office, the decorator accidentally drops a brick on a passerby, the independent contractor, not Ann and Bill, would be liable to the passerby for injuries sustained.

There are, however, some areas where the law still holds a principal liable even though the tort occurred within the scope of the enterprise. For instance, the law generally does not allow a principal to contract away the liability for certain types of dangerous activities such as if someone were injured by an independent contractor's blasting operations.

Contracts

The contracts entered into by an independent contractor bind Ann and Bill only if there has been an agreement to that effect between them and the independent contractor. Otherwise, the independent contractor's contracts are his or her own. Sometimes it can be difficult to tell whether one is actually an employee or an independent contractor. See Box 10–1 ("Common Law Test for Determining Employee Status") for some of the factors the courts use to make the determination.

10–1 CONCEPT SUMMARY

Common Law Test for Determining Employee Status

The rule of thumb for determining whether a worker is an employee is generally determined by the right to control. However, courts, agencies, the IRS, and others have consistently used the 20 factors listed below following the common law test to determine if sufficient control is being exercised such that a worker is considered an employee.

1. **Instructions**: If the worker must take instruction about how to do a job, the worker is usually considered an employee.

2. **Training**: If the worker is trained by the employer, it is generally an indication of being an employee rather than an independent contractor, in that the employer is dealing with instructing the employee in how to do the job.

3. **Integration**: When the success or continuation of a business depends on the performance of certain services, the worker performing those services is subject to a certain amount of control by the owner of the business.

4. **Services rendered personally**: If the services must be rendered personally, the employer controls both the means and the results of the work.

5. **Hiring, supervising, and paying assistants**: If the employer hires, supervises, and pays assistants, this is an indication of the employer's control over the worker, and the worker is thus more likely to be deemed an employee.

6. **Continuing relationships**: If there is a continuing rather than intermittent relationship between the worker and the employer, it generally indicates an employer-employee relationship.

7. **Set hours of work**: If the employer is the one who establishes the hours of work for the worker, it indicates control by the employer and thus that the worker is likely an employee.

8. **Full time required**: If the worker must devote full time to the employer's business, rather than being free to work for whomever the worker wishes, whenever the worker wishes, it is a form of control indicating employee status.

9. **Doing work on the employer's premises**: Control is indicated if the work is performed on the employer's premises rather than wherever the worker wishes to perform it.

10. **Order or sequence set**: If a worker is not free to choose a personal pattern of work, but must perform in the sequence set by the employer, the worker is more likely an employee.

11. **Oral or written reports**: If the worker must submit regular oral or written reports to the employer, the worker is more likely an employee.

12. **Furnishing tools and materials**: If the employer furnishes significant tools, materials, and other equipment needed for the job, the worker is usually an employee.

13. **Payment by hour, week, or month**: Payment of the worker by the hour, week, or month indicates the likelihood of employee status, unless such is simply a convenient way of paying the agreed cost of an independent contractor's job. An independent contractor usually is paid by the job or on commission.

14. **Payment of business and/or traveling expenses**: Payment of the worker's business and traveling expenses indicates the worker is an employee.

15. **Significant investment**: If a worker invests in facilities generally kept by an employer, such as an office or other work premises, generally the worker is not an employee.

16. **Realization of profit or loss**: An employee generally cannot realize a profit or loss over and above wages, through management of resources, but an independent contractor can.

17. **Working for more than one firm at a time**: If a worker performs more than minimal services for unrelated people simultaneously, the worker is more likely an independent contractor.

18. **Making service available to the general public**: A worker is usually not an employee if the worker can make services available to the general public (rather than only to the employer) on a regular or consistent basis.

19. **Right to discharge**: The right of the employer to discharge a worker indicates the worker is an employee rather than an independent contractor who generally has the contractual right to finish the job.

20. **Right to terminate**: A worker is an employee if the worker has the right to end the relationship with the employer at any time without incurring liability; an independent contractor would generally be liable for breach of contract.

AGENCY

Certain parts of Ann and Bill's business enterprise may need the assistance of someone who can enter into agreements on Ann and Bill's behalf for certain purposes. For instance, they may hire someone to act as their **agent** to acquire new clients. This creates an agency relationship in which Ann and Bill would be known as the principals and the person hired would be the agent. Ann and Bill would give the agent the right to enter into agreements to have Ann and Bill's business perform services for clients. Ann and Bill may include in the agreement with their agent whatever limitations they feel are warranted. For instance, they may allow the agent to enter into contracts only up to a certain dollar amount or only for certain types of services.

Whenever an agency relationship is created, three sets of relationships arise with which we must be concerned: the relationship between the principal and agent, the relationship between the agent and the third party with whom the agent is contracting, and the relationship between the principal and the third party with whom the agent contracted. The primary concern for the relationship with third parties is, who will be liable to the third party if something goes wrong with the contract? Does the third party sue the agent with which the third party dealt, or the principal whom the agent represented? The law always tries to protect the third party from being harmed by relationships to which the third party was not privy.

Types of Principals

When the agent enters into agreements for Bill and Ann, those agreements are on Bill and Ann's behalf, with the agent only acting for them. The agreements bind Bill and Ann, not the agent. Ordinarily, the third party knows he or she is dealing with an agent of Bill and Ann and who Bill and Ann actually are. This is a **disclosed principal** situation. If anything goes wrong in the contract, the third party can sue Bill and Ann as disclosed principals, and Bill and Ann are liable to the third party.

It is possible that for some reason Bill and Ann do not wish to have it disclosed that the agent is working for them. This is known as an **undisclosed principal** relationship. If Walt Disney Inc. wanted to acquire land, it would not be uncommon for the company to act through an agent who does not disclose that Walt Disney is the principal. Can you think of why this is true? If you see dollar signs when you hear the name Walt Disney, so will a third-party seller. Thinking that Walt Disney can afford to pay more than an ordinary buyer, the seller often raises the price. There may be nothing illegal about that, but in order to negotiate a fair deal, Disney may wish to remain anonymous.

If anything goes wrong with a contract in which Bill and Ann were undisclosed principals, the third party will be able to elect to sue Bill and Ann as principals (if it is discovered that they exist) or the agent with whom they dealt, but recover from only one or the other, not both. Because there is an agreement between the principal and the agent regarding their own relationship, if the agent is found liable to the third party, the agent can be reimbursed or indemnified by the principal as long as the agent conducted business in accordance with agreed-upon limits.

There is also the possibility of a **partially disclosed principal**. Here the third party is aware there is a principal for whom the agent is contracting, but the third party does not know who the principal is. In the event something goes wrong with the contract, the third party may sue the principal.

Types of Agents

The type of agent Bill and Ann employ will be determined by what they wish the agent to do. If they want the agent to have broad powers to conduct virtually all business for them, they will have a **general agent**. If they want to have the agent conduct only certain kinds of activities for them, they will have a **limited**, or **special**, **agent**. The choice is entirely up to them, and the agent will be liable to them if the agent exceeds the authority given.

Types of Authority

An agent must have authority to act for a principal. Ann and Bill are liable for the authorized acts of their agents. There are two types of authority: **actual authority** and **apparent authority**.

Actual authority is composed of **express authority** and **implied authority**. Express authority is the authority that Ann and Bill give the agent orally or in writing. An agent who has express authority also has implied authority to engage in acts necessary to accomplish the goals of the agency relationship as delineated in the express authority

partially disclosed principal
principal of whom the third party dealing with an agent is aware but does not know for whom the agent acts

general agent
an agent who performs a broad range of duties for the principal

limited agent
an agent for a specific, limited purpose defined by the principal

actual authority
authority given by a principal to an agent

apparent authority
the principal's acts that give the appearance that the agent is acting on the principal's behalf

express authority
oral or written authority given by a principal to an agent

implied authority
authority that an agent has to do acts that are a natural part of the express authority granted by the principal

given. For instance, if Bill and Ann hire an agent to open a branch office for them, that would also include the power of the agent to do things implied in that express authority, such as entering into a lease, purchasing furniture, and hiring staff. Without express authority, there can be no implied authority derived from it.

If Bill and Ann were to clothe an agent with authority, but without express (and, therefore, without implied) authority in fact, they may have created apparent authority in the eyes of a third party. For instance, assume Ann and Bill told an assistant manager that that manager did not have authority to order inventory. However, one day when Bill and Ann are out, a seller comes in and the assistant manager orders replacement stock. When Ann and Bill learn of the order, they call the seller's company to say they will not accept the order because the assistant manager had no authority to place the order.

If the company sues Ann and Bill for breach of contract and Ann and Bill plead the assistant manager's lack of authority as a defense, the seller will argue that the assistant manager had apparent authority to place the order. The apparent authority would flow from the fact that the assistant manager held the title of a manager and was running the store at the time of the order. Thus Bill and Ann had clothed the agent with the apparent authority to order inventory—a normal task in the ordinary course of managing a business. Apparent authority is argued when the principal denies the agent was acting with express authority within the scope of the agency, yet the agent appeared to have authority based on something the principal did.

It is important for Ann and Bill to make sure they comply with the rules of agency in terminating an agency relationship, or they may find themselves liable for contracts the agent entered into without authority after the agency was terminated. After an agency relationship has ended there is no longer any express authority and therefore no implied authority for the agent to act upon. However, until the principal provides **actual notice** by notifying third parties—by letter, phone, fax, or other direct means—of the termination of the relationship, the agent still has apparent authority to bind the principal to contracts. Therefore, at the end of the agency, Bill and Ann should personally notify all parties with whom the agent dealt. Further, they should furnish **constructive notice** to any other parties by publishing a notice in a newspaper of general circulation that is calculated to reach third parties not known to them but with whom the agent could potentially deal. If they give proper constructive notice, then even if the

actual notice
direct communication with third parties the agent dealt with to notify them of termination of the agency relationship

constructive notice
newspaper communication with third parties the agent may deal with to let them know the agency has been terminated

agent does contract with third parties who did not see the notice, Bill and Ann will be protected.

EMPLOYEES

If Ann and Bill want to hire staff to help with the business of the enterprise, chances are that such staff would be considered as employees. Employees are people hired by an employer to perform functions for the employer as per the employer's instructions. Unlike independent contractors, they take directions from the employer and are subject to the employer's control.

If an employee of Ann and Bill's commits a tort while within the scope of employment, Ann and Bill are responsible under the theory of respondeat superior discussed in Chapter 5. The underlying theory is that the employee is actually working for and on behalf of Ann and Bill, so liability should rest with them. This rule does not apply to criminal acts committed by an employee, unless the acts were requested by the employer. Nor does the rule apply to situations in which the employee has gone outside the scope of employment, in which case the employee is liable in his or her own right. For instance, Ann and Bill would probably not be liable if the boyfriend of an employee came onto the work premises and got into a fight with the employee, the employee knocked down the boyfriend, and the boyfriend's head is injured. The rule would, however, encompass situations such as if Bill and Ann's truck driver accidentally runs into someone while driving to make a delivery.

The vicarious liability that holds Bill and Ann liable as principals for torts they did not personally commit is necessary because, as business owners, they are generally in a better financial position to pay (remember the deep-pockets theory?) and the employee committed the act in furtherance of Bill and Ann's business enterprise. Because Bill and Ann receive the benefit, they should be the ones to bear responsibility. In the foregoing truck driver example, the injured person would be able to sue Bill and Ann even though neither Bill nor Ann was driving the truck. The driver is actually liable also, but usually does not have the financial resources with which to pay. Bill and Ann could request reimbursement by the truck driver, but again, an employee generally does not have such funds, and few employees would want to be employed if they were made to pay for accidents that occurred in furtherance of the employer's business.

EMPLOYMENT AT WILL/UNJUST DISMISSAL

THE EMPLOYMENT-AT-WILL DOCTRINE

employment at will
employment of employees at the pleasure of the employer

wrongful discharge
termination of an at-will employee for reasons the law does not allow; also known as abusive termination, abusive discharge, and wrongful termination

What are the parameters of the relationship formed when Ann and Bill hire someone as an employee? Generally, employment relationships are governed by state law. Further, under most state laws, **employment relationships** are **at will**. That is, the employment relationship exists at the will of the parties, and either may terminate the relationship whenever either wishes, with or without a reason. Just as the employee can leave an employer's employ whenever the employee wishes, the employer can terminate the relationship the same way. Most people assume that there is a right to continued employment. However, as the *DeMarco* case rather painfully demonstrates, there generally is no such right.

There are, however, certain limitations on the employment-at-will doctrine: Ann and Bill cannot terminate an employee for reasons forbidden by law. For instance, if they terminate an employee because the employee is of a particular race, gender, or national origin, it would violate Title VII of the Civil Rights Act of 1964. Thus they could not legally do this. There are also other statutes limiting an employer's right to terminate an employee. Some states have statutes that do not allow termination of an employee for reporting for jury duty, filing workers' compensation claims, reporting safety violations, or blowing the whistle on the employer. The latter involves an employee's reporting certain statutorily recognized wrongdoings by an employer. An example would be the case of an employee who reports to the Environmental Protection Agency that the employer is forcing the employee to falsify reports filed with the agency.

Cases brought by terminated employees on these theories are known as **wrongful discharge**, **wrongful termination**, **abusive discharge**, or **abusive termination** cases. In Box 10–2, "The High Cost of Wrongful Termination," on page 311 you will get some idea of how costly it can be for Bill and Ann to wrongfully discharge an employee. In the *Fortune* case, discussed later, the court recognized that the employee had a right to continued employment, and it imposed liability on the employer for not governing himself accordingly.

DEMARCO V. PUBLIX SUPER MARKETS, INC.

384 So.2d 1253 (Fla. 1980)

An employee of a grocery store sued the employer for injuries suffered by his daughter while the child was in the store with the mother shopping. The employer terminated the employee for bringing suit. The court permitted the termination to stand after determining the contract of employment to be at will.

Per Curiam Decision

DeMarco alleged that his employer, Publix, wrongfully terminated his employment solely because he had brought suit against Publix in his daughter's behalf for injuries occurring while she was with her mother shopping in a Publix market. DeMarco contends that the employment termination violated the access-to-the-courts provision of the Florida constitution. The trial court dismissed the complaint with prejudice (i.e., DeMarco could not later try to bring the case again), and the district court affirmed, holding: "[W]here the term of employment is discretionary with either party or indefinite, then either party for any reason may terminate it at any time and no action may be maintained for breach of the employment contract." The district court concluded there is no civil cause of action for interference with the exercise of one's right under the Florida constitution. DeMarco's suit on behalf of the daughter was pending at the time of the district court's opinion; therefore neither he in his representative capacity nor the daughter as beneficiary has been denied access to the courts to vindicate the claim for her injuries. AFFIRMED

Overton, Justice, dissenting

I dissent. In my view, an action for compensatory damages for termination of DeMarco's employment should be allowed to ensure that the individual rights of his minor child will be protected.

The child suffered permanent injuries as a result of the accident. The insurer, acting as an agent of Publix, offered the sum of $200 as full and complete settlement for the injuries. DeMarco rejected the

continued on next page

offer and filed suit on behalf of his daughter against Publix and the manufacturer of the container. DeMarco was notified that he would be fired unless he withdrew the suit. DeMarco refused to withdraw the suit and was terminated.

I would hold that DeMarco has asserted a proper cause of action for interference with that access to the courts necessary to protect the interests of his minor daughter. The termination of discretionary or indefinite employment, solely because of a cause of action filed by an employee against an employer, may be justified in accordance with the views of the majority when the employee files the suit only in his own right. I do not believe that this doctrine is constitutionally valid when its application substantially interferes with the right of access to the courts by a third-party minor child; therefore I would reverse in part and affirm in part.

Case Questions

1. Which decision comes closest to your own thinking: the majority or the dissent? Explain.

2. Do you think the majority decision effectively closes the courts to at-will employees who will not now sue for fear of termination if they do? Does this seem consistent with the constitutional provision? Explain.

The High Cost of Wrongful Termination

A California appeals court recently affirmed a $10.29-million judgment against the WD-40 Co., maker of the multipurpose lubricant WD-40. The judgment was the result of a jury verdict in a suit filed by eight commission sales companies, which sued WD-40 for wrongful termination of their contracts after WD-40 replaced them with an in-house sales force in 1988.

SITUATIONS NOT COVERED BY THE AT-WILL DOCTRINE

Not every employee Bill and Ann have will be an at-will employee. There are certain employment situations that do not fall within the employment-at-will doctrine. When there is a contract between Bill and Ann and an employee, employment is not at will, but, rather, contractual. When there is a collective bargaining agreement between them and a union, it is the agreement that governs the relationship, and the relationship is not at will. Unionization covers about 16% of the working population. Government employees are also generally not at-will employees, because they are governed by applicable employment regulations that set forth specifically how and why their government employment may be terminated.

Ordinarily, when we think of a contract, we may think of the parties' negotiating together and reaching a mutually satisfactory agreement. That has not always been found to be the case in the at-will area—much to many employers' dismay. Contracts have sometimes been implied from the parties' conduct that ordinarily would not be taken as having created a contract. Once the existence of a contract has been determined by a court, the employment relationship is no longer deemed to be at will. Therefore the employee cannot be terminated by the employer without limitation.

In recent years, courts all across the country have dealt with contracts implied from such things as statements contained in employee handbooks and manuals, letters of offer from employers to employees quoting yearly salaries, or comments made by employers to applicants or employees, such as, "You'll be with us as long as you keep your nose clean and do good work." In *Pugh v. See's Candies, Inc.*, the court implied a contract from the duration of employment, as well as commendations and assurances given to the employee, among other things.

PUGH V. SEE'S CANDIES INC.
116 Cal. App.3d 311, 171 Cal. Rptr. 917 (1981)

A 32-year employee was fired from his job at a candy company for no viable reason. He sued alleging unjust dismissal, breach of contract, and termination in violation of public policy. The court agreed and held for the employee.

Grodin, J.: After 32 years of employment with See's Candies Inc., in which he worked his way up the corporate ladder from dishwasher to vice president in charge of production and member of the board of directors, Wayne Pugh was fired. No reason for the termination was provided in his dismissal letter.

When Pugh first went to work for See's, the president and general manager frequently told him, "If you are loyal to [See's] and do a good job, your future is secure." See's had a practice of not terminating administrative personnel except for good cause.

During the entire period of his employment, there had been neither formal or written criticism of Pugh's work. No complaints were ever raised at the annual meetings, and he was never denied a raise or bonus. The preceding Christmas season had been the most successful in See's history, the 1973 Valentine's Day holiday set a new company sales record, and the March 1973 edition of See's newsletter, containing two pictures of Pugh, carried congratulations on the increased production. Pugh received neither a notice there was a problem that needed correction nor any warning that disciplinary action was being contemplated.

An employer's right to terminate employees is not absolute. "The mere fact that a contract is terminable at will does not give the employer the absolute right to terminate it in all cases." Two relevant limiting principles have developed, one of them based on public policy and the other on traditional contract doctrine. The first limitation precludes dismissal "when an employer's discharge of an employee violates fundamental principles of public policy," and the second when the discharge is contrary to the terms of the agreement, express or implied.

"The presumption that an employment contract is intended to be terminable at will is subject, like any presumption, to contrary evidence. In the case at bench, we hold that the longevity of the employee's service, together with the expressed policy of the employer, operates as a form of estoppel, precluding any discharge of such an employee by the employer without good cause." The employer's conduct gave rise to an implied promise that it would not act arbitrarily in dealing with its employees.

There were facts in evidence from which the jury could determine the existence of such an implied promise: duration of the employment, the commendations and promotions Pugh received, the apparent lack of any direct criticism of his work, the assurances he was given, and the employer's acknowledged policies. While oblique language will not, standing alone, be sufficient to establish agreement, it is appropriate to consider the totality of the parties' relationship: Agreement may be shown by the acts and conduct of the parties, interpreted in the light of the subject matter and of the surrounding circumstances. REVERSED

Case Questions

1. Do longevity and satisfactory performance seem to you to be sufficient reasons to deny an employer's at-will rights? Explain.

2. Does the court's decision virtually preclude employers from being able to dismiss at-will employees who have a long record of success with the company? Should it? Discuss.

There are other exceptions to the at-will doctrine that have been carved out by states through statutes or case law. In some states, the at-will nature of the employment relationship is ignored if to do so would promote justice and fair play.

There are also employment relationships that do not come within the at-will concept because exceptions to the doctrine have been created by either statutes or case law when it was deemed necessary to promote justice and fair play. Such cases are generally based on the court's inferring the existence of that implied covenant of good faith and fair dealing between the parties that is inherent in business and contractual arrangements. See if you think justice was promoted in the following decision.

FORTUNE V. THE NATIONAL CASH REGISTER COMPANY

373 Mass. 96; 364 N.E.2d 1251 (1977)

A long-term employee named Fortune was terminated the first working day after securing a contract resulting in a bonus to him of more than $90,000. Although technically the termination did not violate the employee's contract, the court held it to be in bad faith and therefore unlawful.

Abrams, J.: The contract at issue is a classic, terminable, at-will employment contract. It is clear that the contract itself reserved to the parties the explicit power to terminate the contract without cause on written notice. It is also clear that under the express terms of the contract Fortune has received all of the bonus commissions to which he is entitled. Thus, NCR [the National Cash Register Co.] claims it did not breach the contract and that it has no further liability to Fortune. According to a literal reading of the contract, NCR is correct.

However, we hold that NCR's written contract contains an implied covenant of good faith and fair dealing, and a termination not made in good faith constitutes a breach of the contract. We recognize the employer's need for a large amount of control over its workforce. However, we believe that where, as here, commissions are to be paid for work performed by the employee, the employer's decision to terminate its at-will employee should be made in good faith. NCR's right to make decisions in its own interest is not hampered by a requirement of adherence to this.

NCR argues that there was no evidence of bad faith here. We disagree and think that the evidence and the reasonable inferences to be drawn therefrom are that the termination of Fortune's 25 years of employment as a salesman with NCR the next business day after NCR obtained a $5-million order from First National was motivated by a desire to pay Fortune as little of the bonus credit as it could. AFFIRMED

Case Questions

1. Do you agree with the court's assessment of the situation here? Explain.

2. Why do you think an employer would terminate an employee capable of bringing in an order valued at $5 million? Does this seem logical to you? Why or why not?

3. Do you think employees like Fortune and Pugh should be virtually guaranteed their jobs? Explain.

MODEL EMPLOYMENT TERMINATION ACT

The National Conference of Commissioners on Uniform State Laws, in August 1991, issued the Model Employment Termination Act (META) (See Box 10–3, "Model Employment Termination Act, Preferred Version," on page 317 for specific provisions). The purpose was to attempt to bring some degree of uniformity to the patchwork of state laws addressing this area. If adopted by a state, META would supplant the patchwork of various states' cases and laws with a uniform approach to unlawful terminations. Because each state is free to develop on its own the laws governing employment at will, laws vary from state to state. A uniform act would promote predictability and uniformity of at-will termination decisions. For instance, if the model act were adopted by the states, there would not be, as there is now, the possibility of an employee's recovering for unjust dismissal because of whistle-blowing in one state, and not in another, virtually the same facts.

META would not extinguish the rights of an employee against an employer arising from state or federal statutes or administrative rules or regulations having the force of law, collective bargaining agreements, or express oral or written employment agreements not in violation of the law.

Employers could still agree that an employee would be dismissed for not performing as agreed after their establishing appropriate performance standards. The act includes protection against retaliation by the employer, and it decrees the handling of termination complaints by arbitration rather than litigation.

Of course, states adopting this uniform approach would do so voluntarily through their state legislatures and would be able to change provisions to suit their own needs or reflect the particular common law principles they wished to remain intact. States could also pass such a law completely on their own. For instance, the Montana Wrongful Discharge from Employment Act provides that a discharge is wrongful if either it was not for good cause and the employee had completed the probationary period of employment, it was in retaliation for the employee's refusal to violate public policy or for reporting a violation of public policy (very much like whistle-blowing), or the employer violated the express provisions of its own written personnel policies.

 Box 10–4, "The Impact of Employment Litigation," on page 319 gives some indication of how costly litigation can be in the absence of legislation such as META.

DEFAMATION IN THE EMPLOYMENT TERMINATION SETTING

One of the considerations whenever Ann and Bill terminate an employee from employment concerns references. The employee will likely need to receive a favorable reference from Ann and Bill if the upcoming job search is to be fruitful. A recurring problem in this area is what Ann and Bill, as the former employers, may say to a prospective employer who requests information on an applicant who was employed by them.

Ann and Bill, like many employers, are probably afraid of being sued by the former employee for defamation if the employee disagrees with their comments or evaluation given to the inquiring em-

10–3   LEGAL EXCERPTS

Model Employment Termination Act—Preferred Version

A. Applies to employers employing five or more employees for 20 or more weeks in the two years before discharge; applies to employees who have been employed by the same employer for a total period of one year or more and have worked for the employer at least 520 hours during the 26-week period just before termination.

B. An employer may terminate an employee only for good cause, with two exceptions:
- by written agreement an employee accepts a severance pay arrangement in lieu of the act, or
- an employee is hired for a specified term.

C. Termination includes:
- a dismissal (including those resulting from elimination of employee's position by the employer),
- a layoff or suspension by employer for more than two consecutive months, or
- employee's quitting or retiring because of an act or omission by the employer, the employer has been notified of this by the employee and does not provide appropriate relief, and the situation is so intolerable that a reasonable person would quit or retire (constructive dismissal).

D. Good cause means
- a reasonable basis for believing the employee should be terminated in view of the facts and circumstances related to job performance or conduct on the job, or
- in the exercise of good business judgment for good business reasons such as good faith consolidation, reorganizing, discontinuing, or otherwise changing business operations.

E. Employer must provide employee a written statement of the reason for termination within 10 days of terminating the employee. The employee then has 180 days within which to demand arbitration. Before terminating an employee, an employer may request a declaratory judgment in which the employer files a complaint to determine if good cause exists to terminate a specified employee.

F. Employees found to be unjustly dismissed are entitled to be awarded by the arbitrator:
- reinstatement;

continued on next page

- full or partial back pay
  reduced by:
  - interim earning from employment elsewhere,
  - benefits received and amounts that could have been received with reasonable diligence (i.e., there is a duty to mitigate damages)
- a lump-sum payment if there is no reinstatement, equal to the employee's rate of pay in effect before termination, for a period not exceeding 36 months after the date of the award, plus the value of fringe benefits lost during the period and reduced by likely earnings and benefits from employment elsewhere; and
- reasonable attorney's fees and costs.

G. There is no recovery for:
- pain and suffering,
- emotional distress,
- defamation,
- fraud or other common law injury,
- punitive damages,
- compensatory damages, or
- any other monetary award.

H. Either party to the arbitration may seek judicial review to have the award vacated, modified, or enforced by the court. A court may vacate or modify an arbitrator's award only if the court finds:
- it was procured by corruption, fraud, or other improper means;
- the arbitrator was found to have engaged in misconduct or partiality prejudicing the rights of a party;
- the arbitrator exceeded his or her powers;
- the arbitrator committed a prejudicial error of law; or
- there is some other ground for vacating the award under the Uniform Arbitration Act.

10–4   CONCEPT SUMMARY

The Impact of Employment Litigation

The National Conference of Commissioners on Uniform State Laws estimates the expense for defending a single typical wrongful discharge case at $80,000. This cost is not contingent on the resources of the defendant, nor is it diminished if the defendant is successful. The potential loss is devastating if the plaintiff wins. And plaintiffs do win.

In California, using a large state with diverse business activity as an example, plaintiffs won 70% *or more* of all wrongful discharge cases that reached a jury. The verdicts in these cases averaged $300,000–$500,000 (META, 1991).

Nationwide, plaintiffs have received judgments as high as $20 million, $4.7 million, $3.25 million, $2.57 million, and $2 million. "Jury awards exceeding $1 million have been common," and the increase of wrongful termination cases over the past dozen years has been described as a "virtual landslide" (META, 1991).

Source: "Managing the Risk of Wrongful Discharge Litigation: The Small Business Firm and the Model Employment Termination Act," by Robert J. Aalberts and Lorne H. Seidman, *Journal of Small Business Management*, Vol. 31, No. 4, October 1993.

ployer. Recall from Chapter 5 that defamation means intentionally making an untrue statement about someone to a third person, which would lower the first person's reputation and standing in the community. Because of that fear, most employers take the position that they will respond to inquiries only with a confirmation about whether the person worked for the employer and the dates of employment. This does not provide the prospective employer with much information as to whether the applicant will make a satisfactory employee.

Truth is an absolute defense to defamation, and an employer will not be liable if the information provided is found to be true. However, the law actually provides Bill and Ann—as employers in this situation—with a conditional privilege to provide prospective employers with information about former employees. If the conditions of the privilege are met, they will be protected from liability if sued by the former employee for defamation, even if the information they provided turns out to be false.

The conditions are generally that the information be provided in good faith and not be intentionally false and that the inquiry be handled as a reasonable and prudent business person would do. This means that the information should be requested in a businesslike way, such as in a letter on letterhead stationery and asking specific employment-related questions. The response should also be businesslike and given in the regular course of business. The intent of disclosing the information must be to respond to a business inquiry, rather than to retaliate against or seek vengeance on the former employee, thereby causing trouble for the former employee, or simply to gossip.

The conditional privilege would neither be effective nor serve to protect Bill and Ann if, for instance, they gossiped about an ex-employee over cocktails at a party or over the backyard fence to a neighbor who happened to be a prospective employer. If Ann and Bill respond to the prospective employer's inquiry as they should, there should be no liability attached to their information.

SUMMARY

Individuals may contract to work for others in several different capacities. They may act as independent contractors, agents, or employees. Each of these working relationships has its own rules that govern the actions between the parties and between the individual working for someone and third parties with whom that worker may interact.

Employment relationships are generally at the will of the parties, unless otherwise agreed, and may be terminated by either for any reason. That broad rule has recently garnered several exceptions, varying from jurisdiction to jurisdiction. A proposed uniform law on terminations would bring some predictability from one jurisdiction to the next.

Employers terminating employees must be careful that they do not defame the employee when giving references to a prospective new employer. A conditional privilege is given to employers to permit them to provide prospective employers with relevant information about their experience with the employee, which can be used a basis for hiring decisions.

CHAPTER TERMS

actual authority	general agent
actual notice	implied authority
agent	independent contractor
apparent authority	limited agent
constructive notice	partially disclosed principal
disclosed principal	principal
employment at will	undisclosed principal
express authority	wrongful discharge

CHAPTER-END QUESTIONS

1. Joyce and Jacqui are partners who sing professionally. Joyce contracts with Theresa to manage the duo without Jacqui's knowing of the arrangement. When Jacqui discovers the decision, she decides she does not wish to have Theresa manage them. Theresa sues the duo for breach of contract. Jacqui defends on the basis that Joyce was acting on her own and not on behalf of Jacqui; therefore Joyce's act did not bind Jacqui. Will Jacqui win?

2. When Brendan is accidentally run over by a Smith Department Store truck, Ray, the driver, has no injuries, but Brendan does. When Brendan sues, whom will he likely sue for the injuries and why?

3. Donald Ace is a very wealthy and famous entrepreneur. He wishes to purchase some real estate on the boardwalk in Atlantic City, N.J. in order to build a casino. However, he knows that if the seller learns it is Ace who is buying the property, the seller will raise the price because of Ace's ability to pay a high price. The best thing for Ace to do is to be a(n)

   a. disclosed principal.
   b. partially disclosed principal.
   c. undisclosed principal.
   d. respondeat superior.

4. Marcus says that because he hired an independent contractor to put in his new, concrete driveway, he (Marcus) is not responsible for the injuries caused by the contractor backing into the street

and causing an oncoming car to run into a fence while trying to avoid running over the contractor. Marcus is correct. (True or False)

5. Christoff is a noncontractual employee who is dating his boss's wife. When the boss finds out, he fires Christoff. If Christoff sues for unjust dismissal, will he win?

6. If Christoff (in number 5) was a member of the union, would it change your answer? Why or why not?

7. The theory allowing an employer to be liable for the torts committed by an employee within the scope of employment is called

_____.

8. Vernessa is terminated from employment with the Nicole Security Agency after she is suspected of was stealing company funds. Nicole, owner of the Nicole Security Agency, is having drinks at a bar with some friends one evening when one of them, Scott, mentions that he recently interviewed Vernessa for a position. Scott is surprised to learn that Nicole knows Vernessa, as job with Nicole Security was not on Vernessa's resume. Scott is even more surprised when Nicole tells him why she terminated Vernessa. Scott does not hire Vernessa, Vernessa learns of the conversation between Scott and Nicole, and Vernessa sues Nicole for defamation. Discuss the issues.

9. LaToya is hired by Maxima agency as a receptionist. She works at the agency for seven years. During that time she gains 30 pounds. One day LaToya comes in and finds she has received a pink slip notifying her of the termination of her employment, effective at the end of the week. When LaToya inquires as to the reason for her termination, she is told that because she has gained weight, she no longer looks the way the company wants someone to look who represents them to outsiders as a receptionist would do. If LaToya sues for unjust dismissal, will she win? Why or why not?

10. When Diarr files a workers' compensation claim for injuries received while working as a stockbroker for Alexander, Bennett and Keebway, he is terminated. It was the third time Diarr had filed a claim for workers' compensation while working at the firm. The first time he was injured when he slipped on a ragged piece of carpet on the stairs, the second time he was shocked while plugging in the office coffee machine, and the last time, he fell on a slippery lavatory floor. If Diarr brings suit for unlawful termination, what is the likely outcome?

GROUP EXERCISE

Assume that Bill and Ann have become an international corporation. What kinds of business relationships can your group come up with for the various people who work with and for the corporation? Why would those be the kinds you chose? What are the drawbacks for Bill and Ann?

Chapter 11

EMPLOYMENT LAW: WAGES, HOURS, SAFETY, WORKERS' COMPENSATION, AND LABOR LAW

Chapter Preview Summary

In this chapter Bill and Ann are exposed to several other workplace matters that will have a great impact on the legal environment in which their business operates. Wages, hours, workers' compensation, labor law—all are part of the reality that they must address at some time or another when they employ others to work for them.

Chapter Objectives

In studying the chapter, you should learn:
- what the Fair Labor Standards Act is
- minimum wage requirements and exceptions
- the legal provisions for overtime
- what the Occupational Safety and Health Act is and what it requires
- what workers' compensation is, how it works, and who can and cannot receive its benefits
- the requirements imposed on employers under the Family and Medical Leave Act of 1991 and who may take such leave and for what reason
- what the law requires regarding the right of employees to organize and bargain collectively

INTRODUCTION

Several matters arise in the workplace, and Ann and Bill will have to consider them if they employ others. Matters concerning employees' wages, the hours employees can work, workplace safety, and unions are among them. In this chapter we examine some of these issues to see how they may affect Ann and Bill's business.

THE FAIR LABOR STANDARDS ACT (FLSA)

The Fair Labor Standards Act—enacted in 1938 after the devastation of the Great Depression—is a comprehensive piece of legislation that addresses primarily the matter of employee wages and hours. It applies to employers and employees involved in interstate commerce, either individually (e.g., a truck driver who delivers goods from one state to another) or as an enterprise (e.g., manufacturing of computers to be shipped throughout the country). The law exempts certain employees from certain parts of its coverage.

MINIMUM WAGES AND HOURS

In an attempt to prevent workers from sinking into poverty, FLSA sets a minimum standard for the wages of covered employees below which an employer may not pay. Since April 1, 1991, the minimum wage has been $4.25 per hour. When FLSA was enacted in 1938, the minimum wage was 25 cents per hour. Research conducted by the Center for Budget and Policy Priorities using 1990 U.S. Census figures determined that 56% of those officially below the poverty level in the United States live in households in which at least one person works. Poverty was defined as a family of four that earns less than $14,343 per year, or a family of three that earns less than $11,187. (See Box 11–1, "Labor Force Mysteries: The Working Poor and the Underground Economy.")

FLSA has also been said to cause poverty, in that employers will refuse to hire certain groups because it deems the minimum wage figure too high for the skill level of those within the group. As a result, the unemployment rate for, for instance, unskilled minority teens can run as high as 50%. (See Box 11–2, "Pity the Jobless Teenagers.")

11–1   LAW IN THE REAL WORLD

Labor Force Mysteries: The Working Poor and the Underground Economy

According to the commonly used figures produced by the Bureau of Labor Statistics [BLS], some 5.7 million Americans held jobs paying the minimum wage or less. If Washington economist Bruce W. Klein is right, though, the number is much higher—and low-wage jobs may be even more of a problem for the United States than suggested.

Klein, who once worked for the BLS, estimates that in 1988 some 15 million of the nation's 130 million workers were paid at or below the minimum wage ($3.35 then, $4.25 now). Of those, he calculates, nearly 4 million lived in poverty. The BLS data for that year, by contrast, show that 2.5 million workers were paid minimum wages or below, and that just 415,000 were poor.

What accounts for the huge differences? The BLS tallies only people paid by the hour; Klein has tried to take account for those paid weekly, monthly, or by piecework. The agency doesn't entirely disagree with him. "Our numbers *are* the tip of the iceberg," says John E. Bregger, assistant commissioner of current employment analysis. But Bregger argues that Klein's estimates are far from precise, since he uses annual data to approximate hourly rates of pay. That leaves a lot of room for error, which is why the BLS has historically stuck to the hourly data. Moreover, the rise in the minimum wage since 1988 has almost certainly reduced the proportion of workers in poverty.

Other labor economists say that Klein's estimates sound too high, but they agree that he is on the right track in trying to fill out the picture. "The conventional wisdom that all minimum wage workers are white teenagers who work at a mall is not correct," says Princeton labor economist David Card.

11–2   LAW IN THE REAL WORLD

Pity the Jobless Teenagers

According to the latest survey from the National Association of Purchasing Managers, in October of 1993, for the first time in six months, the purchasing survey's overall index exceeded 50 (a level that indicates expansion). The survey also showed that industrial output is up, new orders are on the rise, and export orders are rising, notably from Asian and Latin America.

Unfortunately for President Bill Clinton, there's not much good news in all this for him. He was elected as the jobs president, and precious few new jobs are appearing.

The purchasing managers survey shows that in October manufacturing continued to shed more jobs than were added. What's more, all the new costly mandates, especially health reform, emerging from the Clinton Administration will inevitably keep employers very cautious about adding jobs, warns David Hale, chief economist for Kemper Securities.

One of the groups hit hardest by these mandates is teenagers. The latest threat to their job prospects involves the 50-cent increase in the minimum wage to $4.75 an hour proposed by Labor Secretary Robert Reich. Bowing to the reality that a higher minimum wage will not add jobs for the poor, Reich has put the minimum wage increase on hold.

Reich would do better to dump the idea. Reich's friends, notably Lawrence Katz, formerly of Harvard and now his chief economist at Labor, and Alan Krueger of Princeton, came up with what's called the "new view," which claims a higher minimum wage has no impact on youth jobs. But they are wrong, thunders H. Eric Heinemann, chief economist at Ladenberg, Thalmann & Co. He says that the latest increase in the minimum wage, from $3.35 to $4.25, had an extraordinarily adverse impact on teenage jobs.

Teenagers are always hit hard in any recession, Heinemann says. But in the economic downturn from the second quarter of 1990 to the third quarter of 1991 (which coincided with the increase), teenagers accounted for almost two-thirds of the recession's total employment decline of 1.425 million. "This is off the scale," he says. Moreover, since the 1990 minimum wage increase, what's called the dropout rate (the percentage of teenagers not even bothering to look for work) has increased five points, to a staggeringly high 48% to 49%.

Source: "Pity the Jobless Teenager," by Howard Banks, *Forbes*, November 22, 1993. Reprinted by permission of *Forbes* magazine, ©Forbes Inc., 1993.

FLSA is administered by the Wage and Hour Division of the U.S. Department of Labor. The Wage and Hour Division has the authority to investigate, gather information, issue regulations, and enforce the provisions of FLSA. Violations of the law can be costly. (See Box 11–3, "The High Price of FLSA Violations.") States also have agencies comparable to the Division of Wages and Hours to administer state fair labor standards laws.

As for hours, FLSA does not regulate the number of hours an employee can work. Rather, it requires that if a covered employee works more than a certain number of hours per week (40), then the employee must be paid at the rate of one and a half times the employee's normal pay.

As mentioned, FLSA has exemptions, though more than 40 states cover employees exempted from FLSA in their states' wage and hour laws. Following is a list of exemptions from both the wage and overtime provisions. Note that under FLSA, some employees are exempt from the overtime provisions but not the minimum wage provisions, but because their salaries are generally higher, this does not present a problem (e.g., executives or teachers).

1. Outside salespeople and executive, administrative, and professional employees, including teachers and academic administrative employees in elementary and secondary schools

2. Employees of certain individually owned and operated small retail or service establishments not part of a covered enterprise

11–3   LAW IN THE REAL WORLD

The High Price of FLSA Violations

In August 1993, Food Lion, a major Southern grocery store chain, agreed to pay $16.2 million in the largest-ever settlement from a private employer accused of violating FLSA. The agreement settled claims that Food Lion violated overtime, minimum wage, and child labor laws.

3. Employees of certain seasonal amusements or recreational establishments, messengers, full-time students, employees of certain small newspapers, switchboard operators of small telephone companies, seamen employed on foreign vessels, and employees engaged in fishing operations

4. Farm workers employed by anyone who used more than 500 person-days of farm labor in any calendar quarter of the preceding calendar year

5. Casual baby-sitters and those employed as companions to the elderly

CHILD LABOR

In an effort to rescue America's youth from the debilitating work of the dawn-to-dusk sweatshops that once helped to fuel the U.S. economy, FLSA included restricting the hours and jobs children could work. Most cannot work before age 16, with 18 being the minimum age for jobs deemed hazardous by the Department of Labor. As Box 11–4, "Too Much Work = Poor Grades," demonstrates, things have gone in the opposite direction, with many children working *too* much, though the area is regulated.

Children between the ages of 14 and 16 may work at certain types of jobs that do not interfere with their health, education, or well-being, such as traditional newspaper delivery. Despite the law, there are abuses and violations (See Box 11–5, "Illegal Child Labor Comes Back" on page 333) Certain agricultural work is permitted also. States may have child labor laws that are even stricter than the federal laws, and if so, those state laws override federal law.

Interestingly enough, part of the impetus to clean up child labor violations is coming from business itself. Box 11–6, "The Supply Police," on page 335 details how companies themselves are policing the matter of child labor law violations and other workplace abuses.

11–4   LAW IN THE REAL WORLD

Too Much Work = Poor Grades

Working after school is one of the verities of American life, right up there with baseball and apple pie. But while there's nothing wrong with teaching Junior the value of a buck or Janie self-reliance, too much work can be, well, too much.

Many studies show that, in general, the more kids work, the less time they have for homework, and the worse they perform in school. Says Laurence Steinberg, a psychology professor at Temple University: "We've reached a stage where for many youngsters their main concern is not school but work." Steinberg, who conducted a two-year survey of 10th- and 11th-grade students from nine schools in Wisconsin and California, found that teenagers who toiled more than 20 hours a week cut class more often and were less involved in their studies than those who worked moderate hours. Those who didn't work at all did best.

One teen who overdid it is Ryan Smith, 17, a senior at Shenendhowa High School near Albany, N.Y. Between July and October last year, Ryan worked more than 25 hours a week at a Long John Silver's restaurant. He often got home at 11:30 p.m., found himself falling asleep in class, and rarely had time to do his homework. Ryan now works only ten or so hours a week at the local public library. His grades have improved, and he is looking forward to going to college.

Excessive work also prevents kids from getting a well-rounded education. Carol Harblin, another senior at Shenendhowa, found that a heavy schedule at McDonald's during her junior year kept her from pursuing extracurricular activities. Now she works only Saturdays at Wendy's and has time for ballet classes and field trips, including a jaunt to Washington for the inauguration.

Some critics object not just to how much kids work but to *where* they work: overwhelmingly in fast-food restaurants. Says Joseph Kinney, executive director of the National Safe Workplace Institute: "Fast food is the wrong kind of work. It's repetitive and mindless." Sheer elitism, counters Mark Gorman, senior director for government affairs at the National Restaurant Association: "The argument is, 'If kids are not working, they'll be home studying. They'll go to Harvard and become computer engineers.'"

Still, it's hard to argue against reasonable restrictions on hours worked. In 1991, New York and Maine enacted laws that allow children

continued on next page

under 16, for example, to work no more than 18 hours a week when school is in session. In July, Washington State will impose similar limits. Says Rich Berkowitz, a policy analyst with Washington State's House of Representatives: "What are kids going to learn in 40 hours of work a week that they can't learn in 20?"

Some state industry groups are also joining the charge to convince parents and kids that extra hours on homework offer a better long-term payoff than more time behind the cash register. Since September, Texas Restaurant Association President Bill Daniels has logged 30,000 miles visiting members in his state. The message: "Business must put education first."

11–5   LAW IN THE REAL WORLD

Illegal Child Labor Comes Back

Like tuberculosis and measles, child labor is making a comeback in the United States. From New York to California, employers are breaking the law by hiring children of 7 to 17 who put in long, hard hours and often work in dangerous conditions. Some examples:

- In many states, small fly-by-night candy distributors are hiring young children to sell boxes of chocolates door-to-door, late at night and un-supervised, in strange neighborhoods. In Washington State, one 11-year-old girl selling candy alone at 10 p.m. on a school night, 160 miles from home, was struck and killed by a passing car.
- In New York City and Los Angeles, immigrant children who should be in school work in garment industry sweatshops that are dirty, crowded, and often contain hazards like locked fire doors.
- In the Southeast, the Labor Department is investigating Food Lion, the fast-growing supermarket chain, for hundreds of possible labor viola-tions, most of them safety related. Underage children allegedly used meat-cutting machines and paper-box bailers—machines that compact and crush cardboard cartons and are known to kill.
- In California and Texas—along the Mexican border—and in south Florida, young children still work beside their parents for up to 12 hours a day as migrant farmers. As a 13-year-old, Mexican-American Augustino Nieves started picking olives and strawberries in California. He missed months of school that year, working from 6:30 a.m. until 8 p.m., with a 20-minute lunch break, six days a week, at less than the minimum wage.
- In Miami the Labor Department last December fined Burger King $500,000—the largest child labor penalty in history—for letting 14- and 15-year-olds work late into the night on school days. The Fair Labor Standards Act of 1938 prohibits kids that age from being on the job later than 7 p.m.

Over the past ten years, U.S. government statistics show a marked rise in child labor violations. In 1992 the Labor Department logged 19,443 such offenses, about twice the 1980 level. Most involved kids working too late on school nights in grocery stores and fast-food restaurants or using hazardous equipment like meat saws and slicers.

Why is this problem growing again? Peter Rachleff, an associate pro-fessor at Minnesota's Macalester College and a specialist in the history of child labor, links its reappearance to "the overall deterioration of

continued on next page

working-class life in America." More middle-class families, feeling the jobs pinch, are encouraging their kids to work to supplement family income. Child labor also tends to increase during periods of heavy immigration. In the past decade the number of immigrants—both legal and illegal—has surged. To scrape by, many ask even very young children to help out. Says New York State labor commissioner John Hudacs: "Whenever you have immigrants who don't speak the language and need to make ends meet, employers will take advantage of them."

Child labor laws rarely are enforced. In 1980 the U.S. Labor Department had 1,059 investigators. Today, after several budget cuts, it deploys only 833 agents to enforce not only the child labor laws but a dozen other major regulations, among them minimum wage laws. According to the National Safe Workplace Institute, a Chicago nonprofit group funded by foundations and corporations, a business can expect a visit by a federal labor inspector once every 50 years.

Source: "Illegal Child Labor Comes Back," Brian Dumaine, *Fortune*, April 5, 1993, ©1993 Time Inc. All rights reserved.

THE OCCUPATIONAL SAFETY AND HEALTH ACT

The Occupational Safety and Health Act was passed to provide a safer, more healthful workplace for American workers. To administer the law, the statute created the Occupational Safety and Health Administration (OSHA) within the U.S. Department of Labor.

Among other things, OSHA conducts research on health and safety issues, sets regulatory standards for worker safety, inspects workplaces to determine whether there are regulatory violations, and adju-dicates conflicts over citations and abatement orders issued for the law's violations. Standards of safety are set by the National Institute for Occupational Safety and Health (NIOSH)—established by the act as the research arm of OSHA. See Box 11–7, "OSHA Targets Injury from Repeated Motion," on page 336, which gives an example of a problem OSHA tackled recently.

Under the general-duty clause of the law, employers must adhere to the compliance requirements for safety and health standards and furnish a workplace "free from recognized hazards that are causing or are likely to cause death or serious physical harm." The law includes

11–6   LAW IN THE REAL WORLD

The Supply Police

Companies that make tools and building materials usually love to take orders from Home Depot. But in March 1993 the Atlanta retailer demanded more from its 300 foreign suppliers than the customary shipments of wrenches and lumber. A new questionnaire asked whether any factory in Home Depot's worldwide supply chain employs children or prison convicts. Lest suppliers think the company isn't dead serious about disreputable business practices, Home Depot added an ultimatum: you have 72 hours to respond.

Home Depot desperately wants to avoid a new strain of public relations disaster. The Christmas-week 1992 NBC show asserting that Wal-Mart's "Buy American" program misleads consumers also leveled a more sinister charge: that children as young as 9 churn out clothes for the nation's largest retailer in Bangladeshi sweatshops. Other big-name U.S. importers aren't waiting to see whether the public buys Wal-Mart's denials. Instead they're making sure their own suppliers are free of environmental, human-rights, or other potential embarrassments.

Source: From *Newsweek*, February 15, 1993, Newsweek Inc. All rights reserved. Reprinted by permission.

an antiretaliation provision to protect from detrimental repercussions by the employer any employees who report suspected violations.

OSHA inspectors are authorized to make unannounced visits for inspection of workplace premises. Of course, the visits are unannounced so that the inspectors will be able to see the premises as they actually are. Anyone found to have provided notice of the inspection beforehand can be fined up to $1000. The inspector generally arrives at the site, inspects the premises, and then discusses findings with the employer.

Among other things, OSHA requires employers to provide continual safety training for employees, adequate ventilation and exit in case of an emergency, and medical examination if an employee is exposed to hazardous or toxic chemicals. If violations are found, penalties can range up to more than $10,000 and criminal sanctions, depending on the nature of the offense. Violations found to be willful or repeated carry stiffer penalties.

11–7   LAW IN THE REAL WORLD

OSHA Targets Injury from Repeated Motion

Making workers safer from repetitive stress injuries is a top goal of Joseph Dear, new head of the Occupational Safety and Health Administration [OSHA].

It's a timely goal, because repetitive stress injuries [RSI] are skyrocketing. In 1983, only 27,000 cases of RSI were reported. By 1991, the latest count available, casualties had zoomed to 224,000: 60% of the year's job-related injuries and illnesses.

Under Dear, who took office this month, OSHA is to write broad rules telling U.S. employers how to protect workers. Repetitive stress injuries such as carpal syndrome or tennis elbow can hit those in jobs ranging from data entry to meat packing.

The proposed rules are due in 10 months. Dear says he will push to get them made final as soon as possible.

The rules should "help employers to avoid one of the fastest-rising components of workers' compensation (insurance) costs," Dear says. "You decrease pain and increase performance" in the workplace.

Behind the rise in RSI: More people bang away all day at computer keyboards. Factories speed up production lines. And doctors are getting better at spotting repetitive stress injuries, Dear says.

A team including engineers and doctors will work on the rules. Current thinking is that proper posture, frequent breaks, and switching tasks help avoid RSI. RSI can keep workers off the job from a few days to months. Severe cases call for surgery.

Source: "OSHA Targets Injury from Repeated Motion," by Dale Dallabrida, November 23, 1993. ©1993, *USA Today*. Reprinted with permission.

A hazard may be a recognized one either because the employer actually knows of it through past safety practices indicating the employer knew of the hazard, or because it is so obvious that anyone would know, or through constructive knowledge by way of industry standards such as OSHA regulation about a particular hazard. Employees who reasonably believe that their employer has violated the general-duty clause and the result will be serious injury or death and that there is no less drastic way of avoiding the hazard can rightfully refuse to work or perform a particular hazardous task.

If Ann and Bill do all that is possible to avoid a hazard and an employee disregards them and is injured, Bill and Ann will not be liable. Of course, it is much less likely that they will be held liable if they have a satisfactory safety program in place, as opposed to an employer who does not.

WORKERS' COMPENSATION

It is a fact of life that no matter how careful Ann and Bill are in providing a safe and healthful workplace, employees will probably be injured on the job. There was a time when compensation for on-the-job injury was realized only through either the employer's compensating the employee of its own volition or the employee's suing the employer. The former was rare, and the latter usually resulted in the employee's being terminated and having to incur the expense and time-consuming litigation at a time when money was least likely to be available.

Further, in fighting an employer in the courts, an employee was faced with a formidable foe who generally had more resources and power. Even if employees could afford the expensive and time-consuming avenue of litigation, they were subject to the employer's defenses, which could avoid legal liability for the injury. See Box 11–8, "Common Law Employer Defenses," to learn what the defenses are.

Of course the employer could always also defend by asserting that the situation did not occur in the way the employee asserts it did. For instance, the employer could claim the injury was caused by a fight off the premises and involving a private matter, rather than being a work-related injury for which the employer may be liable.

Workers' compensation statutes were enacted to redress that state of affairs. Under the statutes, employers pay into a fund that serves as a basis for any claims filed for injuries "arising out of and in the course of employment" on a no-fault basis. After the workers' compensation statutes came into existence, common law defenses were no longer effective for the most part. The workers' compensation laws are no-fault. That is, the only thing that matters is that the injury was accidental and arose out of or in the course of employment. If it did, the claim is compensable and the employer has no defense. In those jurisdictions that allow an employee to choose to claim workers' compensation or sue the employer, the defenses may still be used. The law does not include intentionally self-inflicted injuries or those caused by

11–8 LEGAL EXCERPTS

Common Law Employer Defenses

The common law defenses that can be used by an employer to combat claims brought by an employee include:

- The **fellow servant doctrine** in which the employer argues that the accident was not caused by the employer's negligence, but rather by another employee

- **Contributory negligence**, in which the employer argues that the employee's accident was caused by the employee's own failure to meet an appropriate standard of care

- **Assumption of the risk**, in which the employer asserts that the employee knew a risk was present in the situation and acted anyway—and as it turns out, did so to his or her detriment

personal, nonwork circumstances. The fund can either be financed by insurance or be self-insured, depending on state law.

Employees injured on the job who choose to file workers' compensation claims are paid for their injuries according to a schedule of payments that determines the length of payment and the amount of payment for the particular injury. Workers' compensation statutes also have provisions for permanent injuries, death, rehabilitation, and medical and survivor benefits.

In exchange for the security of immediate and guaranteed payment, the employee generally gives up the right to sue Ann and Bill in a civil suit for a larger amount. In exchange for the money paid out, Ann and Bill have the relative security of claim payments of a somewhat predictable amount.

If the injury is caused by a third party rather than by the employer or employee (e.g., the manufacturer of a defective machine that injures the employee), the employee may be able to sue the manufacturer, but the workers' compensation benefit will be reduced by the amount of the compensation. The purpose of the law is to compensate employees for an injury, not allow them a windfall because of it.

It is in an employer's best interest to try to keep down the cost of workers' compensation claims by ensuring that only those employees legitimately injured on the job file claims and that the workplace be as safe as possible to prevent or lessen accidents. Although it is against the law for an employer to retaliate against an employee filing a workers' compensation claim, in an effort to thwart workers' compensation fraud, employers are more and more frequently using claims services that report to employers the number and nature of injuries for which a job applicant has filed workers' compensation claims. Box 11–9, "Workers' Comp Reform: Who's Getting Squeezed?" discusses some of the various interests to be protected in the workers' compensation arena.

The issue of whether a claim arises out of and in the course of employment is constantly litigated: Is an accident considered to be in the course of business if an employee is on the way to or from work? At a work party? On a yearly nonmandatory fishing trip sponsored by the employer? If an employee dies while having sex on the job in a closet? If an employee is raped while being taken home by another employee as per the owner's request? If an employee has an accident on the way from taking the employer's wife home at the employer's request? If the employee is a nurse who steps out of a hospital room, hears the shots of a murder-suicide while closing the door, and becomes stressed out and nervous? If, during an intermission, an orchestra violinist is taken to the playhouse rooftop and murdered by one of the playhouse staff?

All of these have been the subject of cases brought by employees. They may seem bizarre, but to, for instance, the surviving spouse and children of the employee who died while having sex at work, whether the death arose out of and in the course of employment meant the difference between whether or not they collected surviving spouse and children benefits.

Additional questions arise about virtually all aspects of collecting benefits. For instance, would it be a part of rehabilitation benefits for an employee to have bills paid so that the employee's condition is no longer exacerbated by the stress related to financial burden? That, too, is an actual case. See whether you agree that the following case arose out of or in the course of employment.

The recent surge in sexual harassment cases has also affected the workers' compensation area. Because sexual harassment is a workplace violation, claims for workers' compensation for sexual harassment were bound to arise. Look at the case on page 341 and see if you think it is within the spirit of the law.

11-9   LAW IN THE REAL WORLD

Workers' Comp Reform: Who's Getting Squeezed?

In November of 1993, the Florida legislature convened a one-week, special session for the express purpose of overhauling the state's workers' compensation system. Companies in the Sunshine State had seen their premium rates triple since 1979. Democratic Gov. Lawton Chiles had promised business leaders he would fight for a reduction of at least 20%.

The legislators produced a bill in five days, but Chiles threatened to veto it, saying it saved too little money and made too many concessions to special interests. The result was a rewritten version that represented a huge victory for both Chiles and business lobbyists, who praised the governor for his tenacity.

Labor leaders, on the other hand, were furious at the cost-containment provisions, which slashed temporary disability payments from 260 weeks to 104, and they vowed to seek changes in the 1994 session. Nor did the reforms please trial lawyers, whose fee schedules were reduced by 5%.

That is about the way it has gone all over the country lately, as state after state rewrites the rules on workers' comp. Business is a winner. So, to a great extent, is the insurance industry, which claims that for every dollar it collects in workers' compensation premiums, it pays out $1.21.

But labor is a loser in most places, and so are those who have benefited from the relative generosity of workers' comp programs in the past: trial lawyers, doctors, pharmacists, chiropractors, and others who live in the Byzantine workers' comp world. If protections for workers were the paramount concern a few years ago, "in the last year or two the pendulum has swung," says John Burton, a labor management specialist at Rutgers University. "Employers and insurers have dominated the reform effort."

The changes are being driven by harsh economic realities: longtime employers threatening to relocate to cheaper locales, and new businesses deciding not to set up shop at all.

Source: "Worker's Comp Reform: Who's Getting Squeezed?" by Nadine Cohodas, January 1994 *Governing*. Reprinted with permission. *Governing* magazine, ©1994.

BELUE V. PREWETT MILLS DISTRIBUTION CENTER

581 So. 2d 850 (Ala. Civ. App. 1990)

An 18-year-old employee filed for workers' compensation benefits for injuries resulting in her becoming a permanent paraplegic. The injuries had arisen from a car accident she was involved in while on the way home from taking her supervisor's wife home from work. The court permitted recovery.

Ingram, J.: The dispositive issue is whether the employee's accident arose out of and in the course of her employment. Employee, an 18-year-old high school graduate, had been working for her employer pairing socks and turning down the tops for approximately one month prior to the accident. She was trained at her job by Denise Thurman, the wife of the employee's supervisor (Steve Thurman).

On the day of the accident, the employee was working an extra hour and was due to clock out at 11 p.m. Also, Steve, her supervisor, was going to work beyond 11 p.m. The employee drove Denise home and, upon leaving Denise's house, was involved in an accident that rendered the employee a permanent paraplegic.

As a general rule, accidents that occur while the employee is traveling to and from work are not considered "arising out of and in the course of employment." An injury arises in the course of employment when it occurs within the period of employment, at a place where one may reasonably be and while one is reasonably fulfilling the duties of employment or engaged in some incident to it.

Here, the employee contends that her supervisor asked her to take his wife home and because of the mean way he treated employees she believed it was her responsibility to take the supervisor's wife home and that if she did not, she would not have a job. The evidence also reveals that the employee had to go out of her way on an unfamiliar road to take Denise home.

The conclusion to be drawn from this testimony is that the employee believed that she was required as part of her job to take the supervisor's wife home. Therefore, it appears to us that the only reasonable view of the evidence requires a finding that the employee's

continued on next page

injuries arose out of and in the course of her employment. This is especially true in view of the fact that the workmen's compensation act is intended to serve a beneficent purpose and is to be liberally construed so as to effectuate its purpose and humane design. REVERSED and REMANDED

Case Questions

1. Does this decision seem fair to you? Why or why not?

2. What lesson would you take from this decision if you were a manager or supervisor?

3. Do you think the claimant's age was a factor in the court's deciding in her favor? Explain.

THE RAMADA INN SURFSIDE AND ADJUSTCO INC. V. SWANSON

560 So. 2d 300 (Ct. App. Fl., 1st Dist 1990)

Employee received workers' compensation benefits for treatment for her psychiatric condition related to sexual harassment on the job. The employer argued that the claim should not have been allowed because her emotional problems were not caused by the sexual intercourse with her supervisor. The compensation was allowed to stand.

Joanos, J.: Employee testified that she was working in the Ramada Inn lounge when Mr. Schonsheck told her he was going to view another hotel property as a possible business investment and that she should meet him there to look over the property. At his request she accompanied him to inspect one of the guest rooms, and the sexual intercourse employee claims occurred. Mr. Schonsheck denies it took place.

Various witnesses testified that after the date of the intercourse, the employee became very tense and nervous and began drinking on the job. In a three-month period, employee was hospitalized on three separate occasions for psychiatric treatment. Dr. Handel, her treating psychiatrist, diagnosed her condition as a severe major depressive disorder and adjustment disorder.

Florida statutes expressly proscribe workers' compensation benefits for a mental injury due to fright or excitement only. Severe work-related emotional disorders may be compensable when it is shown that the emotional disorder was occasioned by actual physical impact or trauma at the workplace.

We reject the employer's contention that employee's emotional condition and attendant hospitalization were caused by factors unrelated to the workplace sexual encounter. Dr. Handel, the employee's treating psychiatrist, found that her emotional problems and three hospitalizations were caused primarily by the sexual contact with Mr. Schonsheck, within a reasonable degree of psychiatric probability.

Benefits are available under the Workers' Compensation Act for "injuries arising out of and in the course of employment." For an injury to arise out of and in the course of employment, "it must occur within

continued on next page

the period of employment, at a place where the employee may reasonably be and while reasonably fulfilling the duties of employment or engaging in something incidental to it." In other words, "[t]o be compensable, an injury must arise out of employment in the sense of causation and be in the course of employment in the sense of continuity of time, space, and circumstances."

The record in the instant case reflects that the sexual encounter between claimant and her supervisor arose out of and occurred during her employment as lounge supervisor of Ramada Inn Surfside. First, the episode occurred during the period of employment, in that it happened during claimant's normal work hours. Second, the incident happened at the hotel where claimant's supervisor directed her to go. Finally, the incident transpired while claimant was reasonably fulfilling the duties of her employment, in the sense that she purportedly was to assist her supervisor in the evaluation of a hotel property for possible investment purposes. For the foregoing reasons, we AFFIRM.

Case Questions

1. Do you agree with the court's decision? Why or why not?
2. What should the employer have done to avoid liability here?

THE FAMILY AND MEDICAL LEAVE ACT (FMLA)

The FMLA, which provides guaranteed job security for those who take leave for family and medical reasons for a specified time, did not become law without a fight. Twice vetoed by President George Bush, it was the first piece of legislation signed into law by incoming President Bill Clinton after his inauguration in January 1993. The law became effective August 5, 1993.

The FMLA requires that if Bill and Ann have 50 or more employees, they must grant up to 12 weeks of unpaid leave per year to qualified employees for a serious illness of the employee or of the employee's spouse, child, or parents, or for the birth or adoption of a child. Further, employees' health care benefits must be maintained during the absence, and upon return, employees are guaranteed the same or equivalent job as they had before leaving.

Employees must have worked for the employer for at least 12 months and at least 1,250 hours during the year preceding start of the leave. Employers can exempt 10% of their highest-paid employees and need not allow leave for employees in regions with fewer than 50 employees located in a 75-mile radius. Employers can require medical confirmation of an illness. The U.S. Department of Labor regulations define such illness as an illness requiring at least one night of hospitalization.

Employees requesting leave under the law must give Ann and Bill at least 30 days' advance notice for foreseeable leave—otherwise, as soon as is practicable (within a day or two of finding out the need for leave, except in extraordinary cases). Bill and Ann may count FMLA time off against paid vacation time (therefore the leave will be paid, but vacation time lost), and unless Bill and Ann agree otherwise, leave for birth or adoption must be taken all at once. Intermittent or reduced work schedule leave is permitted when medically necessary. Complaints may be made to the U.S. Department of Labor or by private lawsuits.

 As Box 11–10, "The Family Leave Act: Who Benefits?" demonstrates, during the law's proposal, it had many detractors. Those who opposed it fell into two camps. On one hand were those who saw it as a burden on the employer (especially small businesses) and further intrusion into the life of a business owner by the government. They felt that the law preempted an employer's right to offer other work-

11–10 LAW IN THE REAL WORLD

The Family Leave Act—Who Benefits?

Though an estimated 40–50 million workers are now eligible for 12 weeks of leave annually, it's possible that few will take advantage because most cannot afford to. The operative words in the law are "unpaid leave." Some of its opponents have even dubbed it simply the "yuppie relief" act.

"The reason that it might not be well used is that a lot of people live from paycheck to paycheck, and so not getting paid while on leave is not an option for everyone," said Lina Cramer, who recently worked on family issues for the Chicago-based Family Resource Coalition. "If people can't afford it, the choice is not so much of a choice." Others disagree, especially because the new law ensures that important health benefits stay in place during the leave and workers are assured their original or "similar" jobs when they return.

"I think it's going to make a difference very quickly, because knowing you have a job to come back to heightens morale and improves one's ability to produce," said Judith Lichtman, president of the Women's Legal Defense Fund in Washington, D.C.

Research has shown that companies also benefit when some form of family leave is in effect. A study at Johnson & Johnson revealed that employee absenteeism was 50% lower for people who used available family-oriented plans, including flexible hours, child care subsidies, and family leave. At AT&T another study found that the average cost of letting parents off on unpaid leave for one year was slightly more than 30% of an employee's salary compared with the 150% of salary it would cost to replace that employee with a new worker. As far back as 1988, International Business Machines Corp. even offered its workers a generous unpaid leave of up to three years.

But the proof of the new law will be in its use. With only state laws and some corporate policies to go on, some studies indicate that for a variety of reasons, few have taken advantage of leave benefits. A 1991 study from the New York–based Families and Work Institute that looked at some state family leave regulations already in place showed that the percentage of those employees taking leave did not increase after the new laws were in place and fewer still took off the whole time allowed.

Source: "The Family Leave Act: Who Benefits?" by Kara Swisher, *Ms.*, September/October 1993, p. 90. Reprinted by permission of Ms. magazine, ©1993.

place benefits that workers might prefer, such as on-site child or elder care, flexible work hours, better health coverage, and tuition reimbursement programs.

On the other hand were those who opposed it because they did not feel it went far enough. They felt that passing the legislation gave the impression that everything had been taken care of in this sphere, and nothing more need be done. They understood that the law's requirement of unpaid leave meant the law applied only to relatively few employees: those able to take advantage of unpaid leaves of absence. By limiting coverage to employers with 50 or more employees, the law applies only to about 5% of companies and 50–60% of employees. Those in this camp also argued that virtually every other industrialized country offers paid leave under the circumstances set out in the law.

Bill and Ann might be interested to know that despite this, many companies that already have comparable leave policies and think highly of them say that such policies build morale and company loyalty, improve productivity, and decrease absenteeism and turnover. The Small Business Administration and the General Accounting Office (GAO) reported that it costs more to lose an employee permanently than to grant unpaid leaves when needed. The GAO estimated that the new law would cost employers about $5 per employee per year. Employers in states with comparable laws already on their books said they were pleasantly surprised that it had cost them less than expected—and, in fact, little—to have such laws.

There is sufficient limitation in the law to prevent employees from trying to take advantage of an employer. An employer can require appropriate verification of the reason for the leave, and it need not grant it in the absence of verification.

LABOR LAW

If Ann and Bill's employees wish to organize and bargain collectively, they have the right to do so. At one point in U.S. history, it was illegal for employees to work together in concert to gain workplace benefits. You can imagine how repressive this was in light of the advantage many employers took of isolated employees virtually at their mercy. In 1932, in recognition of the toll that increasing labor unrest was levying on interstate commerce, Congress enacted legislation that led the way to organized labor in the United States. In 1953 the percentage of unionized employees was at the all-time high of just under 27%. That percentage has steadily decreased since the 1970s. In 1990, about 13% of the workforce was unionized.

The losses can be blamed in part on factors such as reduction in the labor force of traditionally heavily unionized industries like steel manufacturing, international competition, aggressive nonunionizing campaigns by employers, union concessions during downturns in the economy, and loss of jobs to other countries with cheaper labor, such as Mexico's *maquilladoros.*

There are four main federal laws that form the statutory basis for labor law and unionization. The legislation initiating a move toward collective bargaining in the United States began with restricting court responses to union activity (usually courts enjoined the activity) and establishing the right of employees to form labor organizations and be protected against unfair labor practices by employers. Later legislation prohibited employee unfair labor practices and provided union members with a bill of rights to protect them from union abuses. Box 11–11, "Not with My Money You Don't," discusses how a Hollywood television production was affected by union organizing efforts.

THE NORRIS-LAGUARDIA ACT

The Norris-LaGuardia Act was the first major U.S. labor law statute. When it was illegal for employees to engage in concerted activities like strikes against the employer, courts issued injunctions prohibiting them from continuing such activity. The Norris-LaGuardia Act restricted the right of courts to issue such injunctions.

yellow dog contract
agreements that an employer required from employees promising that the employees did not belong to a union and would not join one while in the owner's employ

The Act also outlawed **yellow dog contracts**, required by many employers, in which employees said that they did not belong to a union and would not join one while employed by the employer. When the Norris-LaGuardia Act removed these two important obstacles to labor's engaging in concerted activity, the way was paved for the National Labor Relations Act.

THE WAGNER, OR NATIONAL LABOR RELATIONS, ACT

This law established the right of employees to form unions, to bargain collectively, and to strike. It also prohibited unfair labor practices and

11–11   LAW IN THE REAL WORLD

Not with My Money You Don't

Earlier this year, Love and War Productions Inc., which Diane English, creator of the wisecracking, Quayle-bashing television character Murphy Brown owns with her husband, Joel Shukovsky, began shooting the pilot for her new show, *Love & War.* A Hollywood craft union, the International Alliance of Theatrical Stage Employees [IATSE], tried to organize some 30 of the show's production people—modestly paid camera operators, sound technicians, makeup workers and such, making maybe $800 a week and up.

Among other things, a union contract would provide health and pension benefits, which Love and War Productions was not offering at the time, according to the union, at a cost of roughly $2 extra an hour. English and Shukovsky summarily replaced the workers. "We had to protect our ability to produce the show," says John Drinkwater, executive vice president and general counsel at Love and War Productions.

Isn't replacing workers during an organizing drive illegal? The IATSE's spokesperson, John Doering, thinks it is. A representative for some of the former crew members filed a charge with the National Labor Relations Board [NLRB], claiming the production company engaged in unfair labor practices. The NLRB is investigating. Meanwhile, *Love & War* is being produced by a nonunion crew.

At the other end of Hollywood's pay scale, English's firm gets an estimated $100,000 per episode—$2.2 million a year—in production fees for *Love & War.* Even in Hollywood, this payout is high. Normal fees for high-end writer-producers range from $50,000 to $75,000 per episode.

English's class consciousness seems to expand the further she gets from blue-collar technical types and the closer she gets to writers, actors, and directors represented by the Directors Guild of America, Writers Guild of America, and Screen Actors Guild. These so-called above-the-line employees account for a production's biggest expenses. Wage costs of technicians like those replaced by English have gone up 4% on average annually since 1989, according to Doering, while nonwage costs for these people dropped 20%. In the same period, rates paid to the most successful writers and directors (who can command above union scale) have escalated an estimated 40%–50%.

Source: "Not with My Money You Don't," by Gretchen Morgenson, *Forbes,* November 23, 1992. Reprinted by permission of *Forbes* magazine. ©Forbes, Inc., 1992.

craft union
a union organized around a specific craft, detached from the particular workplace

industrial union
a union organized around particular jobs at a workplace

business agent
the one who represents the unions to the employer

community of interests
employees who perform similar jobs at the workplace and have similar bargaining issues

bargaining unit
a group of employees with a community of interests who form a unit for bargaining purposes

mandatory subjects of bargaining
wages, hours, and other terms and conditions of employment about which an employer must bargain

permissive subjects of bargaining
nonmandatory terms about which management may bargain with the union

created the National Labor Relations Board (NLRB)—the independent federal agency that enforces labor laws. Among other things, the NLRB conducts elections among employees to determine which union is to represent them, decertifies unions that employees no longer want to represent them, issues labor regulations, hears unfair labor practice complaints at the agency level, and otherwise administers the NLRA.

Employees may unionize either by signing a sufficient number of authorization cards, by voting in a union during a representation election, or, in some cases, by the NLRB's ordering an employer to bargain with a union. Unions are composed of nonsupervisory or nonmanagerial employees, including part-time workers. Specifically excluded are agricultural and domestic workers, independent contractors, and those employed by a spouse or parent.

Employees with a **community of interests**, that is, similar workplace concerns and conditions, come together as a **bargaining unit** the union will represent. The community of interest is based on factors such as similarity of the jobs the employees perform and similar training or skills. Generally, there must be at least two employees in a bargaining unit, but an employer may agree to a one-person unit if necessary—for instance, an on-site carpenter who belongs to a carpenter's union being employed at a work site as the only carpenter.

Unions may be **industrial unions** or **craft unions**. Industrial unions are composed of the employees of a workplace who perform like jobs. They may be part of a larger union network of the same types of employees at other workplaces. Craft unions are not connected to a particular workplace. The **business agent** of the craft union (e.g., carpenters) represents the union craft worker's interest at a given job site. Employers often contact a craft union when they need the type of employees represented by that union.

Good-Faith Bargaining

To prevent management from unilaterally implementing workplace policies that closely affect employees, the NLRA requires employers to bargain in good faith with union representatives over the **mandatory subjects of bargaining** of wages, hours, and other terms and conditions of employment. Employers may also bargain over **permissive subjects** of bargaining, but only a refusal to bargain about mandatory subjects of bargaining may form the basis of an unfair labor practice.

Bargaining in good faith means that the parties act in a responsible, businesslike manner regarding the bargaining process. They must provide necessary information to support their proposals, must attend meetings, and must conduct themselves as if they are engaged in the serious business of bargaining. Bargaining in good faith does not mean that one party must agree to the other's proposal, but only that the parties must seriously negotiate. It would not be bargaining in good faith if a party continually missed negotiation meetings or refused a proposal without seriously considering it or offering any alternatives. If the parties do not reach an agreement, the union may exercise pressure tactics like strikes to try to get management to change its mind.

Duty of Fair Representation

The NLRA imposes on unions the duty of fair representation. The duty of fair representation is not defined in the NLRA and is often used as a catch-all category for grievances against the union. It is clear that as the employees' bargaining representative, the union must fairly represent all members of the bargaining unit, whether or not the unit members belong to the union. Those employees who do not believe their interests have been represented fairly can pursue the matter through an unfair labor practice against the union, alleging a failure of the union in its duty of fair representation.

Collective Bargaining Agreements

If negotiations go well, the end product of the negotiations between management and labor will be a **collective bargaining agreement** for a specified period. There is no set form that such an agreement must take, and it may be any length and contain any provisions agreed to by the parties. Job and union security constitute the main issue for employees; freedom from labor strife such as strikes, slowdowns, and work stoppages is paramount for employers. The agreement also contains provisions regarding strikes, arbitration of labor disputes, seniority, benefits, employment classifications, and so on. Box 11–12, "Selected Collective Bargaining Agreement Clauses," mentions several clauses routinely included in collective bargaining agreements.

collective bargaining agreement
the agreement reached between the employer and the union

11-12   LEGAL EXCERPTS

Selected Collective Bargaining Agreement Clauses

wages—including cost-of-living increases, production increases, learners and apprentices, overtime

benefits—including vacations, sick pay, holidays, insurance

hours—including overtime and determinations as to assignment

seniority—setting forth how employee seniority is determined and used

management security—in which employers may make their own decisions as to how to run the business as long as the decisions are not contrary to the collective bargaining agreement or the law

union security—the union's legal right to exist and to represent the employees involved

job security—how employees will maintain employment, including procedures for layoffs, downsizing, worksharing, etc.

dues checkoff—right of a union to have the employer deduct union dues directly from employees' wages and turn them over to the union rather than have the union try to collect them from members after they get their paychecks.

union shop—requires that all employees join the union within a certain time of coming into the bargaining unit

modified union shop—requires that new employees join the union after an agreement becomes effective, as must any employees who were already union members, but those already working who were not union members and do not wish to join need not do so

maintenance of membership—employees who voluntarily join a union may leave only during a short window period prior to agreement expiration

agency shop—requires that employees of the bargaining unit pay union dues whether union members or not

grievances—sets forth the basis for grievances regarding conflicts over the meaning of the collective bargaining agreement and procedures for addressing them

exclusive representation—the union representative will be the only party who can negotiate with the employer for matters affecting bargaining unit employees

arbitration—that matters that cannot be otherwise resolved will be submitted to arbitration to be resolved by a neutral third party, whose decision is usually binding

midterm negotiations—permits agreed-upon topics to be reopened to negotiation prior to contract expiration

no-strike, no lockout—parties agree that employees either will not strike or will do so only under limited circumstances and employers will not engage in lockouts. Instead, the grievance procedure will be used to handle labor disputes.

Unfair Labor Practices

Activities that would tend to attempt to control or influence the union or interfere with its affairs or that discriminate against employees who join or assist unions may also be **unfair labor practices**. Actual interference by an employer need not be proved in order for it to be considered an unfair labor practice. Rather, the question is whether the activity tends to interfere with, restrain, or coerce employees who are exercising rights protected under the law. Management may not

unfair labor practices
the grounds on which action is brought by labor or management alleging the other party violated the NLRA

11–13 LEGAL EXCERPTS

Management Unfair Labor Practices

- Trying to control the union or interfering with union affairs such as trying to help a certain candidate get elected to a union office
- Discriminating against employees who join a union or are in favor of bringing in a union or who exercise their rights under the law (e.g., terminating, demoting, or giving unfavorable working schedules to such employees)
- Interfering with, coercing, or restraining employees exercising their rights under labor law legislation (e.g., telling employees they cannot have a union or they will be terminated if they do)
- Refusal to bargain or to refusal to bargain in good faith

ELECTROMATION INC. V. NLRB
35 F.3d 1148 (7th Cir. 1994)

In response to employee workplace complaints, Electromation management set up five action committees, which were to meet and try to come up with solutions. Eventually, an unfair labor practice charge was filed claiming that the committees violated the NLRA's prohibition on domination or interference with employees' right to form a labor organization. The court agreed and held for the employees.

Will, J.: To minimize the financial losses it was experiencing at the time, Eletromation decided to cut expenses by revising its employee attendance policy and replacing the next year's scheduled wage increases with lump sum payments based on the length of each employee's service at the company. Electromation informed its approximately 200, mostly female, nonunion employees of these changes at its 1988 Christmas party.

In January 1989, the company received a handwritten request signed by 68 employees expressing their dissatisfaction with and requesting reconsideration of the revised attendance bonus/wage policy. After meeting with the company's supervisors, the company president decided to meet directly with six randomly selected employees at different levels of employment and two other employees who requested to attend. Out of the meeting came complaints in 20–25 areas of concern, which were later distilled to five categories. The president then met with the same employees and proposed that they form action committees to "try [to] come up with ways to resolve these problems." He further proposed that if the solutions were within budget concerns and the [committees] generally felt the [solutions] would be acceptable to employees, the [committees] would implement the suggestions or proposals.

We find that substantial evidence supports the board's factual finding that the action committees were labor organizations within the meaning of the NLRA and that the employer dominated the labor organization. Section 2(5) of the act defines a labor organization as "any organization of any kind, or any agency or employee representation committee or plan, in which employees participate and which exists for the purpose, in whole or in part, of dealing with employers concerning grievances, labor disputes, wages, rates of pay, hours of employment, or conditions of work.

We believe that the determination of what is a labor organization under the act is a factual one to be made in consideration of the specific facts surrounding the formation, function, and administration of each employee involvement or participation organization. Here, the facts clearly warrant the board's conclusion that the action committees were labor organizations within the meaning of the act.

The U.S. Supreme Court has explained that domination of a labor organization exists when the employer controls the form and structure of a labor organization such that the employees are deprived of complete freedom and independence of action as guaranteed by Section 7 of the act and that the principal distinction between an independent labor organization and an employer-dominated one lies in the unfettered power of the independent organization to determine its own action. The Electromation committees, which were created wholly by the employer and whose functions were essentially determined by the employer, lacked the independence of action and free choice guaranteed by Section 7.

This is not to suggest that management was antiunion or had devious intentions in proposing the creation of the committees. But even assuming [the committees] acted from good intentions, their procedure in establishing the committees without employee input, their control of the subject matters to be considered or excluded (chosen without employee input), their membership and participation on the committees, and their financial support of the committees by providing paid time for meetings, meeting places, pencils, paper, phones, [and so forth], all combine to make the committees labor organizations dominated by the employer in violation of the act.

In an effort to succeed in an increasingly competitive global marketplace, many U.S. companies have developed employee involvement structures [that] encourage employee participation in the design of workplace policies and procedures to improve the efficiency and effectiveness of the corporate organization and to create a workplace environment [that] is satisfactory to employees. We recognize the growing importance of such employee involvement organizations. In fact, we applaud the application of such employee participation structures in

continued on next page

appropriate situations. Because the board found no basis to conclude that the purposes of the action committees were limited to achieving increased productivity, quality, or efficiency or that they were designed to function solely as communication devices to promote generally the interests of quality or efficiency, it did not reach the question of whether employer-initiated programs that exist for such purposes may constitute labor organizations [that] violate Sections 8(a) (2) and (1). Accordingly, we AFFIRM the board's findings and ENFORCE the board's order.

Case Questions

1. Do you agree with the court's decision? Explain.

2. What impact do you think the *Electromation* decision had on employers wanting or permitting work concern groups to operate in the workplace?

3. What do you think the employer here could have done differently to avoid being found to have committed an unfair labor practice?

Management may not promise or give benefits or, in the alternative, reduce benefits, in an effort to discourage unionizing efforts; such is an unfair labor practice. Box 11–13, "Management Unfair Labor Practices," on page 353 outlines others.

The NLRB and the courts take seriously any interference with the right of employees to organize and bargain collectively without the interference or pressure of management. In the *Electromation* case, the court surprised many by agreeing with the NLRB that the "workplace action committees" formed at nonunion Electromation Inc. violated the NLRA.

Legitimate strikes may be called by the union either for economic reasons or because of unfair labor practices. If employees strike for legally recognized reasons, their actions are protected under the NLRA and they retain their status as employees. Strikes that are not authorized by the union are called **wildcat strikes** and are illegal if they force the employer to deal with the employees rather than the union or impose the will of the minority rather than the majority.

wildcat strike
a strike not authorized by the union

11-14   LEGAL EXCERPTS

Union Unfair Labor Practices

- Refusal to bargain or bargaining in bad faith (e.g., not attending bargaining sessions)
- Coercing or restraining employees in exercising their rights to join (or not join) a union: If the union and employer have a provision in their collective bargaining agreement that states that a nonunion member coming into the bargaining unit must join the union within a certain amount of time, then union members performing that activity does not represent a problem.
- Charging discriminatory or very high dues or entrance fees for admittance into the union
- Threatening, encouraging, or influencing employees to strike in an effort to pressure the employer to join an employer organization, or to get the employer to recognize an uncertified union, or to stop doing business with an employer because of the employer's not doing this.
- Influencing employers to discriminate against, or otherwise treat differently, employees who do not belong to the union or are denied union membership for some reason other than nonpayment of union dues or fees

Unauthorized strikes have been found not to be unlawful if they are merely to make a statement of some sort. Many collective bargaining agreements contain **no-strike, no-lockout clauses**, which either prohibit or limit the availability of such action and instead agree to use the grievance process to handle issues.

no-strike, no-lockout clause clause prohibiting or limiting employee strikes and employer lockouts

THE TAFT-HARTLEY ACT

The Taft-Hartley Act of 1947 was enacted as an amendment to the NLRA to curb excesses by unions. Unfair labor practices by unions include such activities as the union's refusing to bargain or refusing to do so in good faith, as mentioned previously; coercing employees to join unions (or not join, as the case may be); and charging members discriminatory dues and entrance fees. Box 11–14, "Union Unfair Labor Practices," tells of other such violations.

11-15   LEGAL EXCERPTS

Union Members' Bill of Rights

Among other things, the law provides that
- union members have the right to attend union meetings, vote on union business, and nominate candidates for union elections;
- members may bring an agency or court action against the union after exhausting union procedures;
- certain procedures must be followed before any dues or initiation fee increases; and
- except for the failure to pay dues, members must have a full and fair hearing when being disciplined by the union.

THE LANDRUM-GRIFFIN ACT

The Landrum-Griffin Act, also called the Labor Management Reporting and Disclosure Act, was enacted to establish basic rules of union operation that would ensure a democratic process, provide union members with a minimum bill of rights attached to union membership, and regulate the activities of union officials and the use of union funds. The bill of rights was enacted in response to union abuses found during a two-year congressional investigation. The act set forth procedures unions must adhere to in union elections, including voting for officers by secret ballot, elections at least every three years (other frequencies for various levels of the union, such as international officers), candidates' being allowed to see lists of eligible voters, and provisions for members having an election. See Box 11–15, "Union Members' Bill of Rights," for other provisions of the law.

LABOR RELATIONS IN THE PUBLIC SECTOR

Much of what has been discussed relates to the private sector. Of more recent vintage is the matter of collective bargaining in the public sector. The NLRA applies only to the private sector. Federal, state, and local government employees (e.g., public employees) are governed by other laws. Federal employees are covered by the Civil Service Reform Act of 1978, which established the Federal Labor Relations Authority to administer federal-sector labor law. State and local employees are covered by their state's public employee relations statute, usually administered by a state public employees relations commission. Of course, because Ann and Bill's business is a private one, this would not be a concern for them.

The most significant differences between public and private collective bargaining is that government employees are generally not permitted to strike or to bargain over wages, hours, and benefits. The former prohibition is grounded in the need to protect public health and safety (i.e., police officers or firefighters out on strike and crime rising or buildings burning), as well as in the sovereignty doctrine that deems striking against a government employer as inconsistent with the federal government's being the highest authority.

SUMMARY

Employers like Ann and Bill must take into consideration several factors that are required by law to be incorporated into the employment relationship. Employees have the right to form and join unions, they may not be made to work for less than a certain minimum wage, and they must be paid time and a half if they work more than a certain number of hours in a given week. In addition, some employers must provide leave for qualified employees who need to take time off for family or medical reasons. Employers must also provide a safe and healthful workplace for their employees. Failure to do what is required by law has serious repercussions and should be avoided.

CHAPTER TERMS

bargaining unit	industrial union
business agent	mandatory subjects of bargaining
collective bargaining agreement	no-strike, no-lockout clause
community of interests	permissive subjects of bargaining
craft union	unfair labor practices
fellow servant doctrine	wildcat strike
industrial union	yellow dog contract

CHAPTER-END QUESTIONS

1. Dan's mother breaks her hip. Dan is an only child and his father is dead. Dan works as a prosecutor and is head of his division. Dan's wife, Deb, works at the state courthouse as a computer diagnostics engineer. Dan wants his mother cared for in his home, and due to the nature of their jobs, it is easier for Deb to take off from work than Dan. They decide that Deb will take off four months to care for Mom. Deb requests leave under the FMLA, and her supervisor rejects the leave request. Deb protests. Who is correct? Why?

2. Charmaine owns a large pharmaceutical manufacturing firm and is very successful in the market. When OSHA comes to perform an on-site visit, the inspectors find several violations for which Charmaine is heavily fined in penalties. When Charmaine discovers that the reason the inspectors came to visit was that they had been called by Michael, an employee in the mixing division, she becomes angry and fires Michael. Michael sues Charmaine and her firm for unjust dismissal. Who wins and why?

3. Branch is working at a mixing vat at Charmaine's pharmaceutical firm when he is injured by slipping on a puddle of oil left by the machine mechanic who had been working on the machine earlier. Branch is injured in the fall and files for workers' compensation. Charmaine protests, saying that she should not have to be responsible because the injury was not caused by her, but rather by another employee. Rule on Charmaine's argument.

4. There are 34 members in Clerical Workers Union #79. However, there are 35 members in the bargaining unit. One of the employees in the unit refuses to join the union. One day Sarafina, the nonunion employee, tells the shop steward that a supervisor has assigned her tasks not within her job description and which she is not required to do. Sarafina asks the steward to intercede on her behalf. The steward refuses, saying that because Sarafina is not a member of the union, she does not get the union's protection. Discuss.

5. Jones Sanitation workers are in an uproar. They have been told they must work ten-hour days during Christmas week because of the extra trash generated by the holiday. They will be working approximately ten hours a day for six days. The employees say they

cannot be required to work more than 40 hours a week, by law. Are they correct? Explain.

6. If a union wants to ensure that all employees join the union within a certain time after coming into the workplace, the union would request that its collective bargaining agreement include a _____ clause.

7. If management wants to ensure that it has the right to make its own decisions as to how to run the business, it would likely request that the collective bargaining agreement include a

   a. union security clause.
   b. maintenance-of-membership clause.
   c. management security clause.
   d. modified union shop clause.

8. During a unionization drive, management sends out to employees memos and flyers describing the evils of unionism. The flyers say that unions bring in and promote the idea of organized crime, that expenses of running a business go up when unions come to a workplace, and that there is often violence associated with unions. Is this an unfair labor practice? Explain.

9. Discuss some of the ways an employer can cut workers' compensation costs.

10. Management unilaterally removes the candy and soft drink machines from the employees' lunchroom and lounge areas. The union charges that this is an unfair labor practice in that management failed to bargain over the issue before removing the machines. Is it?

GROUP EXERCISE

For each of the areas of the chapter, have a group find out what is needed for someone starting up a business in the jurisdiction you are in. For instance, what would someone in your jurisdiction need to know about payment of minimum wages, workers' compensation, and OSHA? Each group should be responsible for finding out whom to contact to get the information and for getting needed information, including any applicable forms. Share the results with the class.

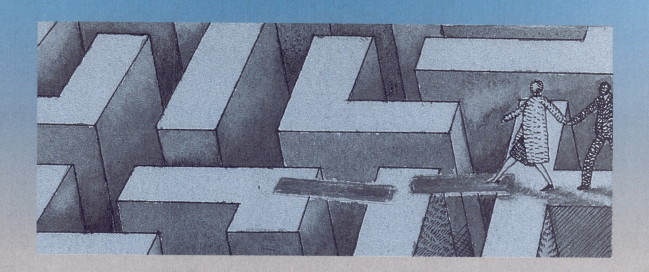

Chapter 12

DISCRIMINATION IN EMPLOYMENT

Chapter Preview Summary

In this chapter Ann and Bill learn about employment discrimination laws and the impact of those laws on employment. In addition, they learn how to avoid potential liability for violating such laws.

Chapter Objectives

In studying the chapter, you should learn:
- why there is a need for employment discrimination laws
- the requirements of Title VII of the Civil Rights Acts of 1964 and 1991
- the two theories of recovery under Title VII
- the five protected categories of Title VII
- the provisions of the Age Discrimination in Employment Act
- the provisions of the Americans with Disabilities Act
- the employer defenses of bona fide occupational qualification, business necessity, and legitimate nondiscriminatory reason
- what affirmative action is and is not

INTRODUCTION

When Bill and Ann employ 15 or more employees, hiring, firing, promotion, compensation, benefits, training, discipline, and other workplace decisions must be made in accordance with appropriate federal civil rights laws. Equivalent state fair employment practice laws may set the minimum number of employees limit even lower. Under such laws, for instance, Ann and Bill will not be able to refuse to hire qualified males as secretaries because they think it inappropriate for males to hold that position.

In this chapter we explore the different laws Ann and Bill must consider in making workplace decisions consistent with fair employment practices and equal employment opportunity law. We want to ensure that they will not make employment decisions that may later serve as the basis for costly, time-consuming, and embarrassing discrimination litigation. We will do so by making sure that Bill and Ann know what the law requires and how to avoid common pitfalls.

APPLICABLE LAWS

The single most important law Bill and Ann must understand is the Civil Rights Act of 1964, a federal law that prohibits employment discrimination in any way on the basis of race, color, gender, national origin, or religion. Gender discrimination includes discrimination on the basis of pregnancy, as well as sexual harassment. States and municipalities have comparable laws that may be called human rights laws, equal employment opportunity laws, or fair employment practice laws. State and municipal laws generally track federal law, but many expand coverage to include in their prohibitions other categories such as marital status, affinity orientation (homosexuality), receipt of public assistance benefits, and physical appearance.

With the passage of the Civil Rights Act of 1991, Title VII now permits jury trials as well as the recovery of compensatory and punitive damages for employment discrimination. Title VII originally limited damages to make-whole relief, including back pay, reinstatement, injunctions, and retroactive seniority and benefits. The Civil Rights Act of 1991 was hotly contested and in fact was vetoed by President George Bush before its eventual passage, because it sought to overturn by legislation several 1989 U.S. Supreme Court cases that were

12–1   LEGAL EXCERPTS

Civil Rights Act of 1991

The 1991 Civil Rights Act represented a major overhaul for Title VII. The law's long history was closely scrutinized, and Congress chose to strengthen the law in many ways rather than weaken it. Among other things, the new law:

— for the first time in Title VII cases permitted:

- jury trials in which compensatory or punitive damages are sought,
- compensatory damages in religious, sex, and disability cases (such damages were already allowed for race and national origin under related legislation),
- punitive damages for the same, and
- unlimited medical expenses;

— limited the extent to which reverse discrimination suits could be brought;

— authorized expert witness fees to successful plaintiffs;

— codified the disparate impact theory;

— broadened protections against private race discrimination in 42USC section 1981 cases (see later discussion);

— expanded the right to bring actions challenging discriminatory seniority systems;

— extended extraterritorial coverage of Title VII to U.S. citizens working for U.S. companies outside the United States, except when it would violate the laws of the country;

— extended coverage and established procedures for Senate employees;

— established the Glass Ceiling Commission; and

— established the National Award for Diversity and Excellence in American Executive Management (known as the Frances Perkins–Elizabeth Hanford Dole National Award for Diversity and Excellence in American Executive Management) for businesses that "have made substantial efforts to promote the opportunities and development experiences of women and minorities and foster advancement to management and decision-making positions within the business."

perceived by many as eroding the long-standing protections of Title VII. See Box 12–1, "Civil Rights Act of 1991," for its provisions.

Subsequent to the passage of Title VII, other federal laws were passed with similar intents for other categories of differences. There are now federal laws prohibiting discrimination on the basis of age (Age Discrimination in Employment Act, or ADEA), disability (Americans with Disabilities Act, or ADA, and the Rehabilitation Act), and Vietnam veteran status (Vietnam Veterans Readjustment Act). There is also Executive Order 11246, which requires those who contract to provide the federal government with goods or services worth $10,000 or more to refrain from employment discrimination on the same basis as set forth in Title VII. In addition, a contractor who has a contract of $50,000 or more must as a contractor/employer, develop an affirmative action plan, which we will discuss later.

These laws exist to ensure equal employment opportunity to all qualified applicants and employees regardless of immutable characteristics such as race or gender. The intent of the law is to provide equal employment *opportunity* for all, *not* equal *employment*, as many take the law to mean. Ann and Bill do not have to hire a candidate simply because the candidate is female, African American, Hispanic, and so on, if she is not qualified for the job. Rather, they must ensure that if she is qualified, she be allowed an equal opportunity to be employed. They may not keep her out based on her gender, race, or ethnicity. Because fair employment laws vary from state to state and federal laws apply the same across the country, it is federal law that will be addressed primarily in this chapter, though most of the considerations are the same.

Because most of today's students have lived only in a time when employment discrimination has been illegal, some may wonder why antidiscrimination laws are needed—especially when the laws received such a lambasting in the 1980s and 1990s regarding the issue of affirmative action. The reason is as complex as it is simple. We need such laws because people discriminate. Although this can be one's choice in one's personal life, it is illegal when it comes to the workplace.

Due primarily to the history of slavery in the United States, and its aftereffects, Title VII of the 1964 Civil Rights Act—the first significant employment discrimination law enacted—was needed to address the reality that was still present 99 years after the Thirteenth Amend-ment to the U.S. Constitution abolished slavery in 1865. That reality, expressed in the legislative history of the law as well as in many subsequent cases, was that a hundred years after slavery ended, African-Americans were nowhere near parity with whites in virtually any facet of society.

Before passage of the Civil Rights Act, several states had legalized discrimination and segregation in housing, education, employment, and public accommodations. Even though it had been a hundred years since slavery ended, it was perfectly legal to refuse to hire based purely on race. Newspaper classified ads were divided into help wanted ads for "colored" and white, as well as for males and females.

Since the U.S. Supreme Court's decision in *Brown v. Topeka Board of Education*,[1] which desegregated the public schools, the civil rights struggle to end legalized discrimination had been fought in earnest. In 1963, on the 100th anniversary of the Emancipation Proclamation, the famous March on Washington took place, at which Rev. Dr. Martin Luther King Jr. gave his "I Have a Dream" speech. It was past the time to start breaking down the barriers to full participation by all Americans in the American dream of equality for all. A year later, Title VII was passed. Title VII and the later antidiscrimination laws were some of the tools used to dismantle the barriers of discrimination.

Before we leave this section, we want Bill and Ann to be aware that refusal to hire, unfairly disciplining an employee, sexually harassing employees, or other violations of the equal employment opportunity laws may also serve as the basis for tort or even criminal claims. For instance, sexual harassment is a violation of Title VII, but if the harasser attempts to have forced sex with the harassee, it may constitute civil and criminal assault or battery or both. Preventing an African-American employee from getting a deserved promotion may be an interference with contractual relations in addition to employment discrimination based on race. The distinction was probably more pronounced and threatening when Title VII permitted only the recovery of make-whole relief. Now that it also permits compensatory and punitive damages much like civil cases, the difference between suing under Title VII and state civil laws is less significant.

Finally, if the employer is the federal, state, or local government, employment discrimination may also be redressed by the state or federal constitution. For instance, if a federal agency refused to hire females as engineers, that refusal may well be a denial of equal protection of the laws, a deprivation of due process, or both—in violation of the Fifth and Fourteenth Amendments to the U.S. Constitution.

DISCRIMINATION THEORIES UNDER TITLE VII

Employees who feel they have been discriminated against may file a claim with their state human rights or fair employment practice office or with the Equal Employment Opportunity Commission (EEOC). The EEOC is the federal agency charged with enforcing Title VII and other equal employment opportunity laws. By law the EEOC is required to accept and address all complaints filed with it—and do so free of charge.

Ann and Bill should be aware that it is easy and economical for employees to assert their rights under Title VII—at least initially. If the claimant is not satisfied with the EEOC's disposition of the case, the employee may bring suit in federal court after exhausting administrative remedies. At this point, the employee will have to bear the cost of litigation. The cost will also be on the employee if the employee brought a civil suit or a suit on constitutional grounds.

disparate treatment intentionally treating an employee different from those similarly situated because of a prohibited Title VII factor

disparate impact effect of facially neutral policy that is deleterious for Title VII group

Employees or applicants who feel they have been discriminated against in employment must be able to prove it in one of two ways: **disparate treatment** or **disparate impact**. The former is used when an employee alleges intentional treatment different from others similarly situated. The latter is used when a seemingly neutral employment policy adversely affects virtually an entire group of employees.

DISPARATE TREATMENT

In disparate treatment the employee alleges that he or she was treated differently from other similarly situated employees regarding some aspect of employment based on one of the prohibited reasons, that is, based on race, gender, and so on. The allegation is that but for the employee's race, color, gender, religion, or national origin, the employee would not have been treated differently. Disparate treatment is an individual concept of discrimination. That is, the employee alleges that he or she as an individual was treated differently from others of a different group based on a prohibited reason.

Intent to discriminate must be shown, but it can be shown directly or indirectly. For instance, for direct proof, the employee may allege that Bill and Ann said, "I do not hire women." Or Bill and Ann's discrimination may be shown indirectly by the employee's establishing that Bill and Ann refused to hire a woman who was qualified for the open job and upon rejecting her, that they continued to search to fill the job. The latter, indirect approach, demonstrates discrimination by ruling out all of the usual reasons that a person would not be hired (e.g., no job is available, lack of the necessary qualifications, etc.) so that all that is left is the applicant's membership in a protected class. Bill and Ann must therefore be sure that their treatment of all employees is consistent and fair, so that the basis for a disparate treatment claim does not exist.

DISPARATE IMPACT

Disparate impact is not quite so simple. With disparate impact the employee must show that an employment policy that is neutral on its face actually has a harsher impact on a group protected by the law. Disparate impact is a group concept of discrimination rather than an individual concept. No intent to discriminate need be shown. Rather, the result which is important.

For instance, Ann and Bill may have a policy requiring that anyone who works for them in a security capacity be at least 5 feet 4 inches and weigh at least 140 pounds. The policy applies across the board to anyone applying for the job. Statistically, women as a group are not as likely as men to fit such requirements because most are shorter and lighter. Therefore the policy has the effect of screening out women from security jobs at a higher rate than men, thus creating a disparate impact on women. It also creates a disparate impact on certain ethnic groups that tend to be shorter and slighter in their physical bearing, such as Asians.

Therefore, while Ann and Bill's policy appears on its face to be neutral, courts actually have found such a policy has a disparate impact on women and Asians. To continue to apply the policy Ann and Bill would be required to show that the policy is job related, that is, that in order to perform necessary security functions, employees must be at least 5 feet 4 inches and at least 140 pounds. This is difficult to do, because many who do not fit those requirements routinely perform quite well as security personnel.

Disparate impact is generally defined as the employer's using a **screening device** to choose employees, whereby a minority group does not do at least 80% as well as the majority group. But courts have not held that theory to strictly numerical terms. Because of the many ways in which policies may have disparate impacts on different groups, it

screening device
factor used to weed applicants out of the pool of potential hires

may be difficult for Ann and Bill to discern that a given policy has a disparate impact. Listening to the concerns of employees can greatly aid in that discernment, as the following case somewhat startlingly demonstrates.

BRADLEY V. PIZZACO OF NEBRASKA, INC. D/B/A DOMINO'S

939 F.2d 610 (8th Cir. 1991)

Domino's Pizza, the employer, had a policy requiring all male employees to be clean shaven. An African-American employee who did not wish to shave because it exacerbated a common African-American male skin condition was terminated for failure to comply with the policy. The court held that the policy had a disparate impact upon African-Americans and thus violated Title VII.

Fagg, J.: Domino's grooming policy prohibits employees from wearing beards. Pizzaco, a Domino's franchisee, hired Bradley to deliver pizzas, but fired him within two weeks because he would not remove his beard. Bradley is a black man who suffers from pseudofolliculitis barbae (PFB), a skin disorder affecting almost half of all black males. The symptoms of PFB—skin irritation and scarring—are brought on by shaving, and in severe cases PFB sufferers must abstain from shaving altogether. Domino's policy, however, provides for no exceptions. As Pizzaco's owner explained, "You must be clean shaven to work for Domino's."

This case then, is about a seemingly neutral employment policy that discriminates against black males when applied. Title VII forbids employment policies with a disparate impact unless the policy is justified by legitimate employment goals. Through expert medical testimony and studies, the EEOC demonstrated Domino's policy necessarily excludes black males from the company's workforce at a substantially higher rate than white males. In so doing, the EEOC has shown Domino's facially neutral grooming requirement operates as a "built-in headwind" for black males (*Griggs*, 401 U.S. at 432).

The record shows PFB affects black males almost exclusively and that white males rarely suffer from PFB or comparable skin disorders that may prevent a man from appearing clean shaven. Dermatologists for both sides testified that as many as 45% of black males have PFB. The EEOC's dermatologist offered the opinion that approximately 25% of all black males cannot shave because of PFB.

PFB prevents a sizable segment of the black male population from appearing clean shaven, but does not similarly affect white males. Domino's policy—which makes no exceptions for black males who are medically unable to shave because of a skin disorder peculiar to their face—effectively operates to exclude [such] black males from employment with Domino's. REVERSE in part, AFFIRM in part, and REMAND

Case Questions

1. Why do you think there was a no-beard policy? Does it make sense to you? Should it, when you think of someone being hired to deliver pizza? Is it enough reason to keep a qualified pizza deliverer from working?

2. Do you agree with the court's decision? Why or why not?

3. Can you think of a better legal approach to this situation? If so, what? If not, why not?

PROTECTED CATEGORIES UNDER TITLE VII AND RELATED LEGISLATION

Title VII protects everyone from employment discrimination, but the discrimination prohibited falls into certain categories. Those categories are race, color, gender, religion, national origin, age, and disability. The sections that follow outline the requirements for each of these. In addition, other protected categories from similar laws are provided.

RACE

Because of the particular history of the United States, with its more than 300 years of slavery and slavery's inevitable vestiges, racial discrimination is an ongoing concern in the workplace. Even though Title VII was enacted specifically to address the 99-year post–Thirteenth Amendment segregation and codified discrimination against blacks (called Jim Crow laws), Title VII applies to everyone equally. Whites are protected, just as are blacks and others. Bill and Ann must ensure that all employees are treated equally or comparably regardless of their race.

Discrimination on the basis of race may be overt or covert, disparate impact or disparate treatment, but it should not be tolerated in any of its manifestations. *Bradley* was a good example of the subtle ways in which the issue of race can enter into the workplace. At times it is totally unintentional, but it has a devastating impact on minorities nonetheless. For instance, Bradley, a qualified pizza deliverer, was terminated for what amounted to racial reasons. Ann and Bill should not look for discrimination only in its more obvious manifestations. They should look for the subtle as well, and have zero tolerance for it. Not only does it waste precious resources, but it also lowers productivity, sends the wrong message to other employees, and is simply not good business.

GENDER

Gender is another of those areas where the treatment and policies have been generally accepted for a long period of time and Title VII attempted, much as with race, to change such ingrained notions. Ann and Bill both must guard against such ingrained notions' finding their way into employment policies that discriminate on the basis of gender. Again, because of the particulars of U.S. history, most of the discrimination in the workplace has been against the female gender rather than the male gender. However, the law equally protects men from gender discrimination.

Gender discrimination has many different manifestations, of which Ann and Bill must be aware. The problem does not lie in ignorance that one cannot discriminate on the basis of gender, but as we see in Box 12–2, "The Many Faces of Gender Discrimination," on page 374, it lies in recognizing when it occurs.

MCDONALD V. SANTA FE TRAIL TRANSPORTATION
427 U.S. 273 (1976)

Two white employees were discharged for misappropriating cargo from one of the employer's shipments. A black employee who also misappropriated cargo at the same time was not discharged. The Supreme Court held for the white employees when they sued the employer for race discrimination.

Marshall, J.: We hold that this unequal discipline based on race violates Title VII even though the employees bringing suit are white. Title VII of the Civil Rights Act of 1964 prohibits the discharge of "any individual" because of "such individual's race." Its terms are not limited to discrimination against any particular race. Thus, although we were not there confronted with racial discrimination against whites, we described the Act in *Griggs v. Duke Power Co.* as prohibiting "[d]iscriminatory preference for any [racial] group, minority or majority."

This conclusion is in accord with uncontradicted legislative history to the effect that Title VII was intended to "cover white men and white women and all Americans"—110 Cong. Rec. 2578 (1964)—and create an "obligation not to discriminate against whites"—id., at 7218.

Santa Fe, while conceding that "across-the-board discrimination in favor of minorities could never be condoned consistent with Title VII," contends nevertheless that "such discrimination in isolated cases which cannot reasonably be said to burden whites as a class unduly," such as is alleged here, "may be acceptable." We cannot agree. There is no exception in the terms of the act for isolated cases; on the contrary, "Title VII tolerates no racial discrimination, subtle or otherwise."

While Santa Fe may decide that participation in a theft of cargo may render an employee unqualified for employment, this criterion must be applied alike to members of all races, and Title VII is violated if, as employees allege, it is not. REVERSE and REMAND

Case Questions

1. Discuss why you think the employer did what it did here.
2. Did you realize that Title VII applied equally to whites as well as nonwhites?
3. Do you agree with the Court's decision? Why or why not?

In General

The list in Box 12–2 can go on. The important thing to note is that Ann and Bill must ensure that their workplace policies do not consider what is "appropriate" work or activity for one gender or the other, but instead limit consideration to qualifications for the job. As *Price Waterhouse v. Hopkins* demonstrates, liability can ensue when that

---

12–2   BLACK LETTER LAW

The Many Faces of Gender Discrimination

Gender discrimination has been found by courts to exist in such diverse situations as:

- refusal to hire males as airline flight attendants
- refusal to hire females as bartenders
- not hiring women with preschool-aged children, but hiring men with such children
- Not hiring unmarried women who have children, but hiring unmarried men who have children
- refusing to hire anyone not at least 5 feet 4 inches and weighing 140 pounds or more
- having only "filthy" toilets on the worksite premises and refusing to allow the female employee access to an off-limits, cleaner rest room
- refusal to hire males as servers at a restaurant
- refusal to hire males at an all-women's health spa
- prohibiting women of childbearing age from working in jobs with exposure to lead and not prohibiting men of childbearing age from doing so, when both were at reproductive risk
- requiring men to wear so-called business attire, but requiring similarly situated women to wear uniforms or smocks
- requiring that in order to be acceptable as a partner, the female (who had outperformed her male competition) dress more femininely, have her hair styled, wear jewelry, not use curse words, and be less aggressive
- requiring that female flight attendants be unmarried, but not requiring the same restriction of male flight attendants

PRICE WATERHOUSE V. HOPKINS
490 U.S. 228 (1989)

A female associate who was refused admission as a partner in an accounting firm brought a gender discrimination action against the firm. The U.S. Supreme Court held that the gender stereotyping that had taken place was impermissible under Title VII.

Brennan, J.: In a jointly prepared statement supporting her candidacy, the partners in Hopkins's office showcased her successful two-year effort to secure a $25-million contract with the Department of State, labeling it "an outstanding performance" and one that Hopkins carried out "virtually at the partner level." None of the other partnership candidates had a comparable record in terms of successfully securing major contracts for the partnership.

The partners in Hopkins's office praised her character and her accomplishments, describing her as "an outstanding professional" who had a "deft touch," a "strong character, independence, and integrity." Clients appeared to have agreed with those assessments.

Virtually all of the partners' negative comments about Hopkins—even those of partners supporting her—had to do with her "interpersonal skills." Both supporters and opponents of her candidacy indicate she was sometimes "overly aggressive, unduly harsh, difficult to work with, and impatient with staff."

There were clear signs, though, that some of the partners reacted negatively to Hopkins's personality because she was a woman. One partner described her as "macho"; another suggested that she "overcompensated for being a woman"; a third advised her to take "a course at charm school." Several partners criticized her use of profanity; in response, one partner suggested that those partners objected to her swearing only "because it['s] a lady using foul language." Another supporter explained that Hopkins "ha[d] matured from a tough-talking somewhat masculine hard-nosed manager to an authoritative, formidable, but much more appealing lady partner candidate." But it was the man who bore the responsibility for explaining to Hopkins the reasons for the Policy Board's decision to place her candidacy on hold

continued on next page

who delivered the coup de grace: in order to improve her chances for partnership, Thomas Beyer advised, Hopkins should "walk more femininely, talk more femininely, dress more femininely, wear makeup, have her hair styled, and wear jewelry."

As for the legal relevance of gender stereotyping, we are beyond the day when an employer may evaluate employees by assuming or insisting that they matched the stereotype associated with their group, for "[i]n forbidding employers to discriminate against individuals because of their gender, Congress intended to strike at the entire spectrum of disparate treatment of men and women resulting from sex stereotypes." An employer who objects to aggressiveness in women but whose positions require that trait places women in the intolerable and impermissible catch-22: out of a job if they behave aggressively and out of a job if they don't. Title VII lifts women out of that bind. REVERSED and REMANDED

Case Questions

1. What was Price Waterhouse's fatal flaw?
2. Does Hopkins's treatment here make good business sense?
3. How would you avoid the problem in this case?

advice is not followed and employees are instead stereotyped based on gender.

Affinity Orientation

same gender affinity orientation gender an individual is attracted to for primary relationships is same as individual's

Bill and Ann should recognize that the gender classification of Title VII has been deemed *not* to include a prohibition against discrimination on the basis of **same gender affinity orientation**. Even though lesbians, gays, bisexuals, and transsexuals are not covered under Title VII, many state and municipal governments have laws protecting them from job discrimination, and the list changes quickly, both as to those laws that do and those that try to limit job protections.

To date, state laws extending employment protection and benefits to gays and lesbians have been enacted in Wisconsin, California,

Massachusetts, Hawaii, Connecticut, New Jersey, Maine, Minnesota, and Vermont. More than 125 municipalities also have such enactments. See Box 12–3 for a partial list of jurisdictions with such laws. In addition, the Fifth and Fourteenth amendments to the U.S. constitu-

---

12–3   BLACK LETTER LAW

Municipalities with Antidiscrimination Laws Banning Discrimination against Gays and Lesbians

- At least 14 states have executive orders.
- At least 71 cities and counties have civil rights ordinances.
- At least 41 cities or counties have council or mayoral proclamations banning discrimination in public employment.

Jurisdictions include:

Berkeley, CA	Marshall, MN
Davis, CA	Minneapolis, MN
Laguna Beach, CA	St. Louis, MO
Los Angeles, CA	Essex County, NJ
Oakland, CA	Albany, NY
Sacramento, CA	Alfred, NY
San Diego, Ca	Ithaca, NY
San Francisco, CA	New York, NY
West Hollywood, CA	Tompkins County, NY
Washington, DC	Watertown, NY
Key West, FL	Columbus, OH
Miami Beach, FL	Yellow Springs, OH
Champaign, IL	Portland, OR
Chicago, IL	Harrisburg, PA
Ames, IA	Lancaster, PA
Iowa City, IA	Philadelphia, PA
New Orleans, LA	Pittsburgh, PA
Gaithersberg, MD	Austin, TX
Howard County, MD	Alexandria, VA
Rockville, MD	Seattle, WA
Detroit, MI	Madison, WI

Source: National Gay & Lesbian Task Force.

tion may also protect government employees as a denial of equal protection unless it is justified by a legitimate state interest.

Equal Pay and Comparable Worth

Whereas Title VII prohibits discrimination in any aspect of employment, the matter of gender discrimination in wages was actually addressed even before Title VII was passed. The Equal Pay Act (EPA) was passed in 1963, the year before Title VII. The act prohibits discrimination in pay on the basis of gender, except in certain circumscribed situations such as when the difference in pay is based on the amount produced, quality of production, and so forth. Employers may not circumvent the law to justify wage differentials by simply calling the same job by different titles when it is performed by males and females (e.g., a male "orderly," but a female "nurse's aide," though both perform the same tasks).

comparable worth employer's comparison of the worth of jobs to determine its rate of pay

Since Title VII came into being so soon after the Equal Pay Act and also addressed the matter of gender-based wage discrimination, the Equal Pay Act has not been used as much as it might have otherwise. However, its biggest contribution may well be that it also gave rise to the concept of **comparable worth**.

Comparable worth permits jobs that are not the same, but are of comparable worth to the employer, to be examined for wage disparities. For instance, one can argue that secretaries are paid less because the profession is female dominated, while construction workers are paid more because the profession is male dominated, and yet both are of comparable value to the employer. It thus gets around the EPA limitation on comparing jobs that are essentially the same. It permits arguments for those situations when pay within a profession may not be discriminatory among males and females, but the profession itself, being, say, female dominated, may pay lower wages for reasons more related to gender than anything else.

Comparable worth has not been fully accepted by the courts, and legislation does not require it. However, Bill and Ann should ensure that the wages paid to their employees are free of possible claims in this area.

Pregnancy

Although many have notions regarding the so-called frailty of pregnant employees, the law takes the position that it is gender discrimination on the basis of pregnancy to treat pregnancy differently from any other short-term disability that other employees have. Pregnant employees cannot be made to leave work early to take maternity leave at a certain arbitrarily set date, as was once the case with teachers. They also cannot have their job duties taken away unless there is some basis for doing so, such as inability to perform.

Even though pregnant employees must be treated like any other employee with a short-term disability, as the following case indicates, it is not a violation of the Pregnancy Discrimination Act (PDA) to pro-

CALIFORNIA FEDERAL SAVINGS AND LOAN ASS'N. V. GUERRA
479 U.S. 272 (1987)

The U.S. Supreme Court held that California's law guaranteeing pregnant employees maternity leave and reinstatement to jobs upon return, much like the Family and Medical Leave Act, did not violate Title VII even though it did not extend such benefits to others suffering short-term disabilities.

Marshall, J.: We hold that the California statute does not violate Title VII or the PDA. Title VII's purpose is to achieve equality of employment opportunities and remove barriers that have operated in the past to favor identifiable groups of employees over other employees. Rather than limiting Title VII principles and objectives, the PDA extends them to cover pregnancy. California's law also promotes equal employment opportunity. By requiring employers to reinstate women after a reasonable pregnancy disability leave, it ensures that they will not lose their jobs on account of pregnancy. The law does not compel employers to treat pregnant employees better than other disabled employees; it merely establishes benefits that employers must, at a minimum, provide for pregnant workers.

We emphasize the limited nature of the benefits the California statute provides. The statute is narrowly drawn to cover only the period

continued on next page

of actual physical disability on account of pregnancy, childbirth, or related medical conditions. Accordingly, unlike the protective labor legislation prevalent earlier in this century, the statute does not reflect the archaic or stereotypical notions about pregnancy and the abilities of pregnant workers. A statute based on such stereotypical assumptions would, of course, be inconsistent with Title VII's goal of equal employment opportunity. AFFIRMED

Case Questions

1. Do you agree with the Court that the California law does not require that pregnant employees be treated better than other employees?

2. What argument could be made on behalf of an employee who had to take time off to recover from a heart attack, but was not guaranteed a position upon return?

3. Are you surprised by the Court's decision? Why or why not?

vide pregnant employees with more protection than required by the act. Such laws were essentially codified by the Family and Medical Leave Act, previously discussed.

Sexual Harassment

sexual harassment
unwanted gender-based activity directed toward a harassee either requesting sexual activity or creating a hostile or intimidating environment for harassee

antifemale animus
hostile, negative feeling about women—generally exhibited in the workplace

Sexual harassment is also a form of gender discrimination. It is discriminatory to have employees of one gender and not the other be subject to workplace requirements or to oppressive and offensive behavior that interferes with the employee's ability to do his or her job. Both male and female employees are protected from sexual harassment, though well in excess of 90% of sexual harassment claims are brought by females. Contrary to popular thought, sexual harassment need not necessarily involve sex: Courts have found sexual harassment even when the activity was not necessarily sexual in nature, but instead exhibited **antifemale animus** toward the harassee so that because of her gender, she is made to endure a negative work environment. Box 12–4, "EEOC Sexual Harassment Guidelines," provides the specific language that defines sexual harassment.

12–4   BLACK LETTER LAW

EEOC Sexual Harassment Guidelines

Unwelcome sexual advances, requests for sexual favors, and other verbal or physical conduct of a sexual nature constitute sexual harassment when (1) submission to such conduct is made either explicitly or implicitly a term or condition of an individual's employment, (2) submission to or rejection of such conduct by an individual is used as the basis for employment decisions affecting such individual, or (3) such conduct has the purpose or effect of unreasonably interfering with an individual's work performance or creating an intimidating, hostile, or offensive working environment. (29 C.F.R. Section 1604.11 [a])

There are two types of sexual harassment: **quid pro quo sexual harassment** and **hostile environment sexual harassment.** In quid pro quo sexual harassment the employee is directly or indirectly threatened with not receiving workplace benefits or entitlements such as promotions, raises, and training unless the employee engages in sexual activity with the harasser in exchange. Benefits are dependent on the employee's acceding to the sexual demands of the harasser.

Hostile environment sexual harassment is quite different and not always as clear. Under the EEOC sexual harassment guidelines, virtually any unwanted activity directed to one gender but not the other, which creates for an employee a hostile or offensive environment and unreasonably interferes with the employee's ability to perform, can be the subject of a sexual harassment claim. It includes such activities as:

- physical contact
- sexual jokes
- negative or stereotyped gender-based jokes
- teasing
- gestures
- display of nude or sexually explicit photos, drawings, plaques, calendars, magazines, cartoons, or the like in the workplace
- repeated requests for dates or sexual activity

quid pro quo sexual harassment
sexual harassment in which the harasser requests sexual activity from the harassee in exchange for workplace benefits

hostile environment sexual harassment
sexual harassment in which the harasser creates an offensive, hostile, or intimidating environment for the harassee

12–5   LEGAL EXCERPTS

Sexual Harassment Requirements

In order to sustain a finding of hostile environment sexual harassment, it is generally required that:
- The harassment be unwelcome by plaintiff.
- The harassment be based on gender.
- The harassment be sufficiently severe or pervasive to create an abusive working environment.
- The harassment affected a term, condition, or privilege of employment.
- The employer had actual or constructive knowledge of the sexually hostile working environment and took neither prompt nor adequate remedial action.

Although there has been a great deal of attention to the issue of sexual harassment for the past few years, many people, even businesspeople and employers, do not understand sexual harassment. Many think that an allegation of sexual harassment is tantamount to proving it. That is not so. In order to be actionable, the activity alleged must meet certain requirements that ensure that the activity alleged to be sexual harassment is not a mere isolated incident that simply hurt someone's feelings. Box 12–5, "Sexual Harassment Requirements," lists the requirements for sexual harassment.

The requirements make clear that simply asking someone for a date or saying someone looks nice—in an appropriate way (e.g., not staring at someone's breasts while doing so)—is the sort of activity that will serve as a basis for liability for sexual harassment. Even at that, there can be differing opinions as to what is merely inappropriate behavior and what behavior constitutes sexual harassment. As *Rabidue v. Osceola Refining Co.* demonstrates, even judges may differ.

The U.S. Supreme Court recently heard its second sexual harassment case. In 1986 the Court decided *Meritor Savings Bank v. Vinson*, 477 U.S. 57 (1986). *Meritor* established that gender discrimination did, in fact, encompass sexual harassment and that sexual harassment could exist either as quid pro quo or by hostile environment. In 1993 the Court, in reviewing *Harris v. Forklift Systems, Inc.*, 114 S. Ct. 367

RABIDUE V. OSCEOLA REFINING CO.

805 F.2d 611 (6th Cir. 1986)

A female employee alleged sexual harassment and gender discrimination because of vulgarity and nude posters in the workplace in violation of Title VII. The court found for the employer, but there was a strong dissent.

Krupansky, J.: Henry was an extremely vulgar and crude individual who customarily made obscene comments about women generally and, on occasion, directed such obscenities to Rabidue. Management was aware of Henry's vulgarity, but had been unsuccessful in curbing his offensive personality traits. Other male employees from time to time displayed pictures of nude or scantily clad women in their offices and/or work areas, to which Rabidue and other women employees were exposed.

The sexually oriented poster displays had a negligible effect on Rabidue's work environment when considered in the context of a society that condones and publicly features and commercially exploits open displays of written and pictorial erotica at the newsstands, on prime-time television, at the cinema, and in other public places. Henry's vulgar language and the sexually oriented posters did not result in a working environment that could be considered intimidating, hostile, or offensive under the guidelines. AFFIRMED

KEITH, Circuit Judge, concurring in part, dissenting in part.
I dissent for several reasons. The overall circumstances of Rabidue's workplace evince an antifemale environment. In addition to the posters, Henry regularly spewed antifemale obscenity by routinely referring to women as "whores," "cunt," "pussy," and "tits." Of plaintiff, Henry specifically remarked, "All that bitch needs is a good lay," and called her "fat ass." For seven years Rabidue was the sole woman in a salaried management position at Osceola and was routinely excluded from activities she needed [to engaged in] to perform her duties and progress in her career. Unlike male salaried employees, she did not receive free lunches, free gasoline, a telephone credit card, entertainment privileges, or invitations to the weekly golf matches. The district

continued on next page

court dismissed these as fringe benefits. Rabidue's supervisor stated to another worker, "[Rabidue] is doing a good job as credit manager, but we really need a man on that job," adding, "She can't take customers out to lunch."

I conclude that the misogynous language and decorative displays tolerated at the workplace, the primitive views of working women expressed by Osceola supervisors and Osceola's treatment of their only female salaried employee clearly evince antifemale animus. Title VII's precise purpose is to prevent such behavior and attitudes from poisoning the work environment of classes protected under the act. I believe no woman should be subjected to an environment where her sexual dignity and reasonable sensibilities are visually, verbally, or physically assaulted as a matter of prevailing male prerogative.

Nor can I agree with the majority's notion that the effect of pinup posters and misogynous language in the workplace can have only a minimal effect on female employees and should not be deemed hostile or offensive "when considered in the context of a society that condones and publicly features and commercially exploits open displays of erotica."

"Society" in this scenario must primarily refer to the unenlightened; I hardly believe reasonable women condone the pervasive degradation and exploitation of female sexuality perpetuated in American culture. Pervasive societal approval thereof and of other stereotypes stifles female potential and instills the debased sense of self-worth which accompanies stigmatization. I conclude that sexual posters and antifemale language can seriously affect the psychological well-being of the reasonable woman and interfere with her ability to perform her job.

Case Questions

1. Does seeing the judges' differing views make you understand the considerations in sexual harassment any differently? Explain.

2. What, if any, is the merit of the majority's analysis?

3. What do you think of the reasonable-victim standard proposed by Judge Keith? Explain.

(1993), a case from the same circuit in which *Rabidue* was decided, determined that the conduct constituting sexual harassment need not cause severe psychological injury to the harassee, as long as the conduct causes the environment to be reasonably perceived as hostile or abusive.

Supervisory or managerial employees who sexually harass employees may cause the employer to be liable whether or not the employer knew of the harassing activity. Keep in mind that such employees are agents of the employer and act on the employer's behalf. Ann and Bill must be vigilant in choosing supervisory employees to ensure that they are not likely to engage in such costly, unnecessary behavior.

If the harassment is perpetrated by a coworker (rather than a supervisory employee), Ann and Bill are liable if they knew or should have known of the harassment. They should know of it if they are notified by the harassee, they witness it, or the matter is so pervasive and obvious that a prudent employer would be aware of it.

Ann and Bill are also responsible for harassment perpetrated by outsiders who deal with the company and harass its employees, for instance, a computer repairer who comes in to service the office's computers on a regular basis and harasses employees while there.

It is important that Bill and Ann provide immediate corrective action to address sexual harassment once they are notified or otherwise discover it has taken place. The best approach that they or any employer can take in avoiding liability for sexual harassment is to create an atmosphere in which it is not permitted to exist. Box 12–6, "Creating a Nonhostile Work Environment," gives tips on how an employer can do this.

If the steps in Box 12–6 are taken, they will go a long way toward helping Bill and Ann and other employers avoid the unnecessary liability of sexual harassment claims. Considering all of the relevant factors in context, courts address on a case-by-case basis whether a given action constitutes sexual harassment. What may be appropriate in one circumstance or setting may not be in another. Bill and Ann should ensure that employees are aware of what types of activities are more likely to result in liability for sexual harassment and that employees avoid them.

RELIGION

Discrimination on the basis of religion is also prohibited by Title VII. Not only should Ann and Bill refrain from asking applicants or em-

12–6   BLACK LETTER LAW

Creating a Nonhostile Work Environment

Suggestions for creating an atmosphere in which sexual harassment is minimized include:

- Making sure, from the top down, that all employees understand that sexual harassment in the workplace simply will not be tolerated.
- Adopting an antisexual harassment policy discouraging such activity. This should not be part of a general antidiscrimination policy, but should instead be separate.
- Creating and disseminating information about an effective reporting mechanism for those with sexual harassment complaints.
- Providing employees with training or information that apprises them of what sexual harassment is and what specific activities are appropriate and inappropriate to engage in.
- Ensuring that reported incidents of sexual harassment are taken seriously by supervisors and others involved in reporting.
- Ensuring that there is immediate appropriate corrective action to be taken against employees engaging in sexual harassment.

ployees what their religion is, but they should also refrain from treating employees differently based on employees' religion unless the law so permits. Unlike the prohibitions on race or gender we have discussed, the prohibition on discriminating on the basis of religion is somewhat limited. Bill and Ann cannot discriminate on the basis of religion unless to do so would present an undue hardship. What constitutes an undue hardship is determined on a case-by-case basis by the courts. Box 12–7, "Factors in Undue Hardship," provides some of the considerations courts look at to make a determination regarding accommodation. In *TWA v. Hardison* the leading Supreme Court case on religious discrimination—and described next, the Court discussed the undue hardship issue.

Keep in mind that the religion need not be one that Ann and Bill recognize in order for Title VII to apply. As long as the employee's belief is sincerely held and takes the place of religion in his or her life, Bill and Ann cannot attack it as not being a so-called legitimate religion. One thing on Bill and Ann's side is that in their attempts to reach an accommodation, the employee must cooper-

12-7   BLACK LETTER LAW

Factors in Undue Hardship

The EEOC has provided employers with guidelines as to the factors it considers in answering the question of whether the employer's accommodation would cause undue hardship. Such factors include:
- the nature of the employer's workplace
- the type of job needing accommodation
- the cost of the accommodation
- the willingness of other employees to assist in the accommodation
- the possibility of transfer of the employee and its effects
- what is done by similarly situated employers
- the number of employees available for accommodation
- the burden of accommodation upon the union

ate with them rather than putting the full responsibility on them. If it can be shown that they attempted an accommodation and the employee refused to cooperate, there is no liability on the part of Ann and Bill.

NATIONAL ORIGIN

Discrimination on the basis of national origin addresses the reality that in our country of many ethnicities, many employees will not be of the dominant culture. This can present problems when the issue becomes a basis for treating them differently. National origin discrimination addresses that and covers discrimination against employees because of their ethnic origin.

National origin discrimination can take a number of forms. It can be Ann and Bill's refusing to hire or firing those of a particular nationality; having a policy of not permitting those of a different native language to speak their language in the workplace; not permitting those with accents to hold certain jobs; and so forth. None of this is permissible under Title VII.

English-only rules may be permissible if speaking English is a job requirement. However, if the employer imposes such a rule on employees when they take their lunch or breaks or they otherwise do not

TRANS WORLD AIRLINES, INC. V. HARDISON
432 U.S. 63 (1977)

The employee belonged to a religion that did not permit him to work on the Sabbath. Employer TWA alleged it was unable to accommodate employee's religious conflict without undue hardship. The Court set forth the guidelines for making the determination.

White, J.: The employee, Hardison, was employed by Trans World Airlines (TWA), in a department that operated 24 hours a day in connection with an airplane maintenance and overhaul base. Hardison was subject to a seniority system in a collective-bargaining agreement between TWA and the union whereby the most senior employees have first choice for job and shift assignments as they become available.

Because Hardison sought, and was transferred to, a job where he had low seniority, problems began to arise. TWA agreed to permit the union to seek a change of work assignments, but the union was not willing to violate the seniority system, and Hardison had insufficient seniority to bid for a shift having Saturdays off. After TWA rejected a proposal that Hardison work only four days a week on the ground that this would impair critical functions in the airline operations, no accommodation could be reached, and Hardison was discharged for refusing to work on Saturdays.

We hold that TWA, which made reasonable efforts to accommodate Hardison's religious needs, did not violate Title VII, and each of the suggested alternatives would have been an undue hardship within the meaning of the statute as construed by the EEOC guidelines.

When TWA first learned of Hardison's religious observances, and even later, it agreed to permit the union's steward to seek a swap of shifts or days off, but the steward was unable to work out scheduling changes and no one was willing to swap days with Hardison. For TWA to have arranged unilaterally for a swap would have amounted to a breach of the collective-bargaining agreement.

It was also suggested that though it might have left TWA short-handed on the one shift each week that Hardison did not work, [either] TWA could have permitted Hardison to work a four-day week to avoid working on his Sabbath or, TWA could have replaced Hardison on his Saturday shift with other available employees through the payment of premium wages. Both of these alternatives would involve costs to TWA, in the form of either lost efficiency in other jobs or higher wages.

To require TWA to bear more than a *de minimis* cost to accommodate Hardison is an undue hardship. Like abandonment of the seniority system, to require TWA to bear additional costs when no such costs are incurred to give other employees the days off that they want would involve unequal treatment of employees on the basis of their religion. REVERSED

Case Questions

1. In your opinion, were the alternatives suggested by the court of appeals viable for TWA? Why or why not?

2. Does it seem inconsistent to prohibit religious discrimination, yet say that collective bargaining agreements cannot be violated to accommodate religious differences? Why or why not?

3. If you had been Hardison's manager and Hardison came to you with this conflict, what would you have done?

need English, it is probably discriminatory. Likewise, an employer cannot discriminate against employees based on their accents. Having an accent was insufficient basis for an employer not to promote an employee who had previously held the position of laboratory director in the absence of the director, when it could not be shown that the accent interfered with the employee's ability to do the job.

AGE

We live in a society that seems obsessed with youthfulness. Some cultures revere its older members. Our culture, particularly in the work arena, seems to cast them away despite research showing older workers are more reliable, harder working, more committed, and absent less frequently than other employees. To counter this effect of devaluing older workers, Congress passed protective legislation for employees older than 40. If an employee is age 40 or older, the employee cannot be discriminated against in any aspect of employment.

Often employers will attempt to cut costs by terminating older, often higher-paid employees. Or perhaps the employer wishes to bring a more youthful look to a retail establishment and as a part of realizing that wish, terminates older employees or transfers them to lower-paying jobs. This is a violation of the Age Discrimination in Employment Act, or ADEA.

The Employee Retirement Income Security Act (ERISA) also prevents employees from being excluded from a pension plan because of age. In addition, it has vesting requirements protecting older employees from being terminated before vesting of their pension plan.

bona fide occupational qualification
legalized discrimination permitted because it is necessary for the employer's particular business

Although age, like religion, can be a **bona fide occupational qualification** (BFOQ) reasonably necessary for the operation of an employer's business, it is not to be used merely to justify not hiring older employees. If it can be shown that there is a connection between age and performance of the job the employee is hired to do, the BFOQ may be allowed. For instance, airlines and bus companies in the business of safely transporting passengers from one place to another have been able to successfully argue, based on expert medical testimony, that after a certain age, deterioration starts to occur, affecting a pilot's or driver's ability to safely transport passengers. Under those circumstances, making decisions based on age and imposing a maximum age on employability have been upheld. However, the BFOQ cannot be based solely on an employer's perception that the older worker "simply doesn't cut it anymore."

Of course, the ADEA is also not a so-called full employment law for older workers such that they are guaranteed a job regardless of age or level of performance. If an employee can no longer perform a job, then there exists a nondiscriminatory, job-related basis for termination. The trouble comes in assuming that age is the reason for the deteriorating performance and then using the assumption as the basis for stereotyping and subsequent termination. The reality is, the employer should not be as concerned with age as with performance. No matter what age, an employee must be able to perform or termination is in order.

Initially, the ADEA was the only Title VII–type legislation permitting a jury trial. Because of the Civil Rights Act of 1991, however, this is no longer true. However, willful violations of the ADEA may result in treble damages. Bill and Ann should be aware that the employee win rate in ADEA cases is high. Sympathetic jurors tend to put themselves in the place of the employee, and although everyone may not be a female or a minority group member or a different religion, everyone thinks of growing old and fears being cast away without resources. The thought of an employee being dumped by an employer just because the employee grows older does not sit well with jurors.

Bill and Ann should be careful not to allow preconceived notions about age and its relation to ability to creep into their employment decisions and cause potential liability. This is particularly true because treble damages are permitted under the law.

DISABILITY

The passage of the Americans with Disabilities Act (ADA) in 1991 provided Title VII–type relief for those who are disabled. The act was hailed as the "Declaration of Independence" or "Emancipation Proclamation" for the disabled, as well as the most far-reaching civil rights law since the Civil Rights Act of 1964. Disability discrimination is similar to religious discrimination in that it requires that employers with 15 or more employees not discriminate against those qualified applicants who are disabled, unless to do so would present an undue hardship.

The law addresses three types of barriers to those who are disabled: (1) intentional discrimination due to social bias, (2) neutral standards with a disparate impact on those who are disabled, and (3) barriers to job performance that can be addressed by accommodation.

 Under the ADA, a disability is a physical or mental impairment that substantially limits one or more of a person's major life activities. Employers, however, are offered little guidance about the wording, because neither the ADA nor section 504 of the Rehabilitation Act—the forerunner to the ADA—defines with any certainty the terms *physical or mental impairment* or *major life activities*. Box 12–8, "ADA Definitions," gives the definitions contained in the EEOC's ADA- implementing regulations.

Under the law a person is disabled if the person:

- is actually disabled,
- is perceived as disabled, or
- has a record of being disabled.

Although the law covers both mental and physical disabilities, it does not include a definitive list of what is and is not a disability. Rather, courts must address the issue on a case-by-case basis. For in-

12-8   BLACK LETTER LAW

ADA Definitions

The EEOC's regulations provide the following definitions.

Impairment—any physiological disorder or condition affecting one or more of the following body systems: neurological reproductive, musculoskeletal digestive, special sense organs genitourinary, respiratory (including speech organs), skin, cardiovascular, endocrine, hemic and lymphatic, or any mental or psychological disorder that substantially limits one of life's major activities.

Major life activities—functions such as caring for oneself, performing manual tasks, walking, seeing, hearing, speaking, breathing, learning, and working.

Substantially limits—causes the inability to perform a major life activity that the average person in the general population can perform or significantly restricts the condition, manner, or duration under which the person can perform a major life activity.

stance, it has been held that breathing is impaired if an employee has emphysema; learning is impaired when an employee is dyslexic; functioning and procreation are impaired if the employee is HIV positive. Employees are entitled to equal employment opportunity if, aside from the disability, they are otherwise qualified for the job and do not present a risk of harm to themselves or others.

Qualified for the job can include reasonable accommodation of the disability or not, as necessary. The big hurdle for Bill and Ann will be to learn when and what it is they must do to accommodate a disabled employee. Jumping that hurdle will take a substantial effort on the part of them if they think, as many do, the disabled are only people in wheelchairs or who use white canes. Such is not, however, what the law addresses. And in fact it is illegal to act on such presumptions by classifying employees in ways that restrict their status, their opportunities, or what they can do unless those classifications can be shown to be job related and consistent with business necessity.

As with the Title VII categories, Ann and Bill may not discriminate against qualified disabled applicants or employees in recruitment, hiring, promotion, training, discipline, layoffs, pay, terminations, assignments, leave policies, benefits, or any other matter concerning employment. Unlike Title VII, under the ADA Bill and Ann must take a proactive approach rather than waiting until a problem occurs. They must not discriminate against qualified disabled applicants or employees in any aspect of employment; moreover they must also make the workplace accessible to disabled workers. For instance, if necessary, Ann and Bill must restructure their workplace and job descriptions to allow the disabled access.

The law forces us to change not only our perception of who a disabled person is but also our perception of what a disabled person is capable of—both of which may go against our ingrained notions about disabled employees. We must learn to think of employees as being able to perform in a multitude of ways and as having abilities that may be different from those we generally think of. If we learn to so think, we are less likely to be held liable for violating the ADA by failing to accommodate disabled employees.

For instance, a Florida case involved a blind teacher who applied for a position as a physical education instructor. The teacher was denied employment because of blindness, and no attempt was made to accommodate the disability. The teacher was able to show the possibility that the disability could be accommodated by having someone like a work-study student act as eyes to tell whether, for instance, a ball went in the basket or whether everyone was performing as directed. The school system had to at least attempt an accommodation. But it had not done so.

Despite the requirements of the ADA, the latter is not a law that guarantees a job to a disabled person regardless of qualifications. It merely requires that we carefully think of the qualifications actually necessary for the job as well as alternative ways of having the job performed. We may have always thought of typists having fingers, but if an applicant has no arms and can type just as well using toes, then having fingers may not actually be a job requirement after all.

In the *Arline* case, widely perceived to have direct implications for those who have AIDS or are HIV positive, the U.S. Supreme Court was called on to determine whether Arline's contagious disease substantially limited her major life activities and whether she could be terminated simply because of the disease's contagiousness.

In March 1993, the Northern District Court of Illinois issued the first opinion in connection with a case brought under the ADA: *EEOC v. AIC Security Investigations, Ltd.* In that case, Charles Wessel, executive director of AIC, was terminated after being diagnosed with an inoper-

SCHOOL BOARD OF NASSAU COUNTY V. ARLINE
480 U.S. 273 (1987)

Employee Arline, a teacher with tuberculosis, was terminated from her job. The employer argued that the termination was not because of Arline's disease, but instead because of the threat that her relapses posed to the health of others, since tuberculosis is contagious. The Court held for Arline.

Brennan, J.: We must consider whether Arline can be considered a handicapped individual. This impairment was serious enough to require hospitalization, a fact more than sufficient to establish that one or more of her major life activities were substantially limited by her impairment. Thus, Arline's hospitalization for tuberculosis in 1957 suffices to establish that she has a "record of impairment" within the meaning of the regulations and is therefore a handicapped individual.

The board maintains that Arline's record of impairment is irrelevant in this case, since the School Board dismissed her not because of her diminished capabilities, but because of the threat that her relapses of tuberculosis posed to the health of others.

We do not agree that, in [the definition of] a handicapped individual, the contagious effects of a disease can be meaningfully distinguished from the disease's physical effects on a claimant in a case such as this. Arline's contagiousness and her physical impairment each resulted from the same underlying condition, tuberculosis. It would be unfair to allow an employer to seize upon the distinction between the effects of a disease on others and the effects of a disease on a patient and use that distinction to justify discriminatory treatment.

The fact that *some* persons who have contagious diseases may pose a serious health threat to others under certain circumstances does not justify excluding from the coverage of the act *all* persons with actual or perceived contagious diseases. It would mean those accused of being contagious would never have the opportunity to have their condition evaluated in light of medical evidence and a determination made as to whether they were "otherwise qualified." The fact that a person with a record of a physical impairment is also contagious does not suffice to remove that person from coverage under the law.

The remaining question is whether Arline is otherwise qualified for the job of elementary school teacher. The basic factors to be considered should include findings of facts based on reasonable medical judgment given the state of medical knowledge about (a) the nature of the risk (how the disease is transmitted), (b) the duration of the risk (how long the carrier is infectious), (c) the severity of the risk (what the potential is to harm third parties), and (d) the probabilities the disease will be transmitted and will cause varying degrees of harm. The next step in the "otherwise-qualified" inquiry is for the Court to evaluate whether the employer could reasonably accommodate the employee under the established standards for that inquiry.

Because there were few factual findings by the district court, we are unable at this stage to resolve whether Arline is otherwise qualified for her job. We remand the case to the district court to determine whether Arline is otherwise qualified for her position. REMANDED

Case Questions

1. Do you agree with the Court's decision? Why or why not? Would your answer change if the contagious disease was AIDS or HIV? Explain.

2. If it is shown that Arline could perform some other function in the school system besides teaching, and contact with others were not as prevalent as in the classroom, would you allow her to stay on? Discuss.

3. Do you think there is adequate protection of both the employee and the public in this case? What should the courts do to diminish discrimination against the disabled built upon myth and misconceptions?

able, malignant brain tumor, though still able and willing to perform the essential functions of his job. He was terminated for fear he would no longer be able to perform as his health deteriorated. The jury awarded Wessel $572,000 after concluding that the termination violated the ADA because Wessel was otherwise qualified to perform the job.

The ADA takes very seriously the issue of equal employment opportunity for the disabled, and therefore Bill and Ann must do so also. According to the preamble to the legislation, Congress's intent in enacting the law was to open opportunities for a fuller life to the nation's 43 million disabled citizens. Bill and Ann should be aware that compliance with the law will take thinking about disabilities and the disabled in a different way. That thinking should not be, "How can they perform if they are disabled?" but instead, "How can we accommodate disabled employees in ways that enables them to do the job?"

DEFENSES TO EMPLOYMENT DISCRIMINATION CASES

If Bill and Ann are sued for discrimination, they have several defenses available to them to avoid being found liable. Not all defenses may be used for every case, but they provide at least a modicum of protection if they meet the requirements for their usage. For instance, it is a defense to a discrimination action if Ann and Bill are using a bona fide seniority plan, even though the plan may have an adverse impact on a group protected by Title VII. Generally, having a bona fide plan means the plan was not enacted for the purpose of discrimination.

BFOQ

Title VII and, as we saw, the ADEA permit Ann and Bill to use a defense of the discriminatory characteristic's being a bona fide occupational qualification that is reasonably necessary for the employer's particular business. Because the BFOQ defense is actually legalized discrimination, you can imagine that it is very narrowly interpreted.

The BFOQ defense is used in situations when, for instance, authenticity is necessary, such as being female as a BFOQ for modeling women's clothes or playing a female part in a theater production. It can also be used when safety may be at stake, for instance, using males to guard male prisoners in a maximum security facility. As we saw, courts have upheld a maximum age as a BFOQ in such occupations as airline pilot and bus driver, both of whose business is to safely transport passengers from one point to another. Employers were able to demonstrate through expert testimony their necessity for putting an age cap on job applicants by showing that after a certain age, attributes important to the transportation task began to deteriorate.

It is also required to show that the older workers' attributes being challenged are such that they occur so frequently within the targeted population that it would be unwieldy to test each applicant for the problem, so the rule is permitted to be applied to all. Race cannot be the subject of a BFOQ.

Although Ann and Bill can use the BFOQ if the requirements are met, they should do so sparingly. Courts are not fond of permitting legalized discrimination under a law intended to prevent discrimination.

BUSINESS NECESSITY

Employers can also use the defense of **business necessity** to defend against discrimination claims. If an employee establishes a **prima facie case** of discrimination using the disparate impact theory, Bill and Ann can counter by demonstrating that the offending policy is necessary for performance of the employee's job.

business necessity
a nondiscriminatory reason for an employer's policy that seems to discriminate against a protected class

For instance, if Bill and Ann had an employment policy requiring all employees to have a good credit history of at least 20 years' duration, it might adversely affect females, who, as a group, have tended to have shorter credit histories because of the way family structures are set up. If Ann and Bill can show that they need the credit history requirement because the position necessitates responsible handling of money or finances, the policy might be justified by business necessity.

prima facie case
proof of all the legal elements needed for a cause of action

However, even when Bill and Ann can demonstrate business necessity, the employee is still able to show that there is a way that Bill and Ann can get what they need (stable credit experience) with less of a disparate impact upon women than their present policy involves. This forces Bill and Ann's policies to be as narrow as possible to accomplish their purpose.

Business necessity permits an employer whose workplace policies are necessary for performance, but that have an adverse impact, to still use them if the requirements are legitimate. In this way, an employer is more likely to have policies with a disparate impact only when those policies are necessary to performing the employer's business.

AFFIRMATIVE ACTION AND REVERSE DISCRIMINATION

Before we leave the area of employment discrimination, we will address one other issue of major importance. As stated at the outset, Executive Order 11246 prohibits government contractors from discriminating in the workplace on the same bases as Title VII. If a contract is for $50,000 or more, in addition to not discriminating the employer must conduct an audit of the workplace to determine whether there is an underrepresentation of women or minorities in several job categories including those traditionally closed to those groups.

If there exists such an underrepresentation, the employer/contractor must also develop a way to remedy it. The employer must establish goals that will make the workforce more representative of the population from which the employees are drawn and timetables within which to accomplish the goals. This is called an **affirmative action plan**, and the area is called **affirmative action**.

Affirmative action plans may also arise as remedies imposed by a court after discrimination is found, or such plans can be voluntarily adopted by an employer to redress underrepresentation. The latter must be done in strict conformity with certain requirements ensuring that the rights of other employees are not unnecessarily trammeled.

When an affirmative action plan is instituted, often other employees who belong to the group not discriminated against may feel discriminated against. For instance, a court may find that an employer has a long history of discrimination against women in hiring and promotions. The court may order the employer to promote one woman for every man promoted until the percentage of women in the managerial ranks reflects their availability for such positions in the workforce drawn from. The men who would have been in line for promotion may then feel they are being discriminated against because they must now wait longer to be promoted. They may bring a suit alleging **reverse discrimination**.

Actually, there is only one type of discrimination under the law. Everyone is protected equally. Suits alleging reverse discrimination

affirmative action
intentional inclusion—generally in the workplace—of historically excluded groups such as women and minorities

affirmative action plan
a plan developed to intentionally include minorities and females in the workplace after a showing of illegal discrimination or underrepresentation

reverse discrimination
belief of majority group members that they were adversely affected by affirmative action implementation

UNITED STEEL WORKERS OF AMERICA, AFL-CIO V. WEBER
443 U.S. 193 (1979)

A white employee sued under Title VII alleging race discrimination in that the union and the employer adopted a voluntary affirmative action plan reserving for black employees 50% of the openings in a training program until the percentage of black craft workers in the plant approximated the percentage of blacks in the local labor force. The U.S. Supreme Court held that the program was permissible under Title VII.

Brennan, J.: At Kaiser's Gramercy plant, prior to 1974, only 1.83% of the skilled craft workers were black, even though the local workforce was approximately 39% black. Kaiser established a training program to train its production workers to fill craft openings. During the first year of the plan, seven black and six white craft trainees were selected, with the most senior black trainee having less seniority than several white production workers whose bids for admission to the program were rejected. Weber, one of those more senior white workers, sued for violation of Title VII of the Civil Rights Act of 1964, which made it unlawful to discriminate on the basis of race.

The question is whether Title VII left employers and unions in the private sector free to take such race-conscious steps to eliminate manifest racial imbalances in traditionally segregated job categories. We hold that it does.

Weber's argument overlooks the significance of the fact that the plan is an affirmative action plan voluntarily adopted by private parties to eliminate traditional patterns of racial segregation. Weber's reliance upon a literal construction of Title VII is misplaced. The prohibition against racial discrimination must be read against the background of the legislative history of Title VII and the historical context from which the act arose. An interpretation that forbade all race-conscious affirmative action would "bring about an end completely at variance with the purpose of the statute" and must be rejected.

Congress's primary concern in enacting the prohibition against racial discrimination in Title VII of the Civil Rights Act of 1964 was with "the plight of the Negro in our economy." Before 1964, blacks were

continued on next page

largely relegated to "unskilled and semiskilled jobs." Because of automation, the number of such jobs was rapidly decreasing. As a consequence, "the relative position of the Negro worker [was] steadily worsening."

The purposes of Kaiser's plan mirror those of the statute. Both were designed to break down old patterns of racial segregation and hierarchy and structured to "open employment opportunities for Negroes in occupations which have been traditionally closed to them." The plan does not unnecessarily trammel the interests of the white employees, require their discharge and replacement with new black hires, nor create an absolute bar to the advancement of white employees; half of those trained in the program will be white. Moreover, the plan is a temporary measure intended to eliminate a manifest racial imbalance and will end as soon as the percentage of black skilled craft workers in the plant approximates the percentage of blacks in the local labor force.

We conclude that the adoption of the plan falls within the area of discretion left by Title VII to the private sector. REVERSED

Case Questions

1. Does this decision make sense to you? Why or why not?

2. If, because of discrimination, blacks were not in a workplace for as long as whites and therefore did not have as much seniority as whites, does it seem reasonable to allow blacks with less seniority than whites to join the training program?

3. As a manager in a firm thinking of instituting a voluntary affirmative action plan, what factors would you consider?

will be successful only if the employer or court either did not establish the goals with a sufficient basis to do so or did not do so in the least harmful way, as explained in the case on the following page.

Johnson v. Transportation Agency, Santa Clara County, California,[2] a 1987 Supreme Court decision that relied heavily upon *Weber,* determined that under circumstances similar to those in *Weber* but involving a public employer rather than private and gender rather than race, the employer can appropriately take gender into account as one factor of a promotion decision under its voluntary affirmative action plan. The Court said the plan—voluntarily adopted to redress a "conspicuous imbalance in traditionally segregated job categories"— represented a "moderate, flexible, case-by-case approach to effecting a gradual improvement in the representation of minorities and women."

The plan was acceptable because it did not unnecessarily trammel male employees' rights or create an absolute bar to their advancement; set aside no positions for women; expressly stated that its goals should not be construed as quotas to be met; unsettled no legitimate, firmly rooted expectation on the plaintiff's part; was only temporary in that it was for purposes of attaining, not maintaining, a balanced workforce; and caused only minimal intrusion into the legitimate expectations of other employees.

SUMMARY

Title VII and other antidiscrimination laws ensure that employers afford all qualified employees an equal opportunity for employment. Rather than be viewed as a nuisance that interferes with an employer's right to hire and fire however the employer wishes, Ann and Bill should view the law as a necessary part of doing business. It forces them to use all available resources rather than screen out, for arbitrary reasons, those of certain groups, who may be productive members of the workplace.

CHAPTER TERMS

affirmative action   affirmative action plan antifemale animus

bona fide occupational
   qualification

business necessity

comparable worth

disparate impact

disparate treatment

hostile environment sexual
   harassment

prima facie case

quid pro quo sexual
   harassment

reverse discrimination

screening device

sexual harassment

same gender affinity
   orientation

CHAPTER-END QUESTIONS

1. Betty and Laura, two females, apply for a position at Walter Construction Co. as flag holders at construction sites. Walter has a policy of not hiring females. If Betty and Laura sue Walter Construction Co. for gender discrimination, it will likely be under the theory of

   a. disparate impact.
   b. hostile environment.
   c. quid pro quo.
   d. disparate treatment.

2. An African-American firefighter is transferred to a different engine company. The fire captain at the engine company the firefighter is being transferred from tells him to take his bed with him. The captain says the other firefighters, who are white, will not want to sleep on his bed. Would the firefighter have a cause of action under Title VII? Explain.

3. List the states that have enacted state legislation protecting gays and lesbians from discrimination.

4. Richard retires from the post office after a 35-year career. After being at home and dealing with his wife for a few days, he's sorry he retired. Richard then applies for a position with the local recreation center as an after-school recreation coordinator. The superintendent does not hire Richard, however, because he feels Richard is too old to be able to keep up with the children in the recreation program. Does Richard have a cause of action? Explain.

5. Pablo Velasquez, owner of Velasquez Cruise Lines, wishes to make his workplace more reflective of the community in which it is located. Pablo tells Suardana, his personnel director, not to hire any more African-Americans or Hispanics until 20 new whites have been hired. Has Pablo violated Title VII? Discuss.

6. If Suardana, Pablo's personnel director, refuses to hire Christians because workers are required to work on Sunday and Suardana has had a problem with Christians' refusing to work on Sunday because it is their Sabbath, has Suardana violated Title VII? Why or why not?

7. Jay's Transportsit Inc. is in the business of moving office furniture. Jay does not hire women because he believes women shouldn't be doing this kind of work, and anyway, they aren't strong enough to do what he needs done. Debbie, a bodybuilder who can bench-press 350 pounds, applies for a position with Jay's and is not even given an application form. What can Debbie do?

8. Laurabeth comes into work dressed in a business suit because she is going on an interview. Roger, one of the security personnel, approaches her and says, "Is it OK if I tell you that you look very nice today?" Karen, one of Laurabeth's coworkers, overhearing the comment, tells Laurabeth that Laurabeth ought to report Roger to his supervisor for sexual harassment. Should she?

9. An airline hires only female flight attendants, saying it is a marketing tool the company uses as part of its "Love Airlines" logo. If a male sues for gender discrimination and the airline uses the BFOQ as a defense, the airline will win because its marketing plan is protected. (True or False)

10. Assess the validity of this statement. "Affirmative action is a legal way of taking jobs from qualified white males and giving them to unqualified women and minorities. Anyway, I didn't discriminate so why should I have to suffer?"

GROUP EXERCISE

Divide the class into groups based on the areas provided protection by law (e.g., groups for age, gender, disability, race, etc.). For a week, have the students collect news articles, magazine stories, TV or movie stories, and personal stories about the kind of discrimination their group is responsible for. The groups should then report back to the class on what they find.

REFERENCES

1 347 US 483 (1954).
2 480 US 616 (1987).

Chapter 13

EMERGING ISSUES IN THE WORKPLACE

Chapter Preview Summary

The previous chapters have addressed established workplace issues. In this chapter Ann and Bill learn about many of the emerging issues present in the employment setting. Those issues form part of the legal environment of business that, though not necessarily yet fully developed, makes up a part of the employment landscape Ann and Bill may need to navigate. As such, Ann and Bill will be better prepared if they consider these issues, become aware of their pros and cons, and prepare themselves to avoid any legal repercussions that may arise.

Chapter Objectives

In studying the chapter, you should learn:
- why employers are instituting workplace innovations
- what valuing diversity is, how it benefits the employer, and how it can be used to ward off discrimination cases
- what flextime is, how it can help both employers and employees, and the legal considerations for its adoption
- what job sharing is and the legal implications of choosing or not to adopt it

- **the legal considerations in determining the appropriateness of using temporary/leased employees**
- **what domestic partnerships are, what they are not, what their legal implications are, and whether they are appropriate for an employer's workplace**
- **the use of support groups in the workplace, including why they are used, what they can do, and possible legal liability regarding them**
- **the potential legal issues involved in privacy in the workplace**
- **the legal limitations of employment testing**

INTRODUCTION

Employment has had many different incarnations in history. At one time most of those who worked for another were serfs who worked the land of landowners. There have been times even in our own country's history when employment involved the concept of ownership of the worker, such as when slaves worked for masters who owned huge plantations. There were also indentured servitude, sharecropping, sweatshops, and huge industrial complexes, which were monuments to burgeoning technological innovations.

However, at no time in the history of employment has there been such an emphasis as now on trying to integrate the employee with the employer. Innovations such as the four-day workweek, flextime, on-site day care for children and older members of employees' families, workplace health clubs, domestic partnership benefits, valuing diversity programs, satellite workstations, and work-at-home options permitted by the technological innovations of computers, modems, and faxes all are attempts to cause employees to become more productive through the integration of their personal life and their work life.

Today's workplace innovations all have implications for Ann and Bill as employers. Some of them they may wish to adopt; others not. Some are not yet dictated by law, but may be eventually. Some will come upon them whether they want to deal with them or not. Most can have implications from the viewpoint of avoiding liability for work-related litigation. Some of the innovations, if adopted, can help Bill and Ann to avoid lawsuits. Others have implications that may arise from the gender-based perspectives of comparability between male and female employees. It will be helpful to take a look at a few of the emerging issues to see what they involve and how they may affect Ann and Bill, their employees, and the workplace they create for their employees.

VALUING DIVERSITY/ MULTICULTURALISM

In 1987 the Hudson Institute issued a report on research it had conducted for the U.S. Department of Labor. The report, known as Workplace 2000, held a few surprises. Among them was the fact that the United States was about to experience its largest wave of immigration since World War II. But unlike the big immigration wave in the early part of the century, 90% of which was European, this wave would be about 90% Asian and Latin. The report went on to disclose that the number of women in the workplace is increasing, as are the numbers of African-Americans, Hispanics, Asians, and members of other minorities. For the first time in history, white males coming into the workplace will be in the minority. Because all of these employees will come with their own cultural upbringing and values, if adjustments are not made there will be great loss of productivity and serious conflict from potential culturally based misunderstandings.

Valuing diversity tries to turn what could be conflict into a positive, dynamic interchange that values each employee for what that employee brings to the workplace in order to further production, rather than seeing employees' differences as a threat to productivity. The concept of valuing diversity is not just a matter of so-called political correctness. It goes much deeper than that and is not likely to go away in the foreseeable future.

As we saw in Chapter 12, affirmative action forced employers to bring into the workplace employees who, intentionally or unintentionally, had been left out under traditional hiring methods. It is quite another matter to deal with those employees—once they were there— in ways that valued them for who they are rather than try to assimilate them into something they are not. Failing to so value employees takes its toll on an employer's bottom line, for people can rarely produce to their fullest when they do not feel comfortable with who they are for fear of isolation and hostility, either subtle or pronounced. If employers are to maximize production, they must address the ways in which failing to value diversity manifests itself in the workplace. Box 13–1, "Missing People and Others: Joining Together to Expand the Circle," gives some idea of what this is like for those deemed "other." It leaves little doubt as to how such attitudes can result in litigation for Bill and Ann if exhibited in the workplace. Understanding the impact on employees can help Ann and Bill avoid potential liability.

13–1   LAW IN THE REAL WORLD

Missing People and Others: Joining Together to Expand the Circle

I am a citizen of the United States, as are my parents and as were their parents, grandparents, and great-grandparents. I do not, however, fit those mental sets that define America and Americans. My physical appearance, my speech patterns, my name, my profession (a professor of Spanish) create a text that confuses the reader. My normal experience is to be asked, "And where are *you* from?"

I've always known that I was *the other*, even before I knew the vocabulary or understood the significance of being *the other*.

[W]e would always have an accent, however perfect our pronunciation, however excellent our enunciation, however divine our diction. That accent would be heard in our pigmentation, our physiognomy, our names. We were, in short, *the other*.

Being *the other* means feeling different; is awareness of being distinct; is consciousness of being dissimilar. It means being outside the game, outside the circle, outside the set. It means being on the edges, closed out, precluded, even disdained and scorned. It produces a sense of isolation, of apartness, of disconnectedness, of alienation.

Being *the other* involves a contradictory phenomenon. On the other hand, being *the other* frequently means being invisible. Ralph Ellison wrote eloquently about that experience in his magisterial novel *The Invisible Man*. On the other hand, being *the other* sometimes involves sticking out like a sore thumb. What is she/he doing here?

If one is *the other*, one will inevitably be perceived unidimensionally; will be seen stereotypically; will be defined and delimited by mental sets that may not bear much relation to existing realities. There is a darker side to otherness as well. *The other* disturbs, disquiets, discomforts. It provokes distrust and suspicion. *The other* makes people feel anxious, nervous, apprehensive, even fearful. *The other* frightens, scares.

For some of us being *the other* is only annoying; for others it is debilitating; for still others it is damning. Many try to flee otherness by taking on protective colorations that provide invisibility, whether of dress or speech or manner or name. Only a fortunate few succeed. For the majority, otherness is permanently sealed by physical appearance. For the rest, otherness is betrayed by ways of being, speaking or doing.

I spent the first half of my life downplaying the significance and consequences of otherness. The second half has seen me wrestling to understand its complex and deeply ingrained realities; striving to fathom why otherness denies us a voice or visibility or validity in American society and its institutions; struggling to make otherness familiar, reasonable, even normal to my fellow Americans.

Source: From "Diversity and Its Discontents," by Arturo Madrid, *Academe*, November-December 1990, Volume 76, Number 6. Reprinted with permission of Arturo Madrid.

Often, without realizing it, we think differently about those who speak differently from us, act differently from us, eat or have fun differently from ourselves. *Different from* too often in the workplace is translated into *less than*. That ends up meaning fewer promotions, less frequent raises, less training, more discipline, and quicker lay-offs and terminations for the others. And all of these can lead to litigation.

Employees may claim discrimination under Title VII of the 1964 Civil Rights Act, the ADEA, or other protective legislation. You may recall that Title VII prohibits discrimination on the basis of race, color, gender, religion, or national origin. And even though we may have moved away from obvious, open discrimination, for the most part, subtle discrimination constitutes the new frontier. Because the overall effect of differences in treatment can deeply impact the experience of similarly situated employees, redress will inevitably come through the courts. Box 13–2, "Valuing Diversity: Preparing for the Reality of Multiculturalism," outlines some of the considerations this will mean for the workplace.

In addition to the possibility that employee diversity may be the basis of unequal treatment that in turn leads to discrimination suits, Ann and Bill must ensure that information gathered for dealing with this issue is not used in any unauthorized or negative way. In a recent case, a manager who admitted to feelings of prejudice in a multiculturalism training session sued after he was terminated because of his revealing that information. Needless to say, such training sessions will be virtually useless if the participants do not feel safe to be frank in trying to pinpoint any trouble they may be having finding ways to alleviate it.

13-2   LAW IN THE REAL WORLD

Valuing Diversity: Preparing for the Reality of Multiculturalism

Make a circle with your thumb and forefinger. What does it mean? In America we know it primarily as meaning "okay." But how many of us know that it may also mean the equivalent of "flipping someone the bird", "give me coin change," "I wish to make love with you," or "I wish you dead, as my mortal enemy?" The objective act has not changed, yet the meaning has. The interpretation the act is given depends upon the cultural conditioning of the receiver. Welcome to multiculturalism. Knowing what is meant becomes a necessity in processing the act; otherwise, the act has little meaning. Culture is what provides that information, and thus meaning, for virtually everything we do, say, wear, eat, value, and where and in what we live, sit, and sleep. Imagine how many other acts we engage in every day which can be misinterpreted based upon differences in cultural conditioning. Yet our cultural conditioning is rarely given much thought. Even less is given to the culture of others. That will not be true much longer.

In the Fall 1992 issue of the magazine of the American Assembly of Collegiate Schools of Business, the accrediting body of schools of business, the cover story and lead article was "Teaching Diversity: Business Schools Search for Model Approaches." In the article, it stated that "without integrating a comprehensive diversity message into the entire curriculum, the most relevant management education cannot occur." Multiculturalism is learning to understand, appreciate, and value (*not* just "tolerate") the unique aspects of cultures different from one's own. The end product is learning to value others who may be different for what they contribute, rather than rejecting them simply because they are different.

The concept of "culture" encompasses not only ethnicity, but also gender, age, disability, affinity orientation and other factors which may significantly affect, and in many ways define, one's life. Multiculturalism is learning that "different from" does not mean "less than." It is getting in touch with one's cultural conditioning and working toward inclusion rather than conformity.

Learning to value diversity opens people up to more. A major workplace concern is maximizing production and minimizing liability. Multiculturalism and valuing diversity contribute to this. To the extent that each person, regardless of cultural differences, is valued as a contributor in the workplace, he or she is less likely to sue the employer for transgressions (or perceived transgressions) stemming from not being valued. To the extent they are valued for who they are and what they can contribute in society, they are much less likely to end up engaging in acts such as the Los Angeles riots causing death and destruction in the spring of 1992 after the Rodney King verdict.

The U.S. Department of Labor's Workforce 2000 study conducted by the Hudson Institute and released in 1987 held a few surprises that galvanized America into addressing the issue of multiculturalism. According to the widely cited study, by the year 2000 we will experience the greatest influx of immigrants since World War II. At the same time, the percentage of women entering the workforce is increasing. The net result, according to the study, is that 85% of the net growth in the workforce will comprise women and non-Europeans. For the first time, white males will be a minority entering the workforce. This need not be viewed as a threatening circumstance, but rather an opportunity for innovation and progress.

These factors, alone, reveal that the workplace (and by implication, schools, universities, recreational facilities and everything else) will be very different from before. It will no longer do to have a white, European, male standard of operation. Others will be pouring into the workplace and will come with talent, energy, ideas, tenacity, imagination and other contributions the United States has always held dear as the basis for the "American Dream." They will come expecting to be able to use those qualities to pursue that dream. They will come feeling that they have much to offer and are valuable for all their uniqueness and the differences they may have from "the norm." And what will happen? There is no choice but to be prepared. It is a simple fact that the workplace cannot continue to operate in the same way and remain productive.

Studies have shown that when the same problem is given to homogeneous groups and heterogeneous groups to solve, the heterogeneous groups come up with more effective solutions. When people feel valued for who they are and what they can contribute, rather than feeling pressed into conformity as if who they are is not good enough, they are more productive. Energy and creativity can be spent on the task at hand rather than on worrying about how well they fit into someone's idea of who they should be. A significant number of the problems we face as a society and on which are spent millions in precious tax dollars come from rejecting multiculturalism and not valuing diversity. If people were judged for who

continued on next page

they are and what they contribute, there would not be a need for a civil rights act, affirmative action plans, riot gear, human rights commissions, etc.

There are, of course, naysayers on the topic of multiculturalism—those who think it is just an attempt at being "politically correct." It has been said that the term "politically correct" is an attempt to devalue, trivialize, demean and diffuse the substantive value of the issues spoken of. That once something is deemed to be an issue of "political correctness," then there is no need to worry about the real import or impact of it, because it is only a passing fad which need not be taken seriously, as it will die its own natural death soon enough.

Multiculturalism is here to stay. People have evolved to the point where it will not go away. Self-worth and valuing oneself is a lesson that takes many [people] a long time to learn. Once learned, it is hard to give up. And, of course, why should it be given up? Again, "different from" does not mean "less than." Learning to value others as unique human beings whose culture is an integral part of who they are, rather than something to be shed at the work or school door, and learning to value the differences rather than to try to assimilate them will benefit everyone.

Source: Reprinted from *Columns*, University of Georgia faculty-staff newspaper, Dawn Bennett-Alexander, Esq., author. March 1993, with permission.

FLEXTIME

flextime
variable hours employees can work and still be full-time employees.

Many employers have adopted the notion of **flextime**. Rather than have all employees report, for instance, from 9 a.m. to 5 p.m., Monday through Friday, employers adopting flextime allow their employees the option of maintaining flexible hours. The extent to which an employer can adopt this alternative depends, to a great extent, on the nature of the business as well as the positions the employer must maintain. Flextime may have legal implications for Bill and Ann regarding its examination as an alternative that may be available in addressing the issue of gender equity in the workplace.

Many employers have certain core hours during which employees must be present; then the rest of the hours may consist of flextime. In this way, the employer is fairly certain of a full complement of employees for all positions during a given time period. Determining whether flextime is right for a given employer requires a good deal of thought about the nature of the jobs held and how the jobs are affected by the change in hours.

If Ann and Bill have a workplace at which much of the work to be done involves interacting with outside businesses, most of which operate from 9 to 5, then Ann and Bill will be limited in their ability to adopt flextime. But if some of the jobs merely require that the employees get the job done and for the most part, time is not of the essence, flexibility may be a viable option.

A large law firm in Oregon adopted flextime for members of its typing pool after discovering that many of the employees wanted flexibility concerning child-rearing issues. Productivity went up—and frustration down—after the employer allowed the typists to choose their hours as long as the typing was done by the deadline. Many were able to come in and work for several hours in the evening after their children were settled. Others were there during the time their children were at school. Because their jobs required minimal interaction with the rest of the staff (which was there for regular business hours) and they were required to have the work done by the deadline, flexibility was not a problem.

Flextime is not appropriate for every employer. However, for those who entertain it as a possibility, it may well be worth the effort. With employees being able to choose their own hours, within a certain range, absenteeism and turnover tend to be lower and loyalty higher.

JOB SHARING

Job sharing is another of the flexible approaches to the workplace that have been necessitated by the business owner's realization that more and more employees wish to have a life outside the workplace. Whereas much of the job sharing that goes on is done by female employees who are attempting to coordinate their parental responsibilities with their job, males are also using this option where it is offered, in an effort to take the emphasis off work as the center of their lives.

Job sharing involves the employee's sharing one or several jobs among one or more people, so that the job is always covered. Yet each of the employees has separate responsibilities or times of responsibility that result in the employee's not being tied to the job all day, every day. With job sharing, for instance, one employee may have the job in the morning and another in the afternoon. One employee may

job sharing
more than one employee employed in the same job, with sharing of responsibilities so that the job is always covered

have the job on certain days of the week, and another on the remaining days. Bill and Ann get two employees at about the price of one, and the employees are each responsible totally for the job when they are on duty. Employees receive the benefit of the job without being tied to it full-time. See Box 13–3, "Two Reporters, One Post: NBC Tries Job Sharing," for an idea of how it worked at NBC News.

Not all jobs lend themselves to being shared. Before establishing the option, Bill and Ann need to look closely at what the particular job requires and whether it lends itself to sharing. When permitted, the option can represent a win-win situation for Bill and Ann as well as the employee. Bill and Ann have the job covered, and the employees receive the flexibility they need to attend to both professional and personal concerns.

If Ann and Bill are approached by employees who ask them to consider the possibility of flextime, Ann and Bill should carefully examine the option. Instituting such a policy goes a long way to building employee loyalty, productivity, diversity and morale while providing an atmosphere in which it is less likely that gender claims will arise or will result in litigation. As more employers explore and implement the option, more employees will come to expect it, and employers who can institute the policy and do not may find themselves agreeing that a proactive approach may have saved them time, trouble, and litigation.

TEMPORARY/LEASED EMPLOYEES

More and more employers are taking advantage of the benefits of the burgeoning phenomenon of temporary or leased employees. This arrangement might be particularly attractive to Bill and Ann because of the nature of the work their business is engaged in. They have a need not only for clerical workers to do office work but also for employees who will clean, keep their books, be responsible for waste management, and so on. Their business may have cyclical or ad hoc needs also, engendered by being busier, say, during holidays or the need to hire extra workers during a catastrophe such as an oil spill or nuclear facility accident.

During the workforce cutbacks of the 1980s, employees many times found themselves out of work with no prospect of a full-time job. Many connected themselves with temporary agencies, which then found themselves with employees who did not fit the traditional pro-

13–3   LAW IN THE REAL WORLD

Two Reporters, One Post: NBC Tries Job Sharing

Lisa Rudolph always wanted to be a network correspondent. "But I was hesitant because of the travel involved," she says. "I wanted a family but traveling all the time wasn't something I felt comfortable doing—living out of a suitcase at this point in my life."

Victoria Corderi could relate: She had quit CBS News after 7½ years when her daughter was born 20 months ago. "I didn't want to travel." Instead, she took a local anchor job at WABC, but quit after 11 months. "Those hours were really long."

Today, both women have found a home at NBC News in New York, where they share the work normally performed by one correspondent. They're assigned to two newsmagazines: *Now* and *Dateline NBC.* Both say word of their deal spread fast throughout the TV news industry and beyond, among friends and colleagues who themselves are struggling to juggle work and parenthood.

"The response has been tremendous," says Corderi, who points out that the mind-set in both local and network news—when it comes to reporters and anchors—has been: "You work full-time or nothing."

(In a celebrated case, at CBS, *60 Minutes* canned correspondent Meredith Vieira after she tried to work out a part-time schedule so she could spend more time with her kids. ABC News, where she now is a correspondent on the upcoming newsmagazine *Turning Point*, is said to be more flexible on the issue.)

Rudolph, formerly an anchor/reporter at WCBS in New York, says her new job "is the closest to ideal you can get. This is something many families are struggling with."

The arrangement came about "not through plotting or scheming or heavy-duty planning. These two women became available at the same time and we had a job to fill," says NBC News vice president Cheryl Gould. "They didn't want to work full-time and we looked at each other and said, 'Why not? Let's make this work.' I don't think there's going to be a problem.

"I think managers are beginning to see that it's a wise business move," Gould says. "It's good business to have employees happy and allow for a more diverse workplace. It enables you to attract more people to your ranks. What is difficult to understand is why it was never done before."

file of those wishing to be placed with an employer. At one point most temporary employees were clerical workers. Not anymore: During the 80s, the agencies had a number of professionals available. Nowadays, Bill and Ann can lease anyone from a temporary company president to a temporary window washer. Box 13–4, "More Firms Hire White-Collar Temps," speaks to that issue.

To Bill and Ann the advantage of temporary employees is that such employees are not actually employed by the company. Thus Bill and Ann are not responsible for the usual benefits, such as health and life insurance and pensions, which add a great deal to the cost of hiring. There is also less downtime devoted to learning, for leased employees can be handpicked to fit Bill and Ann's needs by coming fully equipped for the positions to be filled.

 Employees can use their skills on a temporary basis, can change jobs from time to time, can stop whenever they wish, and are not bound to a company out of loyalty or other considerations. However, Ann and Bill should be aware that if they are going to consider the use of temporary employees, potential legal implications are present. Box 13–5, "Temporary Solutions," mentions a number of these.

Temporary employees will allow Ann and Bill to have a continuous cadre of workers to fill virtually any of the company's human resources needs, and Ann and Bill also will be relieved of the burden of having to offer benefits, make pension contributions, be constrained by possible limitations on discharging the employees, and handle other matters. Some of the temp agencies offer partial benefits; others none. Changes in the health care system may cause this to change. President Clinton's proposed health care reform bill, for example, included part-time health benefits, and even though the bill did not make it into law, given the increase in part-time workers, the issue will not go away.

As more companies engage temporary employees who earn less wages and benefits, many such positions may be taken from female employees whose lower-end jobs tend to be most vulnerable. The temps taking those jobs at lower wages and with few or no benefits are also largely female. Thus, if Bill and Ann decide to move to temps, the decision has the potential of creating a disparate impact on females. Bill and Ann should also be aware that as the trend toward the use of temporary workers takes hold, those very same advantages will create disadvantages for the workers. Eventually politicians will respond. That was, in part, what prompted the inclusion of part-time employees in President Clinton's health care package. If this happens,

13–4   LAW IN THE REAL WORLD

More Firms Hire White-Collar Temps

The revolving door to the executive suite is spinning faster these days as more companies hire temporary top managers.

Of the 1 million temporary employees working on any given day in the U.S.A., about 12%, or 125,000, are executives, *Executive Recruiter News* says.

Since 1990, the number of companies placing temporary executives earning more than $75,000 a year has more than tripled, says editor David Lord, to 140 from 40. Revenue has doubled to $100 million in 1992 from 1990 levels.

"It's the fastest-growing segment of the industry," says Bruce Steinberg of the National Association of Temporary Services.

What's fueling the trend toward high-priced temps? Many companies are reluctant to hire permanent staffers because of the uncertainty over higher taxes and the cost of proposed health care reform. Plus, they are trying to stay lean after years of restructuring and layoffs.

Meanwhile, temporary hiring at all levels—including clerical, technical, professional and medical—rose 17% from 1991 to 1992, says Steinberg. It is still going strong.

Compared with clerical temps, who make as little as $5 an hour, executive temping is lucrative. For instance:

- Accountants are paid $20 to $40 an hour.
- Middle managers, $50 to $60.
- Top-notch senior executives, $150 to $200 an hour.

Executive temp assignments typically last four to six months.

Source: "More Firms Hire White-Collar Temps," by Julia Lawlor, *USA Today*, July 20, 1993. ©1994, *USA Today*. Reprinted with permission.

13–5   LAW IN THE REAL WORLD

Temporary Solutions

Belle, who has been a consultant for 10 years, makes $45 an hour for what averages out to be a 35-hour week. At the moment, she is helping Wells Fargo Bank develop and market a new software program that will enable customers to bank through their computers, doing everything but getting cash out of the machine.

But a more common example of the new contingent worker is the woman who had been on the Bank of America payroll for 14 years when the bank offered her a choice: She could reduce her 30-hour workweek to 19 hours, with no benefits, or leave with a modest severance package. She stayed, and now depends on a second job at a convenience store for survival.

Such a "choice" was offered in 1993 to thousands of Bank of America employees, mostly women. When the restructuring at the giant bank is complete, only 19% of the workforce will be full-time. A similar downsizing is rippling through Wells Fargo and other banks and companies across the country. Scratch a large corporation today and it may well be in the process of reducing its full-time, or core, employees and replacing them with lower-paid disposable workers, the ultimate in just-in-time inventory control.

Still, as troubling as the growth of throwaway workers is, it would be a mistake to conclude that the trend toward contingent work is all bad. Even those concerned about it agree that a significant, although relatively small, number of contingent workers are highly skilled, well paid and/or happy with their arrangements. And for many companies, the flexibility and lower labor costs may be critical to future prosperity. The big question is: Can it work for employers and employees alike and enhance the economy as a whole?

Source: First appeared in *Working Woman* in February 1994. Written by Ann Crittenden. Reprinted with the permission of *Working Woman* magazine. ©1994, by Working Woman, Inc.

Bill and Ann must concern themselves not only with the possibility of gender-based litigation from the use of temps but also with the legislative responses that may change the picture in ways adverse to their choice of using them.

DOMESTIC PARTNERSHIPS

If Ann and Bill wish to extend equal benefits to unmarried employees who live with others of the same or a different gender in a mutually supportive household, it may be done by extending benefits to domestic partners. Several municipalities have made provisions for domestic partnerships, but such provisions need not be in place in order for an employer to recognize and extend benefits to domestic partners. Among others, Ithaca and New York, New York; Madison, Wisconsin; Ann Arbor, Michigan; Minneapolis, Minnesota; and Los Angeles, San Francisco, Berkeley, Laguna Beach, and West Hollywood, California, provide for the registration of unmarried couples as domestic partners.

domestic partnership a process of registering with the state or local government those who wish to have some of the benefits of the marital relationship, without the relationship itself

Most domestic partnership provisions include both relationships between people of the opposite gender as well as between those of the same gender. Domestic partnerships serve as the basis for permitting those involved to receive certain benefits that have heretofore been open only to married couples, though the partnerships themselves are not considered marriages.

For instance, some employers permit employees to put their domestic partner on an insurance policy. Delta Air Lines has extended its frequent-flier-miles transfer of benefits to encompass not only the traditional notion of family members but also domestic partners. In February 1994 Avis Car Rental eliminated its second-driver car rental charge for unmarried couples who live together; previously, only spouses and business colleagues were exempt from the charge.

The concept is not without its detractors. Apple Computer recently withdrew its decision to build an $80-million, 700-employee customer service center in Williamson County's Round Rock, Texas, when the city council refused to grant the company business concessions after it learned Apple provided benefits for domestic partners. The city later withdrew its opposition. In addition to companies such as Apple, AT&T, Hewlett-Packard, and Coors Brewing addressing such issues, Box 13–6, "Employers Adopt Domestic Partnership Benefits," discloses that domestic partnership benefits have been extended to gay and lesbian employees by cities and universities as well.

The legal considerations for Ann and Bill on the issue of domestic partnerships stems from the increased litigation surrounding the issue of gays and lesbians striving for rights that are routinely extended other employees. Gay and lesbian employees have challenged certain workplace antidiscrimination policies that include same-gender affinity orientation as a category but that do not then recognize long-term relationships or domestic partnerships for purposes of bereavement leave, life and health insurance, or even infirmary care or other benefit programs. If Bill and Ann either choose to or are required by law to have an antidiscrimination policy encompassing gays and lesbians, they should be aware of the existence of domestic partnerships and investigate how they will actually implement such a policy with gays and lesbians. Some employers choose to apply it through domestic partnerships; others, not. Box 13–7, "Domestic Partner Law Debate: Domestic Partner Law Protects Personal Wishes," on page 422, gives some of the pros and cons an employer looking at the issue may wish to consider.

If Bill and Ann decide to extend benefits to domestic partners, they should be certain first to investigate thoroughly whether their benefit carriers permit such arrangements and whether state law has been interpreted to allow it. At least one state's attorney general (Michael Bowers of Georgia) has opined that the state constitution does not allow insurance carriers to cover domestic partnerships. If state law allows it but the insurance carriers do not, and Bill and Ann still want such benefits offered to their employees, they should search for carriers who can handle their needs.

Litigation can also arise if Bill and Ann have an antidiscrimination policy that includes gays and lesbians, but then the policy is not construed to include them for purposes of certain benefits. AT&T had a policy against discrimination on the basis of affinity orientation and marital status. Under AT&T's pension plan, the surviving partner of an employee receives a year's salary upon the employee's death. When Marjorie Forlini, an AT&T employee, died, Sandra Rovira, her partner of 12 years, applied for the benefits and was refused. Rovira filed suit against AT&T, and the federal district court judge ruled that the policy applied only to spouses. Although New York did not have legally sanctioned same-gender marriages, private industries can opt to guarantee such benefits.

13–6 LAW IN THE REAL WORLD

Employers Adopt Domestic Partnership Benefits

Columbia University has joined several other big universities in offering medical benefits to domestic partners of the same sex for its full-time faculty members and administrative officers. The policy will go into effect on January 1, 1994, said the university's provost, Jonathon R. Cole.

Prof. James Hoover, the university's law librarian and a gay member of the study group that developed the package, said, "I think the fact that the university has offered the package is important. It is the first time the university has actively taken steps to implement nondiscrimination policies."

To qualify for benefits, couples must have shared a household for six months and meet two criteria of common financial obligation, including sharing a mortgage or lease; declaring the partner a primary beneficiary in a life insurance policy, retirement benefits, or will; assigning the partner a durable power of attorney; or owning a joint bank account.

Professor Hoover said university officials studied the packages offered by Stanford University and the University of Chicago.

"I think there is a concern that this is a community that would have higher AIDS costs than the general population," Professor Hoover said. "The Stanford study did a lot to show that there were not significant cost considerations. The university benefits consultants were able to corroborate that."

Source: "Employers Adopt Domestic Partnership Benefits," *New York Times*, November 3, 1993. ©1993 by the New York Times Company. Reprinted by permission.

Partners of gay and lesbian city employees in Baltimore will get the same health benefits as workers' legal spouses under a policy city officials adopted unanimously, with no public opposition. The new policy adopted December 15, 1993, takes effect January 1, 1995. Baltimore joins several major cities, including New York, San Francisco and Seattle, in recognizing gay and lesbian partnerships.

Source: *USA Today*, December 17, 1993. ©1993, *USA Today*. Reprinted with permission.

13–7   LAW IN THE REAL WORLD

Domestic Partner Law Debate: Domestic Partner Law Protects Personal Wishes

USA Today **editorial: Our View**

Shouldn't you be able to decide who should care for you in crisis or [should] benefit if you die?

Unmarried couples should keep an eye on California. A bill awaiting the governor's signature would bring some needed changes to Californians' lives. The concept could, and should, spread to other states.

There's nothing earthshaking about the bill. In fact, it's surprising no state yet offers three basic protections to unmarrieds:

- The right to have your partner visit if you're hospitalized
- The right to have your partner act as guardian if you're incapacitated
- And the right to leave your money and property to whom you wish in your will, avoiding nasty court battles with relatives

Spouses, of course, already have these rights. But there are plenty of couples—nearly half a million in California alone—who aren't married, 93% of them heterosexual. Many will marry later; some never will, for a variety of reasons. And for gay couples, marriage is out of the question.

Domestic partner programs have expanded rapidly in the past decade. Two states and several cities grant full health benefits to employees' partners.

Others offer domestic partner registration, which offers varying degrees of legal protection. Ordinances in Minneapolis, Minn., and West Hollywood, Calif., for example, allow hospital visitation. In other places, registration provides psychological benefits but not legal ones.

How important is legal recognition of a partnership? Anyone who pooh-poohs it could use a lesson from Karen Thompson and Sharon Kowalski. The two women, teachers in Minnesota, began living together in 1979. In 1983, Kowalski was injured in an accident caused by a drunken driver. She was brain damaged and comatose for five months.

Thompson battled Kowalski's parents over guardianship, and when the parents won in 1985, they banned Thompson from even visiting their daughter. The case went to the Minnesota Court of Appeals, and Thompson, who had built a wheelchair-accessible home for Kowalski, finally gained custody in 1991.

When it comes to the law, spouses and blood relatives come first regardless of the wishes of the victim. That's why legislation such as the one in California [is] so important.

[It allows] people to say, in effect, "Hey, world. This is my life partner. This is the person I want when I'm sick or need to be taken care of, and it's the person I want taken care of if I die first."

The California proposal is such a little step in the legal scheme of things, But it's an important one.

Growth of Benefits

More than 70 firms and organizations offer some type of domestic partner benefits. Two states, Vermont and New York, have granted health and dental benefits to domestic partners of state employees. Some cities with similar provisions:

Health benefits: Ann Arbor and East Lansing, Mich.; Berkeley, Calif.; Cambridge, Mass.; Seattle, Wash.; New York, New York, N.Y.

Registration and/or sick and bereavement leave: Atlanta, Ga.; Madison, Wis.; Takoma Park, Md.; Los Angeles, Calif.; West Palm Beach, Fla.

Source: Lambda Legal Defense and Education Fund, Inc.

Opposing View

This law isn't necessary. Stop this campaign to legitimize cohabitation.

Hold on to your checkbook, because the liberal/left is pushing another nearsighted social experiment called "domestic partners," which will cost taxpayers and redefine the institution of marriage.

The goal of the homosexual special interest lobby is to change the public policy of this nation by expanding the definition of marriage and family to include two homosexuals or heterosexuals living together. This new quasi-marital union impacts the way our judges make their rulings on issues that relate to marriage and family, and it devalues the concept of marriage.

So far, courts have denied marital status to cohabiting homosexuals. But this could change. If government expands the definition of marriage, the courts will then be compelled to force businesses to pay benefits for the domestic partners of employees just like benefits for employees' spouses. And governments could be forced to use scarce tax dollars for benefits for domestic partners of government employees. Most states allow consenting adults to live together, but that doesn't mean taxpayers should have to subsidize this arrangement.

Also, domestic partnerships weaken the institution of marriage and encourage relationships without the responsibility of marriage. Some may argue this new legislation promotes monogamous relationships, but these

continued on next page

laws typically allow for a new "partner" every six months and erode the cultural support for the permanency of marriage.

Homosexual activists are good at marketing. They have tried to mainstream themselves by garnering some senior citizens' support. But domestic partners is an unnecessary shotgun approach to remedy some senior-citizen concerns.

Moreover, medical facilities already allow visitation in intensive care units and hospital rooms by friends or relatives. Existing law allows a testator to will property to anyone—friend or stranger. Existing law allows any "interested person" to file petitions or receive notice regarding conservatorship or guardianships.

The man/woman marriage relationship is best for society.

Rev. Louis P. Sheldon, chairman of Traditional Values Coalition, Anaheim, Calif.

Source: "Domestic-Partner Law Protects Personal Wishes," August 31, 1994. ©1994. *USA Today.*

If Ann and Bill decide to have an antidiscrimination policy, they should be sure to govern themselves consistently with the policy. If they intend to discriminate for some purposes and not others, they should be sure it is clear in the policy. In many cases, litigation can be avoided simply by being clear about policies from the outset.

Extending benefits to registered domestic partners will allow Bill and Ann to have some measure of control over the limitations regarding to whom benefits can be extended. There is nothing to prevent Bill and Ann from having a company-wide domestic partnership registration system of its own or from permitting the extension of benefits even though their state or local government has no such system in place yet. If there is no such system, Bill and Ann should be aware that it is a potential point of litigation for gay and lesbian employees to ask for it.

Because most of the state and local gay and lesbian antidiscrimination laws are fairly new, as is increasingly frequent litigation surrounding gay and lesbian issues, there is little Bill and Ann can turn to in the way of guidance. However, if the laws are going to be implemented, rather than simply exist on paper, part of it will inevitably cover the area of benefits. In the alternative, Bill and Ann may decide, for whatever reasons, that they do not wish to adopt this benefit. It is their prerogative to do so.

SUPPORT GROUPS

Support groups are now being offered at many workplaces. With the constant pressure of social and personal concerns of one type or another, some employers have found it beneficial to offer such groups as an inexpensive but effective way to provide some measure of assistance to help turn out more productive employees. Workplace groups have been organized for working mothers, gays and lesbians, incest survivors, women, men, and others.

The support groups need only a minimum of administrative support from the employer and often offer large rewards. By employees' meeting in the workplace with others who share their concerns, many times issues are worked out before becoming problems. Employees are often less isolated, less distracted, and more productive and loyal when there is a feeling of support for issues of importance to them. The employer benefits by having more productive and loyal employees, who tend to have less absenteeism and turnover.

As an example, a growing number of employers, acknowledging that they do not quite know what to do about gay and lesbian concerns but wishing to do something positive, have established gay and lesbian support groups within their companies. Among such companies are Apple, Digital Equipment, AT&T, Boeing, Coors, DuPont, Hewlett-Packard, Lockheed, Sun Microsystems, Pacific Gas and Electric Co., and USWest. The groups tackle such issues as workplace hostility, and they extend employee benefits to domestic partners, making sure that partners are welcome at company social functions and generally making the workplace more hospitable to gays and lesbians.

If a growing number of employees seem to have similar problems that affect or interfere with their ability to do the job, Bill and Ann may consider suggesting a support group. The employees will appreciate the suggestion and probably attempt to help, yet value the autonomy of being able to deal with the issue without interference from Bill and Ann. Of course, support groups are not intended to take the place of qualified professional counseling when such is called for. However, groups on dealing with work and family responsibility conflicts, ethnicity or affinity orientation, and so on, may be appropriate.

Bill and Ann should be aware, however, that while support groups may have the effect of preventing lawsuits in certain areas by addressing matters proactively, privacy is a possible area of litigation in terms of support groups. Information brought out during support group sessions should be kept confidential and neither used by Bill and Ann to make adverse employment decisions nor spread to others in or outside the workplace with no need to know. Employees have sued employers when information has come out of such sessions and been used for other purposes. Bill and Ann can attempt to avoid that problem by giving the groups sanction and autonomy, but providing strict guidelines for participation—and serious consequences for violations.

WORKPLACE PRIVACY

We covered one aspect of employee privacy previously in discussing Bill and Ann's giving references to potential employers about present or ex-employees. Employees who feel Bill and Ann's comments go beyond the limits of what is necessary to give an employment recommendation can sue Bill and Ann for some type of invasion of privacy (recall that there are several types).

Employee privacy is becoming a more frequent source of litigation against employers, with the advent of technology that permits sophisticated surveillance to gather information on employees for purposes of evaluating efficiency and quality. State and federal government employees are protected from privacy invasion by the government under federal and similar state constitutional guarantees under the Fourth (freedom from unreasonable search and seizures), Fifth, and Fourteenth (right to due process) amendments. Federal employees are also afforded the protection of the Privacy Act of 1974 (restricts the availability of information given out about federal employees by federal agencies). Private employees, however, do not have as much protection from unwarranted intrusions by an employer. The Constitution prohibits excessive *government* intrusions upon privacy; private employers like Bill and Ann, engaging in the same activity, will not be viewed the same way.

Tort claims can be brought by employees on the theories of invasion of privacy through publication of private facts, intrusion upon seclusion, appropriation of name or likeness, or false light. These were covered in the previous chapter on torts and can be used in the employment setting as appropriate. For instance, if Ann and Bill gathered information about an employee, found the employee had a history of drug abuse, and unnecessarily disseminated that information to the workplace in general, the employee will have a cause of action for publication of private facts.

As Bill and Ann use more sophisticated technology to gather more types of information on employees, what they do with such information is important. They must be sure to disseminate it only on a need-to-know basis, gather as little information as required, and not unnecessarily invade employees' privacy in doing so.

Closely related to this is the matter of how far Ann and Bill can go in regulating the off-duty activities of their employees. Employees have sued employers for privacy invasions and other legal violations such as unjust dismissal, when an employer has made a workplace decision based on activity taking place outside work hours. For instance, in *Rulon-Miller v. IBM Corporation*, 162 Cal. App. 3d 241 (1984), a managerial employee at IBM received $100,000 of compensation and $200,000 in punitive damages after she was terminated for dating an employee who worked for a competing business, despite the company's policy guarding employees' right to personal privacy.

Ann and Bill should take a conservative view of regulating employees' after-hours behavior. If the activity actually constitutes a conflict of interest or is detrimental to the employee's ability to perform on the job, regulation would be more justifiable than not. It should be made clear to employees beforehand what is regulated, why, and what the consequences will be.

WORKPLACE TESTING

With the advent of increased recreational drug use in society, it was inevitable that such use would affect the workplace. Drug use can cost Ann and Bill significant dollars in lost efficiency, accidents, increased workers' compensation premiums stemming from on-the-job injuries, and lowered productivity. You may recall that the Exxon *Valdez* accident was alcohol related and that certain recent train accidents have been drug related.

In an effort to avoid such costs, employers like Ann and Bill began testing their employees to determine whether they had been taking drugs and thus would suffer from impaired workplace competence. Employees who have felt the tests invasive and a violation of their right to privacy have sued employers. In determining the propriety of the tests, courts have balanced the employer's interest in having a drug-free and alcohol-free workplace against the employee's right to privacy and constitutional Fifth Amendment protection against self-incrimination.

Preemployment testing for competency has also been a significant employment screening tool for nearly 50 years. Employers test employees before hiring in order to ensure that they are hiring people who can perform the work and who will be well placed based on their abilities. For instance, employers give a typing test to an applicant for a position as a typist and a truck driving test to an applicant for a position as a truck driver.

But not all preemployment tests have been so directly related to the job to be performed. In administering such tests, Ann and Bill run the risk of being sued by employees in groups protected by Title VII who feel they are adversely affected, without counterbalancing employer need for the test. An example is a general intelligence test that can be shown to be unrelated to the work the employee is to perform but that screens out a disparate number of female or minority applicants.

In ruling on the propriety of preemployment tests, the courts have used the four-fifths rule discussed in Chapter 12. Under the rule, a test that screens out female or minority applicants is presumed to have a disparate impact if the females or minorities do not do at least 80% or four-fifths as well as the majority applicants. The employer must then show that the test is job related and that there exists no way to screen employees that has less of an adverse impact. If Ann and Bill can show this, then the test will be allowed even though it has a disparate impact on groups protected by Title VII. Most employers who are sued, however, cannot show this.

In *Griggs v. Duke Power Co.*, 401 U.S. 424 (1971), the employer required a high school diploma or a passing score on a general intelligence test before allowing employees to transfer from the all-African-American labor section—where employees made less than the lowest-paid white worker in any other section—into any other division of the workplace. Employees already in all the other sections were grandfathered in and not made to meet the diploma or intelligence test requirement. The U.S. Supreme Court held that the employer could not have the test imposed as a requirement. The reason was that the test was obviously not job related, because employees in those sections were currently holding positions and had neither a diploma nor a passing score on the intelligence test. Thus the only thing the requirement accomplished was that it acted as a screening device to weed out African-Americans looking to move up in the organization.

Bill and Ann can also have their tests professionally validated, but as this is very expensive with no guarantee of success in the courts, few employers do it; consequently, professional validation has represented very little of what courts have faced in cases challenging test impact.

In instituting preemployment tests, Bill and Ann must be sure that such tests—which can be screening devices of any kind whatsoever and not just paper-and-pencil exams—test employees on their qualifications for the job. For drug and alcohol testing, Bill and Ann should be sure there is a need for such testing based on the job the employee performs and that it is no more invasive than necessary.

SUMMARY

With employees' wanting a better quality of work life and the employer's learning of the benefits this has for workplace productivity and harmony, workplace innovations are being tried as never before. Employers wishing to gain the advantages of such innovations are cautioned to be willing to gather information about the effect—before instituting big changes—and to remain flexible. Picking and choosing which innovations are best and which will give the most return may represent a time-consuming task, but it will be well worth it if the innovations bring the expected rewards.

CHAPTER TERMS

domestic partnership   job sharing

flextime

CHAPTER-END QUESTIONS

1. Dawn's Aunt Ruth calls Dawn, a lawyer, for legal advice. Ruth is employed by the county library as a book processor. Ruth found out that the library administrators, in an effort to see whether the books and videos she takes from the library form any "patterns the administrators should be aware of," have been monitoring those books and videos. What will Dawn likely tell her? Why?

2. Kurlen, a high school football hero now in an undergraduate pre-medicine program, applies for a summer job as a hospital medical technician. In the position, Kurlen will have access to the hospital's drugs and pharmaceuticals. The hospital requires Kurlen to take a drug test before deciding on his application. Kurlen does not see the need for such an exam and does not wish to take it. He feels his rights are being violated. Are they?

3. David tells Jack that if the state does not have a domestic registration statute, then his employer cannot provide domestic partner benefits. Is David's statement true or false?

4. Randall has a consulting business that employs 25 people, 15 of whom have children. Within a two-month span, 10 of the 15 say they will need to make some workplace accommodation in September, when their children return to school. What are the legal implications for Randall to consider?

5. In order to determine whether a matter of employee testing is an invasion of workplace privacy, courts balance _____ against the right _____.

6. Julian, an architect, is married and has two young children. His wife, a lawyer, is pregnant with a third. Julian decides he wants to become more involved in parenting. He goes to his supervisor and says so. Most likely, if the decision is made to allow Julian some measure of job flexibility, then due to the nature of Julian's job it will likely be

   a. job sharing.
   b. flextime.
   c. temporary employee.
   d. support group.

   Why? If the employer refuses Julian's request, will Julian have a cause of action? Explain.

7. Christie is in a workplace support group for abusive relationships. One day Elmer, a secretary at the workplace and someone who has been trying to get Christie to go out with him, brings refreshments into the meeting for the end-of-meeting social hour. Elmer is shocked to see Christie in the group. He leaves the meeting and in the next few days tells several employees that Christie "has *some* nerve spurning him when she is in a relationship with an abusive spouse and [he Elmer] would be a great improvement."

Word of this gets back to Christie, and she sues the company for invasion of privacy. Will she win? Explain.

8. When Ms. Marks is hired by an employer and puts down the names of others to be covered by her health insurance, her form is rejected by Carrie, the human resources worker who says that the designation is not permissible because it is a person of the same gender—Ms. Wooley. Ms. Marks explains that she and Ms. Wooley have lived together for 15 years and are domestic partners. Carrie says that this is highly irregular and that she has never heard of such a thing. When Carrie checks with the state registration office as Ms. Marks tells her to do, she finds that Ms. Marks and Ms. Wooley are indeed registered as domestic partners. Is the employer required to cover domestic partners under the employees' health care plan? Explain.

9. Elaine says that if the employer does not offer flextime or job-share options to employees who wish to have them, then it is a violation of law. Is Elaine's statement true or false?

10. John is frustrated with Yin Su, a female Asian employee who came to this country from China three years ago. John finds that when he is talking with Yin Su, she rarely looks at him. He also finds that she never disagrees with him, even though he later discovers that he was wrong about something he said to Yin Su. John takes Yin Su's failure to look him in the eye as an indication that she is not honest. He interprets her failure to tell him when he is wrong as her wish to sabotage and undermine him. John finally terminates Yin Su. Does Yin Su have a cause of action against John for her dismissal? What issues should John have considered in order to avoid possible litigation?

GROUP EXERCISE

Break into groups and split up the local phonebook's business section. Call business personnel offices and ask which, if any, of the innovations discussed in the chapter they have, why they adopted them, and how they have worked out. Report back to the class. In the alternative, have each group take one innovation and make calls related only to that innovation.

Chapter 14

LEGAL RESPONSIBILITY OF THE BUSINESS TO ITS CUSTOMERS AND CLIENTS

Chapter Preview Summary

Regardless of how much a product or service is needed in the market, Ann and Bill can be successful only if they earn a profit. The competitive nature of the market, however, can lead some businesses to take advantage of consumers who are less than knowledgeable about business tactics and the intricacies of the marketplace. Not only can such practice be unethical; it can also be illegal.

Primarily for consumers' protection and benefit, the government has implemented regulations that help to level the playing field by requiring that businesses disclose matters consumers commonly deal with. Those matters include the true cost of products, money (loan interest), and services that regulate the amount of credit information and advertising between a business and its customers. By requiring every business to disclose the same kind of information to each consumer, the idea is that the consumer will benefit by being able to comparison shop for the best value.

Not only are Bill and Ann in business themselves, but they are customers of other businesses as well. They purchase office and industrial supplies, contract with institutions to handle their finances, and buy advertising space. Although many of the regulations apply only to nonbusiness consumers, some apply to all consumers. Therefore, Bill and Ann's knowledge of regulations is imperative from both a customer and a business viewpoint. Unquestionably, fair treatment of Bill and Ann's customers not only will help to ensure the success of their business, but it also will prevent them from running afoul of the law.

Chapter Objectives

In studying the chapter, you should learn:
- what the Federal Trade Commission is and what it does
- business owners' duties to consumers
- what bait-and-switch tactics are
- the limitations on advertising
- which federal acts regulate lending and billing
- which collection practices are unlawful
- what lemon laws are and how they protect consumers
- the laws governing electronic fund transfers
- which laws regulate your credit reporting and opportunity

INTRODUCTION

Not only must Bill and Ann address the internal matters of how to do business—which type of business organization is best, how to safely hire and employ workers, and how to deal with disputes that may arise—but they must also deal with external business matters. One of the most important of those matters is the business's legal responsibility to consumers.

The legal responsibilities imposed on Bill and Ann may come from a number of sources, including federal and state government rules that regulate how Bill and Ann can advertise, how they must deal with those who ask for credit, how they can collect debts, and how they must handle the credit information of consumers. In this chapter we explore some of the legal responsibilities Bill and Ann have to their customers or clients as consumers.

THE FEDERAL TRADE COMMISSION

The Federal Trade Commission (FTC) was established by Congress in 1914, primarily for the purpose of supplementing antitrust laws; it was not specifically designed to protect consumers. However, the statute gave the FTC the power to prohibit unfair methods of competition, and it did not take long for its interpretation to include deceptive trade practices as unfair methods. As early as 1922, the U.S. Supreme Court recognized that to mislabel products diverted customers from suppliers who actually produced the real thing, hurting competition. Thus, by 1938, the act was amended to include specifically the language "unfair or deceptive acts or practices," clearly extending the act to consumer-related issues.

It was not until the 1970s, however, that the FTC became a vocal defender of consumers' rights, and that resulted largely in response to Ralph Nader and his Nader's Raiders group. The group began to issue reports criticizing the Federal Trade Commission for not defending the rights of the general consumer. In response to that criticisms, and others, the FTC began expanding its initiatives to include regulation of advertising, credit practices, and other areas. In 1975, Congress expanded the FTC's duties through passage of the Magnuson-Moss Warranty Act and gave the FTC the power to issue binding trade regulation rules defining unfair or deceptive acts or practices.

By the early 1980s, the FTC began to be criticized again, this time for going too far in protecting the rights of consumers, and there were some efforts to curb the power of the commission. However, so far, no substantial changes to the commission's rules have been implemented.

In the area of consumer protection, the FTC act garners most of its power from section 5, which forbids unfair methods of competition via regulation of **unfair or deceptive acts or practices**. Although section 5 does not define the word *deceptive*, through judicial interpretation it has been broadly applied to mean a practice that has a tendency to mislead a substantial number of consumers in a material way. Actual deception need not occur; even only the likelihood of deception can trigger an action.

Unfair acts are also prohibited. Bill and Ann will do well to know that the commission of an unfair act is determined by considering whether the act offends public policy; whether the practice is immoral, unethical, oppressive, or unscrupulous; and whether the practice causes substantial injury to consumers. Thus, the prohibition against unfairness is broader than that against deception.

deceptive practices
practices that have a tendency to mislead a substantial number of consumers in a material way

unfair acts
acts that offend public policy; are immoral, unethical, oppressive, or unscrupulous; or cause substantial injury to others

EXEMPT INDUSTRIES

Almost every type of business is covered within the scope of the authority of the FTC. Some industries are exempted under the act due

ORKIN EXTERMINATING CO., INC., V. FEDERAL TRADE COMMISSION

849 F.2d 1354 (11th Cir. 1988)

The FTC issued an administrative complaint charging that Orkin, the largest termite and pest control company in the world, committed an unfair act or practice by unilaterally raising annual renewal fees on its lifetime guarantee termite extermination contracts in violation of no-increase fee clauses in the contracts. The 21,500 customers who called to complain had their increases rolled back. Another 42,000 canceled their contracts. Orkin defended the increase by asserting that the contracts were ambiguous, that the FTC exceeded its authority, and that the FTC erred in not considering Orkin's reliance on legal counsel in raising its fees. The court affirmed the findings of the FTC and ordered Orkin to cease and desist its unfair practices.

Clark, J.: Under well-established principles of contract law, where the language of a contract is unambiguous, an ambiguity will not be created by the mere assertion of a party to it. It is undisputed that the pre-1975 contracts refer to lifetime services and guarantees. They specify an annual renewal fee and contain no language that suggests in any way that the renewal fee may change during the lifetime of the treated structure—assuming timely annual payments. The fact that the contracts Orkin used after 1975 contain express language which allows for such an increase strongly suggests that these contracts at issue are properly read to provide for a fixed renewal fee.

As to Orkin's contention that the FTC exceeded its authority, it alleges that a mere breach of contract cannot serve as a basis for deceptive or fraudulent conduct. Under the FTC's definition of unfairness, the injury must satisfy three tests: it must be substantial; it must not be outweighed by any countervailing benefits to consumers; and it must be an injury that consumers could not have avoided. Therefore, the question is whether one company's breach of 207,000 contracts could meet the FTC's definition of unfairness.

The finding of substantial injury is supported by the fact that Orkin's breach amounted to over $7 million in revenues over a four-year period for Orkin, to which they were not entitled. Although the actual injury to individual customers may be small on an annual basis, this does not mean that such injury is insubstantial.

As for the second prong, the increase in the fee was not accompanied by an increase in the level of service provided or the enhancement of its quality; therefore there was no benefit to consumers. With regard to the third prong, consumers could not have anticipated the impending harm; nor could they have mitigated any subsequent harm; therefore, they could not have avoided the harm. Anticipatory avoidance was impossible because the consumers had no way of knowing that Orkin would increase its renewal fees, and subsequent mitigation was available only to those customers who complained about the increase and thus had their increases rolled back.

Orkin's final argument—that it relied on counsel for its actions—is irrelevant because an unfairness action does not take into account the mental state of the party accused of the violation. Therefore, whether its violation was a willful breach or whether it was a calculated move suggested by its lawyers is a nonissue. Earlier cases have established that proof of a party's intent has no bearing on the question of whether a violation has occurred. For the foregoing reasons, we AFFIRM.

Case Questions

1. What do you think of the court's interpretation of *insubstantial* as focusing on the amount of money paid to Orkin from all of its affected customers, rather than the traditional focus of unjustified customer injury?

2. What do you think the incentive was for Orkin to offer lifetime contracts to its customers without the ability to raise prices to account for inflation? How could the company have avoided this problem?

to their extensive regulation by other agencies. Those businesses are banks, common carriers, airlines, meat packers, and poultry dealers. Also excluded is the insurance industry, but that exemption comes from the McCarran-Ferguson Act and not from the FTC statute itself. The FTC is also limited in its regulation of food and drugs, to the extent that the U.S. Food and Drug Administration (FDA) has coverage.

REGULATION OF ADVERTISING PRACTICES UNDER THE FTC

The FTC has issued guidelines for advertising so that sellers of goods can steer clear of deceptive practices in their advertisements. Two such practices that are commonly litigated are bait-and-switch advertisements and door-to-door sales.

Bait and Switch

bait and switch
method of advertisement in which an advertiser offers a product it has no intention of selling in order to lure in customers

Bait and switch occurs when an advertiser offers a product or service it has no intention of selling. The advertisement is usually an eye-catching ad intended to get the purchaser into the store, but once there, the purchaser is subject to a sales tactic that attempts to persuade the buyer to purchase another, usually higher-priced, item.

Bait-and-switch techniques that are prohibited by the FTC are as follows: refusal to show the advertised item, disparagement of the advertised item, failure to have sufficient stock of the advertised product (absent a clearly stated limited number in the ad), refusal to take orders for the advertised goods (absent a statement saying "no rainchecks"), show or demonstration of a defective or unusable sample of the advertised product, or penalization of the salesperson of the advertised product.

Door-to-Door Sales

door-to-door sales
a sales technique in which a salesperson solicits sales by going directly to the consumer's home

In 1974, the FTC adopted a trade regulation sales rule that involves sellers who sell goods by going to people's homes rather than at a retail outlet. The regulations for **door-to-door sales** included a cooling-off period during which one has time to decide after the sale whether one wishes to abide by the terms of the sale.

The rule came about in response to complaints of high-pressure sales tactics being used by salespersons who trapped people inside their homes with the intent to make a sale. Under the rule, the purchaser of goods in excess of $25 who purchases a seller's goods from a location other than the seller's place of business has three business days from the date of the sale to rescind the contract.

The FTC also specifies guidelines for notifying a purchaser of the right to rescind. The guidelines state that the seller must provide the buyer with a Notice of Cancellation that must be in at least 10-point type, the Notice of Cancellation must contain the date by which the notice must be received (but not less than three business days from the date of the sale) and the name and address of the seller, the seller must inform the buyer orally—at the time of the purchase—of the buyer's right to rescind, and the seller may not misrepresent in any way the buyer's right to cancel.

The door-to-door rule does not apply to sales made entirely by telephone with no personal contact between the buyer and the seller, to sales involving real property, to sales when property is sold by a member of the Securities and Exchange Commission, or when the buyer has initiated the contract and the goods are needed for immediate personal use by the buyer. Certain other exceptions apply to sellers at auctions and tent sales and at arts and craft fairs.

900 Numbers

After a rash of minors calling adult 900 numbers and so-called phone-sex numbers, the Federal Communications Commission was given the power to enact regulations dealing with pay-per-call services (900 numbers). It enacted the Telephone Disclosure and Dispute Resolution Act of 1992, which also directs the Federal Trade Commission to police the industry for unfair and deceptive practices under section 5 of the FTC Act. (See Box 14–1, "New Regulations for 900 Numbers.")

Large numbers of minors were making calls to 900 numbers without their parents' permission and without their parents even realizing it until the phone bill came, in some cases billing hundreds of dollars' worth of phone calls to 900 numbers that children did not realize charged. The new law prohibits 900 services from advertising to children under 12 years of age unless such a 900 service is a bona fide educational service. Further, it requires disclosure that a parent's permission be obtained before use of services is permitted. And it requires a disclosure message be played before any service is advertised.

14–1 LAW IN THE REAL WORLD

New Regulations for 900 Numbers

A new FTC rule concerning 900-number (pay-per-call) telephone services went into effect in November 1993. Companies that offer these services will be required to disclose the costs of these services in their advertising, and to begin calls costing more than $2 with a "preamble" stating, among other things, the cost of the call. Consumers will not be charged for the call if they hang up shortly after hearing the preamble. The new rule also establishes requirements for resolving consumer billing disputes for pay-per-call services.

Under the new rule, companies that offer pay-per-call services will have to disclose certain information in any print, radio, or television advertisements they run for the service. For flat-fee services, the company must disclose the total cost of the call. For time-sensitive services, companies must disclose:

- the cost-per-minute,
- any minimum charges,
- the maximum charge if it can be determined in advance.

For services billed at varying rates depending on which options callers select, companies must disclose:

- the cost of the initial portion of the call,
- any minimum charges,
- the range of rates that may be charged,
- all other fees charged for these services,
- the cost of any other pay-per-call services to which the caller may be transferred.

The rule requires that these and other mandated disclosures be clear and conspicuous. The cost disclosures generally will have to be made adjacent to the telephone number, in the same format, and at least half the size of the phone number. For services directed to consumers under the age of 18, the rule requires:

- a statement that parental permission is required before calling the service (this statement is also required to be in the preamble).

Another provision will ban the services from targeting children under 12 years old, unless that service is a bona fide educational service dedicated to areas of school study. The rule adopts a two-part test for children's advertising. The first part is whether the advertisement appears during programming or in publications for which 50% of the audience or readership is under 12. The second part allows for an independent determination where demographics are not available to meet the first part of the test.

The billing dispute resolution portion of the rule requires services to give consumers written notice at least once a year of their billing rights, requires services to investigate complaints free of charge, prohibits services from reporting disputed calls to a credit bureau or other third parties pending the dispute, and requires forfeiture of the bill if any consumer right is violated. Finally, companies that offer these services are liable for refunds or credits to consumers if they violate this rule.

Source: "New Regulations for 900 Numbers," *Consumer's Research* magazine, October 1993. Reprinted with permission of Consumer's Research Inc.

FEDERAL STATUTORY PROTECTION FOR THE CONSUMER

In 1968, Congress passed the Consumer Credit Protection Act, which provides a series of subchapters all designed to inform consumers about the full payment of their purchases through mandatory disclosures of the cost of credit and about all of their rights regarding the deal. The subchapters and what each is designed to do are discussed next.

TRUTH-IN-LENDING ACT

Congress believed that consumers could make the best choices only after they were completely informed of the total cost of a product. The Truth-in-Lending Act (TILA) was designed to facilitate that. It is essentially a disclosure statute requiring a seller to tell a buyer in clear and precise language the credit terms of the agreement.

Prior to the passage of TILA, there was no consistency in the way creditors quoted the cost of credit. Terms such as the dollar add-on quotation, discounted rate, monthly rate, and interest-free rate (but with hidden closing costs or finance charges) made comparison of the true costs of credit difficult for consumers. TILA requires that any finance charge made in connection with the loan or extension of credit be disclosed to the debtor.

TILA also requires that all interest rates be calculated using the same formula and that all interest rates and finance charges be stated in terms of an annual percentage rate (APR). Because all APRs have to be calculated the same way, consumers become able to realistically compare advertised rates of interest. Failure to properly inform a consumer of the terms of an agreement can result in the liability of the seller.

The Federal Reserve Board (the Board), through Regulation Z, interprets and enforces TILA. Regulation Z is simply the regulation issued by the Board that states the authority, purpose, coverage, organization, enforcement, and liability as interpreted by the Board to enforce the TILA. The Board has been designated as the official interpreter of TILA and is authorized to issue regulations and interpretations.

The Board defines a **creditor** as one who regularly extends credit that is subject to a finance charge or is payable by written agreement in more than four installments whether or not a finance charge is imposed. A creditor may also be one who honors a credit card or who issues a credit card. **Credit** is defined as a right granted by a creditor to a consumer to defer payment of a debt.

Under TILA, a **consumer** is a cardholder or natural person to whom consumer credit is offered or extended. A **consumer credit transaction** is credit offered or extended to a consumer primarily for private, family, or household purposes. Neither TILA nor Regulation Z has any effect if a transaction does not involve consumer credit. Thus, an extension of credit for purposes that are primarily business, commercial, or agricultural are outside the scope of the act.

In 1980, Congress passed the Truth-in-Lending Simplification and Reform Act, which changed the original TILA significantly, for the benefit of both the consumer and the creditor. For the benefit of the creditor, the Simplification Act reduced the amount of information a creditor needed to give to the consumer, reduced the liability for noncompliance with nonsignificant terms, and allowed avoidance of liability altogether by use of forms issued by the Federal Reserve Board. On behalf of the consumer, it strengthened enforcement of TILA by the administration.

TILA provides for three types of enforcement: private, criminal, and administrative. The primary burden for administrative enforcement is on the FTC; however, no fewer than nine agencies are authorized to enforce TILA. Because of this, the Federal Reserve Board, which, through Regulation Z of the act, interprets and enforces the act, has been designated the official interpreter of the act and is authorized to issue regulations and interpretations.

---

creditor
one who regularly extends credit that is subject to a finance charge or is payable by written agreement in more than four installments whether or not a finance charge is imposed

credit
a right granted by a creditor to a consumer to defer payment of a debt

consumer
a cardholder or natural person to whom consumer credit is offered or extended

consumer credit
credit offered or extended to a consumer primarily for private family or household purposes

Criminal enforcement is handled by the U.S. attorney general's office. For violations of the act that are willfully and knowingly committed, the act imposes penalties of up to $5,000, or imprisonment of 1 year, or both. Private enforcement generally takes the form of a private suit, but may also take the form of a class action suit.

FAIR CREDIT BILLING ACT

The credit card is a consumer boon, as well as a consumer nightmare. Since BankAmerica issue its first national credit card in 1966 (now known as VISA), Americans' use of their cards has increased from $4 billion per year in 1971 to $351.7 billion in 1993 (on MasterCard and VISA only). That figure represented a 20.7% increase over the 1992 figure of $291.3 billion.

The act requires creditors to comply if the credit is payable in more than four installments or if a financing charge is imposed. An important section of the Fair Credit Billing Act is the section providing for the resolution of errors. It states that errors must be reported in writing by the consumer within 60 days of receipt of the bill. When errors are reported to the credit card issuer, the issuer must acknowledge the claim within 30 days, and must investigate the claim. The issuer has up to 90 days to resolve it. Prior to any resolution, the issuer cannot take any negative action that reflects on the contested claim, such as closing the account, making adverse credit reports about the debt, threatening the debtor, or attempting to collect the debt. Merely maintaining the charge on the debtor's bill, however, does not violate any of these restrictions.

FAIR CREDIT REPORTING ACT

In today's society, because of the critical importance of maintaining a good credit rating, the publication of false or inaccurate credit information can be financially crippling. However, under the common law, a consumer's remedies were limited to tort actions in the form of defamation or invasion of privacy, which did not adequately redress the harm. Defamation actions were hard to prove, because a mistake made by a credit bureau was generally an honest mistake that exempted the bureau from liability. Proving invasion of privacy was an equally inadequate measure, because the limited number of subscribers who received the false information generally did not rise to the level of unreasonable public exposure required for a sufficient recovery.

In 1970, Congress responded to the special needs of the consumer in this area by passage of the Fair Credit Reporting Act. The act, enforced by the Federal Trade Commission, is narrow in scope and includes only **consumer reports**. It attempts to define the types of situations in which a report can be given to a third party. Such purposes include employment, insurance, and credit, but contains a catch-all phrase that allows for a report to be given to anyone who has a legitimate business need for the information in connection with a business purpose.

Because of the vagueness of the wording of the statute, most of the litigation has surrounded the definition of a consumer report. In 1990, the Federal Trade Commission defined a consumer report as any report furnished by a consumer reporting agency (as defined by section 603[f] of the statute) if that report contained information bearing on the creditworthiness, character, general reputation, personal characteristics, or mode of living of a person. The 1990 definition specifically excludes from that definition any report that is coded so that the consumer is not identified; law enforcement bulletins; directories such as telephone, city, and trade directories; and reports limited to actual transactions between the consumer and the agency making the report.

If a consumer disputes information contained on the credit report, the reporting agency must investigate the reported error. If the objectionable information is not deleted, then the consumer may provide the reporting agency with an explanation of the disputed facts; that explanation must be attached to the credit report and disseminated along with any subsequent report furnished by the reporting agency. If the consumer requests it, the explanation must be sent to anyone who received the report within the prior six months.

Users of the credit report are entitled to a copy of the report and are required to use it in a lawful manner. Reporting agencies that provide the credit report for illegitimate purposes are subject to criminal penalties and may incur civil liability for their negligent or willful violations.

EQUAL CREDIT OPPORTUNITY ACT

In 1974, Congress enacted the Equal Credit Opportunity Act to combat discrimination in awarding credit based on sex and marital

consumer report
any report furnished by a consumer reporting agency if such report contains information bearing on the creditworthiness, character, general reputation, personal characteristics, or mode of living of a person

status. This made a tremendous difference for single and divorced women, because it eliminated the requirement—that had theretofore been imposed by many lending institutions—for disclosure of the earned income of a husband when a wife was being considered for credit.

In 1976, Congress amended the act to prohibit discrimination based on sex, race, age, national origin, color, religion, receipt of public assistance, or good-faith use of the Consumer Credit Protection Act. Thus far, the act has not been extended to acts of discrimination based on alienage, and thus, creditors may deny credit on the ground that the applicant is an alien, even if a permanent resident. The act is regulated by the Federal Reserve Board.

The act states that consumers should be evaluated in a nondiscriminatory manner when applying for credit. It applies only to the extending of credit and not to all aspects of credit transactions. Under the act, the term *creditor* means one who, in the regular course of business, regularly participates in the decision of whether or not to extend credit. Excluded from the scope of coverage are credit transactions involving public utilities, securities credit, business credit, credit extended to government, and incidental credit—defined as credit not to exceed four months, not subject to a credit card account, or not subject to a finance charge.

FAIR DEBT COLLECTION PRACTICES ACT (FDCPA)

The FDCPA was enacted in 1977 for the purpose of eliminating abusive debt collection practices by **debt collectors**. Such abuses had been noted to contribute to personal bankruptcies, marital instability, loss of employment, and invasion of privacy. Enforced by the Federal Trade Commission, the act states that any violation of the act results in unfair or deceptive practices, thereby invoking all the enforcement powers of the FTC.

debt collectors
those who use any instrumentality of interstate commerce or the mails in any business whose principal purpose is the collection of any debts owed or due another

The act applies principally to debt collectors, defined as "any person who uses any instrumentality of interstate commerce or the mails in any business the principal purpose of which is the collection of any debts . . . owed or due another." The definition does not include a creditor that collects its own debts, but does include a creditor that uses a name other than its own, indicating that a third party is actually collecting the debt.

The act also excludes any in-house collector, one whose principal business is not debt collection, any federal or state debt collector per-

14–2   LAW IN THE REAL WORLD

FTC Charges Payco with Harassment

Payco American, one of the largest collection agencies in the U.S., was charged by the FTC with collecting debts the old-fashioned way—by harassment. The FTC charged that Payco:

- told third parties, such as employers, about consumers' debt problems;
- used obscenities;
- pretended to be lawyers;
- threatened to sue, even though Payco didn't intend to sue.

  Under the Fair Debt Collection Practices Act, agencies can:

- call only from 8 a.m. until 9 p.m.;
- use strong language, but not foul language;
- call employers, but only if the employers allow such calls;
- threaten to sue, but only if the agency really plans to do so.

  The FTC sued Payco to keep it from breaking the law. The FTC also would make the company tell consumers about their right to tell collection agencies to stop contacting them. Consumers still would owe the debt, but the agencies would have to go to court or try to repossess the goods to get the debt repaid.

Source: "FTC Charges Payco with Harassment," *USA Today*, August 3, 1993. ©1993, *USA Today*. Reprinted with permission.

forming his or her duty, a legal-process server who is serving papers concerning the collection of a debt, any nonprofit organization that assists with debt collection, and an assignee of commercial paper.

   The practices of some debt collectors amounted to deception and outright harassment (see Box 14–2, "FTC Charges Payco with Harassment"), and therefore the practices prohibited by the act are specifically designated so as to eliminate harassment, intimidation, and threats to the debtor in connection with debt collection.

  Prohibited practices include limitations on how a debtor can be located, what a debt collector can tell a third party, how many times a third party can be called to obtain information about the debtor, and otherwise harassing, abusing, misleading, or deceiving the debtor.

garnish
action directed against debtor's assets in the hands of a third party, such as an employer

UNITED STATES V. ACB SALES AND SERVICES INC.

683 F. Supp. 734 (D.C. Ariz. 1987)

The FTC brought this action against ACB Sales and Services alleging violations of the Fair Debt Collection Practices Act. ACB is engaged in the collection of debts as third-party collection agents. In December 1974, the FTC issued a cease and desist order to ACB Sales requiring it to cease-and-desist from (1) representing that legal action had been taken, (2) representing that wages would be **garnished**, (3) misrepresenting remedies available to ACB, (4) representing that criminal action would be taken, (5) calling debtors' at work, (6) . . . , (7) placing phone calls between 9 p.m. and 8 a.m., (8) threatening to communicate to the debtor's employer the existence of a debt, and (9) communicating the debt to third parties not liable for the debt. ACB was instructed by the FTC to communicate the order to all present and future employees.

In 1978, the Fair Debt Collection Practices Act became effective. Subsequently, the FTC order and the act were combined into a document known as the ACB Rules of Professional Conduct, which all ACB employees were required to read and sign. In addition, all ACB employees were given training in proper methods of collection.

Notwithstanding this, the FTC received hundreds of complaints about improper collection practices, which led to this action being filed.

Hardy, J.: The evidence establishes a pervasive pattern of violations so numerous they cannot be dismissed as simply the work of a few maverick collectors. In many cases, managers or supervisors joined with collectors in committing violations. The very nature of ACB's operations impels its employees to disregard the order and the act in attempting to collect debts. The manager is under pressure to meet his revenue budget. He knows that failure to meet his budget will cost him his job. Consequently, he presses his collectors to collect more money.

A collector is under pressure because his income is based on commissions. If his commissions do not meet his monthly draw, he may lose his job.

continued on next page

Any debtor who was unable or unwilling to make payment as demanded by a collector subjected himself to a torrent of abuse and harassment. He may have been cursed or otherwise verbally abused. Obscene and profane language was used. The collector made repeated telephone calls, many on the same day, often within minutes of each other, many day after day. In some cases collectors threatened violence to the debtors. Additionally, many phone calls were made between 9 at night and 8 a.m.

Another standard tactic was to threaten that legal proceedings would be commenced to enforce collection: filing a lawsuit, garnishing wages, attaching property, or impressing a lien upon property. There were frequent threats to inform the debtor's employer that the debtor was not paying bills. There were also threats to inform others of the debt, and there were times when this information was communicated to third [parties], usually neighbors.

There were frequent phone calls to debtors' places of employment after the debtors requested that they not be called there. Collectors represented that they were attorneys, legal advisers, a friend of the debtor, and an employee of the creditor. A frequent misrepresentation was that an emergency existed that required the collector to get in touch with the debtor immediately.

Altogether, there were over 1,000 violations of the act and the order. Civil penalties are appropriate to deter future violations. Among the factors to consider are the good or bad faith of the defendant, [defendant's] ability to pay; and the necessity of vindicating the authority of the FTC. Good faith is not a defense, but can be a factor in determining the size of the penalty. The Court is not satisfied that the individual defendants have acted fully in good faith. ORDERED, that they be awarded $25,000 in damages from ACB [and] $25,000 from employee Jerry Raker, that the corporate defendants be ordered to pay $150,000 for violations of the FTC order, and that they be required to pay $150,000 for violation of the act.

Case Questions

1. As shown in this case, the training given to employees can conflict with office policies, causing violations of the FTC order to occur. Should the FTC have the ability to examine both the training tools

and the office practices that may lead to such violations during its compliance checks?

2. What is the purpose of holding both the company and individuals within the company financially liable for the violations? Should employees who are carrying out company policies be held financially liable?

ELECTRONIC FUND TRANSFERS

What would life be like without the ATM? Many of you may not even remember when banking *had* to be done inside the bank or at most, at the drive-through window. Gone are the days. With advances in technology and the need to keep up with a population on the move, the banking industry combined with the computer industry and has created the idea that society can operate on a cashless basis. (See Box 14–3, "Carry-Out Cash.") That is the idea behind the technology that drives **electronic fund transfers** (EFTs). The uses of such EFTs have grown since their inception (See Box 14–4, "Banking outside Banks"), and the availability of EFTs to consumers has spawned a new area of law and a new Congressional act to regulate the industry and protect consumers. Such availability has also inspired new uses for ATMs. (See Box 14–5, "Charity and Welfare Recipients Both Benefit by ATMs.")

The Electronic Fund Transfer Act (EFTA), enacted in 1980, is administered and enforced by the Federal Reserve Board. Its stated purpose is to provide a basic framework establishing the rights, liabilities, and responsibilities of participants regarding electronic fund transfer systems. The primary objective of this title is the provision of individual consumer rights.

An EFT includes, but is not limited to, ATMs, pay-by-phone systems, direct deposit and automatic payments, and point-of-sale transfers. However, the act includes any transfer of funds—other than a transaction originated by check, draft, or similar paper instrument—that is initiated through a terminal, telephone, computer, or magnetic tape authorizing a financial institution to debit or credit a consumer's account.

electronic fund transfers
transfer of funds—other than transactions originated by check, draft, or similar paper instrument—which is initiated through a terminal, a telephone, a computer or a magnetic tape, authorizing a financial institution to debit or credit a consumer's account

14–3   LAW IN THE REAL WORLD

Carry-Out Cash

More than one-half of all American households now use an automated teller machine (ATM) at least once a month, according to the Electronic Funds Transfer Association (EFTA) of Herndon, Virginia.

The best ATM users are baby boomers. More than one-quarter (27%) of ATM users are aged 35 to 44, and 31% are aged 25 to 34. That's why banks see ATM service as a strategic investment. They hope that cash machines will turn casual young users into regular customers.

ATMs have been in use since 1969. But the number of ATMs increased almost tenfold during the 1980s, as the baby boom generation came of age. The U.S. had 90,000 ATMs in 1990, each of which averaged 5,266 transactions a month. Baby boomers prefer the ATMs because they save time. They are more interested in completing a transaction quickly than they are in receiving personal attention.

But boomers aren't the only group sold on ATMs. In fact, 18- to 24-year-old customers conduct a higher share of their transactions at ATMs than any other group. Most of the youngest ATM users are college students. Thanks to the widespread use of shared banking networks, parents can make a deposit in Connecticut, and their kid can make a withdrawal in California.

Affluent householders also use ATMs to tap into their checking or savings accounts while traveling. Only 11% of householders aged 55 to 64 are frequent ATM users, but the share is higher among affluent older travelers. The average ATM user household earns over $43,000 per year. Sixty percent of householders earning over $75,000 use the machines at least once a month.

Source: "Carry-Out Cash," May 1992, *American Demographics* magazine, ©1992. Reprinted with permission.

14–4   LAW IN THE REAL WORLD

Banking outside Banks

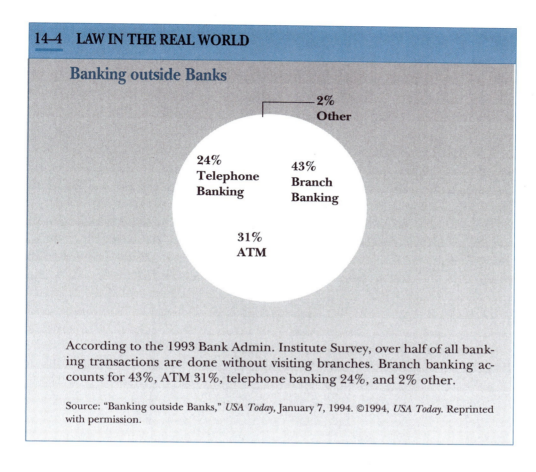

According to the 1993 Bank Admin. Institute Survey, over half of all banking transactions are done without visiting branches. Branch banking accounts for 43%, ATM 31%, telephone banking 24%, and 2% other.

Source: "Banking outside Banks," *USA Today,* January 7, 1994. ©1994, *USA Today.* Reprinted with permission.

The EFTA specifically excludes from its coverage check authorization services, transactions through networks that serve financial institutions, securities transfers, certain automatic transfers such as transfers from a checking to a savings account, and certain one-time-only, telephone-initiated transfers that are not regularly done by the financial institution.

Under the EFTA, financial institutions must disclose to customers the terms and conditions of their electronic fund transfer services—including the cost of using such services, the liability that the consumer has for unauthorized transfers, and the method to use to halt the electronic transfer of funds—and must ask whom they should notify in the event of unauthorized use. The act also mandates that the user receive a receipt for each transaction and that electronic fund transfers appear on the user's bank statement periodically.

14–5   LAW IN THE REAL WORLD

Charity and Welfare Recipients Both Benefit by ATMs

ATMs now accept charitable donations.

Beginning in January 1994, Michigan National Bank began a service that allows users of its 300 ATMs to transfer contributions directly from their accounts to one or more of 20 charities around Michigan, and the machine even provides a receipt for tax records. The new application of technology benefits both customers and organizations that help people in the community.

In St. Paul, Minnesota, welfare has become something of a card trick. Clients of Aid to Families with Dependent Children were given electronically coded, creditlike cards to use at any bank in the county to withdraw their benefits.

The changeover had a powerful impact. The number of stolen checks declined immediately; the county no longer had to replace $250,000 in stolen or lost checks; fewer workers were needed to process paperwork; and welfare recipients no longer had to pay exorbitant rates to check-cashing stores.

In 1991, the county added food stamps to the program, enabling clients to use the cards to buy food in grocery stores equipped with special terminals. The nation's first electronic benefits transfer (EBT) system for people on public assistance has been a win-win situation for all involved.

EBT has caught on nationwide, with at least 33 similar systems under way in other states. New types of automation systems are being tested, which include smart cards (a variation on EBT) and electronic fingerprint verification.

The new technologies are coming at a time of rising demand for public assistance. It is estimated that the demand will increase 25% over the next four years, from nearly $700 million in 1993 to $1.7 billion in 1997.

Source: Social Issues Research Service (SIRS), *Technology*, Vol. 4, Art. #8.

Reported errors must be investigated and the consumer notified of the results of that investigation within 10 days of the reported error (longer if the financial institution is willing to credit the consumer's account pending the outcome of the investigation). If the error turns out to be real, then the institution has one business day to reverse the error. Failure to comply may result in treble damages against the institution.

If there has been unauthorized use of a consumer's electronic fund transfer card, the consumer is liable for up to $50, but must give prompt notification of the unauthorized use. Financial institutions are liable to the consumer for failure to make an authorized transfer, for failure to stop payment when properly ordered to do so, and for other violations of the act.

STATE STATUTORY PROTECTION FOR CONSUMERS

Since the 1970s, states have enacted statutes aimed at protecting consumers against unfair and deceptive practices of sellers. Currently, all 50 states have in place some legislation with this design. Although the content of such statutes varies, they have come to be known as state Unfair and Deceptive Practices Acts, or UDPAs. Most of them have as their model either section 5 of the Federal Trade Commission Act or similar model legislation.

Not all unfair and deceptive practices are covered by state statutes, however. For example, if a federal law exists that regulates the industry, the state law may be preempted by the federal law. What is preempted may not always be clear. For example, the Supreme Court is expected to hear arguments in October 1995 on whether citizens in Illinois can bring suit under Illinois state law against American Airlines for changing the rules concerning the use of frequent flier miles under the airline's AAdvantage Program.

At issue is whether the Airline Deregulation Act of 1978, which governs all regulations relating to rates, routes, or services of any air carrier, preempts such suits brought under state law. The decision could have a major impact on American Airlines, as well as many other airlines that have begun to restrict the use of frequent flier miles.

Most UDPA statutes cover the sale of goods and services. Most also exclude transactions involving credit, realty, leases, insurance, and utilities. Most cover a laundry list of prohibited practices that are fairly consistent. The most prominent ones are discussed next.

DOOR-TO-DOOR SALES

In addition to the requirements imposed on door-to-door sales by the FTC, every state also has imposed regulations on this type of sales technique. Most states require a cooling-off period of at least three days, during which the consumer may cancel the order without any penalty. The cooling-off period does not begin until the seller has informed the consumer of the right to cancel.

One notable exception to the cooling-off period exists. If a buyer requests immediate delivery of the goods, the seller provides those goods before being notified of the cancellation, and the goods cannot be returned in substantially the same condition as when they were delivered to the consumer, then the consumer has waived the right to the cooling-off period.

LEMON LAWS

lemon laws
statutes that act to replace individual contracts between the buyer and seller of an automobile with an objective contract that reflects negotiations between consumer groups and merchants as to what happens in the event a car does not perform as promised

used-car rule
federal rule designed to protect buyers of used cars from unscrupulous practices in the sale of used cars

Lemon laws apply only to the purchase and sale of automobiles and arose as a result of inadequate warranty and other remedies under the terms of the purchase agreement. In essence, the presence of a lemon law in a state statute acts to replace individual contracts between the buyer and seller with an objective contract that reflects negotiations between consumer groups and merchants.

Lemon laws have as a common feature certain guidelines for resolving disputes between the purchaser of the automobile and the seller. Generally, the laws protect only consumers of cars not for resale; in addition, the vehicles must be only passenger cars. Generally, the guidelines determine what has to be done on the part of the buyer to notify the seller of a defect and what constitutes reasonable attempts to fix the defect before the automobile must be replaced or the purchase price refunded. Although lemon laws may sound good in theory, as you will see from Box 14–6, "The Sour Truth about Lemon Laws," at least some people opine that they are not as effective as they were designed to be.

In 1988 the FTC published guidelines for the **used-car rule**, a federal rule enforced by the FTC that is designed to protect buyers of

14–6   LAW IN THE REAL WORLD

The Sour Truth about Lemon Laws

Since 1982, every state but South Dakota and Arkansas has enacted a lemon law. The states' lemon laws establish arbitration procedures designed to make it easier for owners of hopelessly defective automobiles to get a replacement car or refund. Most states define a lemon as a new car that has been in the repair shop for 30 days or has been in for the same problem four times within the first year of ownership.

All state lemon laws work in basically the same way. The dealer and the car owner get to tell their story to an arbitration panel. Sometimes, that panel is state run, some are run by the manufacturers, others are private. Chrysler and Ford run their own program; GM uses the Better Business Bureau's Auto Line Program. Except for Ford, the boards are made up of people with no connection to the manufacturer. Foreign car makers use one of several private arbitration boards.

If your goal is to get a refund or a new car to replace your lemon, it appears that your odds of winning depend largely on who arbitrates your dispute. For example, 55% of the consumers who entered the state-run arbitration program in Florida in 1991 won a refund or replacement car. State-run programs in Connecticut and New York awarded refunds to consumers 48 and 77% of the time, respectively.

By contrast, only 14% received such awards that the Better Business Bureau handled nationally, and the car-manufacturer-sponsored arbitration boards had lower numbers than the Better Business Bureau. Chrysler awarded only 9.6% nationally.

Unfortunately, few states keep records of lemon law cases or even require reporting from the private organizations that run arbitration programs.

Source: "The Sour Truth about Lemon Laws," ©1993 by Consumers Union of U.S., Inc., Yonkers, NY 10703-1057. Reprinted with permission from *Consumer Reports*, January 1993.

used cars from unscrupulous practices in the sale of used cars. The rule requires sellers of used cars to place in the window of the car being sold a Buyer's Guide, which, among other things, requires the seller to specifically state the warranty, if any, the service contract availability, dealer information, and consumer complaint information. A state may be exempt from the rule if the federal government finds there is already in place adequate state protection for consumers that offers substantially the same protection as the used-car rule.

SUMMARY

Ann and Bill must pay close attention to their customers and clients not simply so they will have repeat business and hopefully flourish but also because of certain reasons imposed by law. Under both state and federal regulations, Bill and Ann have a responsibility not to advertise deceptively or engage in other deceptive practices regarding their business. They must correctly bill customers, extend credit to them on an equal basis, disclose all pertinent credit terms to them, and collect their debts without running afoul of the law. While several of these laws must be adhered to by Ann and Bill, Ann and Bill also benefit from them in their capacity as consumers.

CHAPTER TERMS

bait and switch	deceptive practices
consumer	door-to-door sales
consumer credit	electronic fund transfers
consumer report	garnish
credit	lemon laws
creditor	unfair acts
debt collectors	used-car rule

CHAPTER-END QUESTIONS

1. In response to television and newspaper ads, Salizar visits Dorinda Carpet Co. for its big, big closeout sale on carpet at $7 per square

yard. Salizar tells LaToya, the sales associate, what he needs and adds that hearing about the sale he decided to come in and buy. LaToya shows Salizar some carpeting, which he decides to buy. When the bill is figured up, Salizar discovers that the carpeting he chose is $20 per square yard. Salizar tells LaToya he thought the carpeting was $7 per square yard, as advertised. LaToya tells him the carpeting he chose was not on sale. Salizar asks to see the sale carpet, and LaToya shows it to him. It is of very poor quality—so much so that Salizar hardly recognized it as carpeting. LaToya tells him how cheaply made the advertised carpeting is, how it will not last long in his family room, and how much better the carpet is that Salizar originally chose. She also says they are out of stock on the cheaper carpeting and would not be getting any more in. Salizar purchases the original carpeting.

During the next few days, Salizar thought more and more about the transaction with LaToya, and the more he thought about it, the angrier he got. He felt like he had been taken advantage of. Salizar wants to sue Dorinda Carpets. Does he have any basis?

2. The law that prohibits lenders from discriminating in extending credit is the

   a. Fair Credit Reporting Act.
   b. Fair Credit Billing Act.
   c. Truth-in-Lending Act.
   d. Equal Credit Opportunity Act.

3. A mouthwash manufacturer advertises nationally on television and in magazines by showing people gargling with the mouthwash who appear to have a sore throat during cold weather. It says in the ads that the mouthwash kills germs on contact. Is this false advertising? Is it deceptive advertising?

4. Brooks, a water softener seller at WtrClnCo., came to Yana's home to sell her a water softener. Yana was still thinking about whether to make the purchase, when Brooks opened his briefcase to get something. Inside the case Yana saw what appeared to be a section of rusted pipe with about half an inch of minerals built up within the pipe, leaving only a small space for water to pass through. Yana asked what the pipe was and Brooks told her not to worry about it. Intrigued and a bit fearful that it could be an example of what would happen to her pipes if she did not purchase the water softener, she urged Brooks to show her the pipe and tell her what it was. Brooks finally told her it was a piece of

pipe from a house that did not have a water softener. Yana, clearly taken aback, bought the water softener.

A day later, while telling the story to a neighbor, Yana discovered that she had polyvinyl chloride (PVC) pipes, which could not possibly corrode or acquire buildup like the pipe she had seen in Brooks's briefcase. Brooks had inspected Yana's plumbing when he came to the house, but during the discussion of the piece of pipe, mentioned neither that she had PVC—not metal pipes— nor that the PVC would not react as the metal pipe she had seen. Does Yana have a cause of action against Brooks or WtrClnCo.?

5. Amanda takes out a loan to purchase some equipment and supplies for her business. What is Amanda's recourse under the Truth-in-Lending Act when she later finds that the creditor did not fully disclose the terms of the loan before she entered into the agreement?

6. Amp Blans Chaser, a local attorney, is having trouble collecting fees from two of his clients. The fees have been in arrears for several months, and Chaser is frustrated at not receiving anything on the bills, and not even being able to get in touch with the clients. Chaser finally resorts to calling the clients late at night or early in the morning and calling friends of the clients to try to locate the clients. One of the clients, angry at Chaser for "harassing and hassling" him, threatens to report Chaser for violation of the Fair Debt Collection Practices Act. Has Chaser violated the act?

7. Which of the following is *not* a feature of most states' lemon laws?

    a. Guaranteed replacement of a defective vehicle.
    b. Guidelines for resolving disputes between the seller and the purchaser of an auto.
    c. Guidelines for appropriate notice of a defect by buyer to seller regarding defective auto.
    d. Guidelines for what constitutes a reasonable attempt to repair the defect.

8. The FTC's used-car rule requires the seller of a used car to place in the window of a car being sold a _____.

9. Marcia opens her phone bill one month and finds, much to her astonishment, that it is for $857.35. She notices that several of the calls are to the same number and that the charges sometimes run as high as $60 a call. She also notices that the expensive calls are to 900 numbers. Marcia asks Placido, her husband, about the calls

and finds that Placido has been placing the calls to a sports hot line number. The phone and card Placido used are in Marcia's name, but Marcia refuses to pay the bill. Placido says he had no idea the calls would be so expensive. Placido says he does not have the money to pay for the bills. While they are disputing the bill with the 900 company, the 900 company reports to the credit bureau that the bill is unpaid and overdue. Must Marcia pay?

10. Check authorization services are covered by the Electronic Funds Transfer Act. (True or False)

GROUP EXERCISE

Have separate groups in the class each choose one of the laws discussed in the chapter. Have members of each group collect as many documents as they can resulting from the laws discussed. Share them with the class. For instance, "900 numbers" students could collect 900-number ads from various sources, which will probably contain the information required by law to be included in such ads. For the "Equal Credit Opportunity Act" students, the group might go to a bank or other lender (or several lenders) to get credit applications and then see whether they can find in the application the language required by the act to be included. "Door-to-Door Sales" students can contact a company that sells products door-to-door and get copies of their company's sales contracts.

Chapter 15

INTELLECTUAL PROPERTY

Chapter Preview Summary

In this chapter, Bill and Ann learn about the need to protect the intangible property associated with their business, such as their business name, marks or logos they develop to help identify their business, new inventions they create through their research department, and anything they might write in the course of their business. They also learn how to protect themselves from other businesses that might infringe on their protected property as well as how to keep themselves from infringing on others' protected property.

Chapter Objectives

In studying the chapter, you should learn:
- what patents, trademarks, and copyrights are
- the specific requirements for protecting intellectual property based on the type of property protected
- the type of intellectual property that is subject to federal protection
- about protection of intellectual property afforded by state law

INTRODUCTION

intellectual property
concepts, information, symbols, or creative expression that carries the right of exclusive use and ownership

copyright
protection for the works of authors, illustrators, photographers, musical composers, and lyricists from being copied without authorization

patent
absolute protection for inventors and their inventions so they may use, sell, license, or refrain from making, using, or selling their invention for a period of 17 years

trademark
word, name, symbol, or other device used to identify and distinguish one's goods from those manufactured or sold by others

Depending on the nature of Bill and Ann's business, they may need to deal with issues involving intellectual property. Intellectual property issues involve areas such as patents, trademarks, and copyrights. Intellectual property, like all forms of property, embodies the right to exclusive use and ownership. It differs from most other forms of property in that it is intrinsically intangible.

Intellectual property consists of concepts, information, symbols, or creative expression and therefore has no physical boundaries. Such activity becomes property once it is protected by patent, copyright, or trademark. Issues may involve Bill and Ann's patenting of some novel invention, deciding to protect the business name by trademark, copyrighting written information, or some combination thereof.

The Copyright-Patent Clause of the U.S. Constitution, Article I, section 8, clause 8, authorizes the federal government to protect authors and inventors from unauthorized use of their writings and discoveries for limited times. The clause is concerned with the right of the authors and inventors to control the use and reproduction of their original work. This constitutional clause balances the tension between encouraging intellectual, artistic, and technological progress and allowing the dissemination and use of those developments for the enjoyment and betterment of society.

There are three types of federally protected intellectual property: copyrights, patents, and trademarks. **Copyrights** protect authors, illustrators, photographers, musical composers, and lyricists, etc. **Patents** protect inventors and their inventions. **Trademarks** protect goods and services. All three are protected by federal acts. Other types of business information, such as trade secrets, are protected by state statutes or unfair competition laws. In order to best protect Bill and Ann's intellectual property and to prevent themselves from sustaining liability for violating applicable laws, it is important that they know the requirements. (See Box 15-1, "Intellectual Property Characteristics.")

COPYRIGHT

The Copyright Reform Act of 1976 grants to copyright holders the exclusive right to use and authorize use of their work with certain excep-

15–1   BLACK LETTER LAW

Intellectual Property Characteristics

Patent Law	protects mental concepts or creations known as inventions; of three types: design, utility, and plant; example, flip-top can.
Trademark Law	deals with the degree to which the owner of a name used in marketing goods or services will be afforded a monopoly over the use of a name; example, Coke.
Copyright Law	grants authors, composers, programmers, and artists the right to prevent others from copying or using their original creations without permission.
Trade Secret Law	protects private knowledge that gives an owner a competitive business advantage; examples, magic techniques, manufacturing processes, and formulas.
Unfair Competition Law	gives owners of mental creations that don't fall into one of the foregoing four types of protecttion from copying; examples, trade dress (Kodak's yellow packaging), business names, unique advertising slogans, and distinctive packaging label (Duracell's copper top).

tions. A copyright protects "original works of authorship" that are "fixed in any medium of expression, now known or later developed, from which they can be perceived, reproduced, or otherwise communicated, either directly or with the aid of a machine or device." A copyright does not protect an idea itself, but protects the manifestations of the idea. Works of authorship include literary works; musical works, including words; dramatic works, including music; pantomimes and choreographic works; pictorial, graphic, and sculptural works; motion pictures and other audiovisual works; sound recordings; and architectural works.

For works created after 1978 (the effective date of the Copyright Act of 1976), copyright protection lasts for the life of the creator plus 50 years. In the case of joint authorship, the last surviving author plus 50 years is the term of protection. Thus, all of an author's works enter the public domain at the same time.

public domain
works that are not subject to protection against infringement

Works that are in the **public domain** (i.e., works whose copyright has expired or was never requested) are not eligible for copyright protection. Such works are freely usable; there is no restriction whatsoever on the use of the work.

NOTICE AND REGISTRATION

The Copyright Act of 1976 requires three elements to be protected. First, the symbol *c* or the word *copyright* or the abbreviation *copyr.* must appear on the document. Second, the year of first publication of the document or—if the document is unpublished—the year completed must appear. Third, the name of the owner of the copyright should appear. All information should be obvious—not hidden or inconspicuous—on the document.

Although registration with the Copyright Office is not necessary (copyright attaches at the moment of creation), it is required before seeking certain legal remedies, and it is best for legal protection. If a work is filed within five years of creation, the work has the presumption of authenticity; if filed after that, authenticity may have to be proven. Registration requires an application, a fee, and two copies of the work, excluding movies. The Copyright Office of the Library of Congress operates the copyright system.

INFRINGEMENT

To infringe upon a copyright means that the exclusive rights of the copyright owner have been violated. This can be accomplished by either reproducing the copyrighted material; using the copyrighted material in a derivative work, such as a collection, without permission; or distributing, performing, or displaying copyrighted work. If an infringement claim is successful, the copyright owner could elect to enjoin the continued use of the work or could receive either actual damages—including profits made by the infringer—or statutory damages of up to $50,000.

FAIR-USE DOCTRINE

An exception to the unauthorized use of copyrighted material is the **fair-use doctrine**. This judicially created exception to the protection normally afforded copyrighted material recognizes that in certain instances, public policy dictates that use of the material is fair and that its use would not conflict with the constitutional mandate to protect such work for the purposes of promoting intellectual growth and development.

fair-use doctrine
an exception to the unauthorized use of limited copyrighted material used for educational purposes

The Copyright Act lists four criteria to be used in a determination of whether use of material is fair. First, the purpose and character of the use are measured; this considers both how the material is used and the intent for which use was made. Second, the nature of the copyrighted work is measured; this examines both the expectation of the author and whether the work is scholarly or for commercial use. Third, the amount and substantiality of the portion used in relation to the copyrighted work as a whole are measured; this examines both the qualitative and quantitative use of the work. Last, the effect of the use upon the potential market is measured; this examines the value of the copyrighted portions on the potential purchasing market.

The Copyright Act gives six examples of purposes to which the fair-use doctrine normally applies. Those examples are criticism, comment, news reporting, teaching, scholarship, and research. Not listed, but almost always protected by fair use, is the use of copyrighted material in parody and satire. Parody is not protected, however, when the parody is done for commercial advertising. (See Box 15–2, "Parody Defense No Joking Matter.")

FAIR USE AND PHOTOCOPYING

To the specific issue of photocopying (including by audiovisual or computer), three tests apply: brevity, spontaneity, and cumulative effect. Generally considered fair are uses that constitute less than 10% of a total body of work (brevity), are created so quickly that there isn't time to request permission for use (spontaneity), and that the use is limited to one time or such a small number that there is no aggregate use that could harm the potential market (cumulative effect). (See Box 15–3, "Unfair Use of the Fair-Use Doctrine" on page 468.)

15–2   LAW IN THE REAL WORLD

Parody Defense No Joking Matter

When faced with a novelty popcorn product called "Dom Popingnon," packaged in a simulated wine bottle, a federal judge decided he got no kick from a champagne look-alike. A New York judge found that the popcorn product, sold in champagne-style bottles with shield-shaped gold labels, infringed the trademark of the similar-looking bubbly, Cuvee Dom Perignon. Although the popcorn's maker, the Jack Company of Boca Inc., maintained that its product was an obvious parody allowing imitation, the judge found that the claim fell flat. The parody was not sufficiently effective to eliminate likelihood of confusion on the part of customers. The judge ordered the $10-a-bottle popcorn forever corked.

The suit alleged trademark infringement, as well as unfair competition and trademark dilution. The popcorn, which sold 20,000 bottles since its introduction in 1987, comes in a bottle virtually the same size as that of the internationally known champagne. Although the popcorn maker acted in good faith, believing its product to be a parody, that does not shield the maker from liability.

In other parody developments, courts have grappled with the parody problem, with inconsistent results. The court recently upheld a parody of the Nike name and swoosh design marks, in a case where the commercial property was a "Mike" T-shirt marketed by a mail-order business. The court in that case held that there was no likelihood of confusion, because the primary customers were people named Mike, and the product was not sold in stores.

Likewise, a parody of the facsimile of L. L. Bean's well-known mark was upheld in an action against *High Society* magazine, which depicted the mark in an article entitled "L. L. Beam's Back-to-School Sex Catalog." The article featured nude models using "products" in a crudely humorous fashion. The court held that there was no likelihood of confusion, because the magazine had not used the mark to identify any goods or services.

However, Topps Chewing Gum was unable to convince a court that its parody of the "Cabbage Patch Kids," a well-known trademark, was not infringed [by] production of the "Garbage Pail Kids" trading cards. Nor was the producer of "Hard Rain Cafe" T-shirts able to convince a judge that it had not infringed on the "Hard Rock Cafe" trademark, despite the defendant's explanation that it would be understood that the T-shirt would refer to the rain in Seattle, where the T-shirts originated.

American Express failed to convince a court that manufacturers of a condom bearing the logo "Never Leave Home Without It" printed on an American Express look-alike card was likely to cause confusion. Anheuser-Busch was unable to enjoin the sales of beach towels with a striking resemblance to the Budweiser label imprinted; the logo said "King of Beaches" on it. And Universal Studios was unsuccessful in enjoining sales of a T-shirt bearing the designation "Miami Mice," complete with mice dressed like the lead characters in the popular television series, because the court ruled that Universal Studios, the trademark owner, had failed to show a reasonable consumer would believe that Universal Studios had sponsored the T-shirts.

Source: "Parody Defense No Joking Matter," Harold Traub and Robert Erb, *The National Law Journal*, April 24, 1994. Reprinted with the permission of *The National Law Journal*. ©1994, The New York Law Publishing Company.

15–3   LEGAL EXCERPTS

Unfair Use of the Fair-Use Doctrine

In an unusual case in which all the facts and testimony were stipulated to by both parties, the federal court was faced with answering the sole question of whether the making of single copies from scientific journals by individual Texaco scientists is fair use under section 107 of the Copyright Act.

Texaco, which employs between 400 and 500 scientists at six research centers, spends in excess of $80 million annually in carrying on scientific and technological research. To support its research, Texaco subscribes to numerous scientific and technical journals and maintains large libraries of such material. Texaco scientists, in learning of an article that may be helpful or important to their research, regularly make a photocopy to be read, kept in their personal files, and used in the lab in the course of their work.

Texaco argued that the scientists had made these copies for research purposes; that the use was noncommercial and private; that the scope of fair use for factual and scientific work was generally broader; that only a small portion of each journal was copied; and that no harm occurred to publishers, pointing out that the publishers were doing well.

The court ruled against Texaco. The court characterized Texaco's purpose as commercial, which weighed heavily against a finding of fair use. It specifically disagreed with Texaco's characterization of the extent of the copying as insubstantial and of the harm to the publisher as minimal. The decision requires Texaco to seek permission from the individual authors of each article and to pay the copyright fees for each article photocopied, adding thousands of dollars to the cost of research for Texaco and adding thousands of dollars in royalties to the authors.

American Geophysical Union v. Texaco Inc., 802 F.Supp.1 (S.D.N.Y. 1992)

SONY V. UNIVERSAL CITY STUDIOS
464 U.S. 417 (1984)

Sony Corp. manufactured home video tape recorders (VTRs) and sold them through retail outlets. Universal Studios owns the copyrights on some of the television programs that are broadcast on the public airwaves. Universal sued Sony, alleging that VTR consumers had been recording some of Universal's copyrighted works that had been broadcast on commercially sponsored television and thereby infringed Universal's copyrights. It alleged that Sony was liable because Sony had sold the VTRs. The District Court denied Universal's claims, holding that noncommercial home use recording of material broadcast over the public airwaves was a fair use of copyrighted works and that even if such was considered an infringing use, Sony could not be held liable for the infringement. The Court of Appeals reversed, holding that petitioners were liable to Universal for contributory infringement. The Supreme Court reversed the Court of Appeals in an opinion written by Justice Stevens.

Stevens, J.: The average member of the public uses a VTR principally to record a program he cannot view as it is being televised and then to watch it once at a later time. This practice, known as time-shifting, enlarges the viewing audience. The respondents in this case were unable to prove that the practice of time-shifting impaired the commercial value of their copyrights or has created any likelihood of future harm.

Section 107 describes a variety of uses of copyrighted material that are not infringements of copyright, the most pertinent to this case being the doctrine of fair use. The first factor requires that the commercial or nonprofit character of an activity be weighed. If the VTR were used to make copies for a commercial or profit-making purpose, such use would be presumptively unfair. Here the contrary presumption is appropriate, because the District Court's findings clearly establish that time-shifting for private home use is noncommercial and not for profit. In addition, when you consider that time-shifting merely enables a viewer to see a work that was made free to the public at an earlier time, the fact that the entire program was reproduced does not militate against a finding of fair use.

continued on next page

In considering the effect of the use upon the potential market for or value of the copyrighted work, a use that has no demonstrable effect upon the potential market for or the value of the copyrighted work need not prohibit its copying. The prohibition of such noncommercial use would merely inhibit access without any countervailing benefit.

Thus, a challenge to a noncommercial use of a copyrighted work requires proof either that the particular use is harmful or that if it should become widespread, it would adversely affect the potential market for the copyrighted work. What is necessary is a showing that some meaningful likelihood of future harm exists. In this case, respondents failed to carry that burden with regard to home time-shifting.

Case Questions

1. In a dissent by four justices, it was argued that Sony contributed to infringing behavior by inducing purchasers of VTRs to "build a library" of their favorite shows and movies, presumably for repeated viewing, rather than onetime time-shifting. How prevalent do you think this practice has become?

2. Do you personally own any copyrighted program that you have recorded on your VTR (or VCR) that you view on a repeated basis or share with friends? Is this the harm predicted by the Court of Appeals?

3. Although this was a copyright action, consider what effect a so-called home-use exception would have on a patent case. Should there be this exemption for copyrights? Is this a proper question for the courts or should it be the legislature that decides the scope of the fair-use doctrine on television programs?

WORK FOR HIRE

The **work-for-hire doctrine** states that an employer automatically owns copyright in employees' works that are prepared within the scope of employment. The doctrine covers writings, art, photography, music, and computer programs, among other things.

work-for-hire doctrine
a rule that states that an employer automatically owns a copyright in the works of employees that are prepared within the scope of employment

The critical inquiry to be made is whether a person has created the material while within the scope of employment. Generally, absent a written agreement to the contrary, an employer owns any material created while an employee is working at a task directed by the employer, whether that task is performed at home or on the job. Conversely, an employer is not entitled to ownership of material simply because the employer's assets, time, and place of business were used during creation of the material.

A second inquiry revolves around the definition of who is an employee. An employer can more easily claim copyright privileges on material created by an employee than it can on material created by an independent contractor. In fact, some courts suggest that if a person is not a bona fide employee (i.e., an employee for tax and benefit purposes), then the employer is not entitled to any ownership of property created by the independent contractor. Because of the state of flux in this area of the law, the better practice is to have employees enter into contracts that specifically outline the rights of employees and employer regarding works created during employment. A work-for-hire contract that gives an employer the ownership of property created by an individual is generally enforceable. Alternatives are a license to use the product and an assignment of the copyright by the creator of the property to the person who commissioned the work.

COMPUTER SOFTWARE

Because of the increased availability of computer software for public consumption, the Copyright Act of 1976 was amended in 1980 to reflect the specific needs of the new technology. Two specific needs were identified: a program's need to be copied in order to be utilized on a hard drive and a program's need to be copied for protection against destruction.

Two substantive changes to the act were made. First, computer programs were defined as literary works. Second, an owner of a computer program was permitted to make one copy of the program if it was an essential step in the use of the program and if it was for archival purposes only and would be destroyed if the originals were sold or given away. Once a computer program is copyrighted, the accompanying manuals are also protected.

That added section gives specific rights to the producer as well as to the user of the software. The producer has the exclusive rights to:

1. reproduction of copies.
2. production of derivative works.
3. distribution of copies for sale or lease.
4. performance of work in public.
5. display of graphic work in public.

The user has the right to:

1. make one or more copies for archival use.
2. make necessary adaptation to use the program correctly.
3. add features as long as the program is not sold or given away without the owner's permission.

In summary, on one hand, if Bill or Ann or their employees develop a product they wish to maintain exclusive use of, then they or their employees should register the work in order to have the most complete protection from others who may use it without authorization. On the other hand, Bill or Ann may have the opposite problem in that they may wish to use matter that is copyrighted by someone else. In such a case, they must be sure to obtain permission from the copyright holder before using the information, or they risk being sued for damages and injunctive relief. (See Box 15–4, "U.S. Antipiracy Effort Focuses on Home and Foreign Shores.")

PATENTS

The U.S. Patent and Trademark Office grants a patent to inventions and processes under the Patent Act of 1952. Patents provide the strongest protection of any type of intellectual property. (See Box 15–5, "Important Dates in U.S. Patents.") During the term of a patent, its protection is virtually absolute; in exchange, at the end of the term, full disclosure of the patented invention to the public is required. A patent gives the inventor the exclusive right to make, use, or sell (or refrain from making, using, or selling) the invention or design for a 17-year period, which cannot be renewed. The words *patent pending* on an article give no protection at all during the period prior to the ac-

15–4   LAW IN THE REAL WORLD

U.S. Antipiracy Effort Focuses on Home and Foreign Shores

It is estimated that overseas copyright, patent, and trademark piracy costs American businesses some $12 billion to $15 billion annually. The most effective weapon the U.S. has to combat this theft is the trade law "Special 301."

Special 301 requires the U.S. trade representative to determine whether the laws and practices of other countries deny adequate and effective protection of intellectual property rights for American exporters and whether foreign laws or practices deny fair and equitable market access to U.S. persons who rely on intellectual property protection.

Countries that have the most egregious acts, policies, and practices and are not engaged in good-faith negotiations to address those problems are identified as "priority foreign countries." After identification as such, the trade representative must investigate the acts, policies, or practices that were the basis of the identification. If the trade representative determines that such acts are in violation of U.S. trade law, retaliatory action such as increased duties on selected imports must be implemented.

The threat to impose such sanctions in 1992 led to China's signing the Berne Convention and the Universal Copyright Convention and enactment of patent amendments that, it claimed, will provide world-class protection. The trade representative is continuing to monitor the situation there, but remains skeptical that China has the enforcement capability to carry through with its ambitious intellectual property program.

On the home front, the federal government has indicted a California businesswoman on charges of piracy involving software stored on CD-ROMs under felony trademark and import laws. The business is charged with importing 900 counterfeit CD-ROM disks from Hong Kong for sale in the U.S., as well as 18,000 counterfeit user manuals.

U.S. Customs Service agents confiscated the CD-ROM's and user manuals. The CD-ROMs contained copies of software developed by Software Toolworks Inc., a California software publisher. Customs agents said the software was worth in excess of $200,000. [The Customs Service] says it expects more interest in and attempts to pirate this kind of software and hopes to send a discouraging message to those who would make such attempts. The maximum penalty for each count of counterfeit trademark is five years in prison, a $250,000 fine for the individual, and $1 million for the company. This is the first CD-ROM piracy case filed by the federal government.

Source: *Billboard* magazine, Vol. 105, Issue 31, 7/31/93, *-301: A Powerful Antipiracy Weapon*, by Stuart Weinstein. ©1993 BPI Communications Inc. Used with permission from *Billboard*.

15–5   CONCEPT SUMMARY

Important Dates in U.S. Patents

1787   The U.S. Constitution is signed by members of the Constitutional Convention.

1790   The first U.S. patent is awarded to Samuel Hopkins, for his process for making potash and pearl ash.

1794   Eli Whitney receives a patent for his cotton gin.

1809   Mary Kies of Killingly, Conn., becomes the first woman to receive a U.S. patent. Her invention is a process of weaving straw with silk or thread.

1836   The U.S. Patent Office is completely destroyed by fire, with the loss of all patent records.

1842   Congress passes legislation making designs patentable for the first time.

1850   The Supreme Court denies a patent for applying an existing process for making wooden cabinet knobs to the manufacture of clay cabinet knobs. From that point on, to receive a patent, a device or process must show "inventiveness." This is the origin of the requirement that an invention not be obvious.

1861   Congress extends the term of patents to 17 years, with no extensions.

1876   Alexander Graham Bell receives a patent for the telephone.

1878   Thomas Edison receives a patent for the phonograph.

1930   New varieties of plants are added to the list of things that can be patented.

1972   The Supreme Court rules that an algorithm for converting a binary code to pure binary is not patentable, because it was a "hitherto unknown phenomenon of nature."

1980   The Supreme Court rules that a living microorganism is patentable.

1981   The Supreme Court allows a patent on a computer-related invention.

1988   Harvard researchers receive a patent for a mouse genetically engineered to contract cancers.

tual grant of the patent. The monopoly period, during which the patent holder has exclusive use, does not begin to run until the actual issuance of the patent.

TYPES OF PATENTS

There are three types of patents in the United States: utility, design, and plant patents.

A **utility patent** is available for "any new and useful process, machine, manufacture, or composition of matter, or any new and useful improvement thereof." These are the most common types of patents. (See Box 15–6, "U.S. Resumes Granting Patents on Genetically Altered Animals.")

utility patent
a patent that is available for any new and useful process, machine, manufacture, or composition of matter or any new or useful improvement thereof

---

15–6   LAW IN THE REAL WORLD

U.S. Resumes Granting Patents on Genetically Altered Animals

The government has ended a self-imposed moratorium and has again begun approving animal patents, nearly five years after Harvard University made history by patenting a genetically engineered mouse.

The United States Patent and Trademark Office issued patents to three organizations covering "transgenic" mice specially suited to research in human medicine. These were the first new animal patents since Harvard received approval in April 1988 for a genetically altered mouse that was predisposed to getting cancer.

The three new patents are restricted to genetically engineered mice, and each is restricted to a particular set of transplanted genes. Dr. Leder, the Harvard scientist who obtained the original patent, has won a second one with a colleague, William J. Muller. This patent is for a mouse that develops an enlarged prostate, a common problem of older men. Also, researchers at Genpharm International in Mountainview, Calif., patented a mouse without a working immune system, developed for use in AIDS research. And researchers at Ohio University patented a virus-resistant mouse, for use in developing agricultural livestock less vulnerable to disease.

continued on next page

The Harvard mouse prompted a backlash from animal rights groups and some environmentalists, but with the latest approvals industry experts expect a surge of new patents covering mice, pigs, and even cows. More than 180 applications for animal patents are awaiting government action; many of them have been pending for years. And while much of the emphasis in so-called bioengineering was on breeding superior farm animals, the current push seems to be in manipulating animal genes for the benefit of human health.

The most ambitious and very likely the most controversial of these efforts is in "xenografts"—developing animals that can supply organs like hearts, livers, or kidneys for human transplant recipients. The DNX Corporation, a biotechnology company in Princeton, N.J., is working to develop pigs with genes that mask the immunological markers of "pigness," which normally provoke a human immune system to wage war against an alien body part. Officials at DNX said the first swine-to-human transplants could take place by the late 1990s.

"My understanding is that these first few are just the beginning," James McCamant, publisher of the *Ag-biotech Stock Letter* in Berkeley, Calif., said of the recently issued patents. "To me, the most important impact is that it will allow us to find out who's got a strong patent position."

The approval of new animal patents, while good for the United States biotechnology industry, is almost certain to reignite political opposition in Congress from animal rights groups and some farmers. In 1989, the House of Representatives passed a bill that would exempt farmers from paying royalties on the offspring of genetically engineered livestock, but the measure never advanced very far in the Senate.

Industry executives say their shift away from farm animals had little to do with the political controversy. Rather, most say the decision stemmed from technical issues and a concern that farm animals simply would not produce big profits. "The science wasn't ready yet to make it economically feasible," said James Sherblum, president of TSI Corporation in Worcester, Mass. Hoping for more immediate profits, TSI put most of its money into developing mice that could be used as laboratory models and is using them to carve out a position in the drug-testing market. During the past three years, the company bought eight drug-testing laboratories and plans to introduce genetically engineered mice in the next 18 months that develop Alzheimer's disease and AIDS.

Most of the other biotechnology companies that were interested in farm animals have also changed course. Companies involved in "transgenic" animals say that patent protection is crucial, because otherwise they have no way to prevent customers from simply buying one animal and breeding as many others as they like.

Now a new round of attacks is likely, particularly from farmers and animal rights organizations. Such groups say that splicing genes into animals will hurt family farmers, have cruel effects on many animals, and could endanger many species of animals. "This is government giving its imprimatur to the idea that there is no difference between a living thing and an inert object," said Jeremy Rifkin, head of the Foundation on Economic Trends, a nonprofit organization in Washington. "It's the final assault on the sacred meaning of life and life process."

An animal patent covers animals with particular gene sequences that do not exist in any natural animal species and that give the animal identifiable, unique characteristics. The patents also cover the offspring of such animals, even though the chromosomes of offspring are always different from those of parents.

Information made public by the European Patent Office shows that universities and companies are developing an expanding army of small animals that are genetically programmed to suffer. Several European companies have applied for patents covering mice that are prone to get AIDS, tumors, leukemia, and something akin to Alzheimer's.

Except for the United States, no country has approved an animal patent. Indeed, in December 1992, the European Parliament recommended that the European Community reject such patent applications.

The animal rights critics notwithstanding, most experts believe a big wave of animal patents is imminent in the United States.

Source: "U.S. Resumes Granting Patents on Genetically Altered Animals," Edmund Andres, *New York Times*, February 3, 1993. ©1993 by the New York Times Company.

A **design patent** covers any "new, original, and ornamental design for an article of manufacture." (See Box 15–7, "New Holiday Pasta Shaped like Santa.") Design patents differ from utility patents in that (1) they do not cover utilitarian function; (2) the drawing of the design is the focus of the protection; (3) the standards for infringement are different; and (4) the measure of damages is different for infringement.

The **plant patent** covers "distinct and new" varieties of plants that are produced asexually. Thus it excludes seed plants and most commercially valuable crops. Plant patents differ from utility patents in two ways. First, the plant has to be distinct rather than have any utility; thus, a plant may be (and often is) merely an ornamental plant asexu-

design patent
a patent for a new, original and ornamental design for an article of manufacture

plant patent
a patent for a distinct and new variety of plant that is asexually produced

15–7   LAW IN THE REAL WORLD

New Holiday Pasta Shaped like Santa

Over the years patents have been issued for a variety of anthropomorphic and other pasta shapes. One pasta to be issued a patent is designed to look like Santa Claus. The patent was assigned to Kraft General Foods Inc. of Northfield, Ill. The company was assigned design patent 333,546 for the Santa pasta. The company recently shipped to stores a macaroni and cheese product called Santa Mac, which features pasta in six different shapes: a candy cane, bell, Christmas tree, stocking, bugle, and Santa Claus.

Source: "New Holiday Pasta Shaped like Santa," by Teresa Riordan, *New York Times*, December 13, 1993. ©1993 by the New York Times Company. Reprinted by permission.

ally produced. Second, there is a relaxation of disclosure requirements for plants, as their varieties are deemed incapable of accurate description. The description must simply be as complete as possible. (See Box 15–8, "A Dogwood Tree That Resists Disease.")

OBJECTS NOT SUBJECT TO PATENT

Certain things have been judicially deemed unsuitable for patent. Those things are laws of nature and fundamental scientific principles, mathematical formulas and algorithms, and abstract business ideas.

The rationale for excluding such things is that they are discovered, not invented, and therefore patent laws do not protect them.

REQUIREMENTS FOR PATENT PROTECTION

An invention must meet three criteria to qualify for patent protection: novelty, utility, and nonobviousness. Those three criteria, and the strictness with which they are applied, are the reasons why patent protection is the most difficult and expensive to obtain. However, because Bill and Ann will have a monopoly on the use of their patented product for 17 years, the difficulty and expense are well worthwhile if

15–8   LAW IN THE REAL WORLD

A Dogwood Tree That Resists Disease

Dogwood, ash, and sycamore trees across the United States are threatened by a fungus that destroys the ability of their leaves to absorb sunlight and retain sugars. Older trees are especially vulnerable to this blight, known as anthracnose disease. An arboretum in Ohio said it hoped that dead dogwoods would be replaced with a newly patented variety of the tree that appears to be resistant to the disease.

"Anthracnose occurs during damp, wet conditions without good air circulation," said Thomas L. Smith, vice president of the Spring Grove Cemetery and Arboretum in Cincinnati. Landscape and gardening companies say the disease has devastated dogwoods in the Northeast.

"We had been working with a number of different dogwoods," Mr. Smith said. They were breeding trees to survive freezing temperatures and produce more blossoms. When 30 percent of the arboretum's dogwoods succumbed to the fungus, the staff noticed that one breed of the tree seemed impervious. "We put more of them out, in different places, because we thought its location might have given it protection," he said. "But in any of the propagated plants, we didn't see any evidence of the disease." Spring Grove received plant patent 8500.

Source: "Inventions and Inventors, . . . A Dogwood Tree that Resists Disease," Sabra Chartrand. *New York Times*, January 17, 1994. ©1994 by the New York Times Company. Reprinted by permission.

DIAMOND V. DIEHR
450 U.S. 175 (1981)

James Diehr and Theodore Lutton filed a patent application claiming invention for a process for molding raw, uncured synthetic rubber into cured precision products. Although it was possible, using well-known time, temperature and cure relationships, to calculate by means of an established mathematical equation when to open the molding press and remove the cured product, according to the claimants the industry had not been able to precisely measure the temperature inside the mold, making it difficult to know exactly when to open it. The claimants characterized their contribution to the art as residing in the process of constantly measuring the temperature inside the mold and feeding the temperature measurements into a computer that repeatedly recalculates the cure time by use of the mathematical equation and then signals a device to open the press at the proper time. The Patent and Trademark Office examiner rejected the claims on the ground that they were drawn to nonstatutory subject matter. The Court of Customs and Patent Appeals reversed, alleging that the claims were not directed to a mathematical algorithm, but rather recited an improved process for molding rubber articles by solving a practical problem that had risen in the molding of rubber products.

Rehnquist, J.: We granted certiorari to determine whether a process for curing synthetic rubber [that] includes in several of its steps the use of a mathematical formula and a programmed digital computer is patentable subject matter.

Excluded from patent protection are laws of nature, natural phenomena, and abstract ideas. The respondents here do not seek to patent a mathematical formula; they do not seek to preempt the use of that equation. Rather they seek only to foreclose from others the use of that equation in conjunction with the other steps in the process of molding rubber. These include installing a rubber in a press, closing the mold, constantly determining the temperature of the mold, constantly recalculating the appropriate cure time through the use of the formula and a digital computer, and automatically opening the press at the proper time. If the computer is incorporated in the process, it significantly lessens the possibility of overcuring or undercuring; the process as a whole does not become unpatentable subject matter.

We hold that when a claim containing a mathematical formula implements or applies that formula in a structure or process [that], when considered as a whole, is performing a function the patent laws were designed to protect, e.g., transforming or reducing an article to a different state or thing, then the claim satisfies the requirements of the patent law.

Case Questions

1. This case was decided with a four-justice dissent that argued that the mere use of a computer to do a mathematical calculation doesn't make the mathematical calculation patentable and that no other part of the molding process was unknown; therefore, the computerized process was not subject to patent. Do you agree?

2. Aside from the patent requirement that a process be subject to a patent, the idea sought to be protected must be "novel." Do you think, even though the plaintiffs in this case were able to establish their process was subject to patent, that this process would be able to pass the "novel" test?

3. Given the increased use and sophistication of computerized research today, what chance do you think this case would have to be successful if heard today? More of a chance? Less of a chance? Does the fact that this was a five-to-four decision give any indication?

the patented item is viable. Each of these criteria is governed by the Patent Act and consists of a strict and complicated set of rules that guide the issue or nonissue of a patent. (See Box 15–9, "Path from Invention to Patent.")

PATENT INFRINGEMENT

Anyone who, without permission, makes, uses, or sells a patented invention infringes upon the right of the owner. The remedies for infringement are provided by the Patent Act. Those remedies are (1) an injunction, (2) damages, (3) attorney's fees, and (4) costs. As can be seen from Box 15–10, "Microsoft Loses Case on Patent," (page 484) it can be quite costly to litigate patent matters, but also worth the effort.

TRADEMARKS

Think of a refreshing cola drink: what comes to mind? Chances are that you didn't think of an off-brand, but rather, a popular brand of cola. The company's trademark has done its job. It has identified in the minds of consumers its product rather than any other. That is what trademarks are made to do. A trademark includes "any word, name, symbol, or device, or any combination thereof . . . used by a person . . . to identify and distinguish his or her goods . . . from those manufactured or sold by others. . . ." Depending on the nature of the business, it can be extremely important for Bill and Ann to help establish customer loyalty by using a trademark for product or service identification. It is also important for Bill and Ann not to infringe on the trademarks of other businesses.

Unlike the other intellectual properties we have discussed, trademark protection has no limited term, but rather is protected for as long as it is used in commerce. That protection, however, is not absolute. It operates only to avoid confusion resulting from conflicting use of similar words or symbols in the same geographic area, and trademark principles do not protect words or symbols in the abstract, but only as they are used in commerce. Because of the commercial value of trademarks, however, trademark licensing has become enormously profitable business. (See Box 15–11, "Spike Lee versus Mrs. Malcolm X" on page 485.)

Encompassed within the law of trademark are related forms of intellectual property, including service marks, titles and character names, trade names, and trade dress.

15–9   BLACK LETTER LAW

Path from Invention to Patent

Bill and Ann have invented zymgoat, a material used in packaging hazardous waste that is placed inside pressurized barrels of waste and that creates an inner seal that will not allow the waste to spill even if the barrel is broken or fails to seal properly. Bill and Ann seek to do three things to protect their new property: make zymgoat's formula a trade secret, patent zymgoat, and use zymgoat as a trade name. The following diagram follows the path from invention to patent. After reading the sections of this chapter that cover trade names and trade secrets, what must Bill and Ann do to protect zymgoat's name and formula?

1. Invent zymgoat	Done in lab by researchers; make sure work-for-hire contracts cover employees.
2. Record conception building, and testing	Have witnesses sign invention records.
3. Evaluate commercial salability	Before making expensive model, test marketability and commercial feasibility.
4. Evaluate patentability	Determine through research whether the Patent and Trademark Office will issue patent and which kind needed (utility, design, or plant). Request a prefiling search to check existing patents for same inventions.
5. Decide how to proceed	If not commercially feasible, find out what to do.
6. Prepare and file a patent application	This is a technical document involving drawings, formulas, etc.
7. Market the invention	Can place "Patent Pending" sign on it.
8. Wait for the Patent and Trademark Office to issue the patent	If the invention is discovered through reverse engineering, the first filer will own the patent.
9. Use the patent	Once the Patent and Trademark Office issues a patent, the patent holder can sell, license, or use the invention.

15–10   LAW IN THE REAL WORLD

Microsoft Loses Case on Patent

A federal court jury found Microsoft Corp. guilty of patent infringement and awarded $120 million in damages to a small California company that had accused Microsoft of appropriating its technology for increasing the storage capacity of computer disks. The judgment in favor of Stac Electronics Inc. came in the first patent infringement suit against Microsoft ever to reach a trial.

The decision involving Microsoft's MS-DOS 6.0 software, the operating software under which applications systems run, is likely to fuel a controversy about whether the nation's patent process is appropriate for the rapidly changing software industry. The Patent and Trademark Office, which began issuing software patents only a decade ago, has been accused of having inadequate expertise in software to judge what is truly novel. Critics contend that the process too often awards patents for products that are not the first of their kind.

But the jury also found for Microsoft on one of its seven counterclaims against Stac, awarding the larger company $13.6 million in damages for misappropriation of a trade secret. This claim centered on Stac's use of what is known as an undocumented call in MS-DOS—that is, an unpublished feature that allows the operating system to work with compression technology. Stac said it found the feature through reverse engineering.

Source: "Microsoft Loses Case on Patent," by Lawrence M. Fisher, *New York Times*, 2/24/94 and 6/16/94. ©1994 by the New York Times Company. Reprinted by permission.

15–11   LAW IN THE REAL WORLD

Spike Lee versus Mrs. Malcolm X

Malcolm X, the fiery black activist, said he'd achieve his goals "by any means necessary." He probably never expected those means would include licensed T-shirts, jewelry, baseball caps, mugs, posters, sunglasses, board games, and potato chips.

Today, Malcolm X's image has become as hot as his rhetoric was. Retail sales of licensed Malcolm X products, all emblazoned with a large "X" could reach $100 million in 1992. If so, the estate could collect as much as $3 million in royalties.

The estate is controlled by Betty Shabazz, Malcolm X's widow. Until recently, Shabazz had no reason to think the name could sell merchandise: Malcolm X was assassinated in 1965, and the generation born after his death knew little if anything of him. Between 1986 and 1988, Pathfinder Press sold just 58,000 copies of Malcolm X's speeches.

But a proliferation of black history courses at urban colleges has made the name more familiar and helped launch a mini Malcolm X revival. In the past three years, Pathfinder Press has sold 240,000 copies of his collected speeches, and sales of *The Autobiography of Malcolm X* (Ballantine Books) have tripled, to 2.4 million copies.

Shabazz began noticing that Malcolm X shirts were starting to appear on the sidewalks. Figuring she was losing out on licensing revenues, she finally retained a management team. There are now 35 licensees under contract.

The audience for Malcolm X–wear is primarily black. But like rap music and other trends born in the black community, the Malcolm X marketing movement crossed over to a white market. The "X" merchandise has found its way into mainstream retailers like J. C. Penney, Federated, and Montgomery Ward. After basketball star Michael Jordan was seen on television sporting a Malcolm X hat, white fans started stocking up on the hip headgear.

Some of the current interest in the leader comes from the Warner Bros. film *Malcolm X*, directed by Spike Lee. But a fight is brewing. Since 1991, Lee's merchandising company, 40 Acres and a Mule Merchandising, has marketed apparel bearing an "X" logo. Claiming that the "X" is a transparent reference to the Malcolm X trademark, Betty Shabazz is demanding a piece of Lee's merchandising action. Says Jay Lodico, marketing coordinator for Roman Co.: "Spike Lee is where the "X" craze originated. Any others are knockoffs."

continued on next page

Spike Lee isn't the only one trying to get a free ride on the Malcolm X name. Snack Pak, Inc., of Philadelphia markets X Chips, otherwise indistinguishable from normal potato chips but for a big "X" on the bag. The company doesn't have a license and insists it doesn't need one since it argues that the letter *X* has nothing to do with Malcolm X. When pressed, however, Snack Pak admits that the new interest in Malcolm X might help sales.

According to one licenser, Malcolm X products may hit $20 million in 1992. That would have deprived Betty Shabazz of up to $1 million or so in royalties.

Source: "Spike Lee versus Mrs. Malcolm X," by R. Lee Sullivan, *Forbes*, October 12, 1992. Reprinted by permission of *Forbes* magazine. ©Forbes Inc., 1992.

TECHNICAL TRADEMARKS

Trademarks are protected under a federal statute known as the Trademark Act of 1946, amended in 1988 by the Trademark Law Revisions Act and commonly referred to as the Lanham Act. This statute allows owners of trademarks to register them with the Patent and Trademark Office, and it covers a wide variety of things such as the color "pink" for insulation (Owens Corning fiberglass insulation), loop stitching and cloth tabs on pants (Levi Strauss), shapes of bottles (Mogen David wine), and slogans ("Don't Leave Home Without It"— American Express). Although words are probably the principal form of trademarks, names, symbols, and devices can also serve as trademarks. Names such as McDonald's and Pillsbury form trademarks, as do John Hancock and Sam and Libby's. Symbols such as AT&T, 7-Eleven, and V-8 also form trademarks. Devices such as the shape of a Coca-Cola bottle or the shape of a building such as the Fotomat kiosk have been ruled trademarks. (See Box 15–12, "Trademarks Protect the Bizarre and the Sublime.")

SERVICE MARKS

service mark
mark used in the sale or advertising of services to identify and distinguish the services of one producer from those of another

Section 3 of the Lanham Act provides for registration of service marks. It defines the term **service mark** as a mark used in the sale or advertising of services that identifies and distinguishes the services of one person, including a unique service, from the services of others.

15–12 LAW IN THE REAL WORLD

Trademarks Protect the Bizarre and the Sublime

For some people, the $210 it costs to apply for a trademark is a meager outlay compared with what can be earned from protecting the rights to a name or image.

There might not be a better example than the trademark announced for Shaquille O'Neal, the National Basketball Association star of the Orlando Magic, for his nickname, "Shaq." The announcement lists nearly 200 products in three classes of goods.

The inventory leaves little to chance. Mr. O'Neal may never license his name to all of it—from sports trading cards and athletic shoes to cake decorations, bathroom tissue, tuxedos, earmuffs, Halloween costumes, bathtub toys, and kites—but now he can stop others from cashing in.

The law says that a name, a phrase, an image or a logo must be unique. Numbers cannot be reserved, either. Hence the decision by the Intel Corporation to add letters to the names of its computer chips. The company just won a trademark for i386. Getting a trademark for the name and picture of a living individual is easy. Trademarks were announced for a logo bearing a picture of the Miami Dolphins football coach, Don Shula, above the stylized words "Shula's Athletic Club" and for Frank Sinatra's name and picture on a brand of spaghetti sauce.

Being alive is not a trademark requirement: Elvis Presley Enterprises won trademarks for the phrase "Still the King" and for a Graceland mansion logo for soft drinks. And a Los Angeles cosmetics company, the Julie Joubert Corporation, reserved the name of a 15th-century Italian painter, Botticelli, for its perfumes and makeups.

Just as many patents are issued for devices that may never see the light of day, companies offer trademark slogans or logos as a hedge for future products or advertising campaigns. Perhaps hoping for a hit slogan like Nike's "Just Do It," Vida Shoes International Inc. won a trademark for the phrase "Forget the Consequences." The American Express Company may hope to expand the success of its long-standing slogan "Don't Leave Home Without It," with a new trademark for the phrase "Don't Do Business Without It."

Sometimes trademarks can hint where a company might be heading. The McDonald's Corporation has logos for a line of children's toys and an event called "Family FunNight," with the "M" in *Family* spelled with golden arches. Pepsico Inc. wants to name tortilla chips and soft drinks "31 Days of Party Madness" and "Party like a Maniac." The company may

continued on next page

be having a hard time deciding which is best, or it may have abandoned the idea altogether. The trademarks will be valid for 10 years.

Trademarks are often awarded to names or slogans so closely identified with a product or company that they seem superfluous. Recently, the acronym "V.F.W." was awarded a collective membership trademark. Mars Inc., the candy manufacturer, won a trademark for the phrase "The chocolate melts in your mouth, not in your hand." The Coca-Cola Company recently won the rights to use the name "Coca-Cola Classic," which it first began using in 1985.

Within limits, language and innuendo are not obstacles to trademark approval. Sebastian International Inc., for example, won a trademark for hair care products called "Bitchin Do."

Source: "Patents; From 'Shaq' to Sinatra's Spaghetti Sauce, Trademarks Protect the Bizarre and the Sublime," by Sabra Chartrand, *New York Times*, November 22, 1993. ©1993 by the New York Times Company. Reprinted by permission.

Service marks has been given broad meaning, and it differs from a trademark only in that it identifies services rather than goods. Service marks may not be registered for services that are expected, routine, or legally required upon purchase of goods, such as a warranty. Rather, service marks used for such services as motel and hotel services, restaurants, advertising, and insurance services are permitted.

TITLES AND CHARACTER NAMES

Creative property, such as the titles of and the characters in creative works, are commercially important, and trademark principles also protect them. Titles of films, comic book characters, and characters created for commercials or merchandising promotions may be protected. Such well-known characters as Batman, Conan the Barbarian, and the peanut in the Planter's peanut logo have been afforded trademark protection under this theory.

TRADE NAMES

trade name
the name of a firm or business that identifies the producer, rather than the products or services it produces

A **trade name** is the name of a firm or business and differs from a trademark in that it identifies the producer, rather than the products or services produced. Because trade names are not trademarks, they cannot be registered under the Lanham Act, but they are instead protected under nearly identical principles found in the common law. Some states have enacted statutes that provide for registration of trade names. Those states that do not provide for registration generally operate on the theory that the first to use the name in a particular line of activity within a geographic region have the common law right to the name.

TRADE DRESS

The term **trade dress** refers to the total image of a product, including the size, shape, color, texture, graphics, or particular sales technique employed. Almost any feature may be protected under this term if it is distinctive and performs an identifying function. Trade dress is protected by section 43 (a) of the Lanham Act, which refers to unregistered trademarks. This section has been universally applied to trade dress and applies to such items as Rubik's Cube, Le Sportsac luggage, Harlequin romance novels, Hallmark cards, and "adoption" of Cabbage Patch Dolls. (See Box 15–13, "Dictionary Trademark Wars.")

trade dress
the total image of a product, including the size, shape, color, texture, graphics, or sales technique employed

---

15–13   LAW IN THE REAL WORLD

Dictionary Trademark Wars

A verdict against one dictionary publisher in favor of another won't end the public's understandable confusion over what is and what isn't a Webster's.

Despite famed American lexicographer Noah Webster's ardent advocacy of strict copyright laws in the early 19th century, his own name is public domain. The name alone doesn't necessarily mean anything at all on the cover of a dictionary or imply anything about the quality or accuracy of the definitions inside.

A federal jury decided, however, that Merriam-Webster Inc. can lay claim to the Webster name, modifying some form of the word *college* as part of the title of a desk dictionary that has a red cover with *Webster's* in huge white letters down the spine. It was copying the combination that was objectionable.

continued on next page

The jury found that the new *Random House Webster's Collegiate Dictionary* infringed the trademarks and trade dress of Merriam's *Webster's Ninth New Collegiate Dictionary*. It awarded Merriam-Webster $1,774,713 in lost profits plus another $500,000 in punitive damages.

Random House must change its cover and title page under an injunction issued by the judge. Random House has published its well-respected desk dictionary for years under the title *The Random House College Dictionary*. It announced it would add *Webster's* before *College*, reportedly for marketing reasons. Merriam-Webster filed its suit the next month.

The judge allowed Random House to retain the book's disputed title. But the words *Random House* must immediately precede and be in the same typeface as the word *Webster's* on the book cover. The decision protects consumers who were confused by the two dictionaries' similarity.

Merriam has pursued aggressively copycats and alleged infringers since its predecessor company bought the rights to Noah Webster's best-known dictionary upon his death in 1843. At issue in a lawsuit against a California company in 1984 was the "bull's eye" that encircles the dictionary name on Merriam-Webster covers. Merriam-Webster's bright red cover apparently doesn't have the same protection as its bull's eye, though. Random House announced that it is sticking with red, a choice that is permitted under the judge's order.

Source: "Dictionary Trademark Wars," by Don J. DeBenedictis, *ABA Journal*, January 1992. ©American Bar Association. Reprinted by permission of the *ABA Journal*.

JORDACHE V. HOGG WYLD, INC.

828 F.2d 1482 (2d Cir. 1987)

Jordache, the fourth-largest blue jeans manufacturer in the U.S., brought a trademark infringement action against Hogg Wyld, Inc., for manufacturing jeans for larger women with the word *Lardash* on the pocket along with a smiling pig. Jordache appealed a district court ruling that held there was no likelihood of confusion between its product and that of Hogg Wyld's jeans. On appeal, the Court of Appeals affirmed.

Tacha, J.: Two women formed Lardashe for the purpose of marketing designer blue jeans for larger women. Sales were limited to specialty shops in several Southwestern states and to acquaintances or others who heard of the product. The women have not directly advertised their jeans, although several retailers have done so.

Appellant became aware of Lardashe jeans after a TV station broadcast a news segment, which was also broadcast nationally by NBC, highlighting the new product.

The Lanham Act prohibits the unauthorized use of a reproduction, copy, or imitation of a registered trademark in a way that is likely to cause confusion with the registered mark. Confusion occurs when consumers make an incorrect mental association between the involved commercial products or their producers. The party alleging the infringement has the burden of proving likelihood of the confusion.

The District Court found that the two marks in question suggest different images or concepts. Although "Jordache" and "Lardashe" are similar, the pig and the horse design are not. The Jordache horse is a subtle design depicted by a gold horse's head superimposed over the lettering; sometimes the horse's head is used alone, and sometimes the patch has no horse and just lettering. On the other hand, Lardashe's jeans have a brightly colored pig head and two hooves—giving the appearance that the pig is peering over the pocket—with the word *Lardashe* written in script beneath the pig head, below which is embroidered an upside down heart. Far from subtle, we agree with the District

continued on next page

Court that the pig design is humorous, cute, or facetious. The dissimilarities of the design greatly outweigh the similarities of the words.

Another consideration is whether the party had the intent to derive a benefit or goodwill from the reputation or goodwill of the trademark owner. A court generally presumes that the conscious choice of a mark similar to an existing mark intends to confuse the public. However, where a party chooses a mark as a parody of an existing mark, the intent is not to confuse the public but rather to amuse. In one sense, a parody is an attempt to derive benefit from the reputation of the owner of the mark. The benefit to the one making the parody, however, arises from the humorous association, not from public confusion as to the source of the mark. We hold that an intent to parody is not an intent to confuse the public.

Case Questions

1. What harm would come from not allowing the use of trademark parody?

2. Does this case conflict with the general rule that parody for commercial purpose be more strictly scrutinized than parody for noncommercial purpose?

3. Should the owner of a trademark have control over negative parodies if the negative statements are untrue or somehow cheapen the original product?

TRADEMARK INFRINGEMENT

Recall that the underlying purpose for trademarks is to distinguish the trademark holder's products, services, and so on, from those of others. It is not then difficult to understand that the single standard for trademark infringement is likelihood of confusion, whether that infringement action takes federal, statutory, or common law grounds and whether that action is against registered or unregistered trademarks. Basically, under this standard, infringement exists if the two marks, under all the circumstances of the marketplace, make confusion on the part of the consumer likely. The confusion created must be confusion as to the source of origin of a service or product.

How many times have you asked someone if you could "xerox" a document? What you actually wanted to do was photocopy it. The word *Xerox* has come to mean the same thing. In order for Bill and Ann to protect their right to a trademark, efforts must be made to prevent the trademark from falling into general use as a generic term for a product. This often happens with popular products, as when the trademark name of the product becomes so associated with the product that the two have become one in the same in the minds of consumers. For instance, many people simply ask if you have a kleenex, rather than a facial tissue, yet Kleenex is a brand name. The same can be said for Jell-O gelatin, Band-Aid adhesive strips, Frigidaire refrigerators, Pop Tarts toaster pastries, and Kool-Aid powdered drink mix.

If Bill and Ann do not take steps to protect their trademark from general use, they can lose the right to bring suit for trademark infringement. From time to time you may see a magazine advertisement by Xerox that it simply says Xerox is a trade name of the Xerox Corporation and the ad is to serve as a reminder that all photocopies are not xeroxes. That ad can then be used by Xerox to show it has taken steps to prevent general use of its name and can maintain an action for trademark infringement.

certification mark a mark indicating that certain goods or services originated in a particular region, or that they are of a particular nature, quality, or characteristic, or that they were produced by a particular organization

CERTIFICATION MARKS

The Lanham Act also provides for **certification marks**. A certification mark is used to indicate that certain goods or services originated in a particular region, or that they are of a particular nature, quality, or characteristic, or that they were produced by a member of a particular organization. The owner of a certification mark must maintain control over its use, but may not engage in actual production or marketing of the goods.

For example, the mark Good Housekeeping Seal of Approval indicates that particular products meet standards imposed by owners of that certification mark. *Good Housekeeping* magazine, however, as the owner of the mark, must not allow itself to use the certification mark and must design the mark so that it is distinguishable from the magazine itself. Because trademarks indicate origin and certification marks indicate a guarantee of a certain characteristic, a common owner must ensure that the marks are distinguishable.

Another difference between certification marks and trademarks is that use of a certification mark cannot be denied to anyone who maintains the characteristics that the mark certifies. Exclusive ownership, therefore, is contrary to the purpose of certification marks. (See Box 15–14, "Claret-Style Classics.")

COLLECTIVE MARKS

collective mark
a mark indicating that goods or services are produced by members of a collective group or simply indicating membership in a particular group

A **collective mark** indicates that goods or services are produced by members of a collective group or simply indicates membership in a particular group. Ownership of the collective mark is vested in a group, of which each producer or provider is a member. Most of us have seen collective marks in clothing, which often carries a tag stating it was made by the ILGWU or International Ladies' Garment Workers' Union. Those who wish to support unions may assure themselves of it by purchasing only items that contain a union collective mark.

TRADE SECRETS

trade secret
any formula or recipe or client list used in one's business that gives one an advantage over competitors

If Bill and Ann have a secret formula or recipe or client list that is important to the business and not an item of general knowledge, they may wish to protect it as a trade secret. A **trade secret** may be any formula, pattern, device, or compilation of information that is used in one's business and that gives one an opportunity to obtain an advantage over competitors who do not know or use it.

Trade secret protection in the United States is a matter of state law and contains three requirements: (1) limited availability of the se-

15–14   LAW IN THE REAL WORLD

Claret-Style Classics

The Bureau of Alcohol, Tobacco, and Firearms is the federal agency that deals with wine label regulations, and in California it prohibits table wine from being called by its varietal (grape) name unless the wine consists of at least 75% of that varietal.

Unfortunately, most table wines are blends, and those winemakers who opt for the freedom to create premium blends sacrifice the right to use varietal designations on their labels, using instead generic, non-descriptive labels such as "red (or white)" table wine or using proprietary designations such as Trilogy or Cain. The problem is that consumers would prefer to select wines that had the name of the familiar varietal on the label (cabernet sauvignon, merlot, cabernet franc, etc.).

This marketing dilemma created by the 75% rule prompted the formation of the Meritage Association, an organization of approximately 30 wineries that produce Bordeaux-like blends. This association has as its members a majority of wineries in California producing claret-style wines. A special category on retail shelves can help the consumer identify these wines, grouped together under the heading "Meritage" instead of the undistinguished red or white table wines category.

To use the Meritage certification mark, a winery must comply with the following standards:

The wine must be blended entirely from Bordeaux grape varieties. (The Bordeaux red grapes include cabernet sauvignon, merlot, cabernet franc, malbec, and petit verdot; the whites are sauvignon blanc, semillion, and muscadelle.)

It must be among the winery's top-of-the-line wines.

It cannot be designated as a varietal wine (although percentages of each variety may be printed on the label).

The wine must be produced and bottled by a U.S. winery and carry a U.S. appellation of origin. Producers of Meritage wines are limited to 25,000 cases per year per winery.

The association doesn't require its members to carry the term "Meritage" or use special insignia on their labels. Even so, many wineries elect to carry the term on their labels for easy identification.

Source: Reprinted by permission from the February 1992 issue of *Country Living.* ©1992 by The Hearst Corporation. Written by Leslie Martin.

cret to those outside the circle of those who need to know, (2) economic value, and (3) reasonable effort to keep the secret. Once those three requirements are met, the list of things that may qualify for trade secret protection is endless, extending from recipes to customer lists.

Trade secrets differ from other types of intellectual property in several ways. There is no application to or registration by a government office. Trade secrets are creatures solely of state law and may continue indefinitely. Protection exists only against discovery or use by improper means, such as theft, bribery, or espionage. For instance, Bill and Ann may have an employee who leaves their employ and takes a confidential customer list that Bill and Ann wish to regard as a trade secret.

There is no protection against reverse engineering or independent discovery of matters that form the basis of a trade secret. For instance, if Bill and Ann developed a new kind of cleaning agent for hazardous waste containers and an ex-employee experiments with different agents until finding the same combination of ingredients as discovered by Bill and Ann, Bill and Ann would have no cause of action for theft of trade secrets because the ex-employee did not take the formula, but instead discovered it independently through experimentation.

Unlike trademarks or patentable things, trade secrets do not require novelty or nonobviousness to be protected. Like patents and copyrights, however, mere ideas will not be protected as trade secrets; that is, a trade secret must possess concreteness or tangible form.

Recently, some states have moved to enact the Uniform Trade Secret Act (UTSA), which attempts to codify the common law rules under which trade secret violations were previously brought. Thus far, over 20 states have enacted some version of the UTSA. This has helped to define a trade secret violation as well as provide remedies for violations.

STATE V. FEDERAL REGISTRATION

Registration of goods or services not used in commerce or in a wide geographical area are protected either under the common law or by registering the trademark with the state in which the trademark is used. State systems vary from state to state, but generally require registration with the office of the secretary of state. Registration generally provides exclusive use within the jurisdiction of registration.

SUMMARY

Intellectual property is an important area for Bill and Ann to be aware of in establishing and operating a business. Not only do issues in intellectual property involve liability that may be imposed upon Bill and Ann for infringing on the protected rights of others, but such issues also protect them from infringement of legitimate business matters. These may include Bill and Ann's trademark, patents, copyrights, service marks, and trade dress. Knowing the law can help Bill and Ann to grow their business, as well as prevent them from running into legal trouble for infringement.

CHAPTER TERMS

certification mark	public domain
collective mark	service mark
copyright	trade dress
design patent	trademark
fair-use doctrine	trade name
intellectual property	trade secret
patent	utility patent
plant patent	work-for-hire doctrine

CHAPTER-END QUESTIONS

1. How long is a copyright effective?
2. Elizabeth writes a story that Mel thinks is great. Mel urges Elizabeth to send it out for publication. Elizabeth is hesitant to do so because she says the story isn't copyrighted. Must it be in order to be protected?
3. Dror, an industry leader in computer technology, established early the industry standard for computer compatibility. As a part of its computer manufacturing, Dror decides to issue a "seal of approval and compatibility" to other computer companies that request it and meet certain standards Dror thinks are important. The purpose is to inform consumers that the computer meets

what Dror considers to be certain minimal standards for computers. Is Dror's idea a good one? Explain.

4. Sula creates a new type of comfortable pants called Zamis, which can be worn by either gender. Sula registers the name Zami as a trademark. The pants are so comfortable that they quickly become a huge market hit and are known far and wide for their comfort. Within a year, the word Zami becomes a slang term for something that is supremely comfortable. For instance, someone trying on a shoe in a shoe store would say, "Oh yes, this is definitely zami" (meaning that the shoe felt wonderful). The term also starts to be used by the media—in television shows, movies, and the like. Sula does not approve of the widespread use of her trademarked name and wants to protect it. What do you advise her to do?

5. Professor Harrison is gathering materials she will use in an upcoming class she is teaching. The class is new and there is currently no textbook for it on the market. Professor Harrison compiles articles from different sources, which she then takes to a local photocopying establishment to have photocopied for use by her class. The photocopying establishment refuses to copy the materials for Professor Harrison until she provides copyright releases from each of the authors. Professor Harrison argues that no such permission is needed. Who is correct and why?

6. Tess is unhappy with the types of shoes currently available for the active recreational life she leads. Out of frustration, she designs a running shoe for women that better distributes women's weight and is more compatible with the way most women move. Tess decides to patent the design. When she shows the design to Katie, Katie says Tess will not be able to patent the idea because it is not novel in that it only takes advantage of the natural way that most women move. Does Katie's argument have any validity?

7. A national grocery chain has a policy of issuing certain products under its own label. The chain determines which are the top national brands of various items, then designs its packaging to look similar to the national brand—but upon close inspection, one can tell it's the store brand. Is there anything wrong with this practice?

8. A professor at a university purchases a popular computer program he thinks will be helpful for his students. He requests that

each student bring in a blank computer disk and proceeds to copy the computer program onto each one's disk. Then he has the students perform various assignments using the disks. When the software company discovers the professor's actions, it threatens to sue. The professor claims fair use. Who is correct? Why?

9. Derry invents a new device that he duly registers and receives a patent for. Despite the patent, Derry found it difficult to receive financial support for manufacturing and marketing his new product. Three weeks before the end of Derry's 17-year monopoly, Derry finally finds someone who is willing to finance the venture. He applies for an extension of the patent, claiming that his full 17-year, exclusive-use period has not been used because he could not find financing. Will the extension likely be granted? Explain.

GROUP EXERCISE

Your class has decided to go into the business of producing a study guide series consisting of the class notes for every business course offered at your school. You have decided on the name IBM Notebooks (IBM stands for I've Been Mesmerized). Your logo is a superimposed picture of George Washington taken from a dollar bill, and your guide will consist of your classmates' notes condensed into an outline edited by your class. You also intend to include old exams that your professors have placed on file in the library, as well as the relevant portions of the textbook outline used in each course. What will you need to do to protect your intellectual property and what problems do you foresee in securing your rights? Also, who do you expect will challenge the use of your designs?

Chapter 16

LIABILITY FOR PRODUCTS OR SERVICES

Chapter Preview Summary

In this chapter Ann and Bill learn some of the responsibilities they may have that stem specifically from their status as businesspersons. Those responsibilities are wide-ranging, from liability for goods sold, through warranties, to antitrust responsibilities to their competitors, to responsibility for the environment.

Chapter Objectives

In reading this chapter, you should learn:
- what warranties are
- how a seller of goods is responsible under warranty law
- a business owner's responsibilities regarding the environment
- the responsibilities businesspersons have to their competitors and the public

INTRODUCTION

When Bill and Ann endeavor to place their goods or services into the stream of commerce, society will demand that those goods or services do not cause harm; if they do, society will demand that Bill and Ann be held liable for it. This chapter focuses on three types of liability that can potentially affect Bill and Ann's business: liability for products, liability for business practices, and liability for the environment.

Bill and Ann cannot start up and operate a business in a vacuum. First, the goods produced by Bill and Ann must do what they say they will do, or Bill and Ann may be held liable for breach of warranty. If Bill and Ann provide a professional service, the service must meet minimum standards for professional services within their area of expertise.

Second, their goods or services must not compete unfairly with other like goods or services, or Bill and Ann will run afoul of antitrust laws.

And third, Bill and Ann must deal with the regulations that govern manufacture of their products and the environmental impact that that manufacturing process produces. Failure to comply with environmental regulations locally, nationally, or (as seen in earlier chapters) internationally can result in liability to Bill and Ann's business.

LIABILITY FOR GOODS SOLD: WARRANTIES

warranty
an absolute promise

If you have bought any type of consumer good, you have gotten the benefit of the **warranty** laws, whether you know it or not. Many of them will not apply to Bill and Ann as businesspeople because the warranty laws primarily protect consumers. Warranties have long been a part of the sale of goods, and they form an important part of the bargain for most consumers. However, it became more difficult for individual consumers to protect themselves from unscrupulous sellers and less-than-honest merchants who would verbally offer warranties on their products, but rescind them in the fine print of the sales contract. The federal government reacted to protect the consumer by enacting the Magnuson-Moss Warranty Act—federal legislation designed to supplement the protection offered by states under Article 2 of the Uniform Commercial Code (UCC).

Although as businesspeople Ann and Bill will not be operating as consumers who have the UCC warranties open to them, they will still have any contract or tort remedies that cover anything that goes wrong with the products they purchase. If they sell consumer products to anyone else, the law will protect the purchaser.

FEDERAL WARRANTY LAW—THE MAGNUSON-MOSS WARRANTY ACT

The Magnuson-Moss Warranty Act of 1975 was enacted to provide relief from the problems consumers were having regarding warranties. Warranties did not have a specific form they had to take, and as a result, they were so complex they became incomprehensible to the general consumer.

The stated congressional policies of the Magnuson-Moss Warranty Act are to improve the adequacy of information available to consumers, prevent deception, and improve competition in the market. The act was Congress's response to the unequal position between consumers and the large sellers and mass producers of consumer goods. Consumer goods are those normally used for personal, family, or household purposes. The primary purpose of the act was to provide consumers more protection in the area of warranties by placing emphasis on the requirement that a seller clearly disclose all warranties to a buyer before a sale.

Magnuson-Moss is limited to written (not oral) warranties on consumer products. It does not require a merchant to offer a warranty; however, if a warranty is offered, it regulates the warranty's labeling and contents. (See Box 16–1, "Written Warranties.")

While not requiring anyone to offer a warranty, if one is offered, it must provide certain remedies (replacement or refund), it must not disclaim the implied warranties guaranteed by law, and it cannot condition the warranty on the use of any particular product or service of the firm (the anti-tie-in provision).

The act requires that all written warranties must be labeled either full or limited, the terms and conditions of the warranty be disclosed in plain language, the text of the warranty be made available before the sale, and the language of the warranty not mislead the average, reasonable consumer.

written warranties
a warranty given in writing that must be designated as full or limited

---

16–1   CONCEPT SUMMARY

Written Warranties

A **written warranty** is defined as either "any written affirmation of fact or written promise made in connection with a sale of a consumer product by a supplier to a buyer which relates to the nature of the material or workmanship and affirms or promises that such material or workmanship is defect free or will meet a specified level of performance over a specified period of time" or "any undertaking in writing in connection with the sale by a supplier of a consumer product to refund, repair, replace, or take other remedial action with respect to such product in the event that such product fails to meet the specifications as set forth in the undertaking."

Magnuson-Moss requires every seller who supplies a warranty to state the terms of the warranty clearly, conspicuously, and in language that is simple and easily understood. It limits the type of warranty to either a full or limited warranty, with the requirements of each clearly stated.

full warranty
a warranty that meets minimum federal standards for durations, persons covered, remedies available, registration cards, and consequential damages

A **full warranty** must meet the minimum federal standards regulating the duration of the warranty, the persons covered by the warranty, the remedies available, the warranty registration cards, and the exclusion of consequential damages. If a warranty is listed as a **limited warranty**, then the merchant is free to limit the warranty with respect to the federal minimum standards, but must comply with the requirements of Magnuson-Moss regarding disclosure rules, limitations on disclaimers, and tie-in arrangements. (See Box 16–2, "Retailers Caught in Noncompliance with Magnuson-Moss.")

limited warranty
warranty that lessens the minimum standards required by federal law

Both the full and the limited types of warranties prevent a seller from disclaiming or modifying a warranty of implied merchantability. This type of warranty assures the buyer that the goods purchased are suitable for the use for which they were intended. For example, such an implied warranty would require a lawn mower to cut grass, a chair to be suitable to sit in, or a washing machine to wash clothes, when used in the manner in which those items were intended to be used. An implied warranty of merchantability would not, however, ensure that a lawn mower would cut Astroturf, or that a chair would

16–2   BLACK LETTER LAW

Retailers Caught in Noncompliance with Magnuson-Moss

Three major retailers were found to be in violation of the Magnuson-Moss Warranty Act and were ordered to bring their stores within compliance or face $10,000 per incident per day fines for future violations.

Sears, Roebuck & Co., Montgomery Ward & Co., and four subsidiaries of R. H. Macy's entered into a settlement with the FTC [Federal Trade Commission] in July 1994 which required them to instruct employees within 30 days on availability of warranty information which must be offered to the consumer prior to a sale of any product costing more than $15; to continue to train employees for four years; and to furnish the FTC with copies of written instructions for five years.

This was the fourth such FTC-targeted investigation into Magnuson-Moss violations since 1988. In that year, Wiz entered into a compliance agreement, and in 1992, Circuit City and Good Guys were cited for similar violations. The FTC targets large companies for investigation.

Source: *Consumer Electronics*, July 11, 1994.

prop open a door, or that a washing machine would wash small animals, because none of those uses are intended as uses for the products.

Magnuson-Moss provides the consumer with effective remedies when there is a breach of warranty. The Federal Trade Commission may treat breaches of warranty as unfair or deceptive practices, or it may order the warrantor to cease and desist making the warranty. In addition, Magnuson-Moss gives each consumer the right to a federal cause of action to sue for noncompliance with a warranty; in addition, the consumer may seek legal or equitable relief. That grant is hollow, however, because most individual consumer claims cannot meet the federal jurisdiction requirements for monetary damages of $50,000 or more. Therefore, most individual actions are required to be brought in state courts under UCC breach-of-warranty laws.

STATE WARRANTY PROTECTION—THE UNIFORM COMMERCIAL CODE

Consumers who purchase goods that do not live up to expectations have several options under state law that can be taken to remedy such disappointment if they cannot avail themselves of Magnuson-Moss. First, consumers may be able to sue under the common law tort for fraud or deceit. Second, a consumer can sue a seller for breach of contract if the agreement made regarding the goods is not met as promised. Third, most states have enacted legislation giving the consumer rights against a seller who uses unfair or deceptive trade actions as discussed in Chapter 14. Last, a consumer may sue a seller under the UCC for breach of warranty.

Article 2 of the UCC provides the framework for breaches of warranty on consumer goods. There are several types of warranties. Under a **warranty of title**—UCC section 2-312(1)(a)—the seller assures the buyer that seller will provide a clean title (quiet title) that will not expose the buyer to a lawsuit because the goods actually belonged to someone other than the seller. For example, if after a merchant sells goods to a buyer, it turns out that the goods had been stolen, then the party from whom the thief stole the goods can sue the buyer for return of the goods. If a third party sues a buyer, the buyer can bring the merchant into the lawsuit to defend the sale. This form of warranty can be disclaimed only under very specific circumstances in which the seller clearly notifies the buyer that seller does not possess title.

The other form of warranty under the UCC is **warranty of quality**. There are two types: express and implied warranties. Both types create standards that bind sellers, because they form a basis for the bargain.

warranty of title
a promise by the seller that the goods sold have a clean title, that is, that the title will not subject the seller to a lawsuit

Express Warranties

An **express warranty** may be oral or written, and it can be created either by any affirmation or description by the seller or by the use of a model or sample. No special words are required under the UCC. (See Box 16–3, "UCC Section 2-313, Express Warranties.")

Puffery does not constitute an express warranty. Puffery is defined by UCC section 2-313(2) as "an affirmation merely of the value of the goods or a statement purporting to be merely the seller's opinion or commendation of the goods." Thus, such expressions as "excellent condition," "A-1 shape," and "perfect running condition" have been held to be puffery, and not express warranties. However,

puffery
a statement of the seller's opinion about goods, but not a warranty

16–3   CONCEPT SUMMARY

UCC Section 2-313, Express Warranties

(1) Express warranties by the seller are created as follows:
    (a) Any affirmation of fact or promise made by the seller to the buyer which relates to the goods and becomes part of the basis of the bargain creates an express warranty that the goods shall conform to the affirmation or promise.
    (b) Any description of the goods which is made part of the basis of the bargain creates an express warranty that the goods shall conform to the description.
    (c) Any sample or model which is made part of the basis of the bargain creates an express warranty that the whole of the goods shall conform to the sample or model.

experts who give opinions are treated differently. Experts must be careful of what they say because experts are held to a higher standard and their opinion can amount to an actual representation rather than puffing.

Implied Warranties

An implied warranty is one implied by law, even though the seller has not expressed it. There are two types of implied warranties: a warranty of merchantability and a warranty of fitness for a particular purpose. Both of these warranties arise by law; that is, they are implied from the sale itself, if all the conditions for the warranty are met. They arise because the seller has sold the buyer a consumer good.

Warranty of Merchantability

This warranty arises in any sale and need not be explicitly agreed upon by the parties. (See Box 16–4, "UCC Section 2-314," Implied Warranty: Merchantability.") The three requirements that give rise to a **warranty of merchantability** are that

1. there is a sale (although some courts have included leases and bailments, and section 2A of the UCC, currently being reviewed by states and adopted by at least seven—would also cover leases);

warranty of merchantability
promise that goods are fit for ordinary purposes

16–4   CONCEPT SUMMARY

UCC Section 2-314 Implied Warranty: Merchantability

(1) Unless excluded . . . a warranty that the goods shall be merchantable is implied in a contract for their sale if the seller is a merchant with respect to goods of that kind.

(2) Goods to be merchantable must be at least such as

    (a) pass without objection in the trade under the contract description; and . . .

    (c) are fit for the ordinary purposes for which such goods are used; and

    (d) run, within the variations permitted by the agreement, of even kind, quality, and quantity within each unit and among all units involved; and

    (e) are adequately contained, packaged, and labeled as the agreement may require; and

    (f) conform to the promises or affirmations of fact made on the container or label if any.

---

2. the sale is for goods (some courts have included services as well); and

3. the seller is a merchant in goods of that kind.

    In order for the goods to be **merchantable**, they should meet the general definition provided by UCC section 2-314. Generally, goods are said to be merchantable if they pass without objection in the trade, are of fair or average quality, are fit for ordinary purposes, run with even kind within each and all units, are adequately contained or packaged, and conform to the affirmations of fact on the container or label, if any.

    Among the meanings for merchantability stated by the UCC, the most important implied meaning is that the goods be fit for the ordinary purpose for which such goods are used. This warranty essentially holds that merchants are strictly liable for any design defects in their products. To establish that the product is unmerchantable, the consumer must show that a defect, and not misuse by the consumer, caused the problem.

merchantable
goods that can pass without objection in the trade

Implied Warranty of Fitness for a Particular Purpose

For this warranty to arise, three conditions must be present. First, the seller must know the buyer's (or, under UCC 2A, lessee's) purpose for buying (or leasing) the goods. Second, the seller must know that the buyer is relying on the seller's skill and judgment in selecting or furnishing the goods. Third, the buyer must in fact rely on the judgment and skill of the seller. The seller need not be a merchant to be liable under this warranty.

Disclaimers of Warranty Under the UCC

There are different methods required by the UCC to disclaim warranties. A disclaimer of warranty for a particular purpose cannot be made orally. It must be written and conspicuous. A seller may, however, disclaim an implied warranty of merchantability either orally or in writing, but must use the term *merchantability*, and if the warranty is written, the writing must be conspicuous.

The creation of an express warranty can be disclaimed only to the extent that the disclaimer is consistent with the warranty. In other words, if a warranty is expressly given and in writing, then another writing limiting the warranty will not be enforceable, because it is inconsistent with the warranty. The problem arises when an oral, express warranty is negated by a written statement that specifically disclaims all warranties. The buyer in that situation will have to rely on the good faith of the seller to correct whatever problem might arise with the goods.

LIABILITY FOR POSSESSION OF GOODS: BAILMENTS

A bailment is defined as the rightful possession of goods by a person who is not the owner of the goods. The person with the lawful possession of the goods is the bailee. The person who actually owns the property is the bailor. The liability of each is determined by whose benefit the bailment was created for.

TYPES OF BAILMENTS

Bailments arise in numerous contexts and can occur between friends and neighbors as well as customers and businesses. For example, if you borrow a book from your friend, you have entered into a *bailment for the benefit of the bailee*; that is, the book was borrowed so that you could read it, and your friend gains no benefit from it.

A different type of bailment arises when you accept a package from the delivery person for your neighbor who is not home. Here, a *bailment for the benefit of the bailor* is created, because it is only your neighbor, the owner of the property, who will benefit from this bailment.

The third, and most common, business-related bailment is a *mutual benefit bailment.* It occurs when, for example, you take your car into a service station to be repaired. The benefit to you is that your car will be fixed, and the benefit to the repairperson is that you will pay for repairing it. That creates a mutual benefit.

The significance of the different types of bailments is that the liability of the one to whom the property belongs is different for each. In the first example—a bailment for the sole benefit of the bailee—the bailee will be held to the highest standard of care if the property is lost, damaged, or destroyed. It's just like your mother always told you: If you borrow something, take care of it. The law imposes on the bailee in this situation the highest standard of caring for the goods.

In the bailment for the benefit of the bailor, the bailee is held to only a low standard of care and will be liable only if the item was lost, damaged, or destroyed because of gross negligence. In the mutual benefit bailment Bill and Ann are likely to engage in, the bailee must exercise ordinary care and will be held liable only if the property is lost, damaged, or destroyed through ordinary negligence.

In all of the aforedescribed bailments, strict liability will apply if the bailee misdelivers goods by turning them over to the wrong person, that is, someone who has no legal right to the goods. For example, if the book is returned to the wrong person, the package was released to wrong neighbor, and the car was released to a stranger—and none of the parties will release the property to the rightful owner—then the bailee will be strictly liable for the loss suffered by the bailor, to whom the property actually belonged.

DISCLAIMERS

Bailees who are in the business of creating bailments, such as parking lots, dry cleaning establishments, and car repair shops, try to limit their liability for damaged or destroyed property. Parking lots, for example, often have disclaimers written on the receipt, dry cleaners generally have their disclaimers posted on the walls of their business, and repair shops try to limit their liability for damage that occurs as a result of vandalism. Most of these disclaimers, called exculpatory clauses, are disfavored by the courts unless they are known to the customer prior to the creation of the bailment. Some disclaimers, though, are standard, such as disclaimers by photo developers that limit liability for lost film to only the cost of replacement film, rather than the emotional cost to the bailor. A doctor who took to a photo dealer all of the photographs and 8mm film of his whole life to have them put on video was able to recover only the cost of the film when the company lost what he had submitted.

LIABILITY FOR SERVICES: PROFESSIONAL RESPONSIBILITY

When Bill and Ann first merge their two separate businesses into one, they should hire an accountant to handle their business finances. They will be in the market for an auditor who can verify the records and transactions of the firm. They are thinking of soliciting new investors to expand their capital, and they want to be able to show the potential investors just how successful they have been in operating their business. If they develop a business plan as discussed in chapter 9, they will likely rely on the accountant's professional judgment and product for inclusion in the plan.

What happens if, during the course of the audit, it is discovered that the accountant has performed negligently or has intentionally misguided the money or the assets of the firm? Or what if the auditor fails to discover the accountant's misdeeds, causing Bill and Ann to mislead their potential investors about their finances? What recourse do Bill and Ann have against either the accountant or the auditor? This section deals with the liability of professionals who render services that fall below the standard expected of a professional.

COMMON LAW

Although the foregoing scenario involves accountants, the common law provides a remedy in contracts or torts for the rendering of professional services below levels expected by the standards created by the industry in question. The doctrine of the reasonable person that we spoke of in negligence takes into account the knowledge, training, and skills possessed by defendants in negligence cases. In cases involving professionals, rather than being held to the standard of the average person, defendants are held to possess at least the minimum skills and knowledge required to be a member of their profession. This negligence standard applies to those who offer any professional service, including doctors, lawyers, architects, and contractors. In a breach-of-contract action, the suing party would have to show that the delivery of the services of the professional was not in keeping with the contract set forth between the parties.

ACCOUNTANT'S LIABILITY

Probably because of the reliance that business investors place on financial statements concerning business enterprises, accountant's liability has been particularly sharpened by the courts, as investors who suffered losses because of faulty accounting practices sued for professional malpractice. Almost as much as in medical malpractice claims, accountants have found themselves defending their accounting practices to the critical eye of the court. As a result, special emphasis is placed on accounting practices in business.

If the malpractice involves securities, then accountants who violate standards of care may be criminally liable for their actions under the Securities and Exchange Act of 1933 and 1934. You may recall that the act prohibits knowingly making false statements or conspiring with others to make false statements in connection with the sale of securities.

Accountants may also be held liable in civil actions for either breach of contract or negligence. Most civil actions concern negligence, alleging a violation of professional accounting practices. Accountants may be held liable for such things as revealing confidential information, overlooking evidence of fraud, giving incorrect tax advice, or incompetent financial management. Their liability extends to their client as well as any third parties who they reasonably foresee will rely on their work.

In addition to all this, each profession has standards of professional responsibility that members must adhere to. Failure to do so can subject professionals to a full range of actions by the appropriate professional licensing body, up to and including loss of their professional license. Ann and Bill may have standards that apply to their business, which they must adhere to or else they run the risk of losing their professional affiliation.

LIABILITY FOR BUSINESS PRACTICES: ANTITRUST

The heart of the American system of economics is its capitalist approach to business. The basic guiding principle is that the market of goods and services should remain free and open to all who care to enter. Under the theory, those who deliver shoddy goods or services will fall by the wayside, and the market will thus regulate itself. Those circumstances, in turn, inure to the benefit of consumers, because as long as consumers have a choice and can use personal preference, quality, price, and service to determine their buying decisions, those who must compete for their business will have no choice but to keep up with their competitors or to be one of the ones who fall by the wayside. To that end, our system highly regulates the production and marketing of goods so that those markets stay open and free to whoever wishes to compete. The area of keeping the market open by regulating business activities and practices is called antitrust.

American producers often complain that the American system places them at a competitive disadvantage in the global marketplace. Most of the U.S. laws and regulations were imposed during the period between 1890 and 1950 in an attempt to ensure free competition and to safeguard American workers and consumers. Here we will look at laws that regulate competition between U.S. businesses.

Earlier in this text you were introduced to white-collar crimes and some of the statutory law making certain business practices illegal. Many of those white-collar crimes involve marketing practices. Marketing involves many factors such as the pricing, packaging, promotion, and placement (distribution) of goods and services. Each of these factors is regulated by common law, statutory law, or administrative rules and regulations. The thrust of the laws is to make sure that businesses like Ann and Bill's do not act in ways that will suppress competition, inhibit free trade, and ultimately harm the consumer.

This could include, for instance, Ann and Bill's gobbling up all of their competition so that consumers no longer have a choice, which, of course, means Ann and Bill would be able to charge whatever they want or engage in any kind of shoddy services they cared to. It could also be Ann and Bill's getting together with their competitors so as to reach agreement on what prices they will charge, with no one of them going below, so that they are no longer really competing with each other, and the benefits the consumer receives from competition are thereby lessened. And other practices are covered too. Knowledge of the antitrust laws ensures on one hand that Bill and Ann stay within the law as they market their product and that on the other, the consumer benefits by their doing so.

SHERMAN ANTITRUST ACT

Antitrust law began to develop in 1890 with the passage of the Sherman Antitrust Act. The act was passed after a growth period in our economy led to cutthroat competition and the formation of holding companies, trusts, and monopolies that restrained free competition (see Box 16–5, "Sherman Antitrust Act"). Section 1 of the act prohibits "any contract, combination, or conspiracy in restraint of trade." This language clearly requires at least two participants. Section 2 of the act makes monopolizing or the attempt to monopolize illegal. This section can be applied to a lone participant.

In a landmark case involving the Standard Oil Company, section 1 of the Sherman Act was interpreted by the U.S. Supreme Court to encompass only **unreasonable restraints of trade**. That is, restraints of trade are not in and of themselves illegal, but will be deemed so only if they meet certain requirements. This **rule of reason**, as it is known, requires a two-step analysis. First, there must be proof of a contract, combination, or conspiracy, and second, the combination must be found to be unreasonable under the circumstances, and therefore illegal. Many critics of the rule of reason say that the application of that standard gutted section 1 of the Sherman Act. History does show that there have been relatively few prosecutions under the act, but there could be other reasons for this.

Per Se Violations of the Sherman Antitrust Act

There are a few activities that, if proven, are held by courts to be inherently unreasonable. They are known as per se violations. Per se means in and of itself. Thus, if an act is a per se violation, it is inherently unreasonable, and proof of the prohibited activity is proof of the guilt. Per se violations of section 1 of the Sherman Antitrust Act fall into two categories: **horizontal per se violations** and **vertical per se violations**. Horizontal violations are those that occur between two

unreasonable restraint of trade restraint of trade which violates law

rule of reason rule requiring only unreasonable restraints of trade to be violations of the Sherman Act

per se violation violation of antitrust laws that whether reasonable or not, is illegal

horizontal per se violation antitrust violation among and between competitors

vertical per se violation antitrust violation among and between those in the vertical chain of commerce, that is, seller to buyer

16–5   CONCEPT SUMMARY

Sherman Antitrust Act

Section 1. Trusts, etc., in restraint of trade illegal; penalty.

Every contract, combination in the form of trust or otherwise, or conspiracy, in restraint of trade or commerce among the several States, or with foreign nations, is declared to be illegal. Every person who shall make a contract or engage in any combination or conspiracy declared by sections 1 through 7 of this title to be illegal shall be deemed guilty of a felony, and, on conviction thereof, shall be punished by fine not exceeding one million dollars if a corporation, or, if any other person, one hundred thousand dollars, or by imprisonment not exceeding three years, or by both said punishments, in the discretion of the courts.

Section 2. Monopolizing trade a felony; penalty.

Every person who shall monopolize, or attempt to monopolize, or combine or conspire with any other person or persons, to monopolize any part of the trade or commerce among the several States, or with foreign nations, shall be deemed guilty of a felony, and, on conviction thereof, shall be punished by fine not exceeding one million dollars if a corporation, or, if any other person, one hundred thousand dollars, or by imprisonment not exceeding three years, or by both said punishments, in the discretion of the court.

price fixing
an agreement by marketers of a product to set agreed-to prices for the product

division of territory
agreement between competitors to deal only with certain areas

group boycott
agreement among two or more competitors not to deal with another business or individual

competitors, such as two manufacturers of the same goods or two cleaning companies. Vertical violations are those that occur between buyers and sellers of products.

The most prevalent horizontal per se violation is **price fixing**. Price fixing is an agreement between two or more competitors to set prices. It is illegal for competitors to set prices. It does not matter whether the price as set is high, low, fair, or reasonable to the consumer. The practice is simply illegal. Other types of horizontal per se violations are **division of territory** and **group boycott**. A division-of-territory agreement is an agreement between two competitors to carve up or reserve territory that exclusively they service. A group boycott is an agreement between two or more competitors not to deal with an individual or company. (See Box 16–6, "An Alternative Law School Sues ABA" on page 517.)

resale price maintenance
manufacturer's requirement that buyer resell good at a certain price

exclusive dealing arrangement
supplier agrees to supply buyer with product only if buyer not stock products of supplier's competitor

monopoly
power to control prices and exclude competition

oligopoly
a form of competition in which the products are similar and are distinguished through advertising

Courts have found that agreements whereby a manufacturer tries to dictate to a buyer the price at which an item must be resold (**resale price maintenance**) are examples of a vertical per se violations. Other notable vertical violations are tying arrangements and exclusive dealing contracts. A tying arrangement is one in which a seller tries to tie the sale or lease of one product to the sale or lease of some other product. An **exclusive dealing arrangement** is one in which a supplier agrees to supply a buyer with a product only if the buyer agrees not to stock the product of the supplier's competitors.

All of the aforedescribed per se violations have the anticompetitive effect of prohibiting suppliers from finding buyers for their goods and of prohibiting consumers from having a variety of suppliers to choose from. It is primarily for that reason that such violations are viewed as unreasonable in all circumstances.

Monopolies

Section 2 of the Sherman Antitrust Act makes the monopolization of trade a felony. Not all monopolies are illegal, but monopolization or **monopoly** power can be. Monopoly power is the power to control prices or exclude competition. Merely being successful, beating the competition, and causing the competition to withdraw from the market is not illegal, but possessing a large degree of market power coupled with the ability to reduce competition may lead to monopolization.

THE CLAYTON ACT

Congress passed the Clayton Act in 1914 to plug holes left by the Sherman Act. One of the major changes was a new burden or standard of proof. The Clayton Act's standard is activity that "might substantially lessen competition in a product or geographic market" (see Box 16–7, "Excerpt from The Clayton Act" on page 518). This is a much lower standard of proof than that applied in the Sherman Act, which is more like "beyond a reasonable doubt." There is considerable overlap in coverage under the two acts, and many activities could violate both. In addition, the laws are enforced by different agencies. The Sherman Act comes under the jurisdiction of the Justice Department, whereas the Federal Trade Commission usually enforces the Clayton Act.

The Clayton Act regulates three major areas of competition. **Price discrimination** is regulated in section 2, but was modified by the

16–6   BLACK LETTER LAW

An Alternative Law School Sues ABA

The Massachusetts School of Law at Andover has sued the ABA [American Bar Association] and more than two dozen related parties, alleging antitrust violations stemming from the association's refusal to accredit the 5-year-old alternative private school.

"A small number of law school deans, professors, and law librarians are operating a cartel that has taken charge of the ABA's accreditation process and has abused the ABA's monopoly power," charged MSL Dean Lawrence Velvel. "The purpose of their conspiracy is to promote the economic goals of the professorate, of which they are members."

Filed in federal district court in the Eastern District of Pennsylvania on November 23, 1993, the lawsuit alleges a two-count violation of the Sherman Act, which generally prohibits competitors from collaborating to regulate the costs of goods and services. Velvel estimates damages at $7.5 million.

The first count charges that the ABA's consultant on legal education, James P. White—who has managed the ABA's day-to-day accreditation practices for nearly 20 years—and the other defendants conspired to establish a "group boycott." The second count alleges attempted and actual illegal monopolization of the legal education process, including lawyer licensing.

The lawsuit focuses its attack on the criteria used by the ABA's Section on Legal Education and Admissions to the Bar to review a law school's suitability for accreditation.

Those standards include LSAT [Law School Admission Test] or equivalent standardized test scores for every student, a student/full-time ratio of less than 25:1, limits on faculty workloads and the use of adjunct professors, minimum library requirements, and limitations on how many hours students may work out of school.

Velvel said the ABA's standards lead to "tuition escalation" that places law school out of reach for minorities and other disadvantaged groups. Full-time tuition at MSL is $9,000 a year compared with $15,000–$18,000 at many law schools; MSL does not accept any government aid.

James T. Halverson, a member of the ABA Board of Governors, would not discuss the details of the suit. But, he added, "we emphatically deny the allegations and contend the school has been treated fairly and no differently than any other school that asks for accreditation."

Source: *ABA Journal*, February 94, p. 25, by Richard Reuben.

price discrimination
charging different prices to different buyers of the same product in the same time period

tying arrangement
arrangement whereby the ability to obtain one good is dependent upon taking another, usually less desirable good

merger
two businesses' coming together to form a larger version of one of the businesses

Robinson-Patman Act and therefore will be discussed in the next section. Section 3 of the Clayton Act also governs **tying arrangements**, exclusive dealing contracts (see previous discussion under the Sherman Act), and corporate **mergers** under section 7. A merger under section 7 is the joining together of two companies that were previously separate.

During the 50s, 60s, and 70s the antitrust laws were vigorously enforced. Under section 7 of the Clayton Act, mergers were closely scrutinized and few were allowed, as the courts judged that most of the proposed mergers might substantially lessen competition. During the 80s, antitrust enforcement was almost nonexistent and the United States was swept by mergers and acquisitions, many of which were probably anticompetitive. The antitrust precedents from the period of 50s through the 70s are still law (have not been overruled), and we will have to wait and see if antitrust enforcement will return to former levels. Many believe that our antiquated laws hinder U.S. competition in global markets, because most other countries not only allow, but encourage, joint cooperation between companies as well as the government.

THE ROBINSON-PATMAN ACT

 In 1930, Congress passed the Robinson-Patman Act, which is an amendment to section 2 of the Clayton Act. Section 2 of this act prohibits price discrimination (see Box 16–8, "Robinson-Patman Act"). **Price discrimination** is the charging of different prices to different buyers of the same product during essentially the same time period.

The act allows two defenses to price discrimination: the **cost justification defense** and the **meeting competition defense**. Under the cost justification defense, section 2 states that there shall be no liability when the discount to a buyer reflects the lower cost to the seller of selling to the favored customer. Under the meeting competition defense, section 2 states that there shall be no liability when the seller granted the discount in order to meet a competing seller's price. In addition to the statutory defenses, the FTC recognizes the **practical availability defense**. The FTC will find an absence of competitive injury when discounts are generally and practically available to competitors of the favored customer.

For purposes of the Robinson-Patman Act, the price of a product includes all promotional materials, discounts, or gifts given in connection with the sale of that product. All buyers must be treated the same and thus must be given a proportionate amount of such freebies. Although a company may meet its competitor's price in a specific

cost justification defense
a defense to a violation of the Robinson-Patman Act that allows a seller to give discounts to a buyer if the discount represents a lower cost to the seller

meeting competition defense
a defense to a violation of the Robinson-Patman Act that allows the seller to offer a discount to the buyer if it is done to meet the prices of the competition

practical availability defense
a defense to a violation of the Robinson-Patman Act that excuses a violation if the discount offered the buyer is practically available to competitors of the seller

---

16–8   CONCEPT SUMMARY

Robinson-Patman Act

Section 2. Discrimination in price, services, or facilities.

(a) Price; selection of customers. It shall be unlawful for any person engaged in commerce, in the course of such commerce, either directly or indirectly, to discriminate in price between different purchases of commodities of like grade and quality, where either or any of the purchasers involved in such discrimination are in commerce, where such commodities are sold for use, consumption or resale within the United States or any Territory thereof or the District of Columbia or any insular possession or other place under the jurisdiction of the United States, and where the effect of such discrimination may be substantially to lessen competition or tend to create a monopoly in any line of commerce, or to injure, destroy, or prevent competition with any person who either grants or knowingly receives the benefit of such discrimination, or with customers of either of them. 15 U.S.C. 13(a)

FEDERAL TRADE COMMISSION V. BORDEN CO.
383 U.S. 637 (1966)

The Borden Company produces and sells evaporated milk under the Borden name, a nationally advertised product. At the same time, Borden packs and markets evaporated milk under various private brands owned by its customers. This milk is physically and chemically identical with the milk it distributes under its own brand but is sold at both the wholesale and retail levels at prices regularly below those obtained for the Borden brand milk. The FTC found the milk sold under the Borden and private labels to be of like grade and quality as required for the applicability of section 2 of the Robinson-Patman Act, held the price differential to be discriminatory within the meaning of the section, ascertained the requisite adverse effect on commerce, rejected Borden's claim of cost justification, and consequently issued a cease-and-desist order. Borden appealed this decision, and the Court of Appeals reversed the FTC's findings on the sole ground that as a matter of law, the customer-label milk was not of the same grade and quality as the milk sold under the Borden brand. The Supreme Court reversed the Court of Appeals.

White, J.: The position of Borden and the Court of Appeals is that the determination of the grade and quality, which is a threshold finding essential to the applicability of section 2(a), may not be based solely on the physical properties of the products without regard to the brand names they bear and the relative commercial public acceptance these brands enjoy, stating "consideration should be given to all commercially significant distinctions which affect market value, whether they be physical or promotional." Here, because the milk bearing the Borden brand regularly sold at a higher price than did the milk with the buyer's label, the court considered the products to be "commercially" different and hence of different grade for the purposes of section 2(a), even though they were physically identical and of equal quality. Although a mere difference in brand would not in and of itself demonstrate a difference in grade, decided consumer preference for one brand over another, reflected in the willingness to pay a higher price for the well-known brand, was, in the view of the Court of

Appeals, sufficient to differentiate chemically identical products and to place the price differential beyond the reach of section 2(a).

We reject this construction of section 2(a), as did both the examiner and the FTC in this case. The commission's view is that labels do not differentiate products for the purpose of determining grade or quality, even though the one label may have more customer appeal and command a higher price in the marketplace from a substantial segment of the public. That this is the commission's long-standing interpretation of the present act, may be gathered from the commission's decisions dating back to 1936. These views of the agency are entitled to respect, and represent a more reasonable construction of the statute than offered by the Court of Appeals. REVERSED

Case Questions

1. Borden will either charge the same for both (presumably at the higher price) or add or subtract ingredients to differentiate the products. Is this anticompetitive?

2. What adverse effect on commerce could the FTC have cited in this case? If customers were willing to pay more for the Borden name, but not for the exact same product, isn't that a function of the market?

market in order to remain competitive, as soon as the threat is gone, the seller must raise the price again so that all of the seller's buyers are receiving the same price in all areas of the country.

Price discrimination (charging different prices to different buyers) and **predatory pricing** (selling below cost for the purpose of eliminating competition) have similar effects. In 1994, a small drugstore sued a Wal-Mart pharmacy, alleging that Wal-Mart was using predatory pricing to run it out of business. Wal-Mart alleged that it was not selling below cost but was making money through volume business. There have been numerous suits by small businesses alleging that the corporate giants such as Wal-Mart can obtain huge volume discounts from manufacturers and are therefore able to sell products at retail prices that are lower than even the wholesale prices that manufacturers charge small businesses. This is one of the reasons

predatory pricing
the selling of products below costs, which creates the dangerous probability of creating a successful monopoly

that nowadays we see so few independent pharmacies, department stores, drugstores, supermarkets, and moviehouses.

There are two sides to this argument. On one hand, consumers will benefit in the short run by paying low prices from the big discounters such as Wal-Mart. On the other hand, if giants such as Wal-Mart can put small operations out of business, Wal-Mart may then raise its prices, thus hurting consumers in the long run. However, if we assume that Wal-Mart faces competition from other giants, then the market remains competitive and consumers are well served in both the short and long runs. The inefficient small businesses will leave the market, and thus our scarce resources will be better allocated—so the theory goes.

Antitrust law is important because of the free enterprise system in the United States. The system works because it assumes both that the market will allow all competitors to have an equal shot at securing their share of the market and that market forces will determine who has the best product and whose business ultimately succeeds. The antitrust laws attempt to ensure that smaller enterprises have an opportunity to present their goods on the market and not be forced out by the presence of larger, more established businesses. In the long run, that ensuring of opportunity serves both the free market system and consumers best.

LIABILITY FOR THE ENVIRONMENT: ENVIRONMENTAL PROTECTION

Environmental concerns are not just for "fringies" anymore. During the past 20- to 25-year span, we have seen interest in the environment move from something that only protesters of the 60s and 70s dealt with, to established legislation and a collective consciousness that makes neglect of the environment a crass and unpopular choice. In the years since the advent of the environmental movement, we have learned we cannot ignore the way we treat the planet we live on. We cannot forget the styrofoam hamburger container once we put it in the trash can. We cannot complain about our catalytic converter just because we may not be able to see at the moment the harm not having one does. We now take recycling for granted and think it shamefully indulgent not to do so. We have learned, often through painful lessons, that out of sight is not out of the environment. We now realize that how we handle our wastes, treat our waters, and deal with the air has a direct impact on our quality of life. It is no longer embarrassing to say this in public.

The emergence of environmental law as a major consideration in business originated in the 1970s, along with the horror stories of Love Canal and other places. Recall from Chapter 4 that Love Canal was the environmental disaster in the 1970s that resulted when Occidental Petroleum Corp. used the canal as a sewer for its toxic waste 20 or so years before. It was a wake-up call for us as inhabitors of the planet, who then realized we had to treat it more respectfully.

U.S. government estimates of the number of hazardous waste dump sites ranged from 20,000 to 40,000. Public outcry began to demand that the government clean up those sites and remove the threats to human health and the environment that the dump sites caused. It was against this backdrop that the Environmental Protection Agency (EPA) was created. The law transferred to the federal government the power to control air and water pollution, radiation, and pesticides, each of which previously had been regulated by a variety of agencies in a piecemeal fashion.

Congress also began to enact many of its environmental protection laws, all now administered by the EPA. The powers of the agency are set out in the individual environmental statutes. Under most legislation, EPA has the power to issue regulations and enforce them, both in civil courts and with criminal penalties, which can include incarceration for violators. Of course, since Ann and Bill operate in the areas of waste management and toxic waste management as part of their business, they ought to be particularly sensitive to this subject.

COMPREHENSIVE ENVIRONMENTAL RESPONSE, COMPENSATION, AND LIABILITY ACT OF 1980 (CERCLA)

CERCLA, also known as **Superfund**, is a program designed to clean up facilities (or sites) at which hazardous *substances* are located and either are released or present a threat of release into the environment. CERCLA is intended primarily to target abandoned sites but may be used to clean up facilities that are in current operation. (See Box 16–9, "Your Right to Know.")

At the heart of CERCLA is the accountability of present property owners for hazardous substances that may have been placed on their property by previous owners. Even though at the time the materials were placed on the property it may have been in compliance with accepted professional standards for management of waste materials,

Superfund
another name for CERCLA, a program designed to clean up facilities where hazardous substances are located

16–9   CONCEPT SUMMARY

Your Right to Know

As its name suggests, the new federal Right-to-Know Act is a law about knowledge—knowledge about toxic chemicals stored, used, produced, and released in a community's midst. The law will:

- Help communities reduce the threat of toxic accidents as well as chronic pollution.
- Force companies to keep less hazardous chemicals and reduce emissions.
- Inspire governments at all levels to strengthen and enforce controls on chemical dangers.
- Give victims of toxic hazards crucial information with which to hold polluters accountable.

It's been called "independence from environmental ignorance." Those words from one of Congress's leading environmentalists, Rep. Jim Florio (D-N.J.), describe the Emergency Planning and Community Right-to-Know Act (EPCRA), which was passed by Congress in October 1986 as Title III of SARA (the Superfund Amendments and Reauthorization Act).

The Right-to-Know Act is intended to create a healthier and safer environment for all those who must spend part of their day in the vicinity of the factories, warehouses, refineries, water treatment plants, transportation routes, and other sites that store, use, and manufacture hazardous chemicals.

On July 1, 1988, hundreds of thousands of manufacturing industries nationwide had to disclose, for the first time, the names and amounts of toxic materials they released into the environment in 1987.

By October 17, 1988, local districts (usually a city or county) are required to have an emergency response plan ready in case of a chemical accident.

The Right-to-Know Act is a child of Bhopal. After the December 1984 leak of methyl isocyanate at Union Carbide's India plant killed upwards of 2,500 sleeping townspeople, U.S. citizens and politicians became aware of the potential for similar catastrophic accidents in this country. Some members of Congress drafted legislation modeled on the state and local right-to-know laws that labor and environmentalists had been advocating (and winning) for years and managed to attach it to Superfund. Right- to-Know seeks to reduce both catastrophic chemical accidents and chronic pollution through information and planning.

Source: *Environmental Action*, September/October 1988, pp. 21–28.

UNITED STATES V. SERAFINA

706 F.Supp. 346 (M.D. Pa. 1988)

The government moved for partial summary judgment in an action against the Empire Corporation, seeking recovery of response costs which resulted from a cleanup of a hazardous waste site owned by Empire. Empire had purchased the property from the Parmoff Corporation, which, from 1967 to 1969, had leased the property to the city of Scranton, which had operated the property as a garbage and refuse dump. During the time that the property was leased by Scranton, 1,141 fifty-five-gallon drums were scattered on the site. Many were open, crushed, and in various stages of decay. The inspection done by the EPA revealed that the drums, water, and soil samples taken from the site contained hazardous substances as defined by CERCLA. Empire asserted the third-party defense, alleging that the damages were not the result of either direct or indirect contractual relations with Parmoff, that is, that Empire was an innocent landowner who had no knowledge of the existence of hazardous waste on the property at the time of purchase. The government counters that the failure of Empire to visibly inspect the land precluded Empire from using the innocent landowner defense.

Caldwell, J.: Congress enacted CERCLA in response to the environmental and public health hazards posed by improper disposal of hazardous wastes. The statute established the Superfund, which is financed primarily through excise taxes on the chemical and oil industries. The government is authorized to use the Superfund to finance government responses to hazardous waste problems and to recover those expenditures from those responsible.

Empire admits that it purchased the property from Parmoff, and that the government has made a prima facie case under section 107(a) of CERCLA. Empire's argument is aimed at establishing one of the three defenses available to it under section 107(b), specifically section 107(b)(3), which states that there shall be no liability for a person otherwise liable if that person can establish that the damage resulting from a release of hazardous substances was caused by an act or omission of a third party whose act or omission did not occur in connection with a contractual relationship, existing directly or indirectly with the defendant.

continued on next page

It is not disputed that Empire acquired the land after the disposal of the hazardous substance had occurred. The government contends that at the time [Empire] purchased the land, Empire had reason to know that hazardous substances had been deposited, and thus there exists a contractual relationship between the third party and Empire, [thereby] negating the use of the innocent landowner defense. The government's position is that Empire failed to make "all appropriate inquiry into the previous ownership and uses of the property consistent with good commercial or customary practice" as required by section 101(35)(b). The government contends that a visit to the site would have revealed hundreds of drums on the premises. Empire admits that it did not inspect the land, but that it inspected only maps to ascertain the location of the land. The government posits that SARA's innocent landowner defense does not protect the owner who fails to inspect the land.

Although the government's argument is tempting, the court cannot reach that conclusion on the evidence presented before it. The government has presented no evidence from which the court can conclude that the defendant's failure to inspect was inconsistent with good commercial or customary practices. Thus there exists an unresolved question of fact as to the propriety of the defendant's conduct at the time of the purchase.

For the foregoing reason, the motion for partial summary judgment is DENIED.

Case Questions

1. Is it fair that landowners who have no knowledge of hazardous substances on property they purchase should be held liable for cleanup simply because the previous landowners are no longer around?

2. Empire had already agreed to complete the cleanup started by the EPA on this property, and the federal court had held the city of Scranton liable for response costs. What, then, would be the motivation for seeking response costs from Empire?

3. Why would the judge require the government to prove that it was customary in the industry to visually inspect property purchased under these circumstances? Would a private purchaser (i.e., not a business) be able to escape liability under that standard?

Note: In 1991, the First Circuit Court of Appeals in *U.S. v. Reardon*, struck down the EPA's power to place a lien on private property in order to secure estimated cleanup costs under provisions of CERCLA. Under facts very similar to those presented in *Serafina*, the EPA found hazardous waste on property owned by the Reardons, and the agency placed a lien on the property because of an estimated cleanup cost of $16 million. The Reardons challenged the lien based on due process grounds, arguing that they had not had an opportunity to challenge the imposition of the lien, because the CERCLA provisions did not allow for pre-enforcement actions of this kind. The Court held that because the title and use of the land were significantly encumbered by the lien, the Reardons were entitled to a hearing before the lien was imposed under due process law.

CERCLA may require that an owner, operator, or other responsible party be liable for the acts of others who are insolvent or long forgotten. Remember that in Chapter 9 we said that Ann and Bill should have an environmental audit conducted on any property they plan to buy. This is why. Even though they were not the perpetrators, they can be held liable under the act. CERCLA now includes SARA (Superfund Amendments and Reauthorization Act), which expanded CERCLA and boosted the Superfund to $8.5 billion.

CERCLA imposes strict liability on those potential responsible parties, meaning that a party may be responsible without regard to intent, negligence, or other fault. The only defenses to CERCLA liability are that (1) a hazardous release was caused by an act of God, (2) a hazardous release was caused by an act of war, or (3) the property was obtained by inheritance, bequest, eminent domain, or escheat or was purchased by an innocent landowner. An innocent landowner is one who purchases the property, makes an appropriate inquiry, has no specialized knowledge or experience in the area of hazardous wastes, has no ability to know of the presence of contaminants through inspection, and has not overlooked an obvious presence of contaminants. With the specialized business Ann and Bill will be in, there would be little way they could avoid liability for violations under this law, even if they were not the perpetrators, because the law essentially imposes a duty on purchasers to inquire. This would be especially so with Ann and Bill, for the handling of hazardous materials is the very nature of their business.

RESOURCE CONSERVATION AND RECOVERY ACT (RCRA)

Whereas CERCLA covers hazardous *substances,* RCRA (pronounced "rick-ruh") covers hazardous *wastes.* RCRA provides a comprehensive regulatory scheme for management of hazardous wastes that are currently being generated, stored, transported, or disposed of. Through management of hazardous waste in an environmentally sound manner, RCRA intends to prevent the development of future Superfund sites.

Specifically, RCRA regulates facilities that store, generate, transport, treat, dispose of, or otherwise manage hazardous wastes, and it also regulates underground storage tanks—a major source of contamination. This, of course, is of great importance to Bill and Ann, because they will be in the business of, among other things, hazardous waste disposal.

The EPA has generated voluminous regulations involving many technical and legal complexities for the obtaining of permits to handle hazardous waste. The procedure is costly to those considering the development or acquisition of such property. In addition to the permits that are issued for use of any waste site, businesses that generate hazardous wastes must keep detailed records of such waste. Waste facilities are located in only about one-third of the states. Dumping of waste on those sites by out-of-state facilities has been the subject of several lawsuits challenging the restrictions against such practices.

The original RCRA regulations contained loopholes that allowed many dangerous wastes to go unregulated. To address that, Congress enacted the Hazardous and Solid Waste Amendments in 1984. The amendments greatly expanded the scope of RCRA, which now regulates thousands of facilities, including small businesses such as dry cleaners, service stations, and auto repair shops—all of which may find themselves discarding chemical products. (See Box 16–10, "Pollution Prevention Power to the People," on page 520 and see Box 16–11, "Asbestos and PCBs on page 531.")

CLEAN WATER ACT

Prior to 1972, regulation of water pollution was handled by the individual states, with little involvement by the federal government. This, however, changed quickly after the death of several lakes and after Ohio's Cuyahoga River caught fire (see Box 16–12, "Cuyahoga River on Fire" on page 533).

The deterioration of the nation's waters prompted Congress to enact the Clean Water Act (CWA) to "restore and maintain the chemical, physical, and biological integrity of the Nation's waters." To achieve that result, the CWA prohibits the discharge of any pollutants into the nation's waters without a permit. The discharge permit limits the maximum rate and concentration of pollutants—called **effluent limitations**—from a point source. A **point source** is any discrete point of discharge, such as a pipe, ditch, container, or vessel, that empties directly into receiving waters. The CWA gives the EPA the power to impose criminal sanctions against those who discharge pollutants into protected waters without a permit. (See Box 16–13, "Bankrupted by EPA" on page 534.)

effluent limitations
the maximum rate and concentration of pollutants allowed by a Clean Water Act discharge permit

point source
any discrete point of discharge that empties directly into receiving waters

THE CLEAN AIR ACT

The Clean Air Act (CAA) of 1970 originated as a codification of existing state and federal efforts to control air pollution. Federal prominence in the effort expanded when Congress passed the CAA Amendments of 1977. Under this statutory scheme, the federal government established air quality standards, but left it up to the states to implement plans to achieve those standards. Since that time, the ozone layer, which protects us from the sun's harmful ultraviolet rays, has continued to evaporate due to the continued presence of chlorofluorocarbons, and carbon monoxide levels have remained above mandated levels. As a result, Congress enacted the CAA Amendments of 1990, which cover hundreds of chemical substances, tighten vehicle emission standards, establish a new operating permit program (similar to that authorized by the CWA), and impose costly regulatory requirements on thousands of smaller businesses that previously were exempt under the prior act and amendments.

The CAA regulates only outdoor or ambient air pollution. It regulates emissions from both stationary sources (factories, electric utilities, refineries, boilers, furnace stacks, vents, and valves) and mobile

16–10   BLACK LETTER LAW

Pollution Prevention Power to the People

The Toxic Chemical Release Inventory (TRI) is a database of chemical emissions compiled by the EPA. TRI is part of the Emergency Planning and Community Right-to-Know Act, which requires manufacturing facilities that release any of the 300 chemicals to file a report with the EPA. The TRI database is being made available directly to the public through computer telecommunications and other means. In order to obtain information from the TRI, the public may:

- Dial up the database through a home computer and a modem by calling 301-496-6531. The database is located at the National Library of Medicine in Bethesda, Maryland. The information may be downloaded onto a disk or printer for a nominal fee.
- Call the Emergency Planning and Community Right-to-Know toll-free hot line in Washington, D.C., at 800-535-0202 for the address of the nearest library that has a microfiche copy of TRI data.
- Obtain a CD-ROM with the TRI information on it from one of 400 federal depository libraries, 200 academic and research libraries, and all EPA libraries. The public can locate one of these by using the hot line number.
- Purchase a copy of the TRI information from the U.S. Government Printing Office at 202-275-2091 or the National Technical Information Service at 703-487-4650.
- Obtain copies of TRI reports for individual facilities from state TRI co-ordinators by calling the hot line for the name of the person to contact in each state.
- Obtain data from the TRI Reporting Center in Washington, D.C., which will make data available from individual facilities, and will mail out limited numbers of TRI reports, and will conduct limited searches of the database and provide printouts on request. Contact Title III Reporting Center, P.O. Box 70266, Washington, D.C. 20024-0266 (Attn.: Public Inquiry).

16–11   BLACK LETTER LAW

Asbestos and PCBs

Asbestos is one of the most dangerous substances known to humans. However, before the dangers of asbestos became known, the substance was used extensively to insulate, fireproof, and soundproof the vast majority of commercial buildings constructed between 1920 and 1970. Asbestos fibers, which are often thousands of times thinner than a human hair, can remain suspended in air for extended periods of time. If inhaled, the fibers can become lodged in the lungs and the gastrointestinal tract and cause lung cancer, respiratory disorders, and cancer of the esophagus, stomach, colon, and rectum.

Damage claims by workers exposed to asbestos represent the largest product liability action in the history of U.S. industry. The claimants, however, constitute only the first wave of litigants—the 4.5 million shipyard workers who were exposed in the 30s and 40s. The next wave is likely to increase as those construction workers, custodians, and others who were in places contaminated with asbestos begin to contract asbestos- related illness.

Thus far, litigation has aimed at the manufacturers of asbestos and their insurance carriers. In February 1994, a hearing was held to resolve approximately 100,000 claims in a class-action suit against 20 manufacturers of asbestos products, including Armstrong World Products, GAF Corporation, National Gypsum Company, Pfizer, and Union Carbide Corporation. It is estimated that manufacturers will pay out approximately $3.3 billion in the next decade to asbestos victims. In an unrelated case, a jury ordered Owens-Corning to pay $6.1 million in compensatory damages and $6.5 million in punitive damages to a plaintiff who had worked as a builder of aircraft and other military vessels for seven years at the Navy Yard in Brooklyn, New York, from 1952 to 1959. Although he did not work directly with asbestos, he was exposed to it, and he died at age 60 of a rare cancer of the lining of the lungs caused by asbestos exposure.

Increasingly, however, state and federal regulations are requiring owners and operators of commercial buildings containing asbestos-containing materials (ACMs) to see to costly removal or cleanup operations and may impose liability for personal injury due to asbestos exposure. Lending institutions, such as the Federal National Mortgage Association (Fannie Mae), are requiring comprehensive asbestos inspections of commercial buildings prior to lending.

continued on next page

Currently, asbestos is federally regulated by CERCLA, the Clean Air Act, RCRA, and the Occupational Safety and Health Administration. In addition, there is state regulation of asbestos in the form of inspection, labeling of asbestos debris, right-to-know laws requiring owners to notify certain individuals about the presence of asbestos, and mandatory cleanup.

Polychlorinated biphenyls (PCBs) are a group of extremely stable organic compounds that are nonflammable, are highly resistant to electricity, and because of those properties, were widely used as heat-resistant lubricants, hydraulic fluids, and dielectric fluids in a variety of electrical equipment. PCBs were also often mixed with waste oil and sprayed onto road surfaces to suppress dust.

The danger in PCBs is their toxicity in trace amounts combined with their nonbiodegradability, which tend to let them accumulate in river sediments and soil, where they eventually enter the food chain. After PCBs were detected in dangerous levels in fish, Congress subjected PCBs to special regulation. PCBs are currently regulated under CERCLA, RCRA, and the Toxic Substance Control Act. The federal government now regulates the manufacture, distribution, use, storage, transport, and disposal of PCBs.

16–12   BLACK LETTER LAW

Cuyahoga River on Fire

The blaze did not last long: the monetary damage was fairly small. Yet the 1969 fire on Ohio's Cuyahoga River ignited a public outcry about the state of the nation's environment and, along with oil spills and dying lakes, led to passage of the major environmental legislation of the early 1970s.

Running through Akron and Cleveland, Ohio, into Lake Erie, the Cuyahoga had been polluted for years. In 1881, the mayor of Cleveland called it "an open sewer through the center of the city." The river had burned twice before, in 1936 and in 1952, without much fanfare. But it was the blaze on June 22, 1969, that caught the public's imagination and led many to think, as one local mayor said, "My God, if this is what we can do to our water, then there's got to be a change."

At noon that day, a section of the river covered with oil and debris, just southeast of Cleveland, was ignited by an unknown source. The blaze lasted slightly more than 20 minutes and caused $50,000 in damage to two wooden railroad bridges.

Today, the water quality in the river's 40-mile stretch between Cleveland and Akron has greatly improved. However, the northern part of the river that serves as a ship channel is dredged annually, and the sediments are still contaminated to such an extent that they must be put into a confined disposal facility. Oxygen levels are still very low, and fish that happen into the section of the river in the Cleveland area could go belly-up in the summer.

The Cuyahoga River has come a long way from the sordid state of affairs of 1969. Today, the banks of the river even run through a festive area of restaurants and shops, an example of urban renewal that experts say is a direct result of improved water quality. However, it is the Cuyahoga's misfortune to be a small river located in the midst of a huge population base and the industrial and municipal waste that's produced as a result. As one state official says, "There will never be a trout stream flowing through downtown Cleveland."

Source: *EPA Journal*, Vol. 19, #2, April–June 1993. C/R: U.S. EPA, U.S. Government Printing Office, Public Documents Dept., Superintendent of Documents, Washington, D.C. 20402, 202-512-2262. No permission necessary

16–13   BLACK LETTER LAW

Bankrupted by EPA

In February 1992 the EPA put out a thick "Note to Correspondents" and staged a press conference on what it called its "record-breaking enforcement accomplishments for clean water in 1991." It was a banner year for enforcement, with 3,109 prosecutions, $28 million in penalties, and 346 months of incarceration for the polluters.

"The 1991 numbers [of prosecutions] are more than all the previous years combined," said the EPA. But does this mean justice is being done? Take the case of Lewis "Chuck" Law, 54, of Charleston, West Virginia. Mr. Law was sentenced in U.S. District Court to $160,000 in fines and two years in jail for breaches of the Clean Water Act.

Mr. Law's problems began when he purchased a 260-acre tract of land in 1980 for $160,000, intending to restore the old company store that was on the property. The property had been the site of a coal-washing plant that had closed.

Mr. Law knew nothing of any pollutants when he bought the property, but soon found out that some springs on his property discharged water that is acidic and contains suspended manganese and iron. It is not harmful, but turns water a nasty reddish color, and could hurt aquatic life. Downstream, people started complaining about his water flowing into their reservoir and staining their bathtubs and toilets with a reddish sediment. The problem was fixed by mixing well water into the reservoir, but Mr. Law's problems resurfaced when some fish were found dead in the creek downstream of his property. Mr. Law says the fish were dead when dumped there by the state and actually come from the hatchery.

At trial, Mr. Law did not deny that his water was in violation of the CWA, but contended that he was not the source of the pollution. He argued that it was actually the old coal mine higher up in the watershed that was the source and that the water is seeping underground into his water and subsequently flowing downstream. The government maintained that the pollution came from gob (an overgrown deposit of coal refuse material) left on his property.

The charge under which he was tried was failure to chemically treat the acid water discharges from the coal refuse pile. The government had demanded that he treat the water with soda ash to decrease the acid, but that would have cost him $5,000 per week and would have to be treated indefinitely. Mr. Law earned only $225 per month from rent on the property.

The government argued that under the CWA, the source did not have to be located on the property, just that it had to flow through it to constitute a violation. The government did not even argue that the water was a health hazard, just that it did not meet federal CWA standards.

The judge sentenced Mr. Law to two years in prison for failure to chemically treat his water. Theoretically, if a chemical truck backs onto your property and dumps a load of waste which contaminates water which then flows onto another's property, you would be guilty of a felony if you don't treat it.

Mr. Law has tried to give his land away, but understandably, there are no takers.

Source: *National Review*, by Peter Samuel, March 16, 1992, p. 38. C/R: 150 East 35th Street, New York, NY 10016.

sources (cars, trucks, buses, aircraft, ships, and trains). (See Box 16–14, "What Is Global Warming, and What Does It Have to Do with Trees?")

16–14   BLACK LETTER LAW

What Is Global Warming, and What Does It Have to Do with Trees?

Global warming is a projected increase in worldwide average temperatures caused by excess greenhouse gases in the atmosphere. These include carbon dioxide, released into the air by power plants, factories, and automobiles; methane, from natural gas wells, grass-eating animals, and termites; and nitrous oxide, from agriculture. Man-made gases called chlorofluorocarbons (CFCs) are also believed to play a small role in the greenhouse effect. CFCs are being phased out, however, because they play a big role in depleting the ozone layer.

The greenhouse effect is a natural trapping of heat in the earth's atmosphere. Light from the sun is absorbed by the earth's surface and is then radiated back toward space as infrared energy, which is blocked by greenhouse gases. The trapped energy warms the atmosphere. Without this natural warming, the earth would probably be too cold to inhabit.

The problem is that huge amounts of carbon dioxide are released into the air as we burn coal, oil, and gas, increasing the heat-trapping effect. It is suspected, but not proven, that the whole atmosphere will heat up as a result.

Trees absorb carbon dioxide—in the process called photosynthesis—to make their own tissues, such as leaves, roots, and branches. As a result, they remove large amounts of the most important greenhouse gas from the air. Destroying large numbers of trees increases the likelihood of global warming.

When pollutants are injected into the atmosphere, they are diluted, transported, and mixed with the surrounding air. Some pollutants are also chemically transformed into new substances called secondary pollutants. Examples of secondary pollutants are ozone, which causes smog, and sulfates, which cause acid rain.

SUMMARY

Ann and Bill have liability for several different aspects of their operations as a business. Ensuring that they comply with the applicable laws regarding their liability can greatly lessen the likelihood that they will incur the unnecessary expense of litigation and judgments. In addition, complying with the laws will increase the likelihood that Ann and Bill's business will prosper, because they will build customer loyalty and support for engaging in conduct consistent with the laws. Compliance with even some of the laws will ensure that there will be an earth and inhabitants for Ann and Bill to deal with in the years to come.

CHAPTER TERMS

cost justification defense

division of territory

effluent limitations

exclusive dealing arrangement

full warranty

group boycott

horizontal per se violation

limited warranty

meeting competition defense

merchantable

merger

monopoly

oligopoly

per se violation

point source

practical availability defense

predatory pricing

price discrimination

price fixing

puffery

resale price maintenance

rule of reason

Superfund

tying arrangement

unreasonable restraint of trade

vertical per se violation

warranty

warranty of merchantability

warranty of title

written warranties

CHAPTER-END QUESTIONS

1. Clairina and Moses, owners of a small family-owned pharmacy, complain to the Sabrina Sheila Liles Pharmaceutical Supply Co.,

which they purchase from, that the prices Sabrina charges them for their pharmaceuticals are higher than those they charge Belvinco, a national drugstore chain that also purchases from Sabrina. Because this makes Clairina and Moses have to charge more for their prescriptions than the larger chain, they charge that Sabrina's pricing practice is anticompetitive and illegal. Is it?

2. Clairina and Moses find out that Belvinco lowered its prices on certain items that Clairina and Moses sold to consumers more cheaply than Belvinco. Moses and Clairina think this is unfair, for they know this means Belvinco is not charging even the cost of the items to the consumers and that their small operation cannot afford to cut costs any further. Is it illegal for Belvinco to lower its prices to below cost?

3. Thomasina, who lives in another city, inherits a piece of land that has been in her family for seven generations. Several months later, Thomasina learns for the first time that the land had been used as a toxic waste dump site years ago and is now causing problems in the stream on the property. Thomasina is given a notice to clean up the site, but because it would cost thousands of dollars, which she does not have, she cannot do so. She defends against the citation by saying she just recently inherited the land, she did not know the site had been used to dump waste, and she had nothing to do with it. Is this a good defense?

4. Several pizza parlors are located near a university. Because of the existence of so many of the parlors, owned by different people, none of them is particularly successful. In an effort to become more so, one of the parlors begins to lower prices. The other parlors, seeing the increase in business, do the same. The first parlor continues to lower prices to meet competition. Eventually, though volume has increased, prices are so low at the parlors that none of the owners is really making any money. The owners get together after a local chamber of commerce meeting and decide that they will divide up the area around the school and serve only customers within their area. In this way, all can go back to charging higher prices and not lose out because of undercutting each other to meet competition. They don't feel customers would be harmed because customers will be able to still come to the parlor closest to their area and will have to pay only the prices they paid before for pizza. Can they take care of the problem this way?

5. Tess borrows Julie's bicycle. While she is riding it, Tess falls over and the water bottle holder on the bike comes off. Jenna, Julie's sister, tells Tess that she will have to pay for a new bike because she broke it. Is Julie correct?

6. When Sheila moves out of her apartment into her new house, her roommates—Tan, Dee, and Christie—offer to buy Sheila's space heater, which Sheila had received as a gift but never even took out of the box. When the heater stops working after six days, the roommates tell Sheila that she breached the warranty of merchantability because the heater does not work as it should. Do they have a good case?

7. Odell purchased a new car from Scanman Motors. This is a

   a. bailment for the benefit of the bailee.

   b. bailment for the benefit of the bailor.

   c. bailment for mutual benefit.

   d. none of the above.

8. When Odell purchases the car, he automatically receives a(n)

   a. implied warranty of merchantability.

   b. implied warranty of fitness for a particular purpose.

   c. express warranty.

   d. none of the above.

9. Cedric, a local diamond merchant, sells an engagement ring to Frederico. During the sale, if Cedric tells Frederico which of the following, will it *not* be the basis for breach of an express warranty?

   a. This diamond is real.

   b. This diamond is flawless.

   c. This diamond will last a lifetime.

   d. There's no way your girlfriend won't be happy with this perfect diamond.

10. If an accountant does not perform as agreed for Puhri, because the accountant does shoddy work for Puhri, Puhri has the options of _____, _____, and _____.

GROUP EXERCISE

Look at Box 16–10. Call, fax, or write the TRI and find out the location of the nearest chemical plant. Find out what toxic chemicals are in danger of being released in your area, and what emergency plans are in place in case of such an emergency.

THE CONSTITUTION OF THE UNITED STATES

We the People of the United States, in order to form a more perfect Union, establish justice, insure domestic tranquility, provide for the common defense, promote the general welfare, and secure the blessings of liberty to ourselves and our posterity, do ordain and establish this Constitution for the United States of America.

Article 1

Section 1. All legislative powers herein granted shall be vested in a Congress of the United States, which shall consist of a Senate and House of Representatives.

Section 2. [1] The House of Representatives shall be composed of members chosen every second year by the people of the several States, and the electors in each State shall have the qualifications requisite for electors of the most numerous branch of the State legislature.

[2] No person shall be a representative who shall not have attained to the age of twenty-five years, and been seven years a citizen of the United States, and who shall not, when elected, be an inhabitant of that State in which he shall be chosen.

[3] Representatives and direct taxes shall be apportioned among the several States which may be included within this Union, according to their respective Numbers, which shall be determined by adding to the whole number of free Persons, including those bound to service for a Term of Years, and excluding Indians not taxed, three fifths of all other Persons. The actual Enumeration shall be made within three Years after the first Meeting of the Congress of the United States, and within every subsequent term of ten years, in such manner as they shall by law direct. The number of representatives shall not exceed one for every thirty thousand, but each State shall have at least one representative; and until such enumeration shall be made, the State of New Hampshire shall be entitled to choose three, Massachusetts eight, Rhode Island and Providence Plantations one, Connecticut five, New York six, New Jersey four, Pennsylvania eight, Delaware one, Maryland six, Virginia ten, North Carolina five, South Carolina five, and Georgia three.

[4] When vacancies happen in the representation from any State, the executive authority thereof shall issue writs of election to fill such vacancies.

[5] The House of Representatives shall choose their speaker and other officers; and shall have the sole power of impeachment.

Section 3. [1] The Senate of the United States shall be composed of two senators from each State, chosen by the legislature thereof, for six years; and each senator shall have one vote.

[2] Immediately after they shall be assembled in consequence of the first election, they shall be divided as equally as may be into three classes. The seats of the senators of the first class shall be vacated at the expiration of the second year, of the second class at the expiration of the fourth year, and of the third class at the expiration of the fourth

year, and of the third class at the expiration of the sixth year, so that one third may be chosen every second year; and if vacancies happen by resignation, or otherwise, during the recess of the legislature of any State, the executive thereof may make temporary appointments until the next meeting of the legislature, which shall then fill such vacancies.

[3] No person shall be a senator who shall not have attained to the age of thirty years, and been nine years a citizen of the United States, and who shall not, when elected, be an inhabitant of that State for which he shall be chosen.

[4] The Vice President of the United States shall be President of the Senate, but shall have no vote, unless they be equally divided.

[5] The Senate shall choose their other officers, and also a president pro tempore, in the absence of the Vice President, or when he shall exercise the office of the President of the United States.

[6] The Senate shall have the sole power to try all impeachments. When sitting for that purpose, they shall be on oath or affirmation. When the President of the United States is tried, the chief justice shall preside: and no person shall be convicted without the concurrence of two thirds of the members present.

[7] Judgment in cases of impeachment shall not extend further than to removal from office, and disqualifications to hold and enjoy any office of honor, trust or profit under the United States: but the party convicted shall nevertheless be liable and subject to indictment, trial, judgment and punishment, according to law.

Section 4. [1] The times, places, and manner of holding elections for senators and representatives, shall be prescribed in each State by the legislature thereof; but the Congress may at any time by law make or alter such regulations, except as to the places of choosing senators.

[2] The Congress shall assemble at least once in every year, and such meeting shall be on the first Monday in December, unless they shall by law appoint a different day.

Section 5. [1] Each House shall be the judge of the elections, returns and qualifications of its own members, and a majority of each shall constitute a quorum to do business; but a smaller number may adjourn from day to day, and may be authorized to compel the attendance of absent members, in such manner, and under such penalties as each House may provide.

[2] Each House may determine the rules of its proceedings, punish its members for disorderly behavior, and, with the concurrence of two thirds, expel a member.

[3] Each House shall keep a journal of its proceedings, and from time to time publish the same, excepting such parts as may in their judgment require secrecy; and the yeas and nays of the members of either House on any question shall, at the desire of one fifth of those present, be entered on the journal.

[4] Neither House, during the session of Congress, shall, without the consent of the other, adjourn for more than three days, nor to any other place than that in which the two Houses shall be sitting.

Section 6. [1] The senators and representatives shall receive a compensation for their services, to be ascertained by law, and paid out of the Treasury of the United States. They shall in all cases, except treason, felony, and breach of the peace, be privileged from arrest during their attendance at the session of their respective Houses, and in going to and returning from the same; and for any speech or debate in either House, they shall not be questioned in any other place.

[2] No senator or representative shall, during the time for which he was elected, be appointed to any civil office under the authority of the United States, which shall have been created, or the emoluments whereof shall have been increased during such time; and no person holding any office under the United States shall be a member of either House during his continuance in office.

Section 7. [1] All bills for raising revenue shall originate in the House of Representatives; but the

Senate may propose or concur with amendments as on other bills.

[2] Every bill which shall have passed the House of Representatives and the Senate, shall, before it becomes a law, be presented to the President of the United States; if he approves he shall sign it, but if not he shall return it, with his objections to that House in which it shall have originated, who shall enter the objections at large on their journal, and proceed to reconsider it. If after such reconsideration two thirds of that House shall agree to pass the bill, it shall be sent, together with the objections, to the other House, by which it shall likewise be reconsidered, and if approved by two thirds of that House, it shall become a law. But in all such cases the votes of both Houses shall be determined by yeas and nays, and the names of the persons voting for and against the bill shall be entered on the journal of each House respectively. If any bill shall not be returned by the President within ten days (Sundays excepted) after it shall have been presented to him, the same shall be a law, in like manner as if he had signed it, unless the Congress by their adjournment prevent its return, in which case it shall not be a law.

[3] Every order, resolution, or vote to which the concurrence of the Senate and the House of Representatives may be necessary (except on a question of adjournment) shall be presented to the President of the United States; and before the same shall take effect, shall be approved by him, or being disapproved by him, shall be repassed by two thirds of the Senate and House of Representatives, according to the rules and limitations prescribed in the case of a bill.

Section 8. The Congress shall have the power

[1] To lay and collect taxes, duties, imposts, and excises, to pay the debts and provide for the common defense and general welfare of the United States; but all duties, imposts, and excises shall be uniform throughout the United States;

[2] To borrow money on the credit of the United States;

[3] To regulate commerce with foreign nations, and among the several States, and with the Indian tribes;

[4] To establish a uniform rule of naturalization, and uniform laws on the subject of bankruptcies throughout the United States;

[5] To coin money, regulate the value thereof, and of foreign coin, and fix the standard of weights and measures;

[6] To provide for the punishment of counterfeiting the securities and current coin of the United States;

[7] To establish post offices and post roads;

[8] To promote the progress of science and useful arts, by securing for limited times to authors and inventors the exclusive rights to their respective writings and discoveries;

[9] To constitute tribunals inferior to the Supreme Court;

[10] To define and punish piracies and felonies committed on the high seas, and offenses against the law of nations;

[11] To declare war, grant letters of marque and reprisal, and make rules concerning captures on land and water;

[12] To raise and support armies, but no appropriation of money to that use shall be for a longer term than two years;

[13] To provide and maintain a navy;

[14] To make rules for the government and regulation of the land and naval forces;

[15] To provide for calling forth the militia to execute the laws of the Union, suppress insurrections and repel invasions;

[16] To provide for organizing, arming, and disciplining the militia, and for governing such part of them as may be employed in the service of the United States, reserving to the States respectively, the appointment of the officers, and the authority of training the militia according to the discipline prescribed by Congress.

[17] To exercise exclusive legislation in all cases whatsoever, over such distinct (not exceeding ten miles square) as may, by cession of particular

States, and the acceptance of Congress, become the seat of the government of the United States, and to exercise like authority over all places purchased by the consent of the legislature of the State in which the same shall be, for the erection of forts, magazines, arsenals, dockyards, and other needful buildings; and

[18] To make all laws which shall be necessary and proper for carrying into execution the foregoing powers, and all other powers vested by this Constitution in the government of the United States, or in any department or officer thereof.

Section 9. [1] The migration or importation of such persons as any of the States now existing shall think proper to admit, shall not be prohibited by the Congress prior to the year one thousand eight hundred and eight, but a tax or duty may be imposed on such importation, not exceeding ten dollars for each person.

[2] The privilege of the writ of habeas corpus shall not be suspended, unless when in cases of rebellion or invasion the public safety may require it.

[3] No bill of attainder or ex post facto law shall be passed.

[4] No capitation, or other direct, tax shall be laid, unless in proportion to the census or enumeration hereinbefore directed to be taken.

[5] No tax or duty shall be laid on articles exported from any State.

[6] No preference shall be given by any regulation of commerce or revenue to the ports of one State over those of another: nor shall vessels bound to, or from, one State be obliged to enter, clear, or pay duties in another.

[7] No money shall be drawn from the treasury, but in consequence of appropriations made by law; and a regular statement and account of the receipts and expenditures of all public money shall be published from time to time.

[8] No title of nobility shall be granted by the United States: and no person holding any office of profit or trust under them, shall, without the consent of the Congress, accept of any present, emolument, office, or title, of any kind whatever, from any king, prince, or foreign State.

Section 10. [1] No State shall enter into any treaty, alliance, or confederation; grant letters of marque and reprisal; coin money; emit bills of credit; make anything but gold and silver coin a tender in payment of debts; pass any bill of attainder, ex post facto law, or law impairing the obligation of contracts, or grant any title of nobility.

[2] No State shall, without the consent of the Congress, lay any imposts or duties on imports or exports, except what may be absolutely necessary for executing its inspection laws: and the net produce of all duties and imposts laid by any State on imports or exports, shall be for the use of the treasury of the United States; and all such laws shall be subject to the revision and control of the Congress.

[3] No State shall, without the consent of Congress, lay any duty of tonnage, keep troops, or ships of war in time of peace, enter into any agreement or compact with another State, or with a foreign power, or engage in war, unless actually invaded, or in such imminent danger as will not admit of delay.

Article II

Section 1. [1] The executive power shall be vested in a President of the United States of America. He shall hold his office during the term of four years, and, together with the Vice President, chosen for the same term, be elected as follows:

[2] Each State shall appoint, in such manner as the legislature thereof may direct, a number of electors, equal to the whole number of senators and representatives to which the State may be entitled in the Congress: but no senator or representative, or person holding an office of trust or profit under the United States, shall be appointed an elector.

The electors shall meet in their respective States, and vote by ballot for two persons, of whom one at least shall not be an inhabitant of the same State with themselves. And they shall make a list of all the persons voted for, and of the number of votes for each; which list they shall sign and certify, and transmit sealed to the seat of the government of the United States, directed to the president of the Senate. The president of the Senate shall, in the presence of the Senate and House of Representatives, open all the certificates, and the votes shall then be counted. The person having the greatest number of votes shall be the President, if such number be a majority of the whole number of electors appointed; and if there be more than one who have such majority, and have an equal number of votes, then the House of Representatives shall immediately choose by ballot one of them for President; and if no person have a majority, then from the five highest on the list the said House shall in like manner choose the President. But in choosing the President, the votes shall be taken by States, the representation from each State having one vote; a quorum for this purpose shall consist of a member or members from two thirds of the States, and a majority of all the States shall be necessary to a choice. In every case, after the choice of the President, the person having the greatest number of votes of the electors shall be the Vice President. But if there should remain two or more who have equal votes, the Senate shall choose from them by ballot the Vice President.

[3] The Congress may determine the time of choosing the electors, and the day on which they shall give their votes; which day shall be the same throughout the United States.

[4] No person except a natural born citizen, or a citizen of the United States, at the time of the adoption of this Constitution, shall be eligible to the office of President; neither shall any person be eligible to that office who shall not have attained to the age of thirty-five years, and been fourteen years a resident within the United States.

[5] In the case of removal of the President from office, or of his death, resignation, or inability to discharge the powers and duties of the said office, the same shall devolve on the Vice President, and the Congress may by law provide for the case of removal, death, resignation, or inability, both of the President and Vice President, declaring what officer shall then act as President, and such officer shall act accordingly, until the disability be removed, or a President shall be elected.

[6] The President shall, at stated times, receive for his services a compensation, which shall neither be increased nor diminished during the period for which he shall have been elected, and he shall not receive within that period any other emolument from the United States, or any of them.

[7] Before he enter on the execution of his office, he shall take the following oath or affirmation: "I do solemnly swear (or affirm) that I will faithfully execute the office of President of the United States, and will to the best of my ability, preserve, protect and defend the Constitution of the United States.''

Section 2. [1] The President shall be commander in chief of the army and navy of the United States, and of the militia of the several States, when called into the actual service of the United States; he may require the opinion, in writing, of the principal officer in each of the executive departments, upon any subject relating to the duties of their respective office, and he shall have power to grant reprieves and pardons for offenses against the United States, except in cases of impeachment.

[2] He shall have power, by and with the advice and consent of the Senate, to make treaties, provided two thirds of the senators present concur; and he shall nominate, and by and with the advice and consent of the Senate, shall appoint ambassadors, other public ministers and consuls, judges of the Supreme Court, and all other officers of the United States, whose appointments are not herein otherwise provided for, and which shall be established by law: but the Congress may by law vest the appointment of such inferior officers, as they think proper, in the President alone, in the courts of law, or in the heads of departments.

[3] The President shall have power to fill up all vacancies that may happen during the recess of the

Senate, by granting commissions which shall expire at the end of their next session.

Section 3. He shall from time to time give to the Congress information of the state of the Union, and recommend to their consideration such measures as he shall judge necessary and expedient; he may, on extraordinary occasions, convene both Houses, or either of them, and in case of disagreement between them with respect to the time of adjournment, he may adjourn them to such time as he shall think proper; he shall receive ambassadors and other public ministers; he shall take care that the laws be faithfully executed, and shall commission all the officers of the United States.

Section 4. The President, Vice President, and all civil officers of the United States, shall be removed from office on impeachment for, and conviction of, treason, bribery, or other high crimes and misdemeanors.

Article III

Section 1. The judicial power of the United States shall be vested in one Supreme Court, and in such inferior courts as the Congress may from time to time ordain and establish. The judges, both of the Supreme and inferior courts, shall hold their offices during good behavior, and shall, at stated times, receive for their services, a compensation, which shall not be diminished during their continuance in office.

Section 2. [1] The judicial power shall extend to all cases, in law and equity, arising under this Constitution, the laws of the United States, and treaties made, or which shall be made, under their authority; to all cases affecting ambassadors, other public ministers and consuls; to all cases of admiralty and maritime jurisdiction; to controversies to which the United States shall be a party; to controversies between two or more States; between a State and citizens of another State; between citizens of different States; between citizens of the same State claiming lands under grants of different States, and

between a State, or the citizens thereof, and foreign States citizens or subjects.

[2] In all cases affecting ambassadors, other public ministers and consuls, and those in which a State shall be party, the Supreme Court shall have original jurisdiction. In all the other cases before mentioned, the Supreme Court shall have appellate jurisdiction, both as to law and to fact, with such exceptions, and under such regulations as the Congress shall make.

[3] The trial of all crimes, except in cases of impeachment, shall be by jury; and such trial shall be held in the State where the said crimes shall have been committed; but when not committed within any State, the trial shall be at such place or places as the Congress may by law have directed.

Section 3. [1] Treason against the United States shall consist only in levying war against them, or in adhering to their enemies, giving them aid and comfort. No person shall be convicted of treason unless on the testimony of two witnesses to the same overt act, or on confession in open court.

[2] The Congress shall have power to declare the punishment of treason, but no attainder of treason shall work corruption of blood, or forfeiture except during the life of the person attained.

Article IV

Section 1. Full faith and credit shall be given in each State to the public acts, records, and judicial proceedings of every other State. And the Congress may by general laws prescribe the manner in which such acts, records and proceedings shall be proved, and the effect thereof.

Section 2. [1] The citizens of each State shall be entitled to all privileges and immunities of citizens in the several States.

[2] A person charged in any State with treason, felony, or other crime, who shall flee from justice, and be found in another State, shall on demand of the executive authority of the State from which he

fled, be delivered up to be removed to the State having jurisdiction of the crime.

[3] No person held to service or labor in one State under the laws thereof, escaping into another, shall in consequence of any law or regulation therein, be discharged from such service or labor, but shall be delivered up on claim of the party to whom such service or labor may be due.

Section 3. [1] New States may be admitted by the Congress into this Union; but no new State shall be formed or erected within the jurisdiction of any other State, nor any State be formed by the junction of two or more States, or parts of States, without the consent of the legislatures of the States concerned as well as of the Congress.

[2] The Congress shall have power to dispose of and make all needful rules and regulations respecting the territory or other property belonging to the United States; and nothing in this Constitution shall be so construed as to prejudice any claims of the United States, or of any particular State.

Section 4. The United States shall guarantee to every State in this Union a republican form of government, and shall protect each of them against invasion; and on application of the legislature, or of the executive (when the legislature cannot be convened) against domestic violence.

Article V

The Congress, whenever two thirds of both Houses shall deem it necessary, shall propose amendments to this Constitution, or, on the application of the legislature of two thirds of the several States, shall call a convention for proposing amendments, which in either case, shall be valid to all intents and purposes, as part of this Constitution when ratified by the legislatures of three fourths of the several States, or by conventions in three fourths thereof, as the one or the other mode of ratification may be proposed by the Congress; Provided that no

amendment which may be made prior to the year one thousand eight hundred and eight shall in any manner affect the first and fourth clauses in the ninth section of the first article; and that no State, without its consent, shall be deprived of its equal suffrage in the Senate.

Article VI

[1] All debts contracted and engagements entered into, before the adoption of this Constitution, shall be as valid against the United States under this Constitution, as under the Confederation.

[2] This Constitution, and the laws of the United States which shall be made in pursuance thereof; and all treaties made, or which shall be made, under the authority of the United States, shall be the supreme law of the land; and the Judges in every State shall be bound thereby, anything in the Constitution or laws of any State to the contrary notwithstanding.

[3] The senators and representatives before mentioned, and the members of the several State legislatures, and all executive and judicial officers, both of the United States and of the several States, shall be bound by oath or affirmation to support this Constitution; but no religious test shall ever be required as a qualification to any office or public trust under the United States.

Article VII

The ratification of the conventions of nine States shall be sufficient for the establishment of this Constitution between the States so ratifying the same.

Done in Convention by the unanimous consent of the States present the seventeenth day of September in the year of our Lord one thousand seven hundred and eighty-seven, and of the independence of the United States of America the twelfth. In witness whereof we have hereunto subscribed our names.

AMENDMENTS

First Ten Amendments passed by Congress September 25, 1789. Ratified by three-fourths of the States December 15, 1791.

Amendment I

Congress shall make no law respecting an establishment of religion, or prohibiting the free exercise thereof; or abridging the freedom of speech, or of the press; or the right of the people peaceably to assemble, and to petition the government for a redress of grievances.

Amendment II

A well regulated militia, being necessary to the security of a free State, the right of the people to keep and bear arms, shall not be infringed.

Amendment III

No soldier shall, in time of peace be quartered in any house, without the consent of the owner, nor in time of war, but in a manner to be prescribed by law.

Amendment IV

The right of the people to be secure in their persons, houses, papers, and effects, against unreasonable searches and seizures, shall not be violated, and no warrants shall issue, but upon probable cause, supported by oath or affirmation, and particularly describing the place to be searched, and he person or things to be seized.

Amendment V

No person shall be held to answer for a capital, or otherwise infamous crime, unless on a presentment or indictment of a grand jury, except in cases arising in the land or naval forces, or in the militia, when in actual service in time of war or public danger; nor shall any person be subject for the same offense to be twice put in jeopardy of life or limb; nor shall be compelled in any criminal case to be a witness against himself, nor be deprived of life, liberty, or property, without due process of law; nor shall private property be taken for public use without just compensation.

Amendment VI

In all criminal prosecutions, the accused shall enjoy the right to a speedy and public trial, by an impartial jury of the State and district wherein the crime shall have been committed, which district shall have been previously ascertained by law, and to be informed of the nature and cause of the accusation; to be confronted with the witnesses against him; to have compulsory process for obtaining witnesses in his favor, and to have the assistance of counsel for his defense.

Amendment VII

In suits at common law, where the value in controversy shall exceed twenty dollars, the right of trial by jury shall be preserved, and no fact tried by a jury shall be preserved, and no fact tried by a jury shall be otherwise reexamined in any court of the United States, then according to the rules of the common law.

Amendment VIII

Excessive bail shall not be required, nor excessive fines imposed, nor cruel and unusual punishments inflicted.

Amendment IX

The enumeration in the Constitution of certain rights shall not be construed to deny or disparage others retained by the people.

Amendment X

The powers not delegated to the United States by the Constitution, nor prohibited by it to the States, are reserved to the States respectively, or to the people.

Amendment XI

Passed by Congress March 5, 1794. Ratified January 8, 1798.

The judicial power of the United States shall not be construed to extend to any suit in law or equity, commenced or prosecuted against one of the United States by citizens of another State, or by citizens or subjects of any foreign State.

Amendment XII

Passed by Congress December 12, 1803. Ratified September 25, 1804.

The electors shall meet in their respective States, and vote by ballot for President and Vice President, one of whom, at least, shall not be an inhabitant of the same State with themselves; they shall name in their ballots the person voted for as President, and in distinct ballots the person voted for as Vice President, and they shall make distinct lists of all persons voted for as President and of all persons voted for as Vice President, and of the number of votes for each, which lists they shall sign and certify, and transmit sealed to the seat of the government of the United States, directed to the President of the Senate; The President of the Senate shall, in the presence of the Senate and House of Representatives, open all the certificates and the votes shall then be counted; The person having the greatest number of votes for President, shall be the President, if such number be a majority of the whole number of electors appointed; and if no person have such majority, then from the persons having the highest numbers not exceeding three on the list of those voted for as President, the House of Representatives shall choose immediately, by ballot,

the President. But in choosing the President, the votes shall be taken by States, the representation from each State having one vote; a quorum for this purpose shall consist of a member or members from two thirds of the States, and a majority of all the States shall be necessary to a choice. And if the House of Representatives shall not choose a President whenever the right of choice shall devolve upon them, before the fourth day of March next following, then the Vice President shall act as President, as in the case of the death or other constitutional disability of the President. The person having the greatest number of votes as Vice President shall be the Vice President, if such number be a majority of the whole number of electors appointed, and if no person have a majority, then from the two highest numbers on the list, the Senate shall choose the Vice President; a quorum for the purpose shall consist of two thirds of the whole number of Senators, and a majority of the whole number shall be necessary to a choice. But no person constitutionally ineligible to the office of President shall be eligible to that of Vice President of the United States.

Amendment XIII

Passed by Congress February 1, 1865. Ratified December 18, 1865.

Section 1. Neither slavery nor involuntary servitude, except as punishment for crime whereof the party shall have been duly convicted, shall exist within the United States, or any place subject to their jurisdiction.

Section 2. Congress shall have power to enforce this article by appropriate legislation.

Amendment XIV

Passed by Congress June 16, 1866. Ratified July 23, 1868.

Section 1. All persons born or naturalized in the United States, and subject to the jurisdiction thereof, are citizens of the United States and of the

State wherein they reside. No State shall make or enforce any law which shall abridge the privileges or immunities of citizens of the United States; nor shall any State deprive any person of life, liberty, or property, without due process of law; nor deny to any person within its jurisdiction the equal protection of the laws.

Section 2. Representatives shall be apportioned among the several States according to their respective numbers, counting the whole number of persons in each State, excluding Indians not taxed. But when the right to vote at any election for the choice of electors for President and Vice President of the United States, representatives in Congress, the executive and judicial officers of a State, or the members of the legislature thereof, is denied to any of the male inhabitants of such State, being twenty-one years of age, and citizens of the United States, or in any way abridged, except for participation in rebellion, or other crime, the basis of representation therein shall be reduced in the proportion which the number of such male citizens shall bear to the whole number of male citizens twenty-one years of age in such State.

Section 3. No person shall be a senator or representative in Congress, or elector of President and Vice President, or hold any office, civil or military, under the United States, or under any State, who having previously taken an oath, as a member of Congress, or as an officer of the United States, or as a member of any State legislature, or as an executive or judicial officer of any State, to support the Constitution of the United States, shall have engaged in insurrection or rebellion against the same, or given aid or comfort to the enemies thereof. But Congress may by a vote of two thirds of each House, remove such disability.

Section 4. The validity of the public debt of the United States, authorized by law, including debts incurred for payment of pensions and bounties for services in suppressing insurrection or rebellion, shall not be questioned. But neither the United States nor any State shall assume or pay any debt or obligation incurred in aid of insurrection or rebellion against the United States, or any claim for the loss or emancipation of any slave; but all such debts, obligations, and claims shall be held illegal and void.

Section 5. The Congress shall have power to enforce, by appropriate legislation, the provisions of this article.

Amendment XV

Passed by Congress February 27, 1869. Ratified March 30, 1870.

Section 1. The right of citizens of the United States to vote shall not be denied or abridged by the United States or by any State on account of race, color, or previous condition of servitude.

Section 2. The Congress shall have power to enforce this article by appropriate legislation.

Amendment XVI

Passed by Congress July 12, 1909. Ratified February 25, 1913.

The Congress shall have power to lay and collect taxes on incomes, from whatever source derived, without apportionment among the several States, and without regard to any census or enumeration.

Amendment XVII

Passed by Congress May 16, 1912. Ratified May 31, 1913.

The Senate of the United States shall be composed of two senators from each State, elected by the people thereof, for six years; and each senator shall have one vote. The electors in each State shall have the qualifications requisite for electors of the most numerous branch of the State legislature.

When vacancies happen in the representation of any State in the Senate, the executive authority of such State shall issue writs of election to fill such vacancies: Provided, That the legislature of any State may empower the executive thereof to make temporary appointments until the people fill the vacancies by election as the legislature may direct.

This amendment shall not be so construed as to affect the election or term of any senator chosen before it becomes valid as part of the Constitution.

Amendment XVIII

Passed by Congress December 17, 1917. Ratified January 29, 1919.

After one year from the ratification of this article, the manufacture, sale, or transportation of intoxicating liquors within, the importation thereof into, or the exportation thereof from the United States and all territory subject to the jurisdiction thereof for beverage purposes is hereby prohibited.

The Congress and the several States shall have concurrent power to enforce this article by appropriate legislation.

This article shall be inoperative unless it shall have been ratified as an amendment to the Constitution by the legislatures of the several States, as provided in the Constitution, within seven years from the date of the submission hereof to the States by Congress.

Amendment XIX

Passed by Congress June 5, 1919. Ratified August 26, 1920.

The right of citizens of the United States to vote shall not be denied or abridged by the United States or by any State on account of sex.

The Congress shall have power by appropriate legislation to enforce the provisions of this article.

Amendment XX

Passed by Congress March 3, 1932. Ratified January 23, 1933.

Section 1. The terms of the President and Vice President shall end at noon on the 20th day of January, and the terms of Senators and Representatives at noon on the 3d day of January, of the years in which such terms would have ended if this article had not been ratified; and the terms of their successors shall then begin.

Section 2. The Congress shall assemble at least once in every year, and such meeting shall begin at noon on the 3d day of January, unless they shall by law appoint a different day.

Section 3. If, at the time fixed for the beginning of the term of the President, the President-elect shall have died, the Vice President-elect shall become President. If a President shall not have been chosen before the time fixed for the beginning of his term, or if the President-elect shall have failed to qualify, then the Vice President-elect shall act as President until a President shall have qualified; and the Congress may by law provide for the case wherein neither a President-elect nor a Vice President-elect shall have qualified, declaring who shall then act as President, or the manner in which one who is to act shall be selected, and such person shall act accordingly until a President or Vice President shall have qualified.

Section 4. The Congress may by law provide for the case of the death of any of the persons from whom the House of Representatives may choose a President whenever the right of choice shall have devolved upon them, and for the case of the death of any of the persons from whom the Senate may choose a Vice President whenever the right of choice shall have devolved upon them.

Section 5. Sections 1 and 2 shall take effect on the 15th day of October following the ratification of this article.

Section 6. This article shall be inoperative unless it shall have been ratified as an amendment to the Constitution by the legislatures of three-fourths of the several States within seven years from the date of its submission.

Amendment XXI

Passed by Congress February 20, 1933. Ratified December 5, 1933.

Section 1. The Eighteenth Article of amendment to the Constitution of the United States is hereby repealed.

Section 2. The transportation or importation into any State, Territory, or possession of the United States for delivery or use therein of intoxicating liquors in violation of the laws thereof, is hereby prohibited.

Section 3. This article shall be inoperative unless it shall have been ratified as an amendment to the Constitution by conventions in the several States, as provided in the Constitution, within seven years from the date of the submission thereof to the States by the Congress.

Amendment XXII

Passed by Congress March 24, 1947. Ratified February 26, 1951.

Section 1. No person shall be elected to the office of the President more than twice, and no person who has held the office of President, or acted as President, for more than two years of a term to which some other person was elected President shall be elected to the office of the President more than once. But this article shall not apply to any person holding the office of President when this article was proposed by the Congress, and shall not prevent any person who may be holding the office of President, or acting as President, during the term within which this article becomes operative from holding the office of President or acting as President during the remainder of such term.

Section 2. This article shall be inoperative unless it shall have been ratified as an amendment to the Constitution by the legislatures of three-fourths of the several States within seven years from the date of its submission to the States by the Congress.

Amendment XXIII

Passed by Congress June 16, 1960. Ratified April 3, 1961.

Section 1. The District constituting the seat of Government of the United States shall appoint in such manner as the Congress may direct:

A number of electors of President and Vice President equal to the whole number of Senators and Representatives in Congress to which the District would be entitled if it were a State, but in no event more than the least populous State; they shall be in addition to those appointed by the States, but they shall be considered, for the purposes of the election of President and Vice President, to be electors appointed by a State; and they shall meet in the District and perform such duties as provided by the twelfth article of amendment.

Section 2. The Congress shall have power to enforce this article by appropriate legislation.

Amendment XXIV

Passed by Congress August 27, 1962. Ratified February 4, 1964.

Section 1. The right of citizens of the United States to vote in any primary or other election for President or Vice President, for electors for President or Vice President, or for Senator or Representative in Congress, shall not be denied or abridged by the United States or any State by reason of failure to pay any poll tax or other tax.

Section 2. The Congress shall have power to enforce this article by appropriate legislation.

Amendment XXV

Passed by Congress July 6, 1965. Ratified February 23, 1967.

Section 1. In case of the removal of the President from office or of his death or resignation, the Vice President shall become President.

Section 2. Whenever there is a vacancy in the office of the Vice President, the President shall nominate a Vice President who shall take office upon confirmation by a majority vote of both Houses of Congress.

Section 3. Whenever the President transmits to the President pro tempore of the Senate and the Speaker of the House of Representatives his written declaration that he is unable to discharge the powers and duties of his office, and until he transmits to them a written declaration to the contrary, such powers and duties shall be discharged by the Vice President as Acting President.

Section 4. Whenever the Vice President and a majority of either the principal officers of the executive departments or of such other body as Congress may by law provide, transmit to the President pro tempore of the Senate and the Speaker of the House of Representatives their written declaration that the President is unable to discharge the powers and duties of his office, the Vice President shall immediately assume the powers and duties of the office as Acting President.

Thereafter, when the President transmits to the President pro tempore of the Senate and the Speaker of the House of Representatives his written declaration that no inability exists, he shall resume the powers and duties of his office unless the Vice President and a majority of either the principal officers of the executive department or of such other body as Congress may by law provide, transmit within four days to the President pro tempore of the Senate and the Speaker of the House of Represen-tatives their written declaration that the President is unable to discharge the powers and duties of his office. Thereupon Congress shall decide the issue, assembling within forty-eight hours for that purpose if not in session. If the Congress, within twenty-one days after receipt of the latter written declaration, or, if Congress is not in session, within twenty-one days after Congress is required to assemble, determines by two-thirds vote of both Houses that the President is unable to discharge the powers and duties of his office, the Vice President shall continue to discharge the same as Acting President; otherwise, the President shall resume the powers and duties of his office.

Amendment XXVI

Passed by Congress March 23, 1971. Ratified July 5, 1971.

Section 1. The right of citizens of the United States, who are eighteen years of age or older, to vote shall not be denied or abridged by the United States or by any State on account of age.

Amendment XXVII

Passed by Congress September 25, 1987. Ratified May 18, 1992.

No law, varying the compensation for the services of the Senators and Representatives, shall take effect, until an election of Representatives shall have intervened.

THE UNIFORM COMMERCIAL CODE (EXCERPTS)

Article 1

General Provisions

Part 1 Short Title, Construction, Application and Subject Matter of the Act

§1 102. Purposes; Rules of Construction; Variation by Agreement

(1) This Act shall be liberally construed and applied to promote its underlying purposes and policies.

(2) Underlying purposes and policies of this Act are

(a) to simplify, clarify and modernize the law governing commercial transactions;

(b) to permit the continued expansion of commercial practices through custom, usage and agreement of the parties;

(c) to make uniform the law among the various jurisdictions.

(3) The effect of provisions of this Act may be varied by agreement, except as otherwise provided in this Act and except that the obligations of good faith, diligence, reasonableness and care prescribed by this Act may not be disclaimed by agreement, but the parties may by agreement determine the standards by which the performance of such obligations is to be measured if such standards are not manifestly unreasonable.

. . .

§1 103. Supplementary General Principles of Law Applicable

Unless displaced by the particular provisions of this Act, the principles of law and equity, including the law merchant and the law relative to capacity to contract, principal and agent, estoppel, fraud, misrepresentation, duress, coercion, mistake, bankruptcy, or other validating or invalidating cause shall supplement its provisions.

§1 106. Remedies to Be Liberally Administered

(1) The remedies provided by this Act shall be liberally administered to the end that the aggrieved party may be put in as good a position as if the other party had fully performed, but neither consequential or special nor penal damages may be had except as specifically provided in this Act or by other rule of law.

(2) Any right or obligation declared by this Act is enforceable by action unless the provision declaring it specifies a different and limited effect.

§1 107. Waiver or Renunciation of Claim or Right After Breach

Any claim or right arising out of an alleged breach can be discharged in whole or in part without consideration by a written waiver or renunciation signed and delivered by the aggrieved party.

Part 2 General Definitions and Principles of Interpretation

§1 201. General Definitions

Subject to additional definitions contained in the subsequent Articles of this Act which are applicable to specific Articles or Parts thereof, and unless the context otherwise requires, in this Act:

(1) "Action" in the sense of a judicial proceeding includes recoupment, counterclaim, set-off, suit in

equity and any other proceedings in which rights are determined.

(2) "Aggrieved party" means a party entitled to resort to a remedy.

(3) "Agreement" means the bargain of the parties in fact as found in their language or by implication from other circumstances including course of dealing or usage of trade or course of performance as provided in this Act (Sections 1 205 and 2 208). Whether an agreement has legal consequences is determined by the provisions of this Act, if applicable; otherwise by the law of contracts (Section 1 103). (Compare Contract.)

. . .

(5) "Bearer" means the person in possession of an instrument, document of title, or certificated security payable to bearer or endorsed in blank.

(6) "Bill of lading" means a document evidencing the receipt of goods for shipment issued by a person engaged in the business of transporting or forwarding goods, and includes an airbill. Airbill means a document serving for air transportation as a bill of lading does for marine or rail transportation, and includes an air consignment note or air waybill.

. . .

(8) "Burden of establishing" a fact means the burden of persuading the triers of fact that the existence of the fact is more probable than its nonexistence.

(9) "Buyer in ordinary course of business" means a person who in good faith and without knowledge that the sale to him is in violation of the ownership rights or security interest of a third party in the goods buys in ordinary course from a person in the business of selling goods of that kind but does not include a pawnbroker. All persons who sell minerals or the like (including oil and gas) at wellhead or minehead shall be deemed to be persons in the business of selling goods of that kind. Buying may be for cash or by exchange of other property or on secured or unsecured credit and includes receiving goods or documents of title under a preexisting contract for sale but does not include a transfer in bulk or as security for or in total or partial satisfaction of a money debt.

(10) "Conspicuous:" A term or clause is conspicuous when it is so written that a reasonable person against whom it is to operate ought to have noticed it. A printed heading in capitals (as: NON-NEGOTIABLE BILL OF LADING) is conspicuous. Language in the body of a form is conspicuous if it is in larger or other contrasting type or color. But in a telegram any stated term is conspicuous. Whether a term or clause is conspicuous or not is for decision by the court.

(11) "Contract" means the total legal obligation which results from the parties agreement as affected by this Act and any other applicable rules of law. (Compare Agreement.)

. . .

(15) "Document of title" includes bill of lading, dock warrant, dock receipt, warehouse receipt or order for the delivery of goods, and also any other document which in the regular course of business or financing is treated as adequately evidencing that the person in possession of it is entitled to receive, hold and dispose of the document and the goods it covers. To be a document of title a document must purport to be issued by or addressed to a bailee and purport to cover goods in the bailees possession which are either identified or are fungible portions of an identified mass.

. . .

(18) "Genuine" means free of forgery or counterfeiting.

(19) "Good faith" means honesty in fact in the conduct or transaction concerned.

(20) "Holder" means a person who is in possession of a document of title or an instrument or a certificated investment security drawn, issued or endorsed to him or to his order or to bearer or in blank.

. . .

(25) A person has "notice" of a fact when

(a) he has actual knowledge of it; or

(b) he has received a notice or notification of it; or

(c) from all the facts and circumstances known to

him at the time in question he has reason to know that it exists.

A person "knows" or "has knowledge" of a fact when he has actual knowledge of it. Discover or learn or a word or phrase of similar import refers to knowledge rather than to reason to know. The time and circumstances under which a notice or notification may cease to be effective are not determined by this Act.

(26) A person notifies or gives a notice or notification to another by taking such steps as may be reasonably required to inform the other in ordinary course whether or not such other actually comes to know of it. A person receives a notice or notification when

(a) it comes to his attention; or

(b) it is duly delivered at the place of business through which the contract was made or at any other place held out by him as the place for receipt of such communications.

(27) Notice, knowledge or a notice or notification received by an organization is effective for a particular transaction from the time when it is brought to the attention of the individual conducting that transaction, and in any event from the time when it would have been brought to his attention if the organization had exercised due diligence. An organization exercises due diligence if it maintains reasonable routines for communicating significant information to the person conducting the transaction and there is reasonable compliance with the routines. Due diligence does not require an individual acting for the organization to communicate information unless such communication is part of his regular duties or unless he has reason to know of the transaction and that the transaction would be materially affected by the information.

(28) "Organization" includes a corporation, government or governmental subdivision or agency, business trust, estate, trust, partnership or association, two or more persons having a joint or common interest, or any other legal or commercial entity.

. . .

(31) "Presumption" or "presumed" means that the trier of fact must find the existence of the fact presumed unless and until evidence is introduced which would support a finding of its nonexistence.

(32) "Purchase" includes taking by sale, discount, negotiation, mortgage, pledge, lien, issue or reissue, gift or any other voluntary transaction creating an interest in property.

(33) Purchaser means a person who takes by purchase.

. . .

(37) "Security interest" means an interest in personal property or fixtures which secures payment or performance of an obligation. The retention or reservation of title by a seller of goods notwithstanding shipment or delivery to the buyer (Section 2 401) is limited in effect to a reservation of a security interest. The term also includes any interest of a buyer of accounts or chattel paper which is subject to Article 9. The special property interest of a buyer of goods on identification of such goods to a contract for sale under Section 2 401 is not a security interest, but a buyer may also acquire a security interest by complying with Article 9. Unless a lease or consignment is intended as security, reservation of title thereunder is not a security interest but a consignment is in any event subject to the provisions on consignment sales (Section 2 326). Whether a lease is intended as security is to be determined by the facts of each case; however, (a) the inclusion of an option to purchase does not of itself make the lease one intended for security, and (b) an agreement that upon compliance with the terms of the lease the lessee shall become or has the option to become the owner of the property for no additional consideration or for a nominal consideration does make the lease one intended for security.

(38) "Send" in connection with any writing or notice means to deposit in the mail or deliver for transmission by any other usual means of communication with postage or cost of transmission provided for and properly addressed and in the case of an instrument to an address specified thereon or otherwise agreed, or if there be none to any address reasonable under the circumstances. The receipt of any writing or notice within the time at

which it would have arrived if properly sent has the effect of a proper sending.

(39) "Signed" includes any symbol executed or adopted by a party with present intention to authenticate a writing.

. . .

(46) "Written" or "writing" includes printing, typewriting or any other intentional reduction to tangible form.

§1 203. Obligation of Good Faith

Every contract or duty within this Act imposes an obligation of good faith in its performance or enforcement.

§1 204. Time; Reasonable Time; Seasonably

(1) Whenever this Act requires any action to be taken within a reasonable time, any time which is not manifestly unreasonable may be fixed by agreement.

(2) What is a reasonable time for taking any action depends on the nature, purpose and circumstances of such action.

(3) An action is taken seasonably when it is taken at or within the time agreed or, if no time is agreed, at or within a reasonable time.

§1 205. Course of Dealing and Usage of Trade

(1) A course of dealing is a sequence of previous conduct between the parties to a particular transaction which is fairly to be regarded as establishing a common basis of understanding for interpreting their expressions and other conduct.

(2) A usage of trade is any practice or method of dealing having such regularity of observance in a place, vocation or trade as to justify an expectation that it will be observed with respect to the transaction in question. The existence and scope of such a usage are to be proved as facts. If it is established that such a usage is embodied in a written trade code or similar writing the interpretation of the writing is for the court.

(3) A course of dealing between parties and any usage of trade in the vocation or trade in which they are engaged or of which they are or should be aware give particular meaning to and supplement or qualify terms of an agreement.

(4) The express terms of an agreement and an applicable course of dealing or usage of trade shall be construed wherever reasonable as consistent with each other; but when such construction is unreasonable, express terms control both course of dealing and usage of trade and course of dealing controls usage of trade.

(5) An applicable usage of trade in the place where any part of performance is to occur shall be used in interpreting the agreement as to that part of the performance.

(6) Evidence of a relevant usage of trade offered by one party is not admissible unless and until he has given the other party such notice as the court finds sufficient to prevent unfair surprise to the latter.

§1 206. Statute of Frauds for Kinds of Personal Property Not Otherwise Covered

(1) Except in the cases described in subsection (2) of this section, a contract for the sale of personal property is not enforceable by way of action or defense beyond five thousand dollars in amount or value of remedy unless there is some writing which indicates that a contract for sale has been made between the parties at a defined or stated price, reasonably identifies the subject matter, and is signed by the party against whom enforcement is sought or by his authorized agent.

(2) Subsection (1) of this section does not apply to contracts for the sale of goods (Section 2 201) nor of securities (Section 8 319) nor to security agreements (Section 9 203).

§1 207. Performance or Acceptance Under Reservation of Rights

A party who with explicit reservation of rights performs or promises performance or assents to performance in a manner demanded or offered by the other party does not thereby prejudice the rights reserved. Such words as without prejudice, under protest or the like are sufficient.

§1 208. Option to Accelerate at Will

A term providing that one party or his successor in interest may accelerate payment or performance or require collateral or additional collateral at will or when he deems himself insecure or in words of similar import shall be construed to mean that he shall have power to do so only if he in good faith believes that the prospect of payment or performance is impaired. The burden of establishing lack of good faith is on the party against whom the power has been exercised.

Article 2

Sales

Part 1 Short Title, General Construction and Subject Matter

§2 103. Definitions and Index of Definitions

(1) In this Article, unless the context otherwise requires,

    (a) "Buyer" means a person who buys or contracts to buy goods.

    (b) "Good faith" in the case of a merchant means honesty in fact and the observance of reasonable commercial standards of fair dealing in the trade.

    (c) "Receipt" of goods means taking physical possession of them.

    (d) Seller means a person who sells or contracts to sell goods.

§2 104. Definitions: Merchant; Between Merchants; Financing Agency

(1) "Merchant" means a person who deals in goods of the kind or otherwise by his occupation holds himself out as having knowledge or skill peculiar to the practices or goods involved in the transaction or to whom such knowledge or skill may be attributed by his employment of an agent or broker or other intermediary who by his occupation holds himself out as having such knowledge or skill.

. . .

(3) "Between merchants" means in any transaction with respect to which both parties are chargeable with the knowledge or skill of merchants.

§2 105. Definitions: Transferability; Goods; Future Goods; Lot; Commercial Unit

(1) "Goods" means all things (including specially manufactured goods) which are movable at the time of identification to the contract for sale other than the money in which the price is to be paid, investment securities (Article 8) and things in action. Goods also includes the unborn young of animals and growing crops and other identified things attached to realty as described in the section on goods to be severed from realty (Section 2 107).

(2) Goods must be both existing and identified before any interest in them can pass. Goods which are not both existing and identified are future goods. A purported present sale of future goods or of any interest therein operates as a contract to sell.

. . .

(5) "Lot" means a parcel or a single article which is the subject matter of a separate sale or delivery, whether or not it is sufficient to perform the contract.

(6) "Commercial unit" means such a unit of goods as by commercial usage is a single whole for purposes of sale and division of which materially impairs its character or value on the market or in use. A commercial unit may be a single article (as a machine) or a set of articles (as a suite of furniture or an assortment of sizes) or a quantity (as a bale, gross, or carload) or any other unit treated in use or in the relevant market as a single whole.

§2 106. Definitions: Contract; Agreement; Contract for Sale; Sale; Present Sale; Conforming to Contract; Termination; Cancellation

(1) In this Article unless the context otherwise requires, "contract" and "agreement" are limited to those relating to the present or future sale of goods. "Contract for sale" includes both a present sale of goods and a contract to sell goods at a future time. A "sale" consists in the passing of title from the seller to the buyer for a price (Section 2 401). A "present sale" means a sale which is accomplished by the making of the contract.

(2) Goods or conduct, including any part of a performance, are conforming or conform to the contract when they are in accordance with the obligations under the contract.

. . .

Part 2 Form, Formation and Readjustment of Contract

§2 201. Formal Requirements; Statute of Frauds

(1) Except as otherwise provided in this section, a contract for the sale of goods for the price of $500 or more is not enforceable by way of action or defense unless there is some writing sufficient to indicate that a contract for sale has been made between the parties and signed by the party against whom enforcement is sought or by his authorized agent or broker. A writing is not insufficient because it omits or incorrectly states a term agreed upon but the contract is not enforceable under this paragraph beyond the quantity of goods shown in such writing.

(2) Between merchants, if within a reasonable time a writing in confirmation of the contract and sufficient against the sender is received and the party receiving it has reason to know its contents, it satisfies the requirements of subsection (1) against such party unless written notice of objection to its contents is given within 10 days after it is received.

(3) A contract which does not satisfy the requirements of subsection (1) but which is valid in other respects is enforceable

(a) if the goods are to be specially manufactured for the buyer and are not suitable for sale to others in the ordinary course of the sellers business and the seller, before notice of repudiation is received and under circumstances which reasonably indicate that the goods are for the buyer, has made either a substantial beginning of their manufacture or commitments for their procurement; or

(b) if the party against whom enforcement is sought admits in his pleading, testimony or otherwise in court that a contract for sale was made, but the contract is not enforceable under this provision beyond the quantity of goods admitted; or

(c) with respect to goods for which payment has been made and accepted or which have been received and accepted (Section 2 606).

§2 202. Final Written Expression: Parol or Extrinsic Evidence

Terms with respect to which the confirmatory memoranda of the parties agree or which are otherwise set forth in a writing intended by the parties as a final expression of their agreement with respect to such terms as are included therein may not be contradicted by evidence of any prior agreement or of a contemporaneous oral agreement but may be explained or supplemented

(a) by course of dealing or usage of trade (Section 1 205) or by course of performance (Section 2 208); and

(b) by evidence of consistent additional terms unless the court finds the writing to have been intended also as a complete and exclusive statement of the terms of the agreement.

§2 204. Formation in General

(1) A contract for sale of goods may be made in any manner sufficient to show agreement, including conduct by both parties which recognizes the existence of such a contract.

(2) An agreement sufficient to constitute a contract for sale may be found even though the moment of its making is undetermined.

(3) Even though one or more terms are left open a contract for sale does not fail for indefiniteness if the parties have intended to make a contract and there is a reasonably certain basis for giving an appropriate remedy.

§2 205. Firm Offers

An offer by a merchant to buy or sell goods in a signed writing which by its terms gives assurance that it will be held open is not revocable, for lack of consideration, during the time stated or if no time is stated for a reasonable time, but in no event may such period of irrevocability exceed three months; but any such term of assurance on a form supplied by the offeree must be separately signed by the offeror.

§2 206. Offer and Acceptance in Formation of Contract

(1) Unless otherwise unambiguously indicated by the language or circumstances

(a) an offer to make a contract shall be construed as inviting acceptance in any manner and by any medium reasonable in the circumstances;

(b) an order or other offer to buy goods for prompt or current shipment shall be construed as inviting acceptance either by a prompt promise to ship or by the prompt or current shipment of conforming or non-conforming goods, but such a shipment of non-conforming goods does not constitute an acceptance if the seller seasonably notifies the buyer that the shipment is offered only as an accommodation to the buyer.

(2) Where the beginning of a requested performance is a reasonable mode of acceptance, an offeror who is not notified of acceptance within a reasonable time may treat the offer as having lapsed before acceptance.

§2 207. Additional Terms in Acceptance or Confirmation

(1) A definite and seasonable expression of acceptance or a written confirmation which is sent within a reasonable time operates as an acceptance even though it states terms additional to or different from those offered or agreed upon, unless acceptance is expressly made conditional on assent to the additional or different terms.

(2) The additional terms are to be construed as proposals for addition to the contract. Between merchants such terms become part of the contract unless:

  (a) the offer expressly limits acceptance to the terms of the offer;

  (b) they materially alter it; or

  (c) notification of objection to them has already been given or is given within a reasonable time after notice of them is received.

(3) Conduct by both parties which recognizes the existence of a contract is sufficient to establish a contract for sale although the writings of the parties do not otherwise establish a contract. In such case the terms of the particular contract consist of those terms on which the writings of the parties agree, together with any supplementary terms incorporated under any other provisions of this Act.

§2 208. Course of Performance or Practical Construction

(1) Where the contract for sale involves repeated occasions for performance by either party with knowledge of the nature of the performance and opportunity for objection to it by the other, any course of performance accepted or acquiesced in without objection shall be relevant to determine the meaning of the agreement.

(2) The express terms of the agreement and any such course of performance, as well as any course of dealing and usage of trade, shall be construed whenever reasonable as consistent with each other; but when such construction is unreasonable, express terms shall control course of performance and course of performance shall control both course of dealing and usage of trade (Section 1 205).

(3) Subject to the provisions of the next section on modification and waiver, such course of performance shall be relevant to show a waiver or modification of any term inconsistent with such course of performance.

§2 209. Modification, Rescission and Waiver

(1) An agreement modifying a contract within this Article needs no consideration to be binding.

(2) A signed agreement which excludes modification or rescission except by a signed writing cannot be otherwise modified or rescinded, but except as between merchants such a requirement on a form supplied by the merchant must be separately signed by the other party.

(3) The requirements of the statute of frauds section of this Article (Section 2 201) must be satisfied if the contract as modified is within its provisions.

(4) Although an attempt at modification or rescission does not satisfy the requirements of subsection (2) or (3) it can operate as a waiver.

(5) A party who has made a waiver affecting an executory portion of the contract may retract the waiver by reasonable notification received by the other party that strict performance will be required of any term waived, unless the retraction would be unjust in view of a material change of position in reliance on the waiver.

§2 210. Delegation of Performance; Assignment of Rights

(1) A party may perform his duty through a dele-

gate unless otherwise agreed or unless the other party has a substantial interest in having his original promisor perform or control the acts required by the contract. No delegation of performance relieves the party delegating of any duty to perform or any liability for breach.

(2) Unless otherwise agreed, all rights of either seller or buyer can be assigned except where the assignment would materially change the duty of the other party, or increase materially the burden or risk imposed on him by his contract, or impair materially his chance of obtaining return performance. A right to damages for breach of the whole contract or a right arising out of the assignors due performance of his entire obligation can be assigned despite agreement otherwise.

(3) Unless the circumstances indicate the contrary, a prohibition of assignment of the contract is to be construed as barring only the delegation to the assignee of the assignors performance.

(4) An assignment of the contract or of all my rights under the contract or an assignment in similar general terms is an assignment of rights and, unless the language or the circumstances (as in an assignment for security) indicate the contrary, it is a delegation of performance of the duties of the assignor, and its acceptance by the assignee constitutes a promise by him to perform those duties. This promise is enforceable by either the assignor or the other party to the original contract.

(5) The other party may treat any assignment which delegates performance as creating reasonable grounds for insecurity and may without prejudice to his rights against the assignor demand assurances from the assignee (Section 2 609).

Part 3 General Obligation and Construction of Contract

§2 301. General Obligations of Parties

The obligation of the seller is to transfer and deliver and that of the buyer is to accept and pay in accordance with the contract.

§2 302. Unconscionable Contract or Clause

(1) If the court as a matter of law finds the contract or any clause of the contract to have been unconscionable at the time it was made, the court may refuse to enforce the contract, or it may enforce the remainder of the contract without the unconscionable clause, or it may so limit the application of any unconscionable clause as to avoid any unconscionable result.

(2) When it is claimed or appears to the court that the contract or any clause thereof may be unconscionable, the parties shall be afforded a reasonable opportunity to present evidence as to its commercial setting, purpose and effect to aid the court in making the determination.

§2 303. Allocation or Division of Risks

Where this Article allocates a risk or a burden as between the parties unless otherwise agreed, the agreement may not only shift the allocation but may also divide the risk or burden.

§2 305. Open Price Term

(1) The parties, if they so intend, can conclude a contract for sale even though the price is not settled. In such a case, the price is a reasonable price at the time for delivery if

    (a) nothing is said as to price; or

    (b) the price is left to be agreed by the parties and they fail to agree; or

    (c) the price is to be fixed in terms of some agreed market or other standard as set or recorded by a third person or agency and it is not so set or recorded.

(2) A price to be fixed by the seller or by the buyer means a price for him to fix in good faith.

(3) When a price left to be fixed otherwise than by agreement of the parties fails to be fixed through fault of one party, the other may at his option treat the contract as canceled or himself fix a reasonable price.

(4) Where, however, the parties intend not to be bound unless the price be fixed or agreed and it is not fixed or agreed, there is no contract. In such a case, the buyer must return any goods already received or if unable so to do must pay their reasonable value at the time of delivery and the seller must return any portion of the price paid on account.

§2 306. Output, Requirements and Exclusive Dealings

(1) A term which measures the quantity by the output of the seller or the requirements of the buyer means such actual output or requirements as may occur in good faith, except that no quantity unreasonably disproportionate to any stated estimate or in the absence of a stated estimate to any normal or otherwise comparable prior output or requirements may be tendered or demanded.

(2) A lawful agreement by either the seller or the buyer for exclusive dealing in the kind of goods concerned imposes, unless otherwise agreed, an obligation by the seller to use best efforts to supply the goods and by the buyer to use best efforts to promote their sale.

§2 312. Warranty of Title and Against Infringement; Buyers Obligation Against Infringement

(1) Subject to subsection (2), there is in a contract for sale a warranty by the seller that

(a) the title conveyed shall be good, and its transfer rightful; and

(b) the goods shall be delivered free from any security interest or other lien or encumbrance of which the buyer at the time of contracting has no knowledge.

(2) A warranty under subsection (1) will be excluded or modified only by specific language or by circumstances which give the buyer reason to know that the person selling does not claim title in himself or that he is purporting to sell only such right or title as he or a third person may have.

(3) Unless otherwise agreed a seller who is a merchant regularly dealing in goods of the kind warrants that the goods shall be delivered free of the rightful claim of any third person by way of infringement or the like but a buyer who furnishes specifications to the seller must hold the seller harmless against any such claim which arises out of compliance with the specifications.

§2 313. Express Warranties by Affirmation, Promise, Description, Sample

(1) Express warranties by the seller are created as follows:

(a) Any affirmation of fact or promise made by the seller to the buyer which relates to the goods and becomes part of the basis of the bargain creates an express warranty that the goods shall conform to the affirmation or promise.

(b) Any description of the goods which is made part of the basis of the bargain creates an express warranty that the goods shall conform to the description.

(c) Any sample or model which is made part of the basis of the bargain creates an express warranty that the whole of the goods shall conform to the sample or model.

(2) It is not necessary to the creation of an express warranty that the seller use formal words such as warrant or guarantee or that he have a specific intention to make a warranty, but an affirmation merely of the value of the goods or a statement purporting to be merely the sellers opinion or commendation of the goods does not create a warranty.

§2 314. Implied Warranty; Merchantability; Usage of Trade

(1) Unless excluded or modified (Section 2 316), a warranty that the goods shall be merchantable is implied in a contract for their sale if the seller is a merchant with respect to goods of that kind. Under this section, the serving for value of food or drink to be consumed either on the premises or elsewhere is a sale.

(2) Goods to be merchantable must be at least such as

(a) pass without objection in the trade under the contract description; and

(b) in the case of fungible goods, are of fair average quality within the description; and

(c) are fit for the ordinary purposes for which such goods are used; and

(d) run, within the variations permitted by the agreement, of even kind, quality and quantity within each unit and among all units involved; and

(e) are adequately contained, packaged, and labeled as the agreement may require; and

(f) conform to the promises or affirmations of fact made on the container or label if any.

(3) Unless excluded or modified (Section 2 316), other implied warranties may arise from course of dealing or usage of trade.

§2 315. Implied Warranty: Fitness for Particular Purpose

Where the seller at the time of contracting has reason to know any particular purpose for which the goods are required and that the buyer is relying on the sellers skill or judgment to select or furnish suitable goods, there is unless excluded or modified under the next section an implied warranty that the goods shall be fit for such purpose.

§2 326. Sale on Approval and Sale or Return; Consignment Sales and Rights of Creditors

(1) Unless otherwise agreed, if delivered goods may be returned by the buyer even though they conform to the contract, the transaction is

(a) a sale on approval if the goods are delivered primarily for use, and

(b) a sale or return if the goods are delivered primarily for resale.

(2) Except as provided in subsection (3), goods held on approval are not subject to the claims of the buyers creditors until acceptance; goods held on sale or return are subject to such claims while in the buyers possession.

(3) Where goods are delivered to a person for sale and such person maintains a place of business at which he deals in goods of the kind involved, under a name other than the name of the person making delivery, then with respect to claims of creditors of the person conducting the business the goods are deemed to be on sale or return. The provisions of this subsection are applicable even though an agreement purports to reserve title to the person making delivery until payment or resale or uses such words as on consignment or on memorandum. However, this sub-section is not applicable if the person making delivery

(a) complies with an applicable law providing for a consignors interest or the like to be evidenced by a sign, or

(b) establishes that the person conducting the business is generally known by his creditors to be substantially engaged in selling the goods of others, or

(c) complies with the filing provisions of the Article on secured Transactions (Article 9).

(4) Any or return term of a contract for sale is to be treated as a separate contract for sale within the statute of frauds section of this Article (Section 2 201) and as contradicting the sale aspect of the contract within the provisions of this Article on parol or extrinsic evidence (Section 2 202).

§2 327. Special Incidents of Sale on Approval and Sale or Return

(1) Under a sale on approval, unless otherwise agreed

(a) although the goods are identified to the contract, the risk of loss and the title do not pass to the buyer until acceptance; and

(b) use of the goods consistent with the purpose of trial is not acceptance but failure seasonably to notify the seller of election to return the goods is acceptance, and if the goods conform to the contract acceptance of any part is acceptance of the whole; and

(c) after due notification of election to return, the return is at the sellers risk and expense but a merchant buyer must follow any reasonable instructions.

(2) Under a sale or return, unless otherwise agreed

(a) the option to return extends to the whole or any commercial unit of the goods while in substantially their original condition, but must be exercised seasonably; and

(b) the return is at the buyers risk and expense.

Part 4 Title, Creditors and Good Faith Purchasers
§2 401. Passing of Title; Reservation for Security; Limited Application of This Section

Each provision of this Article with regard to the rights, obligations and remedies of the seller, the buyer, purchasers or other third parties applies irrespective of title to the goods except where the provision refers to such title. Insofar as situations are not covered by the other provisions of this Article and matters concerning title become material the following rules apply:

(1) Title to goods cannot pass under a contract for sale prior to their identification to the contract (Section 2 501), and unless otherwise explicitly agreed the buyer acquires by their identification a

special property as limited by this Act. Any retention or reservation by the seller of the title (property) in goods shipped or delivered to the buyer is limited in effect to a reservation of a security interest. Subject to these provisions and to the provisions of the Article on Secured Transactions (Article 9), title to goods passes from the seller to the buyer in any manner and on any conditions explicitly agreed on by the parties.

(2) Unless otherwise explicitly agreed, title passes to the buyer at the time and place at which the seller completes his performance with reference to the physical delivery of the goods, despite any reservation of security interest and even though a document of title is to be delivered at a different time or place; and in particular and despite any reservation of a security interest by the bill of lading

    (a) if the contract requires or authorizes the seller to send the goods to the buyer but does not require him to deliver them at destination, title passes to the buyer at the time and place of shipment; but

    (b) if the contract requires delivery at destination, title passes on tender there.

(3) Unless otherwise explicitly agreed, where delivery is to be made without moving the goods,

    (a) if the seller is to deliver a document of title, title passes at the time when and the place where he delivers such documents; or

    (b) if the goods are at the time of contracting already identified and no documents are to be delivered, title passes at the time and place of contracting.

(4) A rejection or other refusal by the buyer to receive or retain the goods, whether or not justified, or a justified revocation of acceptance revests title to the goods in the seller. Such revesting occurs by operation of law and is not a sale.

§2 403. Power to Transfer; Good Faith Purchase of Goods; Entrusting

(1) A purchaser of goods acquires all title which his transferor had or had power to transfer except that a purchaser of a limited interest acquires rights only to the extent of the interest purchased. A person with voidable title has power to transfer a good title to a good faith purchaser for value. When goods have been delivered under a transaction of purchase, the purchaser has such power even though

    (a) the transferor was deceived as to the identity of the purchaser, or

    (b) the delivery was in exchange for a check which is later dishonored, or

    (c) it was agreed that the transaction was to be a cash sale or

    (d) the delivery was procured through fraud punishable as larcenous under the criminal law.

(2) Any entrusting of possession of goods to a merchant who deals in goods of that kind gives him power to transfer all rights of the entruster to a buyer in ordinary course of business.

(3) Entrusting includes any delivery and any acquiescence in retention of possession regardless of any condition expressed between the parties to the delivery or acquiescence and regardless of whether the procurement of the entrusting or the possessors disposition of the goods have been such as to be larcenous under the criminal law.

(4) The rights of other purchasers of goods and of lien creditors are governed by the Articles on Secured Transactions (Article 9), Bulk Transfers (Article 6) and Documents of Title (Article 7).

Part 5 Performance

§2 501. Insurable Interest in Goods; Manner of Identification of Goods

(1) The buyer obtains a special property and an insurable interest in goods by identification of existing goods as goods to which the contract refers even though the goods so identified are nonconforming and he has an option to return or reject them. . . .

(2) The seller retains an insurable interest in goods so long as title to or any security interest in the goods remains in him; and where the identification is by the seller alone, he may until default or insolvency or notification to the buyer that the identification is final substitute other goods for those identified.

. . .

§2 503. Manner of Sellers Tender of Delivery

(1) Tender of delivery requires that the seller put and hold conforming goods at the buyers disposition and give the buyer any notification reasonably necessary to enable him to take delivery. The manner, time and place for tender are determined by the agreement and this Article, and in particular

(a) tender must be at a reasonable hour, and, if it is of goods, they must be kept available for the period reasonably necessary to enable the buyer to take possession; but

(b) unless otherwise agreed, the buyer must furnish facilities reasonably suited to the receipt of the goods.

(2) Where the case is within the next section respecting shipment, tender requires that the seller comply with its provisions.

(3) Where the seller is required to deliver at a particular destination, tender requires that he comply with subsection (1) and also, in any appropriate case, tender documents as described in subsections (4) and (5) of this section.

(4) Where goods are in the possession of a bailee and are to be delivered without being moved

(a) tender requires that the seller either tender a negotiable document of title covering such goods or procure acknowledgment by the bailee of the buyers right to possession of the goods; but

(b) tender to the buyer of a nonnegotiable document of title or of a written direction to the bailee to deliver is sufficient tender unless the buyer seasonably objects, and receipt by the bailee of notification of the buyers rights fixes those rights as against the bailee and all third persons; but risk of loss of the goods and of any failure by the bailee to honor the nonnegotiable document of title or to obey the direction remains on the seller until the buyer has had a reasonable time to present the document or direction, and a refusal by the bailee to honor the document or to obey the direction defeats the tender.

(5) Where the contract requires the seller to deliver documents

(a) he must tender all such documents in correct form, except as provided in this Article with respect to bills of lading in a set (subsection (2) of Section 2 323); and

(b) tender through customary banking channels is sufficient and dishonor of a draft accompanying the documents constitutes nonacceptance or rejection.

§2 504. Shipment by Seller

Where the seller is required or authorized to send the goods to the buyer and the contract does not require him to deliver them at a particular destination, then, unless otherwise agreed, he must

(a) put the goods in the possession of such a carrier and make such a contract for their transportation as may be reasonable having regard to the nature of the goods and other circumstances of the case; and

(b) obtain and promptly deliver or tender in due form any document necessary to enable the buyer to obtain possession of the goods or otherwise required by the agreement or by usage of trade; and

(c) promptly notify the buyer of the shipment.

Failure to notify the buyer under paragraph (c) or to make a proper contract under paragraph (a) is a ground for rejection only if material delay or loss ensues.

§2 508. Cure by Seller of Improper Tender or Delivery; Replacement

(1) Where any tender or delivery by the seller is rejected because nonconforming and the time for performance has not yet expired, the seller may seasonably notify the buyer of his intention to cure and may then within the contract time make a conforming delivery.

(2) Where the buyer rejects a nonconforming tender which the seller had reasonable grounds to believe would be acceptable with or without money allowance, the seller may if he seasonably notifies the buyer have a further reasonable time to substitute a conforming tender.

§2 509. Risk of Loss in the Absence of Breach

(1) Where the contract requires or authorizes the seller to ship the goods by carrier

(a) if it does not require him to deliver them at a particular destination, the risk of loss passes to the buyer when the goods are duly delivered to the carrier even though the shipment is under reservation (Section 2 505); but

(b) if it does require him to deliver them at a particular destination and the goods are there duly tendered while in the possession of the carrier, the risk of loss passes to the buyer when the goods are there duly so tendered as to enable the buyer to take delivery.

(2) Where the goods are held by a bailee to be delivered without being moved, the risk of loss passes to the buyer

(a) on his receipt of a negotiable document of title covering the goods; or

(b) on acknowledgment by the bailee of the buyers right to possession of the goods; or

(c) after his receipt of a nonnegotiable document of title or other written direction to deliver, as provided in subsection (4)(b) of Section 2 503.

(3) In any case not within subsection (1) or (2), the risk of loss passes to the buyer on his receipt of the goods if the seller is a merchant; otherwise the risk passes to the buyer on tender of delivery.

(4) The provisions of this section are subject to contrary agreement of the parties and to the provisions of this Article on sale on approval (Section 2 327) and on effect of breach on risk of loss (Section 2 510).

§2 510. Effect of Breach on Risk of Loss

(1) Where a tender or delivery of goods so fails to conform to the contract as to give a right of rejection, the risk of their loss remains on the seller until cure or acceptance.

(2) Where the buyer rightfully revokes acceptance, he may to the extent of any deficiency in his effective insurance coverage treat the risk of loss as having rested on the seller from the beginning.

(3) Where the buyer, as to conforming goods al-ready identified to the contract for sale, repudiates or is otherwise in breach before risk of their loss has passed to him, the seller may to the extent of any deficiency in his effective insurance coverage treat the risk of loss as resting on the buyer for a commercially reasonable time.

Part 6 Breach, Repudiation and Excuse

§2 601. Buyers Rights on Improper Delivery

Subject to the provisions of this Article on breach in installment contracts (Section 2 612) and unless otherwise agreed under the sections on contractual limitations of remedy (Sections 2 718 and 2 719), if the goods or the tender of delivery fail in any respect to conform to the contract, the buyer may

(a) reject the whole; or

(b) accept the whole; or

(c) accept any commercial unit or units and reject the rest.

§2 602. Manner and Effect of Rightful Rejection

(1) Rejection of goods must be within a reasonable time after their delivery or tender. It is ineffective unless the buyer seasonably notifies the seller.

(2) Subject to the provisions of the two following sections on rejected goods (Sections 2 603 and 2 604),

(a) after rejection any exercise of ownership by the buyer with respect to any commercial unit is wrongful as against the seller; and

(b) if the buyer has before rejection taken physical possession of goods in which he does not have a security interest under the provisions of this Article (subsection (3) of Section 2 711), he is under a duty after rejection to hold them with reasonable care at the sellers disposition for a time sufficient to permit the seller to remove them; but

(c) the buyer has no further obligations with regard to goods rightfully rejected.

(3) The sellers rights with respect to goods wrongfully rejected are governed by the provisions of this Article on Sellers remedies in general (Section 2 703).

§2 605. Waiver of Buyers Objections by Failure to Particularize

(1) The buyers failure to state in connection with

rejection a particular defect which is ascertainable by reasonable inspection precludes him from relying on the unstated defect to justify rejection or to establish breach

(a) where the seller could have cured it if stated seasonally; or

(b) between merchants when the seller has after rejection made a request in writing for a full and final written statement of all defects on which the buyer proposes to rely.

(2) Payment against documents made without reservation of rights precludes recovery of the payment for defects apparent on the face of the documents.

§2 606. What Constitutes Acceptance of Goods

(1) Acceptance of goods occurs when the buyer

(a) after a reasonable opportunity to inspect the goods signifies to the seller that the goods are conforming or that he will take or retain them in spite of their nonconformity; or

(b) fails to make an effective rejection (subsection (1) of Section 2 602), but such acceptance does not occur until the buyer has had a reasonable opportunity to inspect them; or

(c) does any act inconsistent with the sellers ownership; but if such act is wrongful as against the seller it is an acceptance only if ratified by him.

(2) Acceptance of a part of any commercial unit is acceptance of that entire unit.

§2 607. Effect of Acceptance; Notice of Breach; Burden of Establishing Breach After Acceptance; Notice of Claim or Litigation to Person Answerable Over

(1) The buyer must pay at the contract rate for any goods accepted.

(2) Acceptance of goods by the buyer precludes rejection of the goods accepted and if made with knowledge of a nonconformity cannot be revoked because of it unless the acceptance was on the reasonable assumption that the nonconformity would be seasonably cured but acceptance does not of itself impair any other remedy provided by this Article for nonconformity.

(3) Where a tender has been accepted

(a) the buyer must within a reasonable time after he discovers or should have discovered any breach notify the seller of breach or be barred from any remedy; and

(b) if the claim is one for infringement or the like (subsection (3) of Section 2 312) and the buyer is sued as a result of such a breach, he must so notify the seller within a reasonable time after he receives notice of the litigation or be barred from any remedy over for liability established by the litigation.

(4) The burden is on the buyer to establish any breach with respect to the goods accepted.

(5) Where the buyer is sued for breach of a warranty or other obligation for which his seller is answerable over

(a) he may give his seller written notice of the litigation. If the notice states that the seller may come in and defend and that if the seller does not do so he will be bound in any action against him by his buyer by any determination of fact common to the two litigations, then unless the seller after seasonable receipt of the notice does come in and defend he is so bound.

(b) if the claim is one for infringement or the like (subsection (3) of Section 2 312), the original seller may demand in writing that his buyer turn over to him control of the litigation including settlement or else be barred from any remedy over and if he also agrees to bear all expense and to satisfy any adverse judgment, then unless the buyer after seasonable receipt of the demand does turn over control the buyer is so barred.

(6) The provisions of subsections (3), (4) and (5) apply to any obligation of a buyer to hold the seller harmless against infringement or the like (subsection (3) of Section 2 312).

§2 608. Revocation of Acceptance in Whole or in Part

(1) The buyer may revoke his acceptance of a lot or commercial unit whose nonconformity substantially impairs its value to him if he has accepted it

(a) on the reasonable assumption that its non-conformity would be cured and it has not been seasonably cured; or

(b) without discovery of such nonconformity if his acceptance was reasonably induced either by the difficulty of discovery before acceptance or by the sellers assurances.

(2) Revocation of acceptance must occur within a reasonable time after the buyer discovers or should have discovered the ground for it and before any substantial change in condition of the goods which is not caused by their own defects. It is not effective until the buyer notifies the seller of it.

(3) A buyer who so revokes has the same rights and duties with regard to the goods involved as if he had rejected them.

§2 615. Excuse by Failure of Presupposed Conditions

Except so far as a seller may have assumed a greater obligation and subject to the preceding section on substituted performance:

(a) Delay in delivery or nondelivery in whole or in part by a seller who complies with paragraphs (b) and (c) is not a breach of his duty under a contract for sale if performance as agreed has been made impracticable by the occurrence of a contingency the nonoccurrence of which was a basic assumption on which the contract was made or by compliance in good faith with any applicable foreign or domestic governmental regulation or order whether or not it later proves to be invalid.

(b) Where the causes mentioned in paragraph (a) affect only a part of the sellers capacity to perform, he must allocate production and deliveries among his customers but may at his option include regular customers not then under contract as well as his own requirements for further manufacture. He may so allocate in any manner which is fair and reasonable.

(c) The seller must notify the buyer seasonably that there will be delay or nondelivery and, when allocation is required under paragraph (b), of the estimated quota thus made available for the buyer.

Part 7 Remedies
§2 701. Remedies for Breach of Collateral Contracts Not Impaired

Remedies for breach of any obligation or promise collateral or ancillary to a contract for sale are not impaired by the provisions of this Article.

§2 706. Sellers Resale Including Contract for Resale

. . . The seller may resell the goods concerned or the undelivered balance thereof. Where the resale is made in good faith and in a commercially reasonable manner, the seller may recover the difference between the resale price and the contract price together with any incidental damages allowed under the provisions of this Article (Section 2 710), but less expenses saved in consequence of the buyers breach.

(2) Except as otherwise provided in subsection (3) or unless otherwise agreed, resale may be at public or private sale including sale by way of one or more contracts to sell or of identification to an existing contract of the seller. Sale may be as a unit or in parcels and at any time and place and on any terms but every aspect of the sale including the method, manner, time, place and terms must be commercially reasonable. The resale must be reasonably identified as referring to the broken contract, but it is not necessary that the goods be in existence or that any or all of them have been identified to the contract before the breach.

(3) Where the resale is at private sale, the seller must give the buyer reasonable notification of his intention to resell.

(4) Where the resale is at public sale

(a) only identified goods can be sold except where there is a recognized market for a public sale of futures in goods of the kind; and

(b) it must be made at a usual place or market for public sale if one is reasonably available and except in the case of goods which are perishable or threaten to decline in value speedily the seller must give the buyer reasonable notice of the time and place of the resale; and

(c) if the goods are not to be within the view of those attending the sale, the notification of sale must state the place where the goods are located and provide for their reasonable inspection by prospective bidders; and

(d) the seller may buy.

(5) A purchaser who buys in good faith at a resale takes the goods free of any rights of the original buyer even though the seller fails to comply with one or more of the requirements of this section.

(6) The seller is not accountable to the buyer for any profit made on any resale. . . .

§2 711. Buyers Remedies in General; Buyers Security Interest in Rejected Goods

(1) Where the seller fails to make delivery or repudiates or the buyer rightfully rejects or justifiably revokes acceptance, then with respect to any goods involved, and with respect to the whole if the breach goes to the whole contract (Section 2 612), the buyer may cancel and whether or not he has done so may in addition to recovering so much of the price as has been paid

(a) cover and have damages under the next section as to all the goods affected whether or not they have been identified to the contract; or

(b) recover damages for nondelivery as provided in this Article (Section 2 713).

(2) Where the seller fails to deliver or repudiates, the buyer may also

(a) if the goods have been identified recover them as provided in this Article (Section 2 502); or

(b) in a proper case obtain specific performance or replevy the goods as provided in this Article (Section 2 716).

(3) On rightful rejection or justifiable revocation of acceptance, a buyer has a security interest in goods in his possession or control for any payments made on their price and any expenses reasonably incurred in their inspection, receipt, transportation, care and custody and may hold such goods and resell them in like manner as an aggrieved seller (Section 2 706).

§2 712. Cover; Buyers Procurement of Substitute Goods

(1) After a breach within the preceding section, the buyer may cover by making in good faith and without unreasonable delay any reasonable purchase of or contract to purchase goods in substitution for those due from the seller.

(2) The buyer may recover from the seller as damages the difference between the cost of cover and the contract price together with any incidental or consequential damages as hereinafter defined (Section 2 715), but less expenses saved in consequence of the sellers breach.

(3) Failure of the buyer to effect cover within this section does not bar him from any other remedy.

§2 713. Buyers Damages for Nondelivery or Repudiation

(1) Subject to the provisions of this Article with respect to proof of market price (Section 2 723), the measure of damages for nondelivery or repudiation by the seller is the difference between the market price at the time when the buyer learned of the breach and the contract price together with any incidental and consequential damages provided in this Article (Section 2 715), but less expenses saved in consequence of the sellers breach.

(2) Market price is to be determined as of the place for tender or, in cases of rejection after arrival or revocation of acceptance, as of the place of arrival.

§2 714. Buyers Damages for Breach in Regard to Accepted Goods

(1) Where the buyer has accepted goods and given notification (subsection (3) of Section 2 607), he may recover as damages for any nonconformity of tender the loss resulting in the ordinary course of events from the sellers breach as determined in any manner which is reasonable.

(2) The measure of damages for breach of warranty is the difference at the time and place of acceptance between the value of the goods accepted and the value they would have had if they had been as warranted, unless special circumstances show proximate damages of a different amount.

(3) In a proper case any incidental and consequential damages under the next section may also be recovered.

§2 715. Buyers Incidental and Consequential Damages

(1) Incidental damages resulting from the sellers breach include expenses reasonably incurred in inspection, receipt, transportation and care and custody of goods rightfully rejected, any commercially reasonable charges, expenses or commissions in connection with effecting cover and any other reasonable expense incident to the delay or other breach.

(2) Consequential damages resulting from the sellers breach include

(a) any loss resulting from general or particular requirements and needs of which the seller at the time of contracting had reason to know and which could not reasonably be prevented by cover or otherwise; and

(b) injury to person or property proximately resulting from any breach of warranty.

§2 719. Contractual Modification or Limitation of Remedy

(1) . . .

(a) the agreement may provide for remedies in addition to or in substitution for those provided in this Article and may limit or alter the measure of damages recoverable under this Article, as by limiting the buyers remedies to return of the goods and repayment of the price or to repair and replacement of nonconforming goods or parts; and

(b) resort to a remedy as provided is optional unless the remedy is expressly agreed to be exclusive, in which case it is the sole remedy.

(2) Where circumstances cause an exclusive or limited remedy to fail of its essential purpose, remedy may be had as provided in this Act.

(3) Consequential damages may be limited or excluded unless the limitation or exclusion is unconscionable. Limitation of consequential damages for injury to the person in the case of consumer goods is prima facie unconscionable but limitation of damages where the loss is commercial is not.

§2 725. Statute of Limitations in Contracts for Sale

(1) An action for breach of any contract for sale must be commenced within four years after the cause of action has accrued. By the original agreement, the parties may reduce the period of limitation to not less than one year but may not extend it.

(2) A cause of action accrues when the breach occurs, regardless of the aggrieved parties lack of knowledge of the breach. A breach of warranty occurs when tender of delivery is made, except that where a warranty explicitly extends to future performance of the goods and discovery of the breach must await the time of such performance the cause of action accrues when the breach is or should have been discovered.

. . .

Article 2A

Leases
Part 1 General Provisions
§2A 103. Definitions and Index of Definitions

(1) In this Article unless the context otherwise requires:

. . .

(e) "Consumer lease" means a lease that a lessor regularly engaged in the business of leasing or selling makes to a lessee, except an organization, who takes under the lease primarily for a personal, family, or household purpose, if the total payments to be made under the lease contract, excluding payments for options to renew or buy, do not exceed $25,000.

. . .

(g) "Finance lease" means a lease in which (i) the lessor does not select, manufacture or supply the goods, (ii) the lessor acquires the goods or the right to possession and use of the goods in connection with the lease, and (iii) either the lessee receives a copy of the contract evidencing the lessors purchase of the goods on or before signing the lease contract, or the lessees approval of the contract evidencing the lessors purchase of the goods is a condition to effectiveness of the lease contract.

. . .

(j) "Lease" means a transfer of the right to possession and use of goods for a term in return for consideration, but a sale, including a sale on approval or a sale or return, or retention or creation of a security interest is not a lease. Unless the context clearly indicates otherwise, the term includes a sublease.

(k) "Lease agreement" means the bargain, with respect to the lease, of the lessor and the lessee in fact as found in their language or by implication from other circumstances including course of dealing or usage of trade or course of performance as provided in this Article. Unless the context clearly indicates otherwise, the term includes a sublease agreement.

(l) "Lease contract" means the total legal obligation that results from the lease agreement as affected by this Article and any other applicable rules of law. Unless the context clearly indicates otherwise, the term includes a sublease contract.

. . .

(o) "Lessee in ordinary course of business" means a person who in good faith and without knowledge that the lease to him [or her] is in violation of the ownership rights or security interest or leasehold interest of a third party in the goods leases in ordinary course from a person in the business of selling or leasing goods of that kind but does not include a pawnbroker. Leasing may be for cash or by exchange of other property or on secured or unsecured credit and includes receiving goods or documents of title under a pre-existing lease contract but does not include a transfer in bulk or as security for or in total or partial satisfaction of a money debt.

. . .

(t) "Merchant lessee" means a lessee that is a merchant with respect to goods of the kind subject to the lease.

§2A 106. Limitation on Power of Parties to Consumer Lease to Choose Applicable Law and Judicial Forum

(1) If the law chosen by the parties to a consumer lease is that of a jurisdiction other than a jurisdiction in which the lessee resides at the time the lease agreement becomes enforceable or within 30 days thereafter or in which the goods are to be used, the choice is not enforceable.

(2) If the judicial forum chosen by the parties to a consumer lease is a forum that would not otherwise have jurisdiction over the lessee, the choice is not enforceable.

Part 2 Formation and Construction of Lease Contract

§2A 209. Lessee Under Finance Lease as Beneficiary of Supply Contract

(1) The benefit of the suppliers promises to the lessor under the supply contract and of all warranties, whether express or implied, under the supply contract, extends to the lessee to the extent of the lessees leasehold interest under a finance lease related to the supply contract, but subject to the terms of the supply contract and all of the suppliers defenses or claims arising therefrom.

(2) The extension of the benefit of the suppliers promises and warranties to the lessee (Section 2A 209(1)) does not: (a) modify the rights and obligations of the parties to the supply contract, whether arising therefrom or otherwise, or (b) impose any duty or liability under the supply contract on the lessee.

(3) Any modification or rescission of the supply contract by the supplier and the lessor is effective against the lessee unless, prior to the modification or rescission, the supplier has received notice that the lessee has entered into a finance lease related to the supply contract. If the supply contract is modified or rescinded after the lessee enters the finance lease, the lessee has a cause of action against the lessor, and against the supplier if the supplier has notice of the lessees entering the finance lease when the supply contract is modified or rescinded. The lessees recovery from such action shall put the lessee in as good a position as if the modification or rescission had not occurred.

§2A 210. Express Warranties

(1) Express warranties by the lessor are created as follows:

(a) Any affirmation of fact or promise made by

the lessor to the lessee which relates to the goods and becomes part of the basis of the bargain creates an express warranty that the goods will conform to the affirmation or promise.

(b) Any description of the goods which is made part of the basis of the bargain creates an express warranty that the goods will conform to the description.

(c) Any sample or model that is made part of the basis of the bargain creates an express warranty that the whole of the goods will conform to the sample or model.

(2) It is not necessary to the creation of an express warranty that the lessor use formal words, such as warrant or guarantee, or that the lessor have a specific intention to make a warranty, but an affirmation merely of the value of the goods or a statement purporting to be merely the lessors opinion or commendation of the goods does not create a warranty.

§2A 219. Risk of Loss

(1) Except in the case of a finance lease, risk of loss is retained by the lessor and does not pass to the lessee. In the case of a finance lease, risk of loss passes to the lessee.

(2) Subject to the provisions of this Article on the effect of default on risk of loss (Section 2A 220), if risk of loss is to pass to the lessee and the time of passage is not stated the following rules apply:

(a) If the lease contract requires or authorizes the goods to be shipped by carrier

(i) and it does not require delivery at a particular destination, the risk of loss passes to the lessee when the goods are duly delivered to the carrier; but

(ii) if it does require delivery at a particular destination and the goods are there duly tendered while in the possession of the carrier, the risk of loss passes to the lessee when the goods are there duly so tendered as to enable the lessee to take delivery.

(b) If the goods are held by a bailee to be delivered without being moved, the risk of loss passes to the lessee on acknowledgment by the bailee of the lessees right to possession of the goods.

(c) In any case not within subsection (a) or (b), the risk of loss passes to the lessee on the lessees receipt of the goods if the lessor, or, in the case of a finance lease, the supplier, is a merchant: otherwise the risk passes to the lessee on tender of delivery.

§2A 220. Effect of Default on Risk of Loss

(1) Where risk of loss is to pass to the lessee and the time of passage is not stated:

(a) If a tender or delivery of goods so fails to conform to the lease contract as to give a right of rejection, the risk of their loss remains with the lessor, or, in the case of a finance lease, the supplier, until cure or acceptance.

(b) If the lessee rightfully revokes acceptance, he [or she], to the extent of any deficiency in his [or her] effective insurance coverage, may treat the risk of loss as having remained with the lessor from the beginning.

(2) Whether or not risk of loss is to pass to the lessee, if the lessee as to conforming goods already identified to a lease contract repudiates or is otherwise in default under the lease contract, the lessor, or, in the case of a finance lease, the supplier, to the extent of any deficiency in his [or her] effective insurance coverage may treat the risk of loss as resting on the lessee for a commercially reasonable time.

§2A 221. Casualty to Identified Goods

If a lease contract requires goods identified when the lease contract is made, and the goods suffer casualty without fault of the lessee, the lessor or the supplier before delivery, or the goods suffer casualty before risk of loss passes to the lessee pursuant to the lease agreement or Section 2A 219, then:

(a) if the loss is total, the lease contract is avoided; and

(b) if the loss is partial or the goods have so deteriorated as to no longer conform to the lease contract, the lessee may nevertheless demand inspection and at his [or her] option either treat the lease contract as avoided or, except in a finance lease that is not a consumer lease, accept the goods with due allowance from the rent payable for the balance of the lease term for the deterioration or the deficiency in quantity but without further right against the lessor.

Part 3 Effect of Lease Contract

§2A 301. Enforceability of Lease Contract

Except as otherwise provided in this Article, a lease contract is effective and enforceable according to its terms between the parties, against purchasers of the goods, and against creditors of the parties.

§2A 303. Alienability of Parties Interest Under Lease Contract or of Lessors Residual Interest in Goods; Delegation of Performance; Assignment of Rights

(1) Any interest of a party under a lease contract and the lessors residual interest in the goods may be transferred unless

(a) the transfer is voluntary and the lease contract prohibits the transfer; or

(b) the transfer materially changes the duty of or materially increases the burden or risk imposed on the other party to the lease contract, and within a reasonable time after notice of the transfer the other party demands that the transferee comply with subsection (2) and the transferee fails to comply.

(2) Within a reasonable time after demand pursuant to subsection (1)(b), the transferee shall:

(a) cure or provide adequate assurance that he [or she] will promptly cure any default other than one arising from the transfer;

(b) compensate or provide adequate assurance that he [or she] will promptly compensate the other party to the lease contract and any other person holding an interest in the lease contract, except the party whose interest is being transferred, for any loss to that party resulting from the transfer;

(c) provide adequate assurance of future due performance under the lease contract; and

(d) assume the lease contract.

(3) Demand pursuant to subsection (1)(b) is without prejudice to the other parties rights against the transferee and the party whose interest is transferred.

(4) An assignment of the lease or of all my rights under the lease or an assignment in similar general terms is a transfer of rights, and unless the language or the circumstances, as in an assignment for security, indicate the contrary, the assignment is a delegation of duties by the assignor to the assignee and acceptance by the assignee constitutes a promise by him [or her] to perform those duties. This promise is enforceable by either the assignor or the other party to the lease contract.

(5) Unless otherwise agreed by the lessor and the lessee, no delegation of performance relieves the assignor as against the other party of any duty to perform or any liability for default.

(6) A right to damages for default with respect to the whole lease contract or a right arising out of the assignors due performance of his [or her] entire obligation can be assigned despite agreement otherwise.

(7) To prohibit the transfer of an interest of a party under a lease contract, the language of prohibition must be specific, by a writing, and conspicuous.

§2A 304. Subsequent Lease of Goods by Lessor

(1) Subject to the provisions of Section 2A 303, a subsequent lessee from a lessor of goods under an existing lease contract obtains, to the extent of the leasehold interest transferred, the leasehold interest in the goods that the lessor had or had power to transfer, and except as provided in subsection (2) and Section 2A 527(4), takes subject to the existing lease contract. A lessor with voidable title has power to transfer a good leasehold interest to a good faith subsequent lessee for value, but only to the extent set forth in the preceding sentence. When goods have been delivered under a transaction of purchase the lessor has that power even though:

(a) the lessors transferor was deceived as to the identity of the lessor;

(b) the delivery was in exchange for a check which is later dishonored;

(c) it was agreed that the transaction was to be a cash sale; or

(d) the delivery was procured through fraud punishable as larcenous under the criminal law.

(2) A subsequent lessee in the ordinary course of business from a lessor who is a merchant dealing in goods of that kind to whom the goods were entrusted by the existing lessee before the interest of the subsequent lessee became enforceable against the lessor obtains, to the extent of the leasehold interest transferred, all of the lessors and the existing lessees rights to the goods, and takes free of the existing lease contract.

(3) A subsequent lessee from the lessor of goods that are subject to an existing lease contract and are covered by a certificate of title issued under a statute of this State or of another jurisdiction takes no greater rights than those provided both by this section and by the certificate of title statute.

§2A 305. Sale or Sublease of Goods by Lessee

(1) Subject to the provisions of Section 2A 303, a buyer or sublessee from the lessee of goods under an existing lease contract obtains, to the extent of the interest transferred, the leasehold interest in the goods that the lessee had or had power to transfer, and except as provided in subsection (2) and Section 2A 511(4), takes subject to the existing lease contract. A lessee with a voidable leasehold interest has power to transfer a good leasehold interest to a good faith buyer for value or a good faith sublessee for value, but only to the extent set forth in the preceding sentence. When goods have been delivered under a transaction of lease the lessee has that power even though:

(a) the lessor was deceived as to the identity of the lessee;

(b) the delivery was in exchange for a check which is later dishonored; or

(c) the delivery was procured through fraud punishable as larcenous under the criminal law.

(2) A buyer in the ordinary course of business or a sublessee in the ordinary course of business from a lessee who is a merchant dealing in goods of that kind to whom the goods were entrusted by the lessor obtains, to the extent of the interest transferred, all of the lessors and lessees rights to the goods, and takes free of the existing lease contract.

(3) A buyer or sublessee from the lessee of goods that are subject to an existing lease contract and are covered by a certificate of title issued under a statute of this State or of another jurisdiction takes no greater rights than those provided both by this section and by the certificate of title statute.

Part 4 Performance of Lease Contract: Repudiated, Substituted and Excused

§2A 401. Insecurity: Adequate Assurance of Performance

(1) A lease contract imposes an obligation on each party that the others expectation of receiving due performance will not be impaired.

(2) If reasonable grounds for insecurity arise with respect to the performance of either party, the insecure party may demand in writing adequate assurance of due performance.

. . .

(4) Between merchants, the reasonableness of grounds for insecurity and the adequacy of any assurance offered must be determined according to commercial standards.

(5) Acceptance of any nonconforming delivery or payment does not prejudice the aggrieved parties right to demand adequate assurance of future performance.

§2A 407. Irrevocable Promises: Finance Leases

(1) In the case of a finance lease that is not a consumer lease the lessees promises under the lease contract become irrevocable and independent upon the lessees acceptance of the goods.

(2) A promise that has become irrevocable and independent under subsection (1):

(a) is effective and enforceable between the parties, and by or against third parties including assignees of the parties, and

(b) is not subject to cancellation, termination, modification, repudiation, excuse, or substitution without the consent of the party to whom the promise runs.

Part 5 Default
A. In General
§2A 501. Default: Procedure
(1) Whether the lessor or the lessee is in default under a lease contract is determined by the lease agreement and this Article.

(2) If the lessor or the lessee is in default under the lease contract, the party seeking enforcement has rights and remedies as provided in this Article and, except as limited by this Article, as provided in the lease agreement.

(3) If the lessor or the lessee is in default under the lease contract, the party seeking enforcement may reduce the parties claim to judgment, or otherwise enforce the lease contract by self-help or any available judicial procedure or nonjudicial procedure, including administrative proceeding, arbitration, or the like, in accordance with this Article.

(4) Except as otherwise provided in this Article or the lease Agreement, the rights and remedies referred to in subsections (2) and (3) are cumulative.

(5) If the lease agreement covers both real property and goods, the party seeking enforcement may proceed under this Part as to the goods, or under other applicable law as to both the real property and the goods in accordance with his [or her] rights and remedies in respect of the real property, in which case this Part does not apply.

§2A 502. Notice After Default
Except as otherwise provided in this Article or the lease agreement, the lessor or lessee in default under the lease contract is not entitled to notice of default or notice of enforcement from the other party to the lease agreement.

§2A 503. Modification or Impairment of Rights and Remedies
(1) Except as otherwise provided in this Article, the lease agreement may include rights and remedies for default in addition to or in substitution for those provided in this Article and may limit or alter the measure of damages recoverable under this Article.

(2) Resort to a remedy provided under this Article or in the lease agreement is optional unless the remedy is expressly agreed to be exclusive. If circumstances cause an exclusive or limited remedy to fail of its essential purpose, or provision for an exclusive remedy is unconscionable, remedy may be had as provided in this Article.

. . .

§2A 506. Statute of Limitations
(1) An action for default under a lease contract, including breach of warranty or indemnity, must be commenced within 4 years after the cause of action accrued. By the original lease contract the parties may reduce the period of limitation to not less that one year.

(2) A cause of action for default accrues when the act or omission on which the default or breach of warranty is based is or should have been discovered by the aggrieved party, or when the default occurs, whichever is later. A cause of action for indemnity accrues when the act or omission on which the claim for indemnity is based is or should have been discovered by the indemnified party, whichever is later.

. . .

B. Default by Lessor
§2A 513. Cure by Lessor of Improper Tender or Delivery; Replacement
(1) If any tender or delivery by the lessor or the supplier is rejected because nonconforming and the time for performance has not yet expired, the lessor or the supplier may seasonably notify the lessee of the lessors or the suppliers intention to cure and may then make a conforming delivery within the time provided in the lease contract.

(2) If the lessee rejects a nonconforming tender that the lessor or the supplier had reasonable grounds to believe would be acceptable with or without money allowance, the lessor or the supplier may have a further reasonable time to substitute a conforming tender if he [or she] seasonably notifies the lessee.

§2A 514. Waiver of Lessees Objections
(1) In rejecting goods, a lessees failure to state a particular defect that is ascertainable by reasonable inspection precludes the lessee from relying on the defect to justify rejection or to establish default:

    (a) if, states seasonably, the lessor or the supplier could have cured it (Section 2A 513); or

(b) between merchants if the lessor or the supplier after rejection has made a request in writing for a full and final written statement of all defects on which the lessee proposes to rely.

(2) A lessees failure to reserve rights when paying rent or other consideration against documents precludes recovery of the payment for defects apparent on the face of the documents.

§2A 515. Acceptance of Goods

(1) Acceptance of goods occurs after the lessee has had a reasonable opportunity to inspect the goods and

(a) the lessee signifies or acts with respect to the goods in a manner that signifies to the lessor or the supplier that the goods are conforming or that the lessee will take or retain them in spite of their nonconformity; or

(b) the lessee fails to make an effective rejection of the goods (Section 2A 509(2)).

(2) Acceptance of a part of any commercial unit is acceptance of that entire unit.

§2A 518. Cover; Substitute Goods

(1) After default by a lessor under the lease contract of or contract to purchase or lease goods in substitution for those due from the lessor.

. . .

§2A 519. Lessees Damages for Nondelivery, Repudiation, Default and Breach of Warranty in Regard to Accepted Goods

(1) Except as otherwise provided with respect to damages liquidated in the lease agreement . . . or determined by agreement of the parties (Section 1 102(3)), if a lessee elects not to cover or a lessee elects to cover and the cover . . . is by purchase or otherwise, the measure of damages for non-delivery or repudiation by the lessor or for rejection or revocation of acceptance by the lessee is the present value as of the date of the default of the difference between the then market rent and the original rent, computed for the remaining lease term of the original lease agreement together with incidental and consequential damages, less expenses saved in consequence of the lessors default.

. . .

(4) The measure of damages for breach of warranty is the present value at the time and place of acceptance of the difference between the value of the use of the goods accepted and the value if they had been as warranted for the lease term, unless special circumstances show proximate damages of a different amount, together with incidental and consequential damages, less expenses saved in consequence of the lessors default or breach of warranty.

§2A 520. Lessees Incidental and Consequential Damages

(1) Incidental damages resulting from a lessors default include expenses reasonably incurred in inspection, receipt, transportation, and care and custody of goods rightfully rejected or goods the acceptance of which is justifiably revoked, any commercially reasonable charges, expenses or commissions in connection with effecting cover, and any other reasonable expense incident to the default.

(2) Consequential damages resulting from a lessors default include:

(a) any loss resulting from general or particular requirements and needs of which the lessor at the time of contracting had reason to know and which could not reasonably be prevented by cover or otherwise; and

(b) injury to person or property proximately resulting from any breach of warranty.

C. Default by Lessee

§2A 525. Lessors Right to Possession of Goods

(1) If a lessor discovers the lessee to be insolvent, the lessor may refuse to deliver the goods.

(2) The lessor has on default by the lessee under the lease contract the right to take possession of the goods. If the lease contract so provides, the lessor may require the lessee to assemble the goods and make them available to the lessor at a place to be designated by the lessor which is reasonably convenient to both parties. Without removal, the lessor may render unusable any goods employed in trade or business, and may dispose of goods on the lessees premises (Section 2A 527).

(3) The lessor may proceed under subsection (2) without judicial process if that can be done without

breach of the peace or the lessor may proceed by action.

§2A 527. Lessors Rights to Dispose of Goods

(1) After a default by a lessee under the lease contract of goods . . . , the lessor may dispose of the goods concerned or the undelivered balance thereof by lease, sale or otherwise.

(2) Except as otherwise provided with respect to damages liquidated in the lease agreement . . . or determined by agreement of the parties (Section 1 102(3)), if the disposition is by lease agreement substantially similar to the original lease agreement and the lease agreement is made in good faith and in a commercially reasonable manner, the lessor may recover from the lessee as damages (a) accrued and unpaid rent as of the date of default, (b) the present value as of the date of default of the difference between the total rent for the remaining lease term of the original lease agreement and the total rent for the lease term of the new lease agreement, and (c) any incidental damages allowed under Section 2A 530, less expenses saved in consequence of the lessees default.

. . .

(4) A subsequent buyer or lessee who buys or leases from the lessor in good faith for value as a result of a disposition under this section takes the goods free of the original lease contract and any rights of the original lessee even though the lessor fails to comply with one or more of the requirements of this Article.

(5) The lessor is not accountable to the lessee for any profit made on any disposition. . . .

§2A 529. Lessors Action for the Rent

(1) After default by the lessee under the lease contract . . . , if the lessor complies with subsection (2), the lessor may recover from the lessee as damages:

> (a) for goods accepted by the lessee and for conforming goods lost or damaged within a commercially reasonable time after risk of loss

passes to the lessee . . . , (i) accrued and unpaid rent as of the date of default, (ii) the present value as of the date of default of the rent for the remaining lease term of the lease agreement, and (iii) any incidental damages allowed under Section 2A 530, less expenses saved in consequence of the lessees default; and

> (b) for goods identified to the lease contract if the lessor is unable after reasonable effort to dispose of them at a reasonable price or the circumstances reasonably indicate that effort will be unavailing, (i) accrued and unpaid rent as of the date of default, (ii) the present value as of the date of default of the rent for the remaining lease term of the lease agreement, and (iii) any incidental damages allowed under Section 2A 530, less expenses saved in consequence of the lessees default.

(2) Except as provided in subsection (3), the lessor shall hold for the lessee for the remaining lease term of the lease agreement any goods that have been identified to the lease contract and are in the lessors control.

(3) The lessor may dispose of the goods at any time before collection of the judgment for damages obtained pursuant to subsection (1). . . .

(4) Payment of the judgment for damages obtained pursuant to subsection (1) entitles the lessee to use and possession of the goods not then disposed of for the remaining lease term of the lease agreement.

. . .

§2A 530. Lessors Incidental Damages

Incidental damages to an aggrieved lessor include any commercially reasonable charges, expenses, or commissions incurred in stopping delivery, in the transportation, care and custody of goods after the lessees default, in connection with return or disposition of the goods, or otherwise resulting from the default.

ANSWERS TO CHAPTER-END QUESTIONS

CHAPTER 1

1. Constitutions, statutes, judicial law, common law, administrative regulations, executive orders, treaties.
2. **Legal positivism**—Law is determined by a sovereign. **Legal realism**—The law should follow what people actually do, rather than what people establish as written law.
   Natural Law—Certain laws of nature exist, and all laws passed must be in conformity with those principles. **Sociological theory of law**—Law should reflect a balance between the competing, constantly shifting interests of society.
3. Precedent means decisions previously rendered by a court. Stare decisis is the theory requiring that precedent be used to determine the outcome in cases like the one presently before the court at the moment.
4. Executive, legislative, judicial.
5. b.
6. Substantive, procedural.
7. Jettie's attorney would likely bring a negligence action against Ratliff Shipping Inc. and Bunn. While Bunn was the one driving the truck, he was doing so while in the scope of employment with Ratliff Shipping, and therefore Ratliff Shipping would be vicariously liable. Jettie would allege that Bunn had a duty to meet a reasonable standard of care for someone driving prudently behind another person and failed to meet that duty when he rear-ended her. She would further allege that his failure was the proximate cause of her injuries.
8. Bill and Ann can find out what agency is issuing the regulations, what type of opportunity to be heard is being provided, and participate in that process.

They may not change the ultimate outcome, but they will have given their input.
9. Law is an absolute that must be obeyed or it is violated. Equity is not a set of absolutes, but rather a balancing of the equities of the specific situation.
   There must be a violation of law alleged to go to a court of law for relief. There need not be a violation of law to go to a court of equity.
   Jury trials are generally permitted in actions at law. They generally are not in a court of equity.
10. True.
11. a.
12. No.

CHAPTER 2

1. c.
2. False. Due process does not apply to most private situations, but rather to actions by the government.
3. True. Congress does not have police power, yet by using its power over transportation funds, it can withhold funds from states that do not raise the drinking age to 21.
4. Yes, the city can legally pass the prohibition on 24-hour businesses under its police power. Chris and Linda can try fighting the law by demonstrating that it is not rationally related to the city's goal of keeping down police protection costs; by showing that keeping down police protection costs is not a legitimate state interest; by showing that there are other, less intrusive ways to accomplish the goal if the goal is found to be legitimate; by showing that the classifications make little or no sense, because bars are allowed to stay open, when, in fact, given the nature of their business, they do not provide the necessary kind of service that health care facilities and gas stations do.

5. a.

6. preempted

7. No. The power of the federal government to tax is often used as a means for the government to do indirectly what it cannot do directly. Here, the government could likely not constitutionally require employers to do what it is requesting, yet it may encourage them to do so by providing financial incentives that employers can take or leave, as they see fit. This is permissible.

8. It depends. Because this is a regulation promulgated by an administrative agency, certain rules must be complied with in promulgation. State administrative agencies generally operate under administrative procedures acts, just as the federal government agencies do. Among other things, such administrative procedures ensure that due process is kept intact when the regulatory function is taken on by an administrative agency. If the reason that Drew's knew nothing of the regulation was not inattention but that the regulation was promulgated without following proper procedures, Drew's may have an argument for denial of due process if the agency did not provide due process by some sort of notice and an opportunity to be heard. This is often provided by notice through the state's counterpart to the *Federal Register*, generally called the state register.

9. Because the ordinance affects business, the challenge to the ordinance based on a denial of equal protection would be analyzed under the rational basis test. Under the test, if the state can show that the ordinance is rationally related to achieving its statutory purpose, then it will be allowed. This is so even if the ordinance is not necessarily the best approach to the issue of decreasing domestic violence. If it is debatable, based on all the considerations of the governing body in considering the issue, it will be upheld. Even though viewing the games in places such as churches, private homes, and schools could also cause domestic violence,

10. The state's police power is very broad. Under it the state has the authority to enact legislation that regulates the health, safety, welfare and morals of its citizens. Here the ordinance did not ban televisions in commercial establishments altogether, but, rather, only at times during which research indicated caused an increase in domestic violence. As such, the ordinance would probably stand.

CHAPTER 3

1. Civil cases are brought by the party injured, for money damages (generally); no jail or prison time is involved; the initiator of the suit pays for it; and the burden of proof is generally a preponderance of the evidence. Criminal cases are brought by the state for punishment of the perpetrator by jail, prison time, and/or fines; the state pays for the suit; and the burden of proof is beyond a reasonable doubt.

2. No, Regine's advice is not good advice. If the perpetrator is prosecuted, it generally does not result in money damages for the victim, but, rather, in prison time for the perpetrator. If Khadizha wishes to receive compensation for her injuries, she must sue the perpetrator in a civil suit.

3. Yes, the fishing industry can engage in regulatory negotiation to try to get the fishers together with the agency administrators to have them hash out some of their differences before the regulation is promulgated.

4. Xie may attempt to conciliate the claim, may have someone mediate the claim, may have someone arbitrate the claim, or may sue Monty in small claims court. All of these options are much less expensive than a full-fledged lawsuit against Monty.

5. Preponderance-of-the-evidence standard used in more serious civil cases, rather than a preponderance of the evidence.

6. No, she will likely not be successful in striking the prospective jurors for cause, because the connection between the cause she alleges and the predisposition of bias she alleges is too tenuous and too many people use computers to allege that they all feel the same way.

7. Ralph's attorney is correct. Although the claim is basically a state personal injury claim, the federal court has diversity of citizenship jurisdiction because the case involves more than $50,000 in damages and the two parties are from different states.

8. No. Barton suffers no compensable injury, because he was able to get virtually the same car at another dealer for the same price. Nominal damages are appropriate here to recognize that a breach has occurred, but no compensatory damages were needed.

9. No. When there is a panel of arbitrators, the majority wins and the award is just as valid as if it were unanimous.

10. Since the sewing machine is unique and irreplaceable, Dawn is in need of equitable remedies rather than money damages. Money damages would be inadequate, because the heirloom sewing machine cannot be replaced. The equitable remedy available would most likely be specific performance to get the repairer to get the machine back and deliver it to Dawn as agreed.

11. False. The jury returns with a verdict. Judgments come from judges.

12. b.

CHAPTER 4

1. Students should recall local events.

2. An ultra vires act is one that is outside the life of the corporation. Therefore it is not directly related to the making of profit for the shareholders. That concept has eroded, however. Today it is legal to make charitable contributions and do other things that are not directly profit related. Once enforced by the courts, today it is rarely enforced.

3. Utilitarianism is the doctrine of the greatest good for the greatest number. It makes one consider how others will be affected. Goodwill requires that the categorical imperative always be followed, without regard to consequence.

4. The suggestion to decrease the amount of lather would appear to "fail" each of the tests. The suggestion to decrease the size of the bottle slightly would also appear to "fail" all three of the tests. However, because consumers can read labels, they could "price" the product by the ounce. However, the attempt appears to make the decrease in size unnoticeable, which is questionable.

5. Ethics are important because a company can lose its reputation, causing decreased sales. Acts that are unethical may also be illegal, leading to jail terms and fines for managers, who will be disgraced.

6. There are many possibilities. It is still legal to emit low amounts of many substances into the air even though such substances may be known carcinogens. Pending regulation, these substances can be legally, though probably not ethically, emitted.

7. If we apply the three tests, we see that it might yield the greatest good for the greatest number. It is arguable that students could concentrate in class, instead of trying to take notes. Those who were ill could get good notes. Those with learning disabilities would have good notes. On the downside, some students will simply sleep or go to the beach and use the notes as a crutch, but overall the service could be positive. The professor would lose out on the ability to teach those students who fail to attend class because of the availability of the notes. It might also cause discomfort in the class, because obviously, the lone student taking copious notes would draw the wrath of the professor. Also, it discriminates against poorer students who can't afford the service. Students should note that this type of service is, in fact, available on many campuses. It is used at some medical schools and law schools.

8. Students discuss their own personal considerations.

9. Students discuss their own personal considerations.

10. Students discuss their own personal considerations.

CHAPTER 5

1. Because the act was an accident rather than an intentional tort and because it was not the serious type of activity prohibited by most strict liability statutes, E.J. and the client will likely sue Roscoe for negligence. They will allege that Roscoe failed to act as a reasonable person by erecting such a thing in his yard, where, even though there was a 10-×-10-foot screen, balls would likely go over or around the screen. Roscoe injured them because of his failure to meet the standard of a reasonable person under the circumstances. Roscoe will likely defend by alleging he used reasonable care by erecting the mesh screen. He would have to show that the screen was of a size and type which generally would provide enough protection from the type of action that occurred. If Roscoe can show that he used reasonable care and met the appropriate standard, he would likely not be held liable for the injuries.

2. Probably not. Cindy saw that the rope appeared to be too weak for the glass, yet because she did not want to be late for work, she took the risk of going under the glass rather than around it. Even though Botticelli was using rope that was too weak for the job, Cindy voluntarily assumed the risk of going under the glass that was being held by a weak-looking rope she thought could break, and therefore Botticelli would not be liable. Botticelli was wrong in creating the risk, but Cindy knew of the risk and voluntarily assumed it.

3. Yes. In this situation, Cindy may be able to show that the Botticelli workers were negligent in not having enough precautions to protect the glass from falling if a worker had to temporarily let go of the glass (such as a pulley system or more rope). However, Botticelli would be able to show contributory negligence on the part of Cindy, in her pinching of the worker. If it is not a comparative negligence jurisdiction, Cindy would not recover, for her contributory negligence would constitute a complete defense to Botticelli's negligence. If it is a comparative negligence jurisdiction, the amount Cindy would receive would be decreased by an amount equal to the percentage of negligence attributable to Cindy.

4. Yes. Ann and Bill are strictly liable for all the damage caused by their keeping Bessie, a wild animal. It does not matter that Ann and Bill had a trainer, used a tame animal with a history of performing under similar circumstances, or had Bessie chained. Because Bessie is a wild animal and Bill and Ann used her for their promotion, they are strictly liable for the harm she does, and therefore the precautions they took are irrelevant. Workers' compensation considerations aside, Ann and Bill would also be liable to Linda for the heart attack she suffered as a result of Bessie's actions.

5. False. Battery is a charge involving harm to a person, not to property, and it is an intentional tort, not a negligence or strict liability offense. If anything, the claim might be for trespass to personal property, but there is still the question of intent.

6. b, battery—an intentional, unpermitted touching. Because an assault charge results from putting someone in fear or apprehension of an immediate bodily touching, Matthew cannot use that charge, because he was asleep and therefore not in fear or apprehension of an immediate bodily touching. Maria's act would likely not be considered outrageous enough to constitute the tort of intentional infliction of emotional distress. Intrusion upon seclusion requires the tortfeasor to go into a private space in some way. That would likely not apply here because they were on a bus. The better answer is battery. Because Maria did not have permission for the intentional kiss and Matthew did not want it or consent to it, the requirements are met.

7. It depends. If on one hand it appeared that the store had a reasonable basis for suspecting Ceilie, held her for a reasonable time, and treated her in a reasonable manner, she will lose. If, on the other hand, it can be shown that the suspicion was unreasonable or that the time limit or manner of treatment was unreasonable, Ceilie will win. The basketball-looking stomach may be reasonable. Holding Ceilie for three hours could be reasonable if the store can show that because of personnel deficiencies or an influx of customers at the time, it could not get to the matter in less time. As for the way in which Ceilie was approached, it was unreasonable. There was no reason Ceilie should have been approached in a way that presumed she had stolen the ball and was unwilling to cooperate if approached correctly. She need not have been grabbed and yelled at unless someone actually saw her steal the ball and put it under her clothing. Even then such an approach is questionable. Because the shopkeeper's rule was not complied with, the shopkeeper lost the defense to false imprisonment, and Ceilie wins. Based on a true situation.

8. *Trespass to personal property.* By taking home the Purvis truck, Carlton is interfering with the possession and use of Purvis's personal property. However, because Carlton brings the truck back every morning, Purvis would likely not want to bring an action for conversion, which is the more serious offense. If Purvis did, he would be forcing Carlton to buy the truck in that Carlton would have to pay Purvis the value of the truck and Purvis would have to convey the truck to Carlton. Because that would serve no purpose here, Purvis's action would likely be for trespass.

9. No. Under the theory of respondeat superior, Bill and Ann are liable for the torts committed by their employees in the scope of employment. They would therefore be responsible for Robert's injuries.

10. Another name for injurious falsehood is *disparagement.*

11. Manuel can sue Deborah for theft of trade secrets. Manuel must show that he took steps to keep the trade secret and that Deborah violated that by sneaking in to watch him, then taking the recipe and using it for her own commercial ends.

12. The contractor probably will not be strictly liable for Mariko's injuries. The strict liability category is generally reserved for activities that are so dan-

gerous until the care the tortfeasor takes in conducting the activity does not matter in recovering for the tort. Here, building a house is not so dangerous an activity that anyone injured at the site can recover. Mariko may be able to recover in negligence, but not on the basis of strict liability.

13. No, it is not a breach of contract for a person involved in a contract not to permit subsequent additions to the contract that would modify the original agreement. If the contractor does not wish to contract to do anything other than what was in the original contract, that is permissible. Mariko's only legal recourse is to get someone else to perform the work and try to get the original contractor to agree to allow someone else to come in and do what Mariko wants done.

CHAPTER 6

1. Yes. This contract is required to be in writing under the Statute of Frauds because it is incapable of being performed within a year from the time it is made. Although the actual period of performance was January to September—less than a year, the contract was formed in July 1994, and that is when the time starts to run for Statute of Frauds purposes. Because the contract is from July 1994 to September 1995, it is incapable of being completed within a year from the time it was made and is therefore required to be in writing in order to be enforced.

2. Chris loses, because gambling is illegal in the state, and therefore it is illegal to contract to gamble. Because the contract is illegal, it is void and has no force or effect; therefore, when Chris sues for breach of contract, because there is no contract, she loses.

3. a. Illegal contracts are void.

4. Because the contract is void, the court will leave the parties where it finds them and thus not enforce the contract.

5. Sheffield wins. If Sheffield can show that the events happened as they did and Gloria mailed the acceptance before she faxed the rejection, then the acceptance, which would be effective when sent, would have created a contract as soon as Gloria mailed it on the 6th. The acceptance is effective when sent, even if it is late or lost. This scenario

should not be confused with an acceptance *after* a prior rejection. There, the first to reach the offeror wins. Here, the acceptance was sent first, rather than the rejection, so the mailbox rule governs.

6. Johnson wins. The Parol Evidence Rule will not allow Weinstein to bring in evidence to show that the contract was different from what was written in the contract. Weinstein wants to use the phone conversation to establish that the agreed-upon color was different from the delivered color. However, because the contract was written and integrated and the agreement reached before the contract was signed, the oral evidence of the phone conversation will not be permitted to vary or alter the terms of the written agreement.

7. Bill and Ann win. There is no consideration to support Ann and Bill's promise to pay Ku the $50,000, and therefore the promise is not enforceable. The consideration, helping Ann and Bill to get the account, was past consideration and therefore not good consideration to support their promise.

8. b, a promise for a promise is a bilateral contract.

9. Prevention. Jekyll's nonperformance will be excused if Hyde, with whom he contracted, prevented him from performing.

10. Alice has the right to train at The Biceps Store. She has been assigned a contract by Sarafina. Because the assignment does not require any change in what The Bicep Store must do, in that it is not more burdensome for the store to allow Alice to come than for Sarafina to come, and the contract is not too personal, The Bicep Store must honor the assignment and perform the contract for Alice. Alice steps into the shoes of Sarafina and is entitled to whatever Sarafina would have been entitled to under the contract.

CHAPTER 7

1. Regional organizations.

2. A custom is a principle or practice that has developed over a course of dealing and is so well recognized that it becomes binding on the parties to the custom.

3. If the political situation in the country to be exported to is unstable, Rondon should be concerned about the possibility of nationalization, expropria-

tion, or confiscation of its goods within that country. Expropriation is the taking of the business by the government. Nationalization is having the government run the business once it is taken. In confiscation, the government takes the property and does not compensate the owner.

4. Suellen should consider how it is she wishes to do business in Rwanda. She must consider whether she will be able to come into the country and operate on her own or whether the laws of the country require her, as a foreigner, to operate only as a part of a joint venture in concert with a Rwandan citizen. She must also think about how she will control what goes on in her Rwandan factory and how she will deal with her Rwandan producers to maintain their efficiency and productivity.

5. Ling Tsu's biggest concern should probably focus on keeping control over the licensing agreement to ensure that the licensing agreement is complied with and not used in unintended ways not compensated for. It should also be a concern that the secret of the paint used for the cartoon design is not given to a competitor of Ling Tsu's.

6. The better type of exporting company for MicroCorp to use would be an export trading company. Such a company handles more types of products and takes title to the goods while they are still in the United States, giving the seller (MicroCorp) the cash it needs even before the goods are actually sold. Export management companies handle smaller amounts of goods and fewer types of products while allowing the seller to retain title to the goods while the goods are still in the United States.

7. c, dumping.

8. d, franchise.

9. d, all of the above.

10. False. The purpose of the GATT is to permit the smooth and efficient exportation of goods between countries that are signatories to the GATT. The signatory nations receive most-favored-nation status, which ensures a fair level of tariffs.

CHAPTER 8

1. Usually, a general partner faces unlimited personal liability for partnership contracts, debts, and torts committed within the scope of the partnership. This liability is said to be joint and several (with the other general partners). In the case of a registered, limited liability partnership, a general partner is not held personally and unlimitedly liable for the debts, obligations, and liabilities chargeable to the partnership arising from negligence, wrongful acts, or misconduct committed in the scope of the partnership business by another partner or an employee, agent, or representative of the partnership. A general partner is, of course, liable for his or her own negligence, wrongful acts, or misconduct or that of a person under the general partner's direct supervision and control. Thus, being a partner in a registered, limited liability partnership is much safer than engaging in the other forms of partnership.

2. Generally, shareholders in corporations are said to have limited liability, in that they face liability only up to the amount of their capital contribution or investment. The corporate veil may be pierced, causing shareholders who participate in management to face unlimited personal liability. Normally, the corporate veil will not be set aside absent wrongful conduct by majority shareholder(s) which amounts to "illegal domination, looting, or failing to treat the corporation as a separate legal entity (alter ego)."

3. A fiduciary duty is the highest duty under the law. It requires honesty and loyalty. It generally runs from an agent to a principal, from a majority shareholder to minority shareholders, and from the Board of Directors to the corporation and its shareholders.

4. No. There may be several things that can be done for the minority shareholders. Preemptive rights, cumulative voting rights, inspection rights, and appraisal rights are all rights that minority shareholders can exercise, if provided by the corporate structure.

5. False. The laws are not made to protect the public from being dumb. Rather, they are to ensure that members of the public have all necessary information available to them before making an investment decision. If they still want to invest in a dumb scheme after knowing all the facts, they are free to do so. Securities laws are basically disclosure laws. It is believed that disclosure of material information about a security and its issuer will allow an opportunity for reasonable investors to make more intelligent investment decisions. Compliance with securities laws does not indicate that any particular security is a good or safe investment.

6. Intrastate exemption (Rule 147); small offering under Reg. A and D (Rule 504); Reg. D. (Rule 505/506)

7. Periodic reports (10K, 10Q and 8K), proxy solicitations (section 14), tender offers (section 13), fraud and insider trading (Rule 10-b-5), and short swing trades (section 16).

8. The FCPA covers payments made to foreign concerns or governments. Bribes are made a violation of the act. "Grease" payments are not illegal, but must be disclosed. In addition, covered corporations must have internal controls in place to account for the disposition of corporate assets.

9. Yes. If the directors carefully analyzed the appropriate information before investing in the venture and the venture turned out badly anyway, Arturo can use the business judgment rule as protection. It covers decisions made in the ordinary course of business by corporate boards of directors and allows them to be protected in making business decisions for the corporation that turn out badly.

10. The factors involved in choice of legal form are the nature and classification of the business that affect the risk of the owners. When there is great potential for risk, a business form providing limited liability will generally be preferable. The tax code and rates in effect will also affect the choice of business form. In addition, management control, need for capital (both financial and human), transferability of interests, and duration of the business are also important factors.

11. Students should discuss the nature of the business and the risk of liability. It appears that because other people's homes and pets are involved, there would be some risks. If each of the business participants wishes to minimize risk due to the others' negligence, then they should select a limited liability company, a limited liability partnership, or a corporation. According to the tax rates, it would appear that the limited liability company, the limited liability partnership, and an S corporation would allow taxation as a partnership. The C corporation would be subject to double taxation.

CHAPTER 9

1. The common law provides protection when a business can prove exclusive use over an extended period of time such that the name has acquired secondary meaning in the minds of consumers and such that use by another company would cause confusion for consumers.

The Lanham Act provides statutory protection for business names that are distinctive or have secondary meaning.

Incorporation provides statewide protection.

2. No, Ziggy is not correct. Zoning laws are part of land-use plans enacted by governments that restrict the types of places and the locations that businesses and homes can locate.

They are a restriction on land even if it is held singly as a fee simple absolute.

3. The business must be able to store and arrange for disposal of whatever wastes it generates. Therefore, the location must be accessible and not restricted by zoning or other legal impediments.

4. The ADA requires that businesses be accessible to the disabled. Thus a business must take accessibility requirements into account when selecting a location. There are tax credits available to help defray the costs of renovation.

5. First, the equipment will probably be repossessed. It will then be sold. The proceeds will be applied to the outstanding balance. The costs of collection will be deducted and the remainder, if any, paid to the debtor.

If a deficiency remains, the debtor will be held liable in the capacity in which the debtor signed. Therefore, if the debtor signed only as a representative of a corporation, he will not be personally liable. A debtor who is a sole proprietor or partner is personally liable, irrespective of the representative capacity. A partner may even be held liable even without having signed it, if the debt was incurred by another of the partners and was within the scope of the partnership.

6. The bulk transfer laws are applicable when a business is sold as a going concern (with stock, inventory, and equipment).

Basically Article 6 requires notice to a seller's creditors so that they may take steps to protect themselves. The buyer will be liable to creditors not notified.

7. Bankruptcy is a legal proceeding in federal court under which debtors who are not paying bills as bills fall due can petition to be discharged from

their debts. Chapter 7 is known as straight bankruptcy; under it, assets will be sold and proceeds, if any, paid to creditors.

Chapter 11 is open to businesses to reorganize or to negotiate the sale of a going concern.

Chapter 13 is known as wage earner bankruptcy and is available to wage earners and self-employed persons. It involves the use of a plan to pay off creditors over an extended period—similar to a composition of creditors.

8. A business license is a revenue producing license imposed by local governments as a requirement to conduct business within the governmental territorial limits.

9. One who is jointly and severally liable can be made to pay the entire indebtedness. If so, one is entitled to contribution from the others who are also jointly liable.

In law, the word *several* means individual.

10. Ann and Bill have the right to sue Lumpkin for breach of the implied warranties that arose upon the sale of the products to them. The warranty of merchantability provides that when a merchant seller (one who deals in goods of that kind) sells a product, the product should be fit for its ordinary purpose. This warranty is imposed by law unless disclaimed or excluded by the seller. Here, because the scrubbing pad and handle came off the scrubber when it was used, the product is not fit for its ordinary purpose and Ann and Bill can recover damages caused by breach of the warranty.

The cleaning product was given to Bill and Ann specifically at their request for something to clean gasoline off floors. Thus the product was supposed to be able to do this, and it did not. Here a buyer tells a seller the purpose for which the buyer seeks goods, relying on the seller's expertise to furnish or select the goods. Therefore there is a warranty that the goods shall be fit for the particular purpose of the buyer. In this case, the product did not perform as promised, so Ann and Bill can recover for breach of implied warranty of fitness for a particular purpose.

11. A franchise is an agreement whereby a franchisee contracts the rights to sell or market goods or services under the name of the franchisor.

McDonald's, Subway, and Burger King

12. Kimmis is correct. The 1933 Securities Act requires that unless the issue falls under an exemption, the issue must be registered. Registration is a disclosure of material information about the corporation, its board of directors, and its officers. One of the exemptions provided by law is for intrastate securities. There is no need for Kimmis to register the securities if the stock issued will be purchased by residents of the same state where the company is incorporated, the stock is issued, the issuer does 80% of its business, 80% of its assets are located, and 80% of the proceeds from the sale of the stock will be used. The residents will not be able to resell the stock for a nine-month period.

CHAPTER 10

1. No. Joyce and Jacqui are partners, and the contracts they both entered into under the scope of the partnership will bind the other.

2. Brendan will likely sue both Snears Department Store; Ray's employer, who is vicariously liable for torts committed by Ray in the course of his employment; and Ray, the tortfeasor. Although there can only be one recovery, it is in Brendan's best interest to sue both parties.

3. c.

4. True. Independent contractors are responsible for their own torts. The principal who hires them is not.

5. No, Christoff will probably not win. As an at-will employee, Christoff can be dismissed by his employer for virtually any reason that does not violate law, including having an affair with the boss's wife.

6. If Christoff is a member of a union, his termination is governed by the collective bargaining agreement between the union and management, and Christoff would not therefore be an at-will employee.

7. Respondeat superior.

8. Vernessa's claim against Nicole for defamation may well succeed. Employers and ex-employers have a limited privilege to disclose information about employees or ex-employees to prospective employers. However, in order to be successful in using the privilege as a defense in a defamation action, employers must see the privilege correctly. The information provided for the prospective employer must come as the result of an inquiry in the regular

course of business and through regular business channels. Because such was not the case here, and instead was the result of social chitchat, Nicole may lose both the privilege and the case, if all other salient defamation elements are proved.

9. LaToya has no wrongful termination cause of action, because her employer can terminate her for any reason as long as it did not violate law. If LaToya can demonstrate that the employer's policy adversely impacts females and is not justifiable as being work related, she may be able to bring a claim under her state's or the federal antidiscrimination statute.

10. Diarr will likely win because it will probably be found that he is being terminated in violation of the workers' compensation statute, which provides protection against employers' retaliating against employees who pursue their rights under workers' compensation laws. Diarr's employment may be at will, but his termination may not violate laws set forth to protect employees. Such laws limit the at-will employer's right to terminate at will.

CHAPTER 11

1. Deb's employer is correct. Under the FMLA, an employee cannot take time off to care for the parent of a spouse, though Deb would be able to take time off to care for her own parent.

2. Michael wins. OSHA contains antiretaliation provisions that protect employees who report violations to the agency.

3. Charmaine's argument carries no weight. Under workers' compensation regulations, the cause of the injury is not at issue. It is a no-fault system, and therefore defenses are neither necessary nor of any consequence.

4. The steward is incorrect. Under the duty-of-fair representation clause, though it is not defined in the law, it has been held that all members of the bargaining unit are entitled to fair representation by the union whether or not they are members of the union.

5. No, the employees are not correct. The FLSA does not establish a maximum time employees can work in a week, but, rather, requires that any hours worked over 40 be paid at the rate of time and a half.

6. union shop.

7. c.

8. No. This is not an unfair labor practice. Management is promising the employees nothing, but, rather, giving its opinion as to what happens in the presence of a unionized workplace. This is permissible.

9. Employers can cut their workers' compensation costs by:
   • ensuring that the workplace is safe in order to minimize accidents
   • training employees in safety matters
   • ascertaining whether claims filed are actually the result of covered injuries, that is, accidents arising out of, or in the course of, business
   • having employees monitor each other for unsafe practices
   • getting employees back to work as quickly as possible

10. No. In order to be the subject of an unfair labor practice, management's refusal to bargain must be over a mandatory subject of bargaining such as wages or hours.

CHAPTER 12

1. d, disparate treatment, because the policy is facially discriminatory in that the company does not hire females.

2. Yes. Because this policy is directed only to African-American firefighters, it constitutes race discrimination in a term or condition of employment, in violation of Title VII. The captain's speculation that white firefighters will not wish to sleep on the black firefighter's bed is not a defense to the action.

3. California, Connecticut, Hawaii, Maine, Massachusetts, Minnesota, New Jersey, Vermont, and Wisconsin.

4. Yes. Richard has a cause of action under the ADEA for age discrimination if that is the reason for the superintendent's decision. We know Richard must be older than 40—the minimum age for application of the ADEA—because he retired from the post office after 35 years. We do not know how much older than 40 he is, and it does not matter, because the important consideration is not his age, but whether he can perform the job. If Richard is able to do the job, it is a violation of the ADEA if he is not hired

simply because someone thinks he may be too old.

5. Yes. Pablo has instituted a voluntary affirmative action plan; however, the chances of its withstanding a reverse discrimination attack are slim. In order for Pablo's plan to withstand judicial scrutiny when challenged by the African-Americans and Hispanics who are not now able to apply for the next 20 slots Pablo has open, Pablo would have to demonstrate that his plan was instituted to address a historical underrepresentation of whites in the workplace, that the plan did not unnecessarily trammel the interests of the nonwhite employees, the the 20 slots chosen were connected to the difference between the percentage of whites available in the area drawn from and the percentage of whites in Pablo's workforce, and that the plan was for the purpose of attaining rather than maintaining the goal percentage. If whites are not historically underrepresented in the workplace or if the goals are not related to their availability in the area drawn from, then Pablo's plan, well intentioned though it may be, will fail.

6. Yes, Suardana has violated Title VII by refusing to hire Christians. Under Title VII, Suardana has a duty to try to accommodate the religious conflicts employees or applicants have. If accommodation attempts fail and there is no other choice except not hiring the Christian applicants, Suardana will have done his duty under Title VII. However, Suardana cannot make a decision to simply not hire any Christians and not provide the attempted accommodation.

7. Debbie can sue Jay's for gender discrimination if Jay's employs 15 or more employees. If not, she may be able to sue under her state fair employment practice statute if the limit is lower. Even though Jay need not hire Debbie if she cannot perform the necessary duties for the job, Jay must allow Debbie to try out for the job, rather than assume she cannot do it simply because she is a female.

8. No. At least not for simply asking that question. If the interchange was done in a suggestive way, or if Roger touched Laurabeth, or if Roger engages in a continual barrage of such comments, it might meet the requirements of sexual harassment. As it is, his behavior does not appear to be severe or pervasive or unduly intrusive such that it meets the requirements of sexual harassment. The fact that Roger is a coworker rather than a supervisor would not mean Laurabeth could not charge him with sexual harassment if his acts met the requirements.

9. No. The BFOQ must be reasonably necessary to the essence of the employer's business. In this case, the business involves the safe transportation of passengers from one point to another. Being female is not a BFOQ for that.

10. False. Anyone who fills a job should be qualified to do so. Affirmative action is appropriate only when there has been a finding of underrepresentation of women and minorities and a reasoned attempt to bring them into the workplace.

CHAPTER 13

1. Dawn will likely tell Aunt Ruth that the library administrators are invading her privacy. The library's use of the information for the nebulous reason of "seeing if they form any pattern" is not sufficient to justify its intrusion into Ruth's privacy concerning the books and videos she checks out.

2. No. Because Kurlen will have access to the hospital's drugs and pharmaceuticals, it is within the hospital's needs to have such a drug test for this type of personnel and thus would probably not be held as an unwarranted invasion of privacy. Of course, the hospital must keep the test results private. In addition, because of the possibility of unauthorized use of the hospital's drug supply, it is probably justifiable for the hospital to require drug tests for this position.

3. False. Unless state law actually prohibits such laws, there is nothing to keep an employer from providing such benefits.

4. Randall should consider the gender implications of the decision he reaches with regard to parenting conflicts. While parenting is not a protected category under federal and most state fair employment practice laws, because females tend to take on the parenting role to a greater extent than males when it comes to workplace conflicts, Randall should ensure that whatever decision he reaches does not have adverse gender implications. He should also ensure that he treats male parents the same or comparably to female parents.

5. The employer's interest in having a drug-free and alcohol-free workplace against the employee's right

to privacy and constitutional Fifth Amendment protection against self-incrimination.

6. Probably b, flextime because as one of the family providers, Julian would likely want to have his full-time job (and therefore job sharing would not meet his needs). If Julian were to become a temporary employee, he would lose the benefits and seniority on his job, which he likely would not wish to have happen now that he has a child. A support group interested in the issue of work and family conflicts may help Julian better handle his conflicting feelings, but it would be only a supplement to the work situation that got worked out.

   If the employer did not allow Julian to use one of these options, then the situation could potentially result in illegal discrimination. If it were shown that similarly situated women were allowed some job flexibility after the birth of a child, yet Julian, a male, was not, then such evidence might well violate Title VII or state fair employment practice laws.

7. Christie may win. If it can be shown that the employer did not institute sufficient workplace guidelines and safeguards for maintaining the privacy of employees in a support group it sponsored, then the employer may well be held liable.

8. Whether an employer is required to cover domestic partners under a health care plan depends. On one hand, if the state or local jurisdiction has some type of law prohibiting discrimination in employment on the basis of affinity orientation, then (1) benefits would be an area in which the employer could not discriminate and (2) not extending partner coverage to an employee with a domestic partner may be deemed illegal discrimination in violation of the applicable law. On the other hand, the court could interpret it as not being illegal discrimination in that the law covers only legal spouses and as the two are not legally married, the law does not apply.

9. False. There is no requirement that employers offer such options to employees. However, employees should be aware of the gender implications of not offering such options, that is, that female employees in particular could effectively argue that a policy of not offering the options adversely impacts females, who thus fare less well than males in progressing in the workplace.

10. Yin Su may be able to sue John under Title VII for discrimination on the basis of national origin discrimination. And she may be able to sue John under the state's wrongful termination law if there is one. John is working with an employee from another culture, and he should have apprised himself of the possible cultural differences that may have accounted for Yin Su's actions. Many Asian cultures consider it extremely rude to look into the eyes of another, and just as rude to correct a supervisor even though they may know the supervisor to be is incorrect. Yin Su's actions have been taken as sabotage by John, when, in fact, in Yin Su's culture, they are merely the way one shows respect to a manager. If John had investigated this first, he would have been able to avoid being sued for discrimination by Yin Su—a suit she may well win.

CHAPTER 14

1. Salizar has a pretty good case of violation of the FTC's prohibition of unfair or deceptive advertising and practices through bait-and-switch tactics. Because deceptive practices are construed to be ones that would tend to mislead a substantial number of consumers in a material way and because the likelihood of deception can trigger an action, Salizar would have a good chance of winning his case. LaToya disparaged the advertised item, failed to have sufficient stock of the advertised product without saying it was in limited supply, only reluctantly showed the advertised product, and offered no raincheck.

2. d, the Equal Credit Opportunity Act.

3. It is deceptive advertising, though it may not actually be false. The mouthwash may well kill germs on contact, but there may be no proof that it kills what it is appearing to be referring to: is cold germs. Even though the ad did not actually say it kills cold germs, by having people who appear to be catching a cold gargle with the mouthwash, it makes the connection. This is basically what happened with Listerine mouthwash.

4. Because the sale of the water softener was a door-to-door sale, Yana has the right to rescind the sale within three days from the date of the contract, whether Brooks misled her or not. She doesn't need to have a reason to rescind the sale if she does it within the cooling-off period.

5. Amanda can do nothing under the Truth in Lending Act, for it applies only to consumer credit—defined as credit extended to a consumer primarily for private, family, or household purposes.

6. No, Chaser has not violated the act. The Fair Debt Collection Practices Act does not include a person whose principal business is not debt collection. Chaser is an attorney, not a debt collector.

7. a. There is no guarantee of replacement of defective auto. Generally, lemon laws provide for repair, replacement, or refund, depending on the circumstances.

8. *Buyer's Guide.* Among other things, the *Buyer's Guide* requires specific statement of the warranty information, if any; service contract availability; dealer information; and consumer complaint information.

9. Marcia may be able to get out of paying the phone bill. Under the FTC rule concerning 900 numbers, the 900-number service is required to disclose the cost of the call—if there is a flat fee—or the cost per minute for time-sensitive calls, as well as any maximum charges. If Placido was not notified of this when he made the calls, causing him not to know how expensive they were, it may be the basis for relief. In addition, the service is prohibited from reporting disputed calls to a credit bureau pending the dispute. Here, the service referred the matter to the credit bureau before the dispute was settled. Under the rule, companies offering 900 services are liable for refunds or credits to consumers if they violate the rule, so Marcia and Placido may be relieved from paying.

10. False. Check authorization services are excluded from the Electronic Funds Transfer Act.

CHAPTER 15

1. Life plus 50 years.
2. No. The work is copyrighted upon creation, though registration is necessary to enforce it.
3. Yes. Certification mark is protected intellectual property.
4. She must litigate each case of infringement in order to protect the trademarked name.
5. The copying company is. It is not simply fair use because it is to be used for the whole class, it is not spontaneous, and it hurts the profitability of the copyright holder.

6. No. Tess's idea for the shoe is novel.
7. Maybe. It depends on how similar the dress is. If it leads to consumer confusion, it may be illegal infringement.
8. The publisher. A purchaser of software can copy it only for safety precautions in case it is erased, or to conform it so that it is useful to the purchaser.
9. No. There are no extensions.
10. Joan. It is a commissioned work and therefore belongs to the one it was commissioned for, not the artist.

CHAPTER 16

1. No. As long as the difference in pricing is justifiable by factors like volume discount, the price justification defense can be used by Sabrina and is not illegal price discrimination in violation of the Robinson-Patman Act.
2. No. If a competitor can show that it has lowered its price to below cost in order to meet the competition, then it will not be subject to liability for predatory pricing in violation of antitrust laws.
3. Yes. Because Thomasina inherited the property, she is able to use this as a defense to the law's violation.
4. No. Price fixing and division of territory—both horizontal per se violations—are illegal per se, whether reasonable or not.
5. Probably not, though because it was a bailment for the benefit of the bailee (Tess), Tess had a high duty of care toward the property. She will have to make good on the drink holder accessory, but will not have to get a whole new bike.
6. No. The warranty of merchantability applies only to goods sold by merchants who deal in goods of that kind. Sheila, as far as we know, is not a space heater merchant, and thus that kind of warranty does not attach to this sale.
7. d. It is a sale when title to goods passes to a purchaser, rather than only possession passing to the recipient of property.
8. a. There are not enough facts to allow b and c. Because an implied warranty of merchantability attaches to the sale, a is correct, not d.
9. d. The other statements are representations of fact, but d is puffery.
10. Suing in tort, suing in contract, or going before the professional licensing association.

GLOSSARY

A

absolute privilege privilege given to engage in certain behavior for which no liability attaches regardless of why the behavior is done

acceptance after a prior rejection an offer that is initially rejected, then later accepted by the offeree

acceptance with varied terms UCC concept allowing offeree to vary the terms of the original offer without terminating it

accounting requirement that one who has fiduciary duty to another account for all money entrusted to a fiduciary

act-of-state doctrine a legal doctrine prohibiting the courts of one country from ruling on the legality of the acts of another country

actual authority authority given by a principal to an agent

actual notice direct communication with third parties the agent dealt with to notify them of termination of the agency relationship

administrative law the law that regulates federal and state agencies and how they conduct their business within constitutional guidelines, as well as the body of quasi-legislative enactments of the agency

administrative law judge (ALJ) one who acts as judge in administrative agency hearings

Administrative Procedures Act the federal law governing the operation of agencies to ensure proper due process and uniform conduct of business among the agencies

adversarial system system of litigation in which cases are handled by attorneys on each side of the case who represent the interest of their client

affirmative action intentional inclusion—generally in the workplace—of historically excluded groups such as women and minorities

affirmative action plan a plan developed to intentionally include minorities and females in the workplace after a showing of illegal discrimination or underrepresentation

affirmative defense defense that may defeat the original claim, such as self-defense or assumption of the risk

agent one who acts for and on behalf of another

alternative dispute resolution nonlitigious ways of resolving legal disputes

annual report the yearly report corporations must make to the SEC, with an audited financial statement and other pertinent information, regarding their business transactions

answer defendant's response to plaintiff's complaint

antifemale animus hostile, negative feeling about women—generally exhibited in a workplace

apparent authority the principal's acts that give the appearance that the agent is acting on the principal's behalf

appeal taking a case that has been decided by a court to the next-highest level for a review of the decision

appellant (or petitioner) one who brings an appeal of a lower court decision

appellate court courts above the trial level that hear cases on review from lower courts

appellee (or respondent) one against whom an appeal is sought

appraisal rights the right of a dissenting minority shareholder to vote no in writing and ask to be bought out at fair market value the day before the sale or disposition of assets as voted by the majority

appropriation of name or likeness intentionally using a picture, drawing or name of someone without the person's permission, generally for economic gain or advantage

arbitration mechanism by which disinterested third party hears dispute between parties and makes a decision based on the findings

arrest warrant legal document issued by a judge indicating enough evidence has been presented to have defendant arrested for and charged with a crime

assault intentionally putting a person in fear and/or apprehension of an immediate harmful or offensive bodily touching

assignee one who receives transferred contract rights

assignment transfer of contract rights to one not a party to the contract

assignor one who transfers contract rights to another

assumption of the risk knowing a risk is present and deciding to take a chance anyway

award decision by an arbitrator

B

bailment relationship created when the owner or legal possessor of personal property gives possession over to another for a period of time for a specific purpose

bait and switch method of advertisement in which an advertiser offers a product it has no intention of selling in order to lure in customers

bankruptcy the process of having property liquidated in order to pay off debts one cannot otherwise repay

bargaining unit a group of employees with a community of interests who form a unit for bargaining purposes

battery intentional unpermitted or offensive touching of the body of another

beyond a reasonable doubt prosecutor's burden of proof in criminal cases

bilateral contract an agreement in which both parties promise something

binding arbitration agreement in advance to be bound by an arbitrator's decision

blue-sky laws state securities laws

board of directors the group that governs a corporation

bona fide occupational qualification legalized discrimination permitted because it is necessary for the employer's particular business

breach of contract party to contract does not perform as agreed

brief written document outlining the points of error that the appellant alleges were made in the trial, along with relevant exhibits

bulk transfer a transfer of virtually all of a seller's interest in materials, supplies, merchandise, or other inventory

business any organization whose objective it is to provide services or goods for profit

business agent one who represents unions to the employer

business ethics the study of what is right or wrong; good or bad human conduct in business

business judgment rule the rule that directors will not be held liable for losses suffered by a corporation if they have used due diligence in making the decision resulting in the loss

business necessity a nondiscriminatory reason for an employer's policy that seems to discriminate against a protected class

business plan a plan that outlines important aspects of a business, generally used to determine feasibility of extending credit to the business

C

C corporation an artificial person or legal entity created by or under the authority of the laws of a state—sometimes composed of a single person and the person's successors, but ordinarily consisting of numerous individuals—which is regarded in law as having a personality and existence distinct from that of its members

case, or controversy two expressions used interchangeably to describe situations sufficiently defined as to be within the power of the court to decide

categorical imperative a universal truth lacking contradictions

certification mark a mark indicating that certain goods or services originated in a particular region, or that they are of a particular nature, quality, or characteristic, or that they were produced by a particular organization

challenge for cause prospective juror does not meet statutory qualifications or is personally unfit for jury service

challenges objections to prospective jurors sitting on jury

Chapter 7 bankruptcy in which the bankrupt's assets are collected, sold, and creditors paid from the proceeds

Chapter 11 bankruptcy also called reorganization; company permitted to file for bankruptcy protection while attempting to reorganize its financial affairs

Chapter 13 bankruptcy also called wage earner bankruptcy; debtor arranges a court-approved plan to repay creditors over an extended period

checks and balances powers one branch of government has over another as a limitation on the powers of the respective branches

circuit jurisdictional area of a court

civil law law governing noncriminal violations of law

clear and convincing evidence burden of proof plaintiff must carry in more serious civil cases in which there has been loss of life or heavy property damage, showing clearly that events occurred as plaintiff alleges

close corporation one whose stock is held by only a few people

closely held corporation a corporation whose shares are held by only a few shareholders

closing argument argument made by lawyers at close of the evidence urging judge or jury to reach the decision each side desires

collective bargaining agreement the agreement reached between the employer and the union

collective mark a mark indicating that goods or services are produced by members of a collective group or simply indicating membership in a particular group

commingle funds received in a professional capacity placed with the professional's personal funds

common law judge-made law and law based on the custom and tradition brought from England by the colonists

community of interests employees who perform similar jobs at the workplace and have similar bargaining issues

comparable worth comparison of the worth of jobs to the employer to determine the rate of pay for the job

comparative negligence comparing the plaintiff's negligence with the defendant's negligence and deducting from plaintiff's award a percentage equal to plaintiff's share of the responsibility

compelling state interest strongest justification for a state to be able to legitimately deny one's constitutional right to equal protection

compelling state interest test test used by courts to determine whether a state may deny a person the constitutional right to equal protection of the law

compensatory damages money given by defendant to plaintiff to compensate for injury

complaint initial pleading alleging a violation of civil law

composition of creditors debtor who cannot repay as promised contacts creditors in an attempt to reach an agreement about repayment without using bankruptcy

conciliation principle by which parties with a dispute attempt to resolve it by trying to reach an agreement between themselves

concurrent conditions acts on the part of each party to a contract that must take place at the same time in order for the parties' duties to perform arise

condition precedent act that must take place before the duty of a party to perform under a contract arises

condition subsequent some act that if it takes place, ends the duty of a party to perform under a contract

conditional fee simple ownership of real estate based on condition that the owner comply with or forfeit the property

confiscation the takeover of private property by a government that does not compensate the owner

consent giving someone permission to do an act

consequential damages damages arising from circumstances that could have been anticipated

consideration a bargained for legal detriment exchanged between parties

constructive notice newspaper communication with third parties the agent may deal with to let them know the agency has been terminated

consumer a cardholder or natural person to whom consumer credit is offered or extended

consumer credit credit offered or extended to a consumer primarily for private family or household purposes

consumer report any report furnished by a consumer reporting agency if such report contains information bearing on the creditworthiness, character, general reputation, personal characteristics, or mode of living of a person

contingency fee arrangement arrangement allowing plaintiff to pay attorney a certain percentage of judgment awarded if plaintiff wins suit

contract lawful agreement between two or more competent parties

contribution the sharing of payment for a debt among the persons liable for it

contributory negligence plaintiff's engaging in an act of negligence that contributes to the harm arising from negligence by another

conversion intentional exercise of dominion and control over the personal property of another

copyright protection for the works of authors, illustrators, photographers, musical composers, and lyricists from being copied without authorization

copyright infringement using the original, copyrighted written material of someone else without permission

corporate culture management philosophy of a business regarding ethics

corporate veil legal protection provided for corporations that protects them as legal entities separate from their owners

cost justification defense a defense to a violation of the Robinson-Patman Act that allows a seller to give discounts to a buyer if the discount represents a lower cost to the seller

counterclaim lawsuit filed against the opposing party

countervailing duty a duty imposed on products manufactured with the help of foreign government subsidies, which are sold for less money in the domestic market, thereby hurting the businesses that are competing in the domestic market

court-annexed ADR ADR done as part of a court's procedures

court of general jurisdiction court without limit as concerns the amount in controversy, the nature of the penalty it may adjudge, or the type of case it may consider within a broad jurisdictional area

court of limited jurisdiction court limited by statute in one or more respects as to what types of cases it may handle

craft union union organized around a specific craft, detached from the particular workplace

credit right granted by a creditor to a consumer to defer payment of a debt

creditor one who regularly extends credit that is subject to a finance charge or is payable by

written agreement in more than four installments whether or not a finance charge is imposed

criminal law law governing criminal matters

crime a violation of criminal law, which may result
in incarceration or a fine or both

cross-claim lawsuit brought by one defendant
against another defendant

cross-examination examination of a witness by the
opposing side

cumulative voting voting in which shareholders
have total votes equal to the number of board
members to be elected times the number of
shares owned

custom a principle or practice that has developed
over a course of dealing that is so well recognized that it becomes binding on the parties to
the custom

D

de novo review court review of agency decision by
court's having a new look at the case through
holding a trial

debt collectors those who use any instrumentality
of interstate commerce or the mails in any business whose principal purpose is the collection of
any debts due another

deceptive practices practices that have a tendency
to mislead a substantial number of consumers in
a material way

decree the decision of a court of equity

deep-pockets theory plaintiff's suing of business
owner, who is thought to have more money
to pay a judgment for tort committed by the
owner's employee in the course of business

defamation intentionally making false statements
about someone to a third person, which has the
effect of lessening the victim's reputation in the
community

defendant one who is sued in a lawsuit

delegation transfer of contract duties to one not a
party to the contract

deposition sworn testimony of witness or party
prior to trial, given before court reporter, for
later use in court

design patent a patent for a new, original and ornamental design for an article of manufacture

direct examination first examination of one's own
witness at trial

direct sale the sale of goods arranged directly between the buyer and the seller

disaffirm exert the legal right to get out of a contract

disclosed principal principal who is known to the
third party with whom the agent acts

discovery learning in advance of trial an adversary's
position on issues raised in the pleadings

disparagement intentionally making false statements about the quality or ownership of someone's goods

disparate impact effect of facially neutral policy
that is deleterious for Title VII group

disparate treatment treating an employee different
from those similarly situated because of a prohibited Title VII factor

dissociation the term used by the RUPA when a
partner leaves (rightfully or wrongfully) a partnership; may or may not be followed by a dissolution

dissolution the ending of a partnership

diversity of citizenship jurisdiction jurisdiction of
federal courts based on controversy between citizens of different states and amount involved

division of territory agreement between competitors to deal only with certain areas

domestic corporation a corporation operating in
the state of its incorporation

domestic partnership process of registering with
the state or local government those who wish to
have some of the benefits of the marital relationship, without the relationship itself

donee one who receives a gift

donee beneficiary one who is to receive benefits
under a contract as a gift from a party to the
contract

donor one who gives a gift

door-to-door sales sales technique in which a salesperson solicits sales by going directly to the consumer's home

double jeopardy doctrine that defendant cannot be tried twice for same crime

due diligence board of directors members' using care and good faith in making decisions for the corporation

due process of law constitutional requirement that all laws be fair rather than arbitrary and provide both notice and an effective opportunity to be heard before the taking of life, liberty or property

dumping sale of goods in a foreign market for a price that is lower than the price of the goods sold in the home market

duress exertion of pressure on a party to influence that party to enter into a contract

E

effluent limitations maximum rate and concentration of pollutants allowed by a Clean Water Act discharge permit

egoism doctrine that an act is morally wrong or right only if it furthers one's own best interest

8K report monthly report corporations must make to the SEC on material matters to update their securities registration

80% rule exemption from SEC registration requirements for offerings in which at least 80% of the investors are from the state, 80% of the issuer's assets are there, and 80% of the proceeds from the issue will be there

electronic fund transfers transfer of funds—other than transactions originated by check, draft, or similar paper instrument—which is initiated through a terminal, telephone, computer or magnetic tape, authorizing a financial institution to debit or credit a consumer's account

eleemosynary corporation set up for charitable purposes

employment at will employment of employees at the pleasure of the employer

environmental audit investigation of a premises to see if there are any existing or potential environmental problems

equal protection constitutional requirement that government treat those similarly situated equally, but if treated differently, the difference be supportable by a legitimate state interest

equitable remedies remedy beyond law, applying equitable principles

equity area of law that goes beyond legalities and instead addresses the fairness of situations

ethics principles of operating in the world that are over and above what is required by law

exclusive dealing arrangement supplier agrees to supply buyer with product only if buyer not stock products of supplier's competitor

executed contract one that has been performed as agreed

executive order the edicts issued by the president or governor that are much like law

executory contract a contract that has been made but not yet performed

exemptions securities that, by statute, do not have to be registered with the SEC

exhaust administrative remedies go through all agency procedures before taking agency decision to court

export a domestically manufactured good or service that is sold in a foreign country

express authority oral or written authority given by a principal to an agent

express contract contract that parties actually discuss and that may or may not be committed to writing

expropriation takeover of private property by a government without paying the owner for the property

F

fair-use doctrine an exception to the unauthorized use of limited copyrighted material used for educational purposes

false imprisonment intentionally confining someone to a place with no reasonable means of exit

false light intentionally publishing something about someone that puts the person in a false light, even though the actual publication may be true

federal district court court established by federal law

federal question jurisdiction judicial power of the United States extending to cases arising under the Constitution, the laws of the United States, and treaties

Federal Register official publication organ of federal agencies, in which the latter publish their business such as rules and regulations

fee simple absolute unconditional ownership of real estate in perpetuity

felony serious crimes resulting in prison time of a year or more

fictitious payee rule the rule that one is liable on a negotiable instrument written on one's account, if it was written by someone in one's employ or control, to a nonexistent person and cashed by the maker

fiduciary one who has the responsibility to act for and on behalf of another's interest rather than that one's own, in making decisions

flextime variable hours employees can work and still be full-time employees

forbearance not doing something one could legally do if one wanted to

foreign corporation a corporation operating in a state other than the state of its incorporation

franchise a licensed business that uses the name of the franchisor's product in the business

fraud in the execution intentional misrepresentation that a writing is something other than the contract it actually is

fraud in the inducement intentional misrepresentation of material facts about a matter in order to induce a party to enter into an agreement

full warranty a warranty that meets minimum federal standards for durations, persons covered, remedies available, registration cards, and consequential damages

G

gap filling UCC concept of court or parties being able to fill in blanks in a contract when UCC provides rules for such

garnish action directed against debtor's assets in the hands of a third party, such as requiring an employer to pay money owed to employee/debtor, directly to creditor

GATT (general agreement on tariffs and trade) agreement between the United States and several other countries about trading among the nations

general agent an agent who performs a broad range of duties for the principal

general partnership a partnership in which all the partners are able to fully participate in the decision making and running of the partnership

good will theory stating that only when we act from duty do we have moral worth

grand jury panel of citizens convened to determine whether a prosecutor has enough evidence to cause an indictment to be issued against a person who allegedly committed a crime

gratuitous promise promise to give someone something without receiving anything in return

gray market goods goods manufactured in a country other than the United States, bearing a valid U.S. trademark, and imported into the United States without the consent of the U.S. trademark holder

group boycott agreement among two or more competitors not to deal with another business or individual

H

horizontal per se violation antitrust violation among and between competitors

hostile environment sexual harassment sexual harassment in which the harasser creates an offensive, hostile, or intimidating environment for the harassee

hung jury in a criminal case, a jury that is unable to decide guilt or innocence of defendant

hypothetical imperative what to do to obtain a certain result or particular outcome

I

implied authority authority that an agent has to do acts that are a natural part of the express authority granted by the principal

implied warranty of fitness for a particular purpose UCC warranty arising from the sale of goods that the goods will perform as the seller represented they would, knowing the particular purpose for which the goods would be used

implied warranty of merchantability UCC warranty arising upon a merchant's sale of goods that the goods will be of fair and average quality and do what such goods should do

implied-in-fact contracts contracts gathered from the acts of parties exhibiting an intent to contract

implied-in-law contracts contracts imposed by law upon parties in an effort to prevent unjust enrichment by one party at the expense of the other

import a foreign-produced good or service that is sold in the domestic country

import duties charges imposed on goods coming into one country from another

imposter rule the rule that one who gives a negotiable instrument to someone who turns out to be an imposter is still responsible payment of for the negotiable instrument

independent contractor one who is employed by a principal to perform work the independent contractor has the authority to direct

indictment decision of grand jury that prosecutor has enough evidence to charge and try defendant for a crime

industrial union union organized around particular jobs at a workplace

information legal document in which prosecutor charges defendant with crime

injunction court order directing something to be done or not to be done

injurious falsehood another term for disparagement

insider 10% shareholder or officer or director of a corporation

insurable interest a legal interest in property that permits one to purchase insurance on the property

intellectual property concepts, information, symbols, or creative expression that carries the right of exclusive use and ownership

intentional infliction of emotional distress intentionally doing an act that goes outside all bounds of common decency, thereby causing serious emotional distress to another

intentional interference with contractual relations intentionally interfering with either established or prospective contractual relations between two or more parties

intentional tort torts based on the intentional acts of others

interrogatories written questions about the case sent to opposing party or witness for answers and for return to sending attorney

intrusion upon seclusion intentionally coming into someone's private space, photographing the person's there, tapping the person's phone, or listening to the person's conversations

invasion of privacy interfering with someone's legitimate expectation of privacy through one of the four recognized means

J

job sharing more than one employee employed in the same job, with sharing of responsibilities so that the job is always covered

joint liability liability in which more than one party is liable for contract breach or tortious activity

joint and several liability liability imposed on individual involved in tort or contract breach or on all of the persons liable

joint tenant with right of survivorship more than one person owning property that will go to the other owners upon their deaths

joint venture a commercial enterprise organized by the participants who control and share its profits and losses

judgment judge's formal determination of a controversy, which details the outcome, how outcome was arrived at, and its consequences

judgment notwithstanding the verdict judgment given in favor of side that lost by verdict

judicial law law derived from cases decided by judges

judicial review review of an agency decision by a court of law

jurisdiction authority of a court over parties and subject matter to hear and determine legal disputes

jurisprudence the study of various theories of law

L

law limitations imposed upon society by government to protect, govern relationships, and provide predictability and security in our persons, possessions, and relationships

legal benefit obtaining a benefit to which one is not otherwise entitled in the absence of contract

legal brief written statement of facts and law supporting one side of a case and presented to a court

legal detriment either doing something one has no legal obligation to do or not doing something one has a legal right to do if one wishes

legal positivism legal philosophy that believes the law is that which the sovereign says it is

legal realism legal philosophy that considers sociology, economics, politics, or other factors in deciding the law

lemon laws statutes that act to replace individual contracts between the buyer and seller of an automobile with an objective contract that reflects negotiations between consumer groups and merchants as to what happens in the event a car does not perform as promised

libel written defamation

license agreement giving the licensee permission to produce or distribute the licensor's product under the licensor's name

life estate real estate conveyed for a time period measured by the life of the transferee or some other party

limited agent an agent for a specific, limited purpose defined by the principal

limited liability company new form of business organization that offers limited liability to its members and taxation as a partnership if certain conditions are met

limited liability partnership new form of business organization that allows the partners to escape joint and several liability in tort

limited partnership an unincorporated association, or firm, in which the limited partners are relieved from liability beyond the amount of capital they contributed

limited review review by court of agency decision to ensure decision was not arbitrary, capricious, or otherwise not in accordance with law

limited warranty warranty that lessens the minimum standards required by federal law

liquidated damages damages predetermined by the parties before breach

M

mailbox, or deposited acceptance, rule rule that once an acceptance is deposited in the system used for communication, it is a valid acceptance which creates a contract

main purpose doctrine enforceability of an otherwise unenforceable oral surety contract if the main reason one acts as a surety is for one's own personal advantage rather than that of the debtor

mandatory injunction court order that a thing be done

mandatory subjects of bargaining wages, hours, and other terms and conditions of employment about which an employer must bargain

marshaling of assets collection of assets, their arrangement in order of priority, then division of the assets to pay claims

mediation disinterested third party attempts to talk with disputing parties to try to help them reach a resolution

meeting competition defense a defense to a violation of the Robinson-Patman Act that allows the seller to offer a discount to the buyer if it is done to meet the prices of the competition

merchant under the UCC, one who deals in goods of the kind under contract

merchantable goods that can pass without objection in the trade

merchant's firm offer merchant's statement in signed writing that offer will remain open for a stated period, not to exceed 90 days

merger two businesses' coming together to form a larger version of one of the businesses

minitrial presentation of conflict before business-people, as a way to enhance settlements and avoid trial

misdemeanor less serious crimes, sometimes resulting in jail time of less than a year or a fine

mock trial pretend trial presented before a group of people to see how they react to presentation of evidence before actual presentation in court

monopoly power to control prices and exclude competition

morality personal opinions concerning right or wrong

most-favored-nation status status given to countries allowing them to enjoy import duties no higher than those of the most favored nation

motion formal request by an attorney that a court decide a matter

motion for new trial request to judge made by the losing party, that new trial be granted because of error committed during trial

moving party the party who makes a motion to the court

multilateral instrument agreement between several nations

multinational enterprise an enterprise that is directed from its countries of origin (or home

countries) and engages in economically significant activities within other states, known as host countries

multinational litigation litigation involving litigants of different countries

mutual ignorance a case of both parties, knowing they do not know one or more factors about the subject matter of a contract, but entering into a contract about it anyway

mutual mistake misunderstanding in which both parties think they are agreeing to the same contract terms, but unbeknownst to them, they are agreeing to different terms

N

nationalization takeover of private property by a government that pays the owner for the property

natural law legal philosophy that believes law is based on certain factors or morals that are universal, unchangeable, and dictated by God

necessaries food, clothing, or shelter contracted for by one lacking capacity

negligence failure to meet the standard of care used by a reasonable person under the circumstances

negotiable instrument legal document, meeting certain requirements and representing a right of the holder of the instrument to receive money or goods

no-strike, no-lockout clause clause prohibiting or limiting employee strikes and employer lockouts

nominal damages damages awarded as acknowledgment that legal right was invaded, but little harm done

nonbinding arbitration agreement to arbitrate a conflict, but not to be bound by the arbitrator's decision

notice due process of law right to be made aware that there is a possibility of loss due to some act of the government

notice of proposed rule making administrative law requirement that before a rule or regulation can be promulgated, notice must be given in the official organ of administrative agencies in the state or national government

novation agreement between obligor, assignor, and assignee to allow assignor to be released from a contract and the assignee be put in the assignor's place

O

obligee one who receives another's performance under a contract

obligor one obligated to perform under a contract

offeree one who receives an offer

offeror one who gives an offer

oligopoly a form of competition in which the products are similar and are distinguished through advertising

on all fours facts before the court are the same in all significant aspects as precedent, thus requiring the precedent be applied in the present case

opening statement statements by lawyers at beginning of trial outlining case and what they expect evidence to prove

opportunity to be heard due process of law right to give input to the government after receiving notice that the government may cause a loss of liberty, rights, economic position, etc

option contract contract of offeror's promising to keep offer open for promisee for a stated period

oral argument verbal presentation by attorneys in court aimed at persuading a judge of their view

ordinance a local law passed for a city, town, or county

organization an international body that is recognized by most countries as having rule-making capabilities to which those nations adhere

original jurisdiction jurisdiction of an appellate court to try a case

P

palming off passing off someone else's goods as one's own

part performance exception enforceability of an oral contract for land if the party moves on, makes improvements and pays part of the consideration

partially disclosed principal principal of whom the third party dealing with an agent is aware but does not know for whom the agent acts

partnership voluntary agreement between two or more people to work together for profit

past consideration the giving of something of value prior to a party's agreeing to give something in return under a contract

patent absolute protection for inventors and their inventions so they may use, sell, license, or refrain from making, using, or selling their invention for a period of 17 years

patent infringement making a product for which an exclusive patent has been given to another

per se violation violation of antitrust laws that whether reasonable or not, is illegal

peremptory strikes objections to prospective jurors made without explanation; usually limited to criminal cases

permanent injunction injunction granted as part of a judgment after full determination of rights of the parties

permissive subjects of bargaining nonmandatory terms about which management may bargain with the union

petit jury jury that hears a case in court

pierce the corporate veil court goes behind the corporate identity shield and imposes personal liability on shareholders for corporate debts

plaintiff party who initiates civil legal proceedings

plant patent patent for a distinct and new variety of plant that is asexually produced

pleadings in civil cases, litigants' written statements of their claims and responses in forms prescribed by a court

point source any discrete point of discharge that empties directly into receiving waters

police power constitutional power of a state to legislate for the health, safety, welfare, and morals of its citizens

political questions issues that do not present a case or controversy, but rather a dispute between two branches of government or within a single branch of government

practical availability defense defense to a violation of the Robinson-Patman Act that excuses violation if discount offered the buyer is practically available to competitors of the seller

precedent judicial decisions that must be looked to in later, similar cases

predatory pricing the selling of products below costs, which creates the dangerous probability of creating a successful monopoly

preemption right of the federal legislature to be the only body to enact legislation in a given area, to the exclusion of the states

preemptive right right of first refusal that a shareholder has in the buying of a portion of new stock issued by the corporation

preexisting contractual or legal obligation a legal requirement imposed by law or contract, which exists prior to the time a party agrees by contract to do what is already required

preliminary injunction injunction granted after hearing before a judge in advance of trial, to last until the granting or denial of a permanent injunction

preponderance of the evidence usual burden of proof that plaintiff must bear in a civil case, showing it was more likely than not that events occurred as plaintiff alleges

pretrial time period between filing of pleadings and trial, during which discovery is completed

price discrimination charging different prices to different buyers of the same product in the same time period

price fixing a agreement by marketers of a product to set agreed-to prices for the product

prima facie case proof of evidence of each element in a cause of action

prima facie obligation obligation that can be overridden by a more important consideration or obligation

principal one who employs an independent contractor; one for whom an agent acts

private corporation one held by private citizens rather than the government

private law law involving rights between private citizens

procedural due process constitutional requirement that government provide appropriate notice and an opportunity to be heard before taking life, liberty, or property

procedural law laws and regulations governing the exercise of substantive rights provided by law

professional corporation (PC) business organization composed of professionals who require a license to practice

promissory estoppel court order prohibiting the use of the lack of consideration defense by someone who made a promise, knowing it would likely be relied upon when the party moves, to their detriment, in reliance on the promise

promissory note note containing a creditor's unconditional promise to repay a loan

proposals for addition to the contract new terms added to an original offer by offeree

prospectus information provided to prospective buyers about a security being offered to the public

proximate cause legal cause of negligence for which law will impose liability

proxy written authorization given by a shareholder permitting someone to vote for him or her when the shareholder is not present to do so

public corporation one held by the government

public domain works that are not subject to protection against infringement

public law law dealing with the government in its operations or the relationship between the government and its citizens

publication of private facts intentionally publishing information about someone that is a private matter

publicly traded securities trading on one of the national stock exchanges

puffery a statement of the seller's opinion about goods, but not a warranty

punitive damages damages awarded in a civil case to punish wrongdoer

Q

qualified privilege no liability for engaging in certain behavior as long as the behavior follows prescribed guidelines

quantum meruit payment of reasonable value of services or goods imposed by law in a transaction where one would otherwise be unjustly enriched by not being required to pay because an element of a valid contract is missing

quasi contract appears to be a contract, but generally lacks mutual assent; another name for contracts implied in law

quid pro quo sexual harassment sexual harassment in which the harasser requests sexual activity from the harassee in exchange for workplace benefits

quorum a minimum number of people necessary to be present to conduct corporate business

R

ratify perform acts or say words evidencing a wish to go through with a contract despite an impediment to contracting

rational basis theory a government can use when denying to a business the equal protection of the law

rational basis test test a court uses to analyze whether denial of equal protection to a business is legal

registration process of disclosing to the SEC or state security agency requested information about a security being offered to the public

regulatory negotiation mediation between agency and interested constituents concerning regulations the agency contemplates promulgating

rejection offeree's nonacceptance of an offer

remedy award of money damages or order to do or refrain from doing something

reply plaintiff's response to defendant's answer

request for production of documents discovery tool whereby relevant evidence is produced for examination by the opposing party

resale price maintenance manufacturer's requirement that buyer resell good at a certain price

rescission contract undone by parties or by court order

respondeat superior legal theory allowing employer to be liable for torts committed by an employee within scope of employment

Restatement of Contracts compilation of states' contract law into one source with suggested approaches that states can adopt if they wish, in whole or in part

restitution giving back something one party gave other under contract

retainer amount paid to an attorney to take a case

reverse discrimination belief of majority group members that they were adversely affected by affirmative action implementation

revocation offeror's rescinding an offer

right to inspect shareholders' right to see corporate books for legitimate purposes

ripeness on the facts and procedurally, the case's realness and readiness for determination by the court

rounds conferences held to rework GATT

rule of reason rule requiring only unreasonable restraints of trade to be violations of the Sherman Act

S

S corporation a small business corporation that may elect to have its undistributed taxable income taxed to its shareholders

same gender affinity orientation gender an individual is attracted to for primary relationships is same as individual's

screening device factor used to weed applicants out of the pool of potential hirees

search warrant legal document issued by a judge indicating enough evidence has been presented to show probable cause that evidence of a crime will be found on premises warrant is issued for

secured transaction credit transaction in which creditor obtains from debtor agreement to use debtor's property as collateral to be taken by creditor in the event debtor defaults on the loan

security any investment in a common enterprise from which the purchaser or holder expects or hopes to make a profit mostly from the efforts of others

security agreement agreement creating a secured transaction that gives creditor a security interest in debtor's goods upon default on a loan

self-defense using appropriate force to protect one-self from an unpermitted touching by another

service mark mark used in the sale or advertising of services to identify and distinguish the services of one producer from those of another

several liability individual liability for an act resulting in need to compensate another

sexual harassment unwanted gender-based activity directed toward a harassee either requesting sexual activity or creating a hostile or intimidating environment for harassee

shopkeeper's rule a shopkeeper's conditional privilege to hold a suspected shoplifter so as to investigate, if the suspicion is reasonable, the time is reasonable and the person receives reasonable treatment

short-swing trade trade of a security within six months of purchase

slander oral defamation

social responsibility responsibility of a corporation to act as a good citizen in the community in which it exists

sociological theory philosophy of law stating that law is a reflection of constantly competing interests of society

sole proprietorship business owned and controlled exclusively by one person

sovereign immunity freedom of a sovereignty from suit in another country without its consent, except for suits involving its commercial activity

specialized courts courts created for handling specific types of cases, e.g., U.S. Tax Court

specific performance equitable remedy ordering party to perform contractual obligation

standing qualification to sue or defend because of having a personal stake in the outcome of a case

stare decisis requirement that prior similar cases be used to determine issues now before the court

Statute of Frauds law requiring that certain contracts be in writing to be enforced

statutory close corporation corporation whose voting shares are held by a single or close-knit group of shareholders

statutory law laws, known as statutes, passed by a legislative body

straight voting voting in which shareholders get to cast the same number of votes that they have in shares in the corporation

strict liability liability regardless of fault

strict scrutiny heightened level of court analysis of laws creating classifications that treat similarly situated people differently

substantive due process constitutional requirement that laws be fair if they are to deprive a person of rights

substantive law laws that provide rights and responsibilities, upon pain of penalty in the form of liability or criminal sanctions

summons legal document issued by a court, demanding that a party under the court's jurisdiction submit to the court's authority

Superfund another name for CERCLA, a program designed to clean up facilities where hazardous substances are located

surety one who agrees to be responsible for debtor's debts if debtor does not pay

T

tariffs charges imposed on a product when imported into a country

temporary restraining order injunction granted without a hearing, usually on a showing of urgency

tenant at sufferance one who overstays a lease period

tenant at will one who leases a premises with no set time period of occupancy

tenant for a stated period one who leases a premises for a given time period (e.g., 5 years)

tenant from period to period one who leases a premises from one date to another (e.g., from 1/1/95 to 12/31/96)

tenants by the entirety a married couple who owns property as joint tenants

tenants in common more than one person's owning property that can be willed to someone other than the other owners upon their death

tender offer offer, usually public, to purchase a certain amount of stock at a set price (generally above market price); generally precedes a takeover (hostile or friendly) of one company by another company or individual

10Q report the quarterly report corporations must file with the SEC to update material aspects of their securities registration statement

theft of trade secrets intentionally taking information that is a business secret and using it for one's own purposes

third-party beneficiary contract contract entered into between two parties for the benefit of a third person

third-party creditor beneficiary one who is to receive benefits under a contract as repayment of an obligation of a party to the contract

tort noncontractual, noncriminal violations of civil law

trade dress total image of a product, including the size, shape, color, texture, graphics, or sales technique employed

trade name the name of a firm or business that identifies the producer, rather than the products or services it produces

trade secret any formula, recipe, or client list used in one's business that gives one an advantage over competitors

trademark any word, name, symbol, or other device used to identify and distinguish one's goods from those manufactured or sold by others

trademark infringement using the trademark registered to another

treaty a negotiated contract between parties who happen to be nations

trespass to personal property intentionally interfering with possession and control of someone's personal property

trespass to real property intentionally coming onto the land of another

tripartite system the system of government that comprises three branches: legislative, executive, and judicial

tying arrangement arrangement whereby the ability to obtain one good is dependent upon taking another, usually less desirable good

U

ultra vires acts outside the power of the corporation

unconscionability UCC concept of refusal of a court to give force and effect to a contract that seems grossly unfair to one of the parties

undisclosed principal one who has another act on his or her behalf without permitting the third party with whom the agent deals to know that the agent is acting in a representative capacity

undue influence presumption created in the case of a dominant-subservient relationship, opportunity for the dominant party to influence the subservient party, and a contract that tends to favor the dominant party

unenforceable contract a contract that is not in writing as required or will not be otherwise made to be completed by the court

unfair acts acts that offend public policy; are immoral, unethical, oppressive, or unscrupulous; or cause substantial injury to others

unfair labor practices the grounds on which action is brought by labor or management alleging the other party violated the NLRA

Uniform Commercial Code (UCC) compilation of state laws covering contracts, with a suggested approach, creating uniformity

unilateral contract agreement in which one party promises to do something if the other party does an act

unilateral mistake mistake that one party makes in contracting, but of which the other party is unaware

unreasonable restraint of trade restraint of trade which violates law

used-car rule federal rule designed to protect buyers of used cars from unscrupulous practices in the sale of used cars

utilitarianism doctrine that we should always act to produce the most good for the most people

utility patent patent that is available for any new and useful process, machine, manufacture, or composition of matter or any new or useful improvement thereof

V

valid contract contract that meets the requirements of mutual assent, consideration, capacity, and legality

valuation determination the worth of business

vertical per se violation antitrust violation among and between those in the vertical chain of commerce, that is, seller to buyer

vicarious liability liability imposed based on legal relationship between tortfeasor and employer rather than upon the liable party committing the tort

void contract an agreement that has no legal effect because it lacks legality or other requirement for a valid contract

voidable contract contract that one of the parties may opt not to go through with, without fault

voir dire questioning of prospective jurors by lawyers to determine who will sit on jury

W

warranty an absolute promise

warranty of merchantability promise that goods fit for ordinary purposes

warranty of title a promise by the seller that the goods sold have a clean title, that is, that the title will not subject the seller to a lawsuit

waste life tenant doing an act inconsistent with the interest of those to take after the life estate is over

white-collar crimes crimes committed against or by a business

wildcat strike strike not authorized by the union

will the capacity to act from principle

work-for-hire doctrine rule that states an employer automatically owns a copyright in the works of employees that are prepared within the scope of employment

writ of certiorari order directing a lower court to send the record of a case to an appellate court for review

written warranties a warranty given in writing that must be designated as full or limited

wrongful discharge termination of an at-will employee for reasons the law does not allow; also known as abusive termination, abusive discharge, and wrongful termination

Y

yellow dog contract outlawed agreements that an employer required from employees promising that the employees did not belong to a union and would not join one while in the owner's employ

INDEX

Coventry University